M000073305

Freaking Romance

Snailords

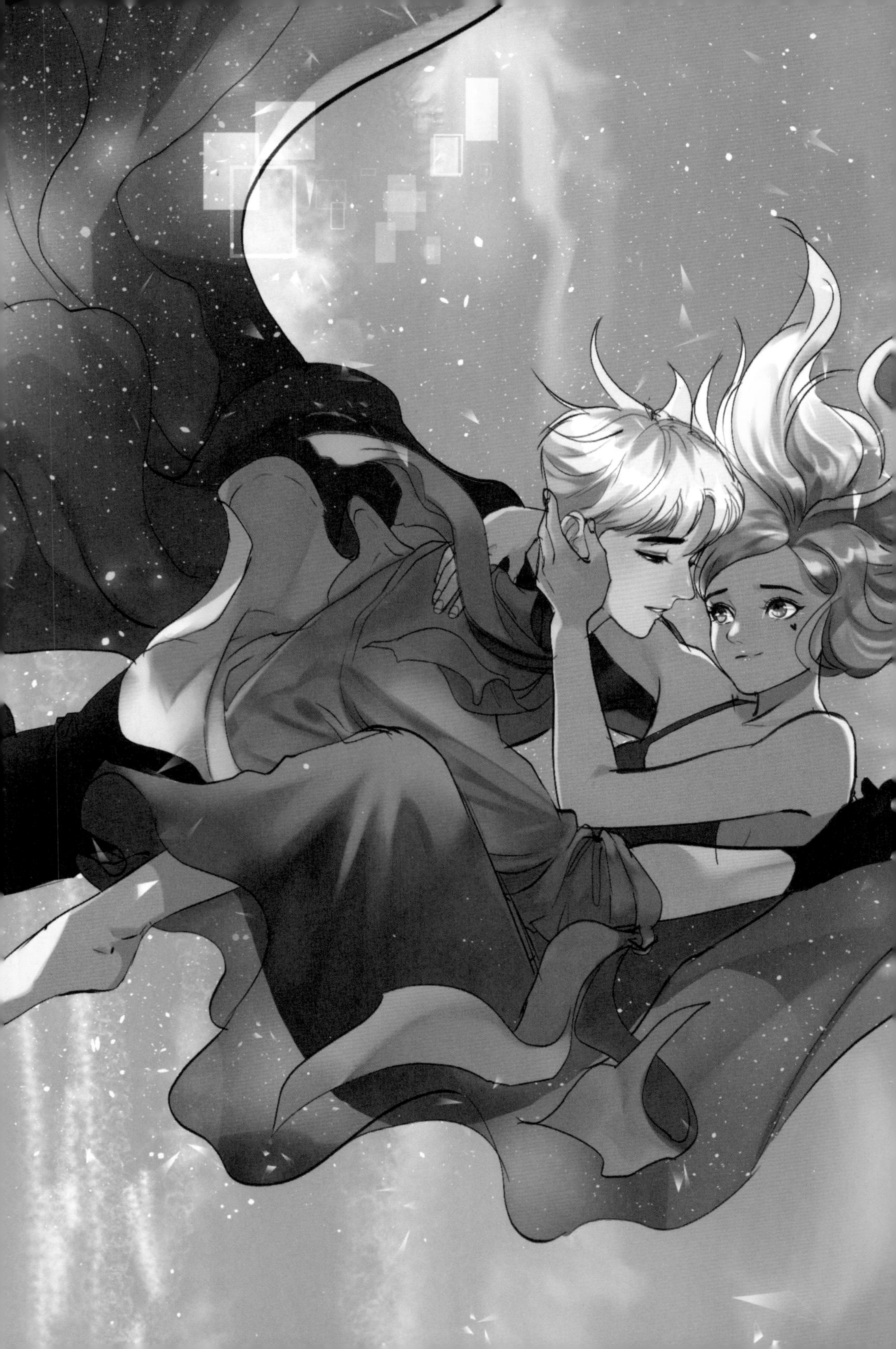

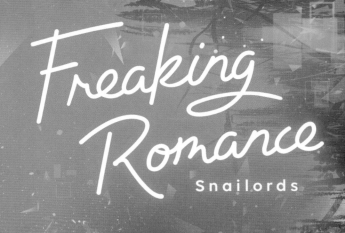

Freaking Romance
Snailords

WEBTOON
UNSCROLLED™

BOBBIE CHASE *Editor*
RENEE NAKAGAWA *Art Director*
RHYS EUSEBIO & MARIA WEHDEKING *Publication Designers*
NIKO DALCIN *Sequential Story Designer*
AMELIA SCHIFFER *Sequential Design Assistance*
PATRICK McCORMICK *Senior Manager, Production*
DELANEY ANDERSON *Production Editor*
PAUL JUN *Original WEBTOON Editor*

ARON LEVITZ *President*
TINA McINTYRE *Interim Head of Publishing, Head of Marketing*
BOBBIE CHASE *Executive Editor, WEBTOON Unscrolled*
DEANNA McFADDEN *Executive Publishing Director, Wattpad WEBTOON Book Group*
DAVID MADDEN *Global Head of Entertainment*
TAYLOR GRANT *VP, Head of Global Animation*
LINDSEY RAMEY *VP, Head of Global Film*
SERA TABB *VP, Head of Global Television*
CAITLIN O'HANLON *Head of Content & Creators*
DEXTER ONG *Managing Director, International*
RYAN PHILP *SVP, Operations*
MAXIMILIAN JO *General Counsel*
AUSTIN WONG *Head of Legal and Business Affairs*
COREY HOCK *Director, Legal & Business Affairs*
KEN KIM *WEBTOON CEO*

FREAKING ROMANCE

Copyright © 2023, Wattpad WEBTOON Studios, Inc. All rights reserved.
Published in Canada by WEBTOON Unscrolled, a division of Wattpad WEBTOON Studios, Inc.
36 Wellington Street E., Suite 200. Toronto, ON M5E 1C7
The digital version of Freaking Romance was originally published on WEBTOON.com in 2018.
Copyright © 2018, Aidyn Arroyal aka Snailords.
www.WEBTOONUnscrolled.com

No portion of this publication may be reproduced or transmitted, in any form or by any means, without
the express written permission of the copyright holders.

First WEBTOON Unscrolled edition: September 2023

ISBN: 978-1-99077-896-4 (Hardcover)
ISBN:978-1-99077-883-4 (Paperback)

Names, characters, places, and incidents featured in this publication are either the product of the
author's imagination or are used fictitiously. Any resemblance to actual persons (living or dead), events,
institutions, or locales, without satiric intent, is coincidental.

WEBTOON, UNSCROLLED, and associated logos are trademarks and/or registered trademarks of
WEBTOON Entertainment Inc. or its affiliates.

Library and Archives Canada Cataloging in Publication information is available upon request.

CONTENT WARNING: This graphic novel contains mature themes, some nudity, strong language, and
depictions of parental abuse.

Printed and bound in Canada

1 3 5 7 9 10 8 6 4 2

TABLE OF CONTENTS

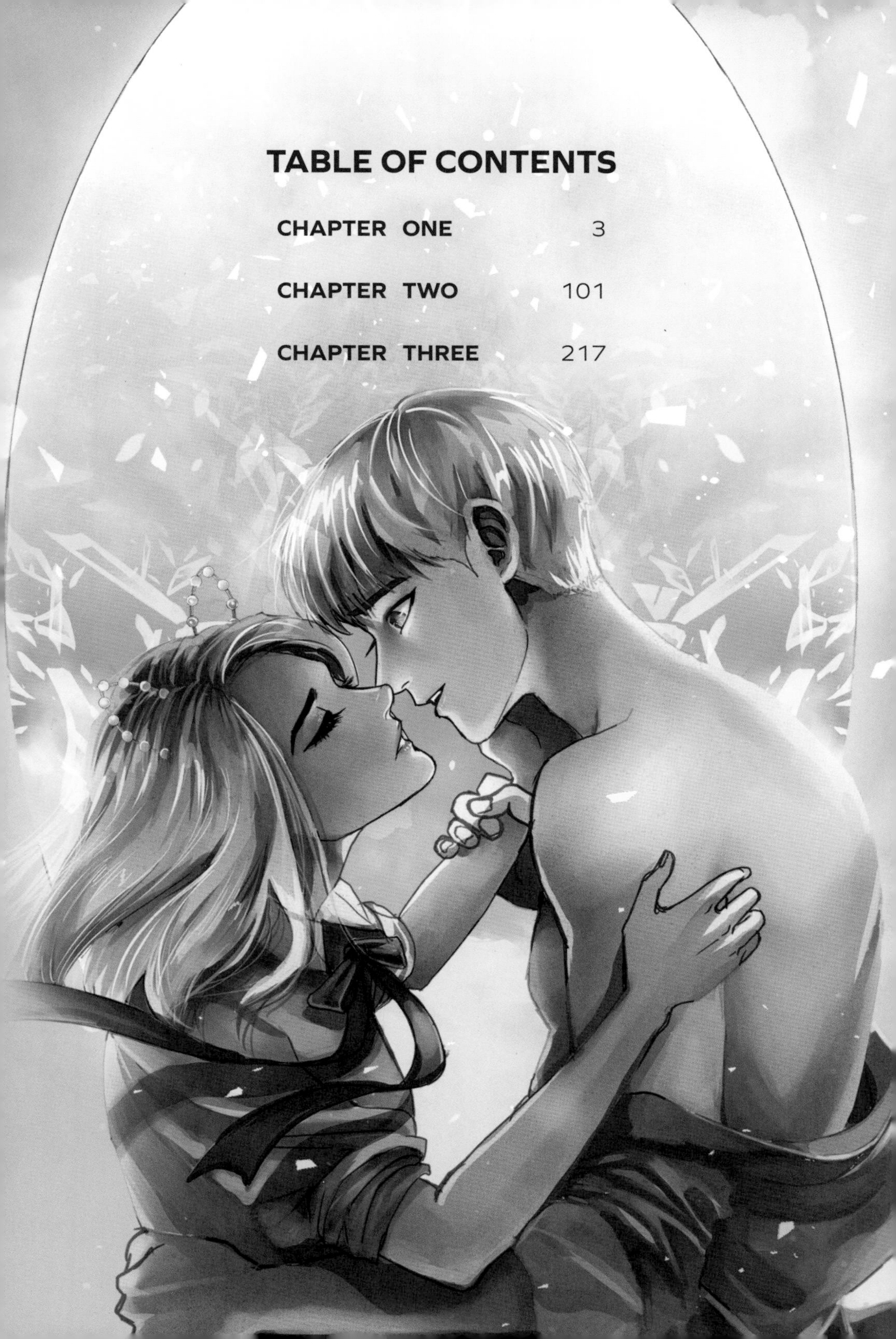

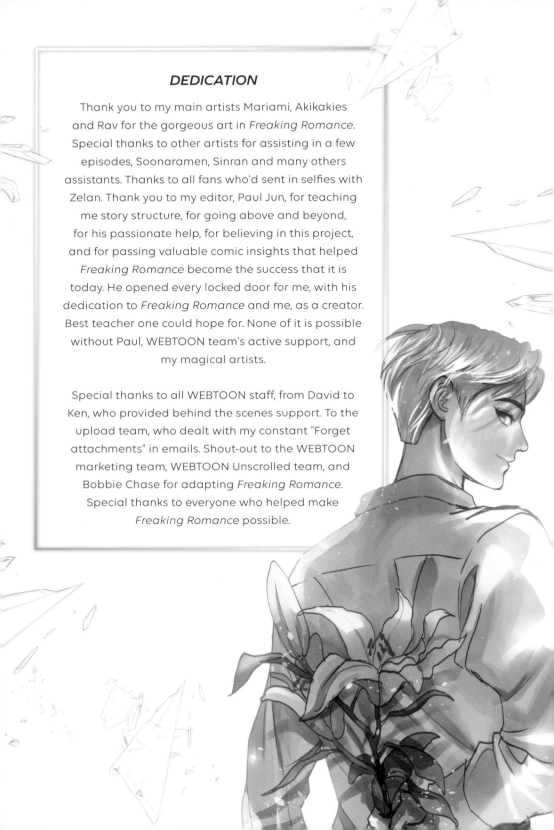

DEDICATION

Thank you to my main artists Mariami, Akikakies and Rav for the gorgeous art in *Freaking Romance*. Special thanks to other artists for assisting in a few episodes, Soonaramen, Sinran and many others assistants. Thanks to all fans who'd sent in selfies with Zelan. Thank you to my editor, Paul Jun, for teaching me story structure, for going above and beyond, for his passionate help, for believing in this project, and for passing valuable comic insights that helped *Freaking Romance* become the success that it is today. He opened every locked door for me, with his dedication to *Freaking Romance* and me, as a creator. Best teacher one could hope for. None of it is possible without Paul, WEBTOON team's active support, and my magical artists.

Special thanks to all WEBTOON staff, from David to Ken, who provided behind the scenes support. To the upload team, who dealt with my constant "Forget attachments" in emails. Shout-out to the WEBTOON marketing team, WEBTOON Unscrolled team, and Bobbie Chase for adapting *Freaking Romance*. Special thanks to everyone who helped make *Freaking Romance* possible.

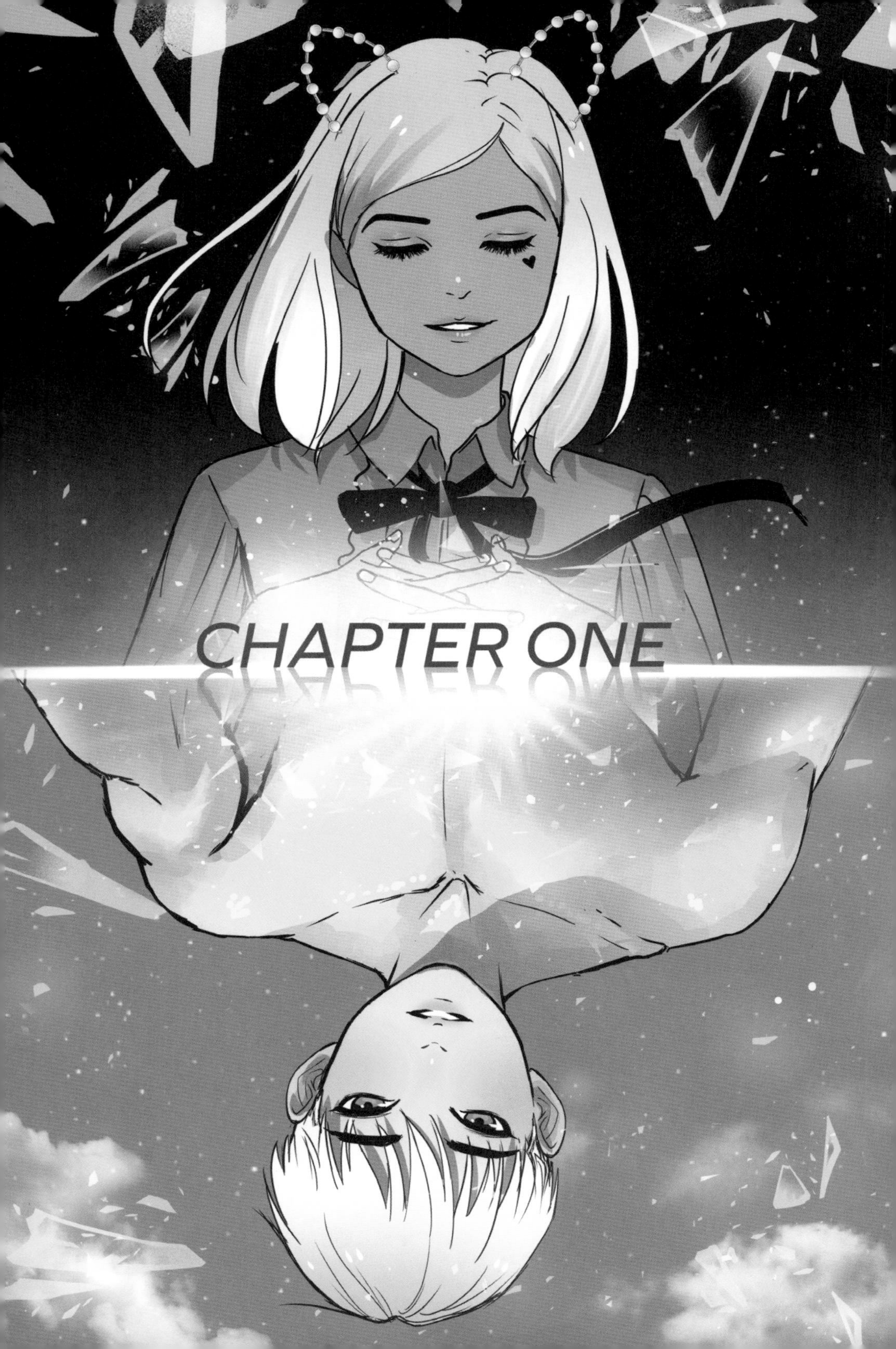
CHAPTER ONE

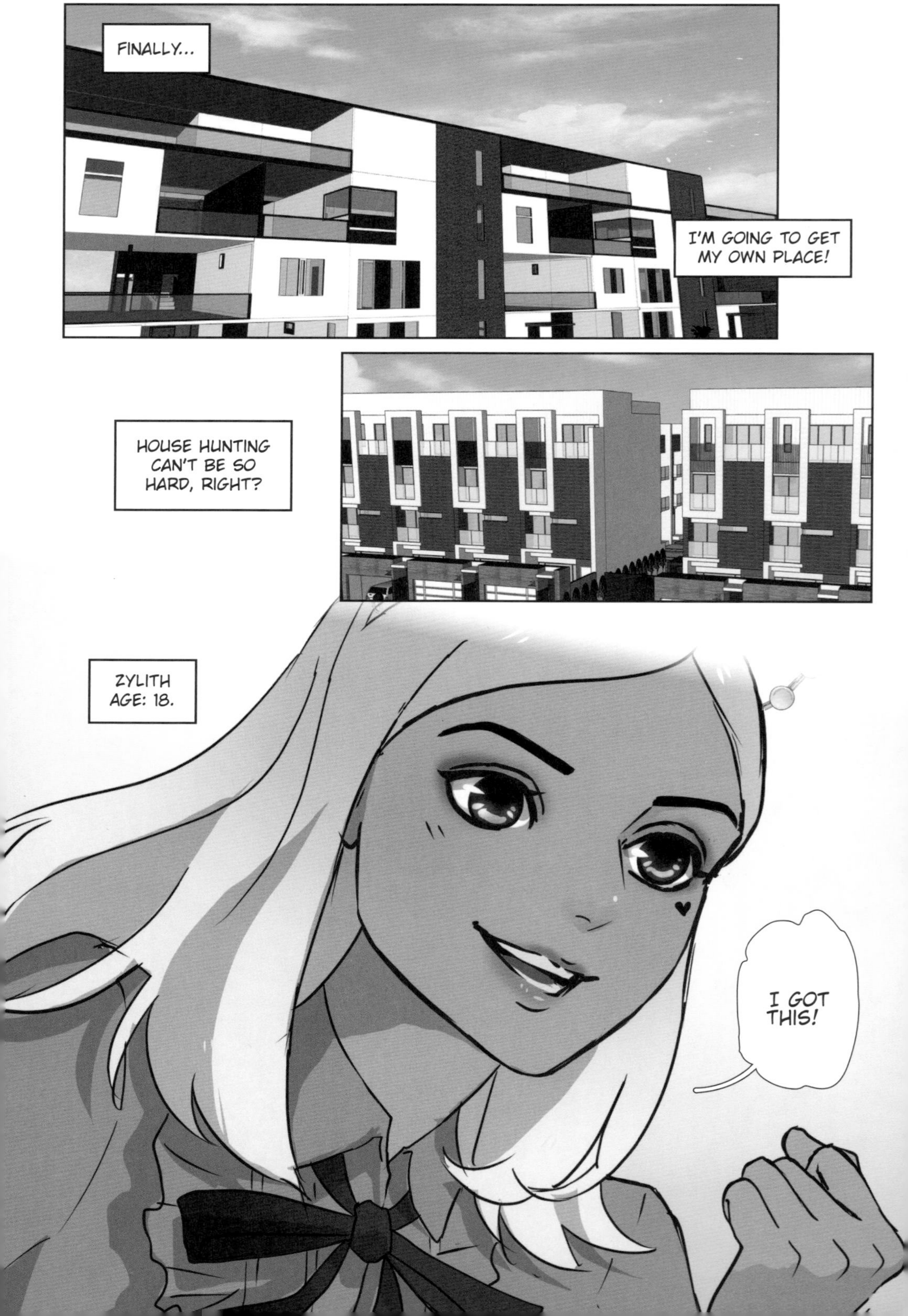
FINALLY...
I'M GOING TO GET MY OWN PLACE!
HOUSE HUNTING CAN'T BE SO HARD, RIGHT?
ZYLITH AGE: 18.
I GOT THIS!

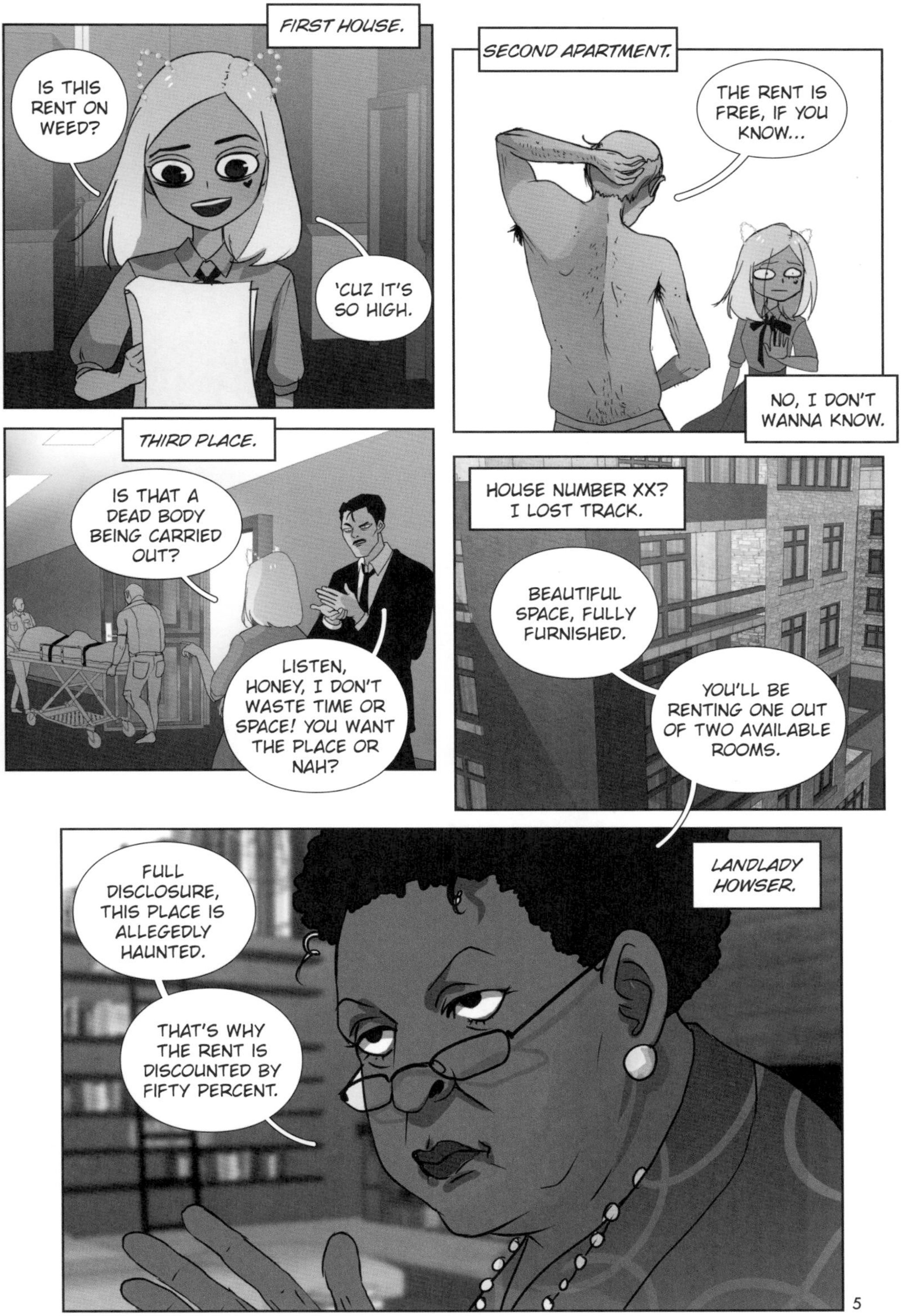
FIRST HOUSE.
IS THIS RENT ON WEED?
'CUZ IT'S SO HIGH.
SECOND APARTMENT.
THE RENT IS FREE, IF YOU KNOW...
NO, I DON'T WANNA KNOW.
THIRD PLACE.
IS THAT A DEAD BODY BEING CARRIED OUT?
LISTEN, HONEY, I DON'T WASTE TIME OR SPACE! YOU WANT THE PLACE OR NAH?
HOUSE NUMBER XX? I LOST TRACK.
BEAUTIFUL SPACE, FULLY FURNISHED.
YOU'LL BE RENTING ONE OUT OF TWO AVAILABLE ROOMS.
FULL DISCLOSURE, THIS PLACE IS ALLEGEDLY HAUNTED.
LANDLADY HOWSER.
THAT'S WHY THE RENT IS DISCOUNTED BY FIFTY PERCENT.

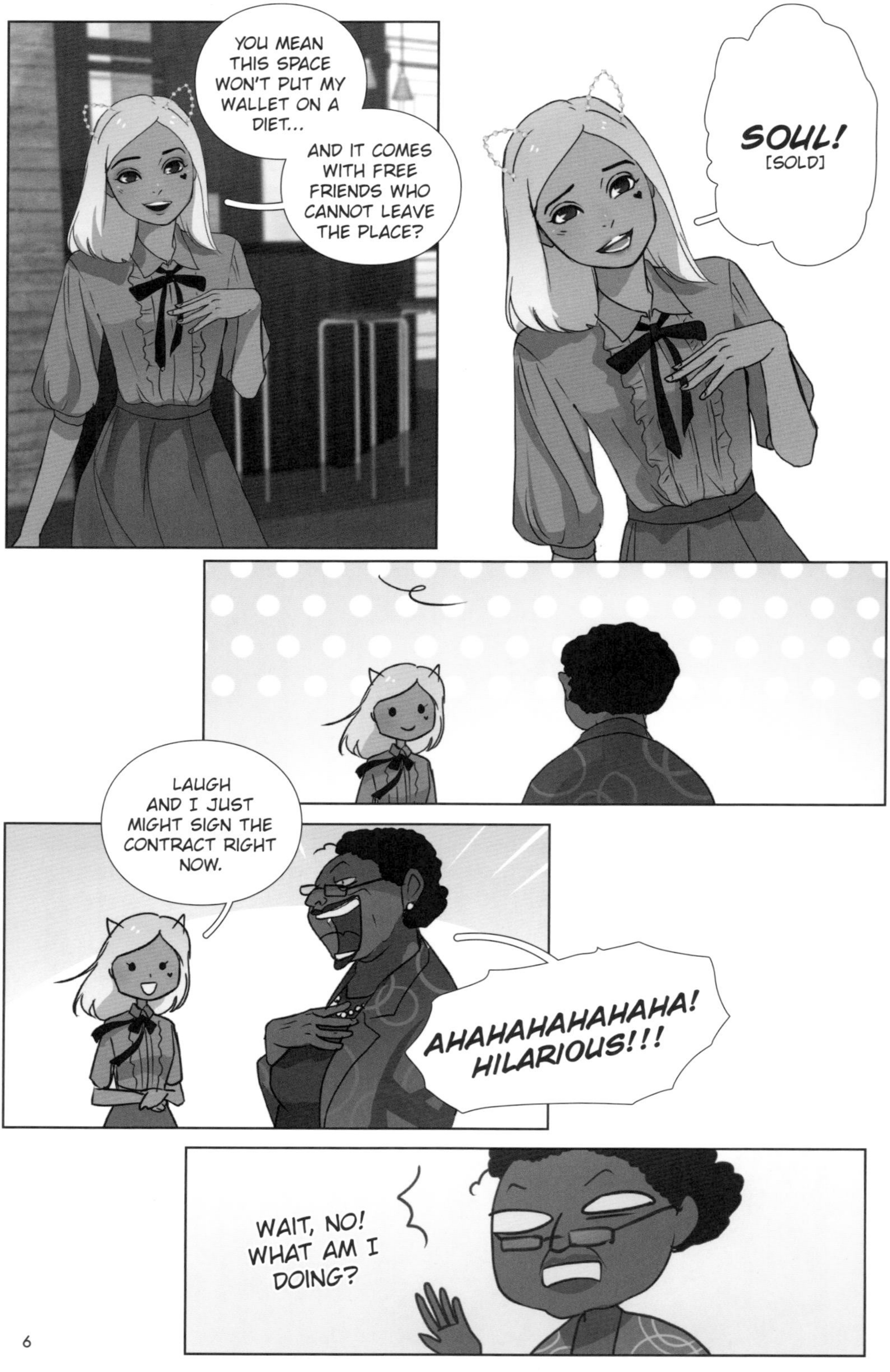
YOU MEAN THIS SPACE WON'T PUT MY WALLET ON A DIET...
AND IT COMES WITH FREE FRIENDS WHO CANNOT LEAVE THE PLACE?
SOUL!
[SOLD]
LAUGH AND I JUST MIGHT SIGN THE CONTRACT RIGHT NOW.
AHAHAHAHAHAHA! HILARIOUS!!!
WAIT, NO! WHAT AM I DOING?

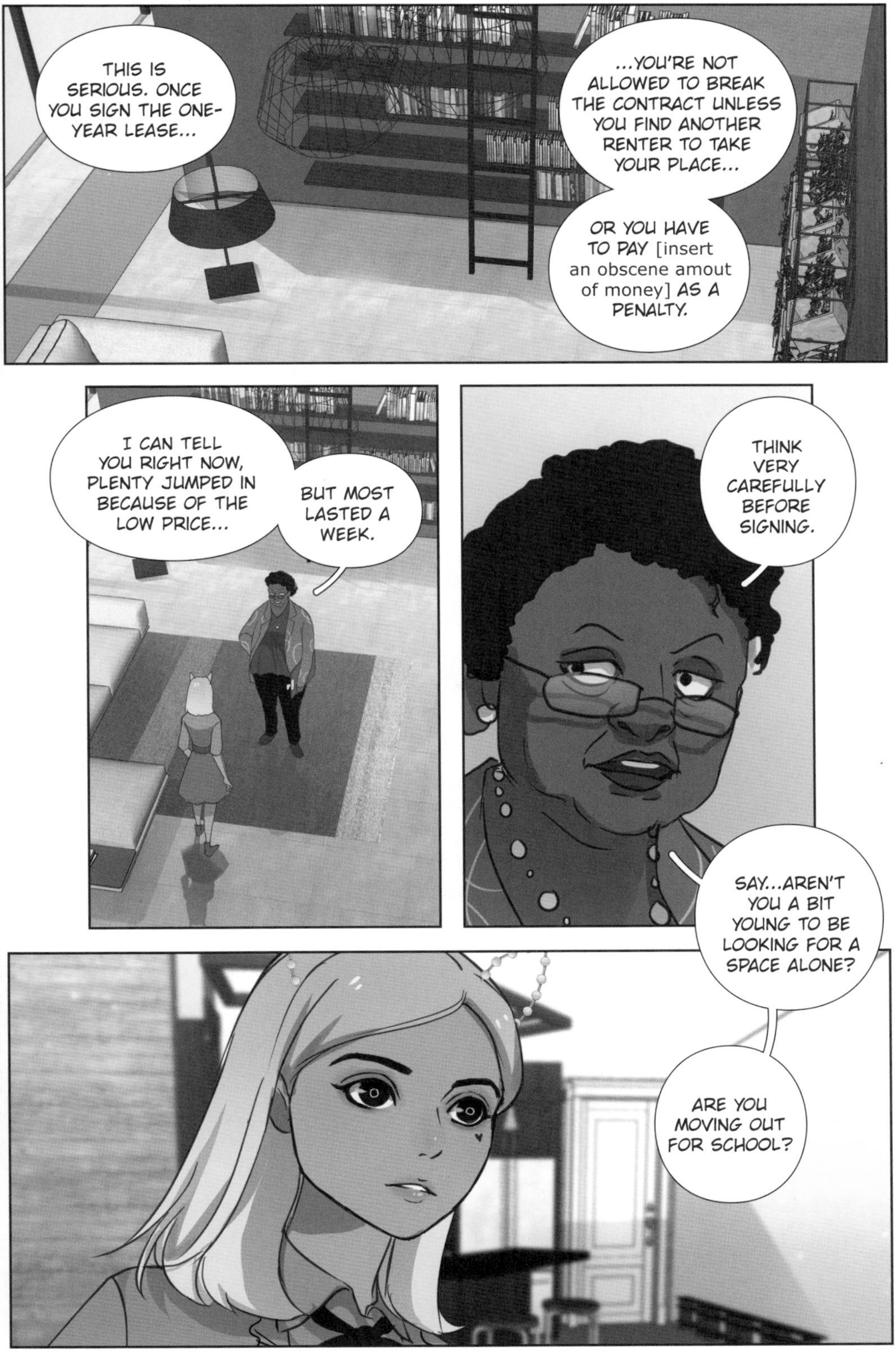
THIS IS SERIOUS. ONCE YOU SIGN THE ONE-YEAR LEASE...
...YOU'RE NOT ALLOWED TO BREAK THE CONTRACT UNLESS YOU FIND ANOTHER RENTER TO TAKE YOUR PLACE...
OR YOU HAVE TO PAY [insert an obscene amout of money] AS A PENALTY.
I CAN TELL YOU RIGHT NOW, PLENTY JUMPED IN BECAUSE OF THE LOW PRICE...
BUT MOST LASTED A WEEK.
THINK VERY CAREFULLY BEFORE SIGNING.
SAY...AREN'T YOU A BIT YOUNG TO BE LOOKING FOR A SPACE ALONE?
ARE YOU MOVING OUT FOR SCHOOL?

I CAME HOME ONE DAY TO MY BELONGINGS PACKED IN BOXES...
...ON THE PAVEMENT IN FRONT OF MY PARENTS' HOUSE.
Good luck Surviving on your own.

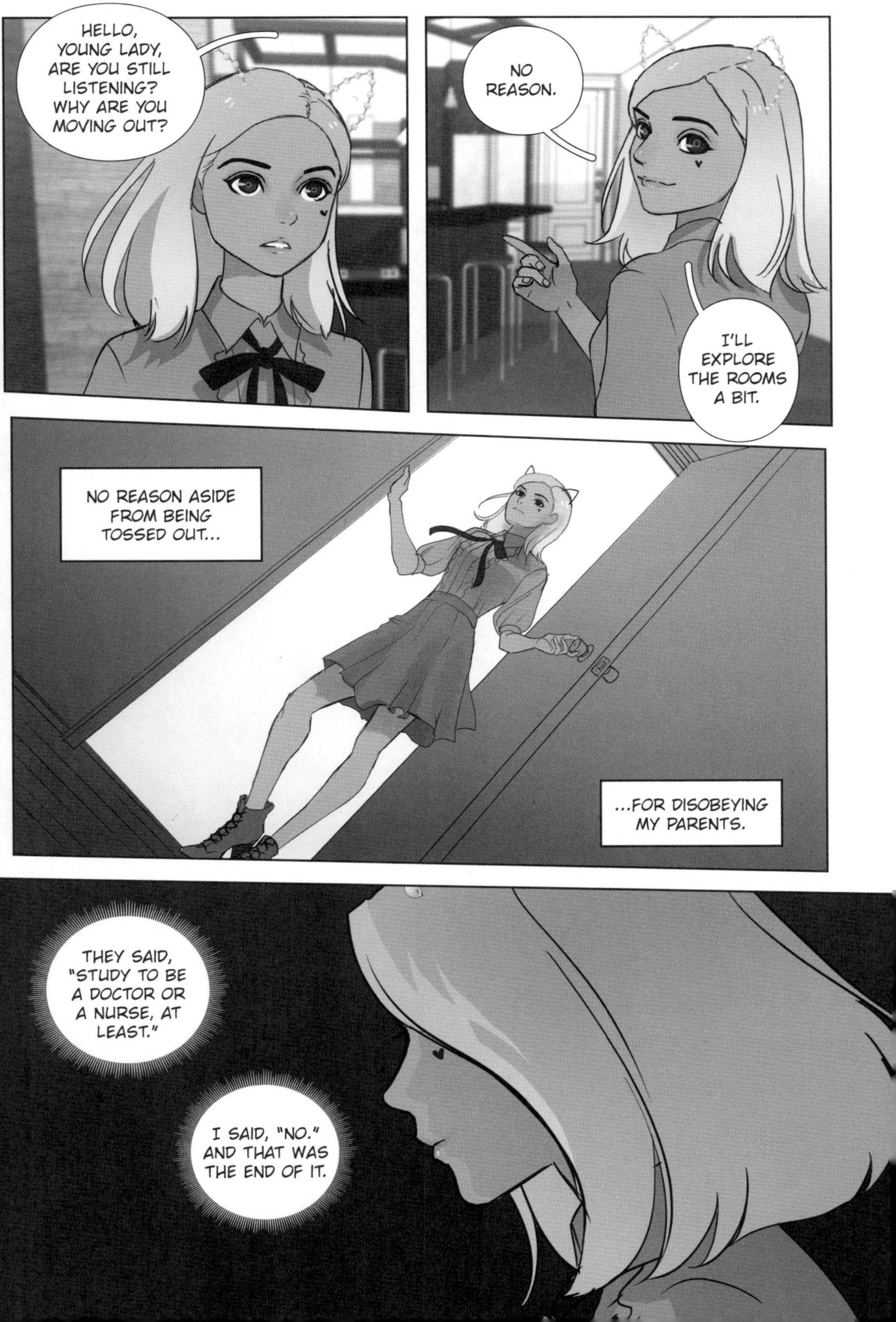
HELLO, YOUNG LADY, ARE YOU STILL LISTENING? WHY ARE YOU MOVING OUT?
NO REASON.
I'LL EXPLORE THE ROOMS A BIT.
NO REASON ASIDE FROM BEING TOSSED OUT...
...FOR DISOBEYING MY PARENTS.
THEY SAID, "STUDY TO BE A DOCTOR OR A NURSE, AT LEAST."
I SAID, "NO." AND THAT WAS THE END OF IT.

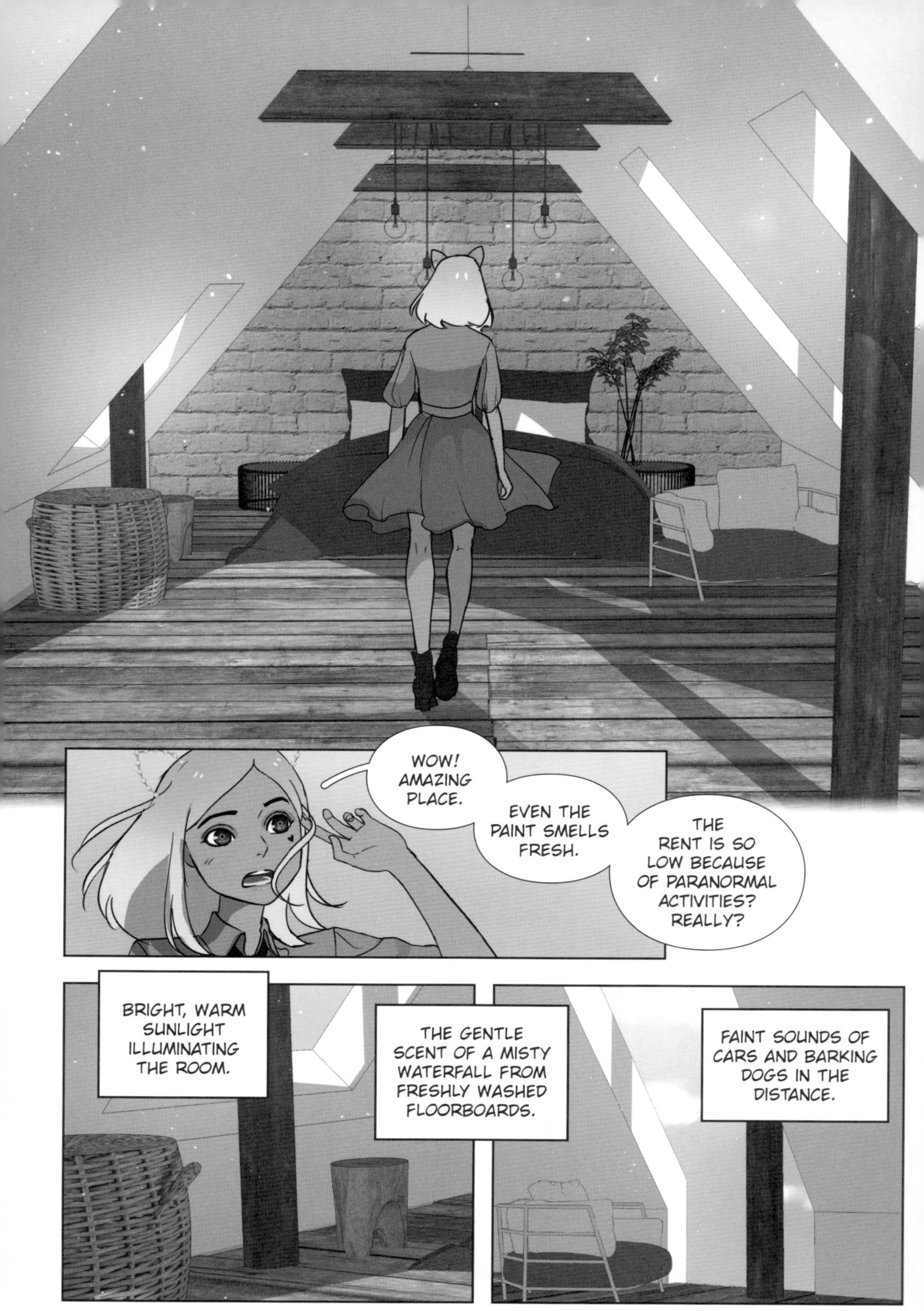

WOW! AMAZING PLACE.
EVEN THE PAINT SMELLS FRESH.
THE RENT IS SO LOW BECAUSE OF PARANORMAL ACTIVITIES? REALLY?
BRIGHT, WARM SUNLIGHT ILLUMINATING THE ROOM.
THE GENTLE SCENT OF A MISTY WATERFALL FROM FRESHLY WASHED FLOORBOARDS.
FAINT SOUNDS OF CARS AND BARKING DOGS IN THE DISTANCE.

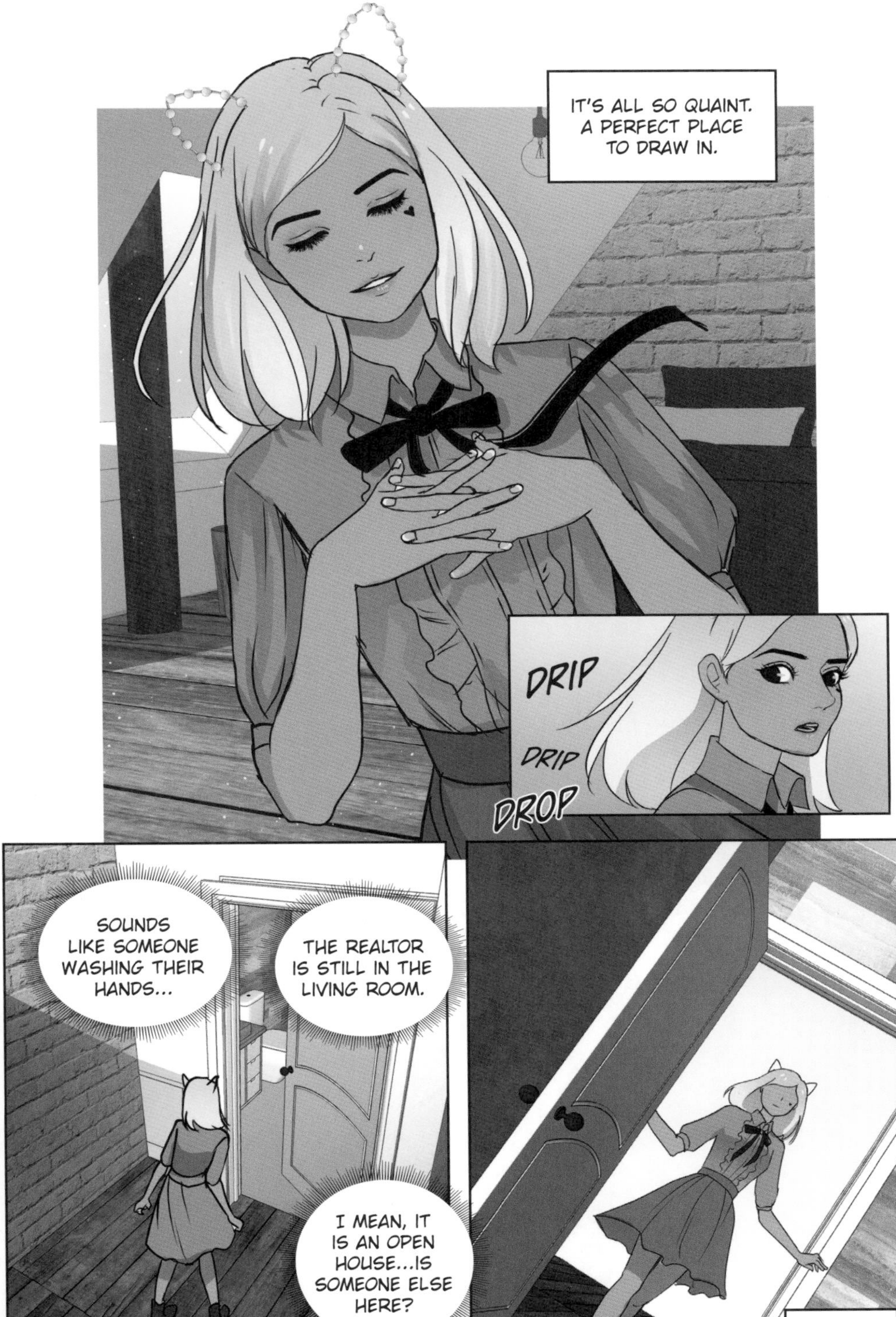
IT'S ALL SO QUAINT. A PERFECT PLACE TO DRAW IN.
DRIP
DRIP
DROP
SOUNDS LIKE SOMEONE WASHING THEIR HANDS...
THE REALTOR IS STILL IN THE LIVING ROOM.
I MEAN, IT IS AN OPEN HOUSE...IS SOMEONE ELSE HERE?
EMPTY.

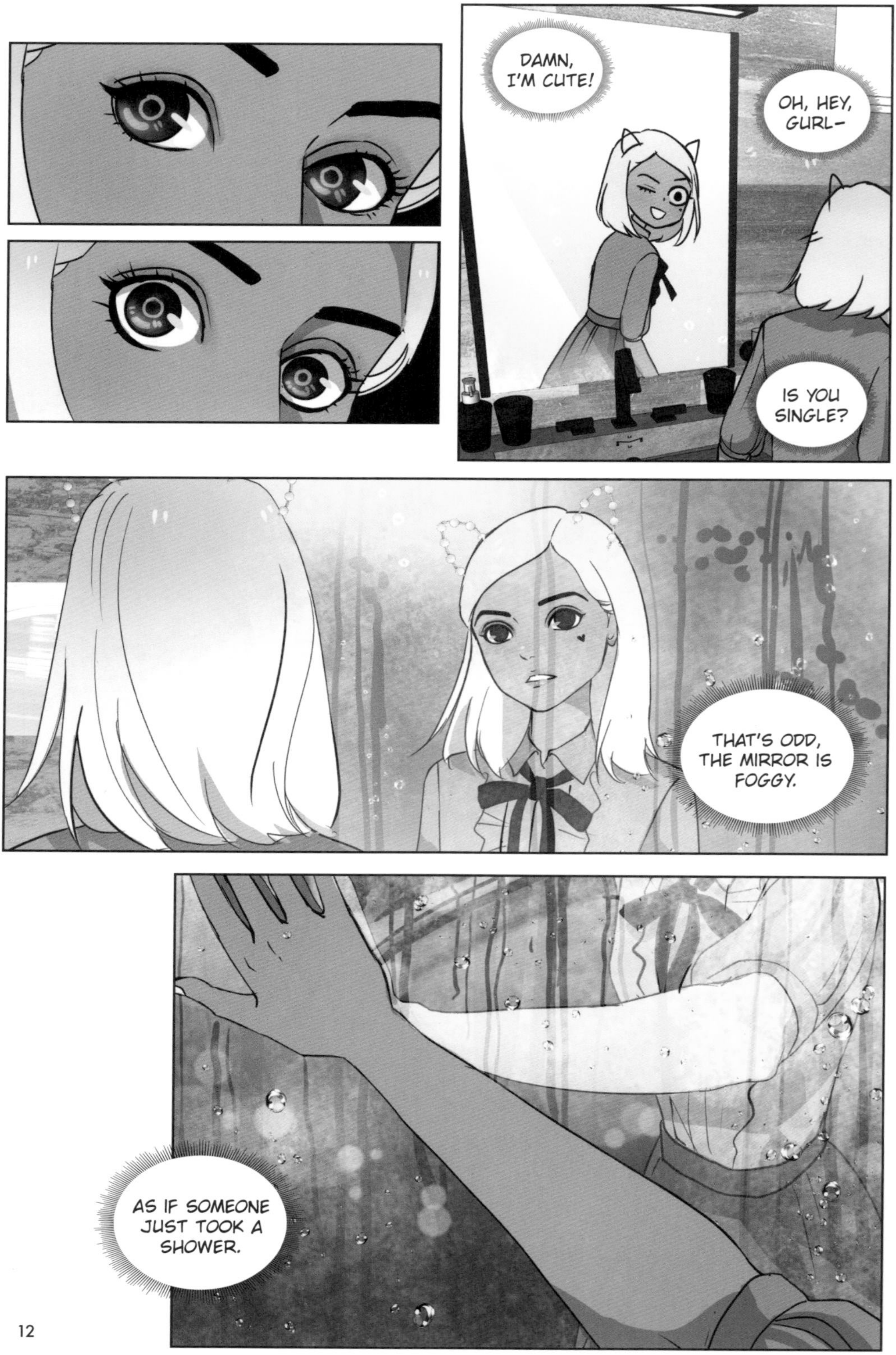
DAMN, I'M CUTE!
OH, HEY, GURL-
IS YOU SINGLE?
THAT'S ODD, THE MIRROR IS FOGGY.
AS IF SOMEONE JUST TOOK A SHOWER.

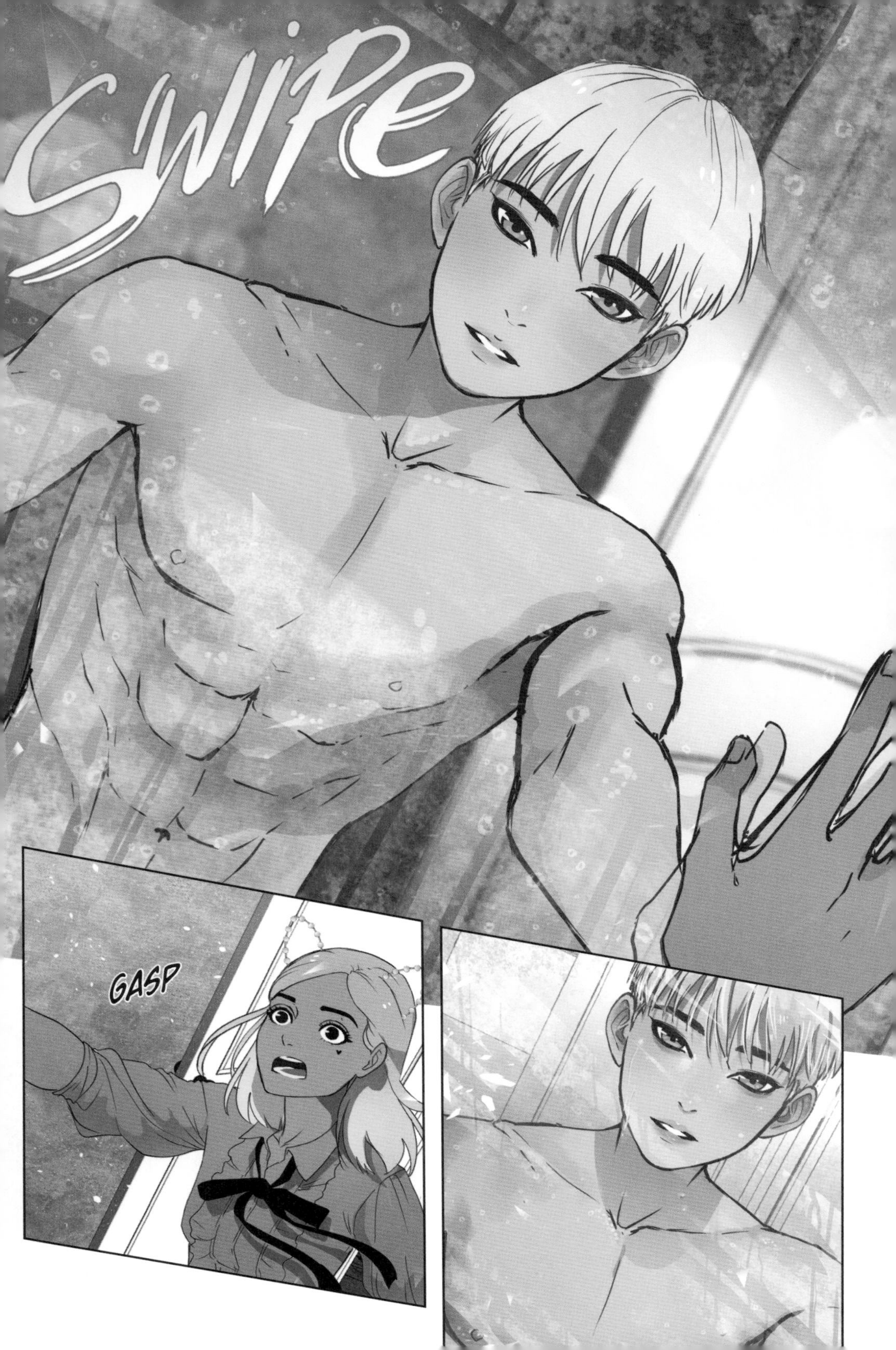
SWIPE
GASP

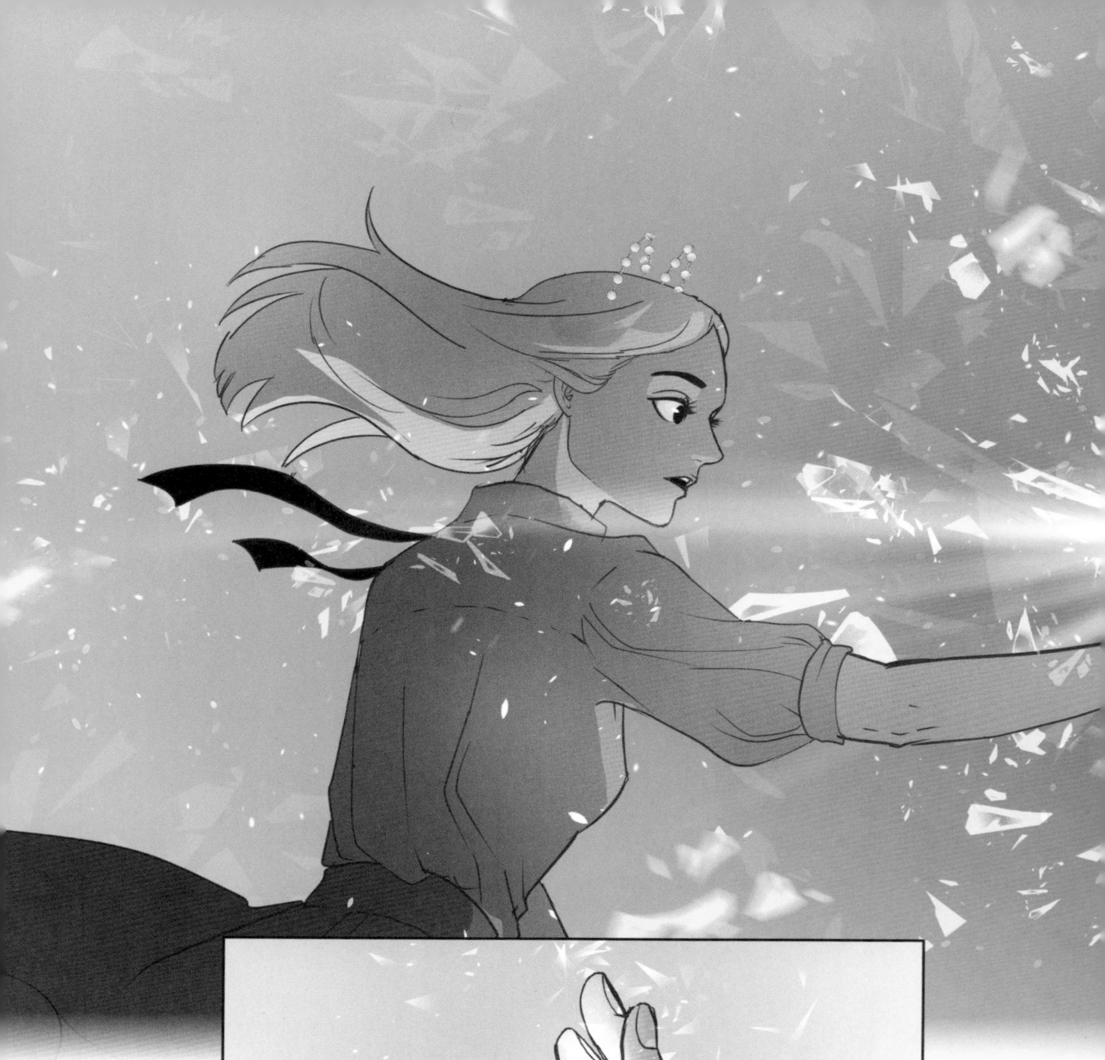

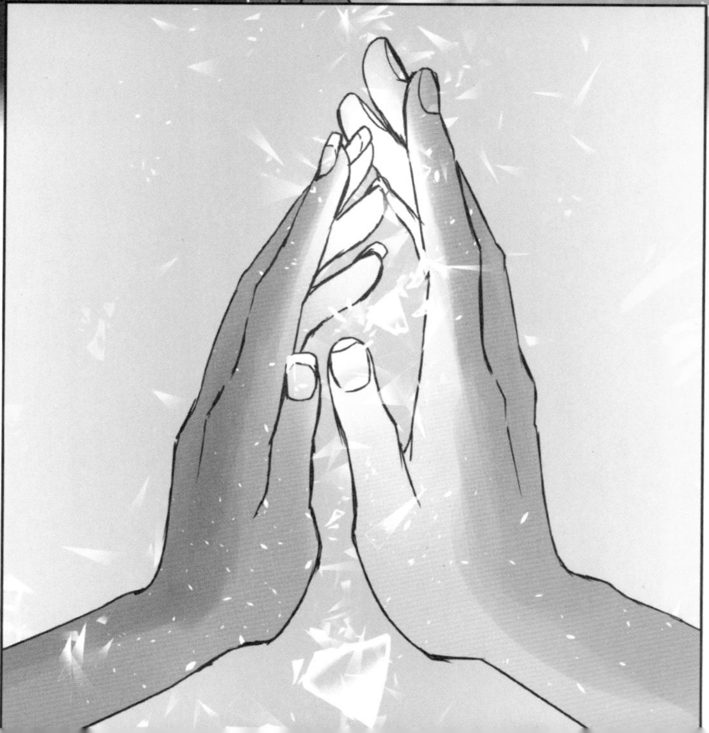

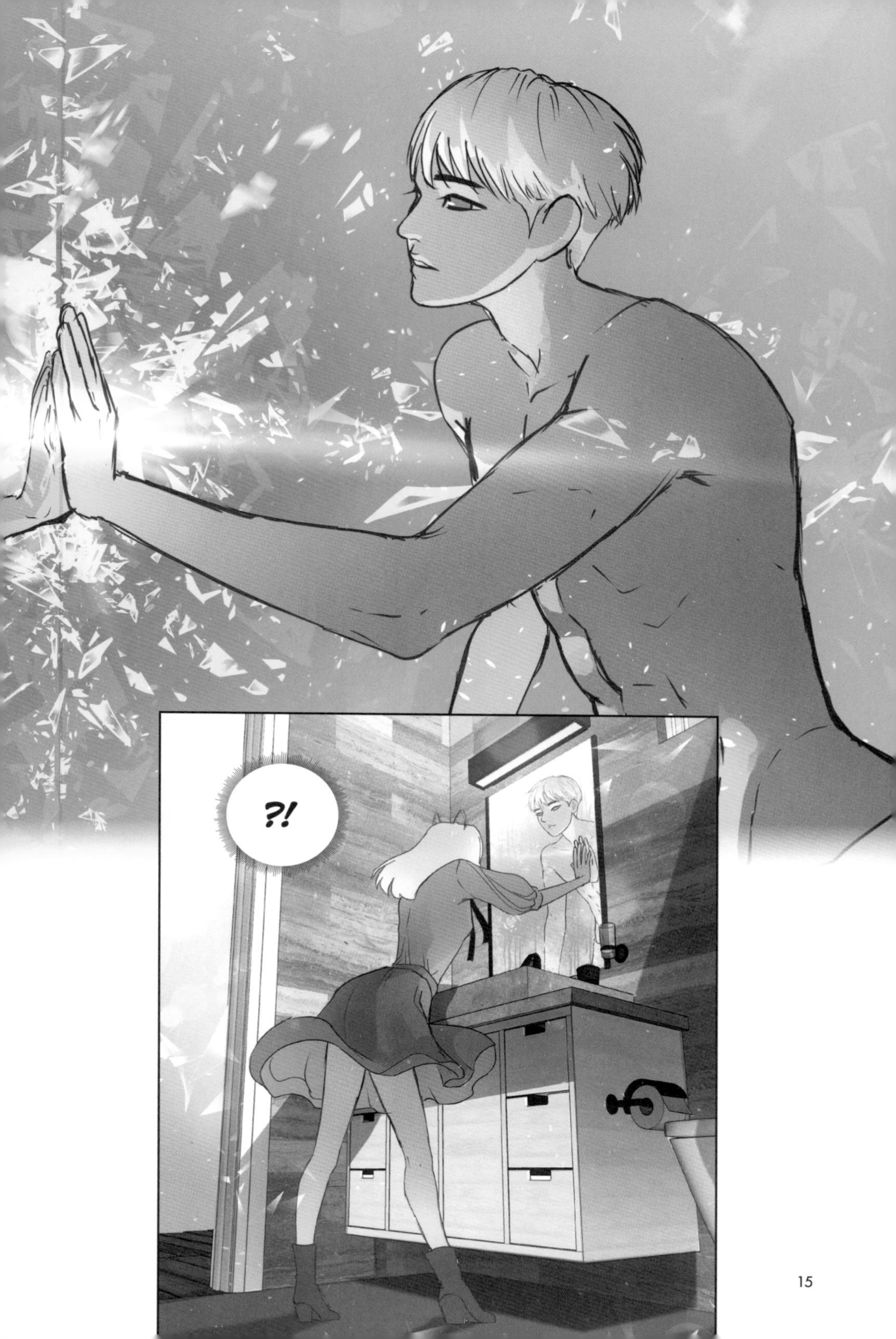
?!

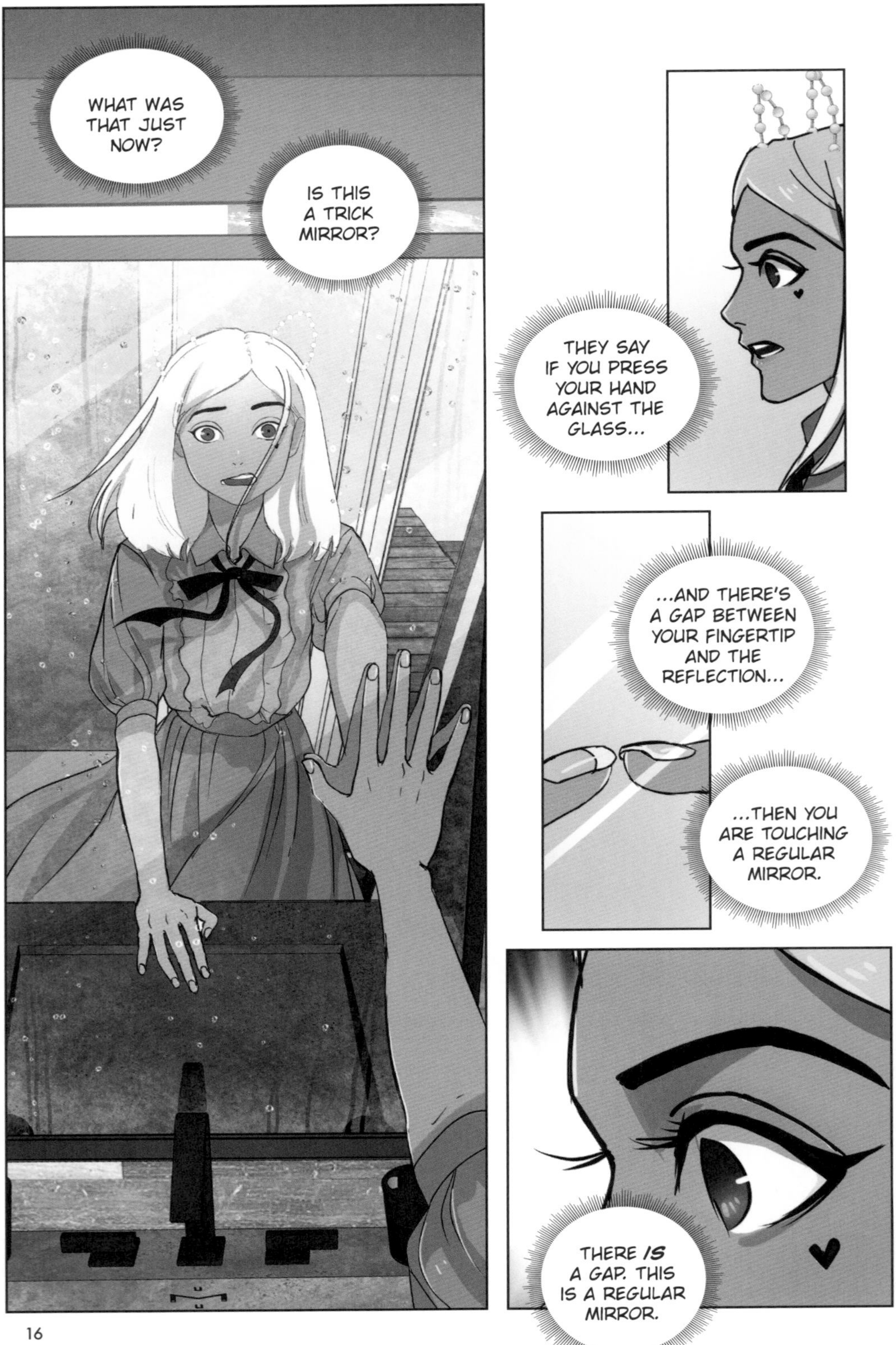
WHAT WAS THAT JUST NOW?
IS THIS A TRICK MIRROR?
THEY SAY IF YOU PRESS YOUR HAND AGAINST THE GLASS...
...AND THERE'S A GAP BETWEEN YOUR FINGERTIP AND THE REFLECTION...
...THEN YOU ARE TOUCHING A REGULAR MIRROR.
THERE *IS* A GAP. THIS IS A REGULAR MIRROR.

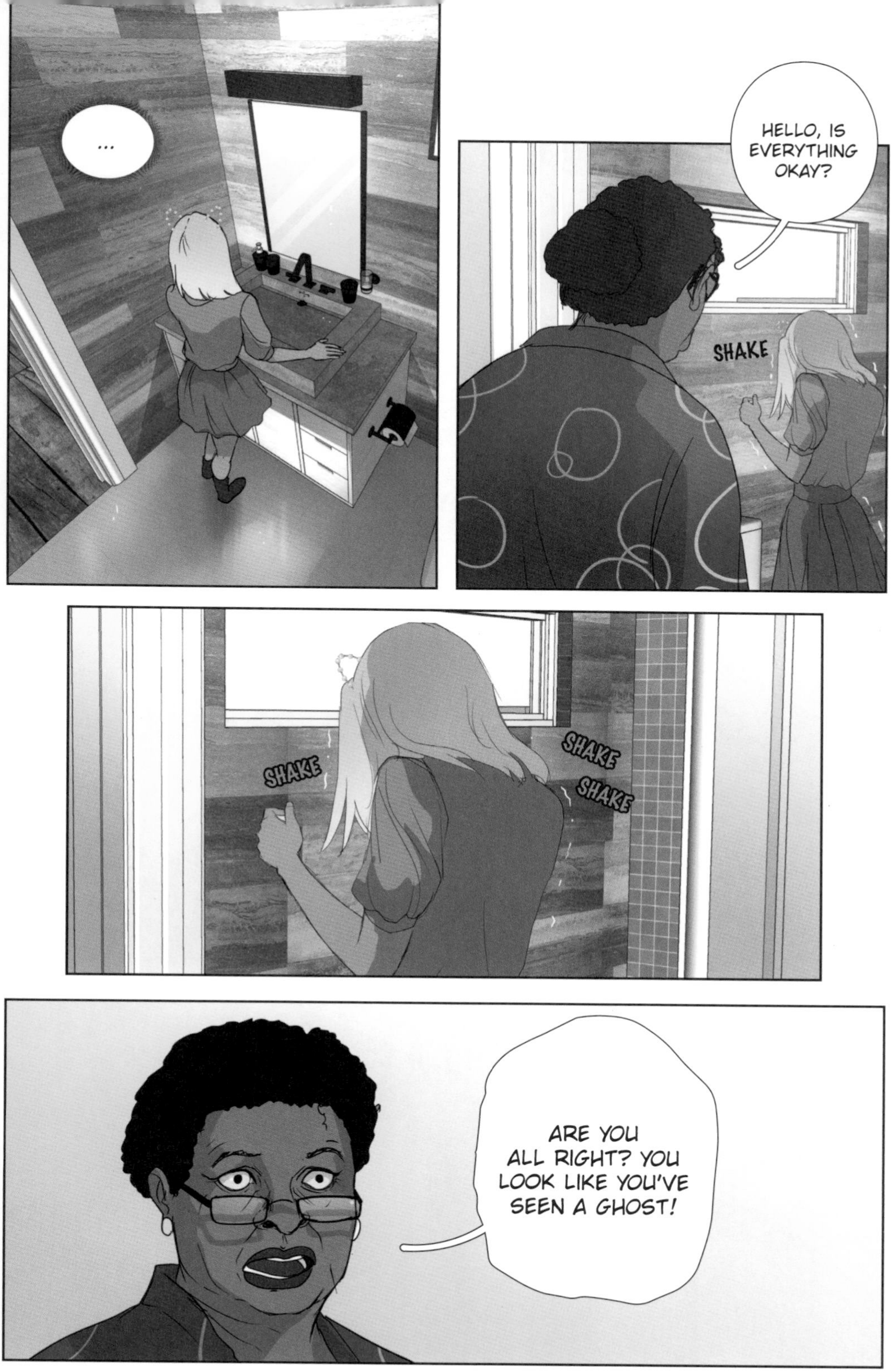
...
HELLO, IS EVERYTHING OKAY?
SHAKE
SHAKE
SHAKE
SHAKE
ARE YOU ALL RIGHT? YOU LOOK LIKE YOU'VE SEEN A GHOST!

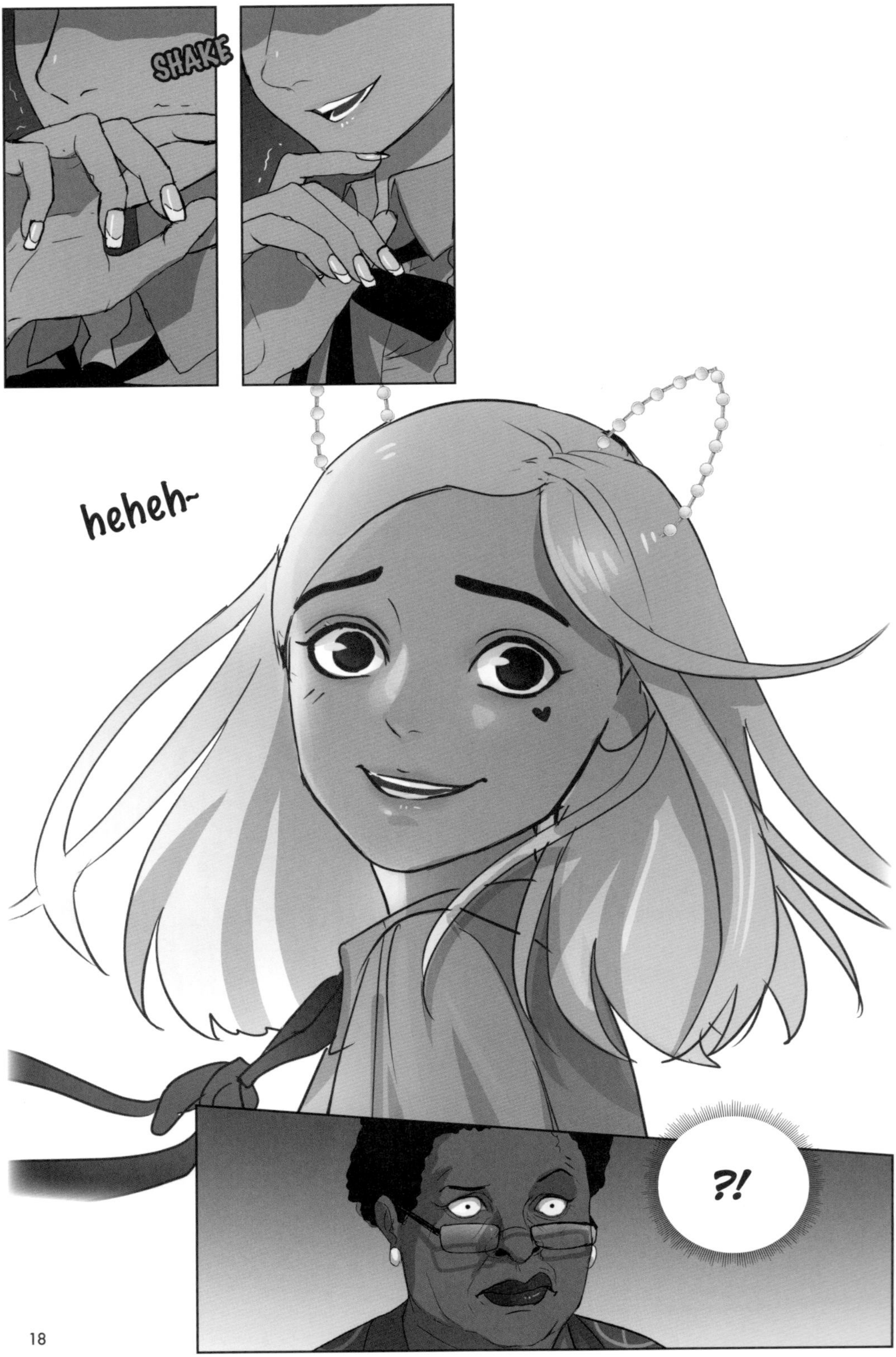
SHAKE
heheh-
?!

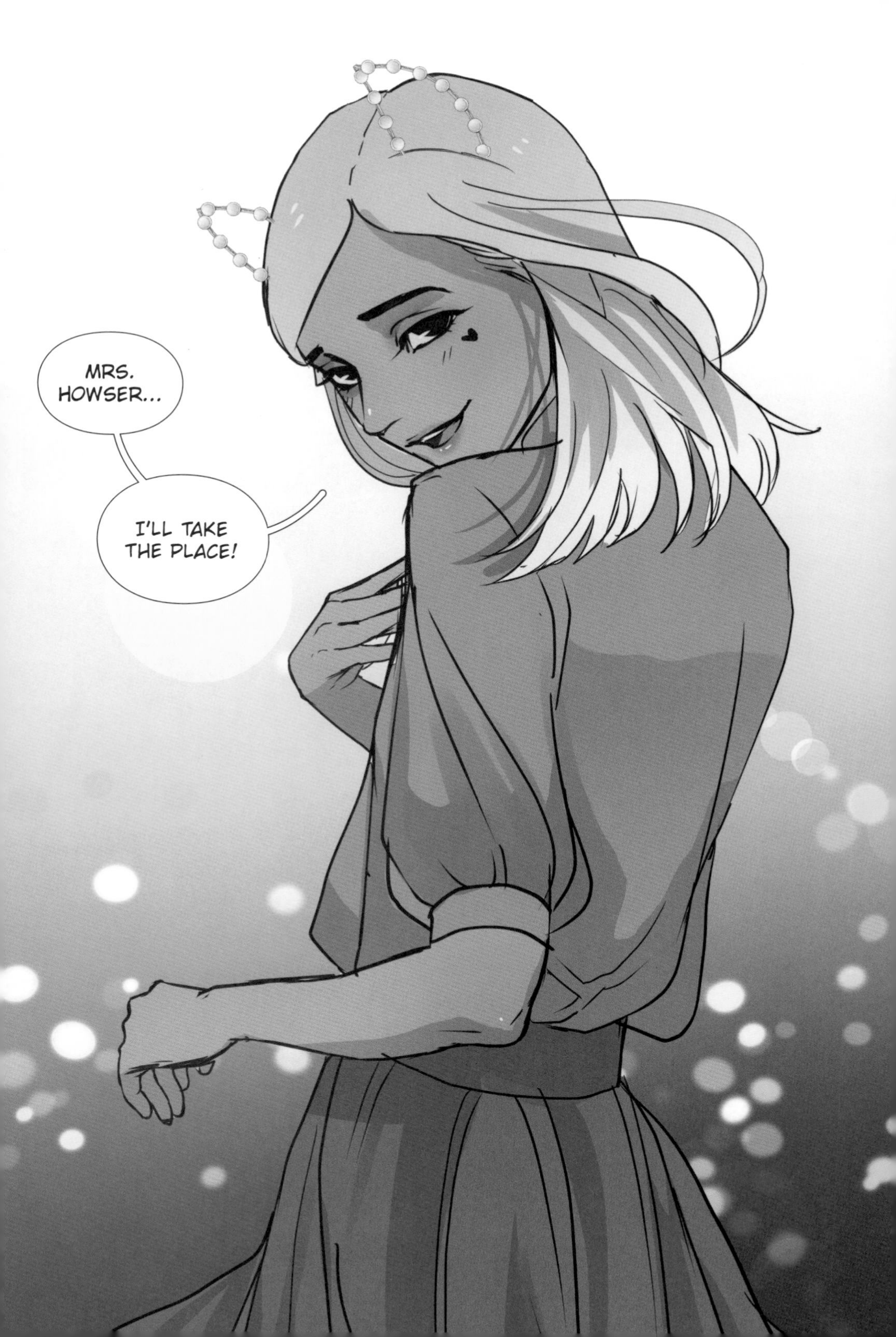
MRS. HOWSER...
I'LL TAKE THE PLACE!

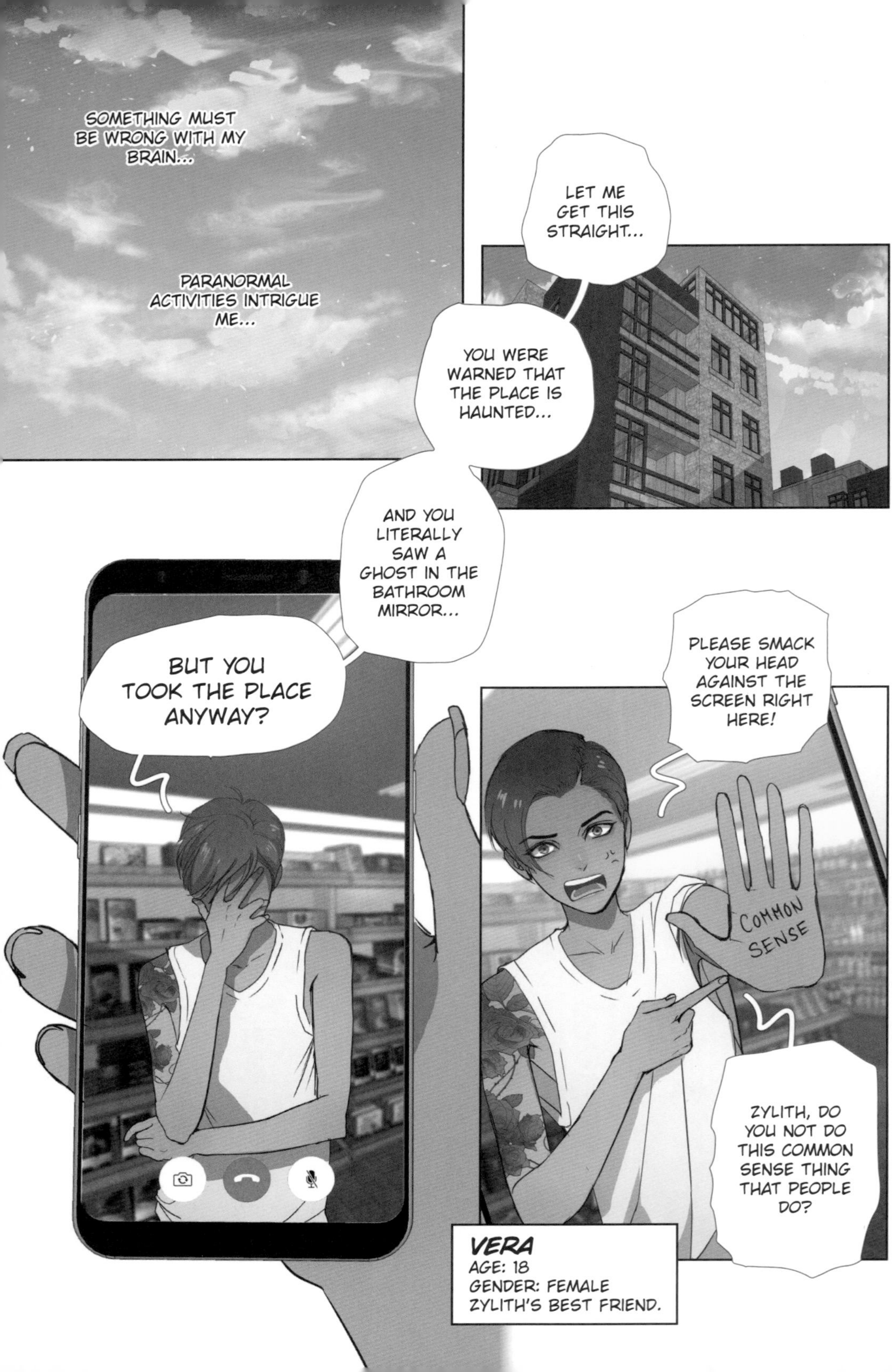
SOMETHING MUST BE WRONG WITH MY BRAIN...
PARANORMAL ACTIVITIES INTRIGUE ME...
LET ME GET THIS STRAIGHT...
YOU WERE WARNED THAT THE PLACE IS HAUNTED...
AND YOU LITERALLY SAW A GHOST IN THE BATHROOM MIRROR...
BUT YOU TOOK THE PLACE ANYWAY?
PLEASE SMACK YOUR HEAD AGAINST THE SCREEN RIGHT HERE!
COMMON SENSE
ZYLITH, DO YOU NOT DO THIS COMMON SENSE THING THAT PEOPLE DO?
VERA
AGE: 18
GENDER: FEMALE
ZYLITH'S BEST FRIEND.

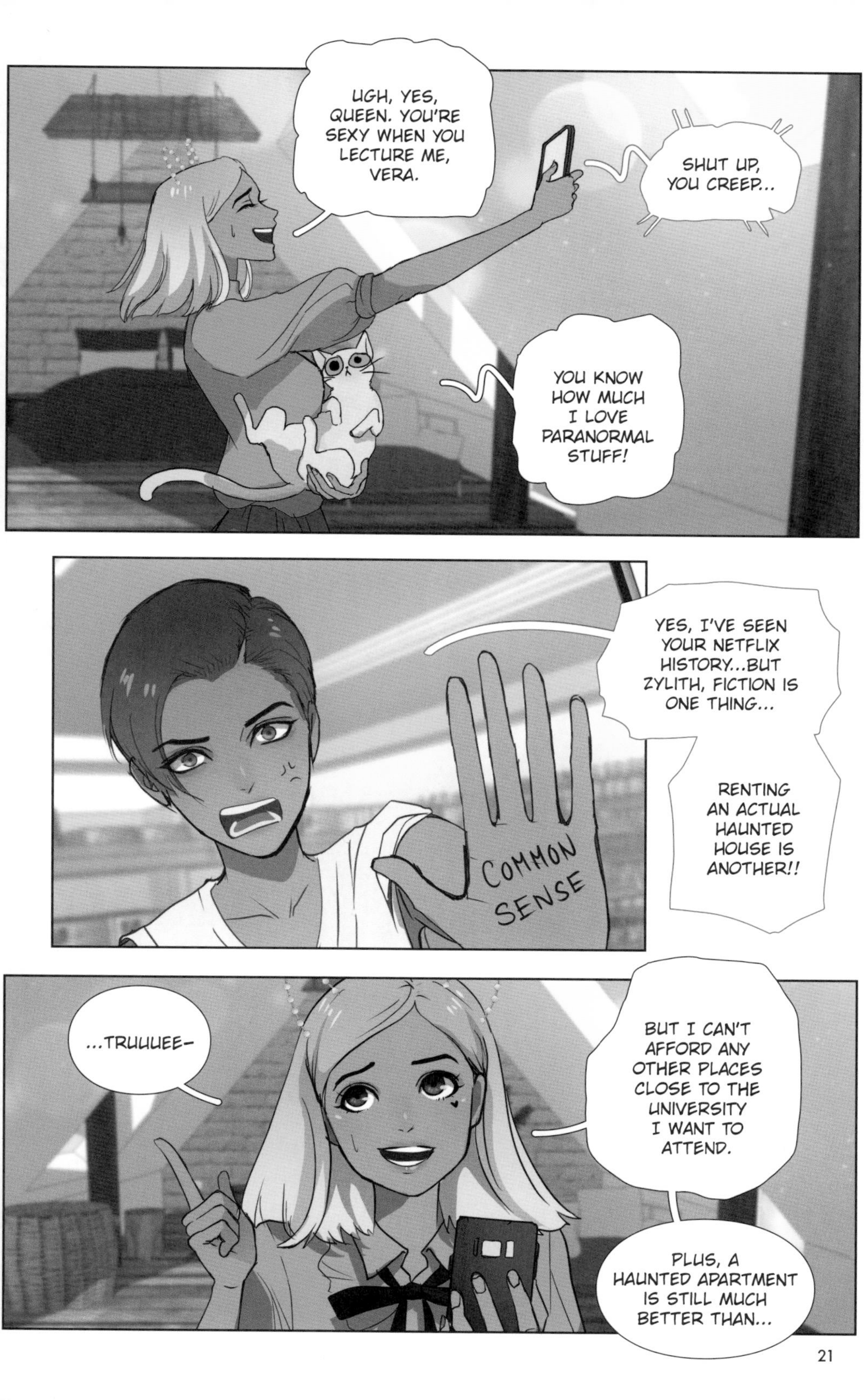
UGH, YES, QUEEN. YOU'RE SEXY WHEN YOU LECTURE ME, VERA.
SHUT UP, YOU CREEP...
YOU KNOW HOW MUCH I LOVE PARANORMAL STUFF!
YES, I'VE SEEN YOUR NETFLIX HISTORY...BUT ZYLITH, FICTION IS ONE THING...
COMMON SENSE
RENTING AN ACTUAL HAUNTED HOUSE IS ANOTHER!!
...TRUUUEE-
BUT I CAN'T AFFORD ANY OTHER PLACES CLOSE TO THE UNIVERSITY I WANT TO ATTEND.
PLUS, A HAUNTED APARTMENT IS STILL MUCH BETTER THAN...

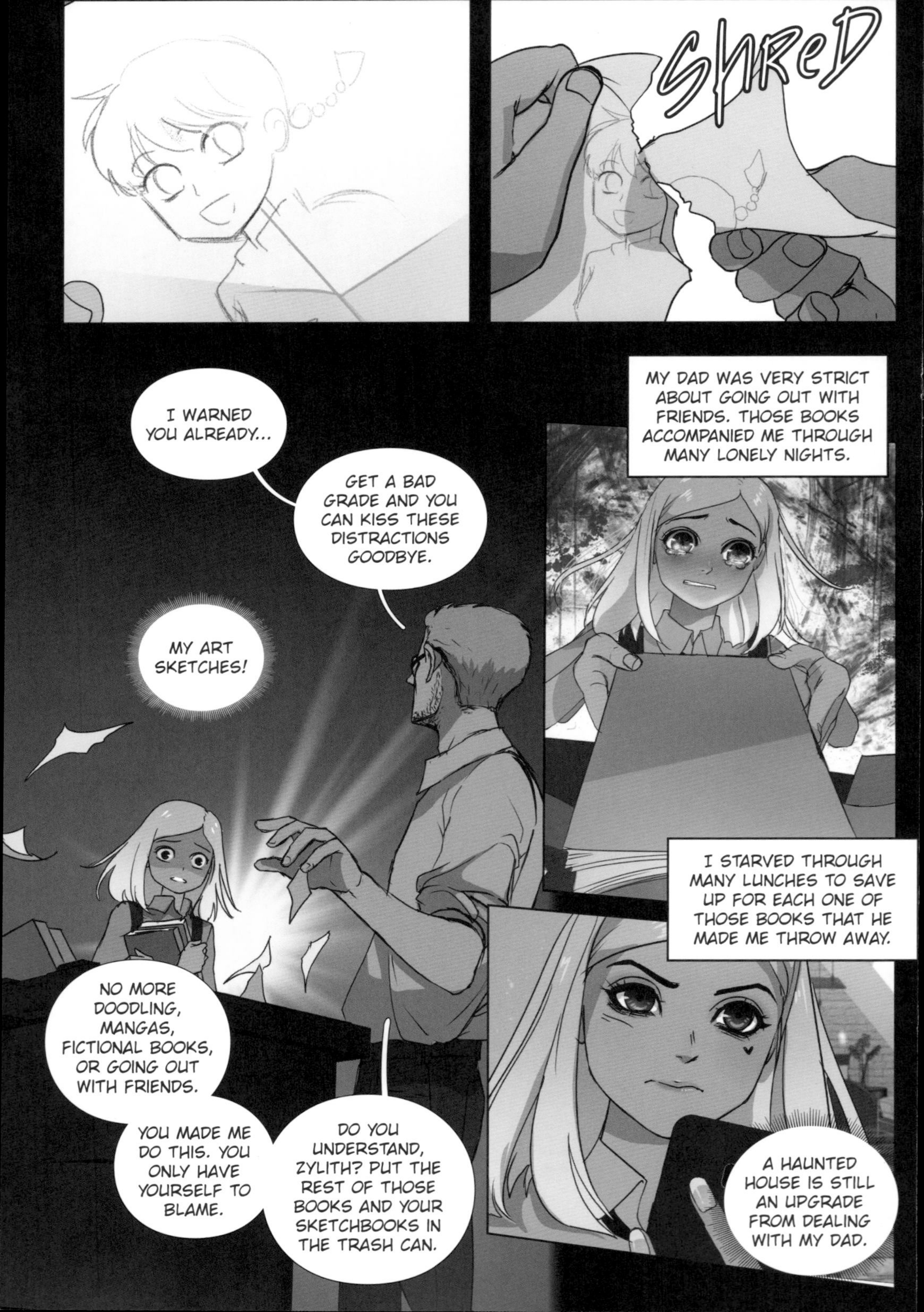
SHRED
I WARNED YOU ALREADY...
GET A BAD GRADE AND YOU CAN KISS THESE DISTRACTIONS GOODBYE.
MY ART SKETCHES!
MY DAD WAS VERY STRICT ABOUT GOING OUT WITH FRIENDS. THOSE BOOKS ACCOMPANIED ME THROUGH MANY LONELY NIGHTS.
I STARVED THROUGH MANY LUNCHES TO SAVE UP FOR EACH ONE OF THOSE BOOKS THAT HE MADE ME THROW AWAY.
NO MORE DOODLING, MANGAS, FICTIONAL BOOKS, OR GOING OUT WITH FRIENDS.
YOU MADE ME DO THIS. YOU ONLY HAVE YOURSELF TO BLAME.
DO YOU UNDERSTAND, ZYLITH? PUT THE REST OF THOSE BOOKS AND YOUR SKETCHBOOKS IN THE TRASH CAN.
A HAUNTED HOUSE IS STILL AN UPGRADE FROM DEALING WITH MY DAD.

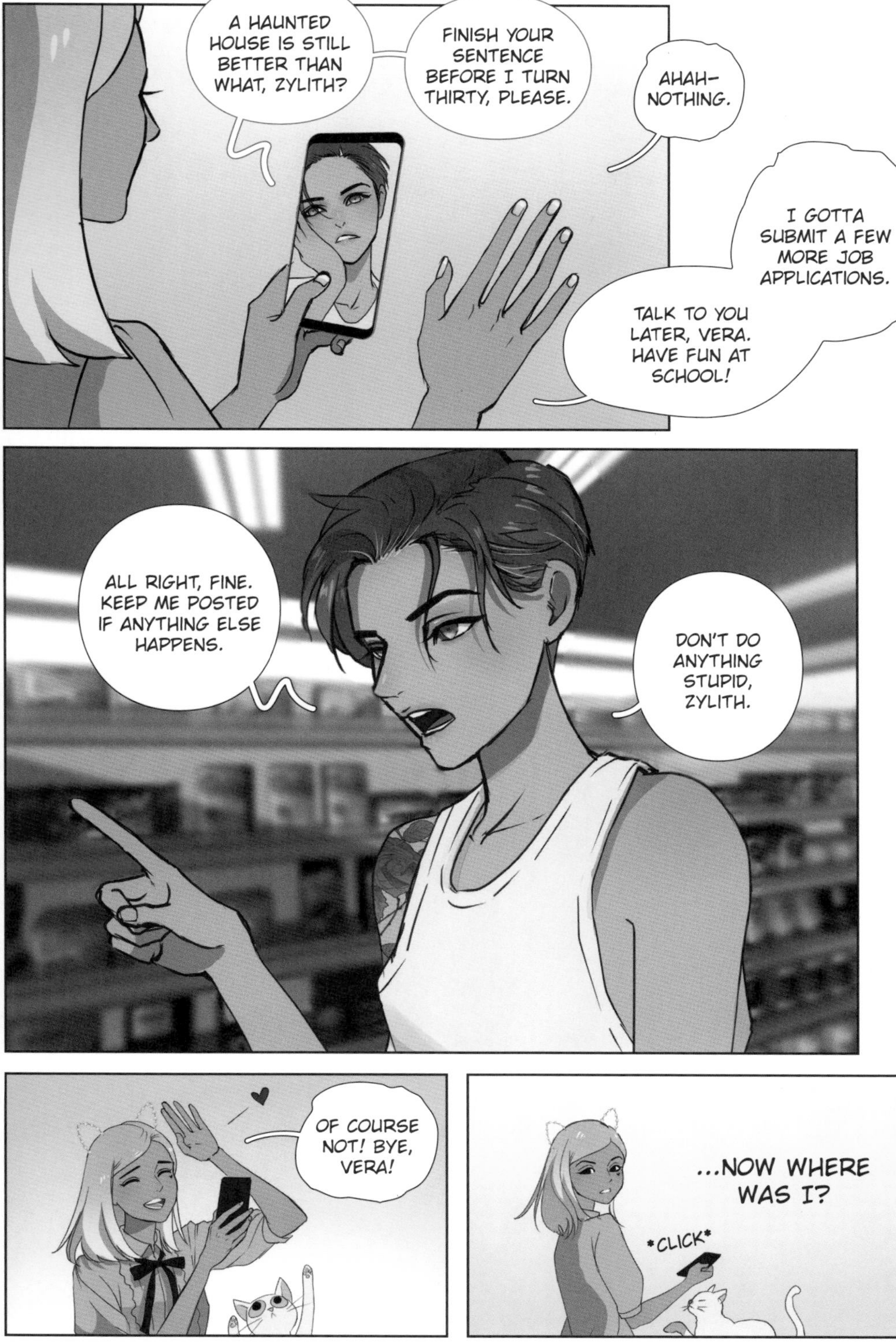
A HAUNTED HOUSE IS STILL BETTER THAN WHAT, ZYLITH?
FINISH YOUR SENTENCE BEFORE I TURN THIRTY, PLEASE.
AHAH- NOTHING.
I GOTTA SUBMIT A FEW MORE JOB APPLICATIONS.
TALK TO YOU LATER, VERA. HAVE FUN AT SCHOOL!
ALL RIGHT, FINE. KEEP ME POSTED IF ANYTHING ELSE HAPPENS.
DON'T DO ANYTHING STUPID, ZYLITH.
OF COURSE NOT! BYE, VERA!
...NOW WHERE WAS I?
CLICK

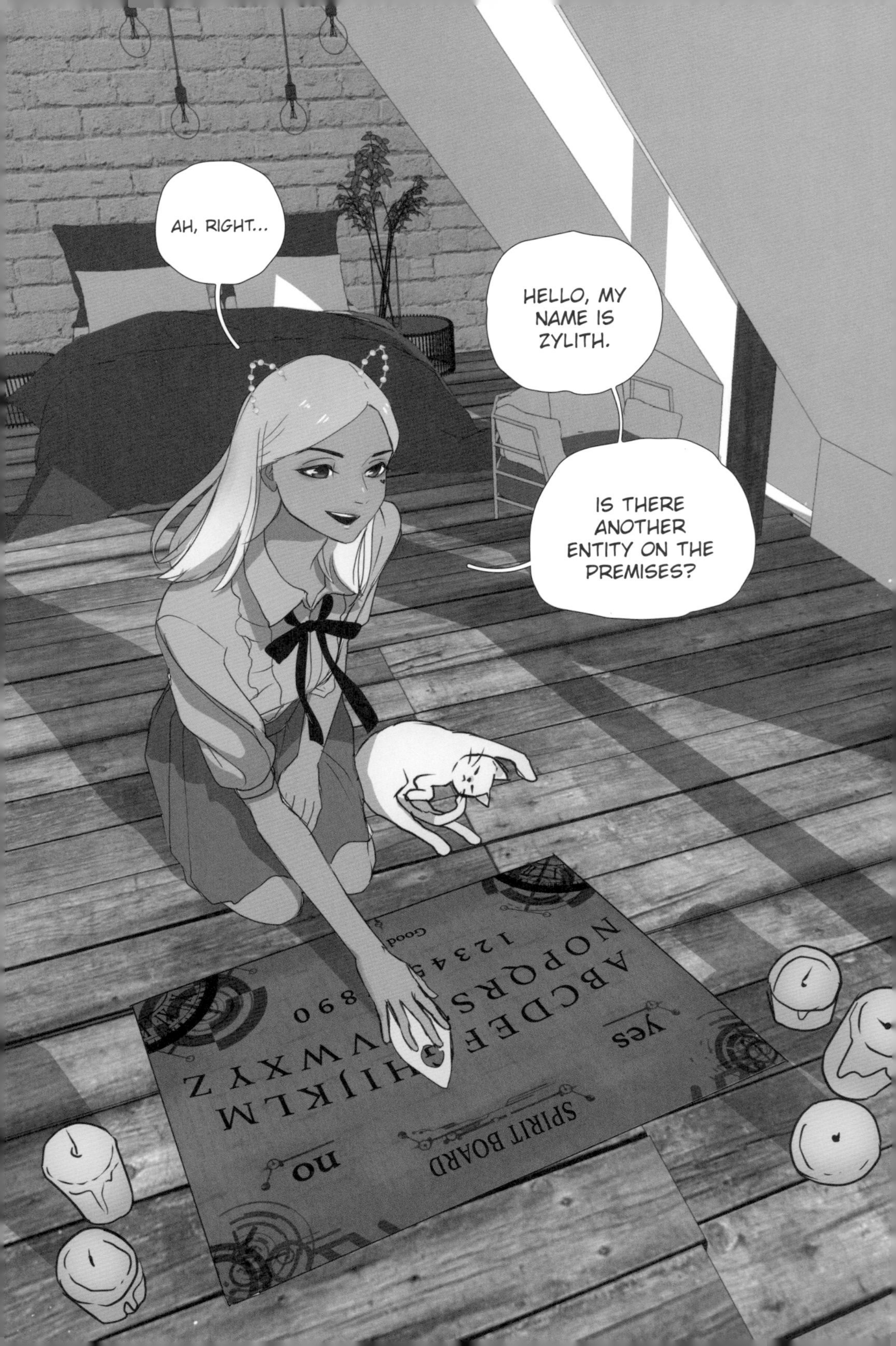
AH, RIGHT...
HELLO, MY NAME IS ZYLITH.
IS THERE ANOTHER ENTITY ON THE PREMISES?
yes
no
SPIRIT BOARD

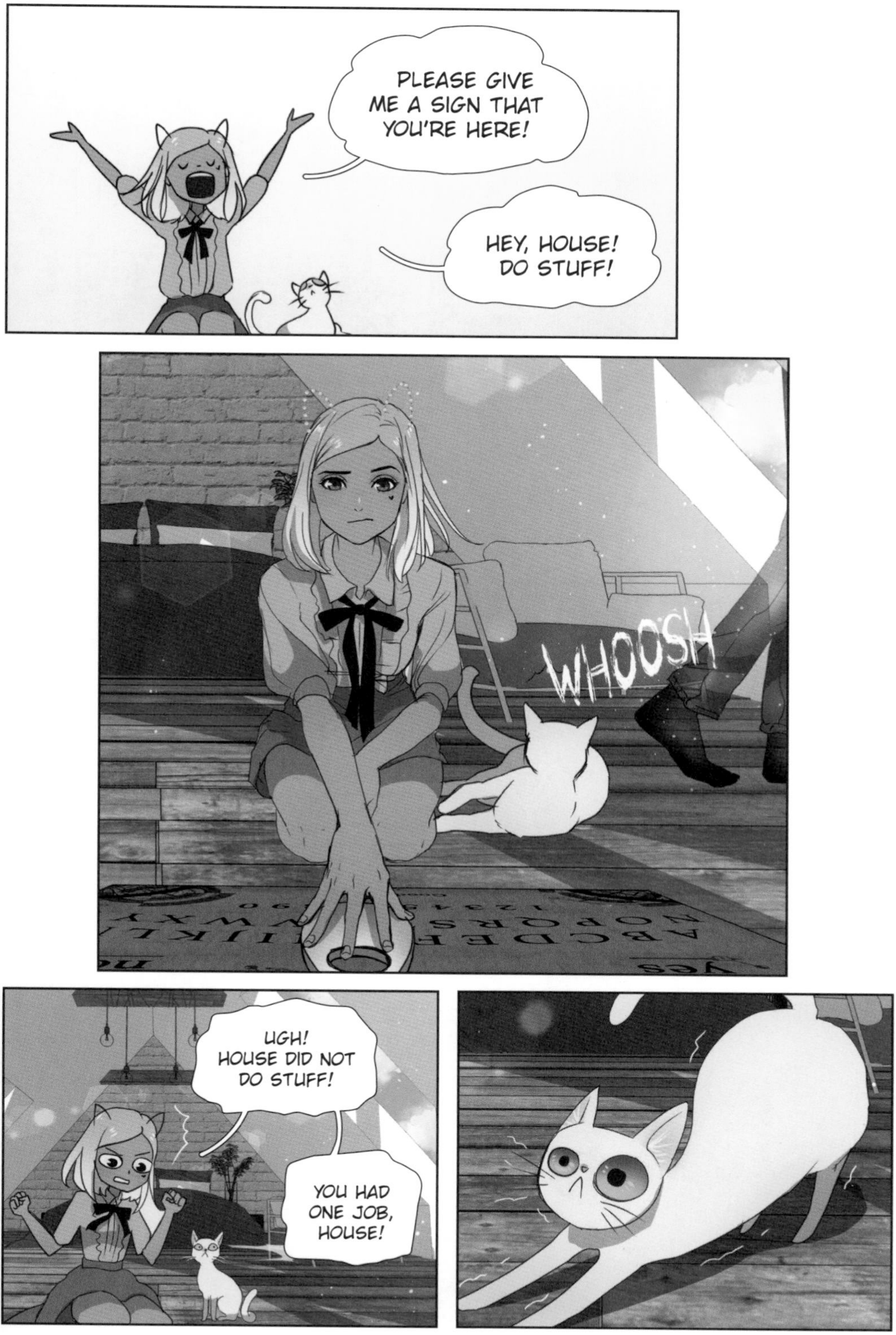
PLEASE GIVE ME A SIGN THAT YOU'RE HERE!
HEY, HOUSE! DO STUFF!
WHOOSH
UGH! HOUSE DID NOT DO STUFF!
YOU HAD ONE JOB, HOUSE!

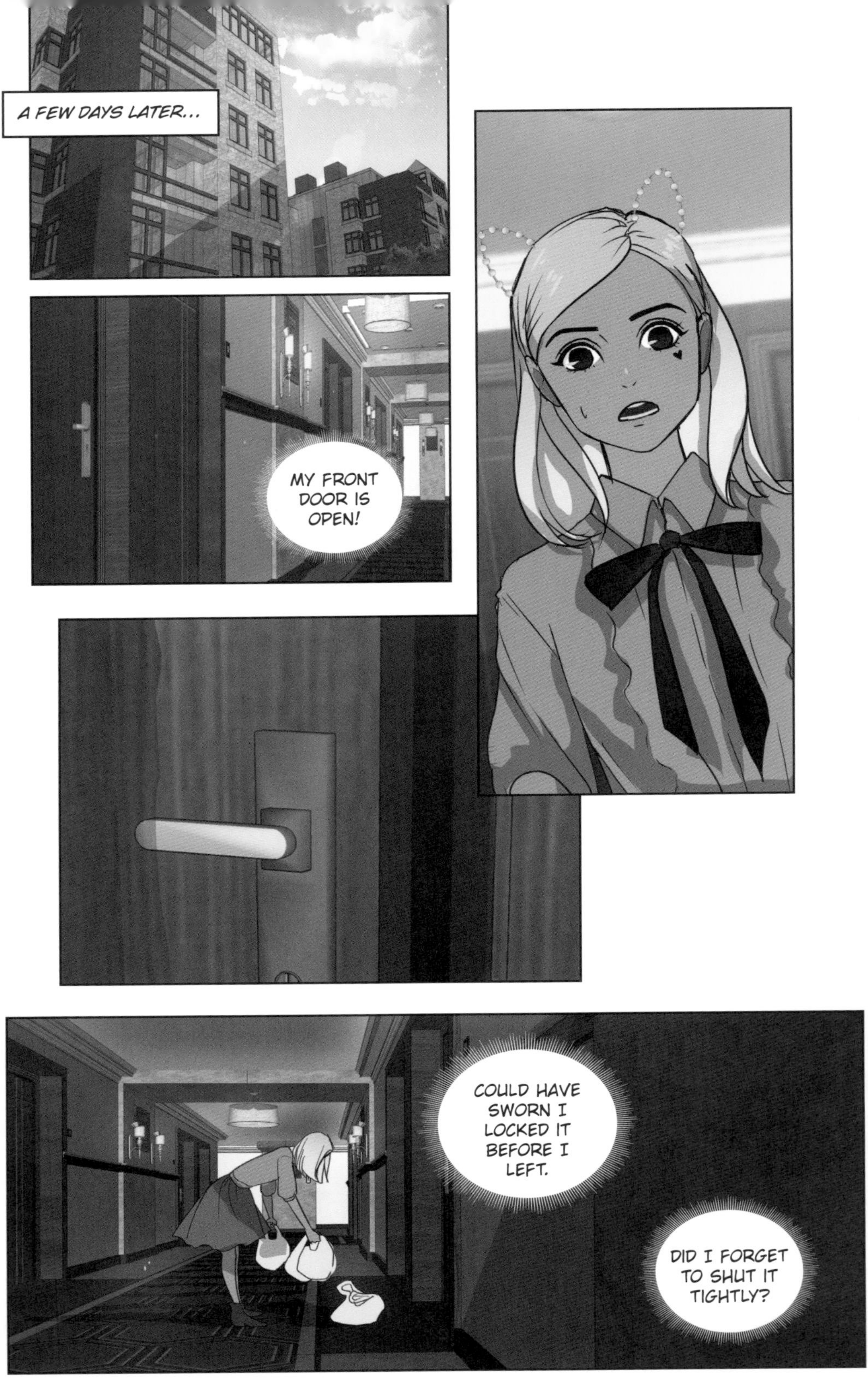
A FEW DAYS LATER...
MY FRONT DOOR IS OPEN!
COULD HAVE SWORN I LOCKED IT BEFORE I LEFT.
DID I FORGET TO SHUT IT TIGHTLY?

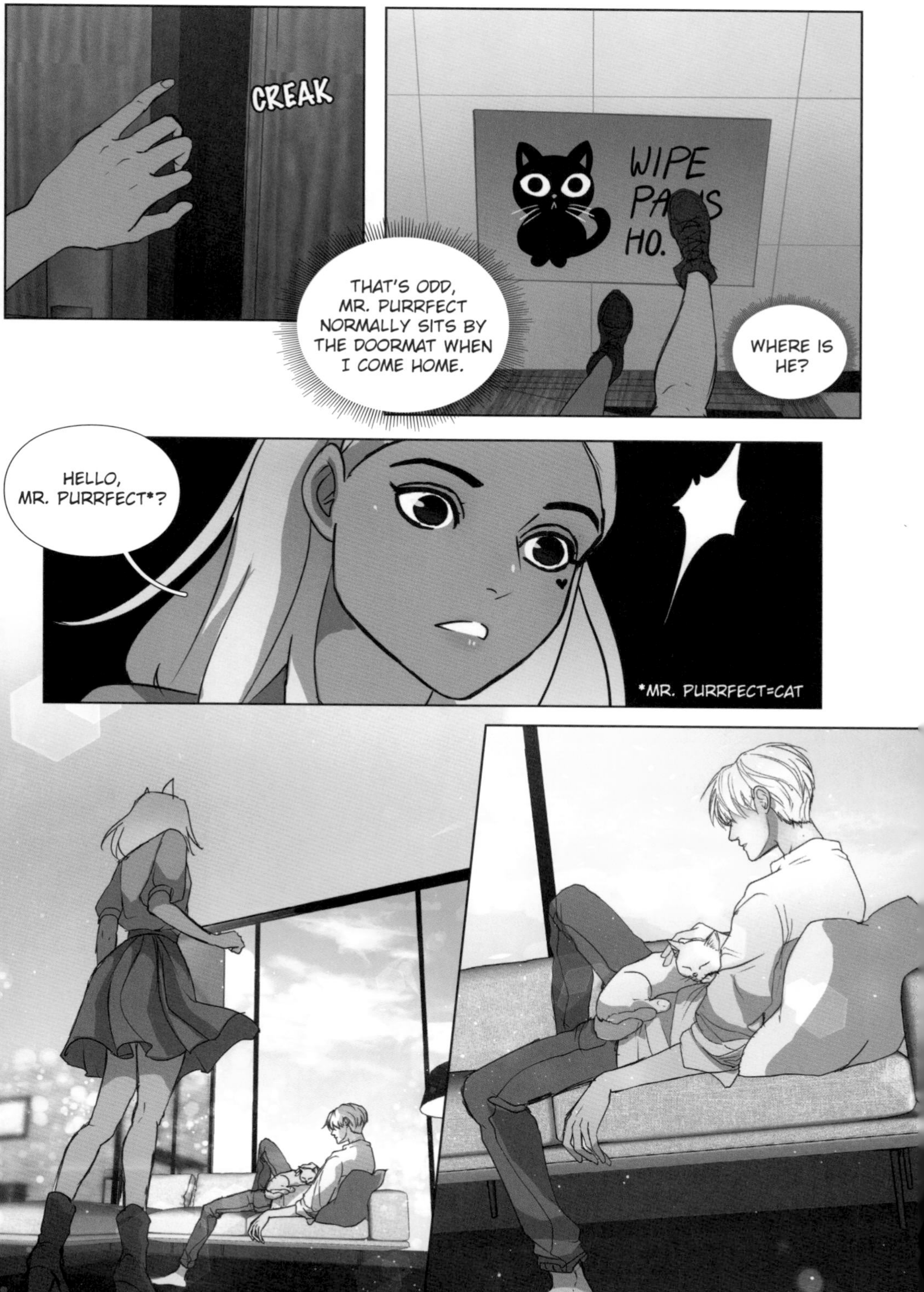
CREAK
WIPE PA S HO.
THAT'S ODD, MR. PURRFECT NORMALLY SITS BY THE DOORMAT WHEN I COME HOME.
WHERE IS HE?
HELLO, MR. PURRFECT*?
*MR. PURRFECT=CAT

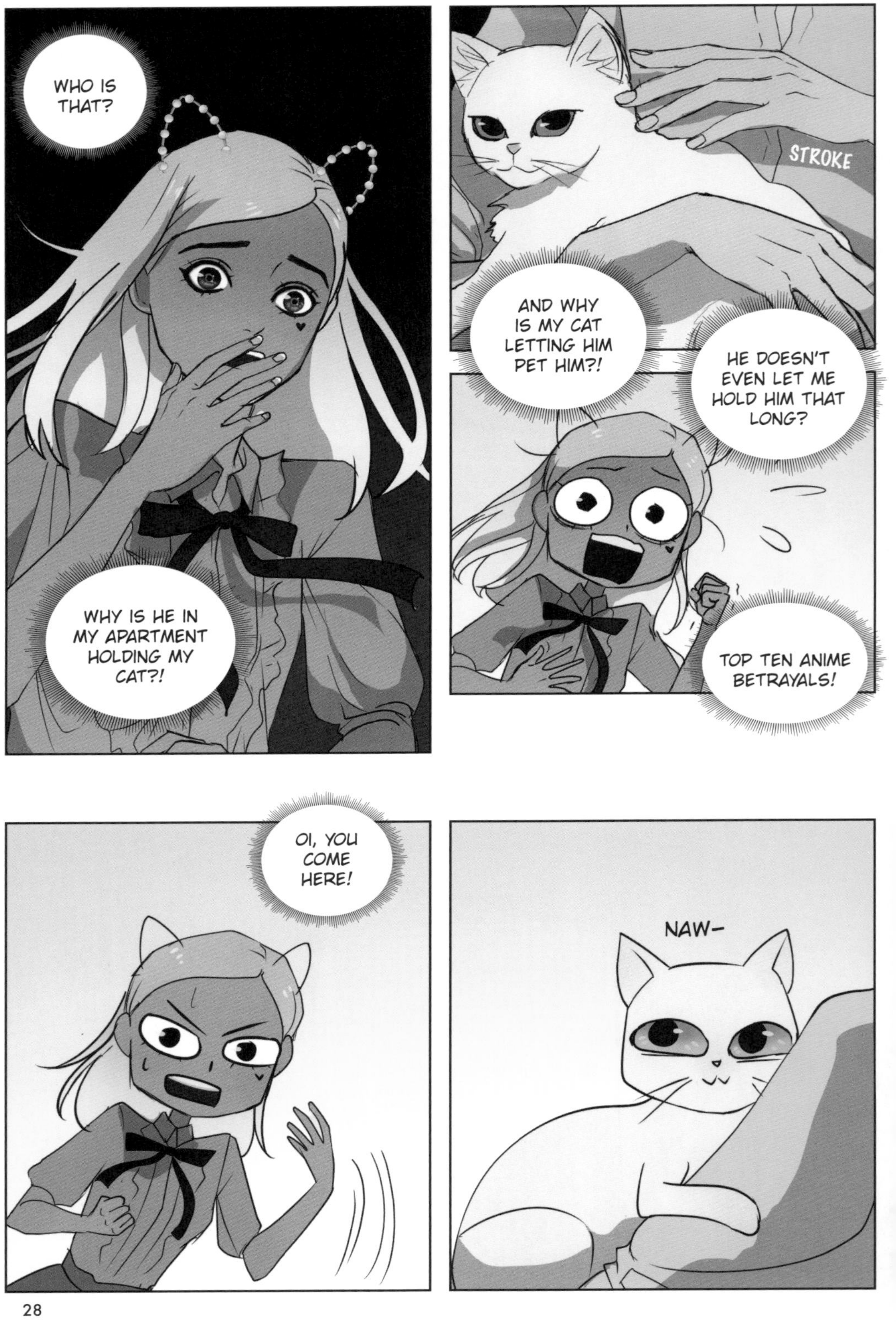
WHO IS THAT?
WHY IS HE IN MY APARTMENT HOLDING MY CAT?!
STROKE
AND WHY IS MY CAT LETTING HIM PET HIM?!
HE DOESN'T EVEN LET ME HOLD HIM THAT LONG?
TOP TEN ANIME BETRAYALS!
OI, YOU COME HERE!
NAW-

AW, C'MON! WHAT IF THAT STRANGER IS DANGEROUS?!

CALM DOWN, ZYLITH!

MAYBE HE WANDERED INTO THE WRONG APARTMENT...

MAYBE HE'S A NEW HOUSEMATE THE LANDLADY MENTIONED I MIGHT GET?

STILL! BETTER SAFE THAN SORRY!

EXCUSE ME, SIR...

WHY ARE YOU IN MY APARTMENT?

TURN

ZAAAAAMMMMMMNNNNNN—

DID A K-POP BOY BAND MEMBER ACCIDENTLY WANDER ONTO MY COUCH???

OKAY, MR. PURRFECT, I FORGIVE YOUR BETRAYAL.

IF I WERE YOU I WOULDN'T CHOOSE ME EITHER.

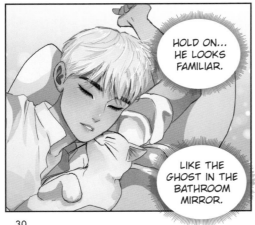

HOLD ON... HE LOOKS FAMILIAR.

LIKE THE GHOST IN THE BATHROOM MIRROR.

THEN...

...WHATEVER LIES IN FRONT OF ME...

BABUM
BABUM

...MIGHT NOT BE HUMAN??

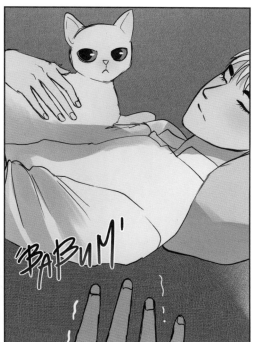

'BABUM'

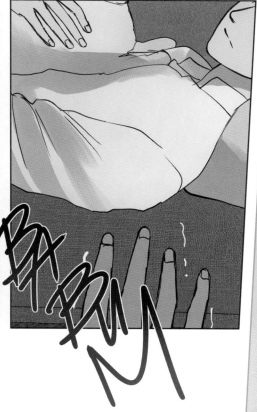

BABUM

BLINK

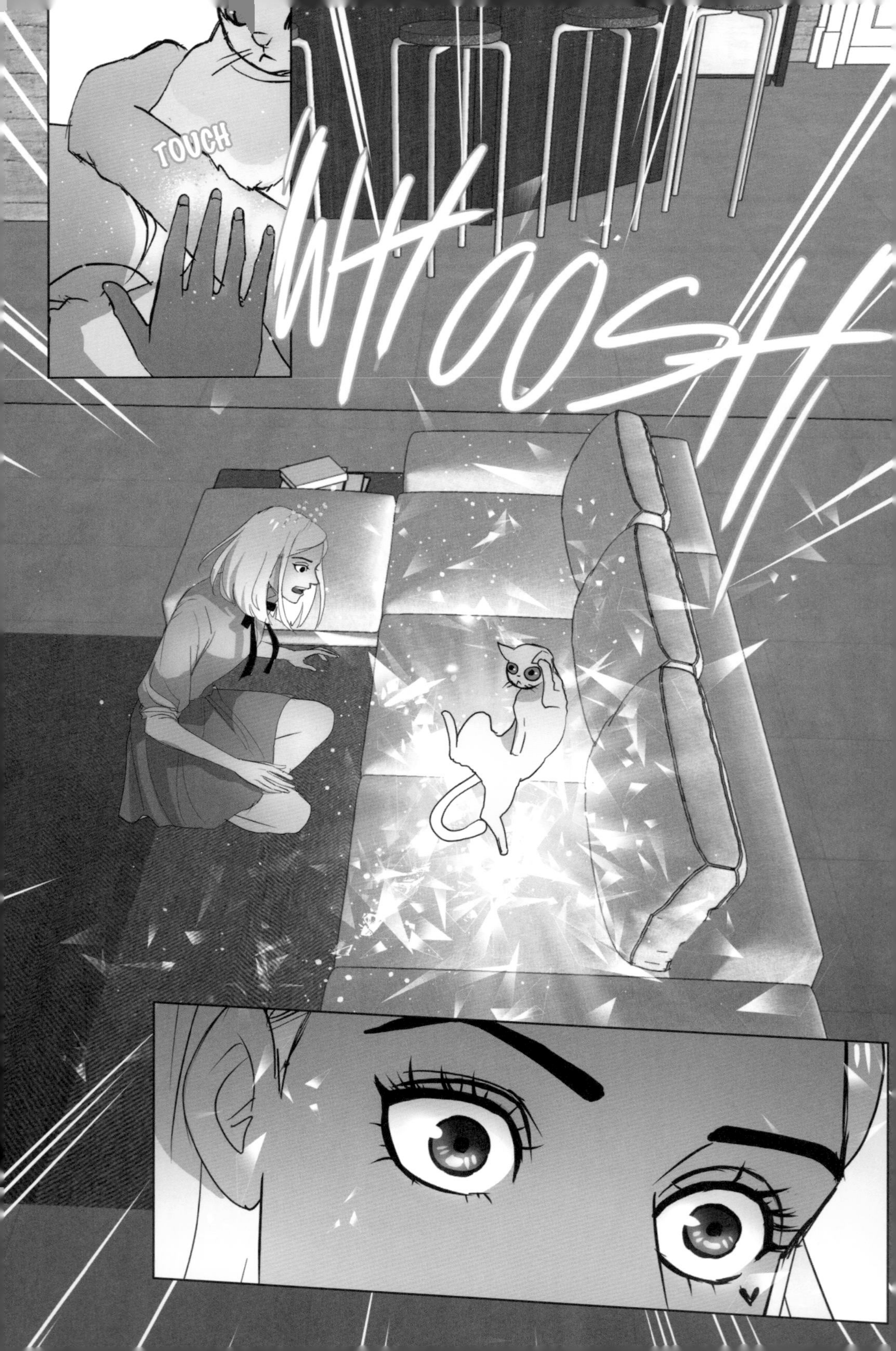
TOUCH
WHOOSH

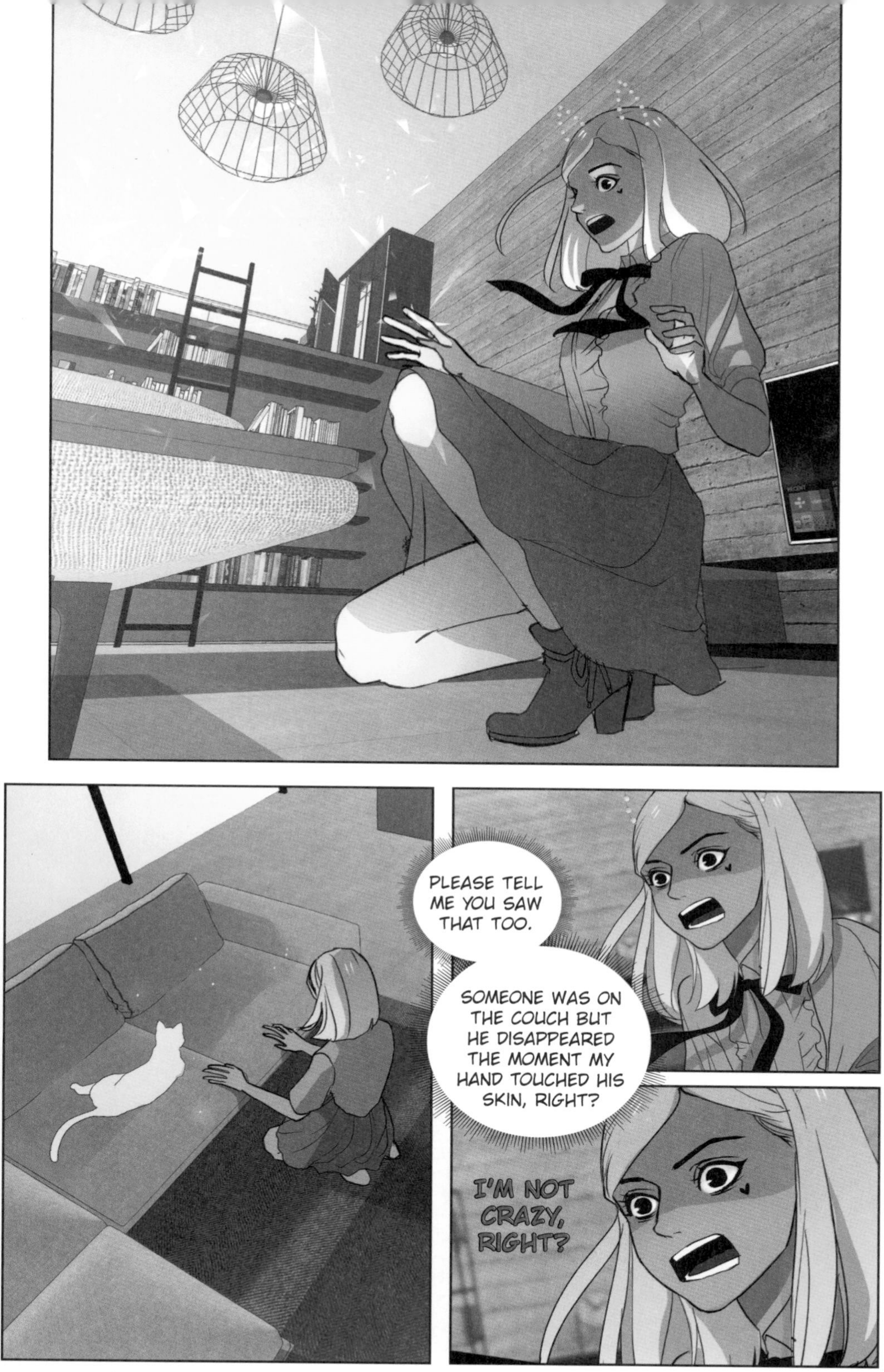
PLEASE TELL ME YOU SAW THAT TOO.
SOMEONE WAS ON THE COUCH BUT HE DISAPPEARED THE MOMENT MY HAND TOUCHED HIS SKIN, RIGHT?
I'M NOT CRAZY, RIGHT?

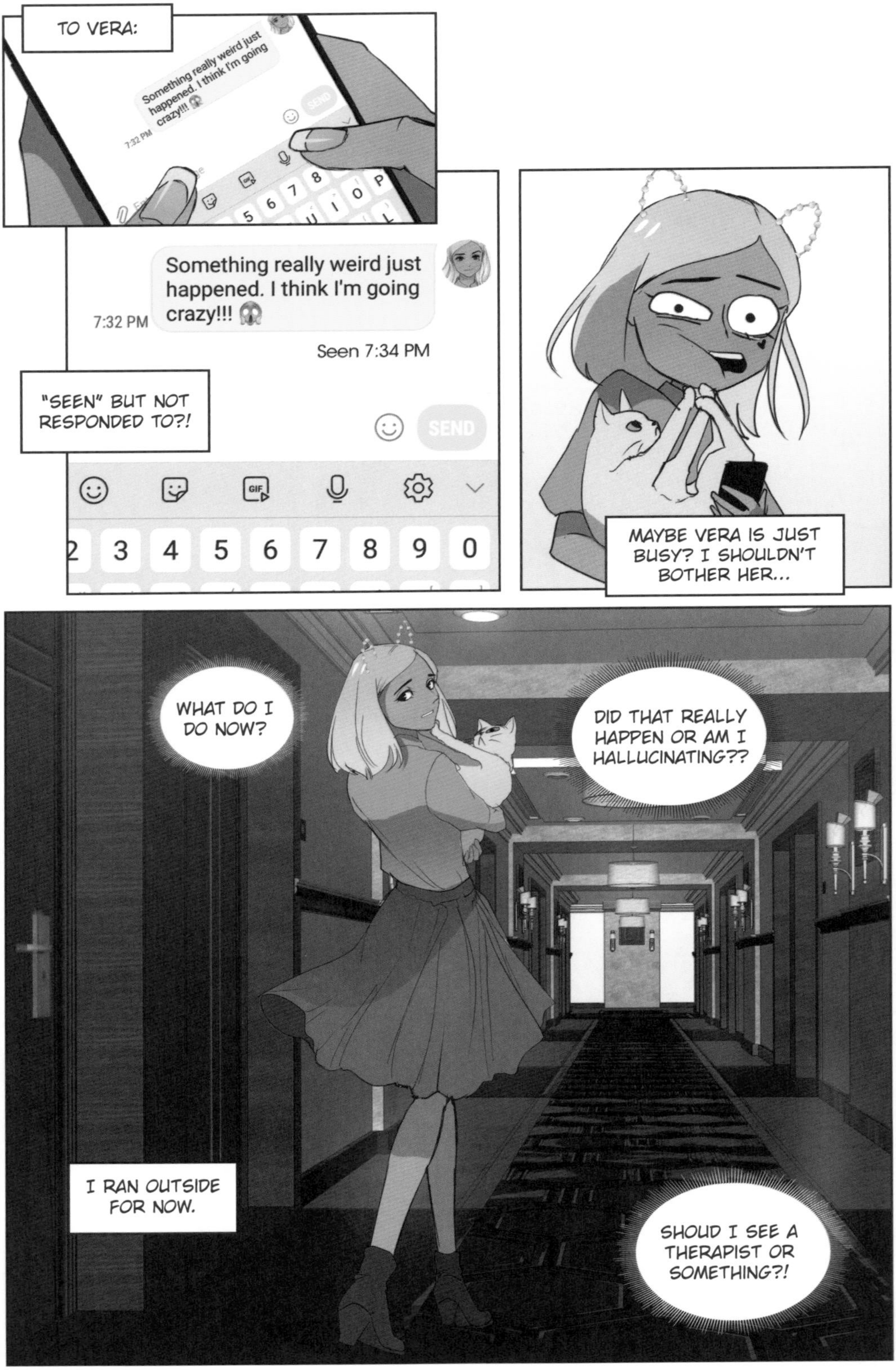
TO VERA:
Something really weird just happened. I think I'm going crazy!!!
7:32 PM
SEND
Something really weird just happened. I think I'm going crazy!!! 😱
7:32 PM
Seen 7:34 PM
"SEEN" BUT NOT RESPONDED TO?!
SEND
GIF
2 3 4 5 6 7 8 9 0
MAYBE VERA IS JUST BUSY? I SHOULDN'T BOTHER HER...
WHAT DO I DO NOW?
DID THAT REALLY HAPPEN OR AM I HALLUCINATING??
I RAN OUTSIDE FOR NOW.
SHOUD I SEE A THERAPIST OR SOMETHING?!

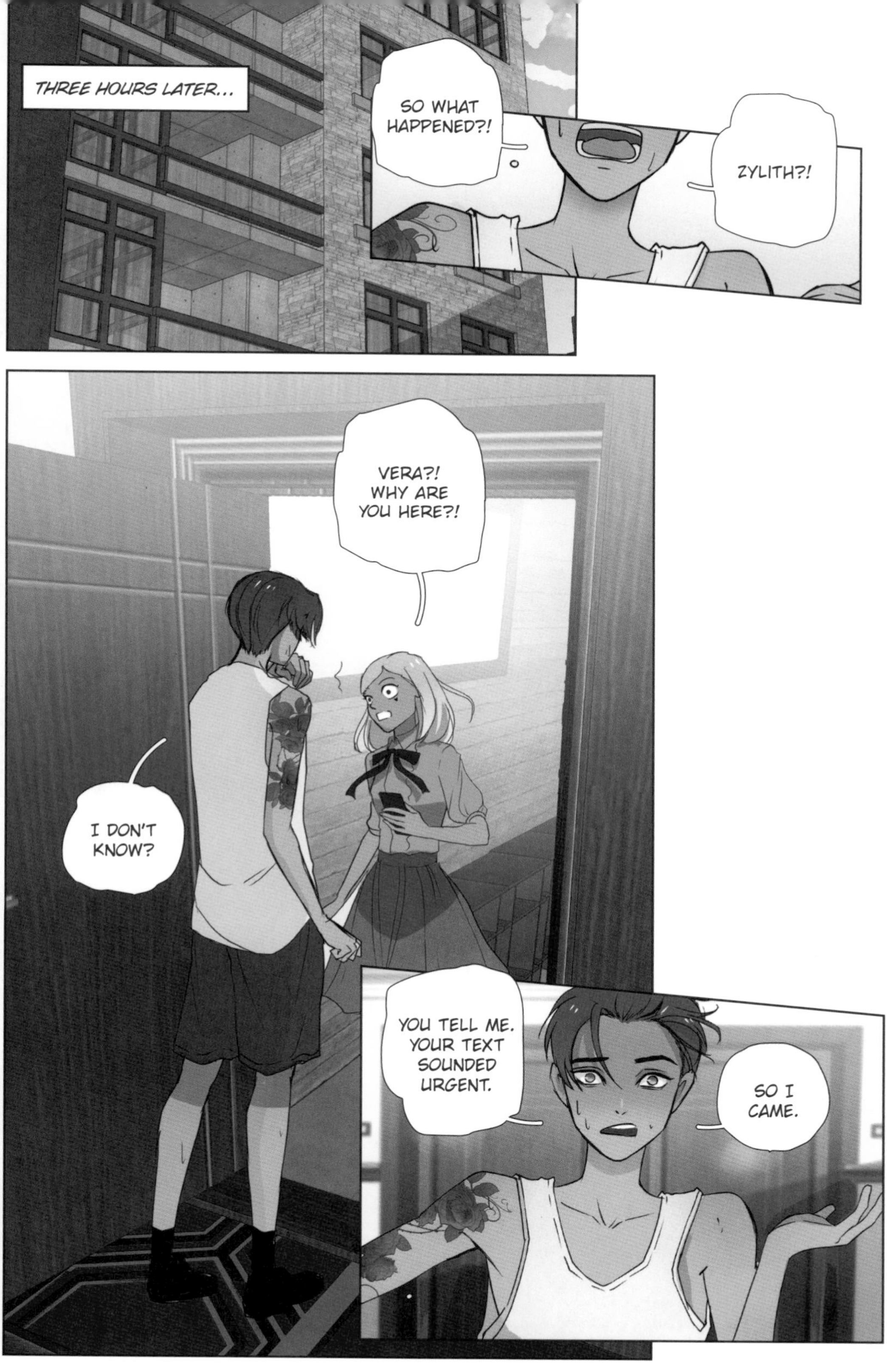
THREE HOURS LATER...
SO WHAT HAPPENED?!
ZYLITH?!
VERA?! WHY ARE YOU HERE?!
I DON'T KNOW?
YOU TELL ME. YOUR TEXT SOUNDED URGENT.
SO I CAME.

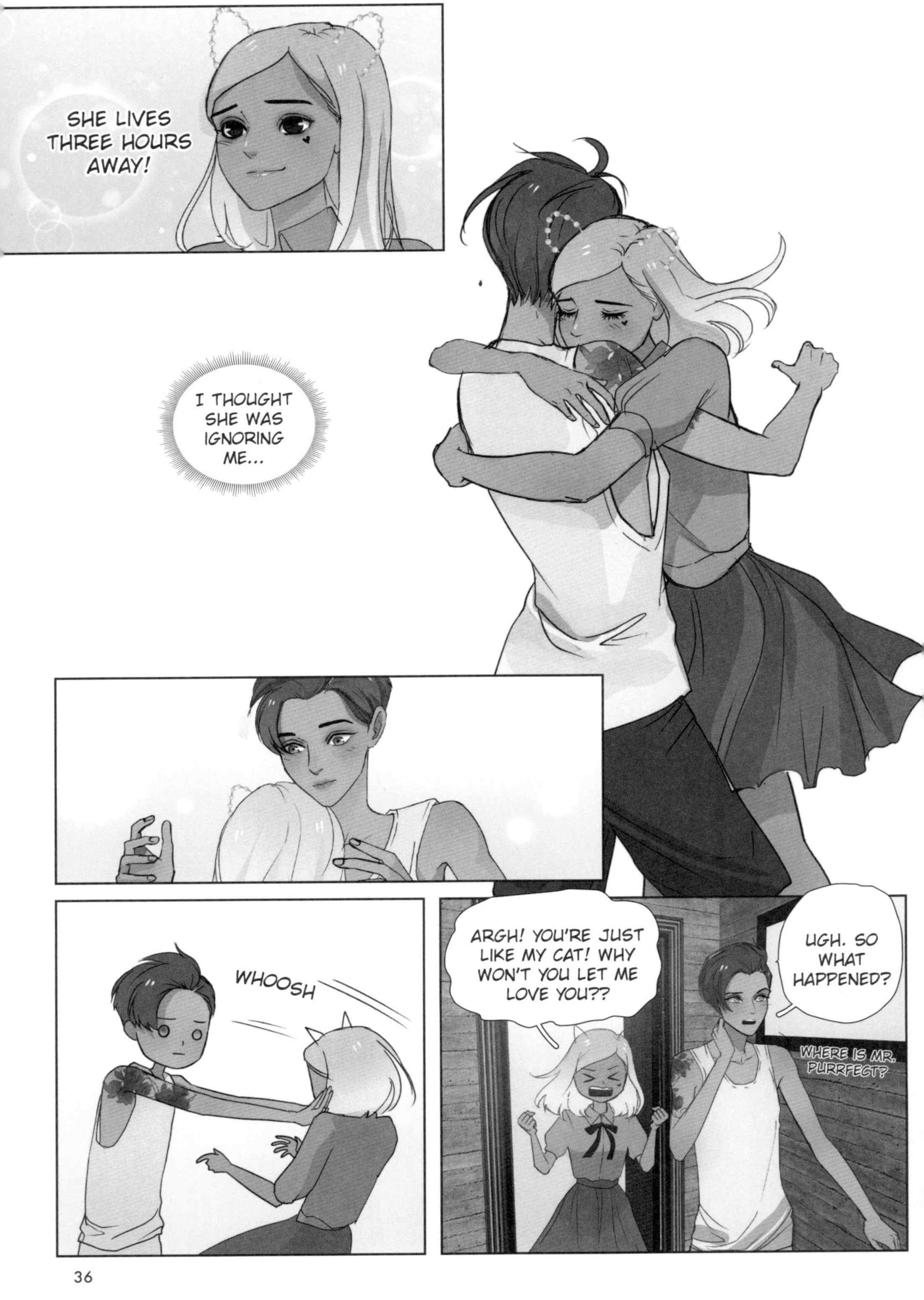
SHE LIVES THREE HOURS AWAY!
I THOUGHT SHE WAS IGNORING ME...
WHOOSH
ARGH! YOU'RE JUST LIKE MY CAT! WHY WON'T YOU LET ME LOVE YOU??
UGH. SO WHAT HAPPENED?
WHERE IS MR. PURRFECT?

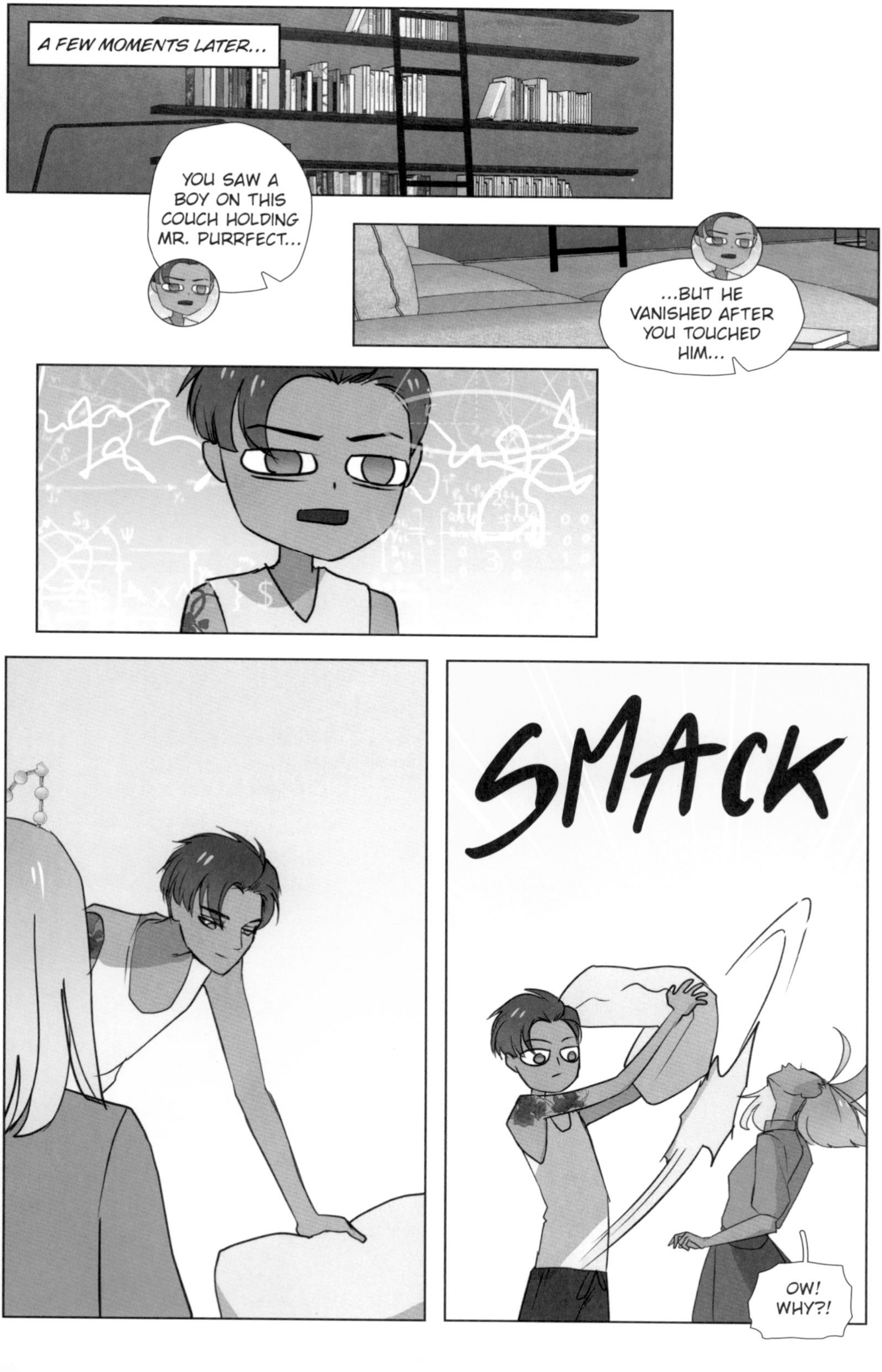
A FEW MOMENTS LATER...
YOU SAW A BOY ON THIS COUCH HOLDING MR. PURRFECT...
...BUT HE VANISHED AFTER YOU TOUCHED HIM...
SMACK
OW! WHY?!

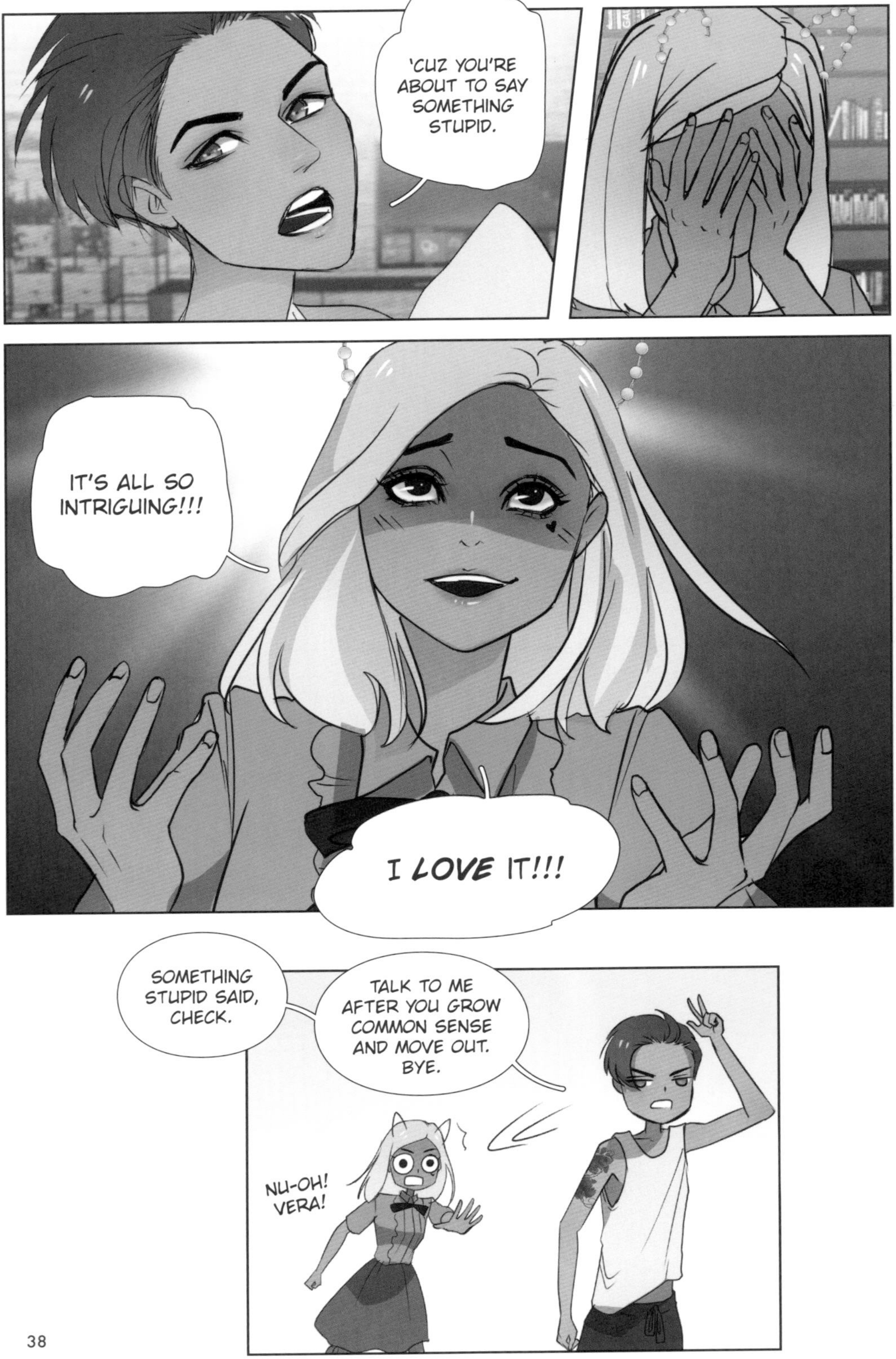

'CUZ YOU'RE ABOUT TO SAY SOMETHING STUPID.
IT'S ALL SO INTRIGUING!!!
I LOVE IT!!!
SOMETHING STUPID SAID, CHECK.
TALK TO ME AFTER YOU GROW COMMON SENSE AND MOVE OUT. BYE.
NU-OH! VERA!

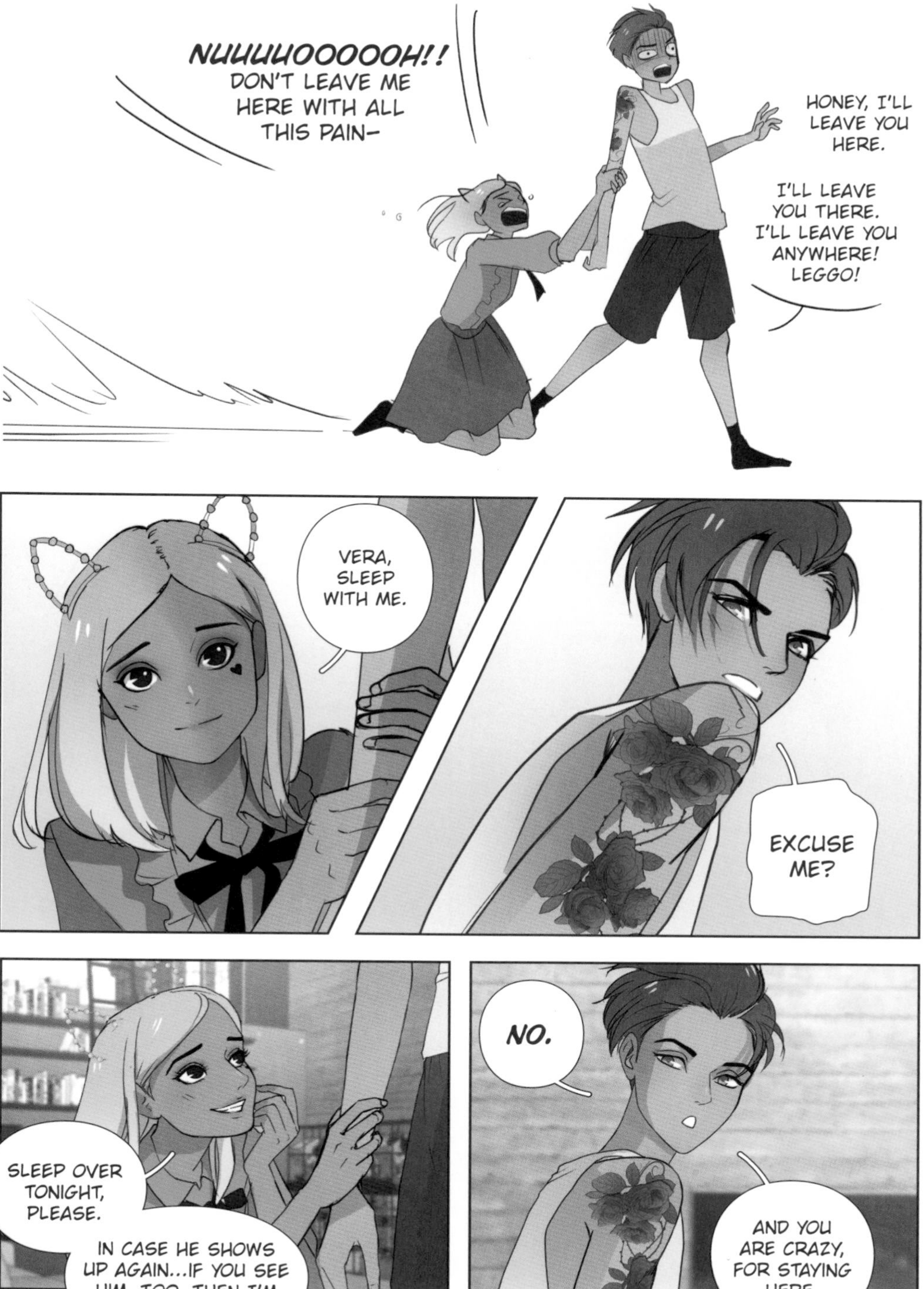
NUUUUOOOOOH!!
DON'T LEAVE ME HERE WITH ALL THIS PAIN–
HONEY, I'LL LEAVE YOU HERE.
I'LL LEAVE YOU THERE. I'LL LEAVE YOU ANYWHERE! LEGGO!
VERA, SLEEP WITH ME.
EXCUSE ME?
SLEEP OVER TONIGHT, PLEASE.
IN CASE HE SHOWS UP AGAIN...IF YOU SEE HIM, TOO, THEN I'M NOT CRAZY.
NO.
AND YOU ARE CRAZY, FOR STAYING HERE.

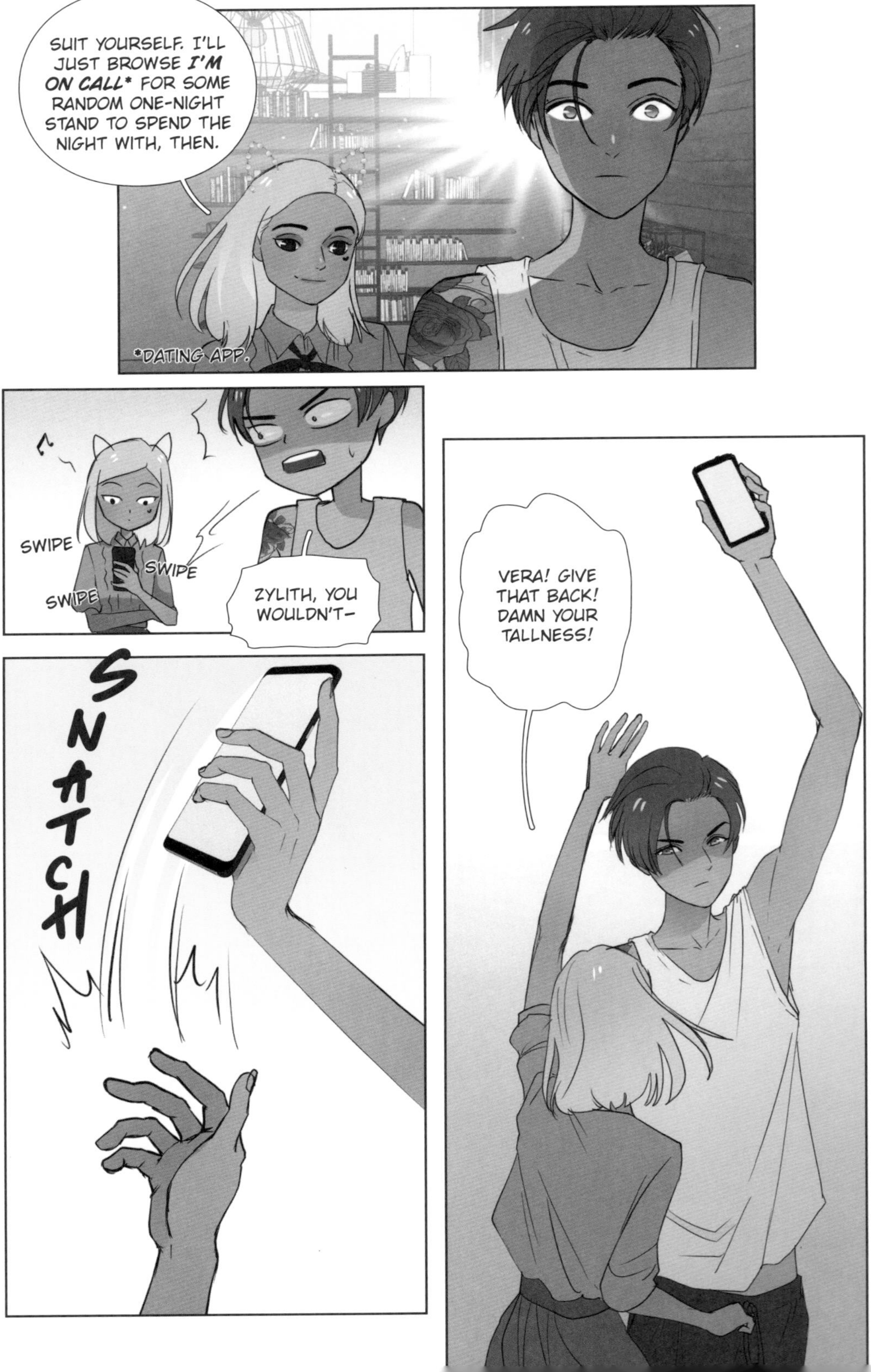
SUIT YOURSELF. I'LL JUST BROWSE ***I'M ON CALL**** FOR SOME RANDOM ONE-NIGHT STAND TO SPEND THE NIGHT WITH, THEN.
*DATING APP.
SWIPE
SWIPE
SWIPE
ZYLITH, YOU WOULDN'T-
SNATCH
VERA! GIVE THAT BACK! DAMN YOUR TALLNESS!

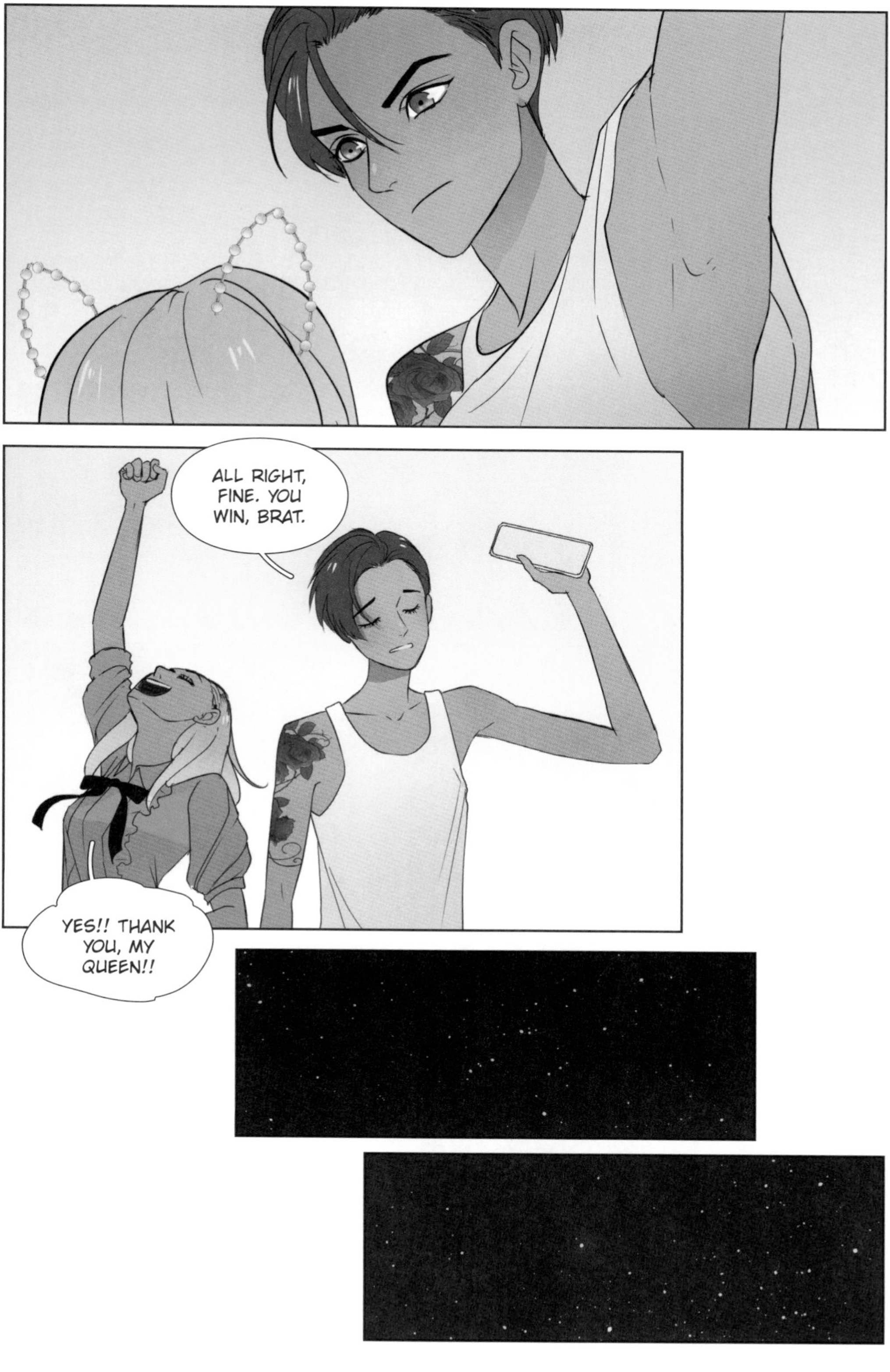
ALL RIGHT, FINE. YOU WIN, BRAT.
YES!! THANK YOU, MY QUEEN!!

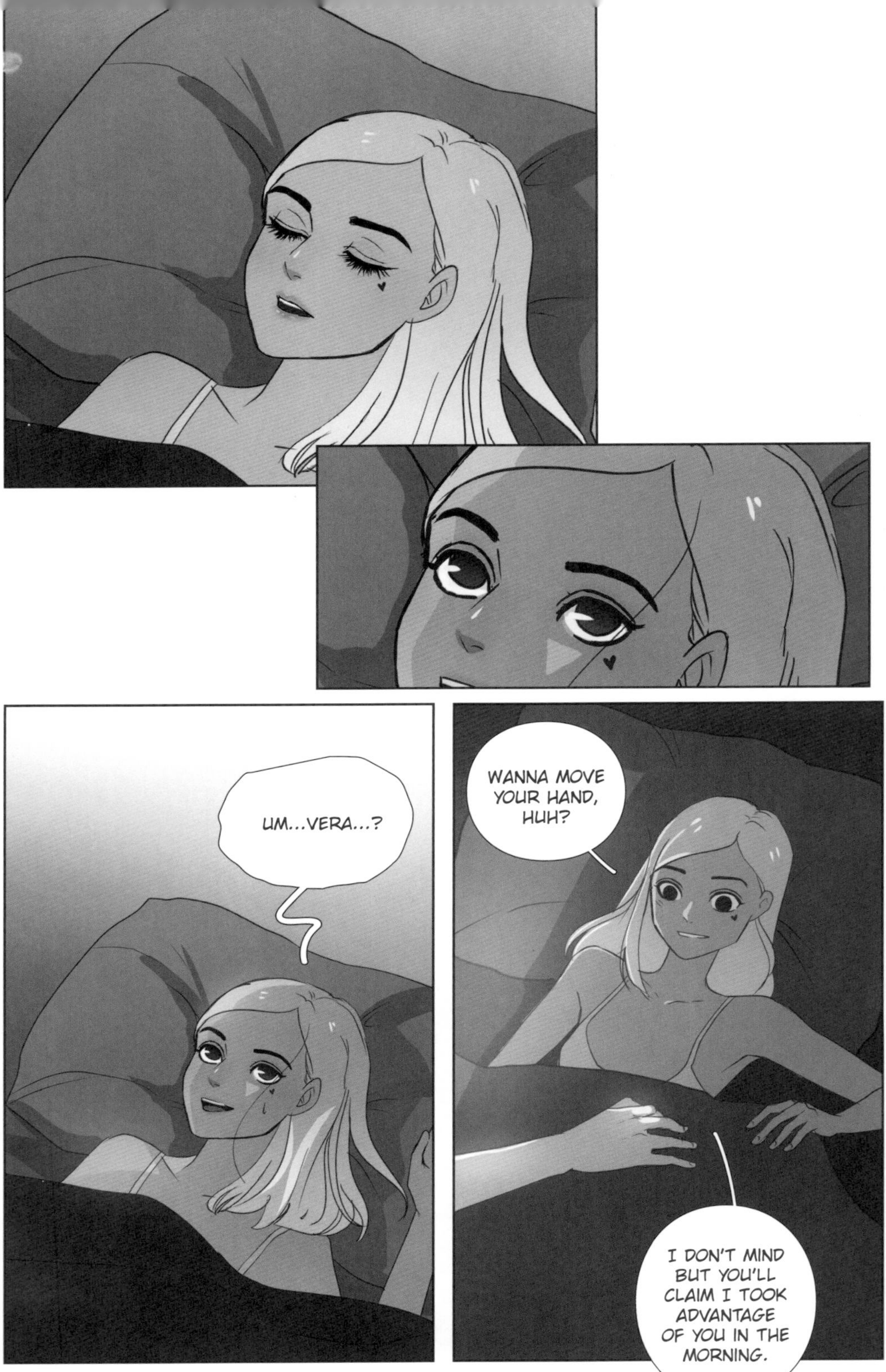
UM...VERA...?
WANNA MOVE YOUR HAND, HUH?
I DON'T MIND BUT YOU'LL CLAIM I TOOK ADVANTAGE OF YOU IN THE MORNING.

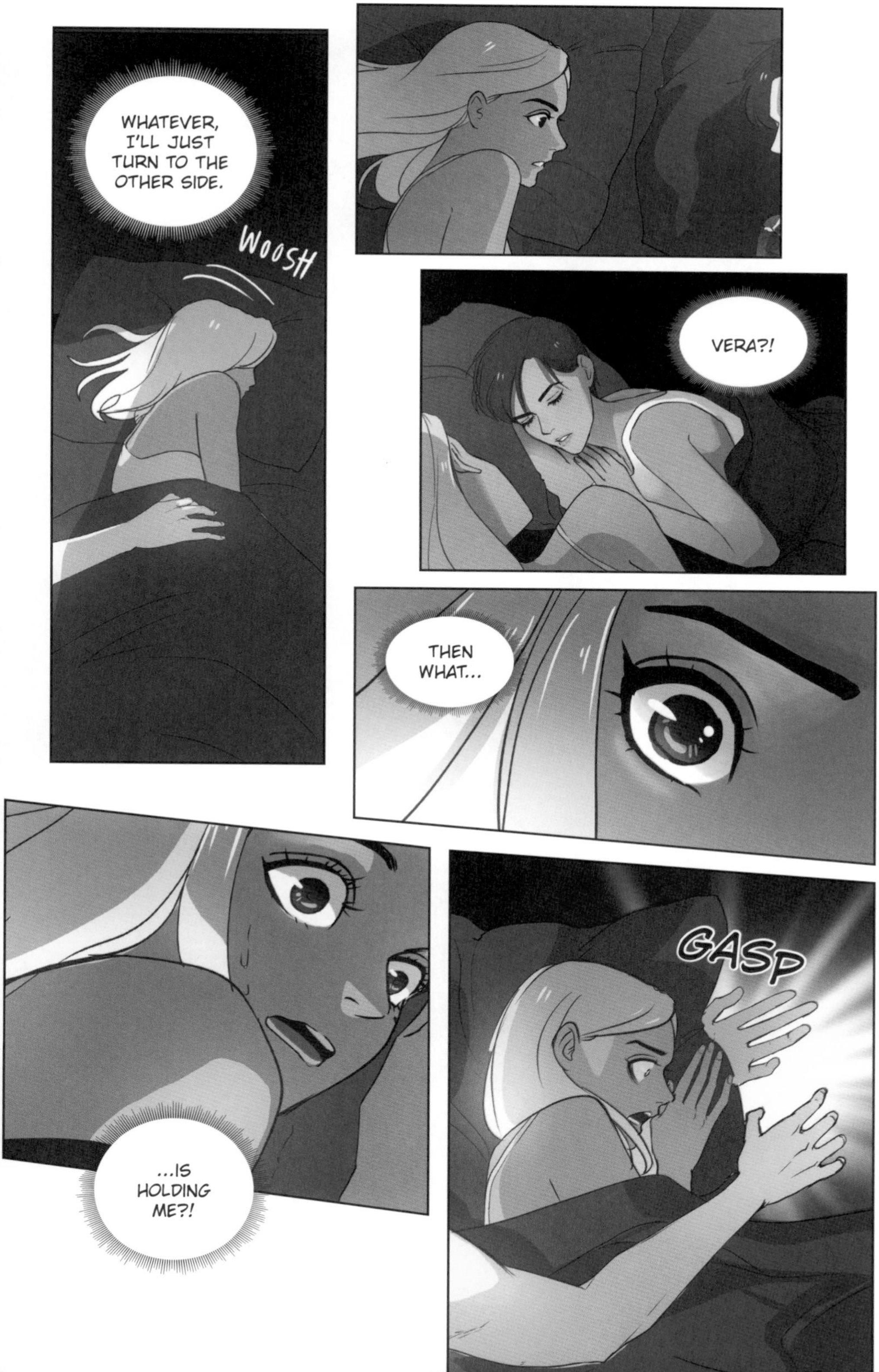
WHATEVER, I'LL JUST TURN TO THE OTHER SIDE.
WOOSH
VERA?!
THEN WHAT...
...IS HOLDING ME?!
GASP

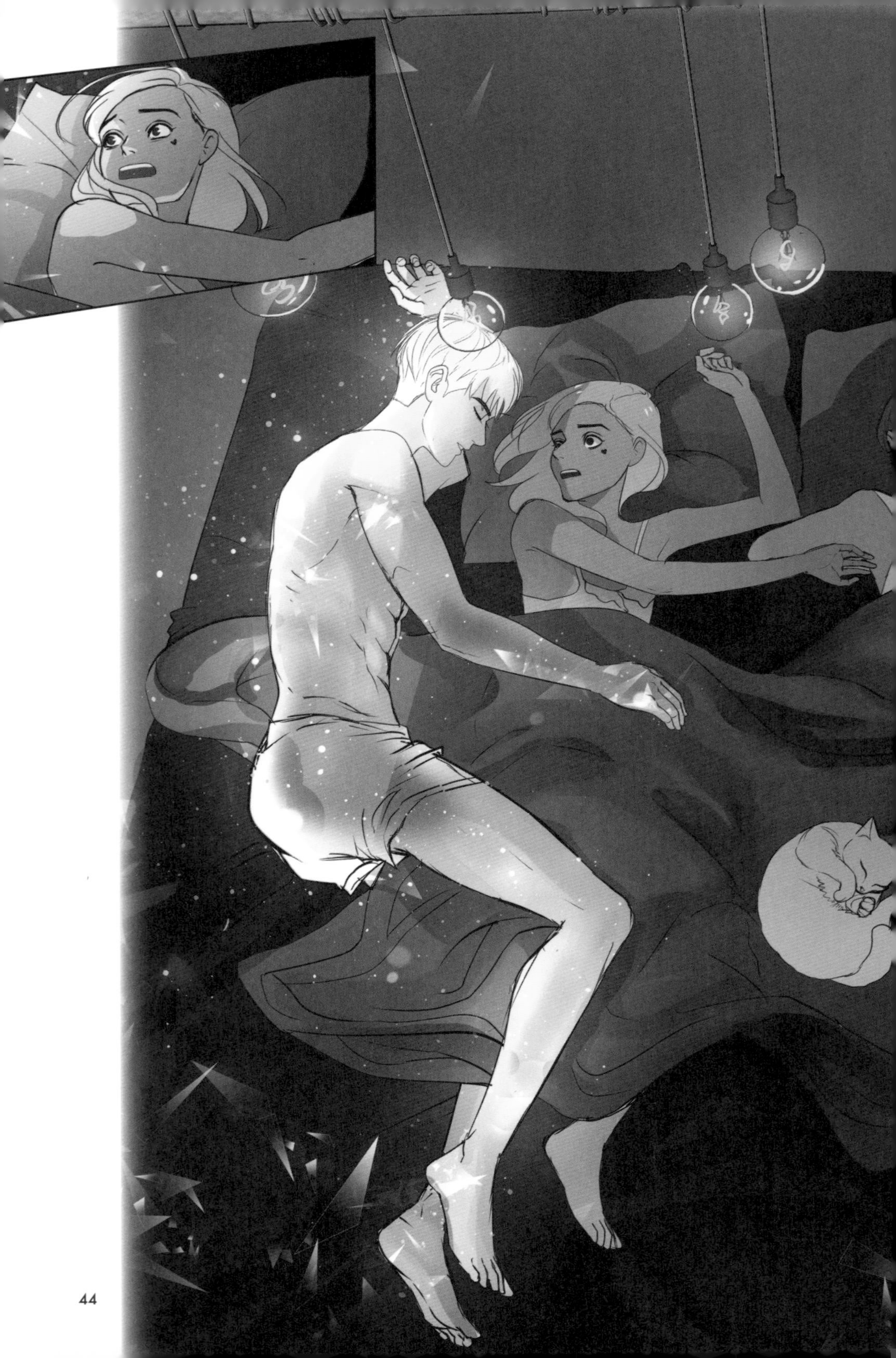

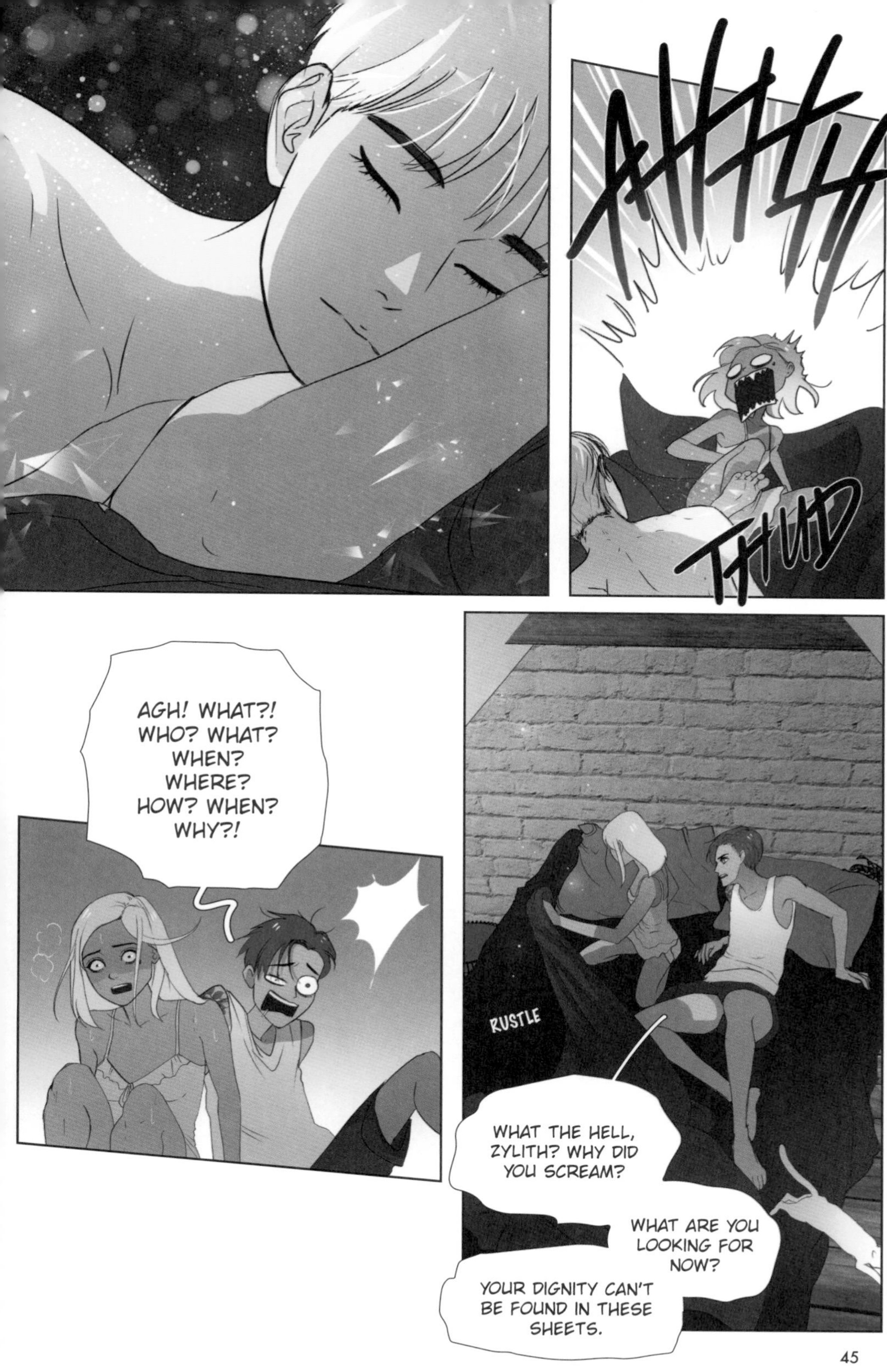
AHHHH
THUD
AGH! WHAT?! WHO? WHAT? WHEN? WHERE? HOW? WHEN? WHY?!
RUSTLE
WHAT THE HELL, ZYLITH? WHY DID YOU SCREAM?
WHAT ARE YOU LOOKING FOR NOW?
YOUR DIGNITY CAN'T BE FOUND IN THESE SHEETS.

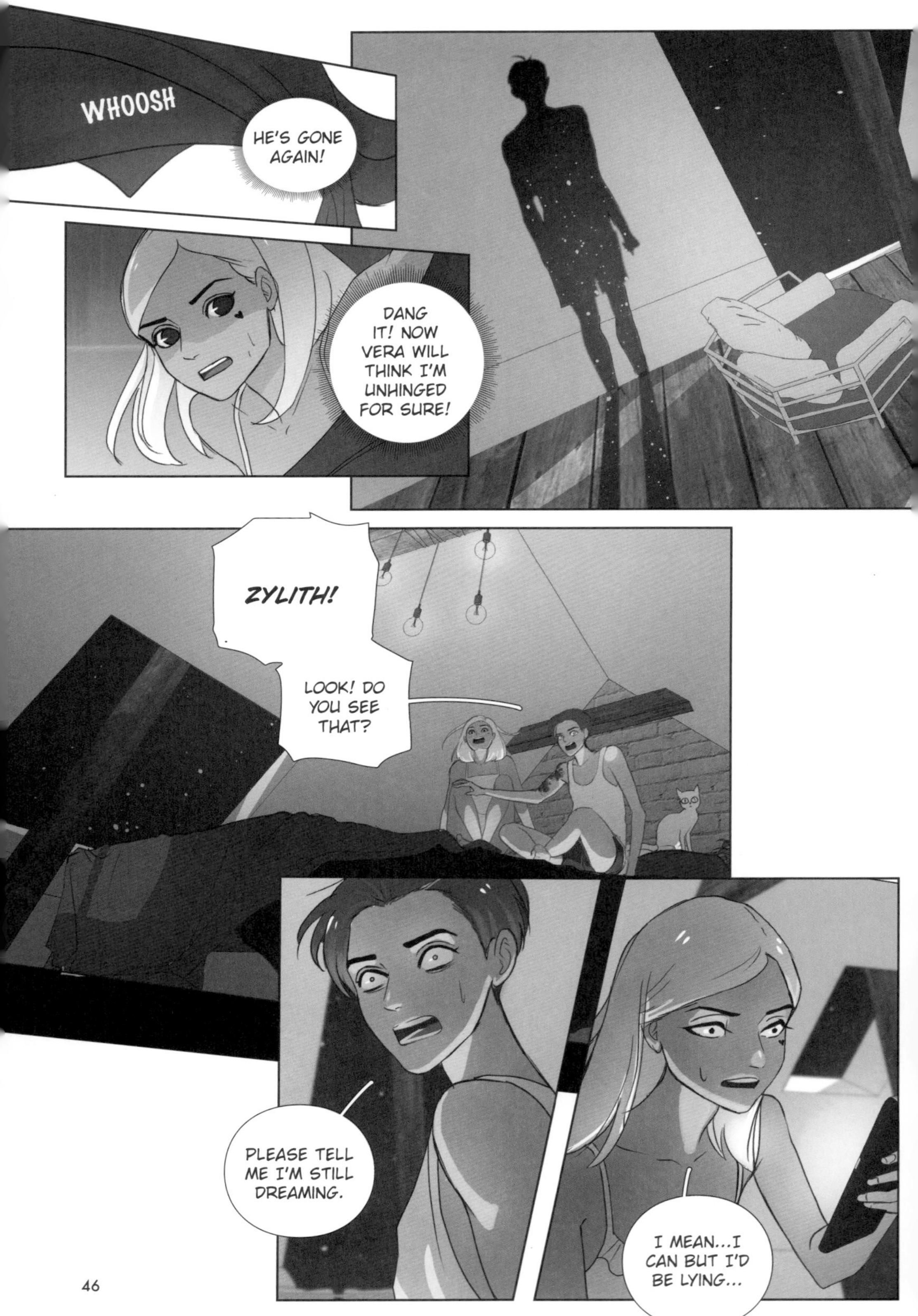
WHOOSH
HE'S GONE AGAIN!
DANG IT! NOW VERA WILL THINK I'M UNHINGED FOR SURE!
ZYLITH!
LOOK! DO YOU SEE THAT?
PLEASE TELL ME I'M STILL DREAMING.
I MEAN...I CAN BUT I'D BE LYING...

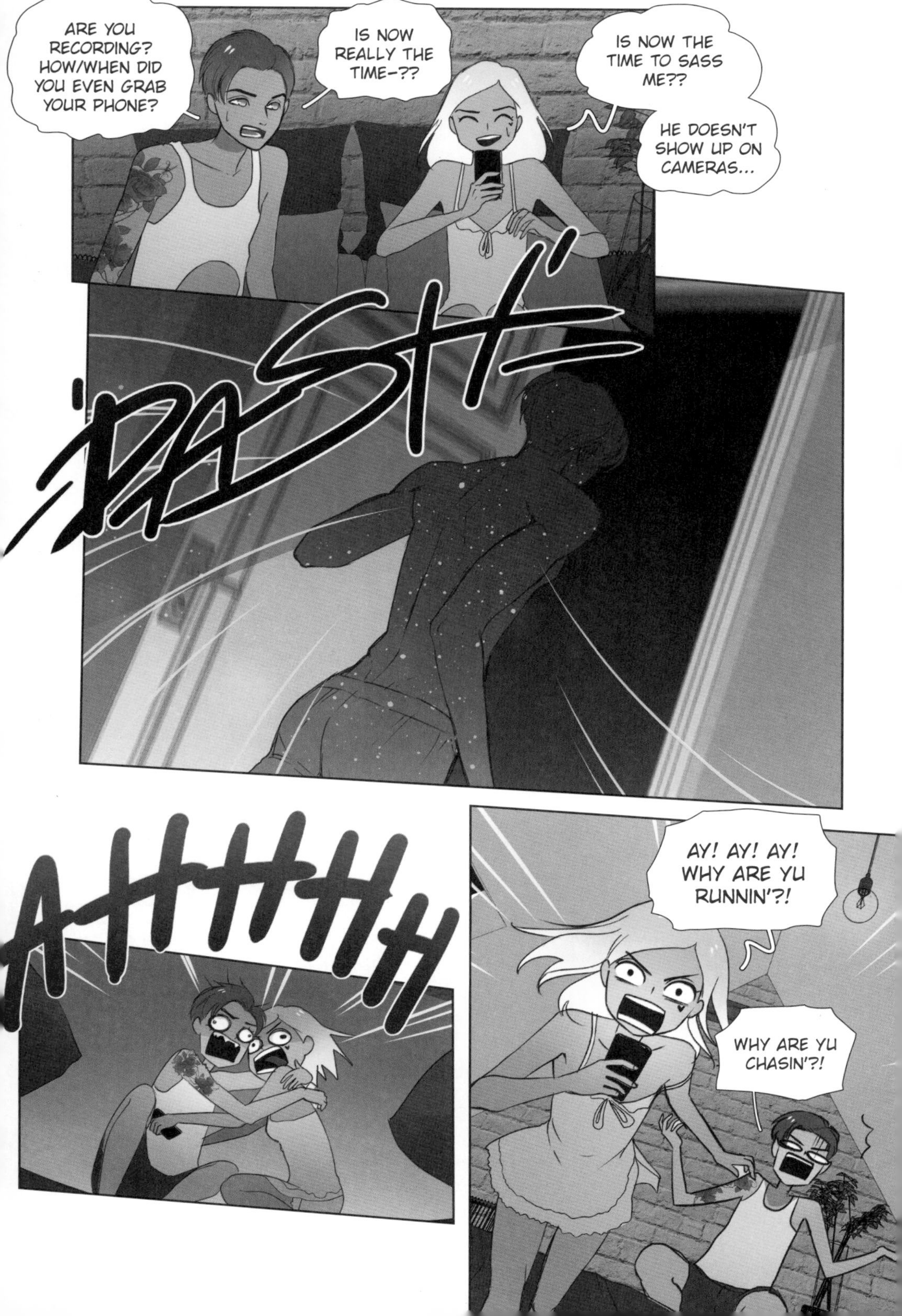
ARE YOU RECORDING? HOW/WHEN DID YOU EVEN GRAB YOUR PHONE?
IS NOW REALLY THE TIME-??
IS NOW THE TIME TO SASS ME??
HE DOESN'T SHOW UP ON CAMERAS...
DASH
AHHHHH
AY! AY! AY! WHY ARE YU RUNNIN'?!
WHY ARE YU CHASIN'?!

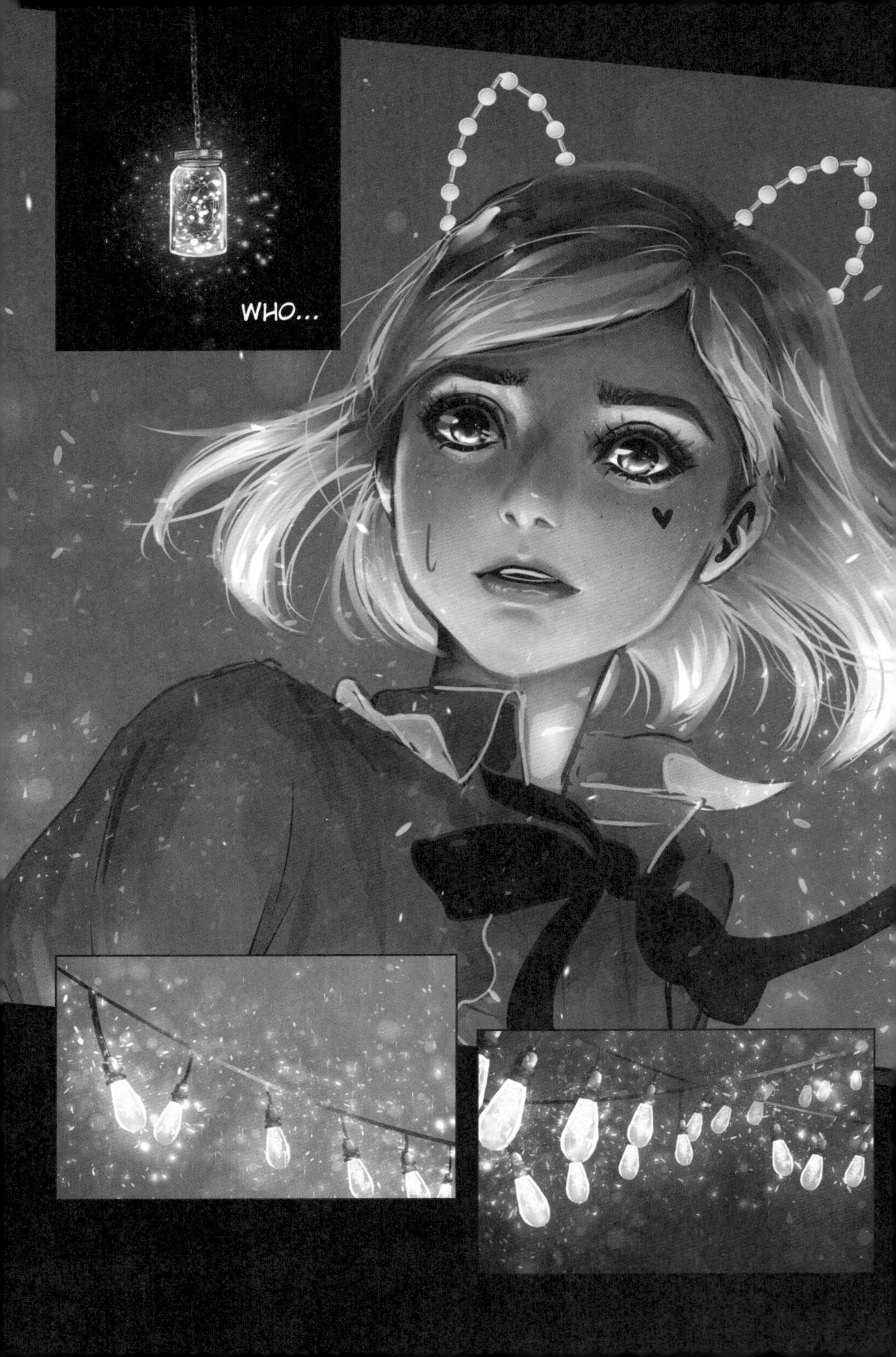
WHO...

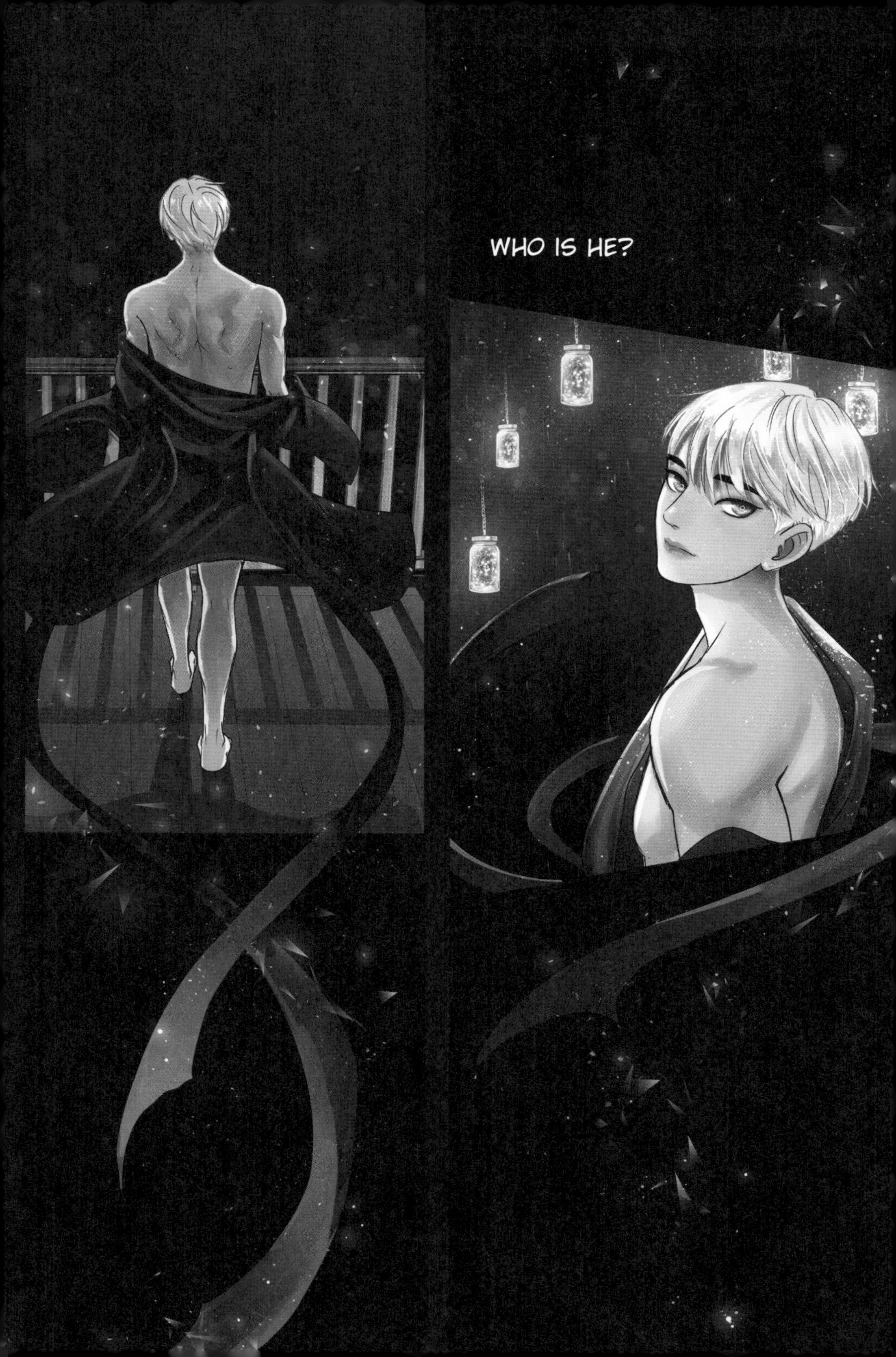
WHO IS HE?

THE NEXT MORNING...

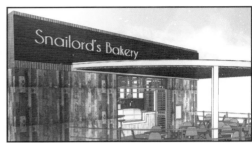

Snailord's Bakery

LET'S TALK ABOUT LAST NIGHT...

...ZYLITH.

YOU HAVE TO MOVE OUT OF THAT PLACE, ZYLITH.

YOU'RE RIGHT, VERA.

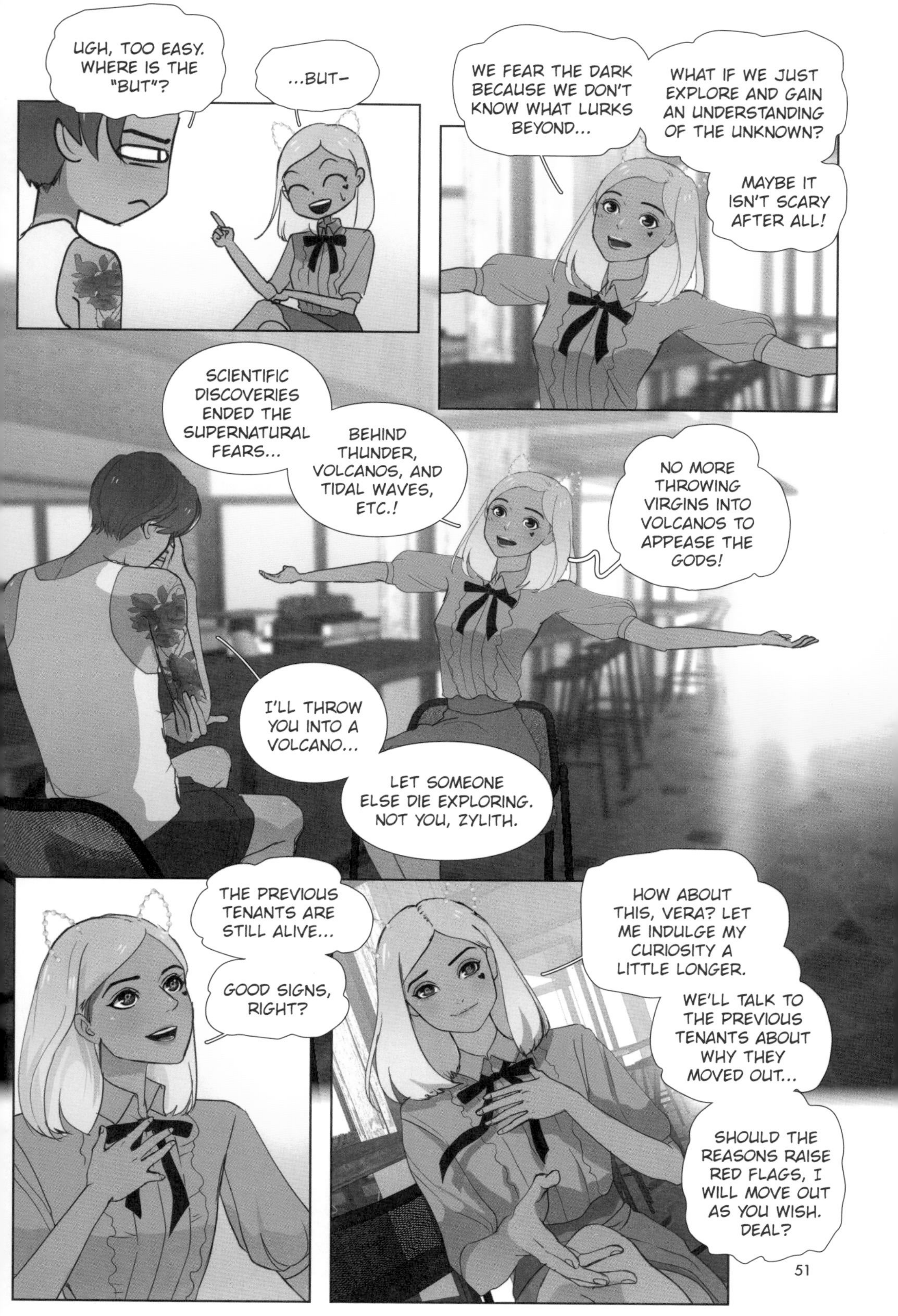
UGH, TOO EASY. WHERE IS THE "BUT"?
...BUT-
WE FEAR THE DARK BECAUSE WE DON'T KNOW WHAT LURKS BEYOND...
WHAT IF WE JUST EXPLORE AND GAIN AN UNDERSTANDING OF THE UNKNOWN?
MAYBE IT ISN'T SCARY AFTER ALL!
SCIENTIFIC DISCOVERIES ENDED THE SUPERNATURAL FEARS...
BEHIND THUNDER, VOLCANOS, AND TIDAL WAVES, ETC.!
NO MORE THROWING VIRGINS INTO VOLCANOS TO APPEASE THE GODS!
I'LL THROW YOU INTO A VOLCANO...
LET SOMEONE ELSE DIE EXPLORING. NOT YOU, ZYLITH.
THE PREVIOUS TENANTS ARE STILL ALIVE...
GOOD SIGNS, RIGHT?
HOW ABOUT THIS, VERA? LET ME INDULGE MY CURIOSITY A LITTLE LONGER.
WE'LL TALK TO THE PREVIOUS TENANTS ABOUT WHY THEY MOVED OUT...
SHOULD THE REASONS RAISE RED FLAGS, I WILL MOVE OUT AS YOU WISH. DEAL?

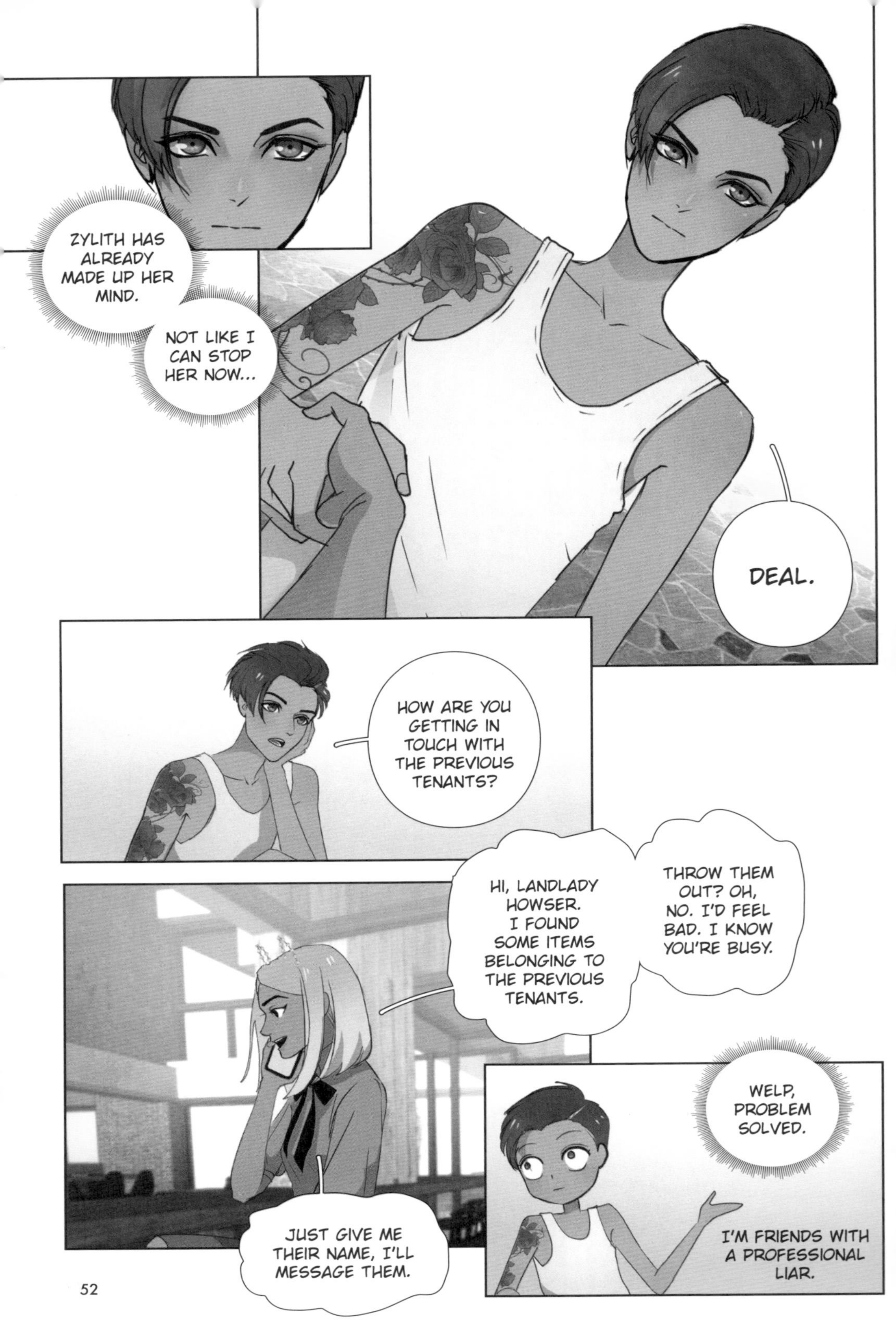
ZYLITH HAS ALREADY MADE UP HER MIND.
NOT LIKE I CAN STOP HER NOW...
DEAL.
HOW ARE YOU GETTING IN TOUCH WITH THE PREVIOUS TENANTS?
HI, LANDLADY HOWSER. I FOUND SOME ITEMS BELONGING TO THE PREVIOUS TENANTS.
THROW THEM OUT? OH, NO. I'D FEEL BAD. I KNOW YOU'RE BUSY.
JUST GIVE ME THEIR NAME, I'LL MESSAGE THEM.
WELP, PROBLEM SOLVED.
I'M FRIENDS WITH A PROFESSIONAL LIAR.

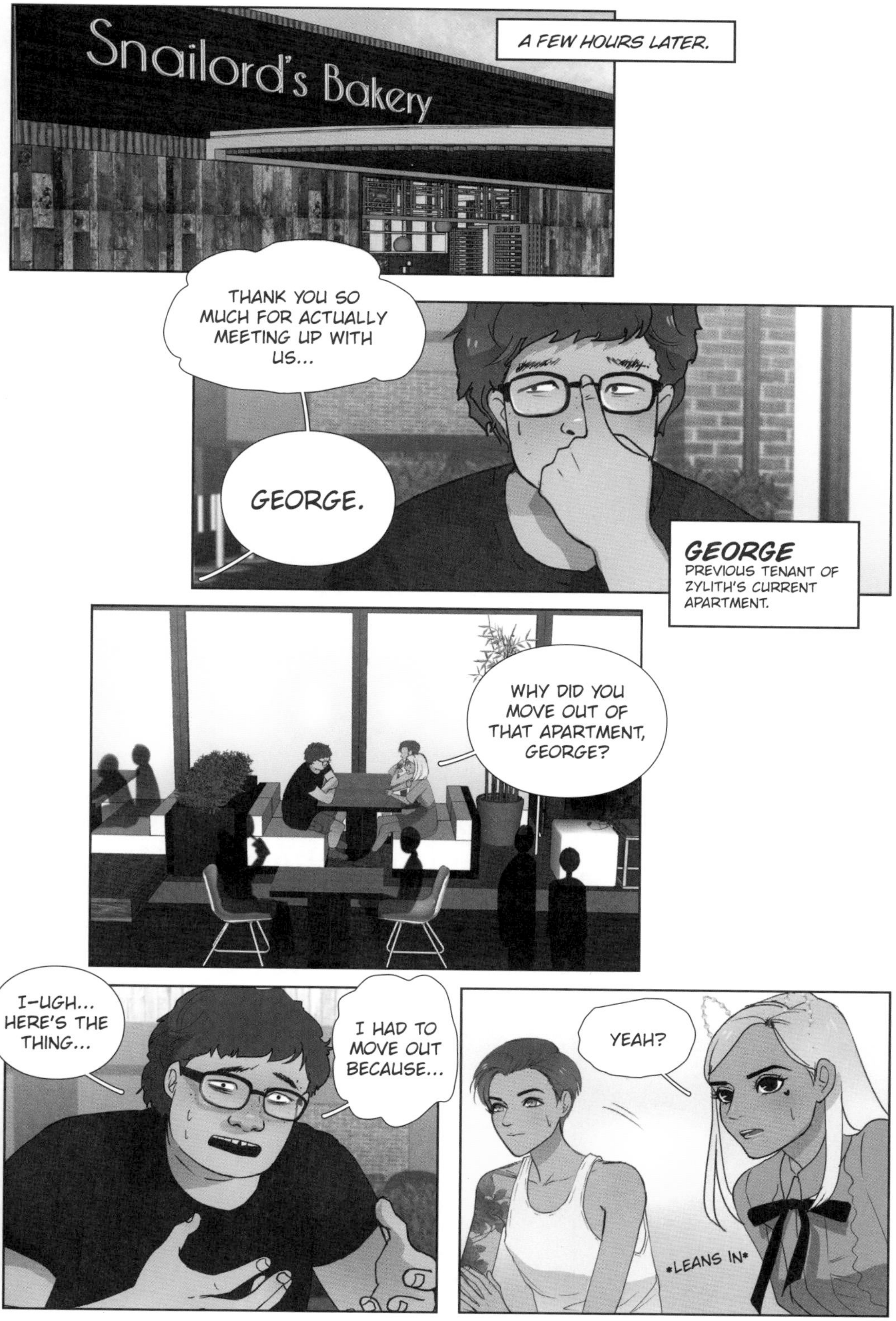
Snailord's Bakery
A FEW HOURS LATER.
THANK YOU SO MUCH FOR ACTUALLY MEETING UP WITH US...
GEORGE.
GEORGE
PREVIOUS TENANT OF ZYLITH'S CURRENT APARTMENT.
WHY DID YOU MOVE OUT OF THAT APARTMENT, GEORGE?
I-UGH... HERE'S THE THING...
I HAD TO MOVE OUT BECAUSE...
YEAH?
LEANS IN

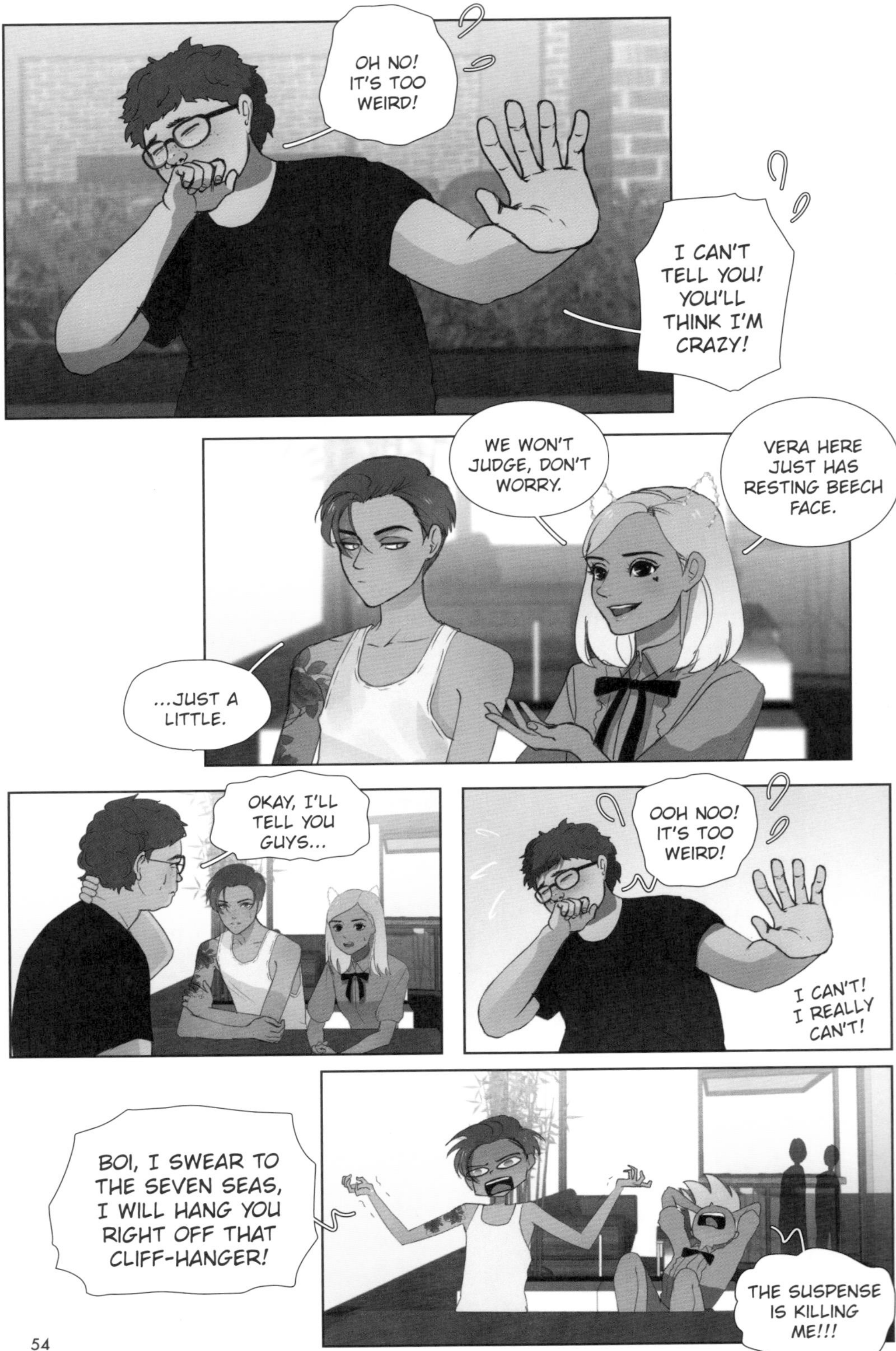
OH NO! IT'S TOO WEIRD!
I CAN'T TELL YOU! YOU'LL THINK I'M CRAZY!
WE WON'T JUDGE, DON'T WORRY.
VERA HERE JUST HAS RESTING BEECH FACE.
...JUST A LITTLE.
OKAY, I'LL TELL YOU GUYS...
OOH NOO! IT'S TOO WEIRD!
I CAN'T! I REALLY CAN'T!
BOI, I SWEAR TO THE SEVEN SEAS, I WILL HANG YOU RIGHT OFF THAT CLIFF-HANGER!
THE SUSPENSE IS KILLING ME!!!

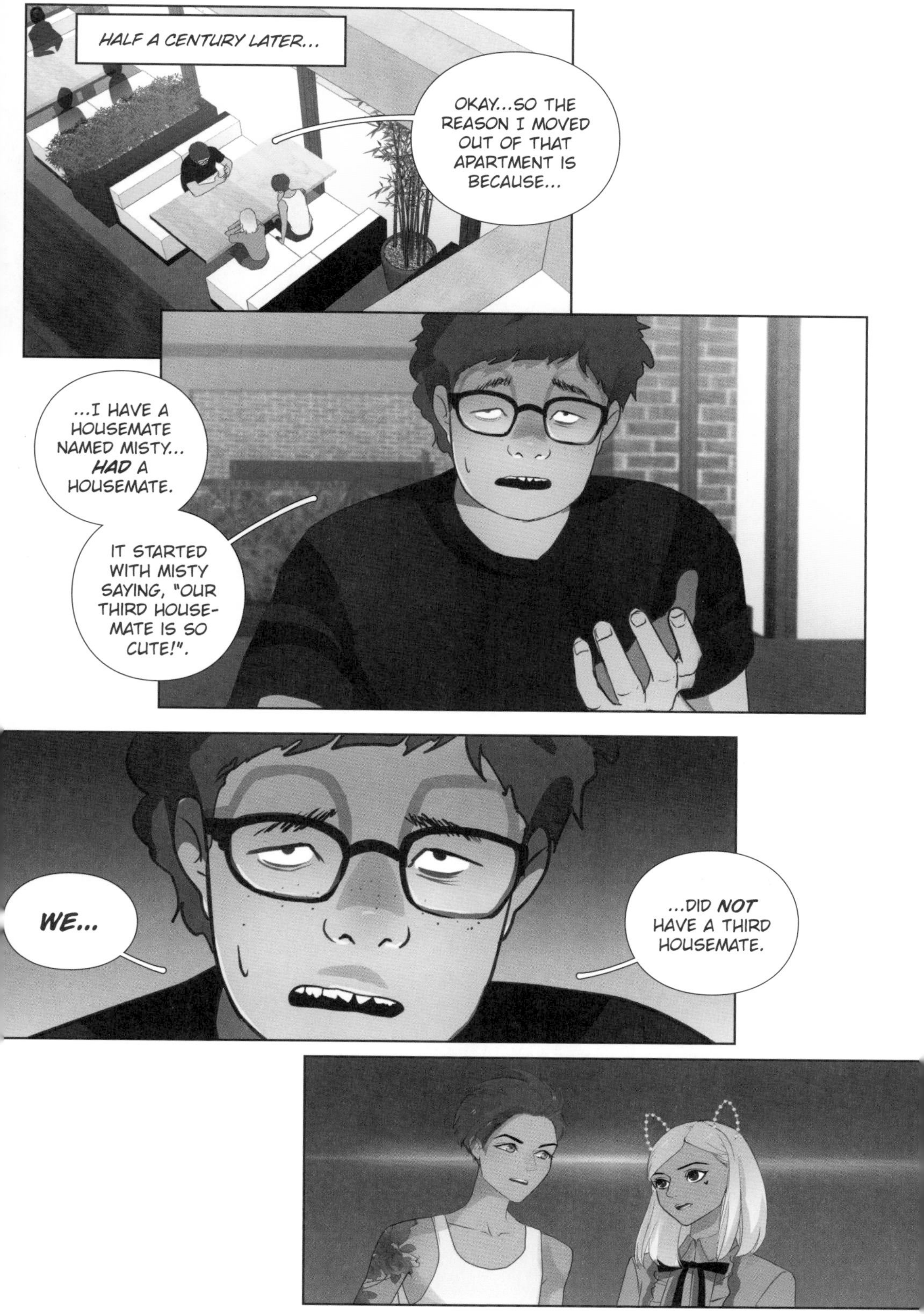
HALF A CENTURY LATER...
OKAY...SO THE REASON I MOVED OUT OF THAT APARTMENT IS BECAUSE...
...I HAVE A HOUSEMATE NAMED MISTY... **HAD** A HOUSEMATE.
IT STARTED WITH MISTY SAYING, "OUR THIRD HOUSE-MATE IS SO CUTE!".
WE...
...DID **NOT** HAVE A THIRD HOUSEMATE.

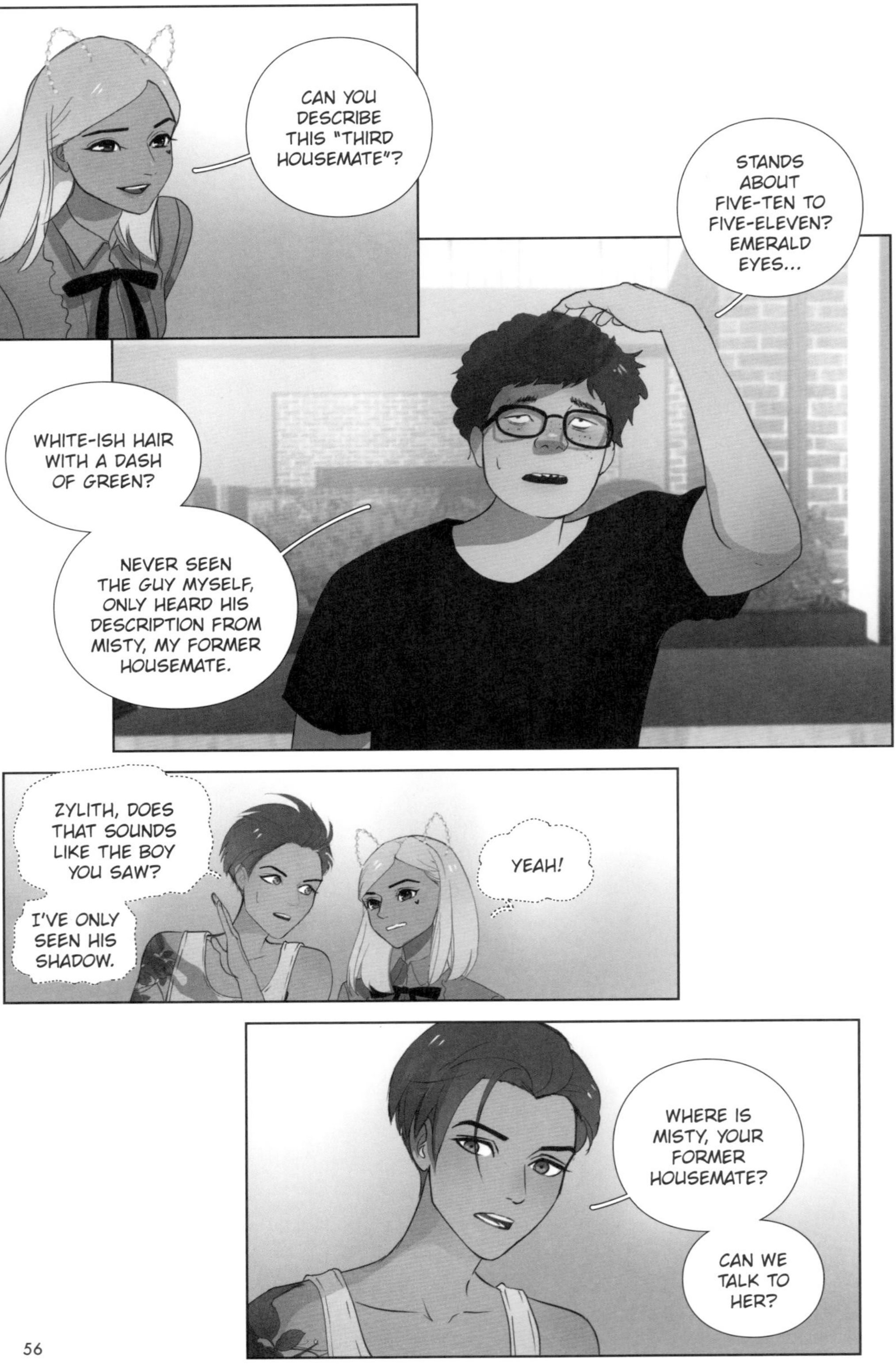
CAN YOU DESCRIBE THIS "THIRD HOUSEMATE"?
STANDS ABOUT FIVE-TEN TO FIVE-ELEVEN? EMERALD EYES...
WHITE-ISH HAIR WITH A DASH OF GREEN?
NEVER SEEN THE GUY MYSELF, ONLY HEARD HIS DESCRIPTION FROM MISTY, MY FORMER HOUSEMATE.
ZYLITH, DOES THAT SOUNDS LIKE THE BOY YOU SAW?
I'VE ONLY SEEN HIS SHADOW.
YEAH!
WHERE IS MISTY, YOUR FORMER HOUSEMATE?
CAN WE TALK TO HER?

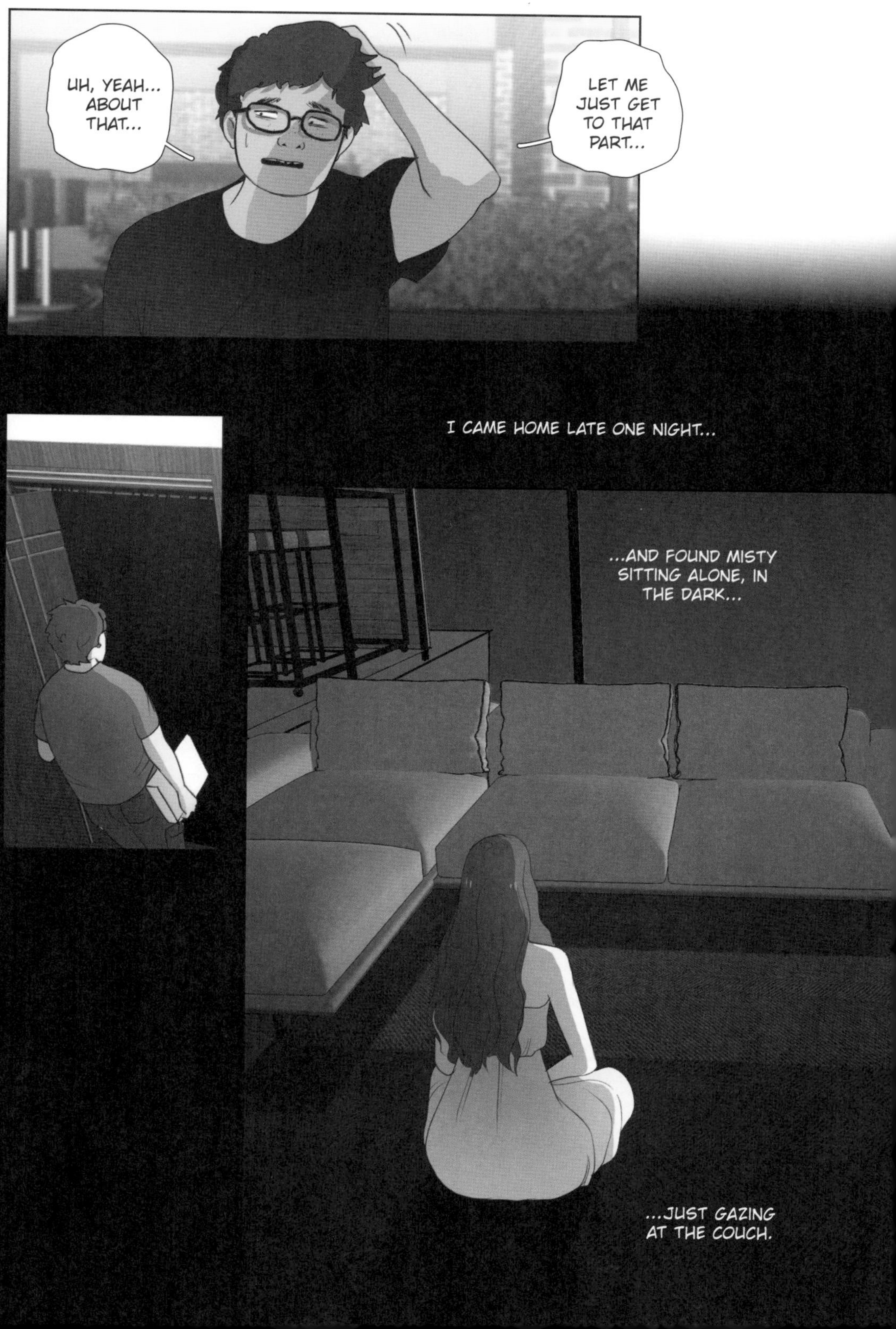
UH, YEAH... ABOUT THAT...
LET ME JUST GET TO THAT PART...
I CAME HOME LATE ONE NIGHT...
...AND FOUND MISTY SITTING ALONE, IN THE DARK...
...JUST GAZING AT THE COUCH.

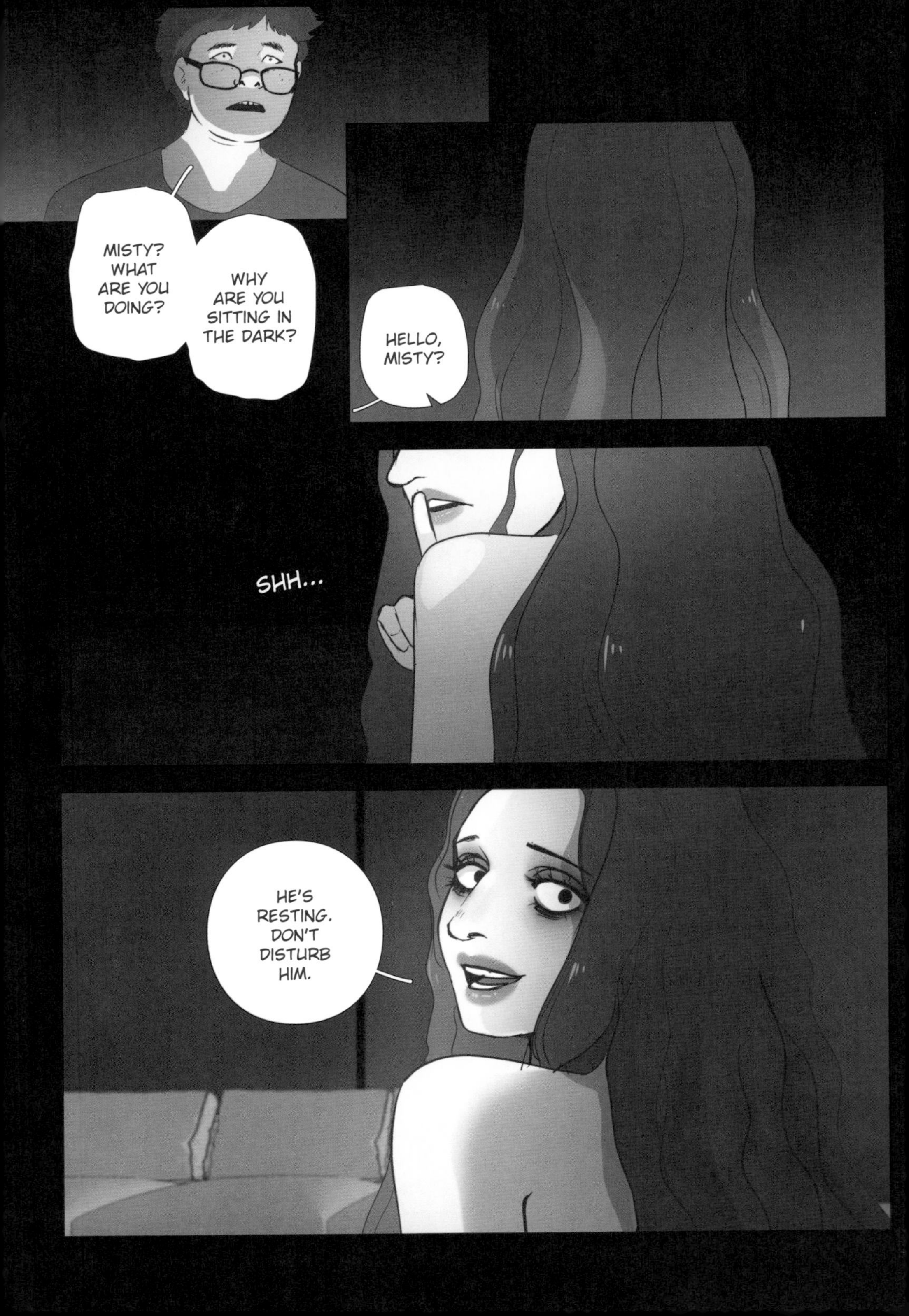
MISTY? WHAT ARE YOU DOING?
WHY ARE YOU SITTING IN THE DARK?
HELLO, MISTY?
SHH...
HE'S RESTING. DON'T DISTURB HIM.

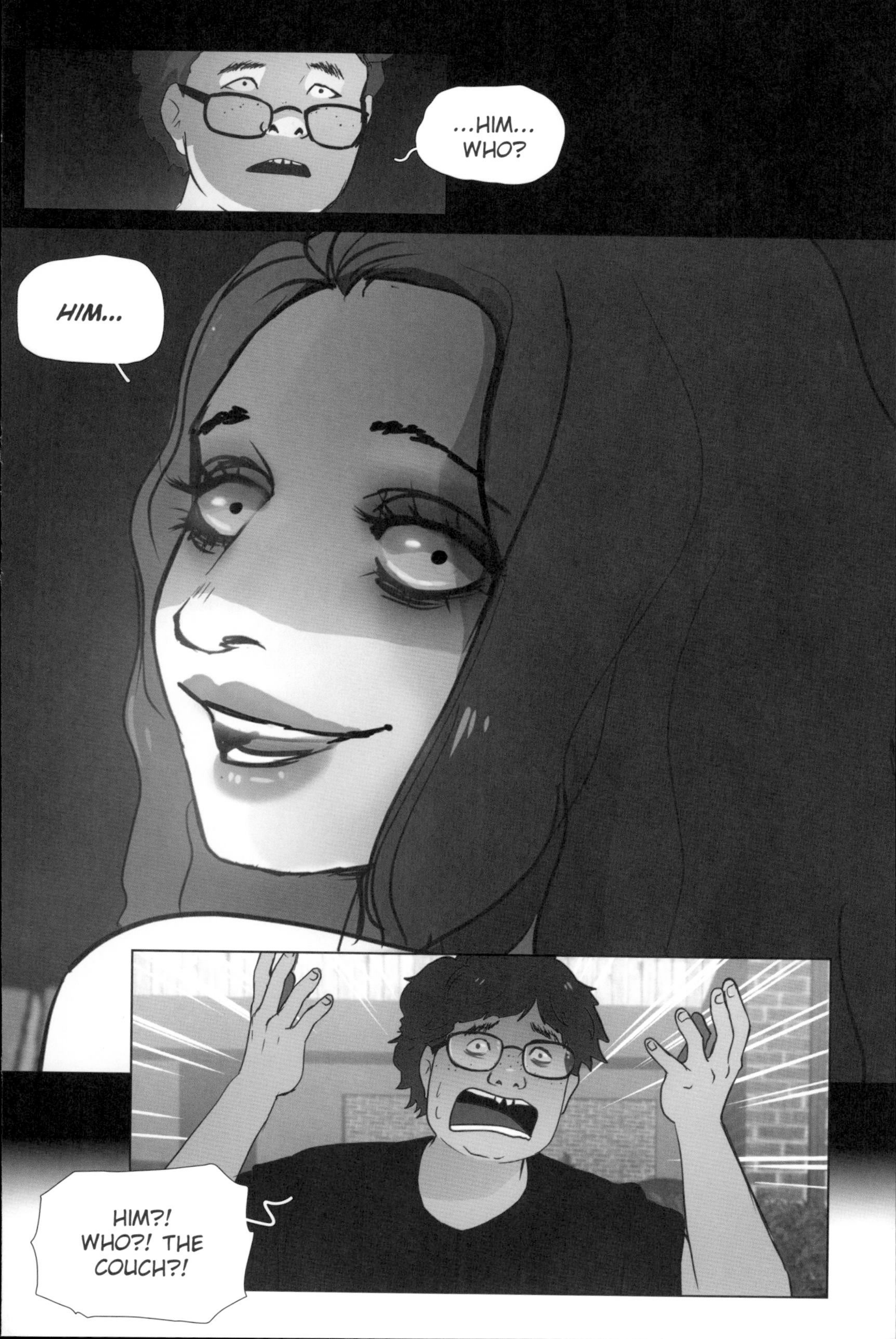
...HIM...
WHO?
HIM...
HIM?! WHO?! THE COUCH?!

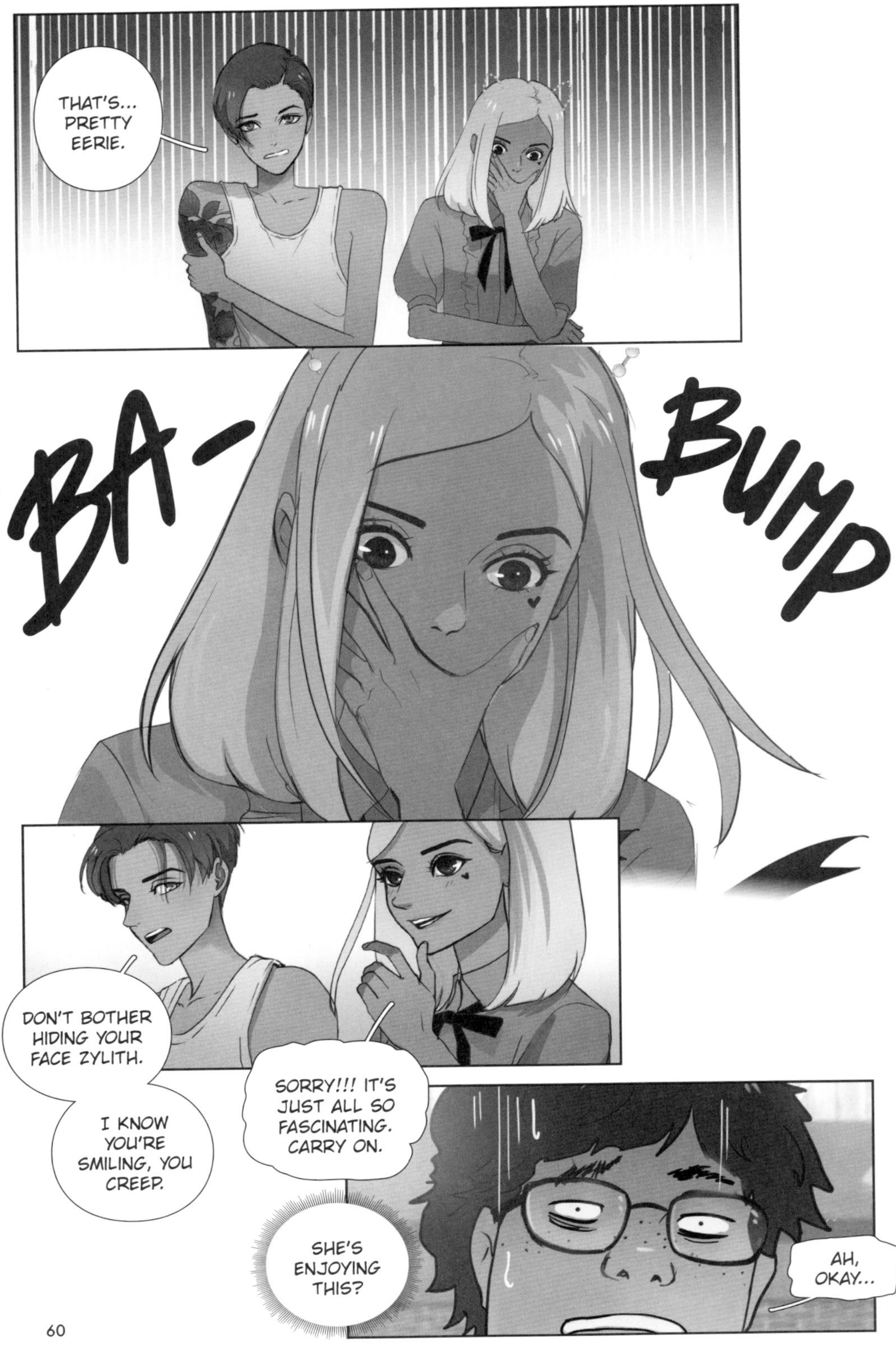
THAT'S... PRETTY EERIE.
BA-BUMP
DON'T BOTHER HIDING YOUR FACE ZYLITH.
I KNOW YOU'RE SMILING, YOU CREEP.
SORRY!!! IT'S JUST ALL SO FASCINATING. CARRY ON.
SHE'S ENJOYING THIS?
AH, OKAY...

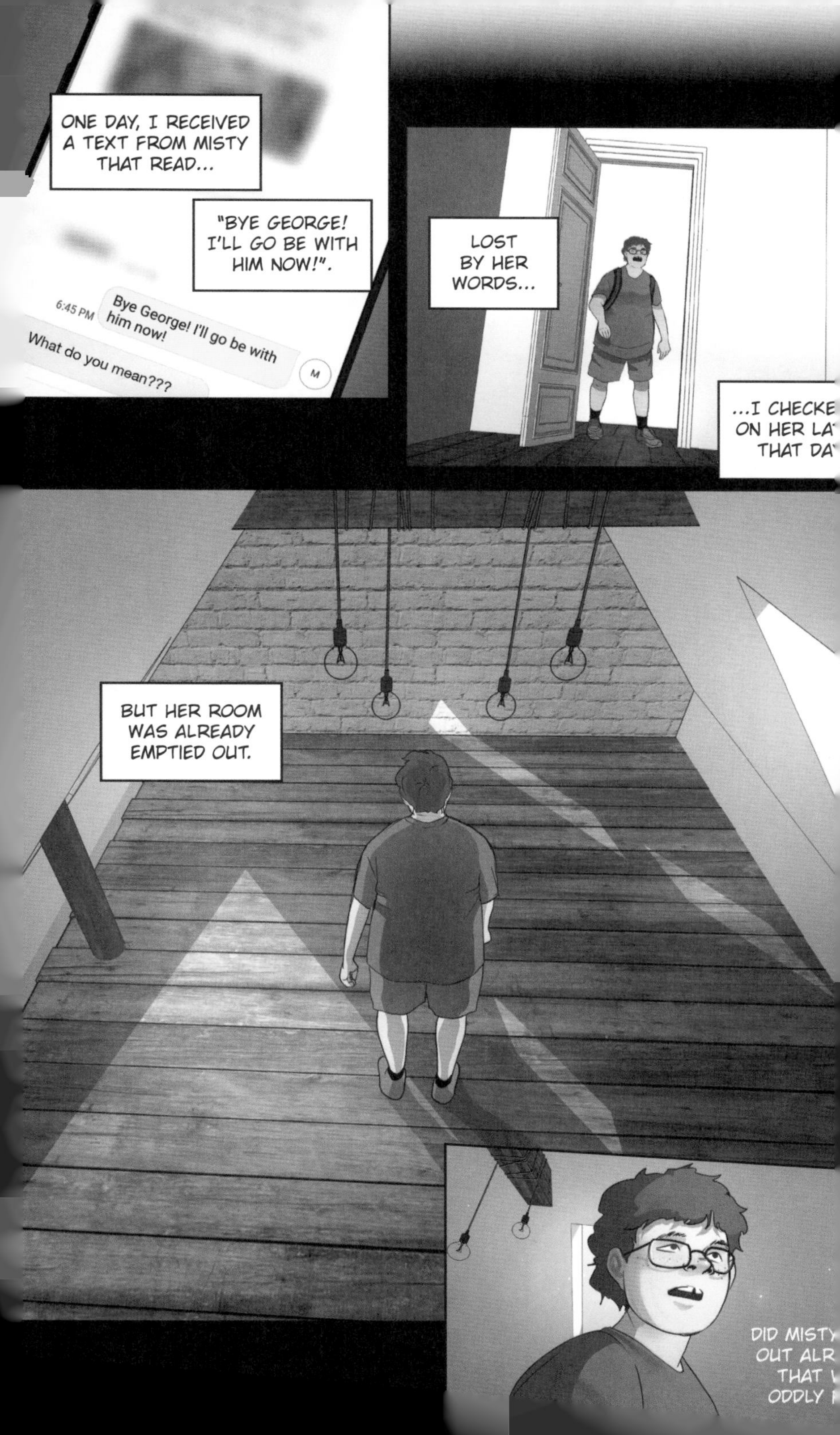
ONE DAY, I RECEIVED A TEXT FROM MISTY THAT READ...
"BYE GEORGE! I'LL GO BE WITH HIM NOW!".
6:45 PM
Bye George! I'll go be with him now!
M
What do you mean???
LOST BY HER WORDS...
...I CHECKE
ON HER LA
THAT DA
BUT HER ROOM WAS ALREADY EMPTIED OUT.
DID MISTY
OUT ALR
THAT
ODDLY

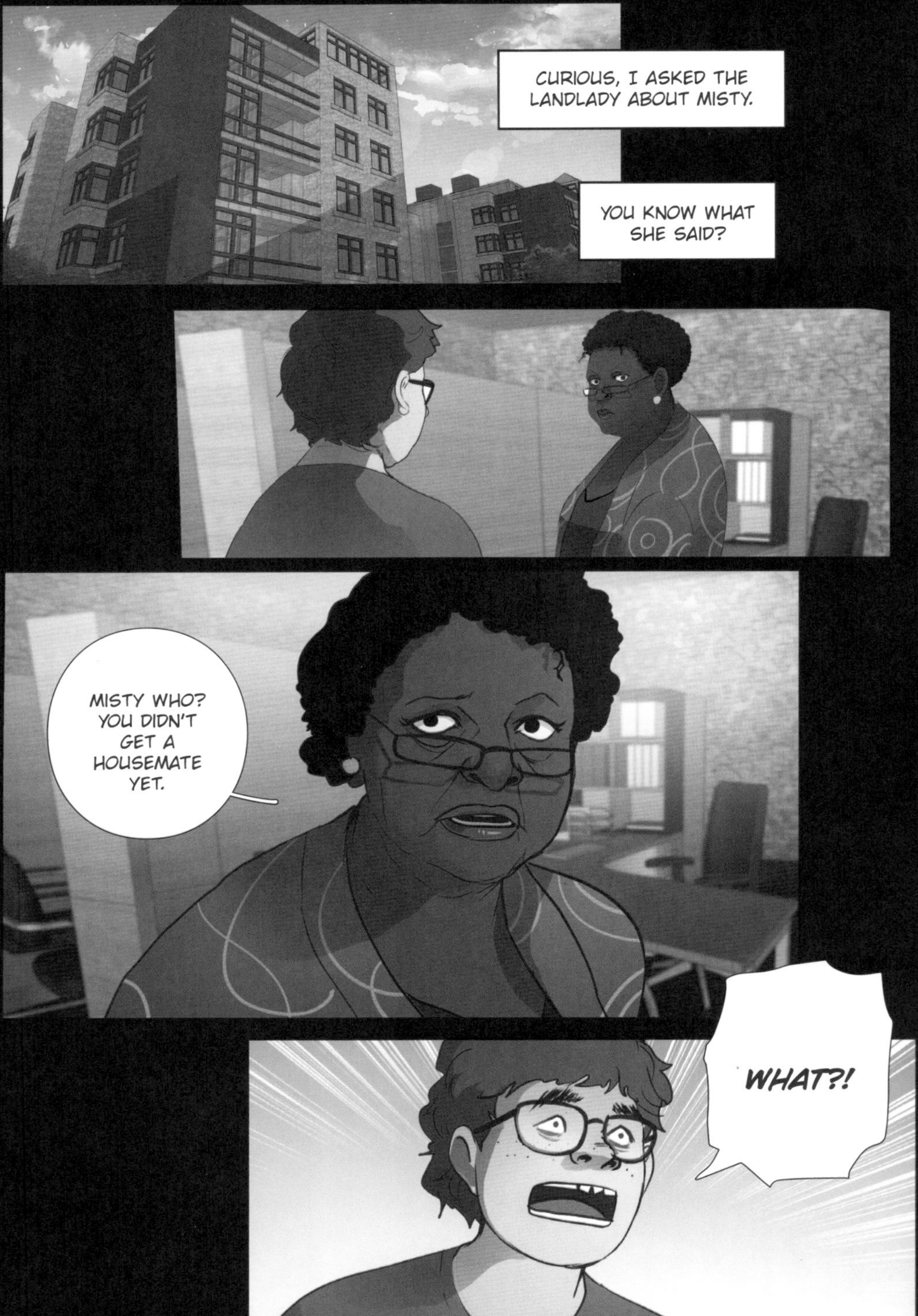
CURIOUS, I ASKED THE LANDLADY ABOUT MISTY.
YOU KNOW WHAT SHE SAID?
MISTY WHO? YOU DIDN'T GET A HOUSEMATE YET.
WHAT?!

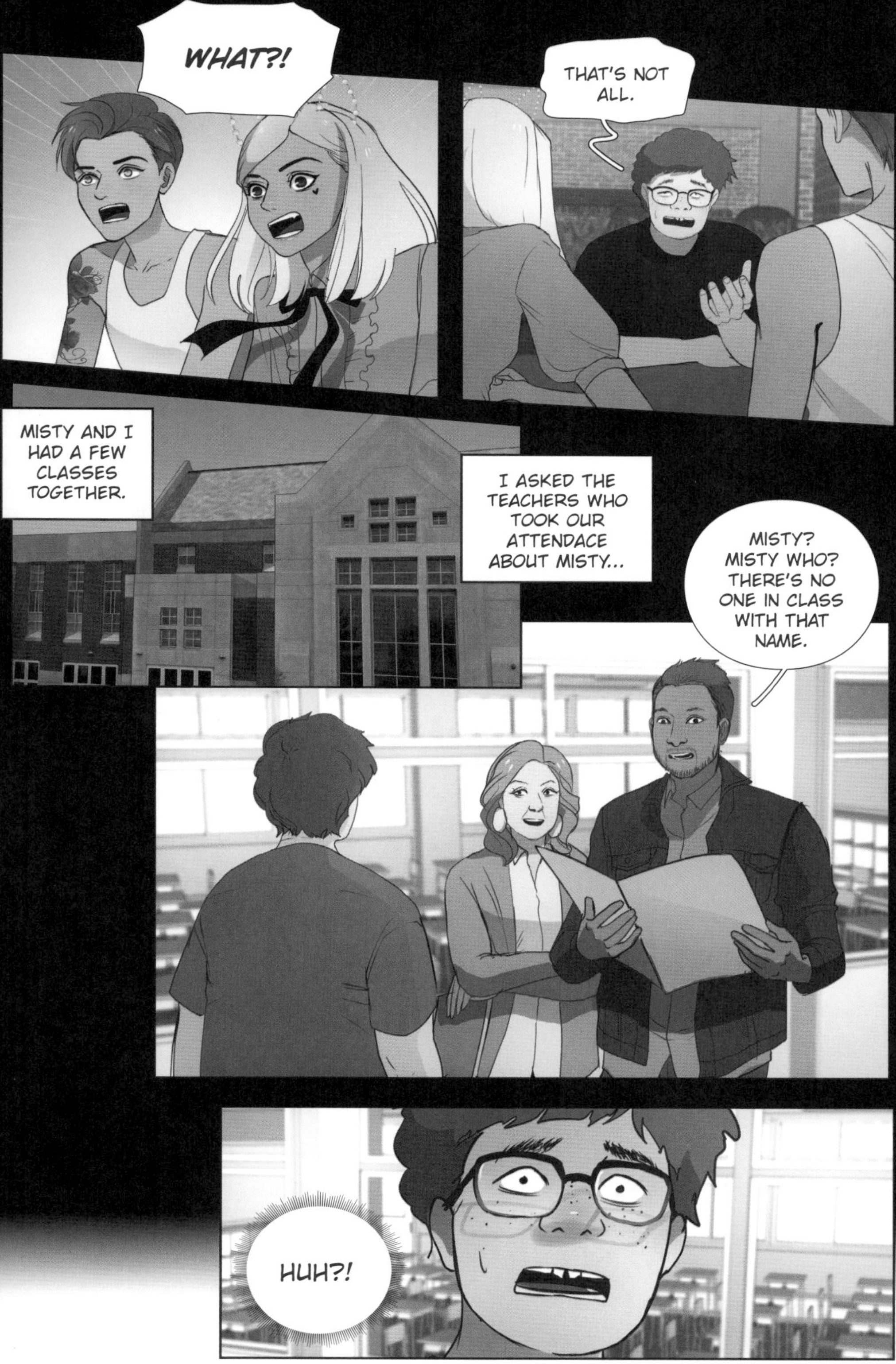
WHAT?!
THAT'S NOT ALL.
MISTY AND I HAD A FEW CLASSES TOGETHER.
I ASKED THE TEACHERS WHO TOOK OUR ATTENDACE ABOUT MISTY...
MISTY? MISTY WHO? THERE'S NO ONE IN CLASS WITH THAT NAME.
HUH?!

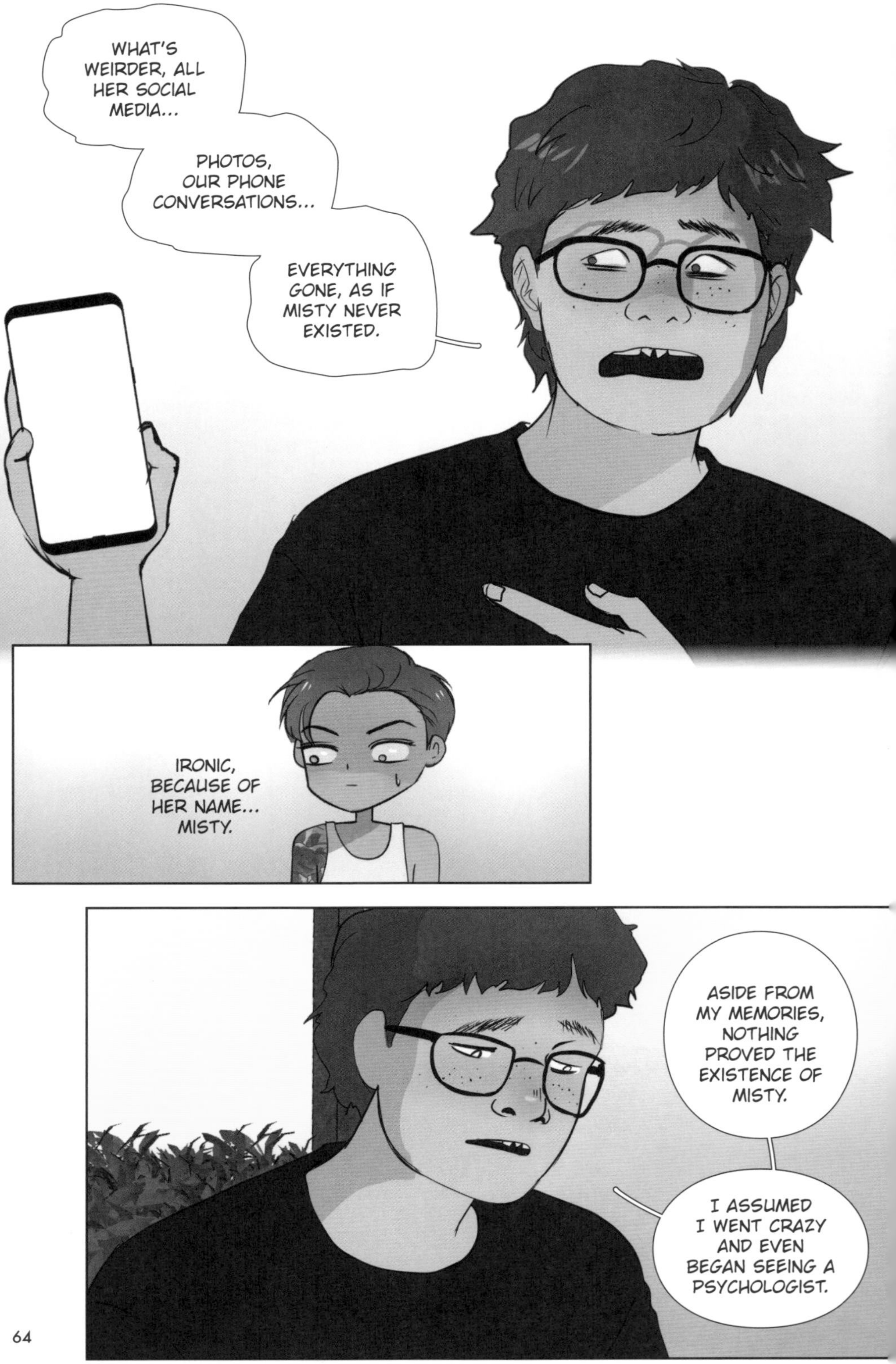
WHAT'S WEIRDER, ALL HER SOCIAL MEDIA...
PHOTOS, OUR PHONE CONVERSATIONS...
EVERYTHING GONE, AS IF MISTY NEVER EXISTED.
IRONIC, BECAUSE OF HER NAME... MISTY.
ASIDE FROM MY MEMORIES, NOTHING PROVED THE EXISTENCE OF MISTY.
I ASSUMED I WENT CRAZY AND EVEN BEGAN SEEING A PSYCHOLOGIST.

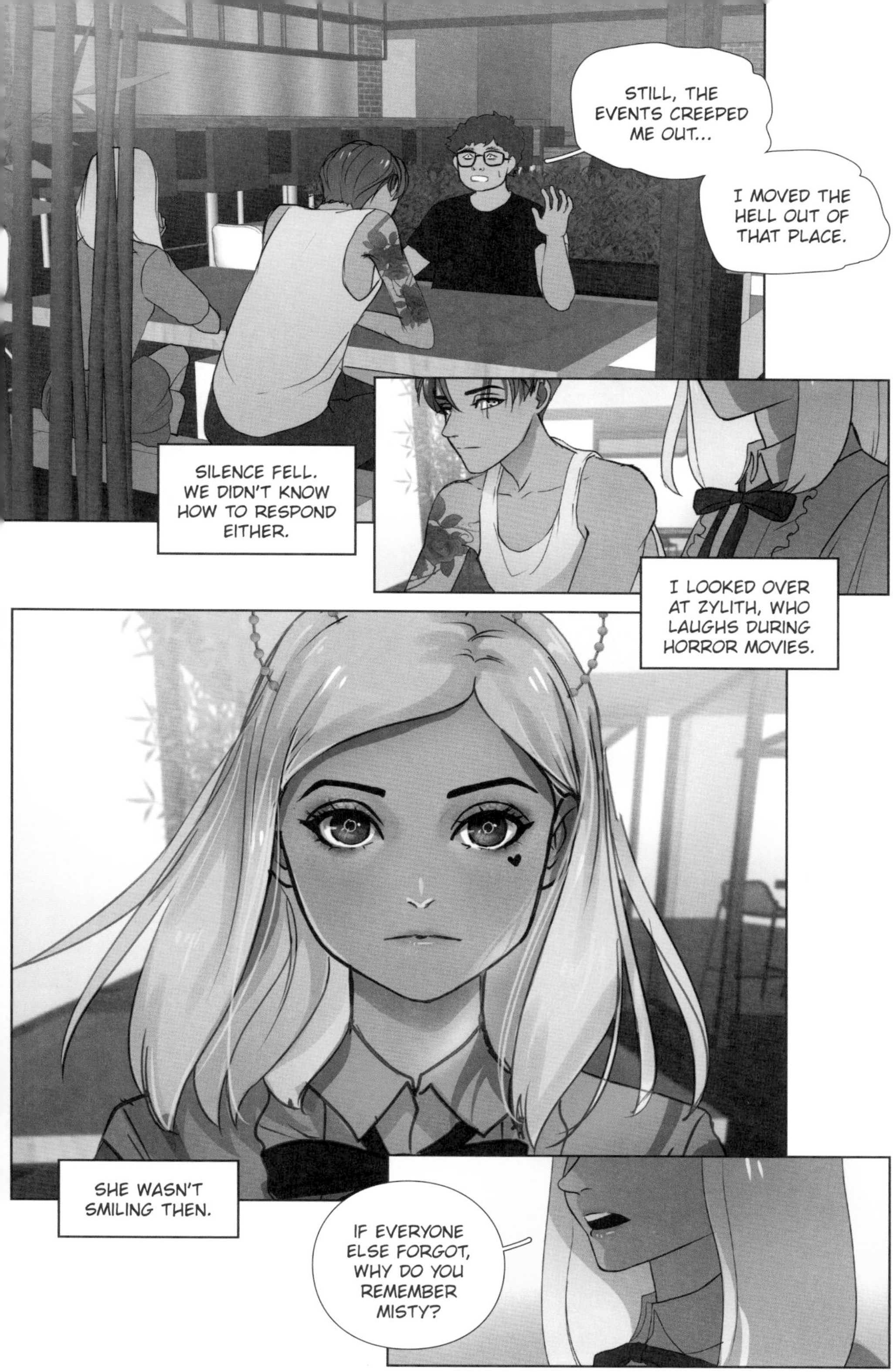
STILL, THE EVENTS CREEPED ME OUT...
I MOVED THE HELL OUT OF THAT PLACE.
SILENCE FELL. WE DIDN'T KNOW HOW TO RESPOND EITHER.
I LOOKED OVER AT ZYLITH, WHO LAUGHS DURING HORROR MOVIES.
SHE WASN'T SMILING THEN.
IF EVERYONE ELSE FORGOT, WHY DO YOU REMEMBER MISTY?

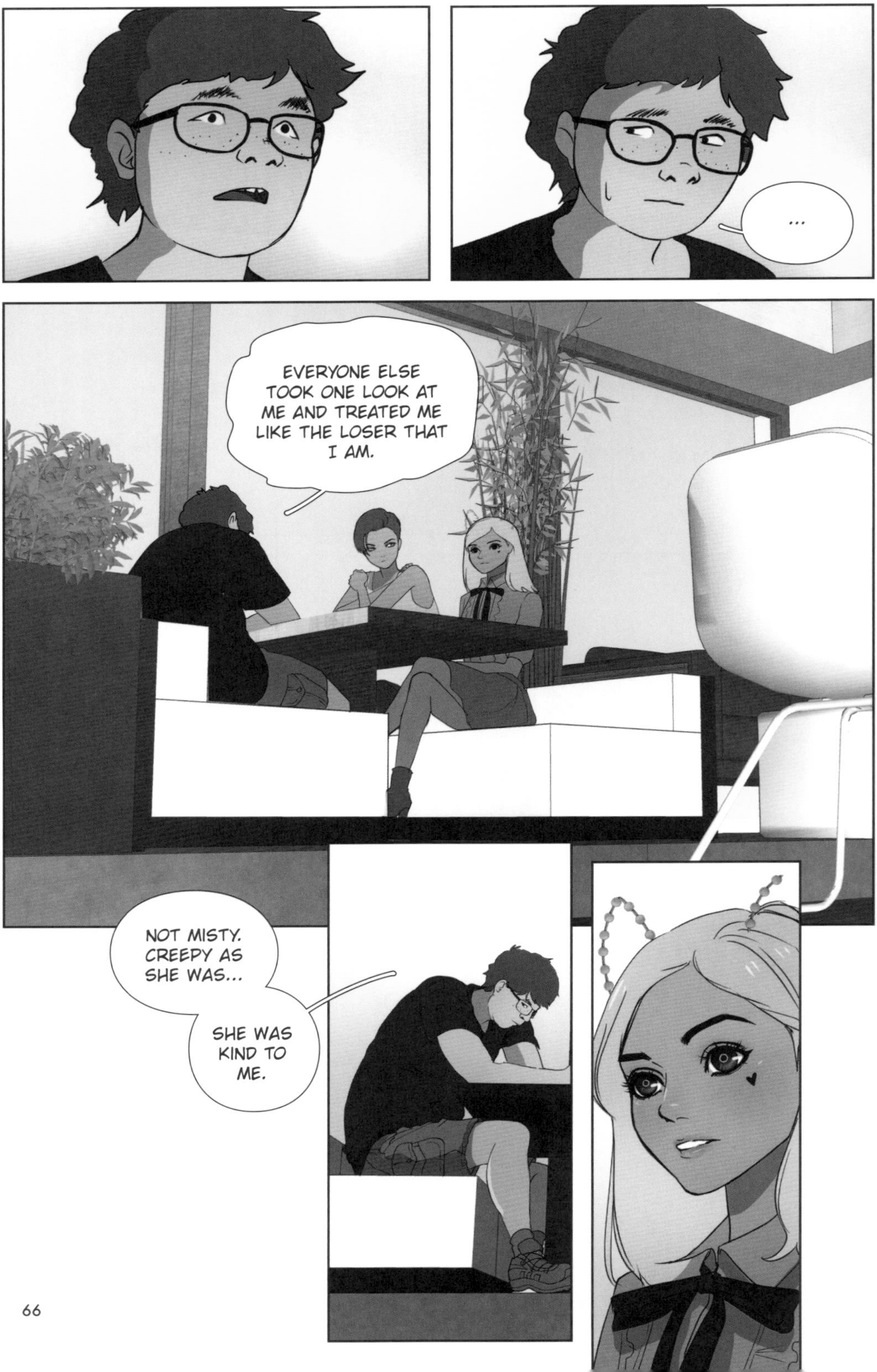
...
EVERYONE ELSE TOOK ONE LOOK AT ME AND TREATED ME LIKE THE LOSER THAT I AM.
NOT MISTY. CREEPY AS SHE WAS...
SHE WAS KIND TO ME.

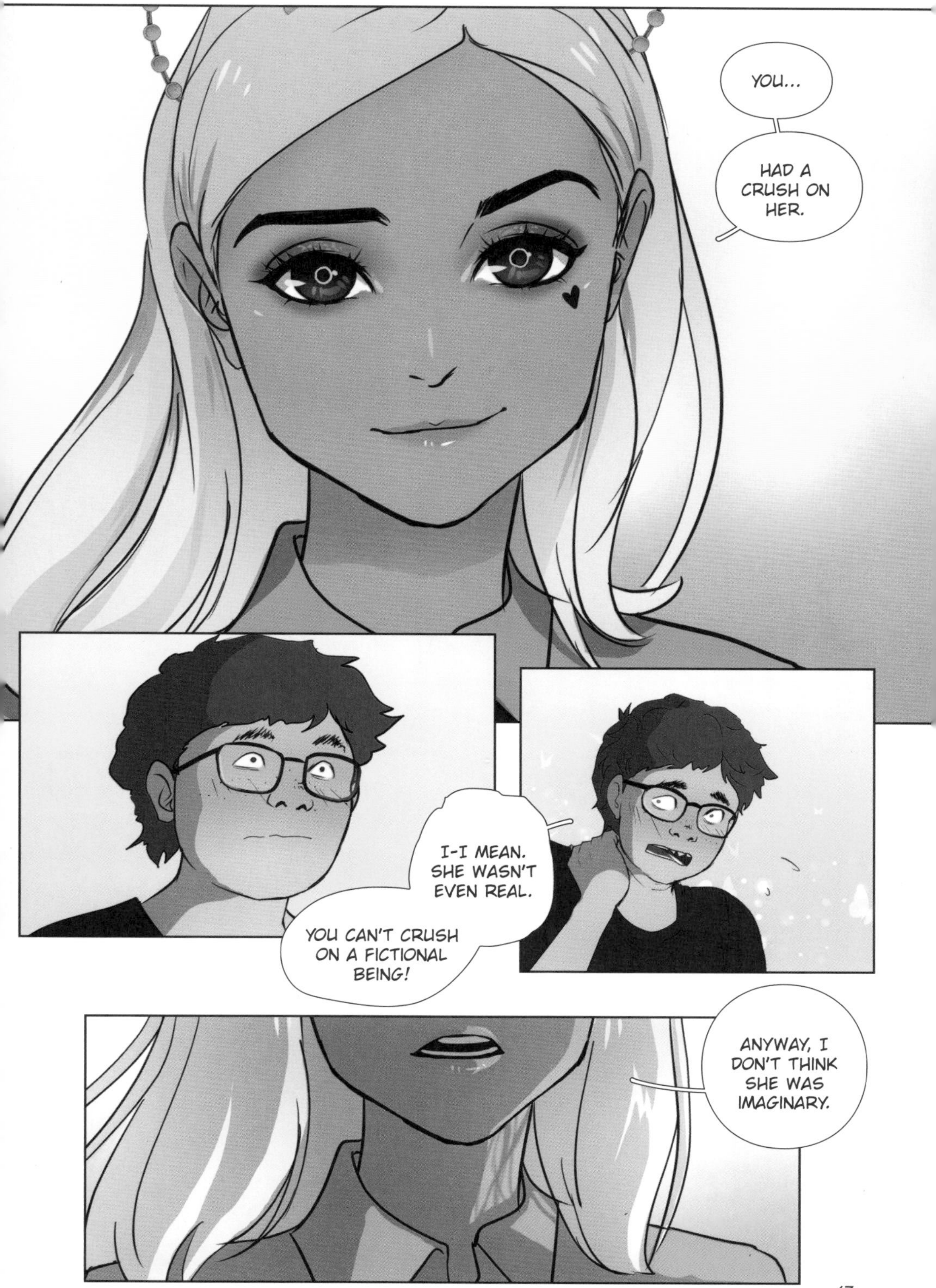

YOU...
HAD A CRUSH ON HER.
I-I MEAN. SHE WASN'T EVEN REAL.
YOU CAN'T CRUSH ON A FICTIONAL BEING!
ANYWAY, I DON'T THINK SHE WAS IMAGINARY.

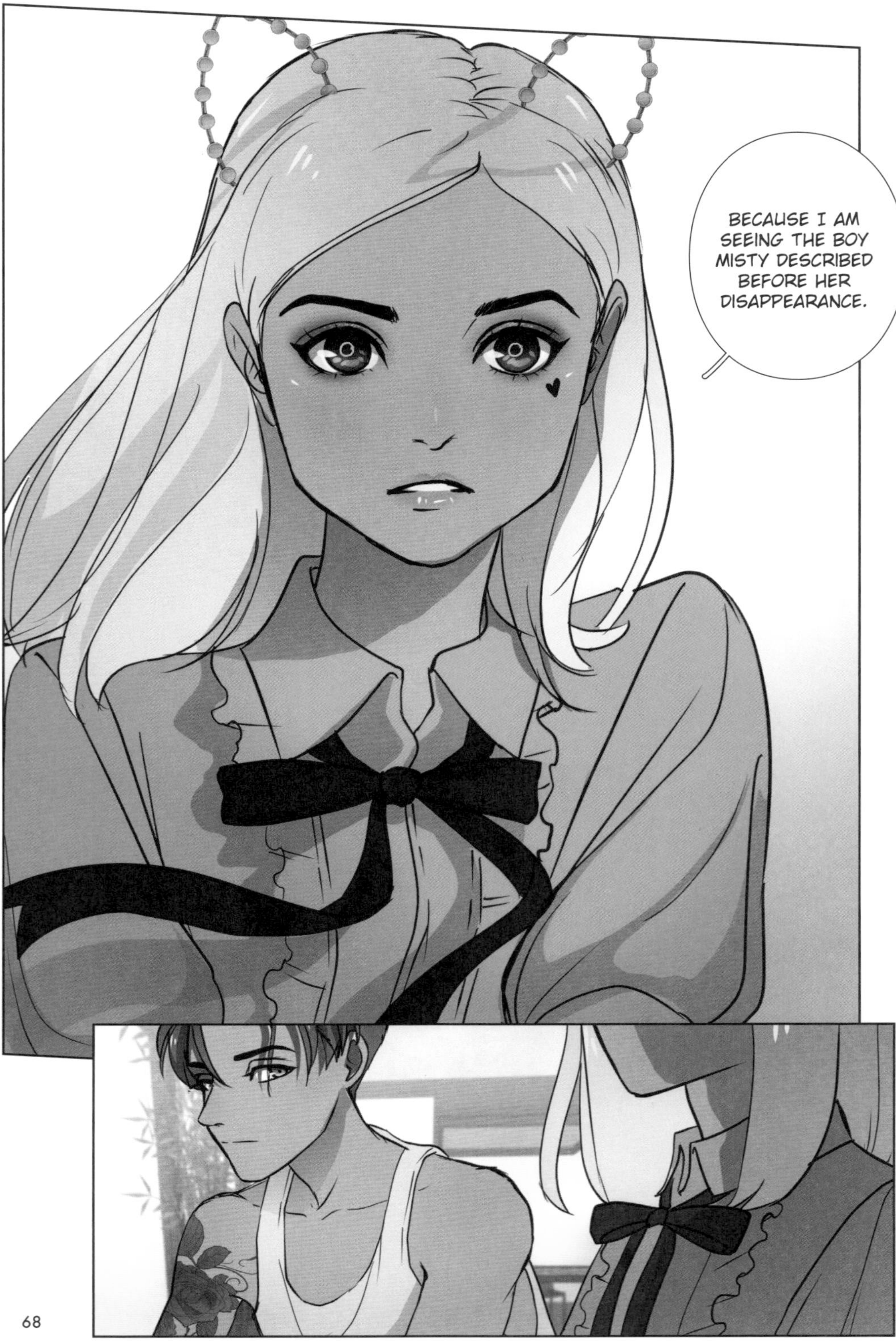
BECAUSE I AM SEEING THE BOY MISTY DESCRIBED BEFORE HER DISAPPEARANCE.

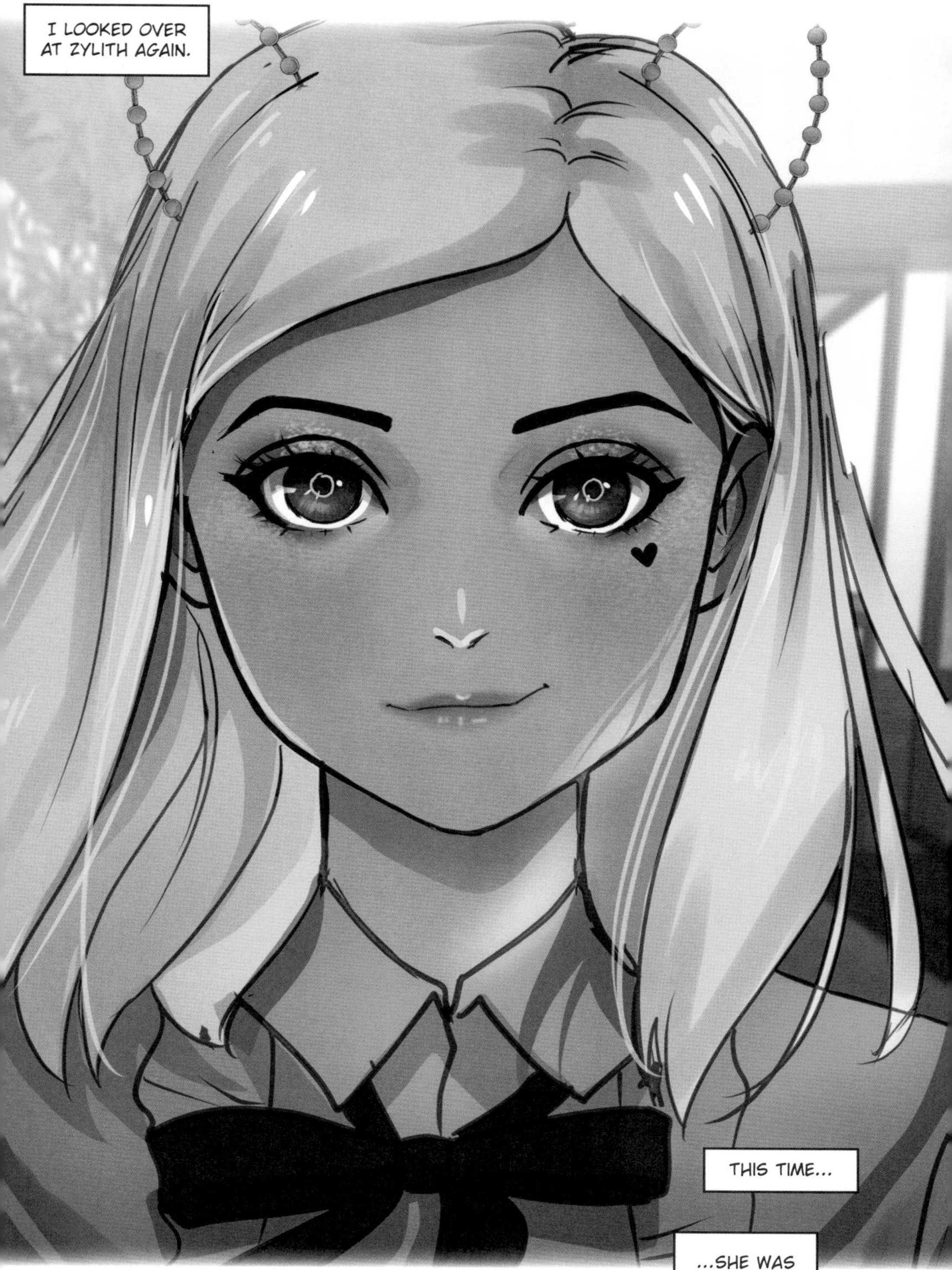
I LOOKED OVER AT ZYLITH AGAIN.
THIS TIME...
...SHE WAS SMILING.

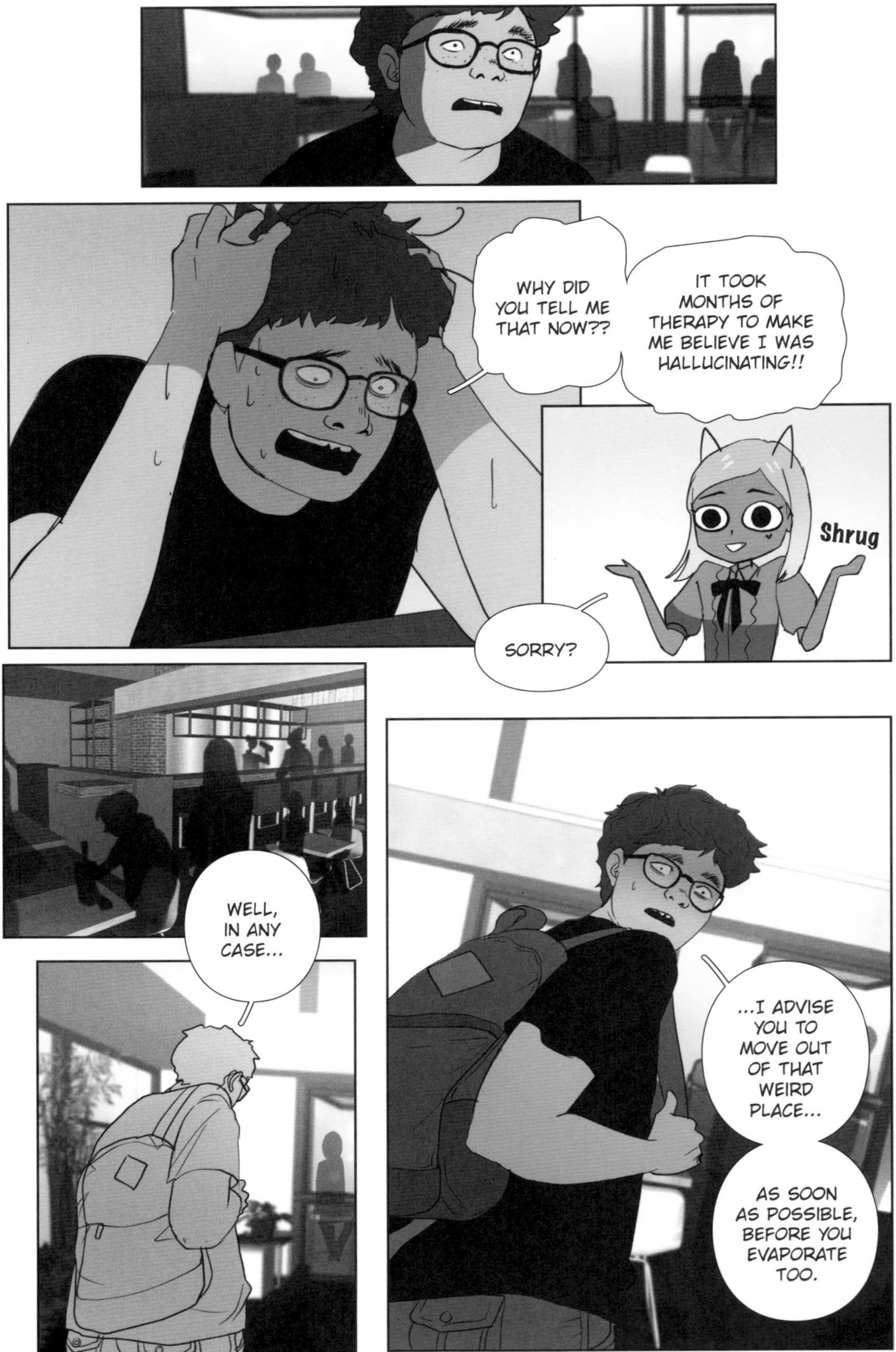
WHY DID YOU TELL ME THAT NOW??
IT TOOK MONTHS OF THERAPY TO MAKE ME BELIEVE I WAS HALLUCINATING!!
Shrug
SORRY?
WELL, IN ANY CASE...
...I ADVISE YOU TO MOVE OUT OF THAT WEIRD PLACE...
AS SOON AS POSSIBLE, BEFORE YOU EVAPORATE TOO.

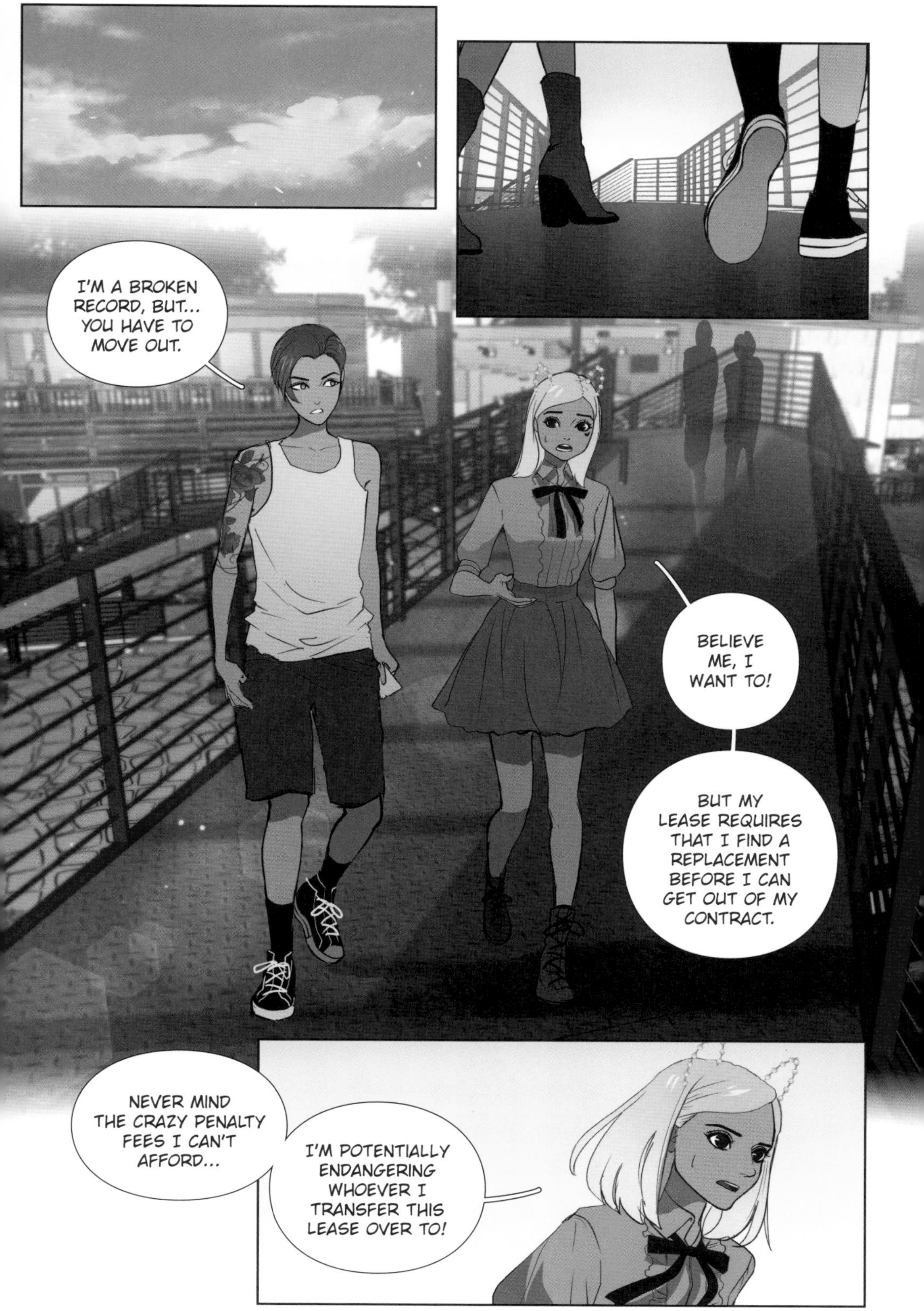
I'M A BROKEN RECORD, BUT... YOU HAVE TO MOVE OUT.
BELIEVE ME, I WANT TO!
BUT MY LEASE REQUIRES THAT I FIND A REPLACEMENT BEFORE I CAN GET OUT OF MY CONTRACT.
NEVER MIND THE CRAZY PENALTY FEES I CAN'T AFFORD...
I'M POTENTIALLY ENDANGERING WHOEVER I TRANSFER THIS LEASE OVER TO!

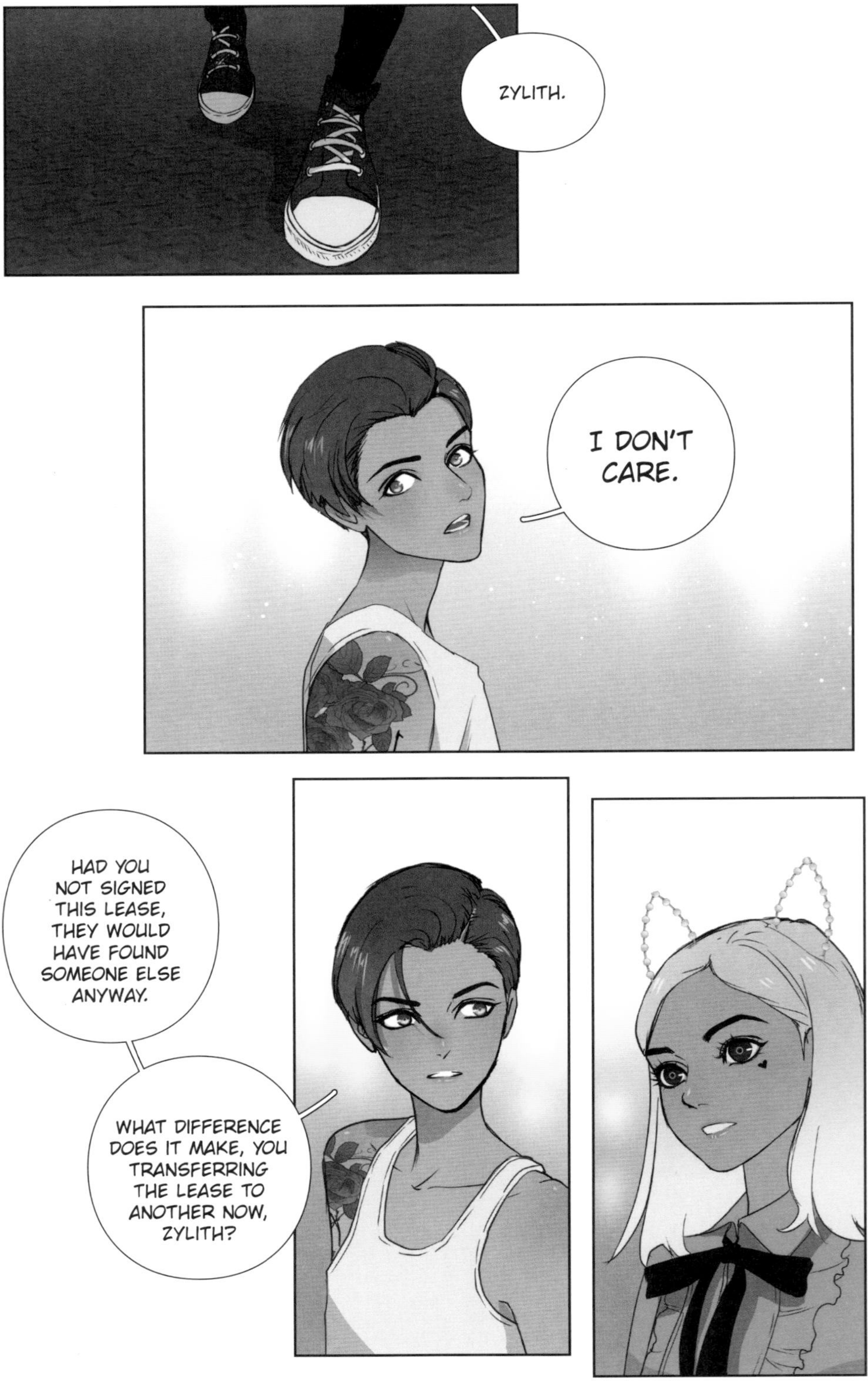
ZYLITH.
I DON'T CARE.
HAD YOU NOT SIGNED THIS LEASE, THEY WOULD HAVE FOUND SOMEONE ELSE ANYWAY.
WHAT DIFFERENCE DOES IT MAKE, YOU TRANSFERRING THE LEASE TO ANOTHER NOW, ZYLITH?

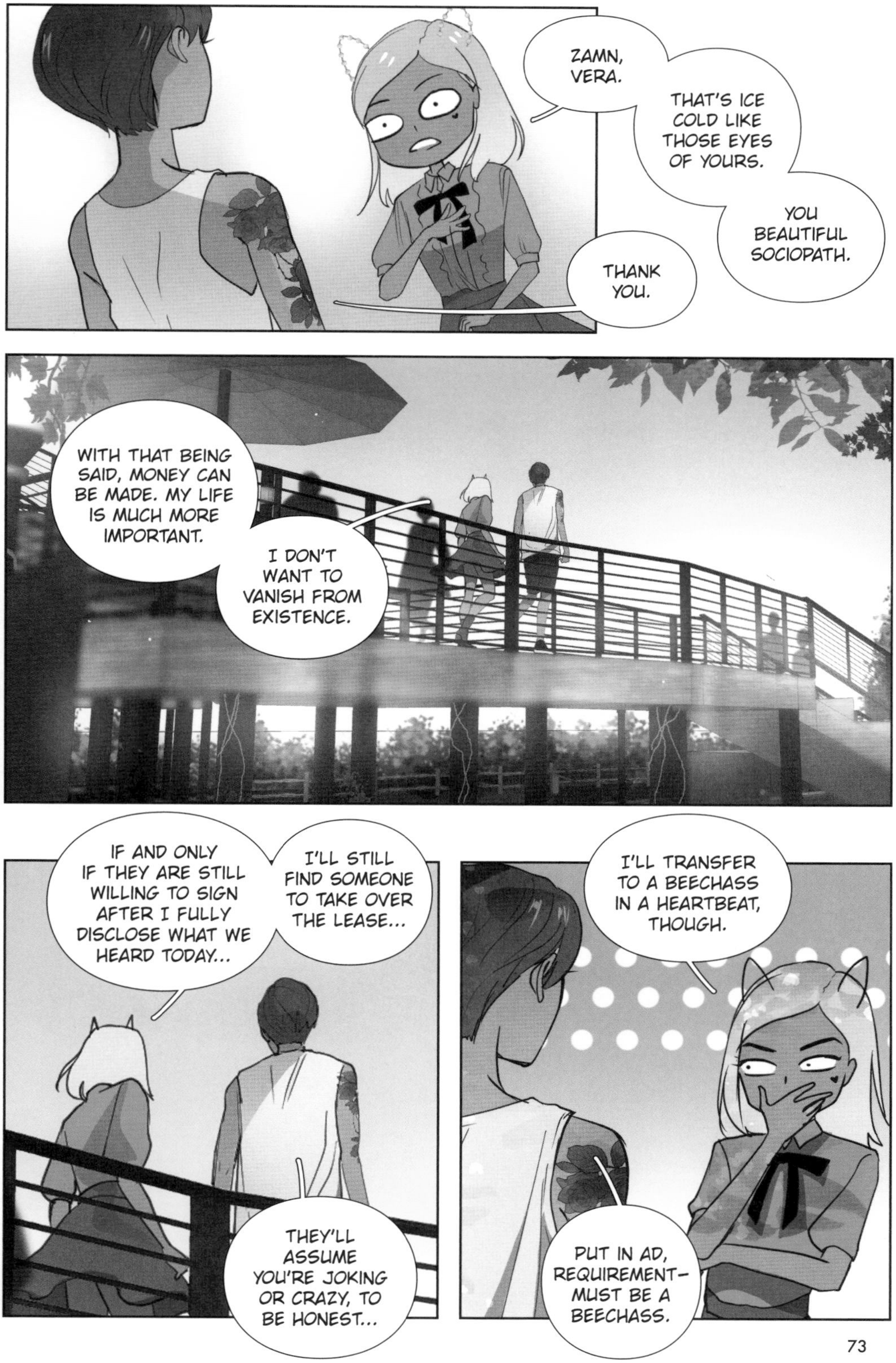
ZAMN, VERA.
THAT'S ICE COLD LIKE THOSE EYES OF YOURS.
YOU BEAUTIFUL SOCIOPATH.
THANK YOU.
WITH THAT BEING SAID, MONEY CAN BE MADE. MY LIFE IS MUCH MORE IMPORTANT.
I DON'T WANT TO VANISH FROM EXISTENCE.
IF AND ONLY IF THEY ARE STILL WILLING TO SIGN AFTER I FULLY DISCLOSE WHAT WE HEARD TODAY...
I'LL STILL FIND SOMEONE TO TAKE OVER THE LEASE...
THEY'LL ASSUME YOU'RE JOKING OR CRAZY, TO BE HONEST...
I'LL TRANSFER TO A BEECHASS IN A HEARTBEAT, THOUGH.
PUT IN AD, REQUIREMENT- MUST BE A BEECHASS.

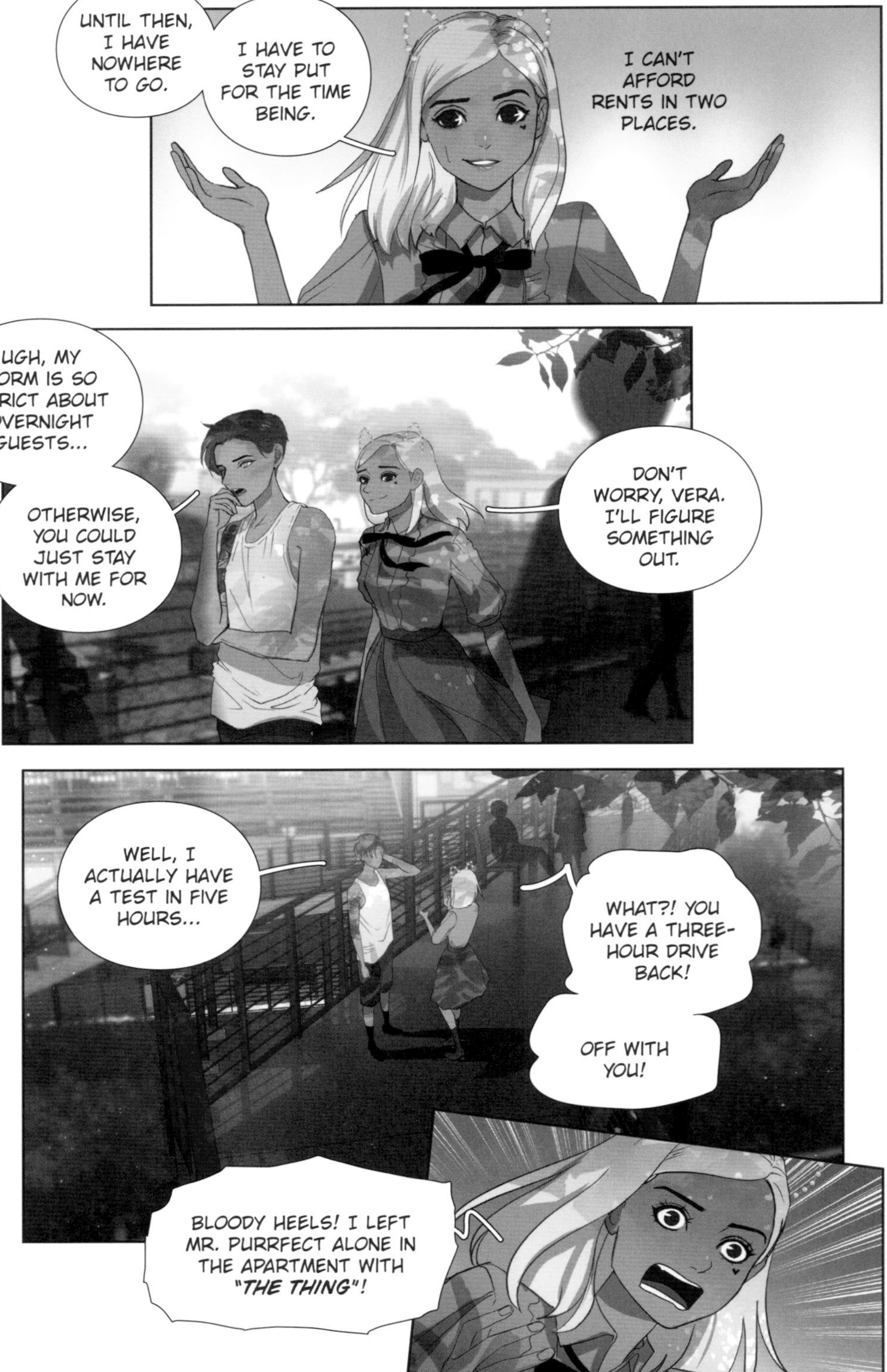
UNTIL THEN, I HAVE NOWHERE TO GO.
I HAVE TO STAY PUT FOR THE TIME BEING.
I CAN'T AFFORD RENTS IN TWO PLACES.
UGH, MY DORM IS SO STRICT ABOUT OVERNIGHT GUESTS...
OTHERWISE, YOU COULD JUST STAY WITH ME FOR NOW.
DON'T WORRY, VERA. I'LL FIGURE SOMETHING OUT.
WELL, I ACTUALLY HAVE A TEST IN FIVE HOURS...
WHAT?! YOU HAVE A THREE-HOUR DRIVE BACK!
OFF WITH YOU!
BLOODY HEELS! I LEFT MR. PURRFECT ALONE IN THE APARTMENT WITH "*THE THING*"!

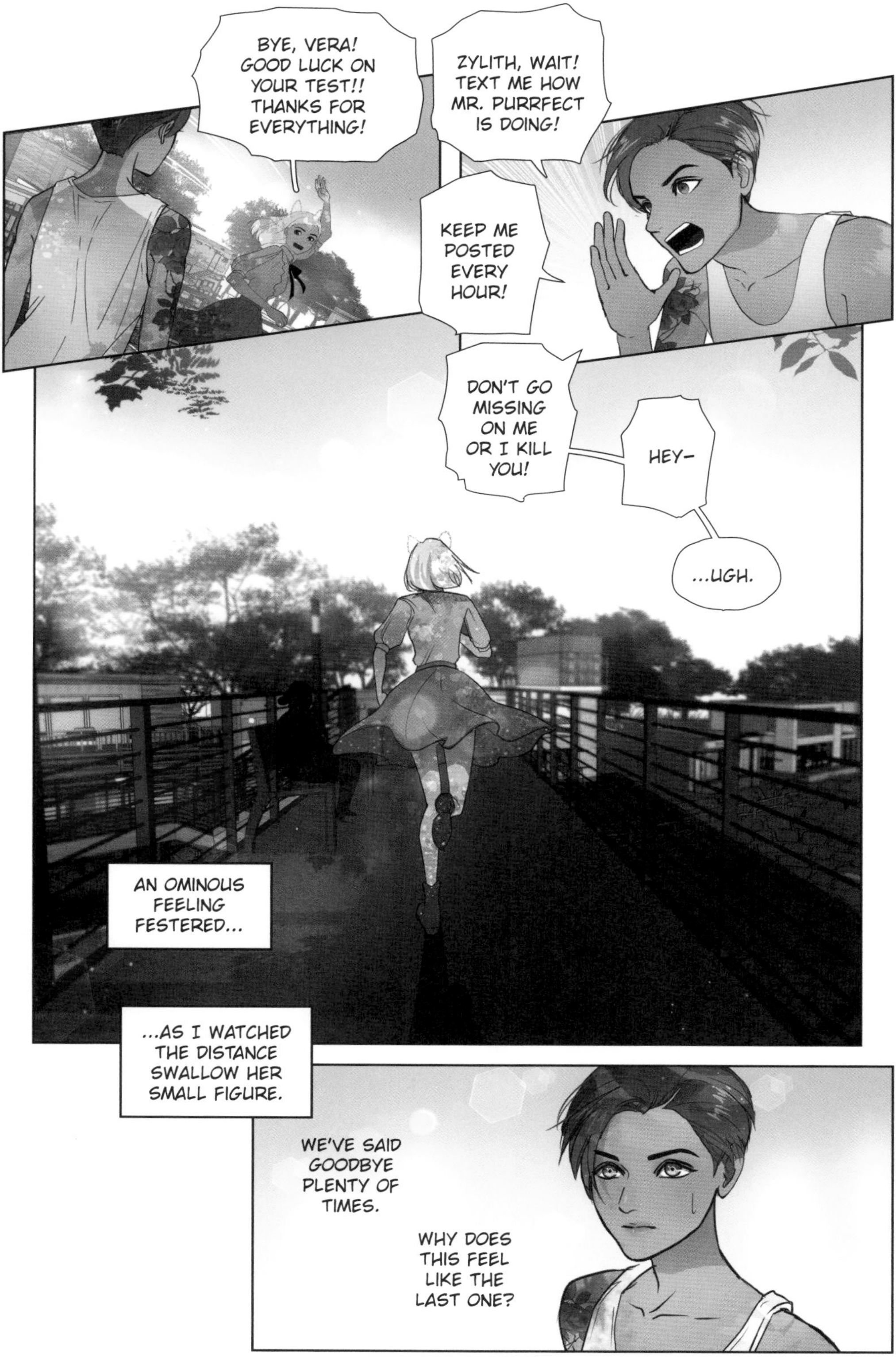
BYE, VERA! GOOD LUCK ON YOUR TEST!! THANKS FOR EVERYTHING!
ZYLITH, WAIT! TEXT ME HOW MR. PURRFECT IS DOING!
KEEP ME POSTED EVERY HOUR!
DON'T GO MISSING ON ME OR I KILL YOU!
HEY-
...UGH.
AN OMINOUS FEELING FESTERED...
...AS I WATCHED THE DISTANCE SWALLOW HER SMALL FIGURE.
WE'VE SAID GOODBYE PLENTY OF TIMES.
WHY DOES THIS FEEL LIKE THE LAST ONE?

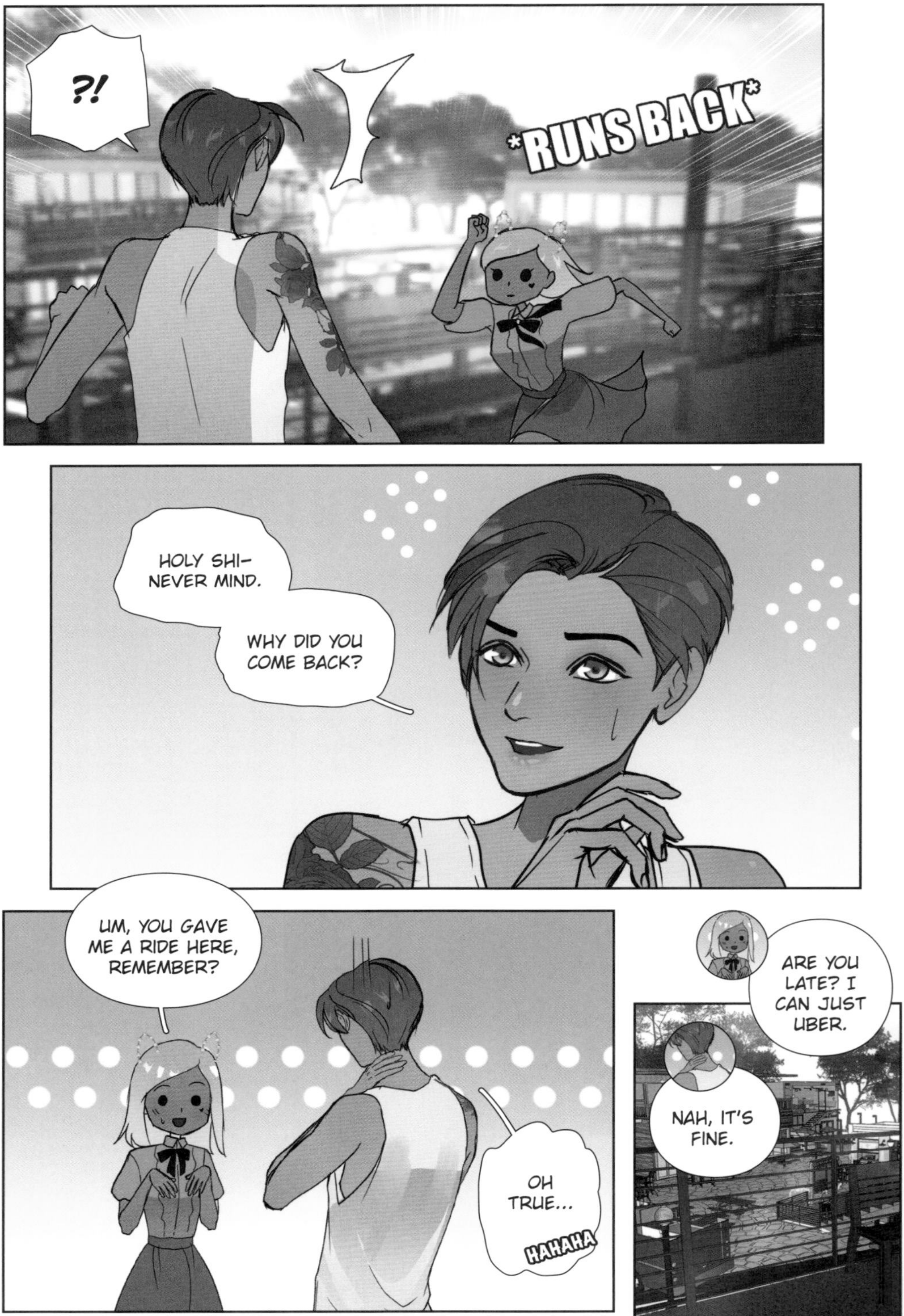

?!
RUNS BACK
HOLY SHI—
NEVER MIND.
WHY DID YOU COME BACK?
UM, YOU GAVE ME A RIDE HERE, REMEMBER?
OH TRUE...
HAHAHA
ARE YOU LATE? I CAN JUST UBER.
NAH, IT'S FINE.

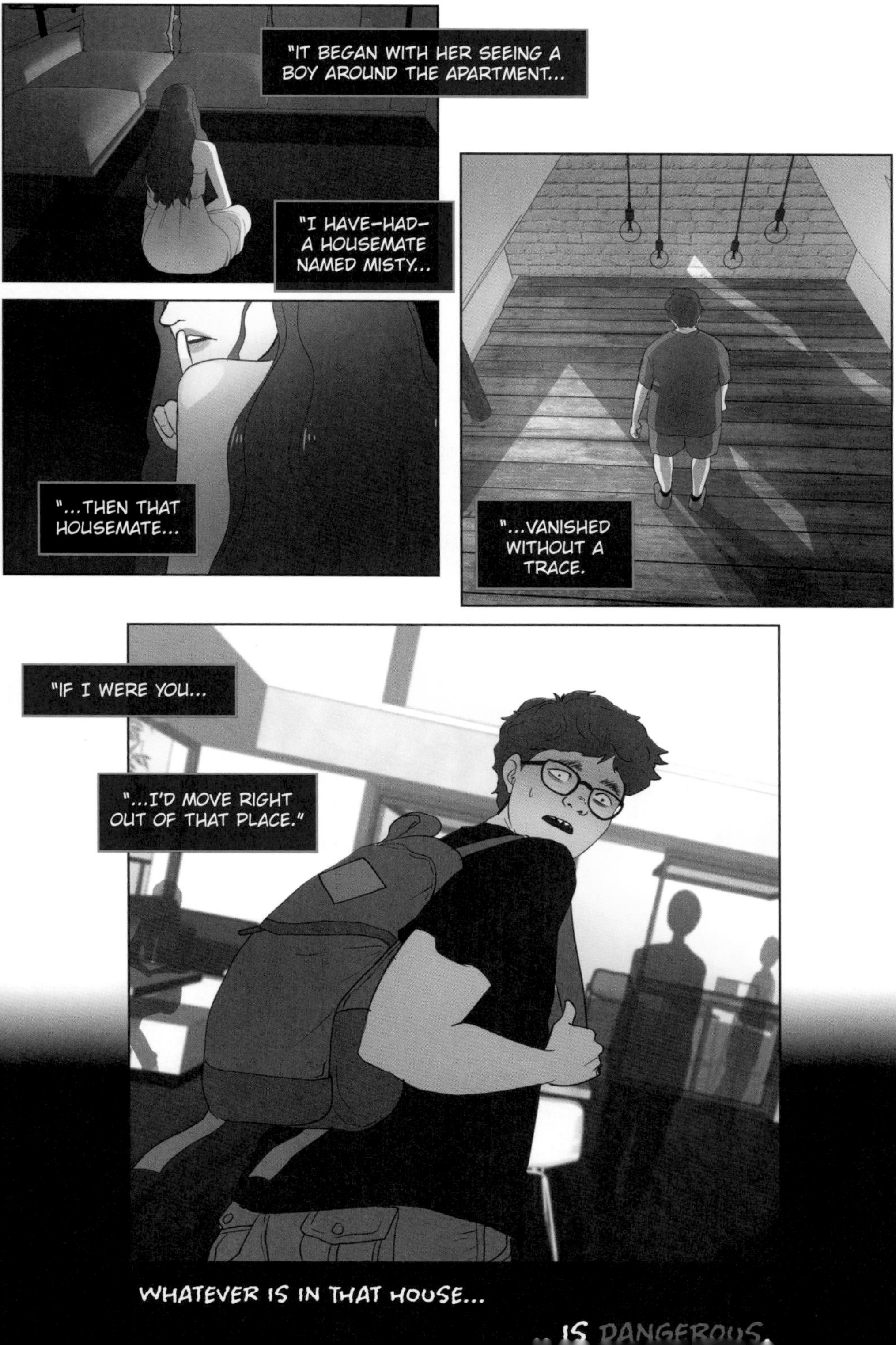
"IT BEGAN WITH HER SEEING A BOY AROUND THE APARTMENT...
"I HAVE—HAD— A HOUSEMATE NAMED MISTY...
"...THEN THAT HOUSEMATE...
"...VANISHED WITHOUT A TRACE.
"IF I WERE YOU...
"...I'D MOVE RIGHT OUT OF THAT PLACE."
WHATEVER IS IN THAT HOUSE...
...IS DANGEROUS.

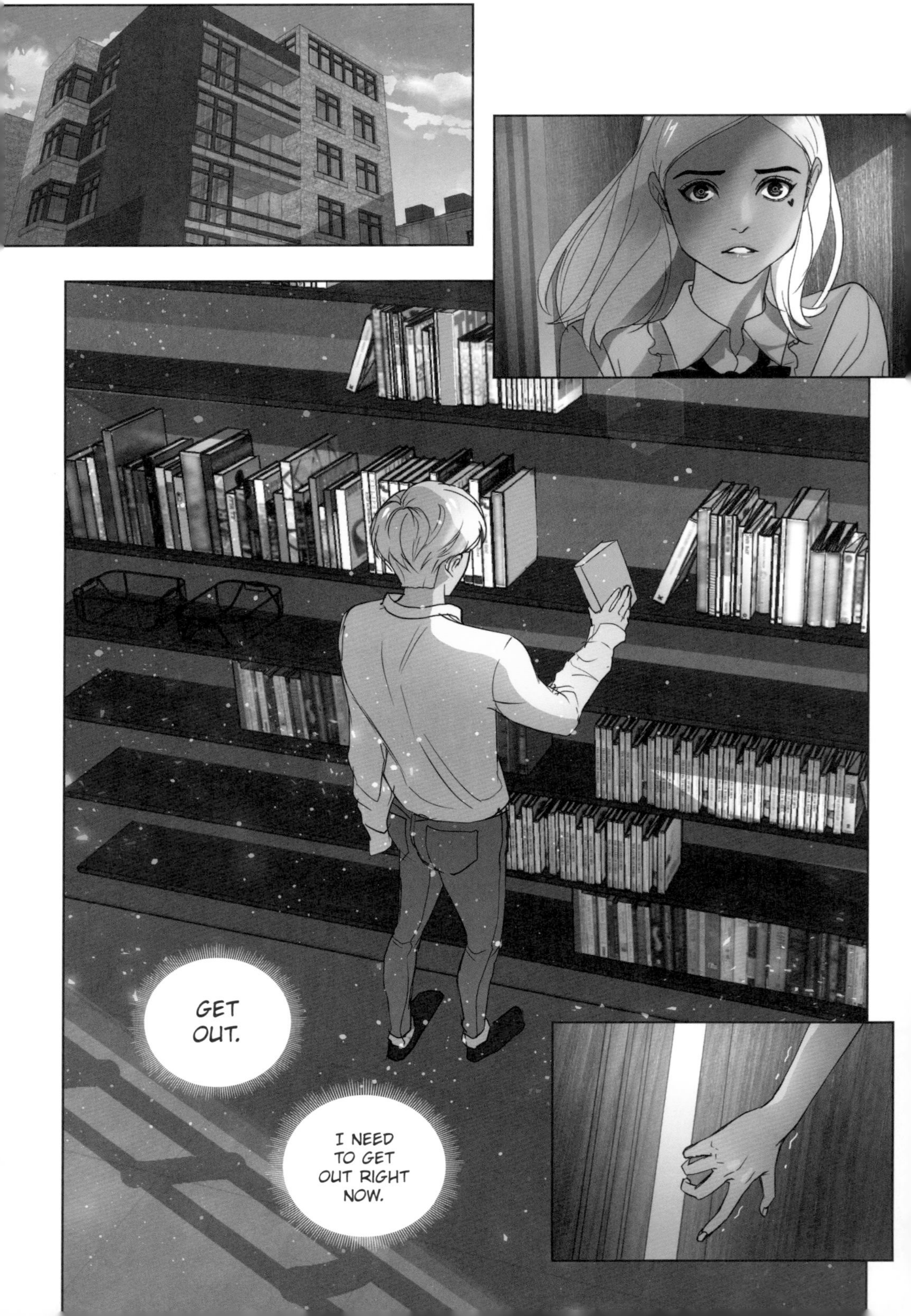
GET OUT.
I NEED TO GET OUT RIGHT NOW.

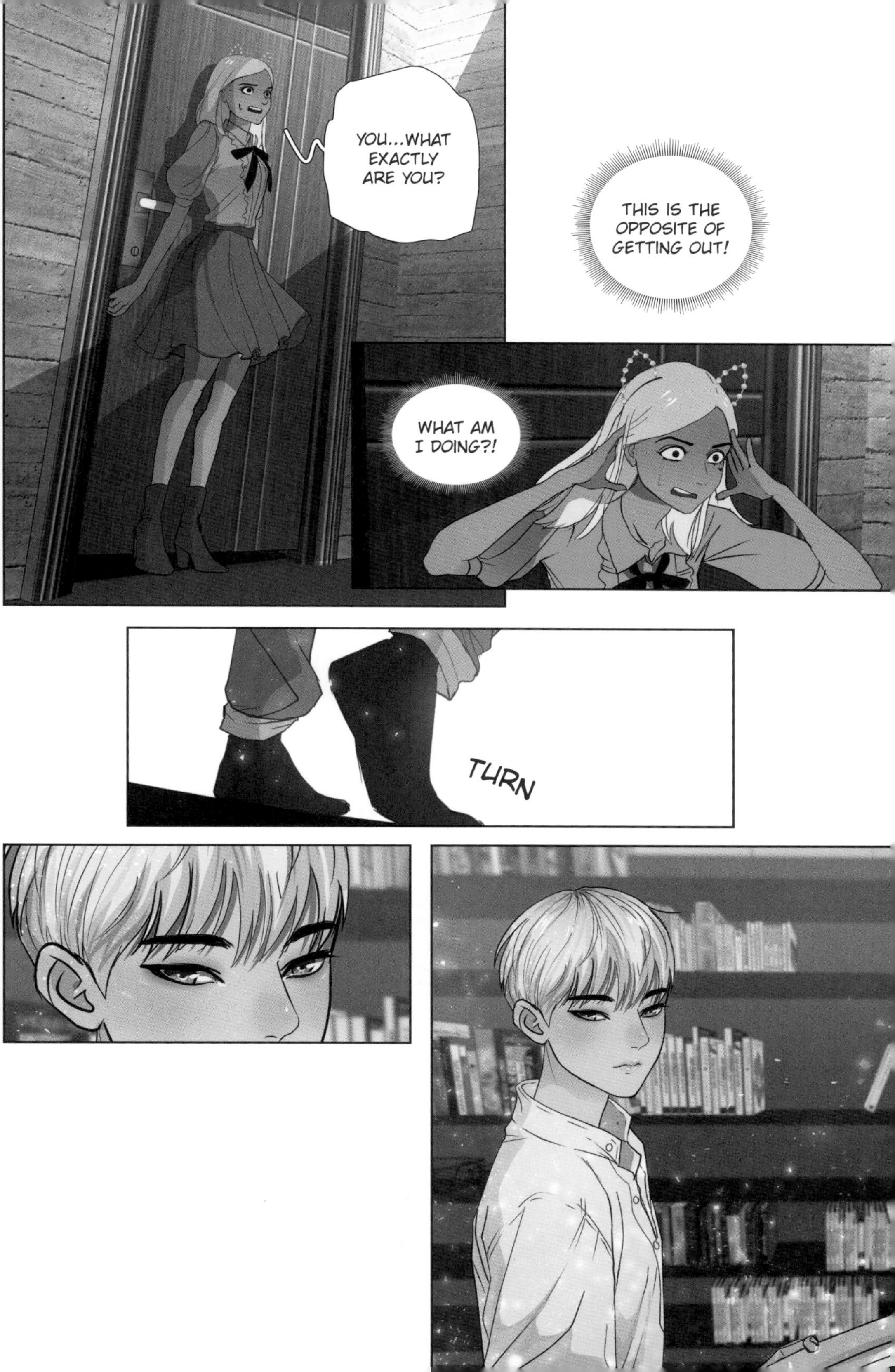
YOU...WHAT EXACTLY ARE YOU?
THIS IS THE OPPOSITE OF GETTING OUT!
WHAT AM I DOING?!
TURN

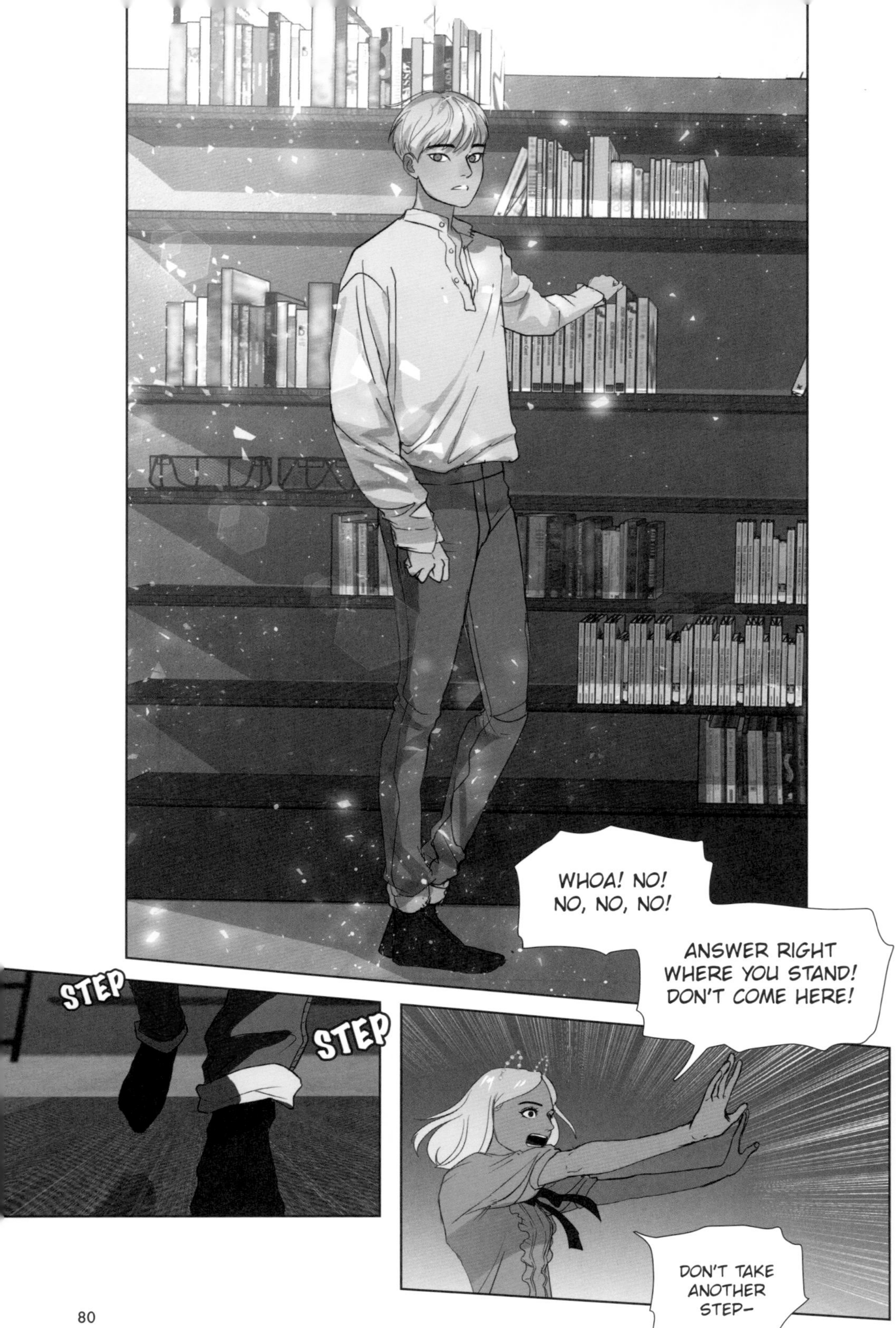
WHOA! NO! NO, NO, NO!
ANSWER RIGHT WHERE YOU STAND! DON'T COME HERE!
STEP
STEP
DON'T TAKE ANOTHER STEP–

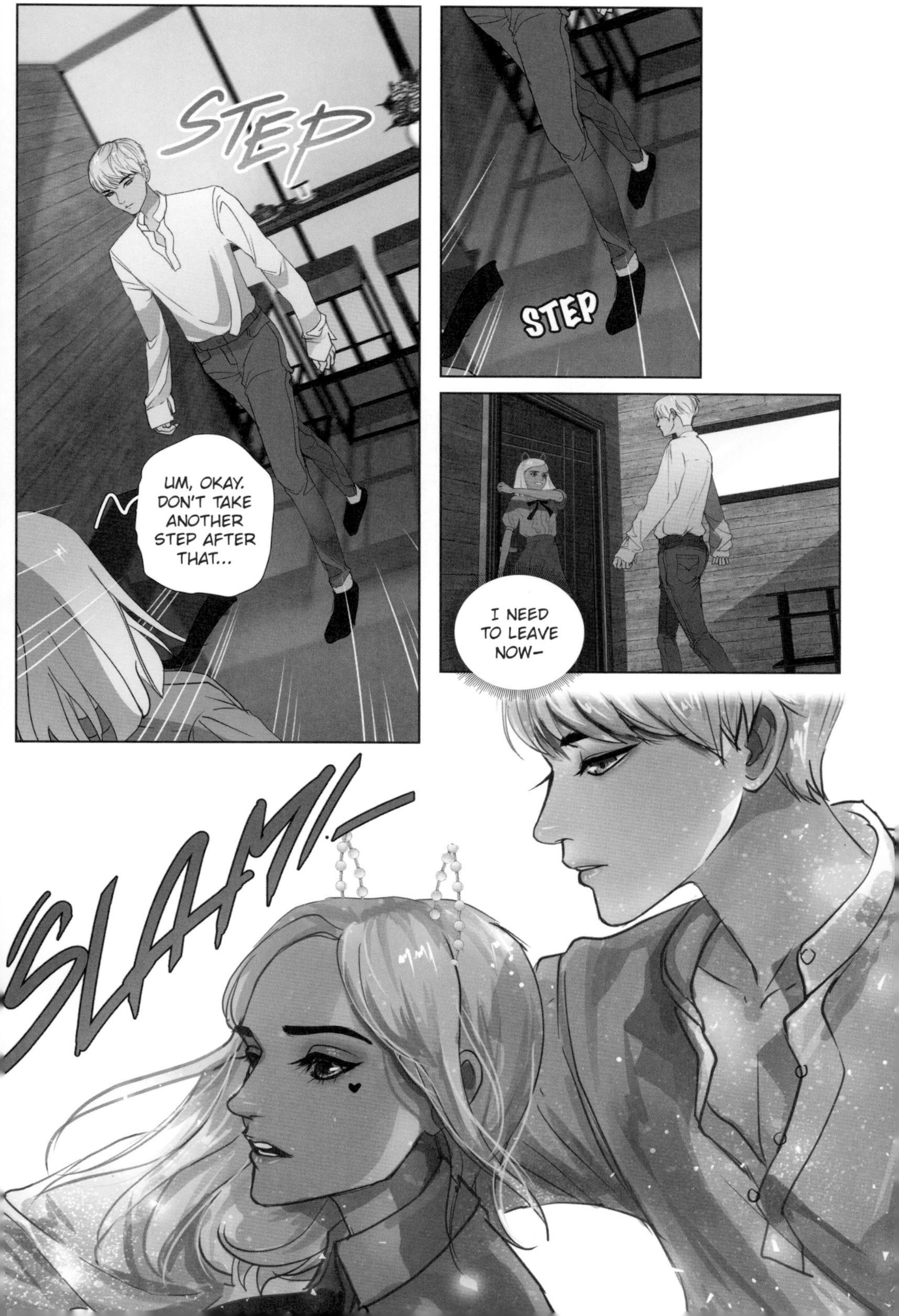
STEP
UM, OKAY. DON'T TAKE ANOTHER STEP AFTER THAT...
STEP
I NEED TO LEAVE NOW-
SLAM!

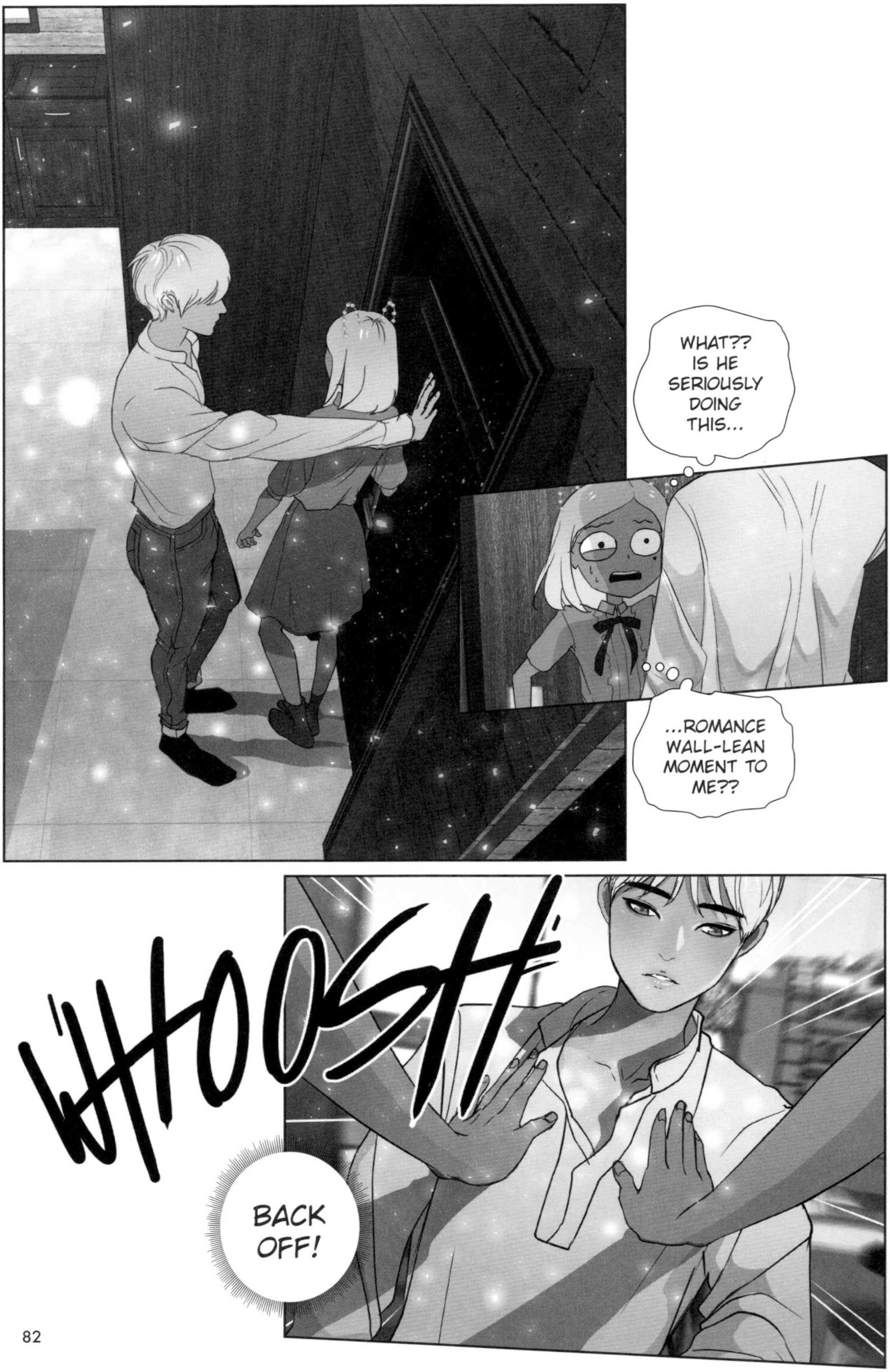
WHAT?? IS HE SERIOUSLY DOING THIS...
...ROMANCE WALL-LEAN MOMENT TO ME??
WHOOSH
BACK OFF!

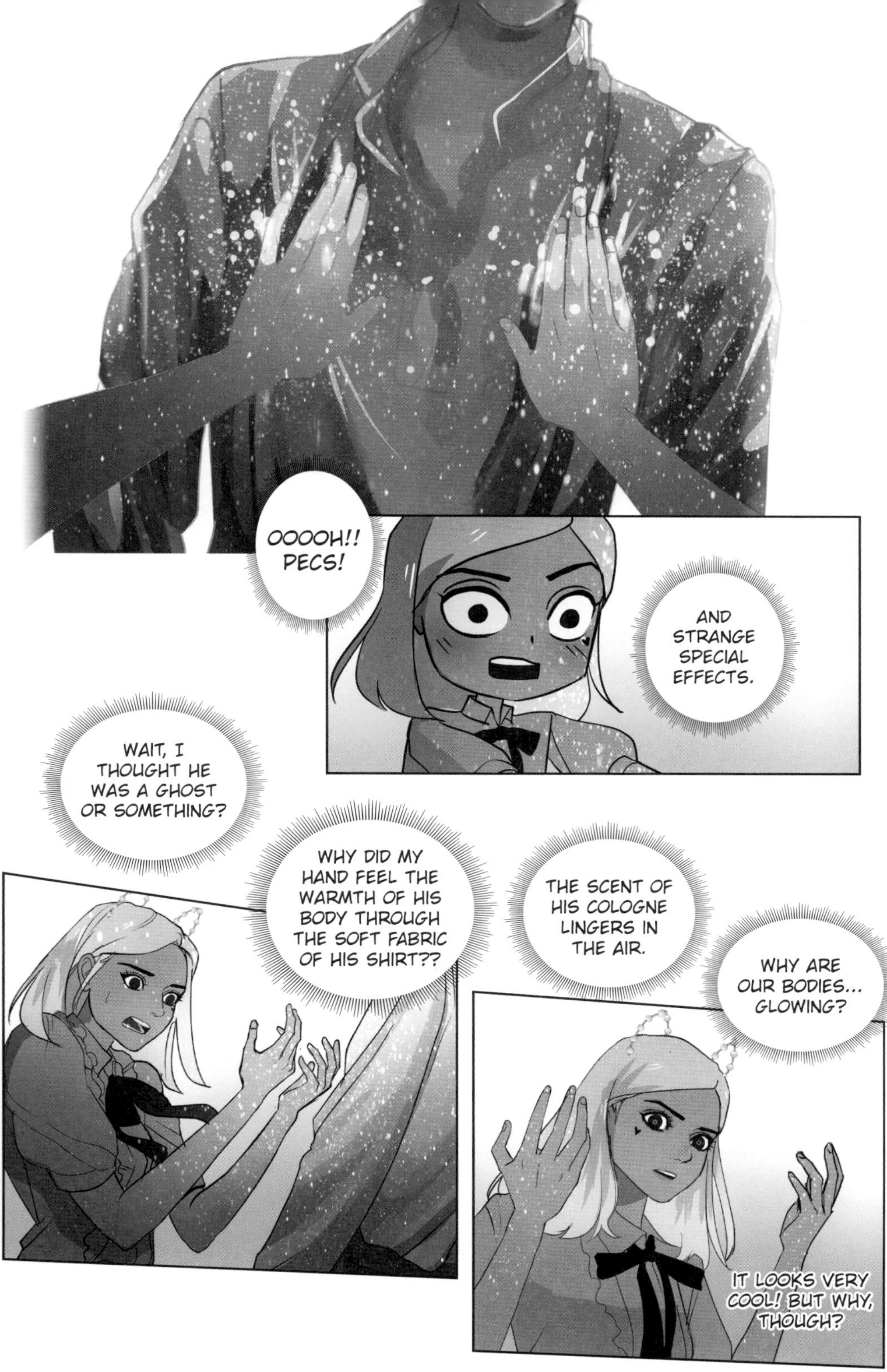
OOOOH!!
PECS!
AND STRANGE SPECIAL EFFECTS.
WAIT, I THOUGHT HE WAS A GHOST OR SOMETHING?
WHY DID MY HAND FEEL THE WARMTH OF HIS BODY THROUGH THE SOFT FABRIC OF HIS SHIRT??
THE SCENT OF HIS COLOGNE LINGERS IN THE AIR.
WHY ARE OUR BODIES... GLOWING?
IT LOOKS VERY COOL! BUT WHY, THOUGH?

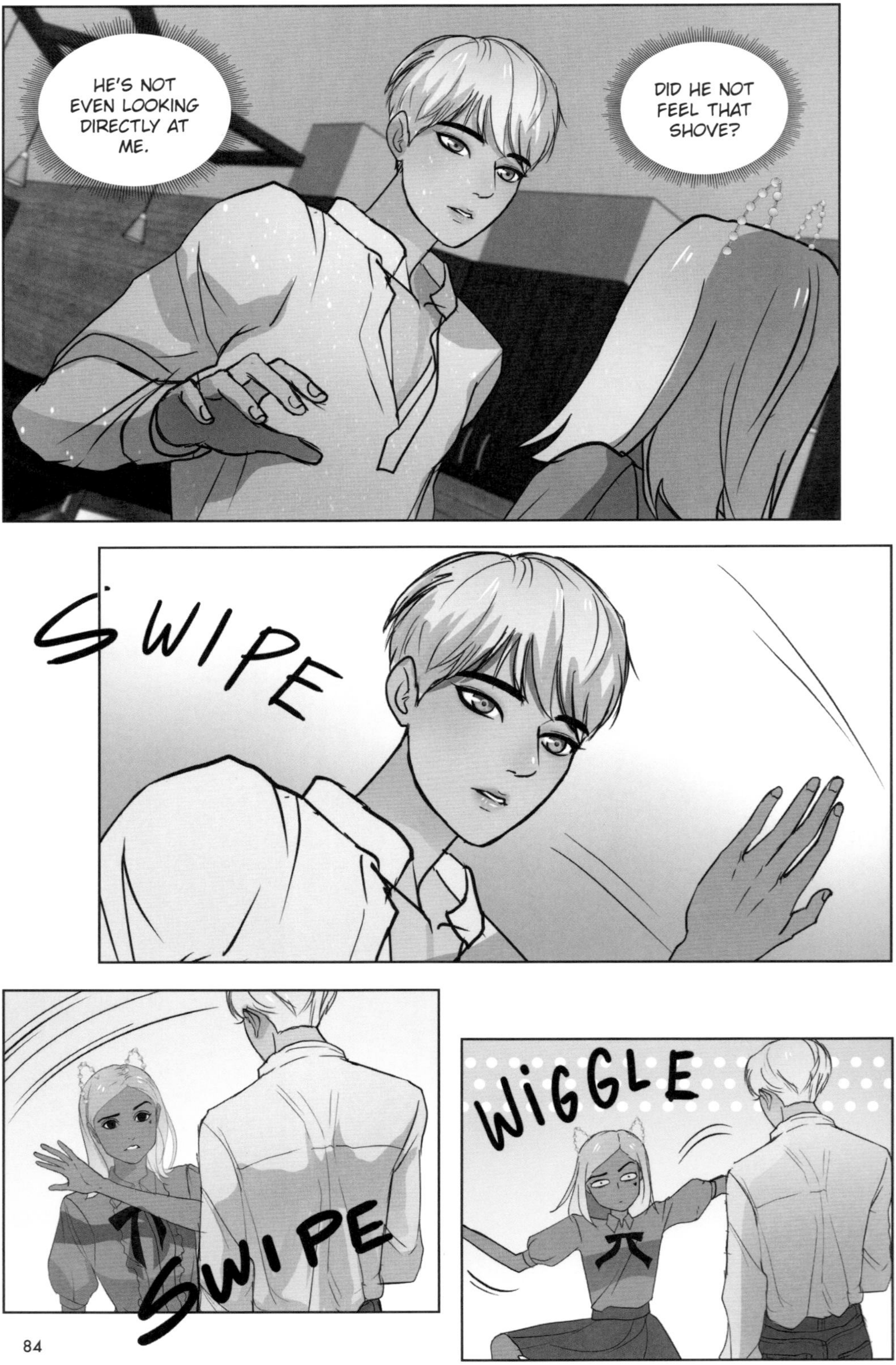
HE'S NOT EVEN LOOKING DIRECTLY AT ME.
DID HE NOT FEEL THAT SHOVE?
SWIPE
SWIPE
WIGGLE

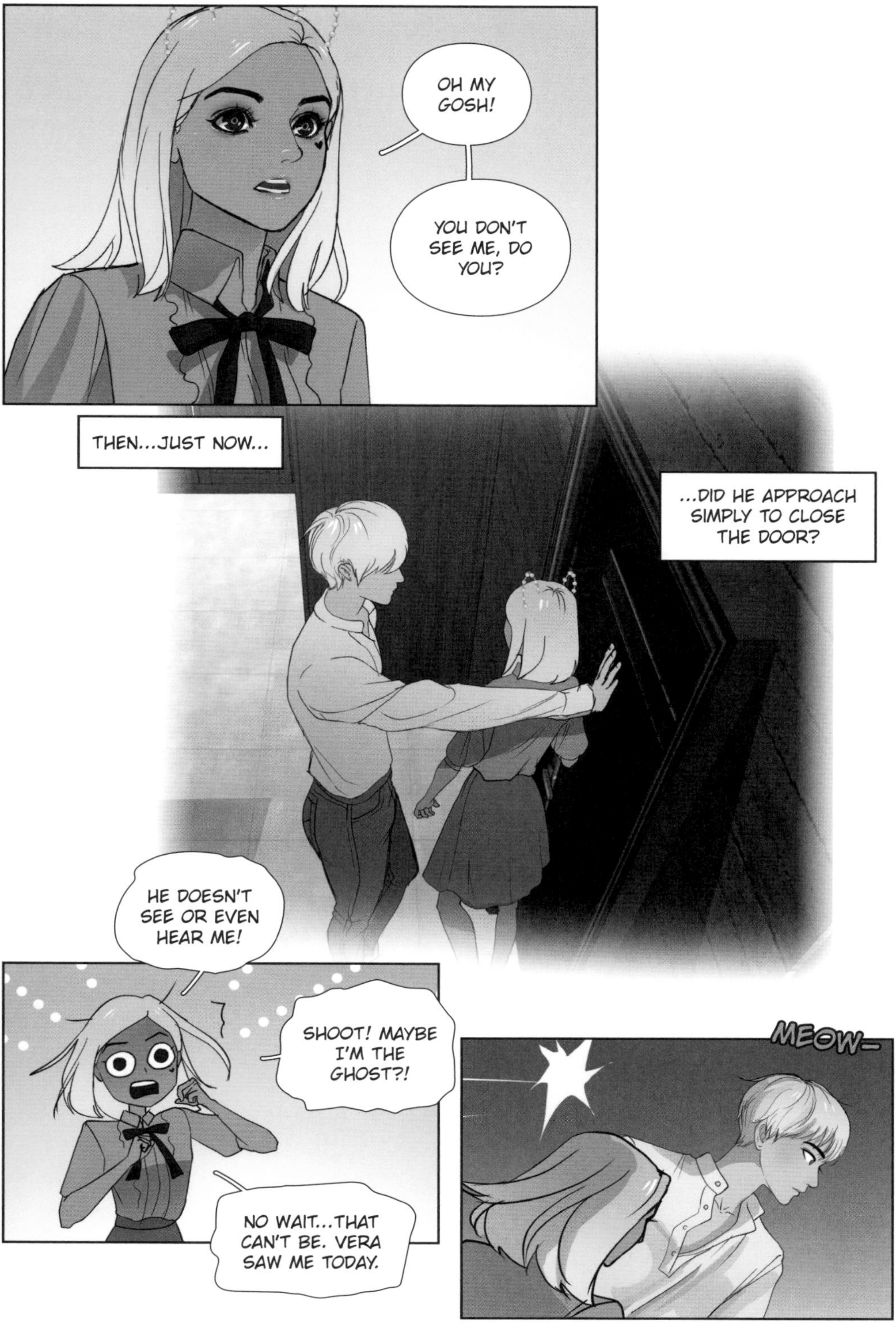
OH MY GOSH!
YOU DON'T SEE ME, DO YOU?
THEN...JUST NOW...
...DID HE APPROACH SIMPLY TO CLOSE THE DOOR?
HE DOESN'T SEE OR EVEN HEAR ME!
SHOOT! MAYBE I'M THE GHOST?!
NO WAIT...THAT CAN'T BE. VERA SAW ME TODAY.
MEOW-

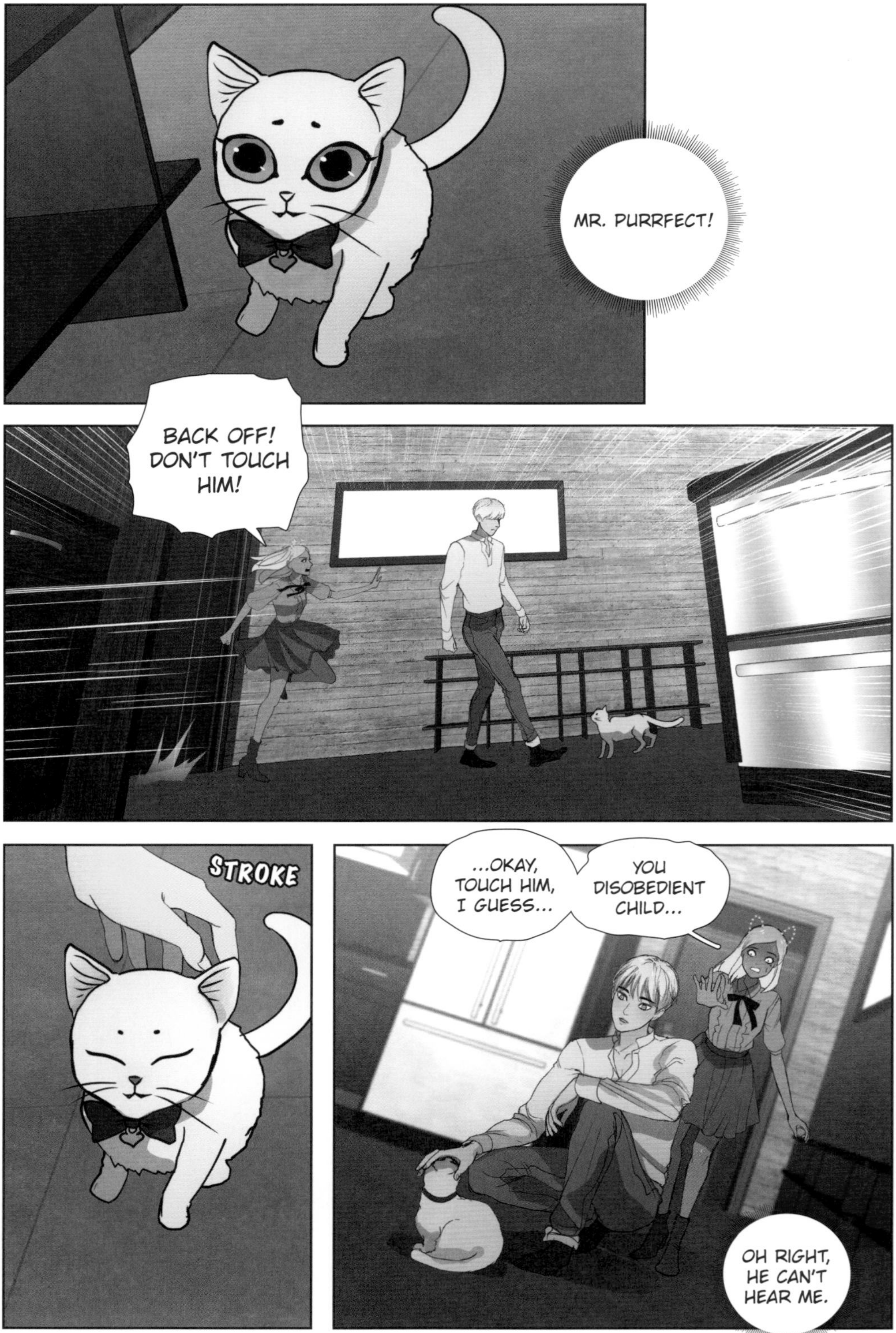
MR. PURRFECT!
BACK OFF! DON'T TOUCH HIM!
STROKE
...OKAY, TOUCH HIM, I GUESS...
YOU DISOBEDIENT CHILD...
OH RIGHT, HE CAN'T HEAR ME.

HE LIKES MY CAT?! HNNN MY HEART!

DO NOT FANGIRL, ZYLITH...

SLAP

A GIRL WENT MISSING BECAUSE OF HIM.

Mr. Purrfect

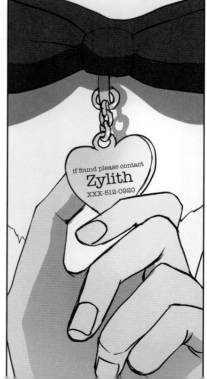

if found please contact
Zylith
XXX-512-0920

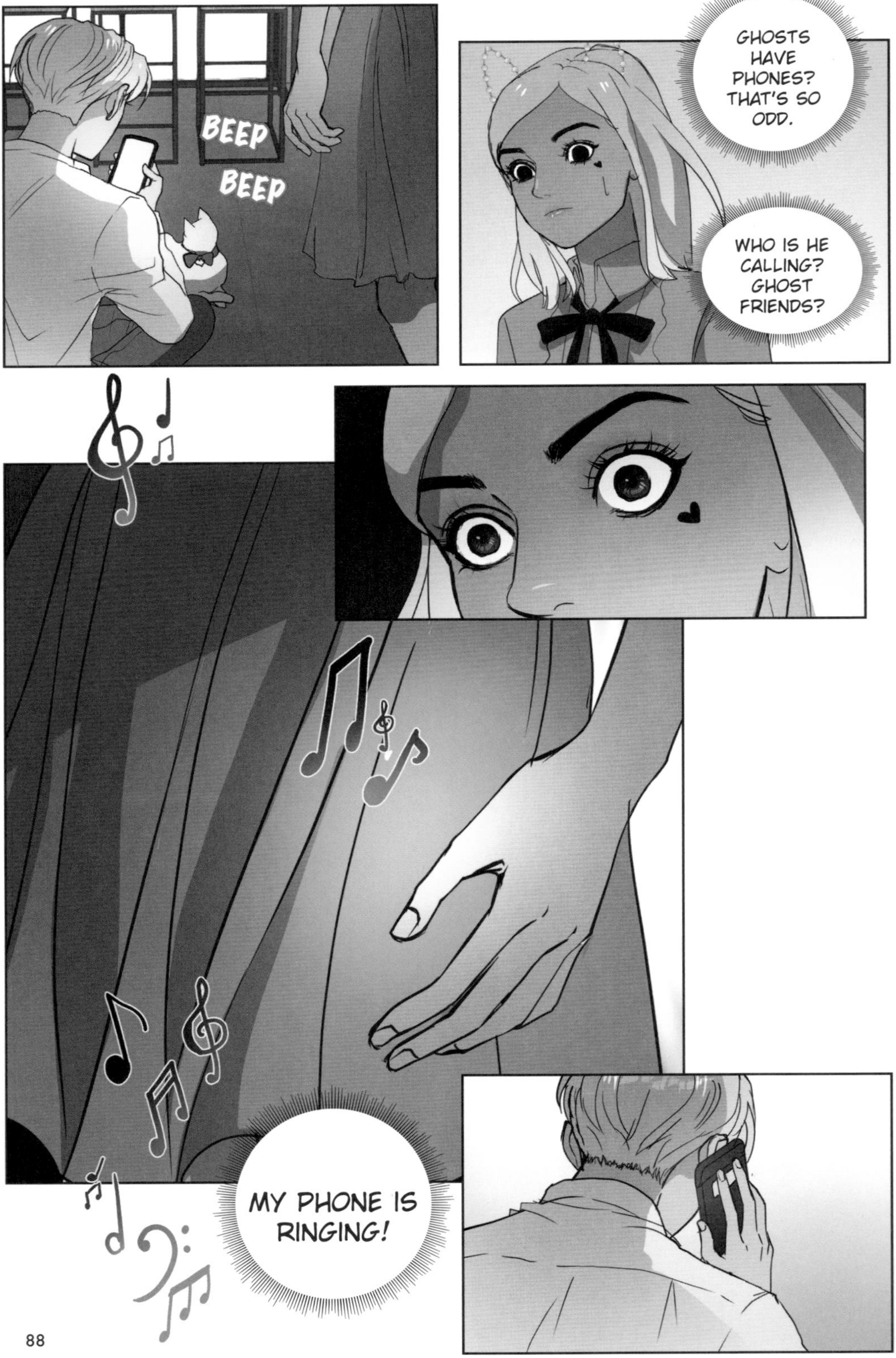
BEEP
BEEP
GHOSTS HAVE PHONES? THAT'S SO ODD.
WHO IS HE CALLING? GHOST FRIENDS?
MY PHONE IS RINGING!

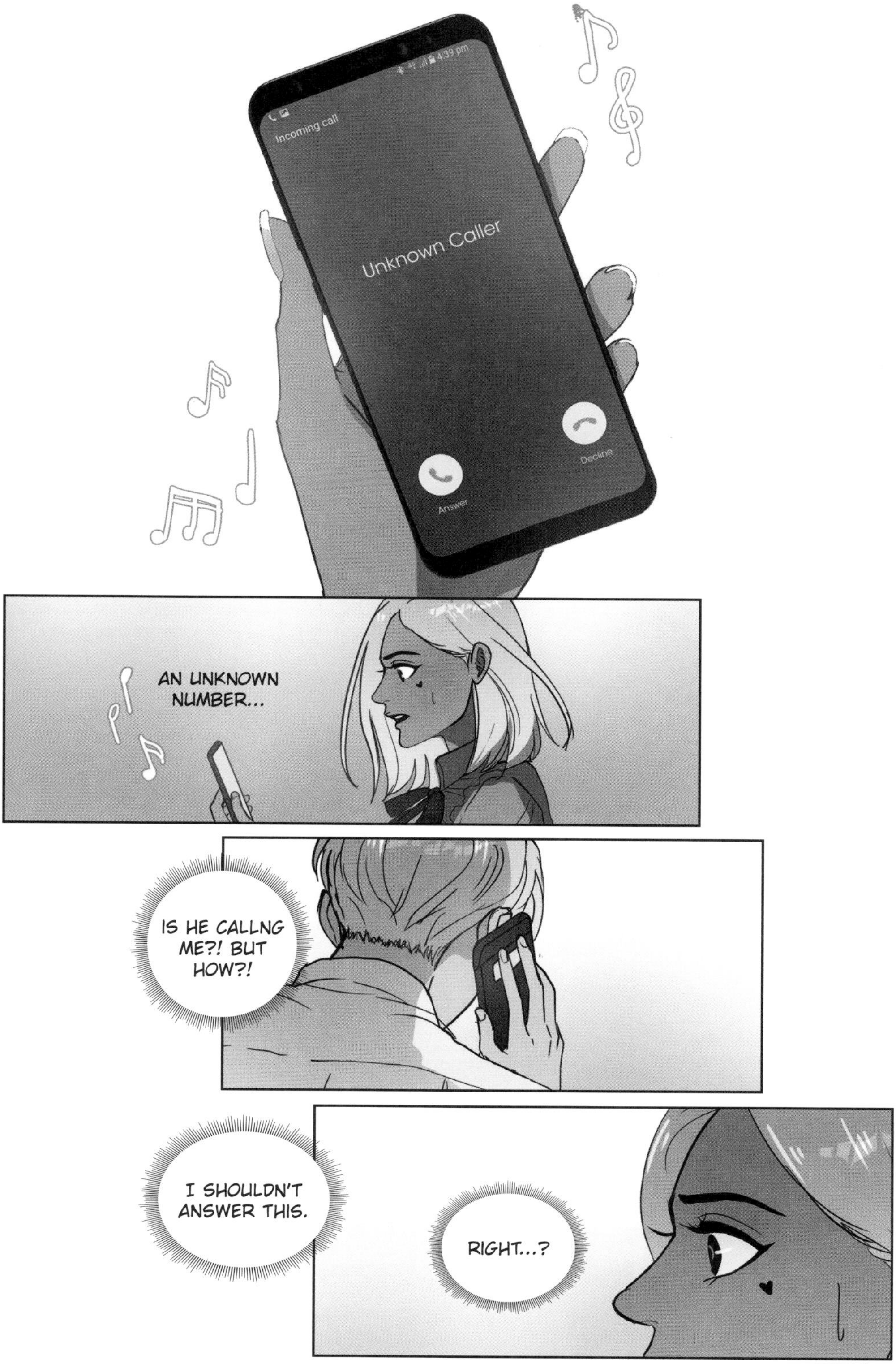
4:39 pm
Incoming call
Unknown Caller
Decline
Answer
AN UNKNOWN NUMBER...
IS HE CALLNG ME?! BUT HOW?!
I SHOULDN'T ANSWER THIS.
RIGHT...?

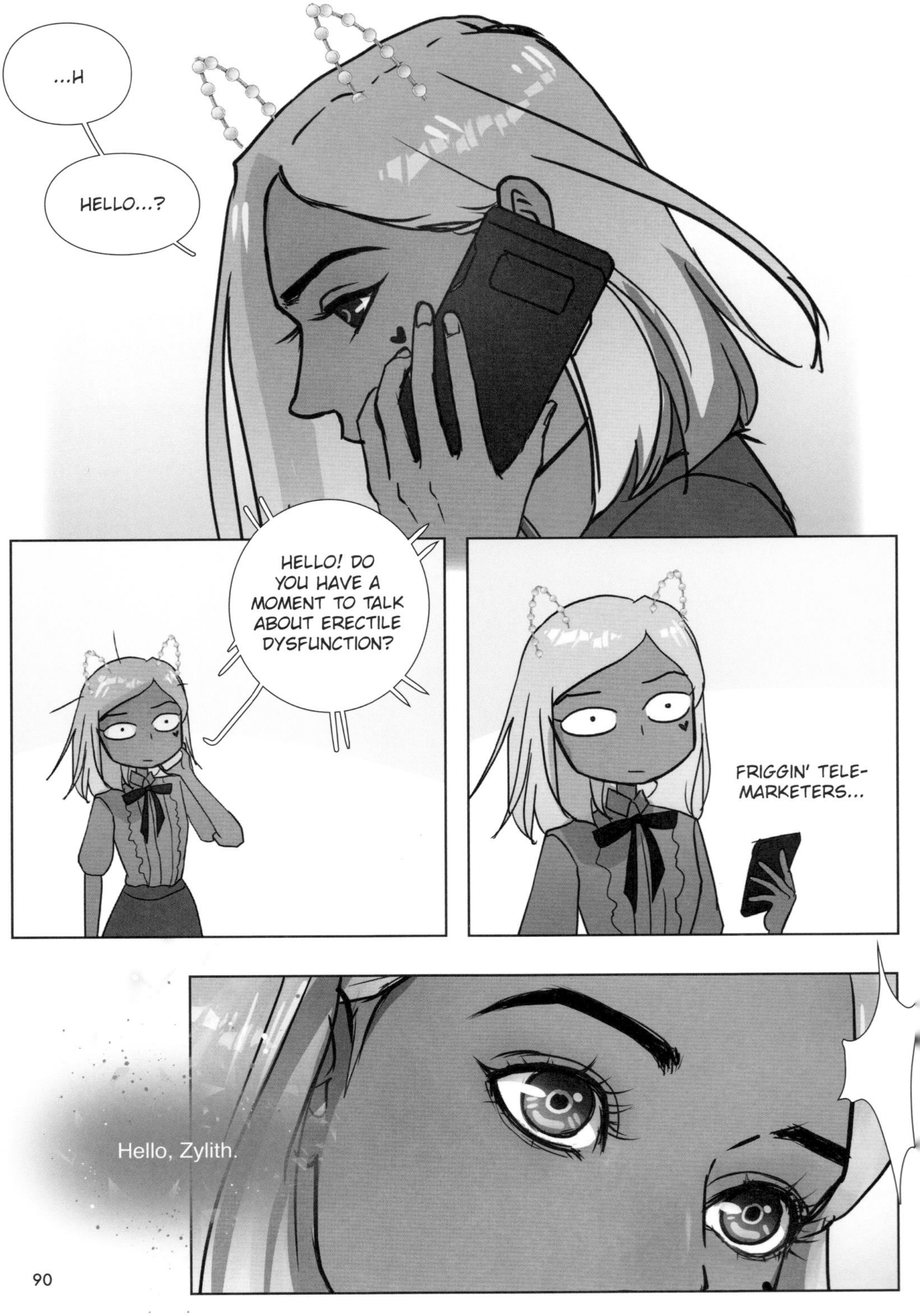
...H
HELLO...?
HELLO! DO YOU HAVE A MOMENT TO TALK ABOUT ERECTILE DYSFUNCTION?
FRIGGIN' TELE-MARKETERS...
Hello, Zylith.

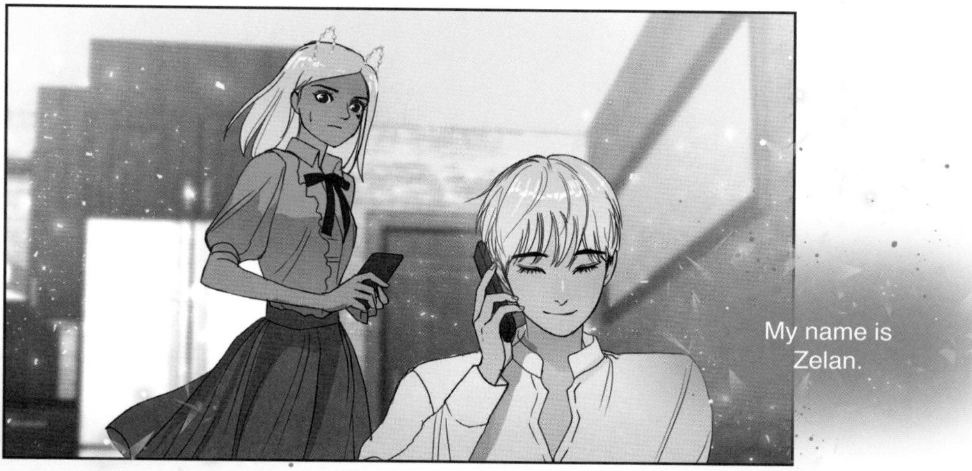
My name is Zelan.

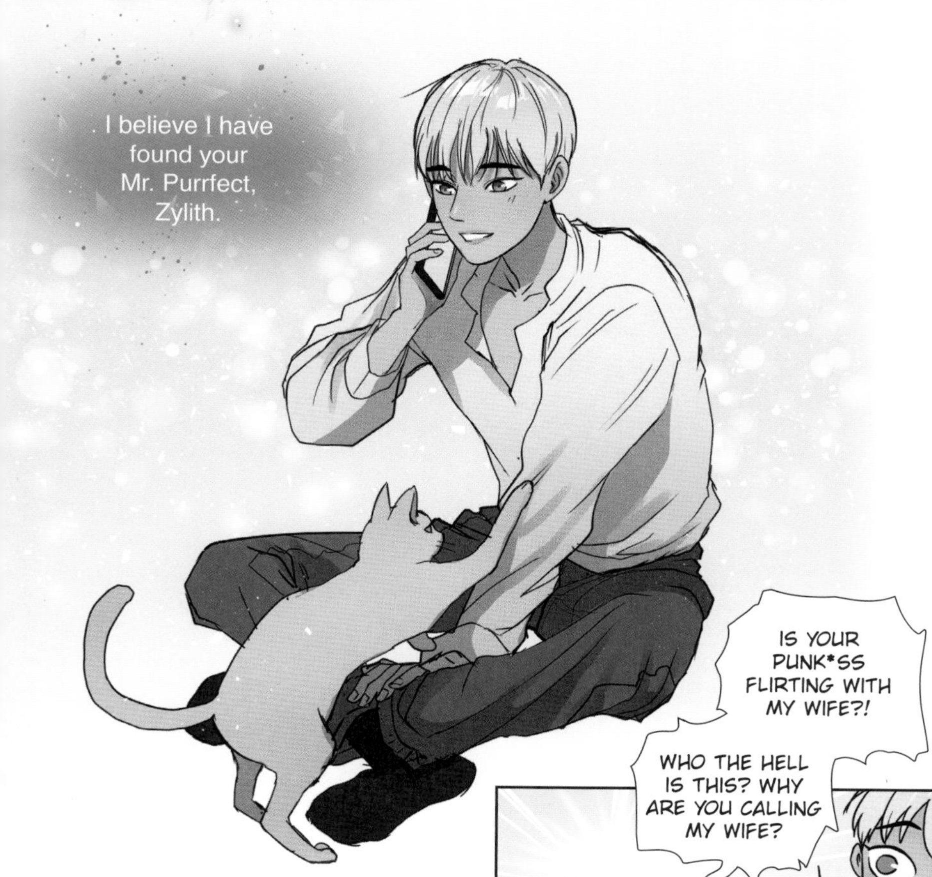
I believe I have found your Mr. Purrfect, Zylith.
IS YOUR PUNK*SS FLIRTING WITH MY WIFE?!
WHO THE HELL IS THIS? WHY ARE YOU CALLING MY WIFE?

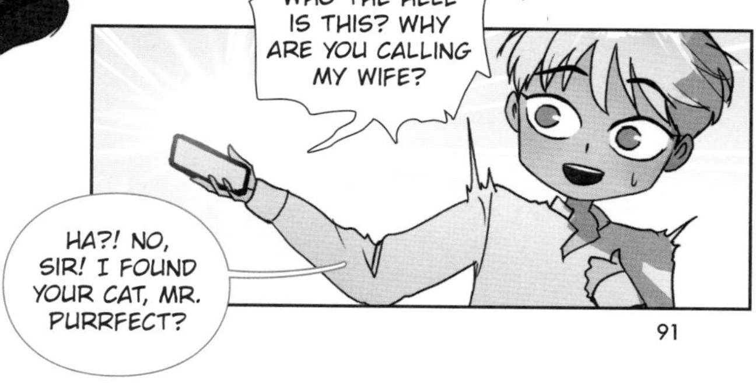
HA?! NO, SIR! I FOUND YOUR CAT, MR. PURRFECT?

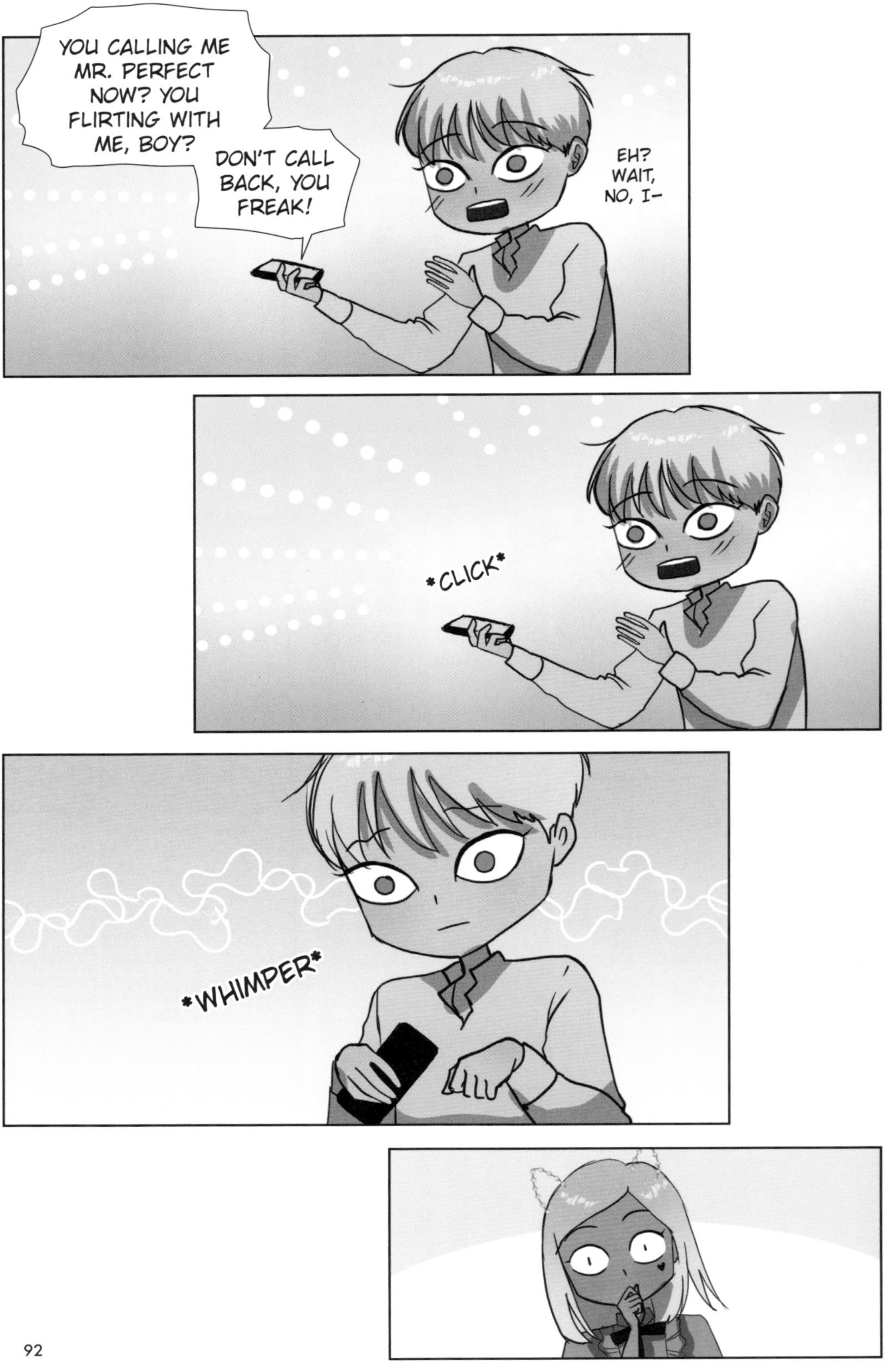
YOU CALLING ME MR. PERFECT NOW? YOU FLIRTING WITH ME, BOY?
DON'T CALL BACK, YOU FREAK!
EH? WAIT, NO, I–
CLICK
WHIMPER

SLAP

SLAP

SLAP

AHAHAH HAH!!!

HOW STRANGE.

YOUR FUR IS BRUSHED, YOUR WHITE COAT AND PAWS HAVE NO GRASS OR OUTDOOR DIRT STAINS.

SOME REMNANTS OF LITTER CAN BE FOUND WEDGED IN YOUR PAWS.

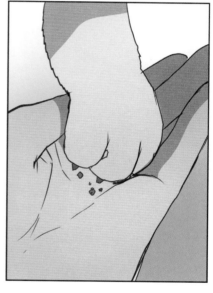

NO SIGNS OF ABUSE OR MALNUTRITION. YOU'RE SOMEONE'S WELL TAKEN CARE OF HOUSE CAT.

HOW ODD THAT A SEEMINGLY RESPONSIBLE OWNER FORGETS TO UPDATE YOUR COLLAR TAG.

DID YOU SNEAK IN WHILE MY DOOR WAS OPEN?

93

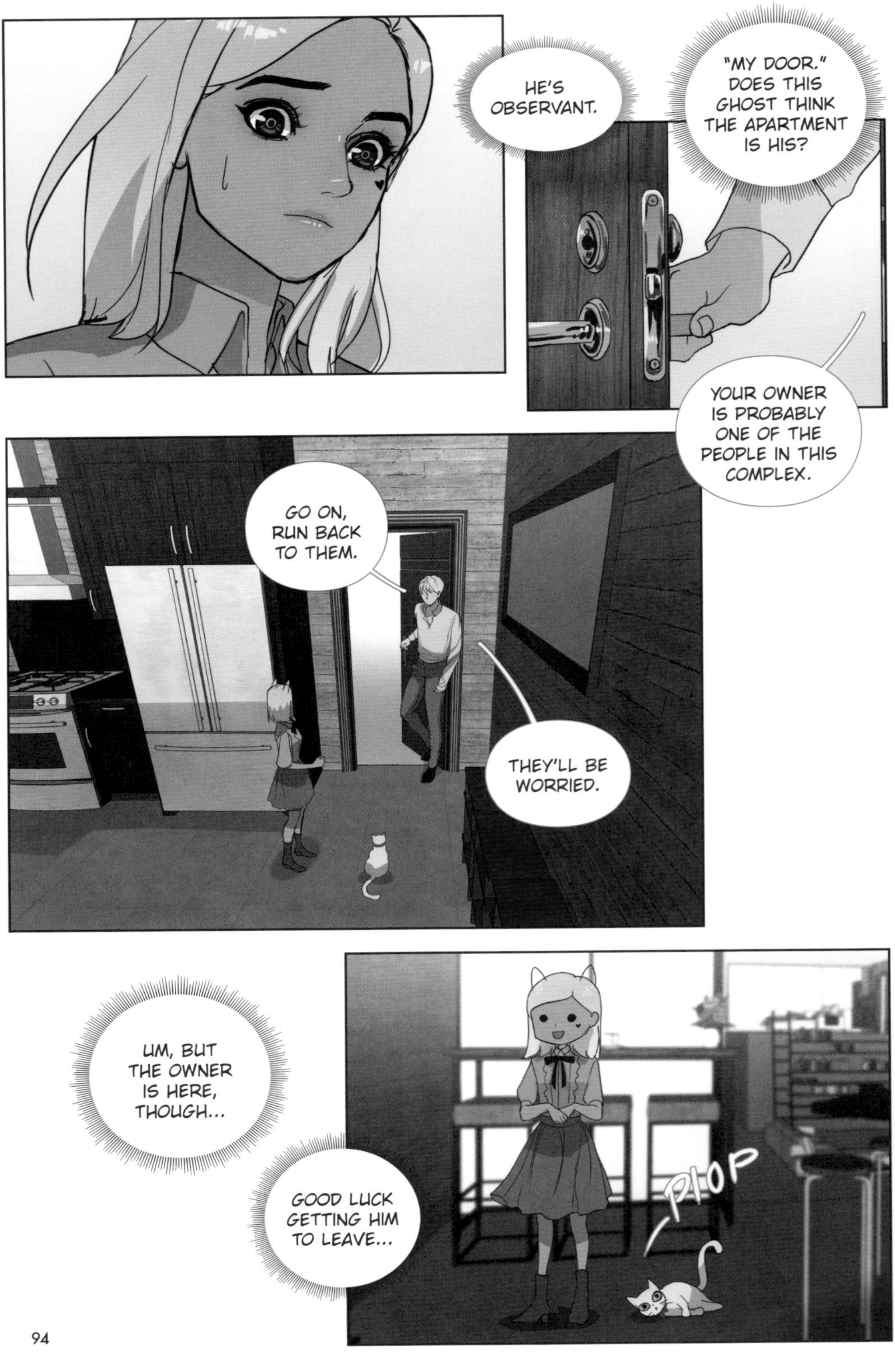
HE'S OBSERVANT.
"MY DOOR." DOES THIS GHOST THINK THE APARTMENT IS HIS?
YOUR OWNER IS PROBABLY ONE OF THE PEOPLE IN THIS COMPLEX.
GO ON, RUN BACK TO THEM.
THEY'LL BE WORRIED.
UM, BUT THE OWNER IS HERE, THOUGH...
GOOD LUCK GETTING HIM TO LEAVE...
PLOP

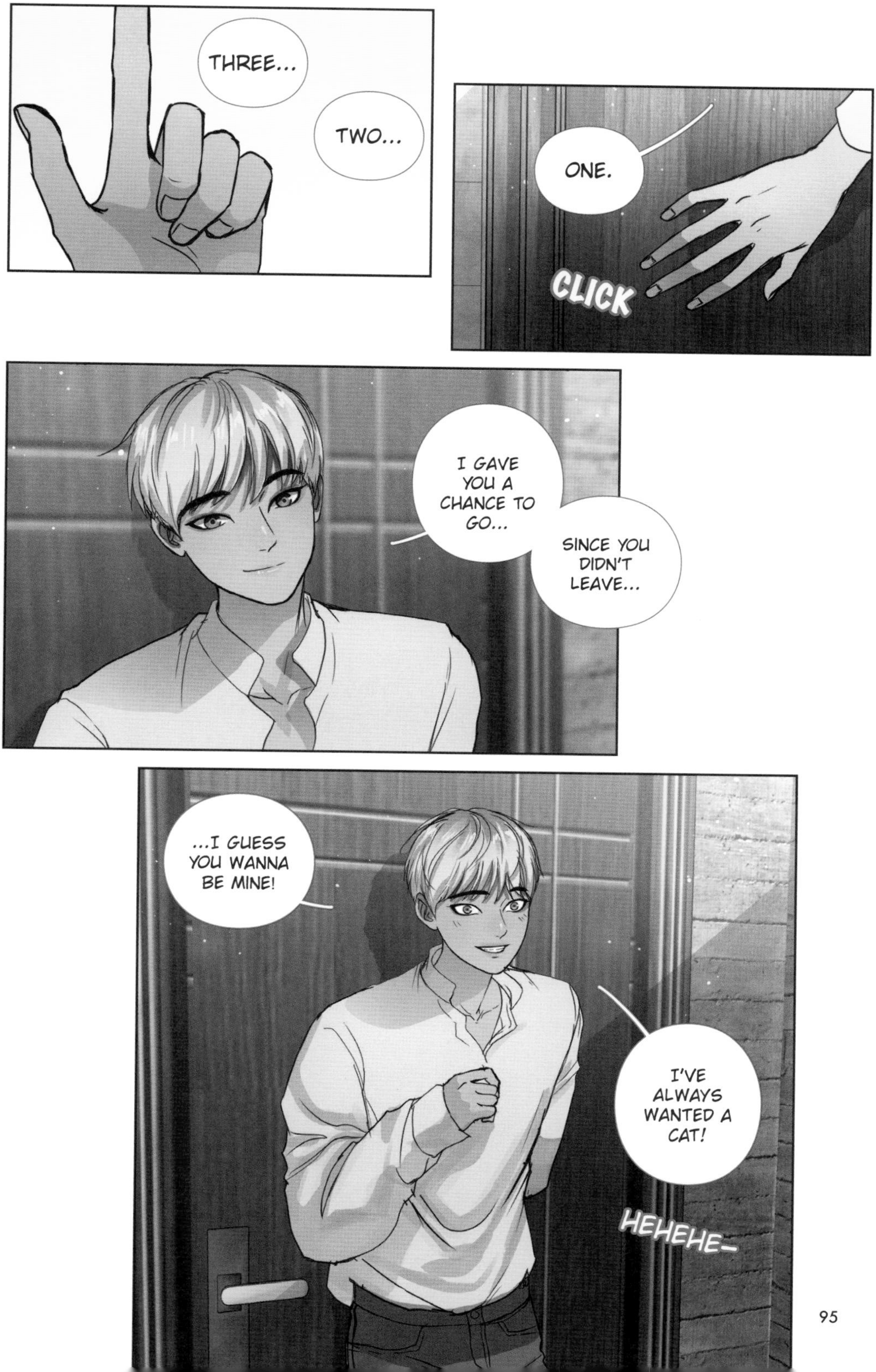
THREE...
TWO...
ONE.
CLICK
I GAVE YOU A CHANCE TO GO...
SINCE YOU DIDN'T LEAVE...
...I GUESS YOU WANNA BE MINE!
I'VE ALWAYS WANTED A CAT!
HEHEHE-

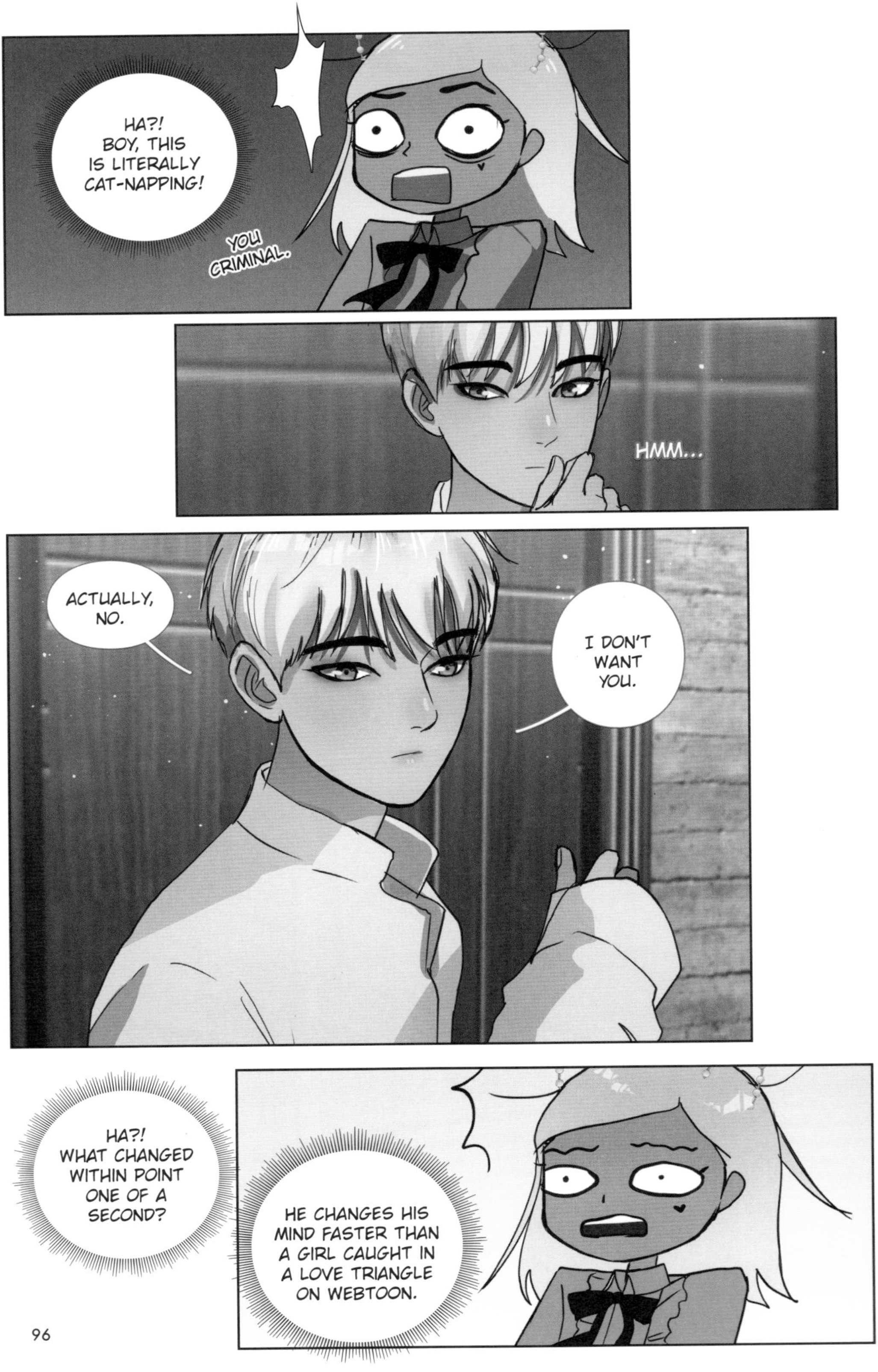
HA?! BOY, THIS IS LITERALLY CAT-NAPPING!
YOU CRIMINAL.
HMM...
ACTUALLY, NO.
I DON'T WANT YOU.
HA?! WHAT CHANGED WITHIN POINT ONE OF A SECOND?
HE CHANGES HIS MIND FASTER THAN A GIRL CAUGHT IN A LOVE TRIANGLE ON WEBTOON.

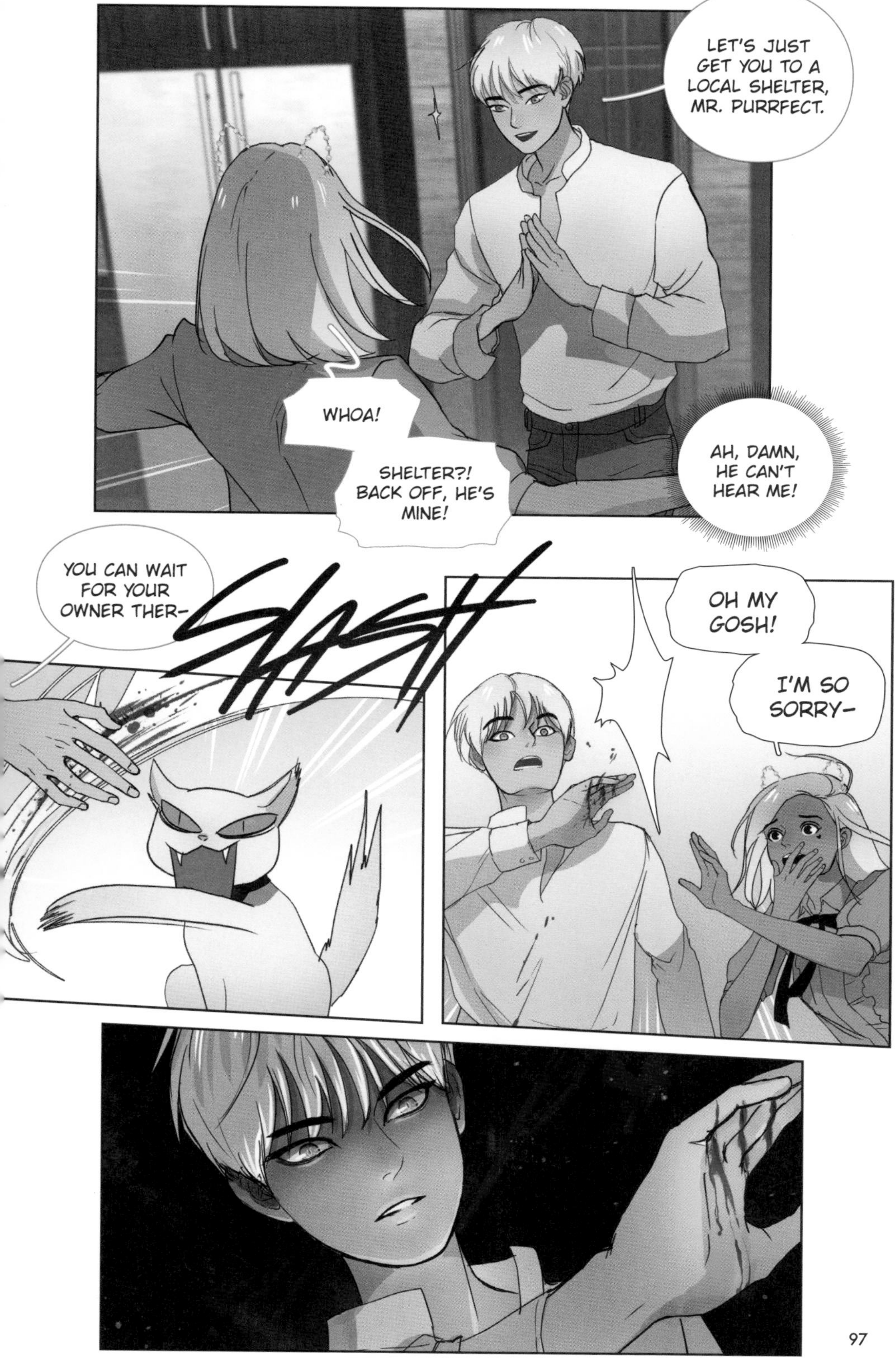
LET'S JUST GET YOU TO A LOCAL SHELTER, MR. PURRFECT.
WHOA!
SHELTER?! BACK OFF, HE'S MINE!
AH, DAMN, HE CAN'T HEAR ME!
YOU CAN WAIT FOR YOUR OWNER THER–
SLASH
OH MY GOSH!
I'M SO SORRY–

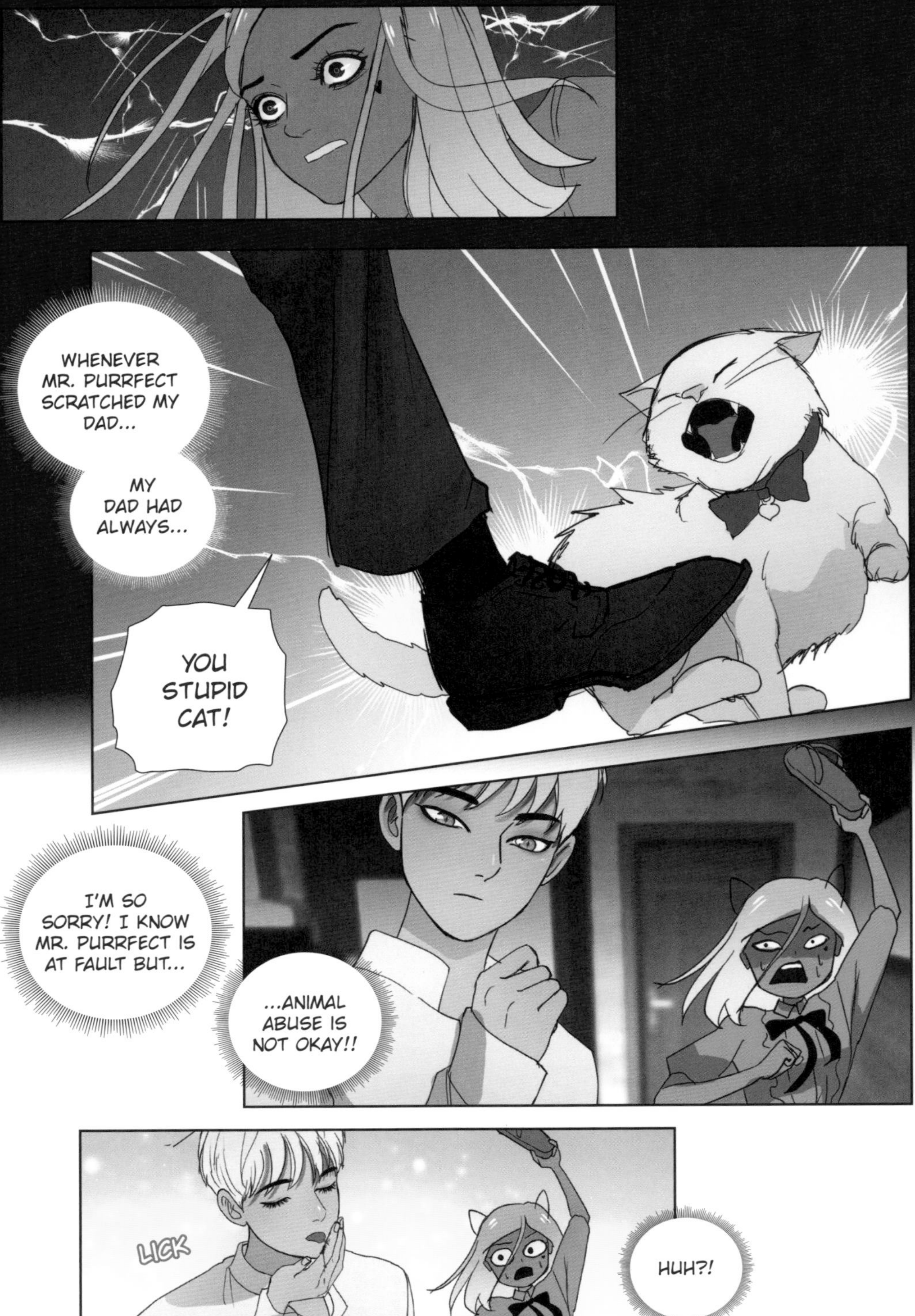
WHENEVER MR. PURRFECT SCRATCHED MY DAD...
MY DAD HAD ALWAYS...
YOU STUPID CAT!
I'M SO SORRY! I KNOW MR. PURRFECT IS AT FAULT BUT...
...ANIMAL ABUSE IS NOT OKAY!!
LICK
HUH?!

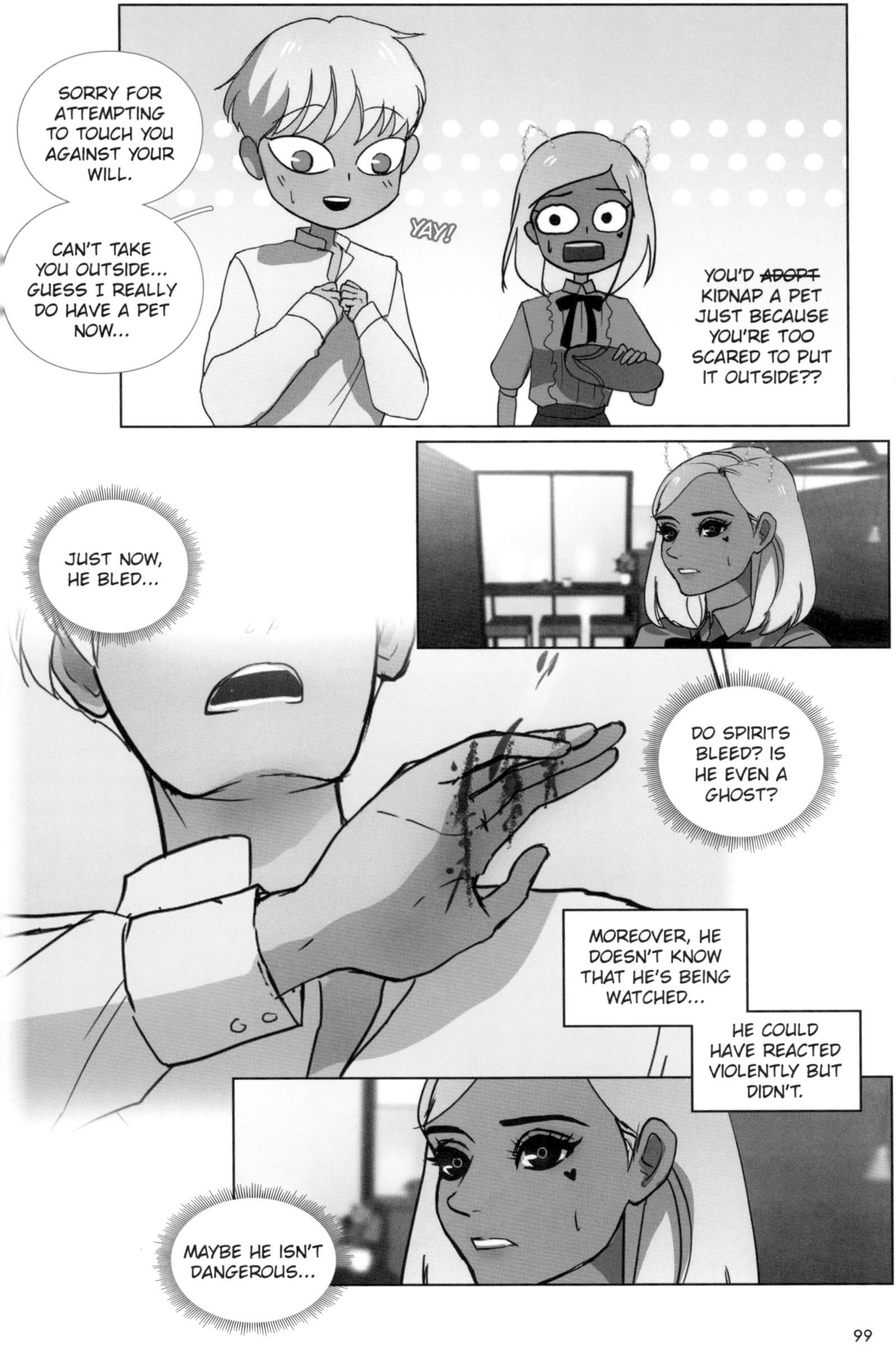
SORRY FOR ATTEMPTING TO TOUCH YOU AGAINST YOUR WILL.
CAN'T TAKE YOU OUTSIDE... GUESS I REALLY DO HAVE A PET NOW...
YAY!
YOU'D ~~ADOPT~~ KIDNAP A PET JUST BECAUSE YOU'RE TOO SCARED TO PUT IT OUTSIDE??
JUST NOW, HE BLED...
DO SPIRITS BLEED? IS HE EVEN A GHOST?
MOREOVER, HE DOESN'T KNOW THAT HE'S BEING WATCHED...
HE COULD HAVE REACTED VIOLENTLY BUT DIDN'T.
MAYBE HE ISN'T DANGEROUS...

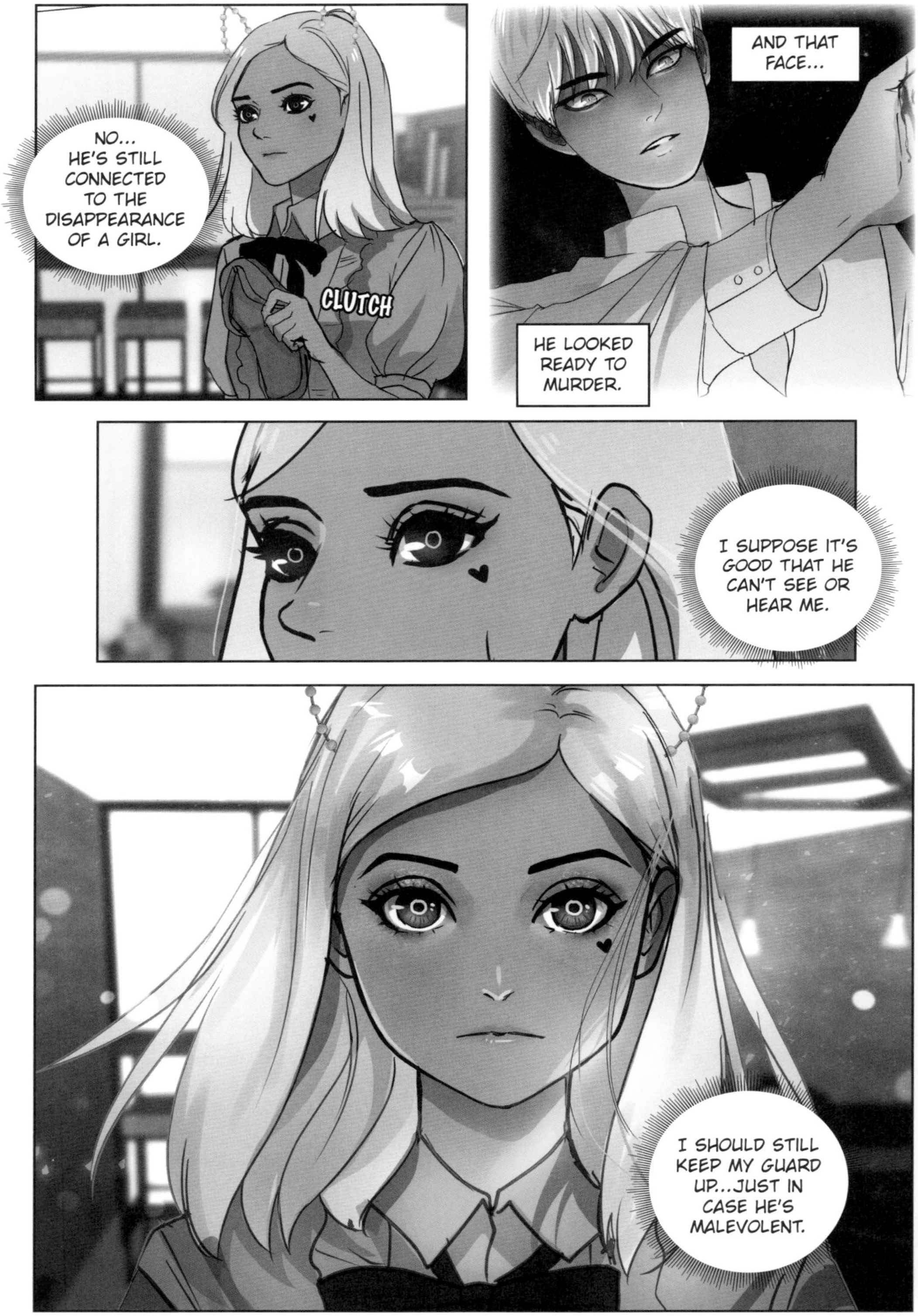
NO... HE'S STILL CONNECTED TO THE DISAPPEARANCE OF A GIRL.
CLUTCH
AND THAT FACE...
HE LOOKED READY TO MURDER.
I SUPPOSE IT'S GOOD THAT HE CAN'T SEE OR HEAR ME.
I SHOULD STILL KEEP MY GUARD UP...JUST IN CASE HE'S MALEVOLENT.

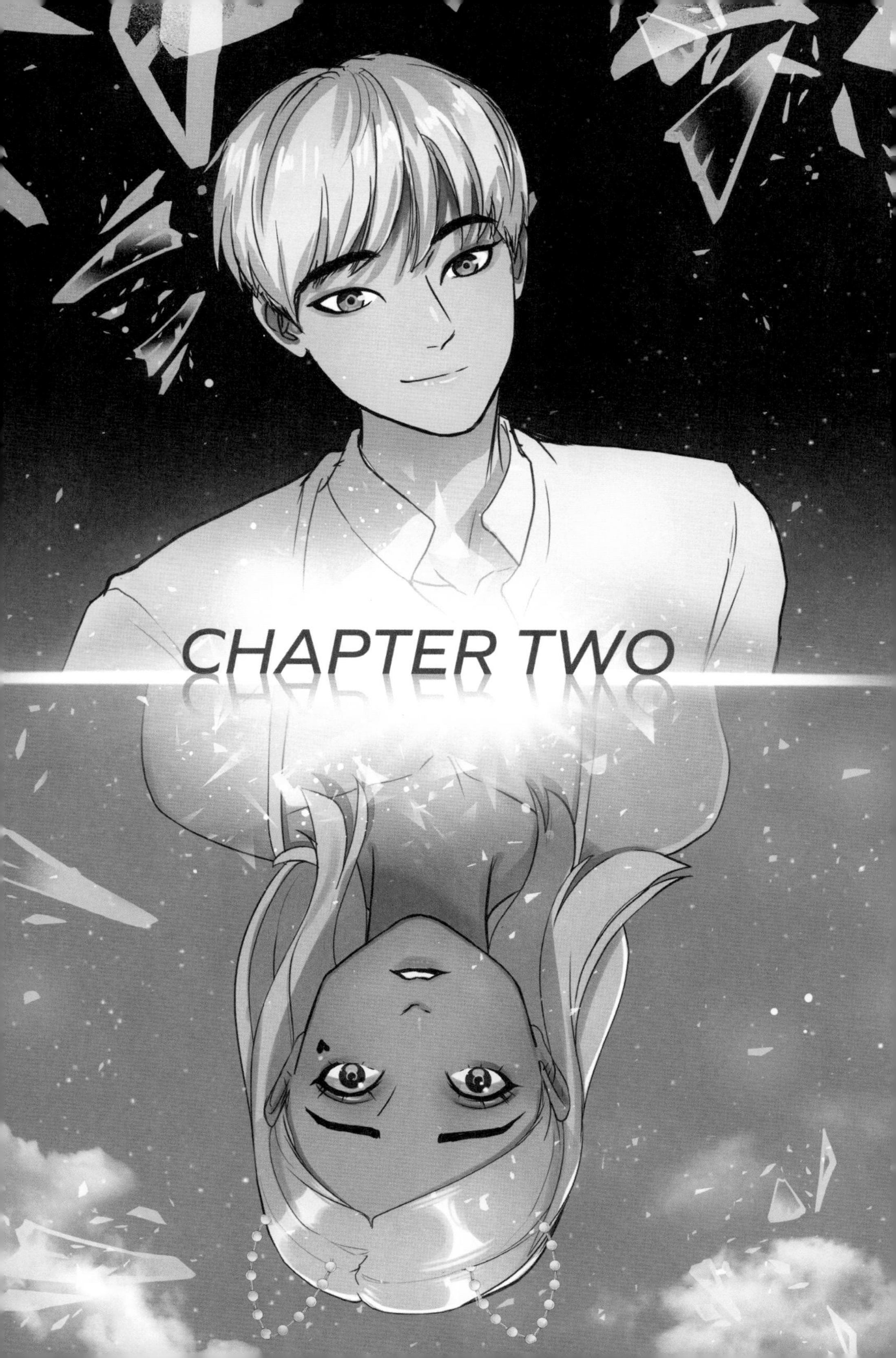
CHAPTER TWO

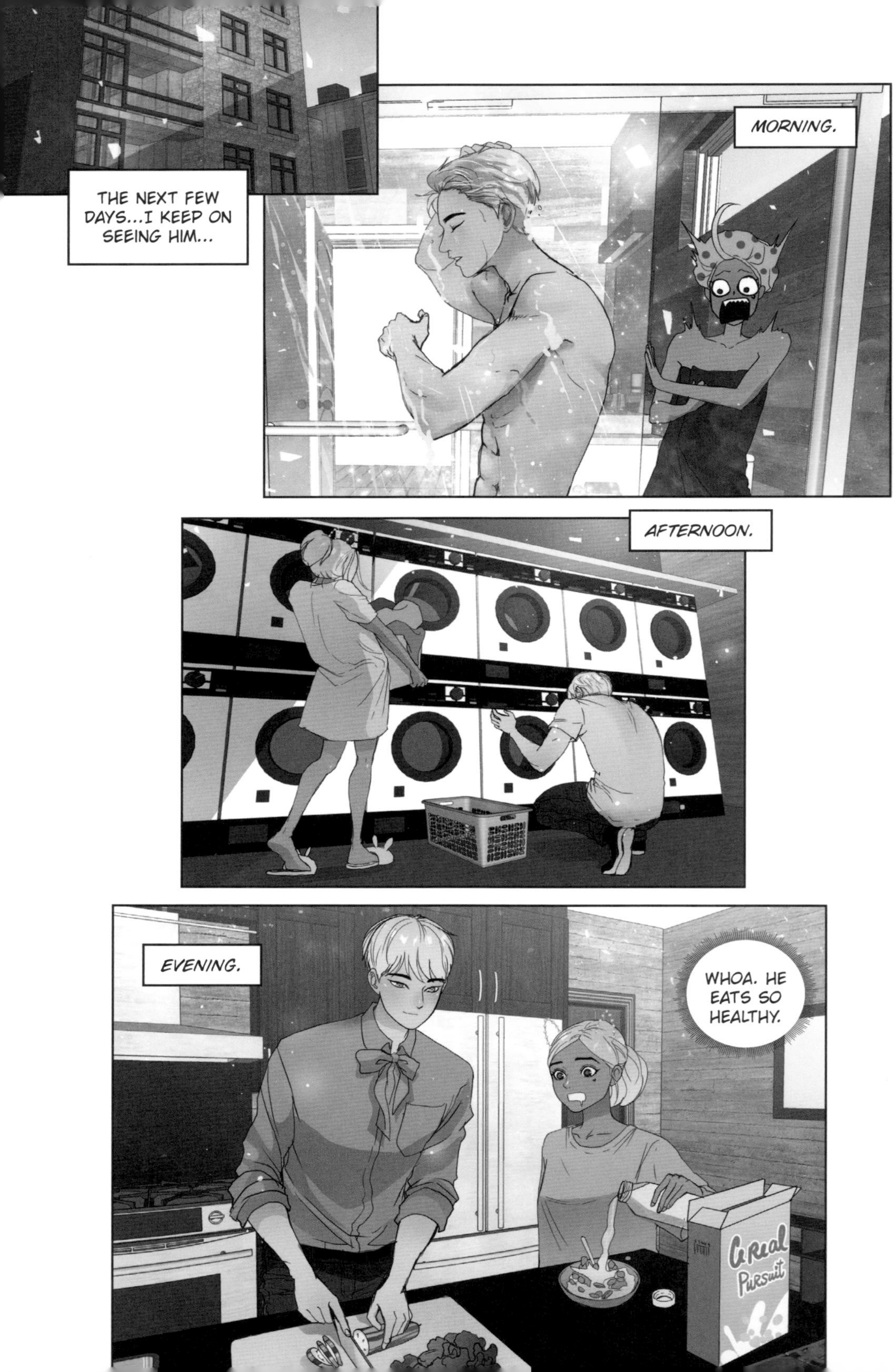
THE NEXT FEW DAYS...I KEEP ON SEEING HIM...
MORNING.
AFTERNOON.
EVENING.
WHOA. HE EATS SO HEALTHY.

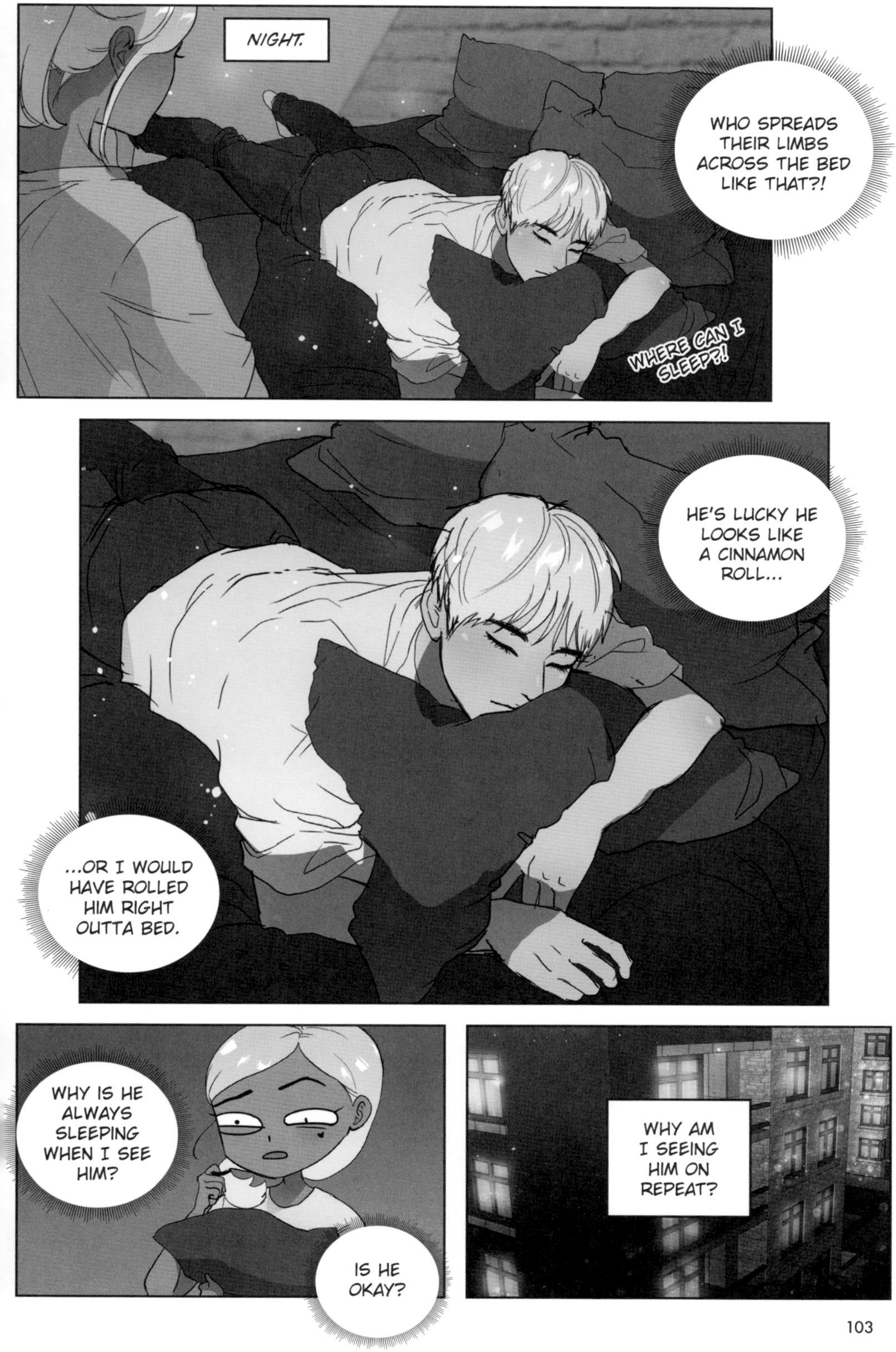
NIGHT.
WHO SPREADS THEIR LIMBS ACROSS THE BED LIKE THAT?!
WHERE CAN I SLEEP?!
HE'S LUCKY HE LOOKS LIKE A CINNAMON ROLL...
...OR I WOULD HAVE ROLLED HIM RIGHT OUTTA BED.
WHY IS HE ALWAYS SLEEPING WHEN I SEE HIM?
IS HE OKAY?
WHY AM I SEEING HIM ON REPEAT?

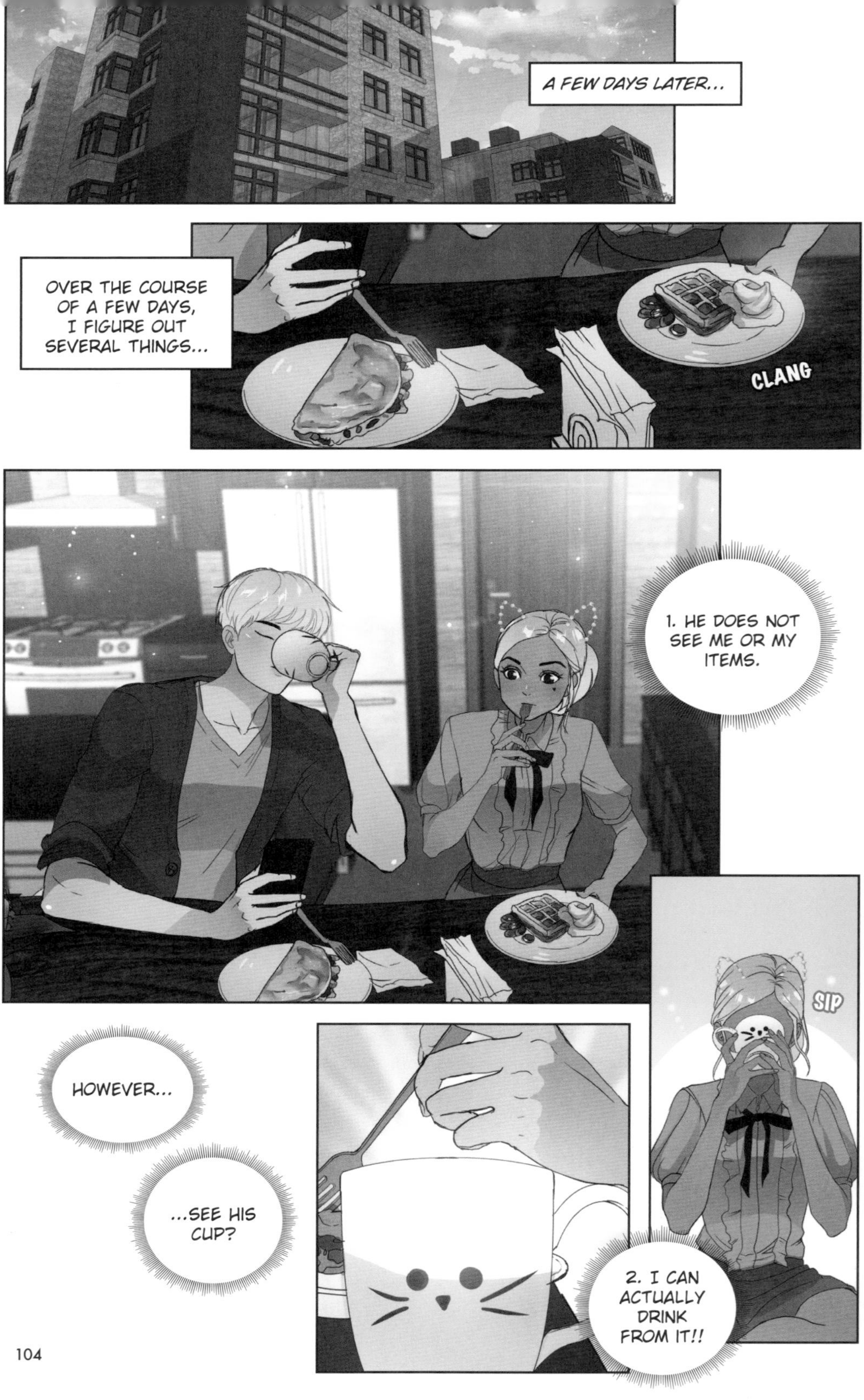
A FEW DAYS LATER...
OVER THE COURSE OF A FEW DAYS, I FIGURE OUT SEVERAL THINGS...
CLANG
1. HE DOES NOT SEE ME OR MY ITEMS.
SIP
HOWEVER...
...SEE HIS CUP?
2. I CAN ACTUALLY DRINK FROM IT!!

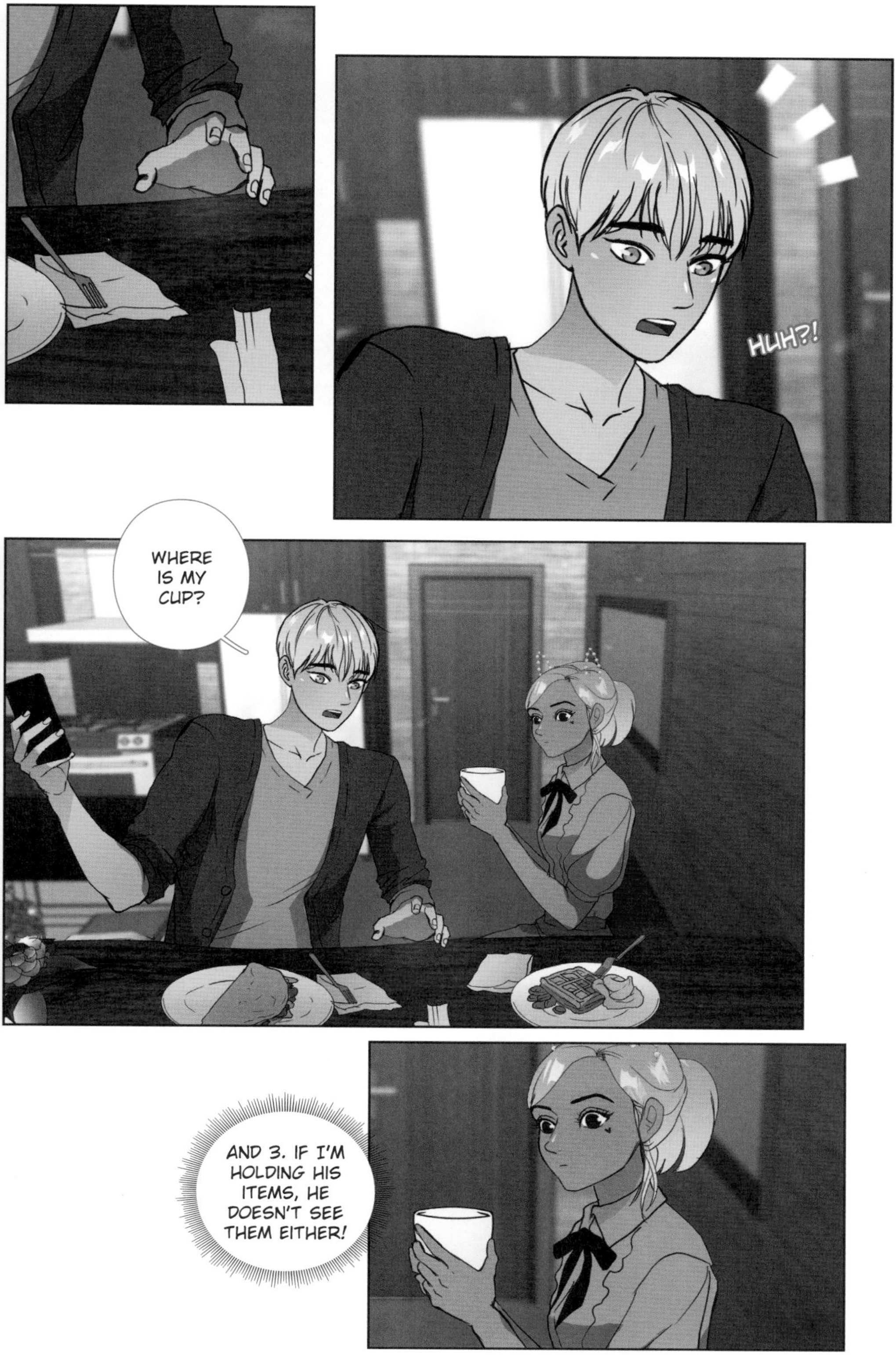
HUH?!
WHERE IS MY CUP?
AND 3. IF I'M HOLDING HIS ITEMS, HE DOESN'T SEE THEM EITHER!

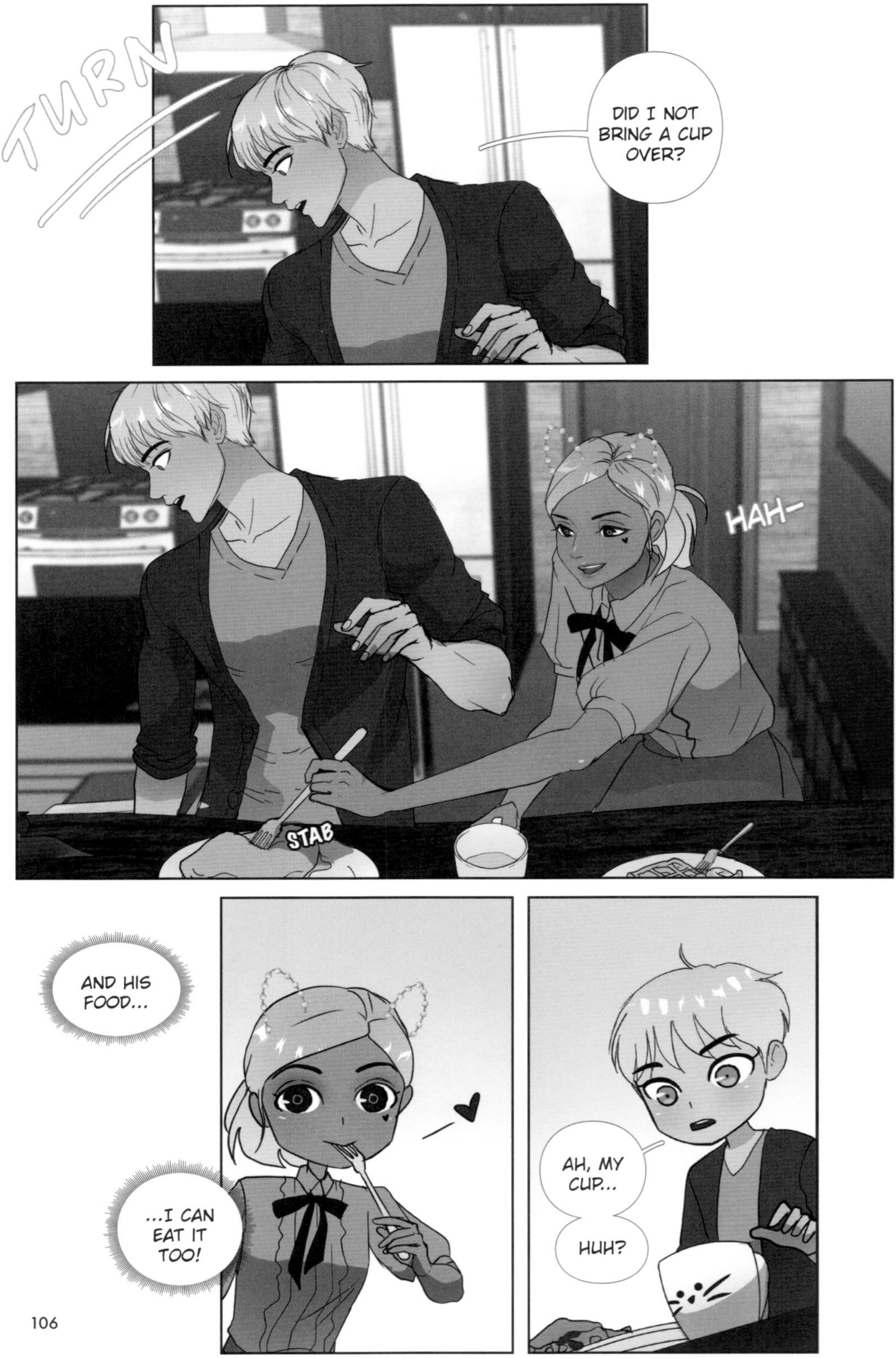
TURN
DID I NOT BRING A CUP OVER?
HAH-
STAB
AND HIS FOOD...
...I CAN EAT IT TOO!
AH, MY CUP...
HUH?

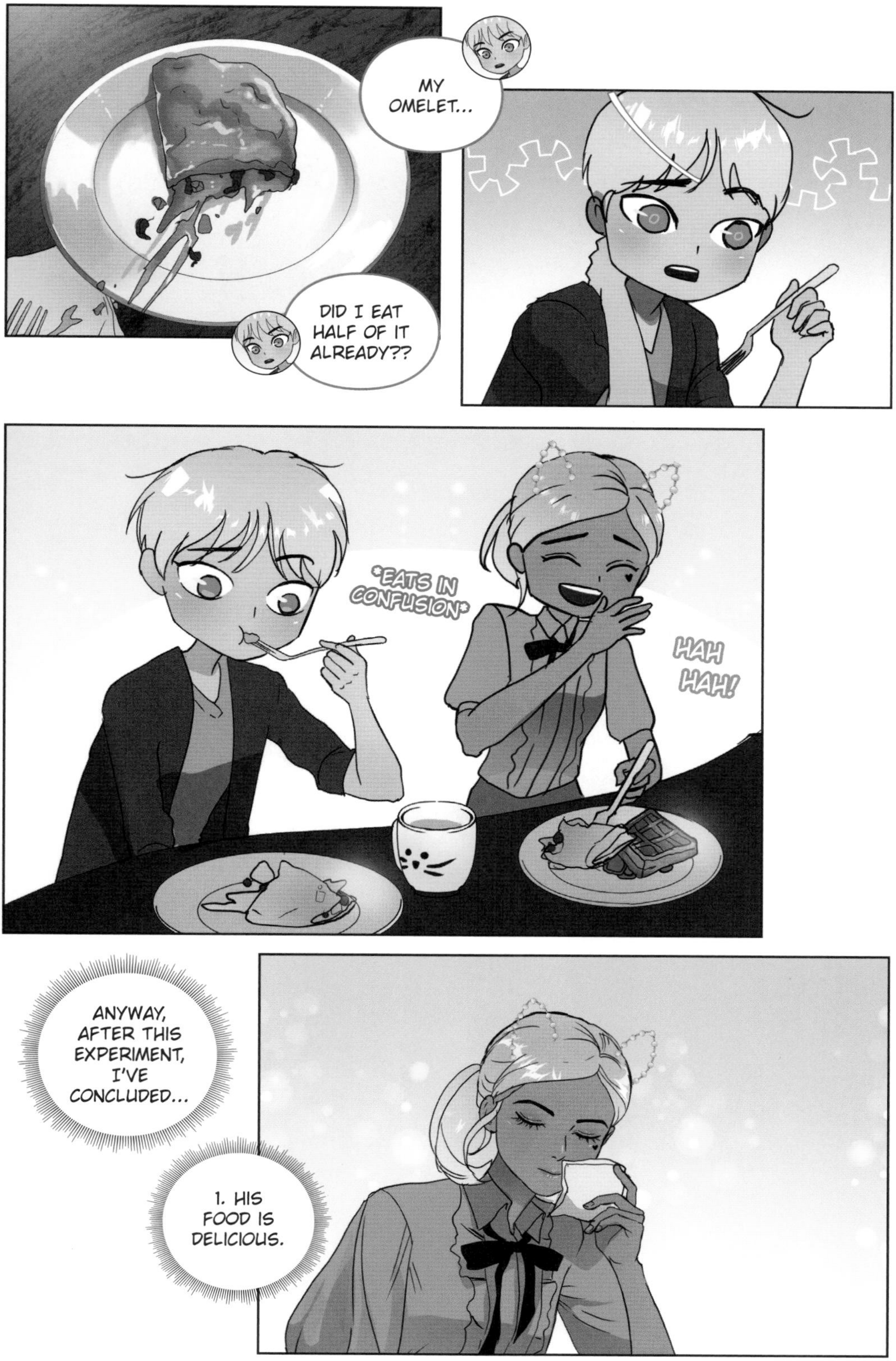
MY OMELET...
DID I EAT HALF OF IT ALREADY??
EATS IN CONFUSION
HAH HAH!
ANYWAY, AFTER THIS EXPERIMENT, I'VE CONCLUDED...
1. HIS FOOD IS DELICIOUS.

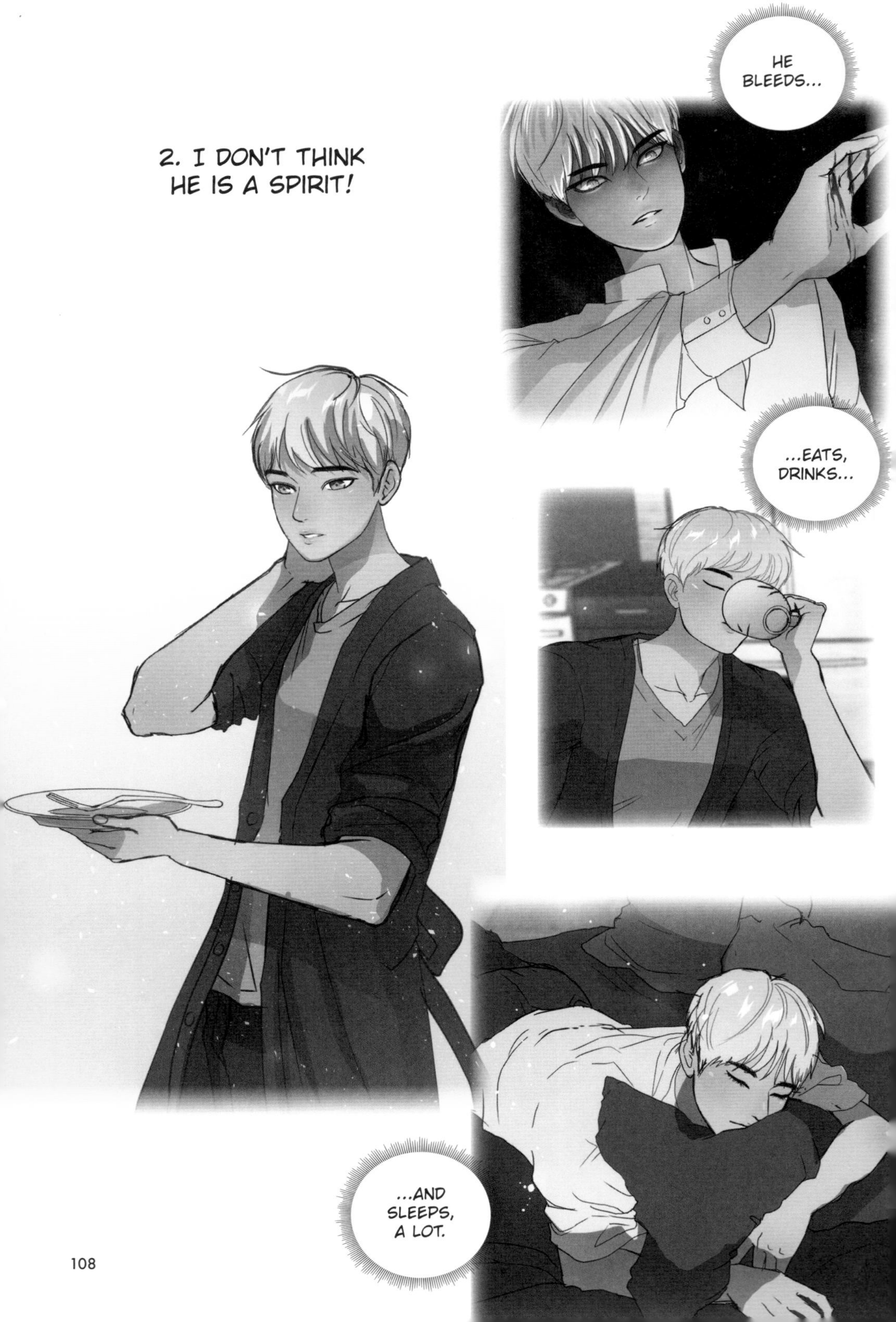
2. I DON'T THINK HE IS A SPIRIT!
HE BLEEDS...
...EATS, DRINKS...
...AND SLEEPS, A LOT.

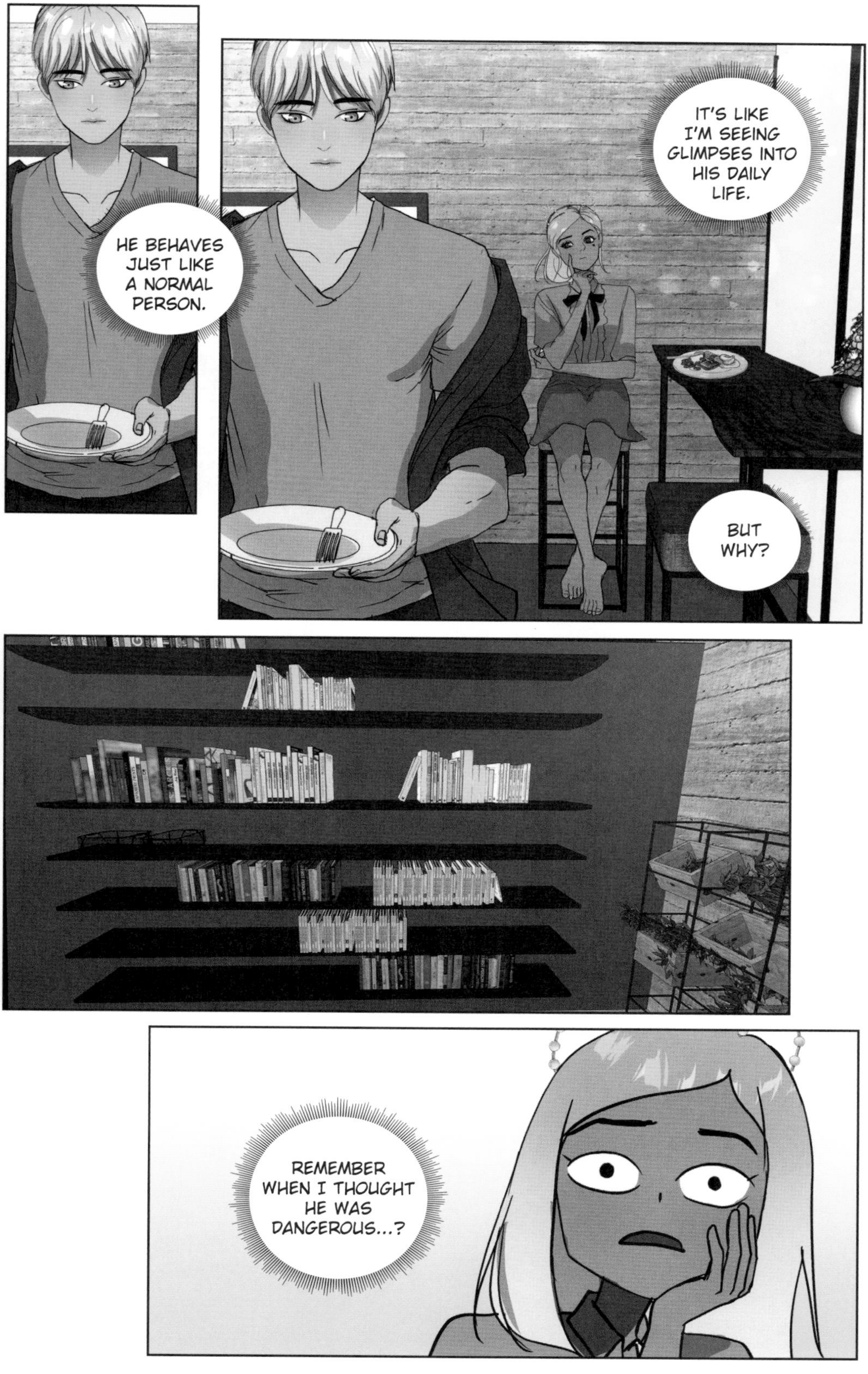
HE BEHAVES JUST LIKE A NORMAL PERSON.
IT'S LIKE I'M SEEING GLIMPSES INTO HIS DAILY LIFE.
BUT WHY?
REMEMBER WHEN I THOUGHT HE WAS DANGEROUS...?

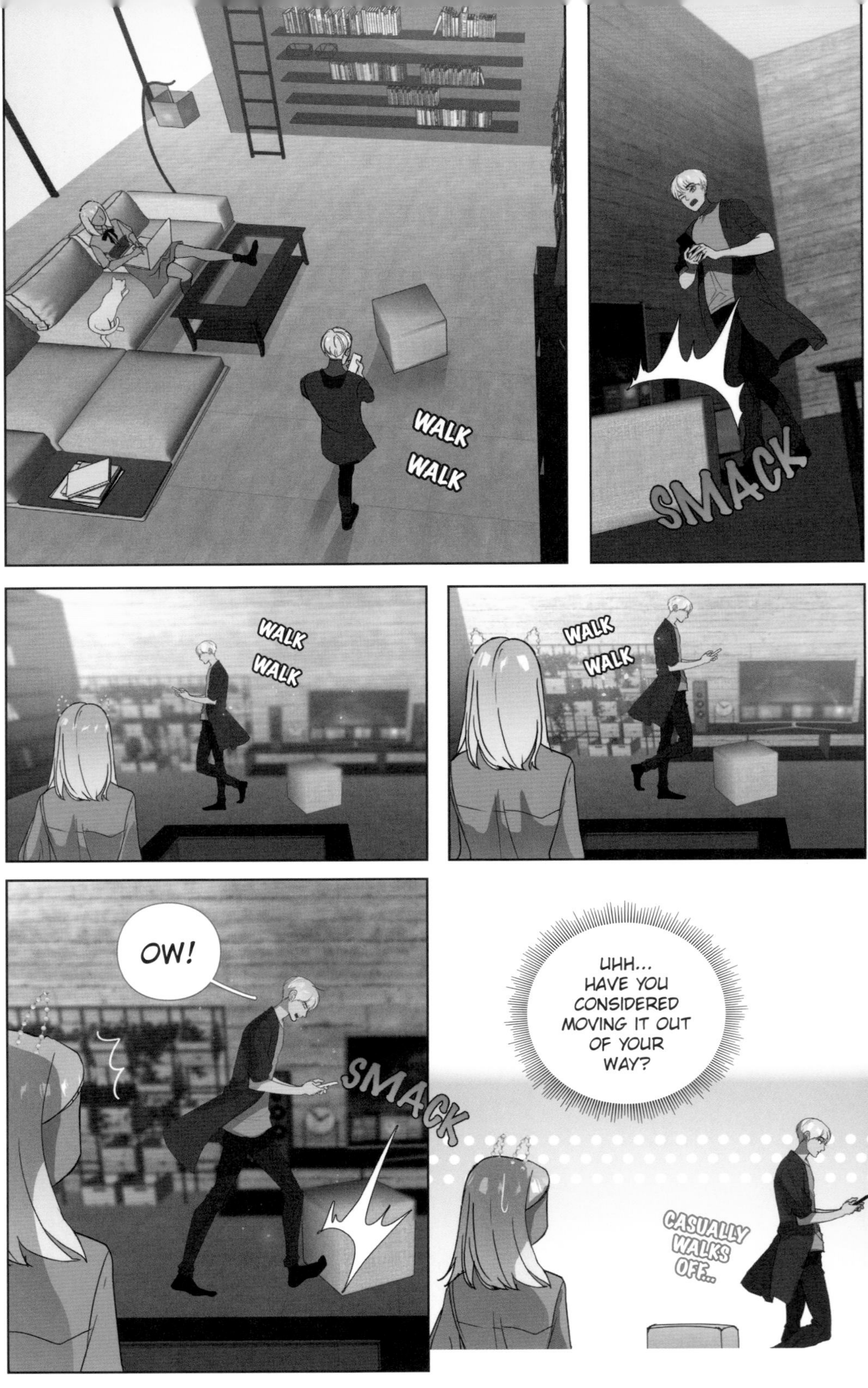
WALK
WALK
SMACK
WALK
WALK
WALK
WALK
OW!
SMACK
UHH... HAVE YOU CONSIDERED MOVING IT OUT OF YOUR WAY?
CASUALLY WALKS OFF...

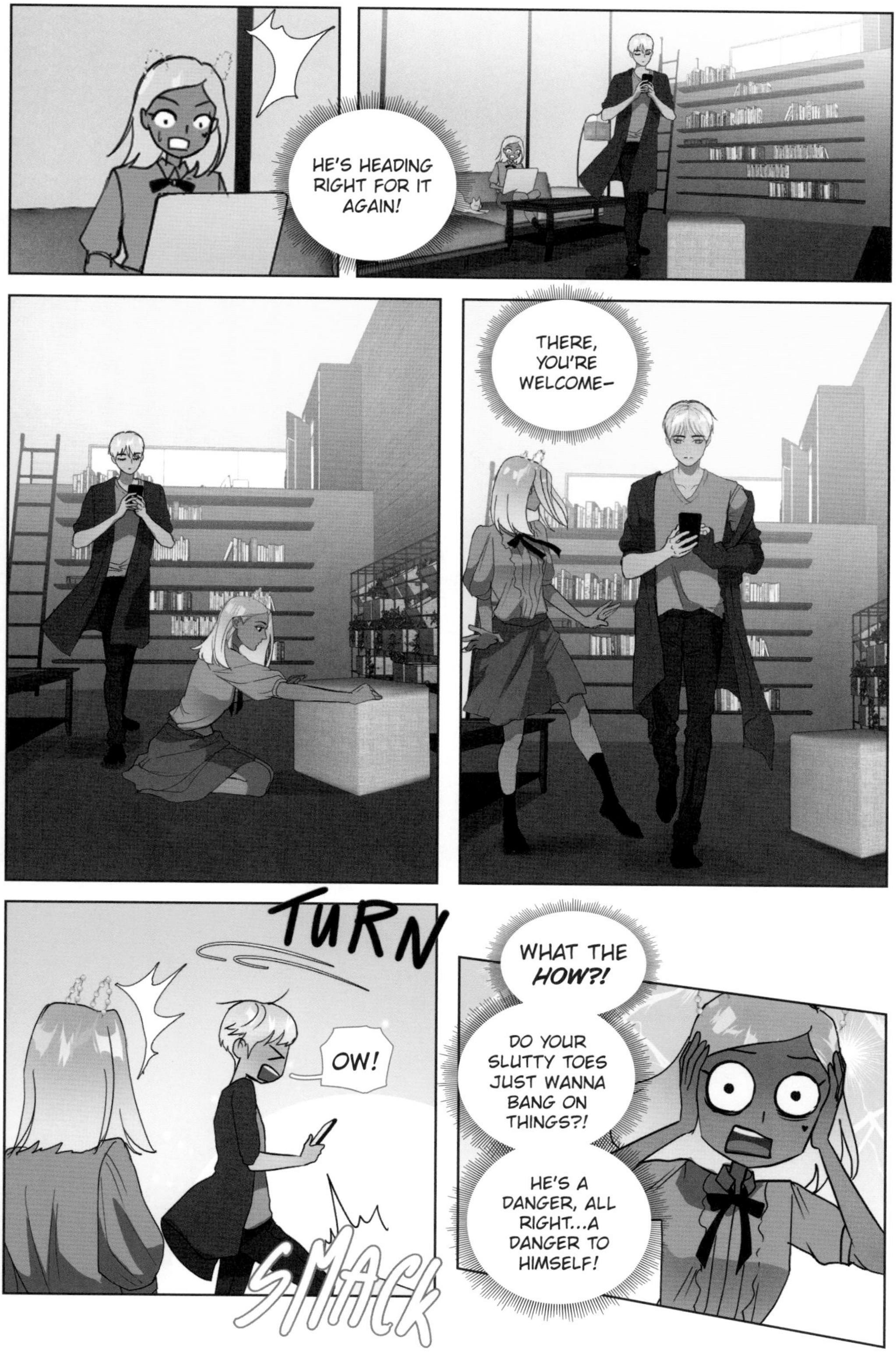
HE'S HEADING RIGHT FOR IT AGAIN!
THERE, YOU'RE WELCOME–
TURN
OW!
SMACK
WHAT THE *HOW?!*
DO YOUR SLUTTY TOES JUST WANNA BANG ON THINGS?!
HE'S A DANGER, ALL RIGHT...A DANGER TO HIMSELF!

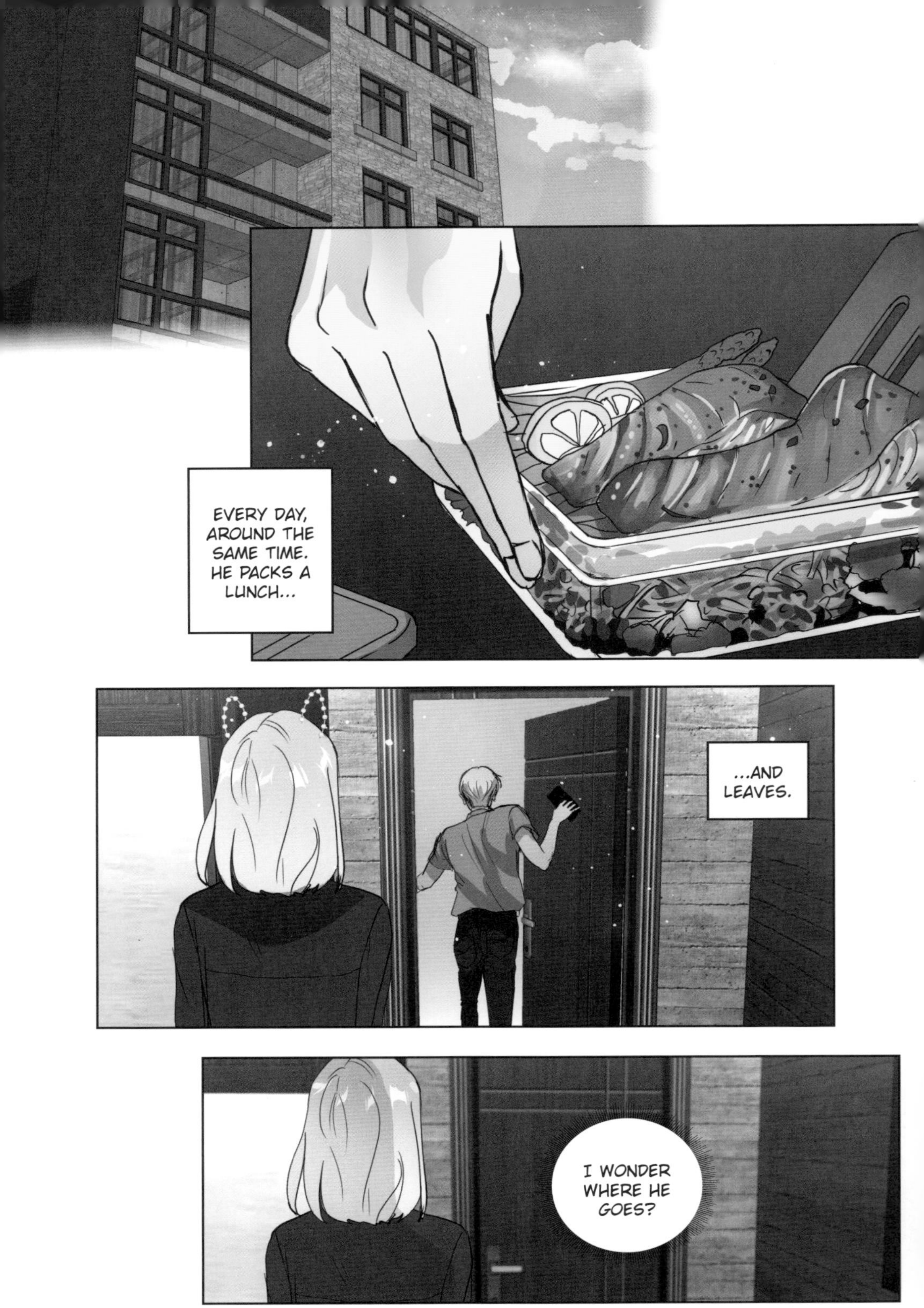
EVERY DAY, AROUND THE SAME TIME. HE PACKS A LUNCH...
...AND LEAVES.
I WONDER WHERE HE GOES?

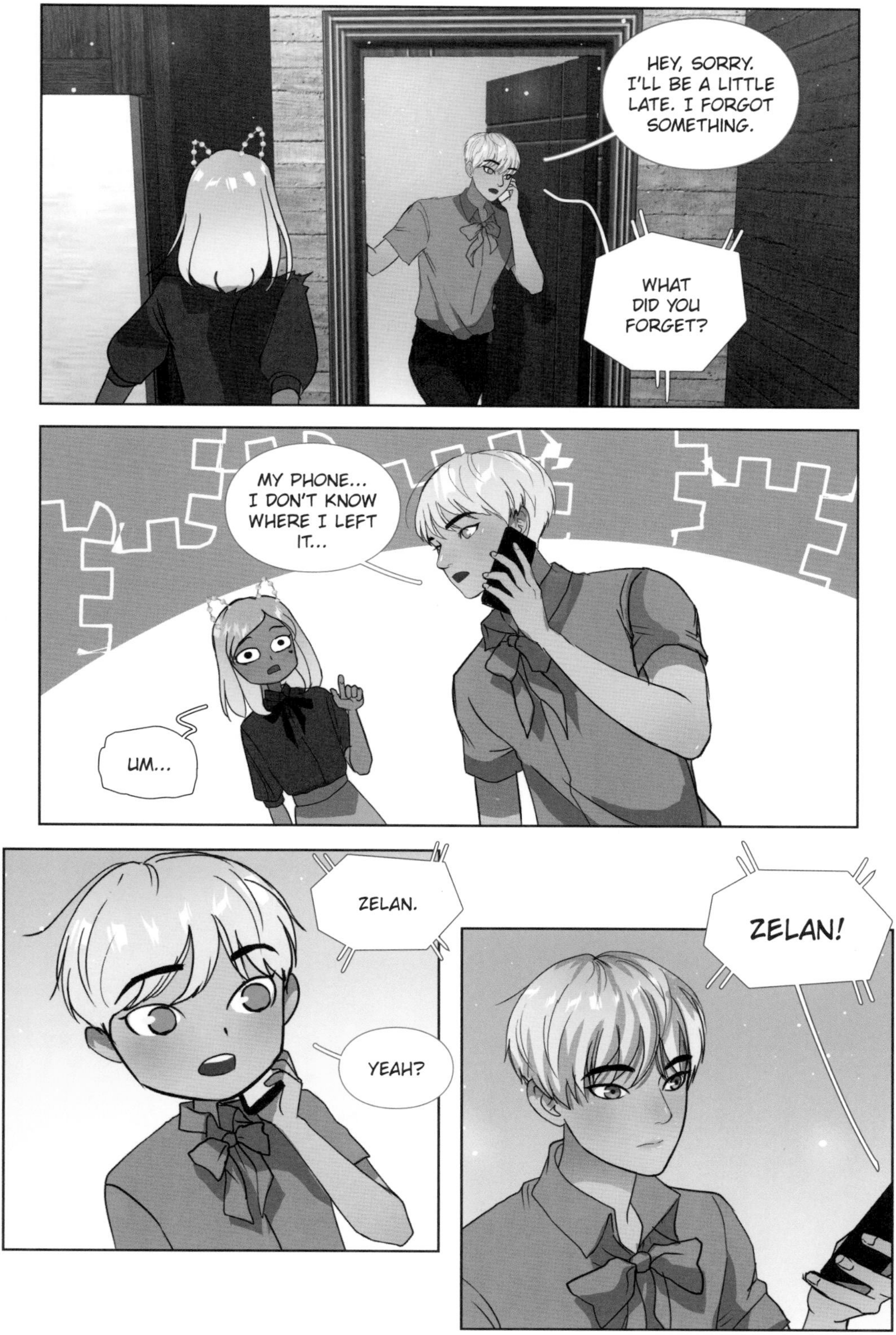
HEY, SORRY. I'LL BE A LITTLE LATE. I FORGOT SOMETHING.
WHAT DID YOU FORGET?
MY PHONE... I DON'T KNOW WHERE I LEFT IT...
UM...
ZELAN.
YEAH?
ZELAN!

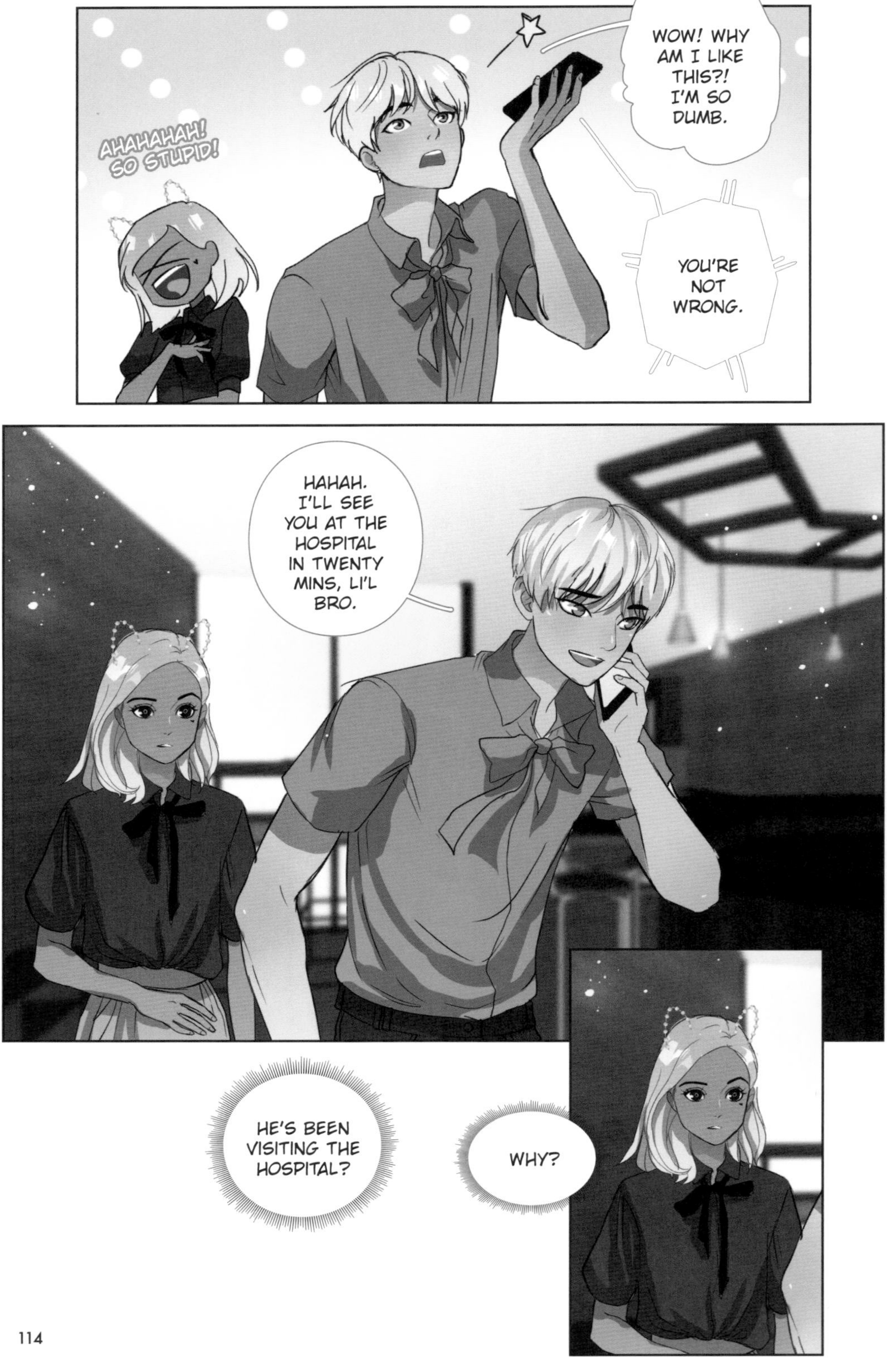
WOW! WHY AM I LIKE THIS?! I'M SO DUMB.
AHAHAHAH! SO STUPID!
YOU'RE NOT WRONG.
HAHAH. I'LL SEE YOU AT THE HOSPITAL IN TWENTY MINS, LI'L BRO.
HE'S BEEN VISITING THE HOSPITAL?
WHY?

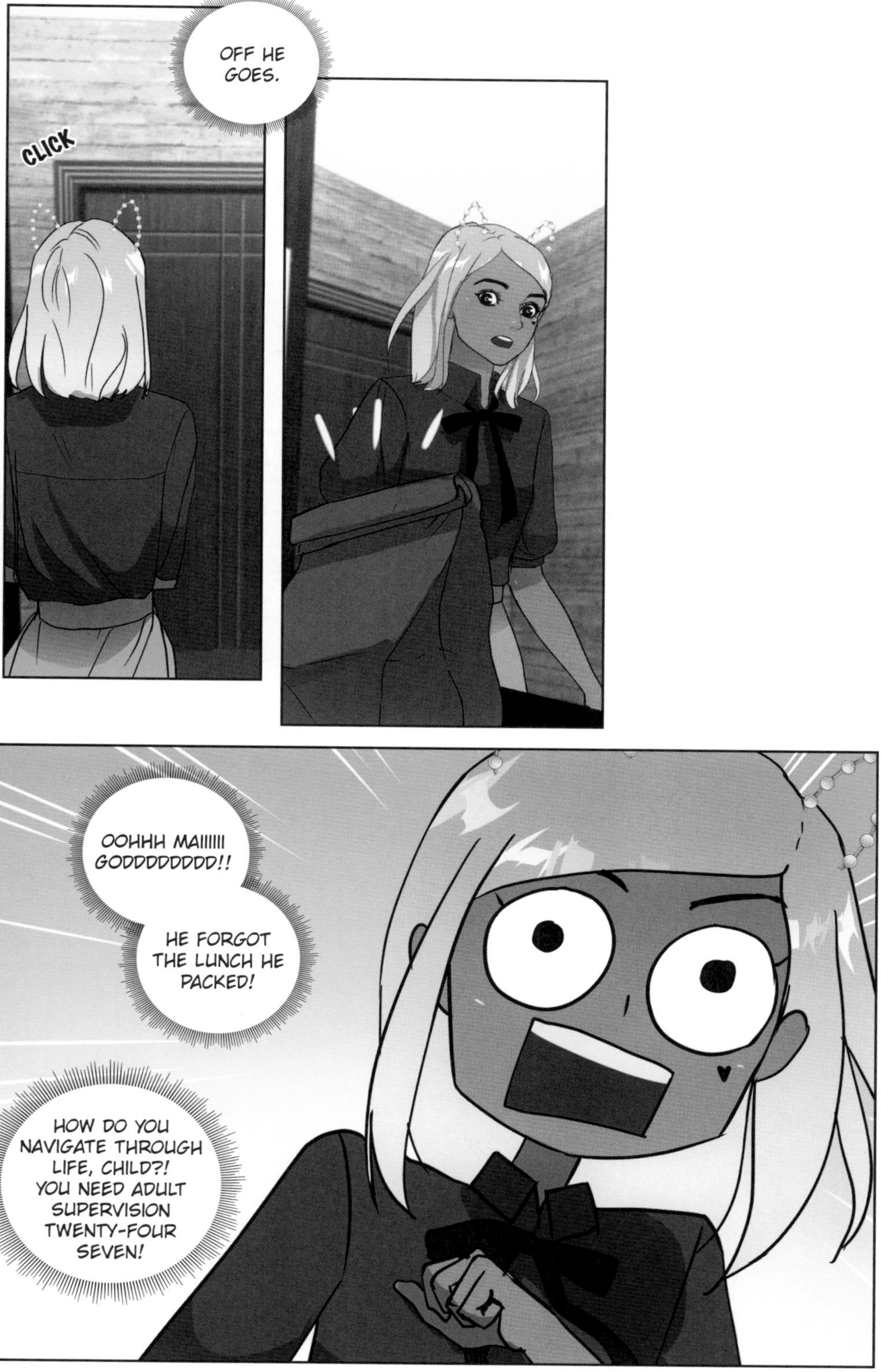
OFF HE GOES.
CLICK
OOHHH MAIIIIII GODDDDDDDD!!
HE FORGOT THE LUNCH HE PACKED!
HOW DO YOU NAVIGATE THROUGH LIFE, CHILD?! YOU NEED ADULT SUPERVISION TWENTY-FOUR SEVEN!

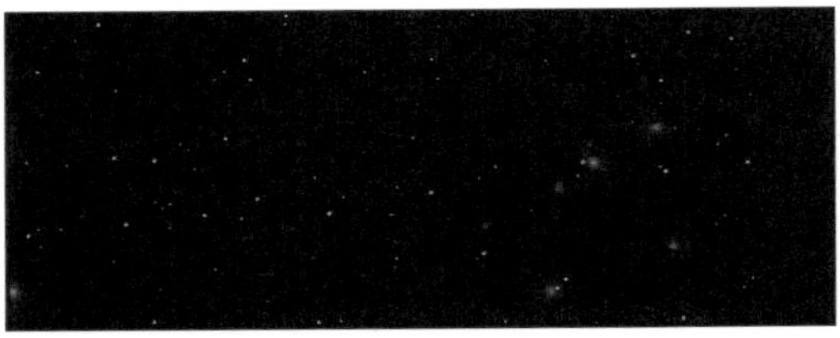

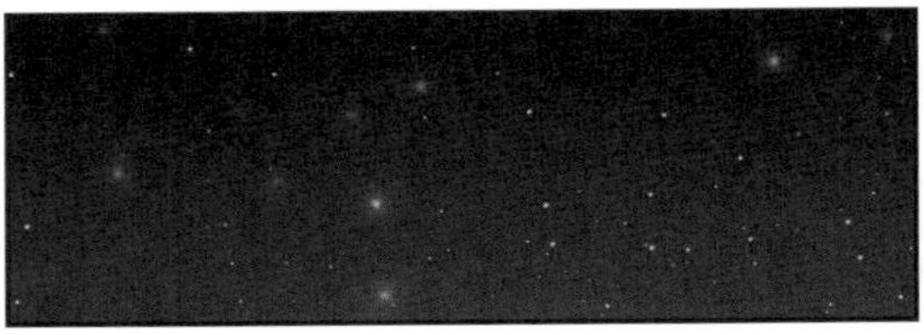

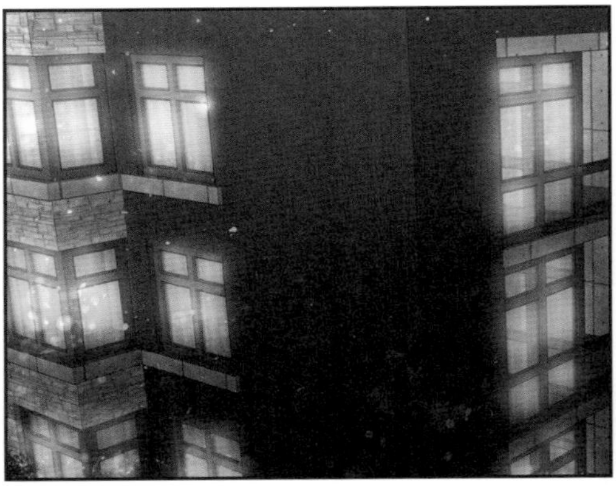

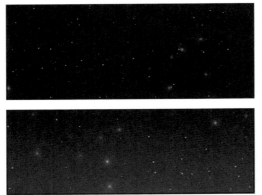

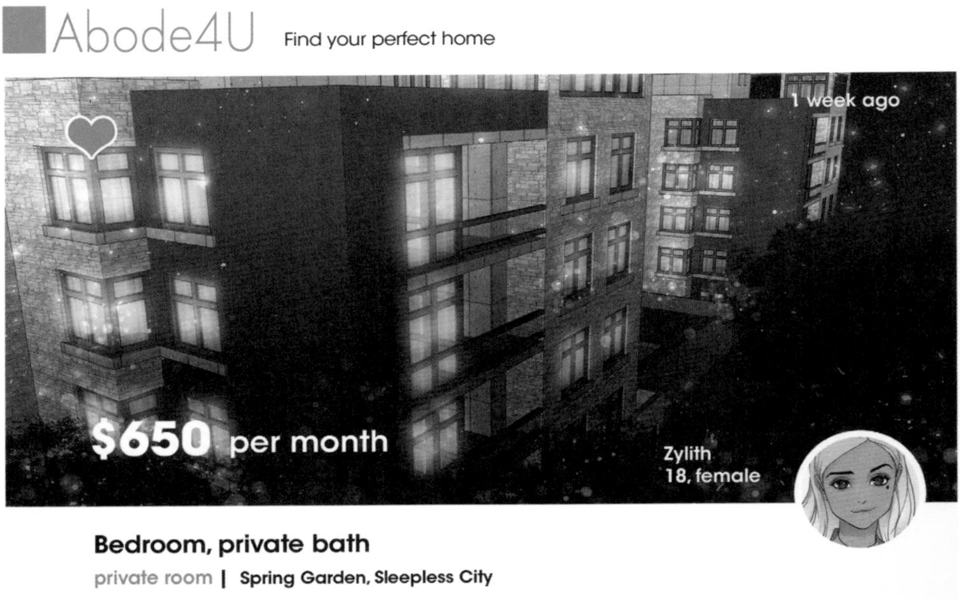
Abode4U
Find your perfect home
1 week ago
$650 per month
Zylith
18, female
Bedroom, private bath
private room | Spring Garden, Sleepless City

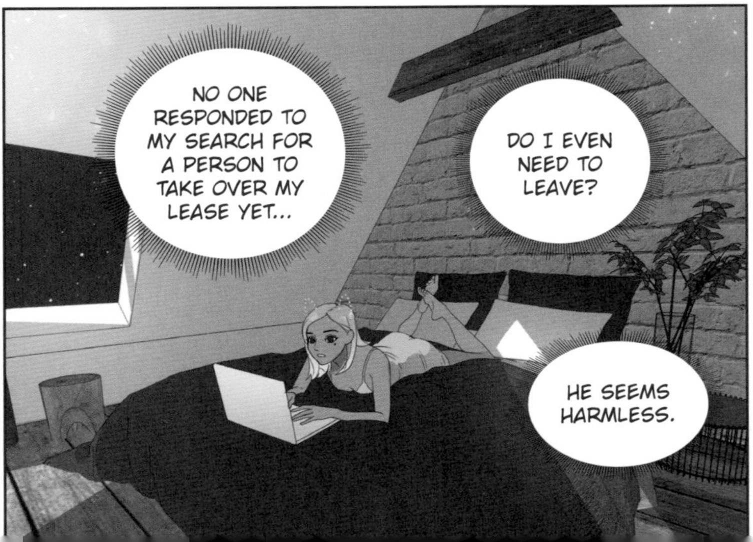
NO ONE RESPONDED TO MY SEARCH FOR A PERSON TO TAKE OVER MY LEASE YET...
DO I EVEN NEED TO LEAVE?
HE SEEMS HARMLESS.

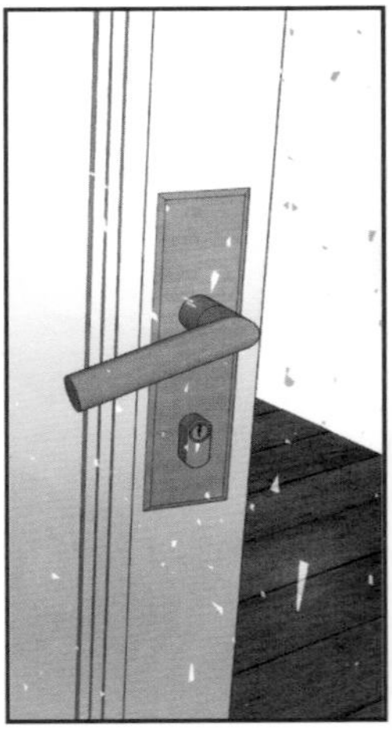

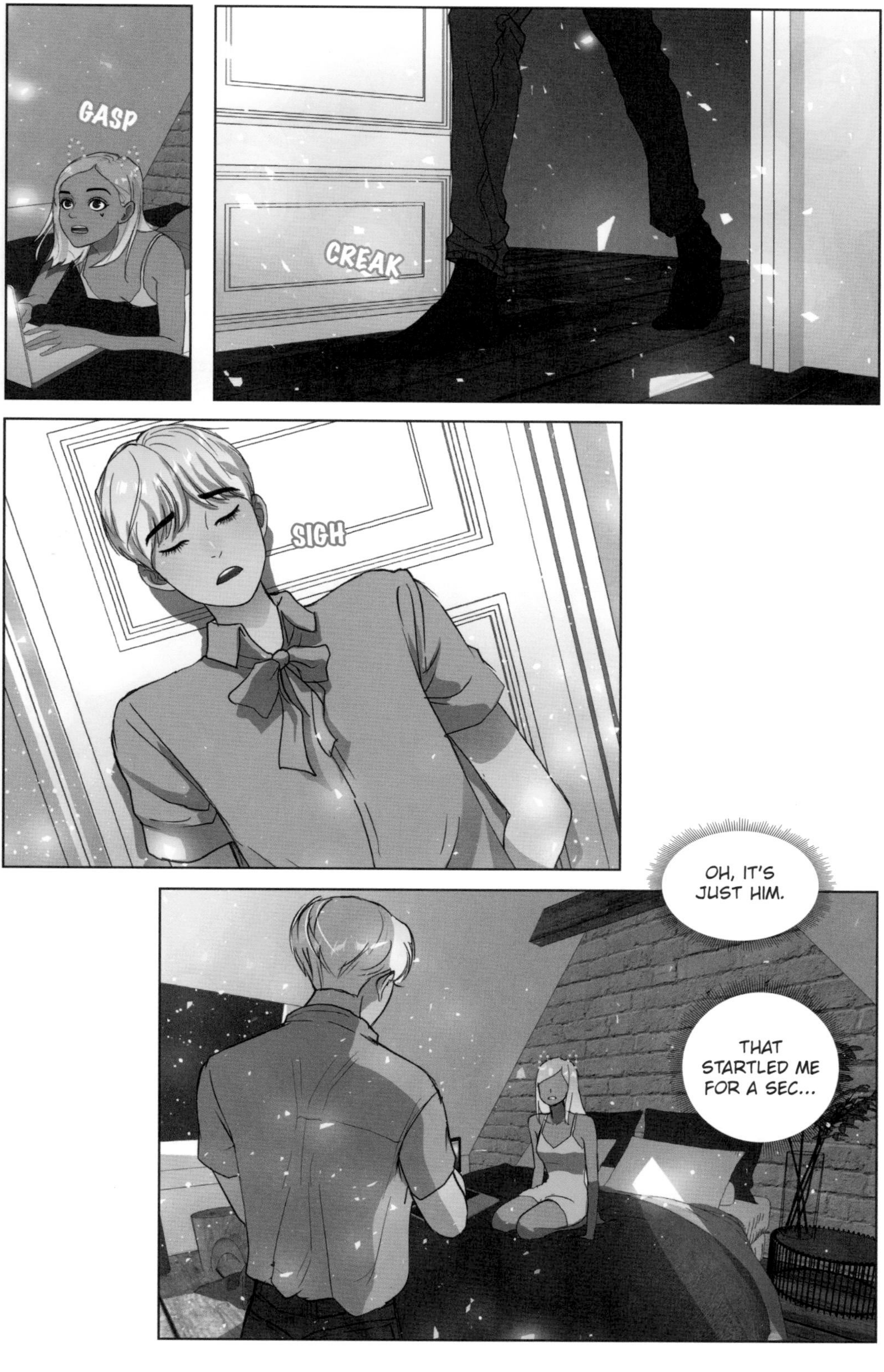
GASP
CREAK
SIGH
OH, IT'S JUST HIM.
THAT STARTLED ME FOR A SEC...

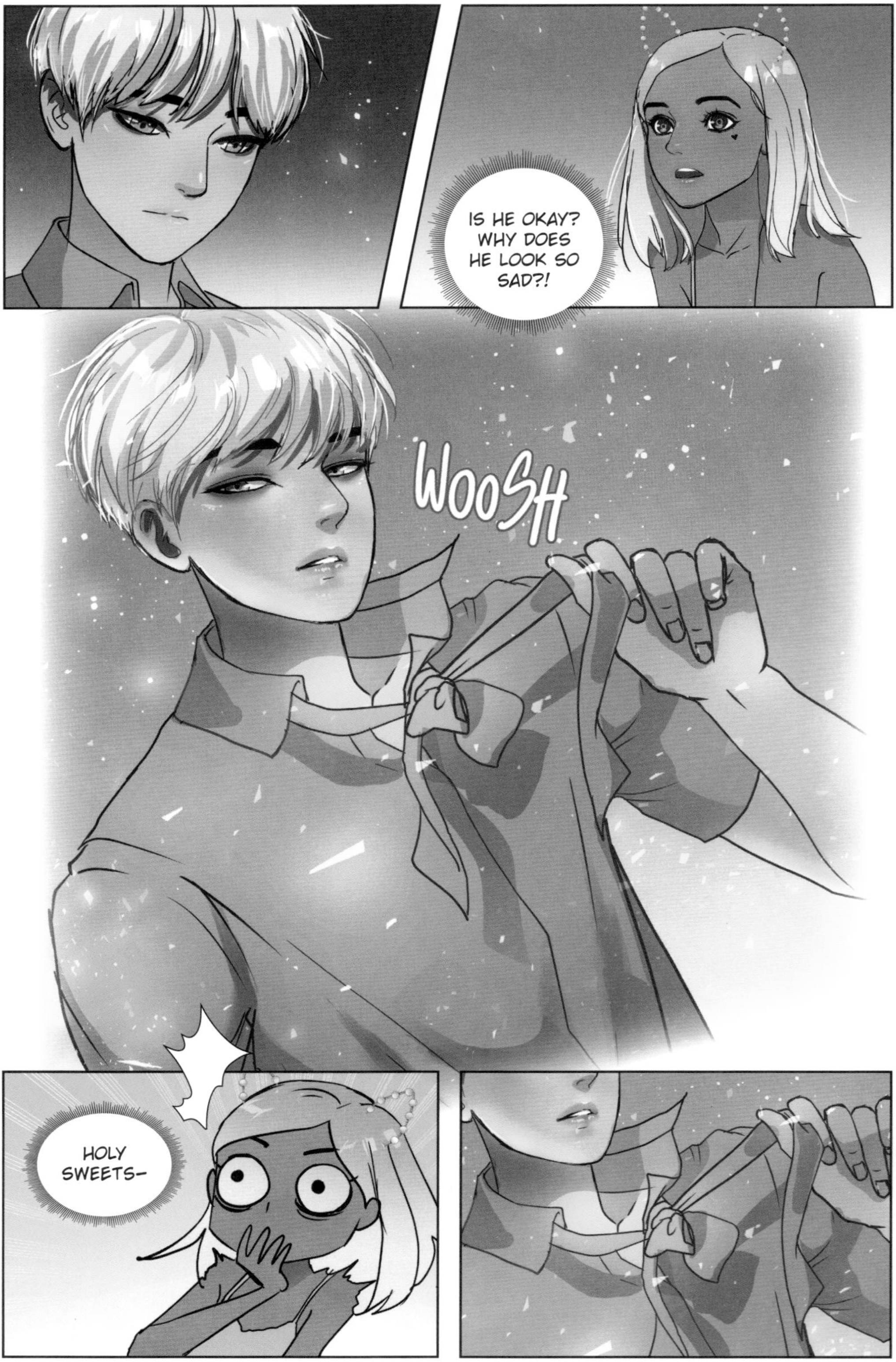
IS HE OKAY? WHY DOES HE LOOK SO SAD?!
WOOSH
HOLY SWEETS-

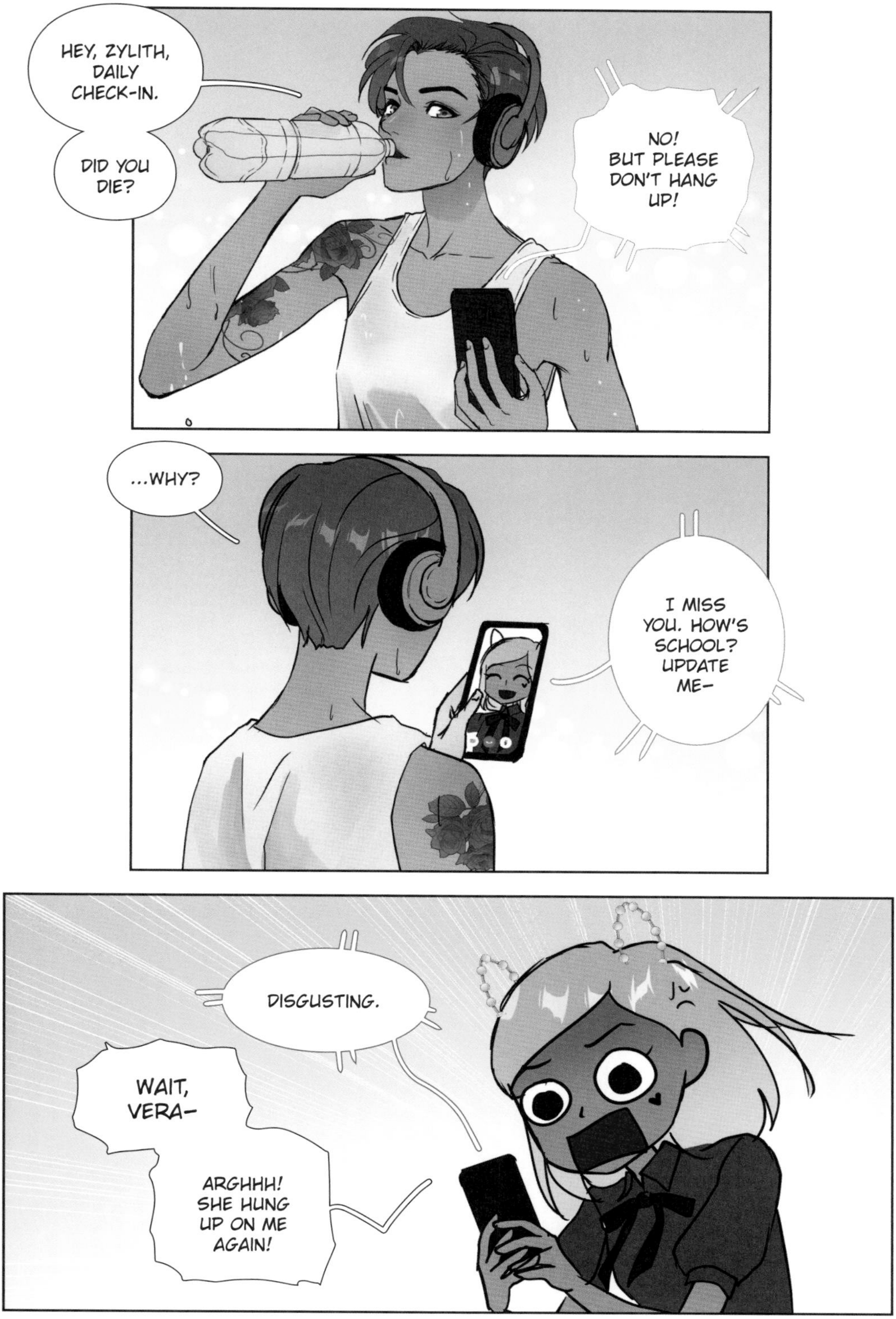
HEY, ZYLITH, DAILY CHECK-IN.
DID YOU DIE?
NO! BUT PLEASE DON'T HANG UP!
...WHY?
I MISS YOU. HOW'S SCHOOL? UPDATE ME-
DISGUSTING.
WAIT, VERA-
ARGHHH! SHE HUNG UP ON ME AGAIN!

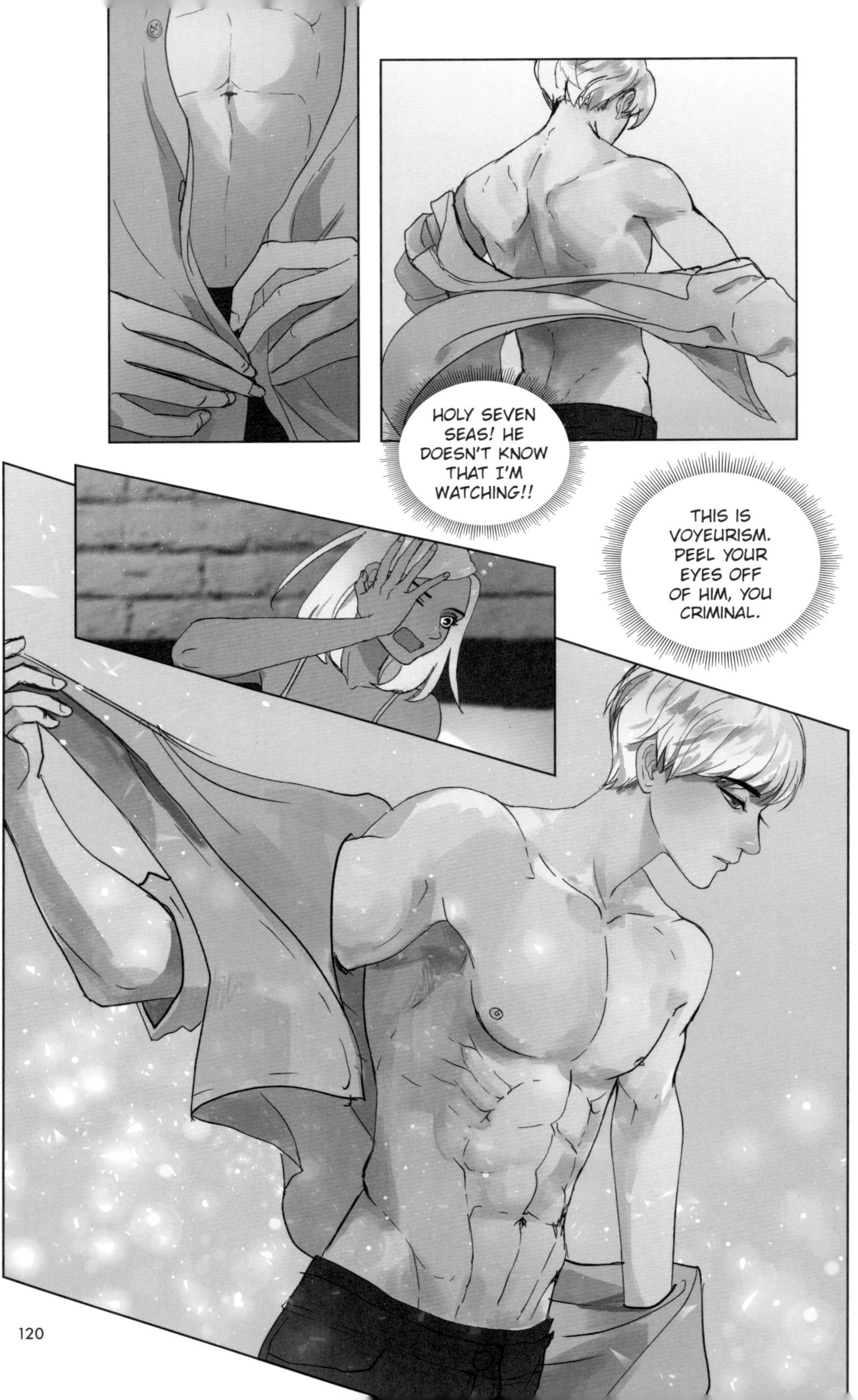
HOLY SEVEN SEAS! HE DOESN'T KNOW THAT I'M WATCHING!!
THIS IS VOYEURISM. PEEL YOUR EYES OFF OF HIM, YOU CRIMINAL.

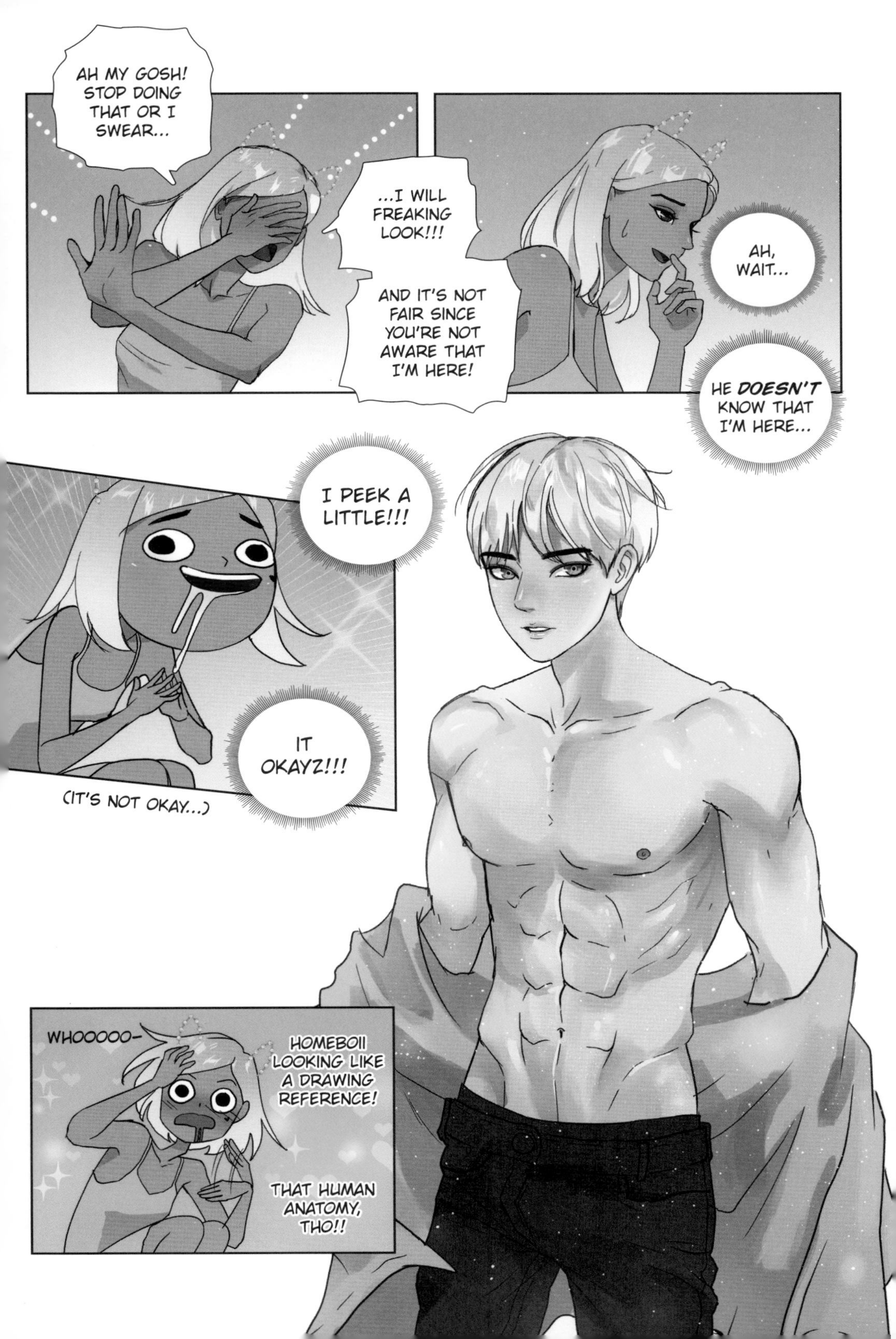
AH MY GOSH! STOP DOING THAT OR I SWEAR...
...I WILL FREAKING LOOK!!!
AND IT'S NOT FAIR SINCE YOU'RE NOT AWARE THAT I'M HERE!
AH, WAIT...
HE DOESN'T KNOW THAT I'M HERE...
I PEEK A LITTLE!!!
IT OKAYZ!!!
(IT'S NOT OKAY...)
WHOOOOO-
HOMEBOII LOOKING LIKE A DRAWING REFERENCE!
THAT HUMAN ANATOMY, THO!!

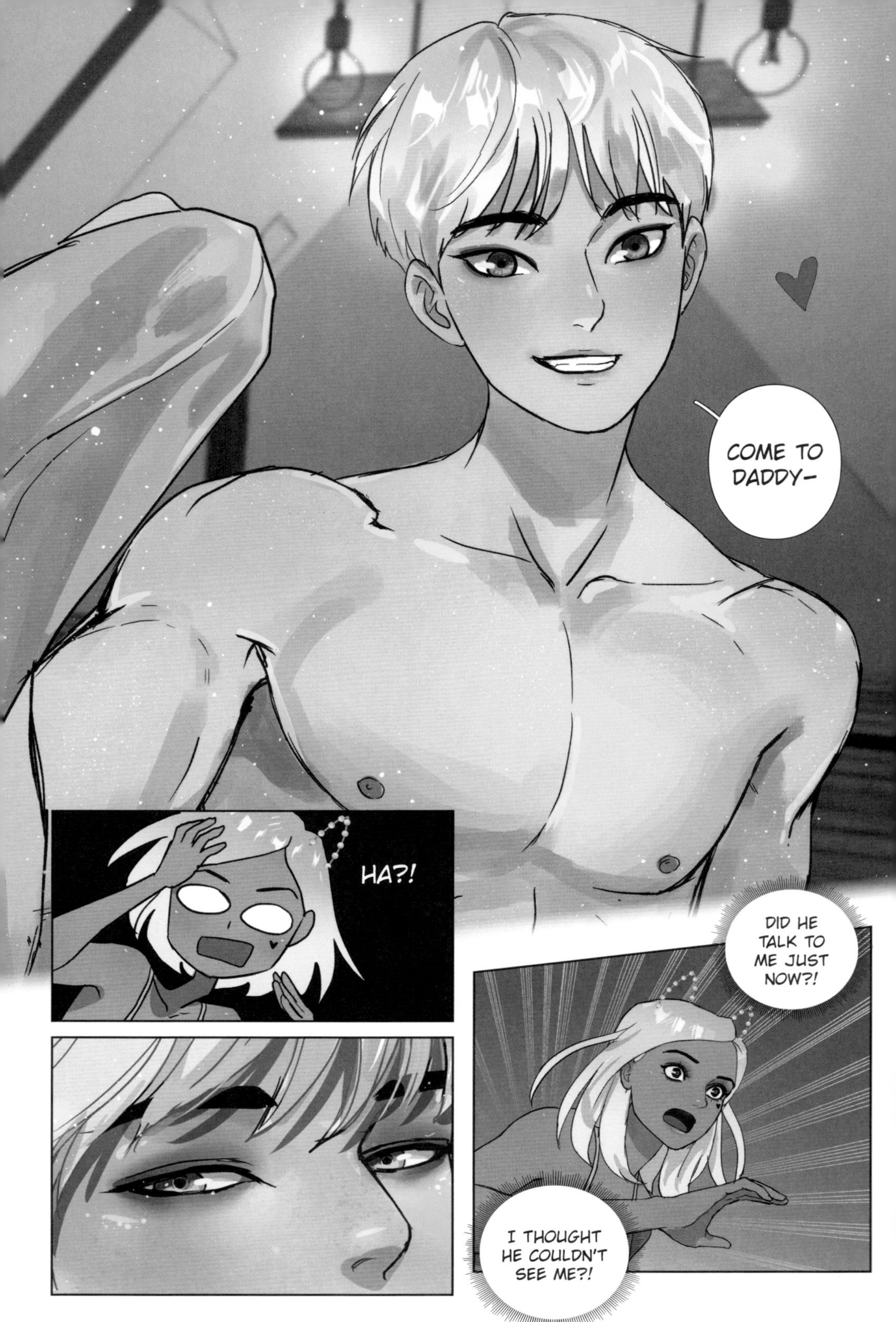
COME TO DADDY-
HA?!
DID HE TALK TO ME JUST NOW?!
I THOUGHT HE COULDN'T SEE ME?!

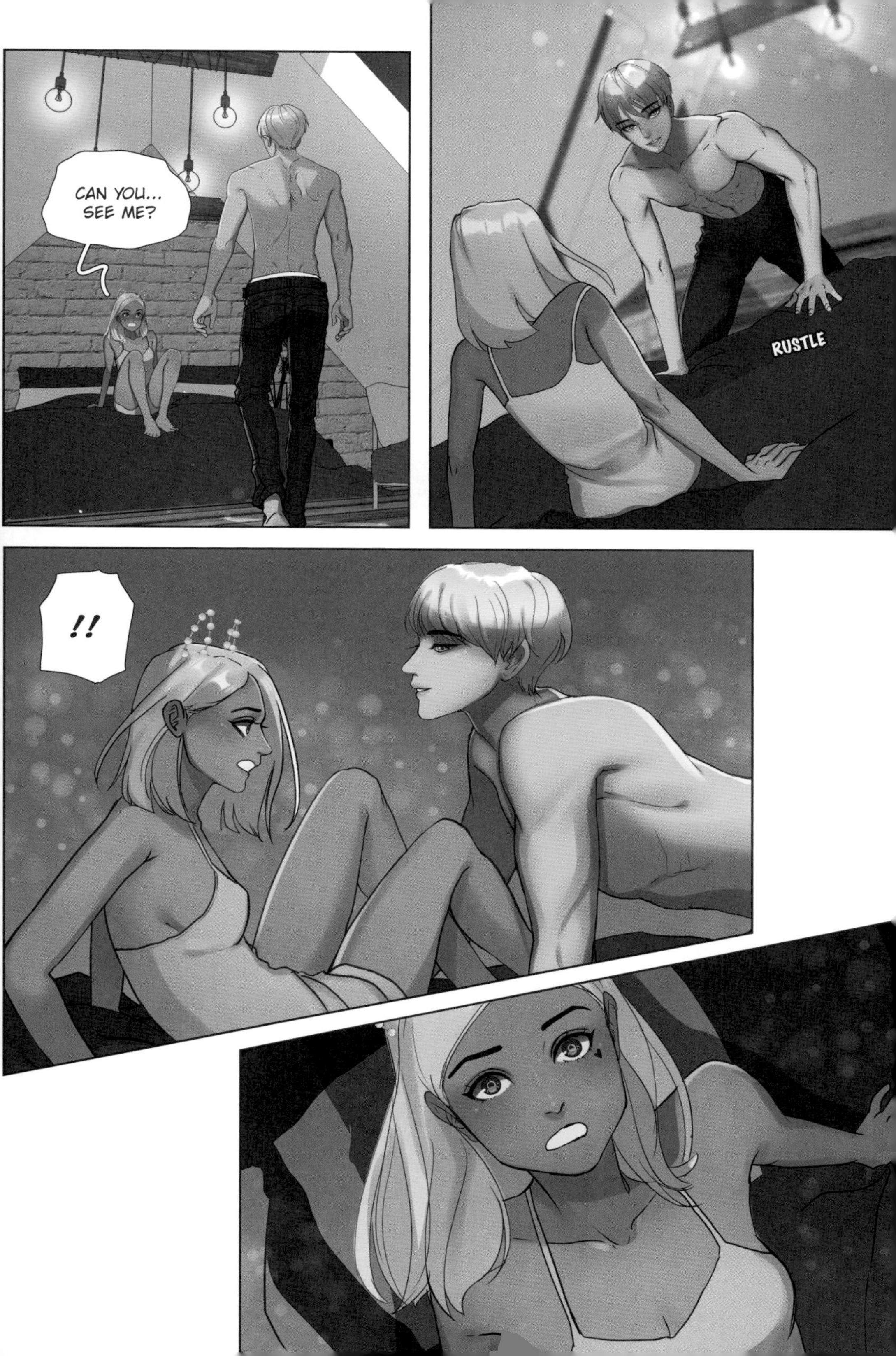
CAN YOU... SEE ME?
RUSTLE
!!

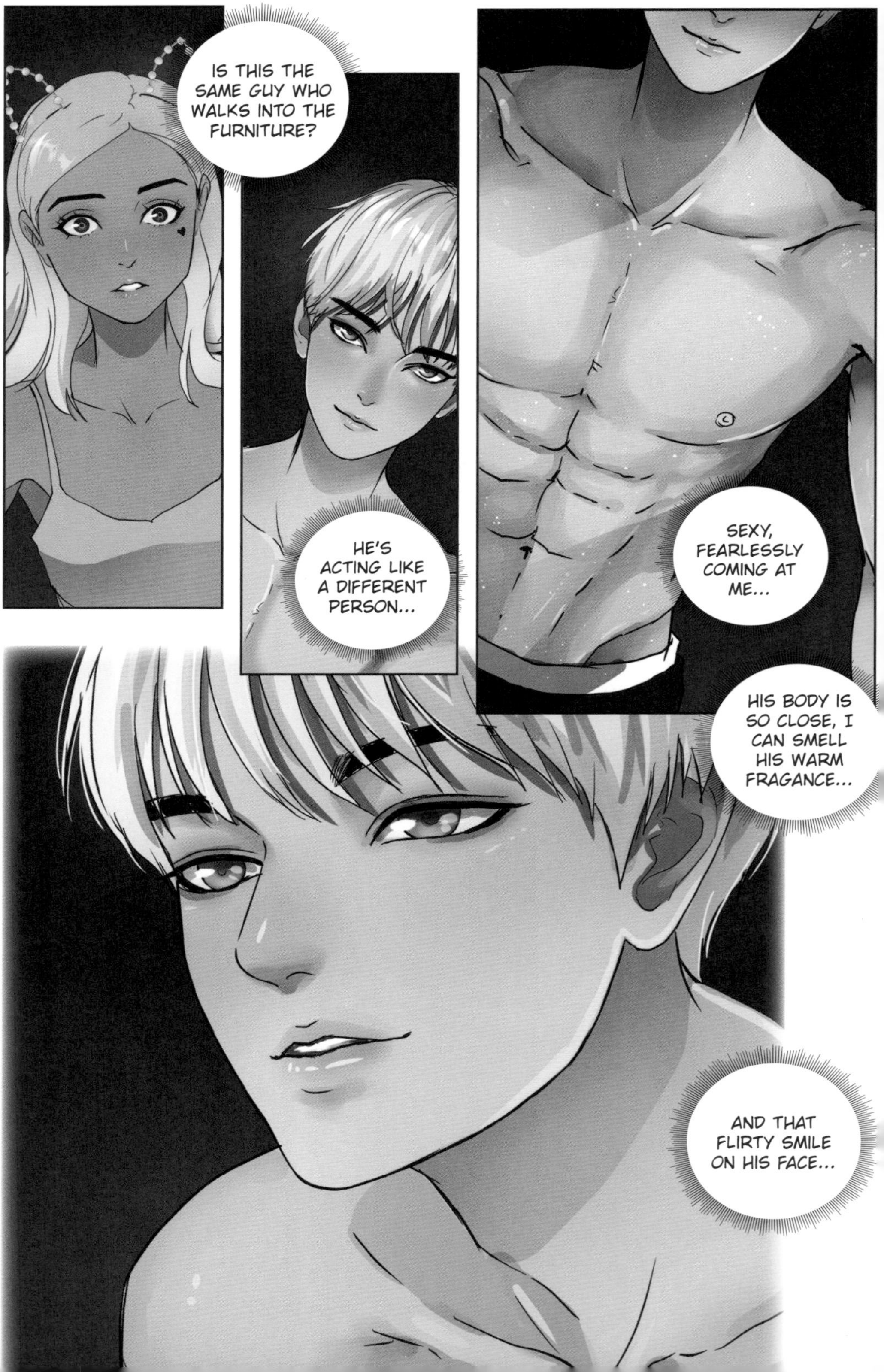
IS THIS THE SAME GUY WHO WALKS INTO THE FURNITURE?
HE'S ACTING LIKE A DIFFERENT PERSON...
SEXY, FEARLESSLY COMING AT ME...
HIS BODY IS SO CLOSE, I CAN SMELL HIS WARM FRAGANCE...
AND THAT FLIRTY SMILE ON HIS FACE...

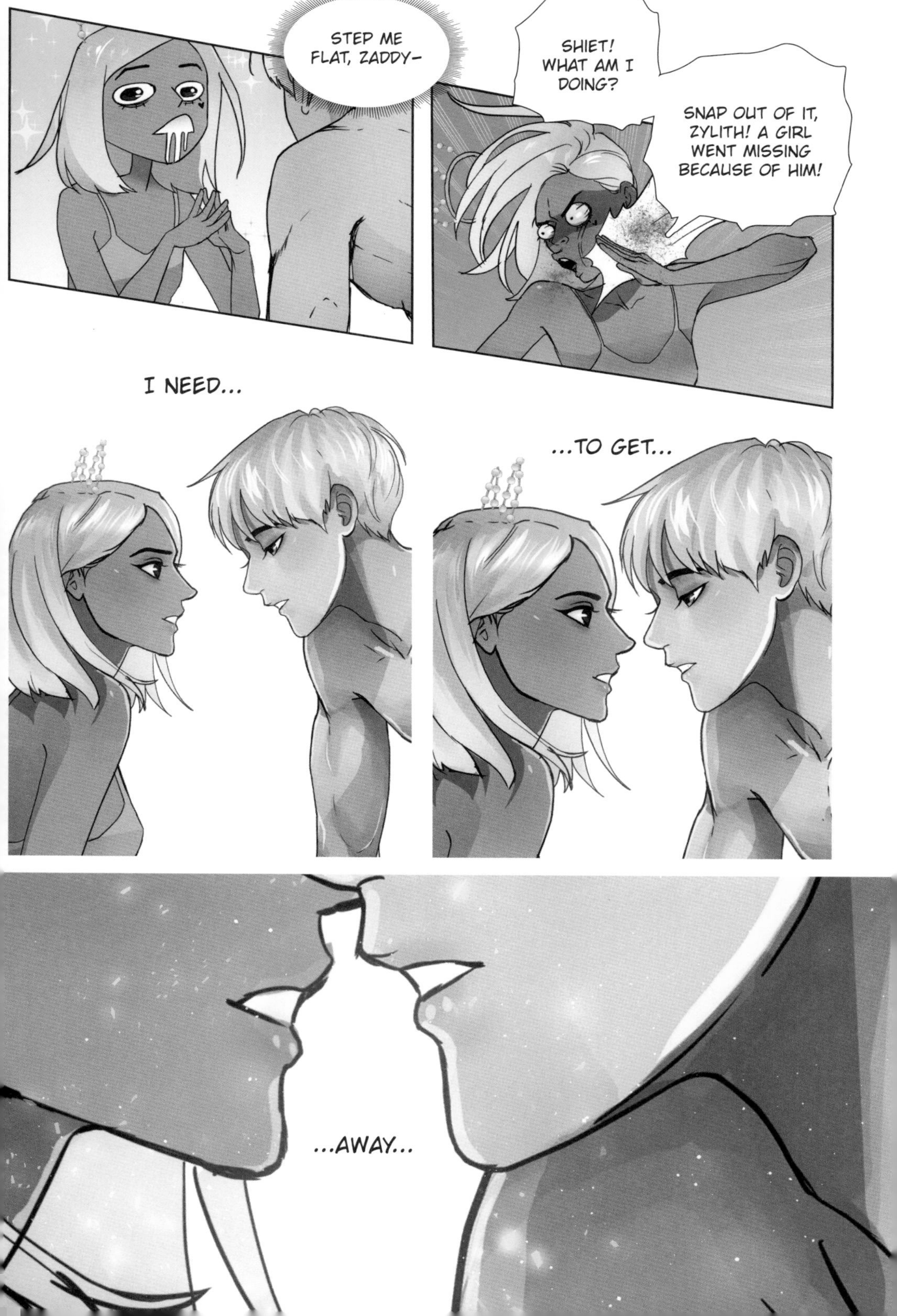
STEP ME FLAT, ZADDY-
SHIET! WHAT AM I DOING?
SNAP OUT OF IT, ZYLITH! A GIRL WENT MISSING BECAUSE OF HIM!
I NEED...
...TO GET...
...AWAY...

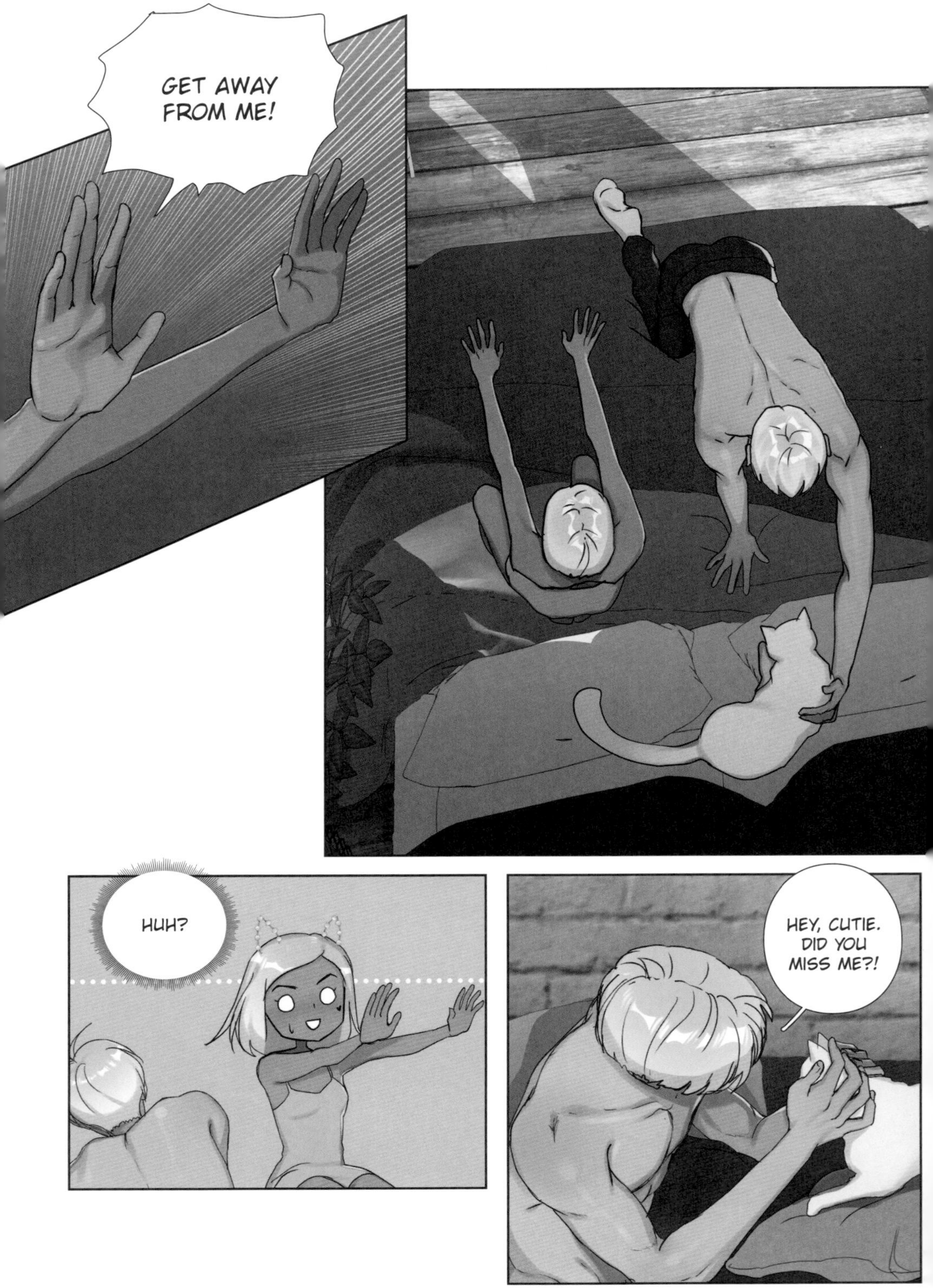
GET AWAY FROM ME!
HUH?
HEY, CUTIE. DID YOU MISS ME?!

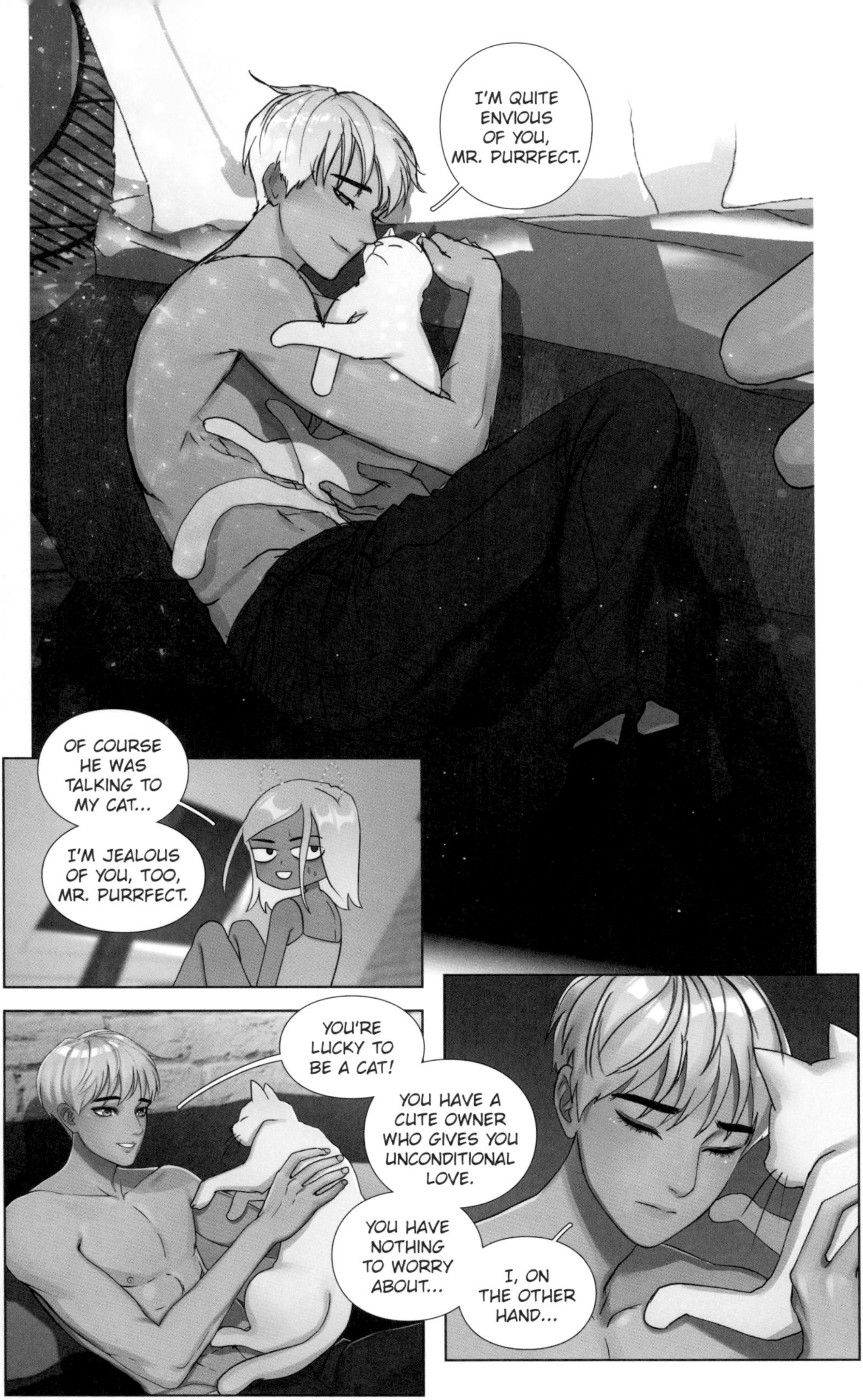
I'M QUITE ENVIOUS OF YOU, MR. PURRFECT.
OF COURSE HE WAS TALKING TO MY CAT...
I'M JEALOUS OF YOU, TOO, MR. PURRFECT.
YOU'RE LUCKY TO BE A CAT!
YOU HAVE A CUTE OWNER WHO GIVES YOU UNCONDITIONAL LOVE.
YOU HAVE NOTHING TO WORRY ABOUT...
I, ON THE OTHER HAND...

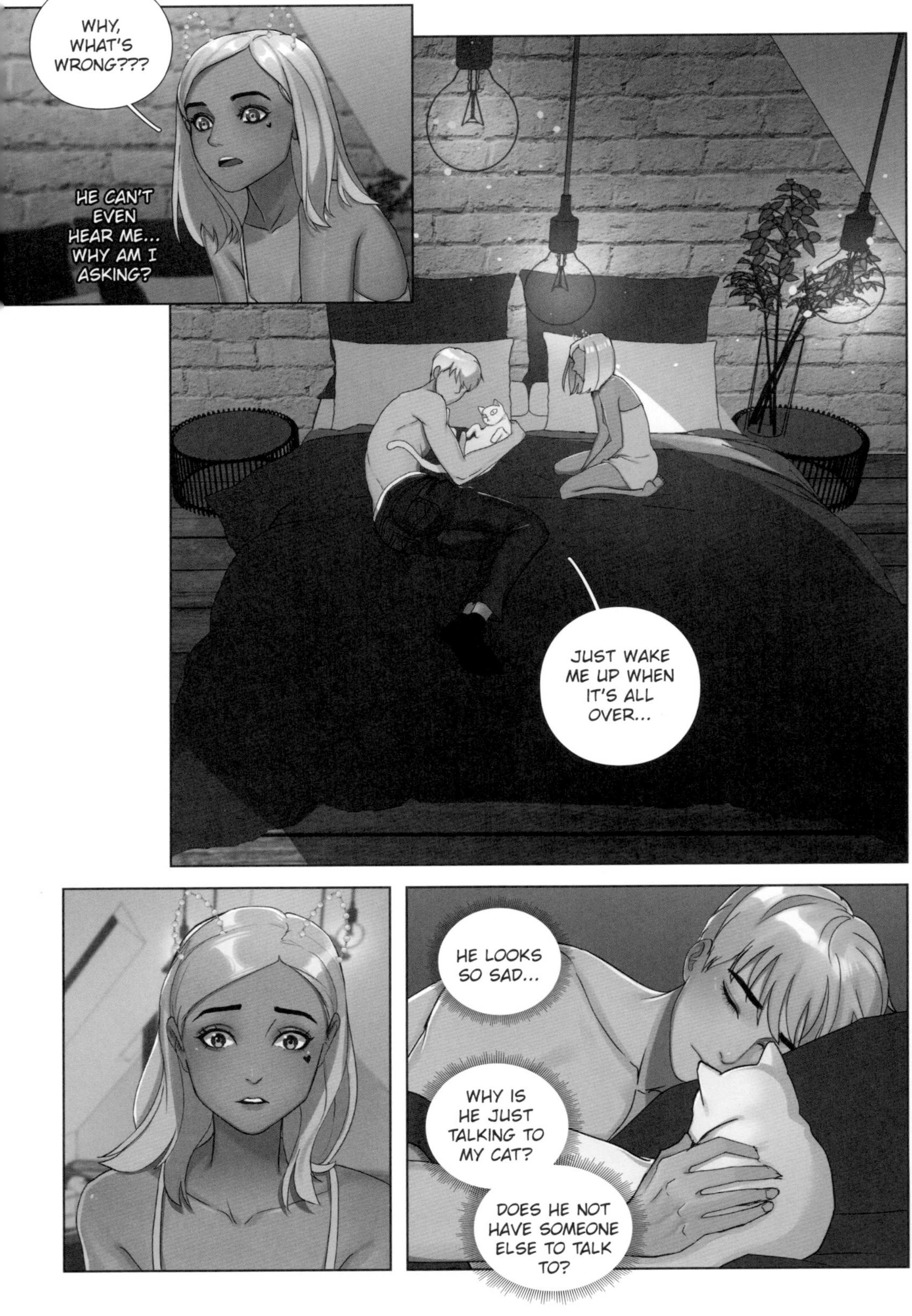
WHY, WHAT'S WRONG???
HE CAN'T EVEN HEAR ME... WHY AM I ASKING?
JUST WAKE ME UP WHEN IT'S ALL OVER...
HE LOOKS SO SAD...
WHY IS HE JUST TALKING TO MY CAT?
DOES HE NOT HAVE SOMEONE ELSE TO TALK TO?

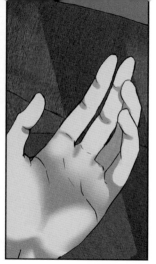

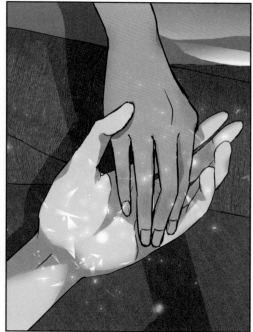

I HAVE NO IDEA WHAT'S HAPPENING...

...BUT I HOPE YOU'LL BE OKAY, ZELAN...

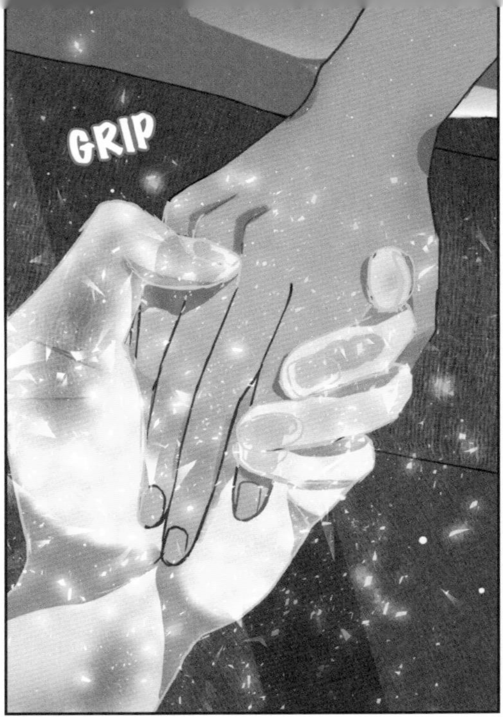
GRIP

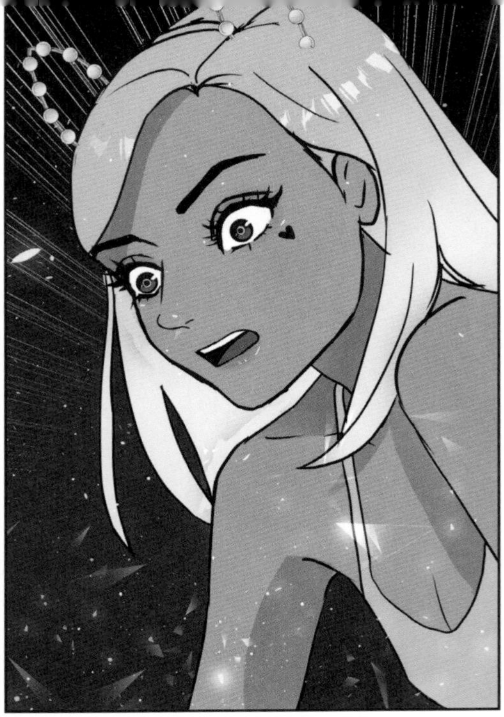

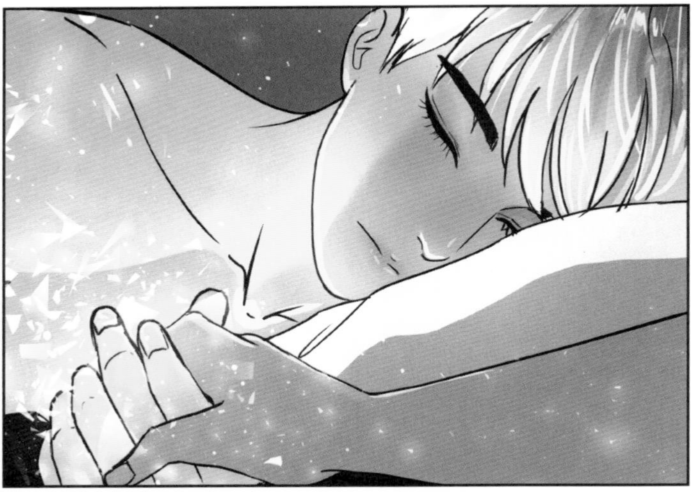

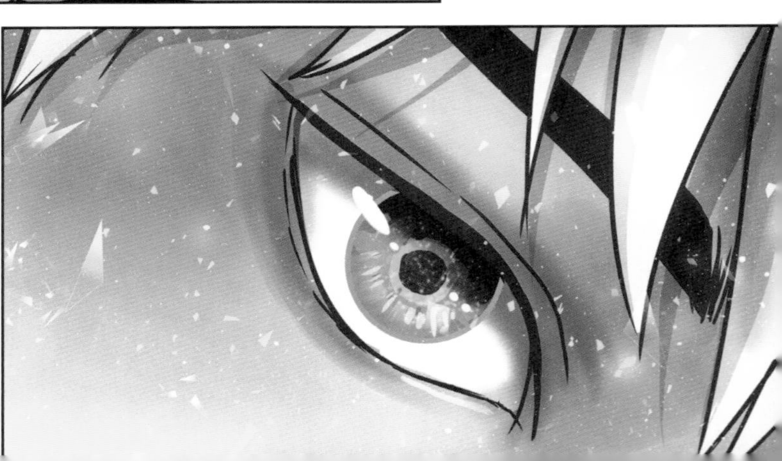

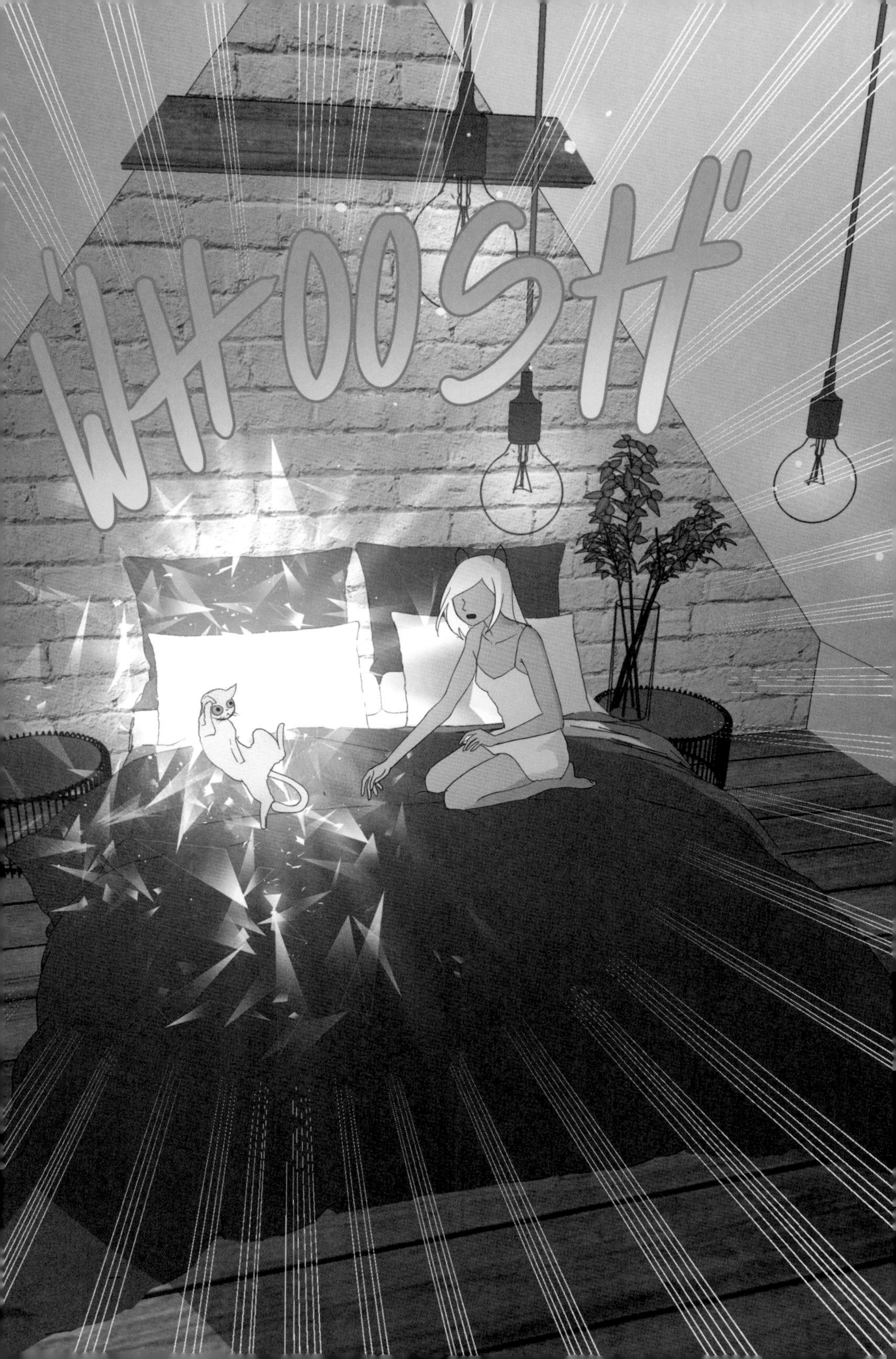
WHOOSH

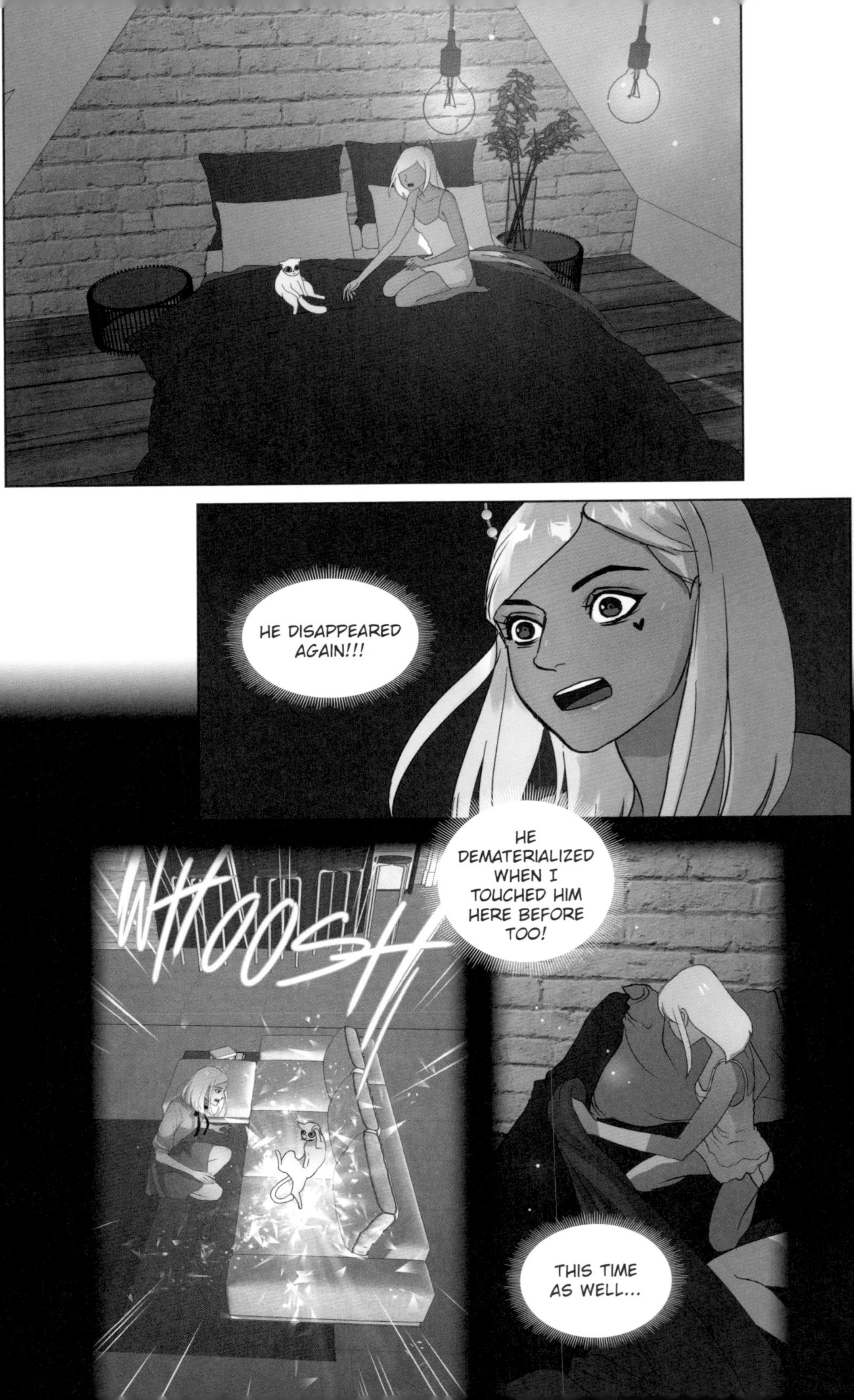
HE DISAPPEARED AGAIN!!!
WHOOSH
HE DEMATERIALIZED WHEN I TOUCHED HIM HERE BEFORE TOO!
THIS TIME AS WELL...

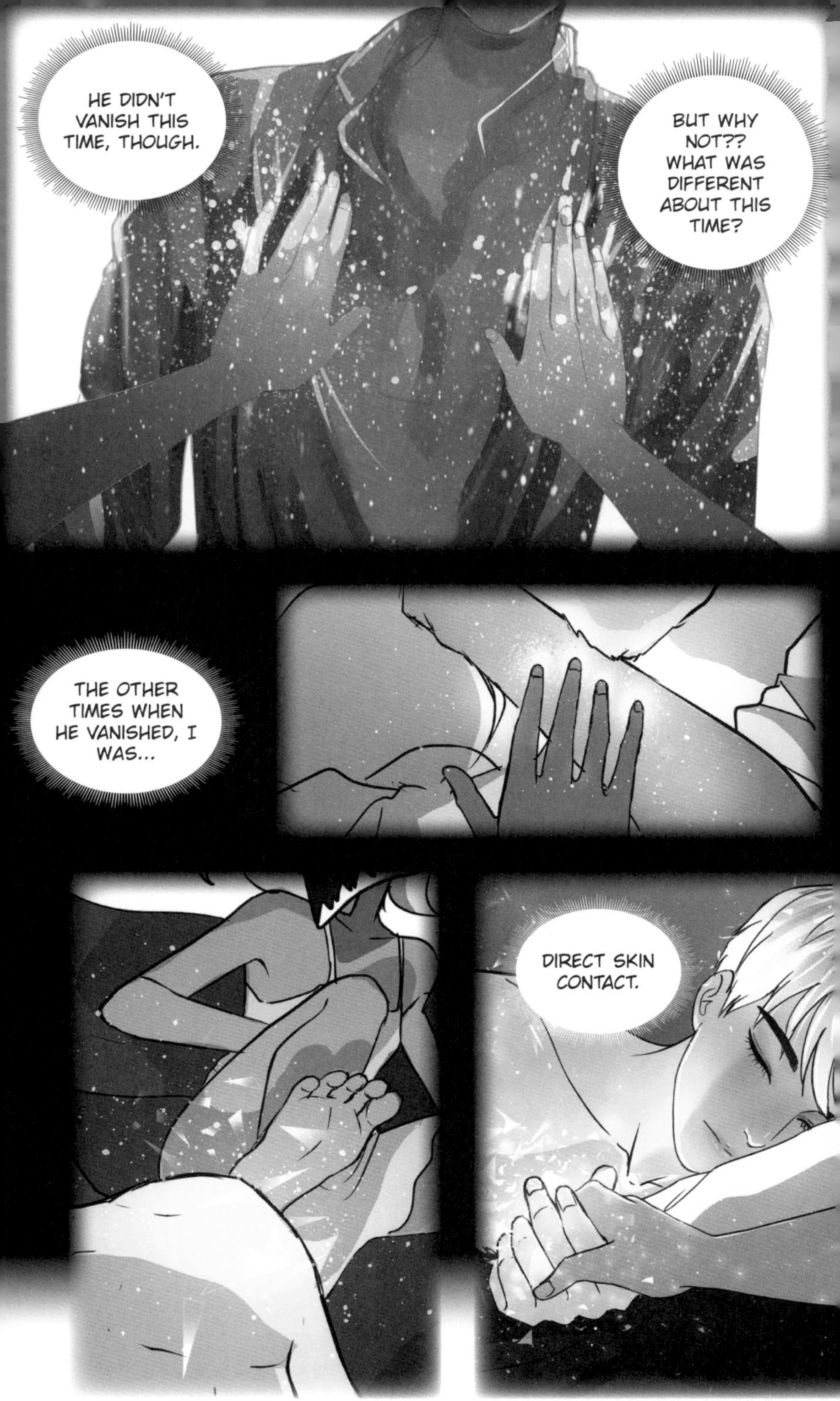
HE DIDN'T VANISH THIS TIME, THOUGH.
BUT WHY NOT?? WHAT WAS DIFFERENT ABOUT THIS TIME?
THE OTHER TIMES WHEN HE VANISHED, I WAS...
DIRECT SKIN CONTACT.

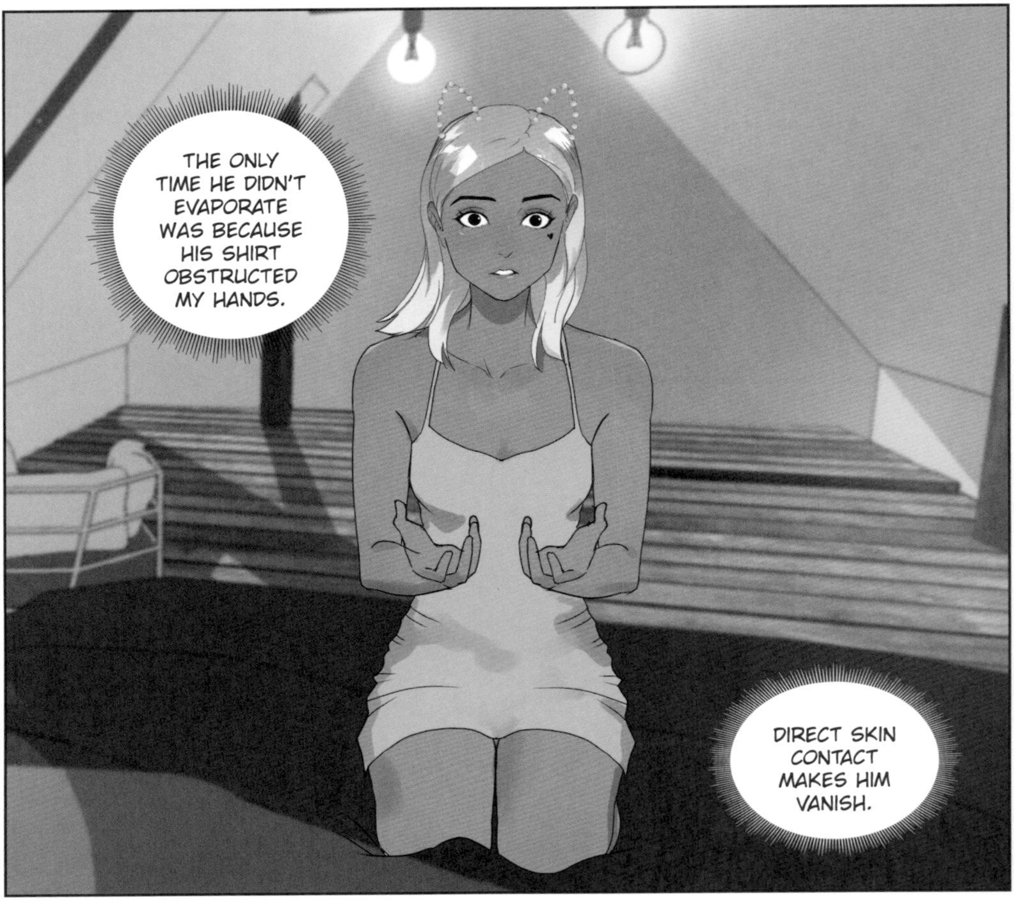
THE ONLY TIME HE DIDN'T EVAPORATE WAS BECAUSE HIS SHIRT OBSTRUCTED MY HANDS.
DIRECT SKIN CONTACT MAKES HIM VANISH.

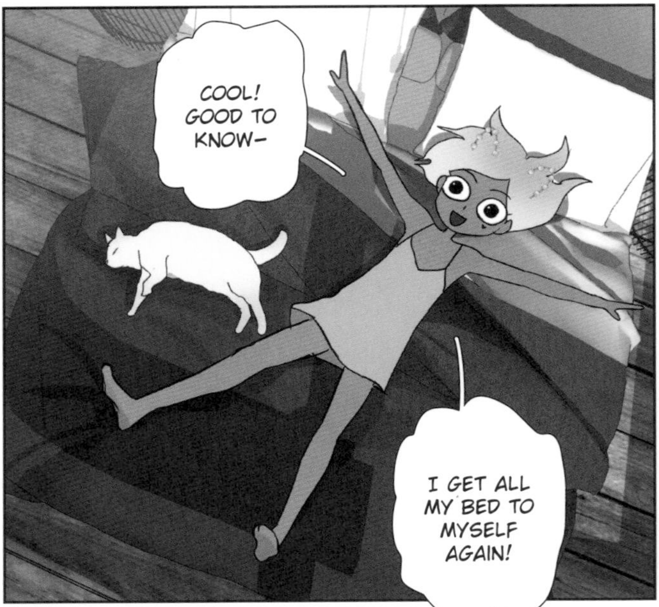
COOL! GOOD TO KNOW–
I GET ALL MY BED TO MYSELF AGAIN!

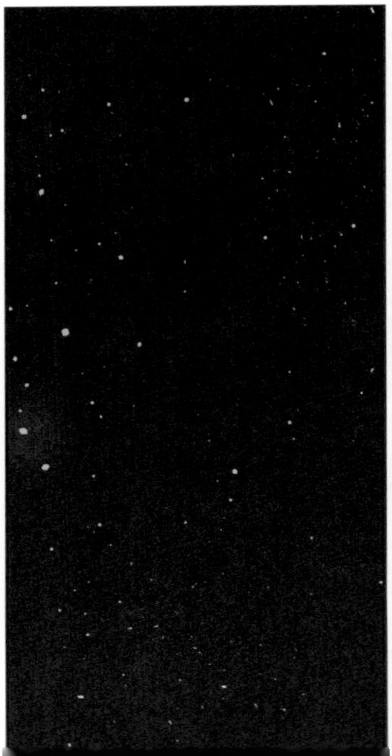

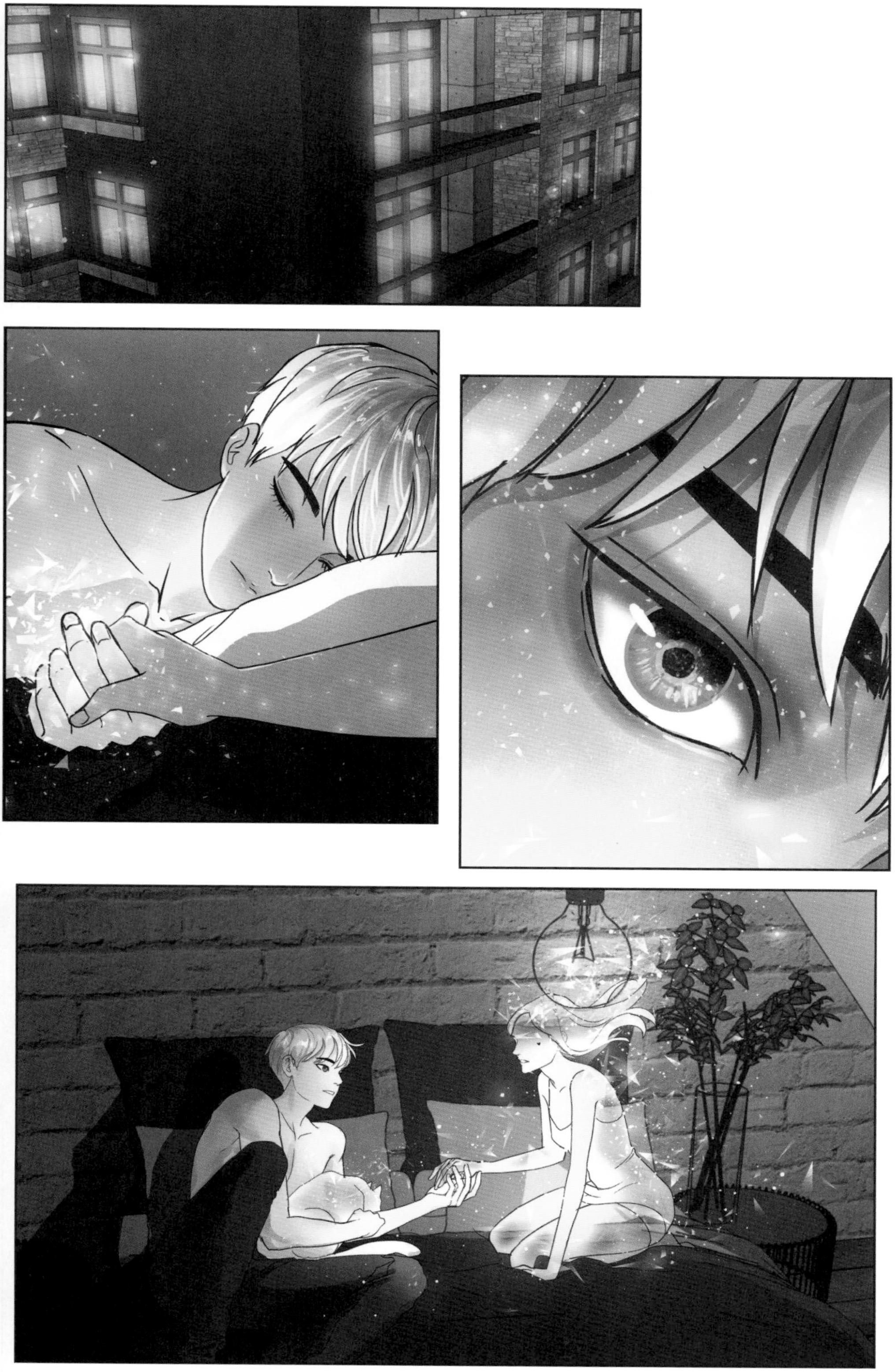

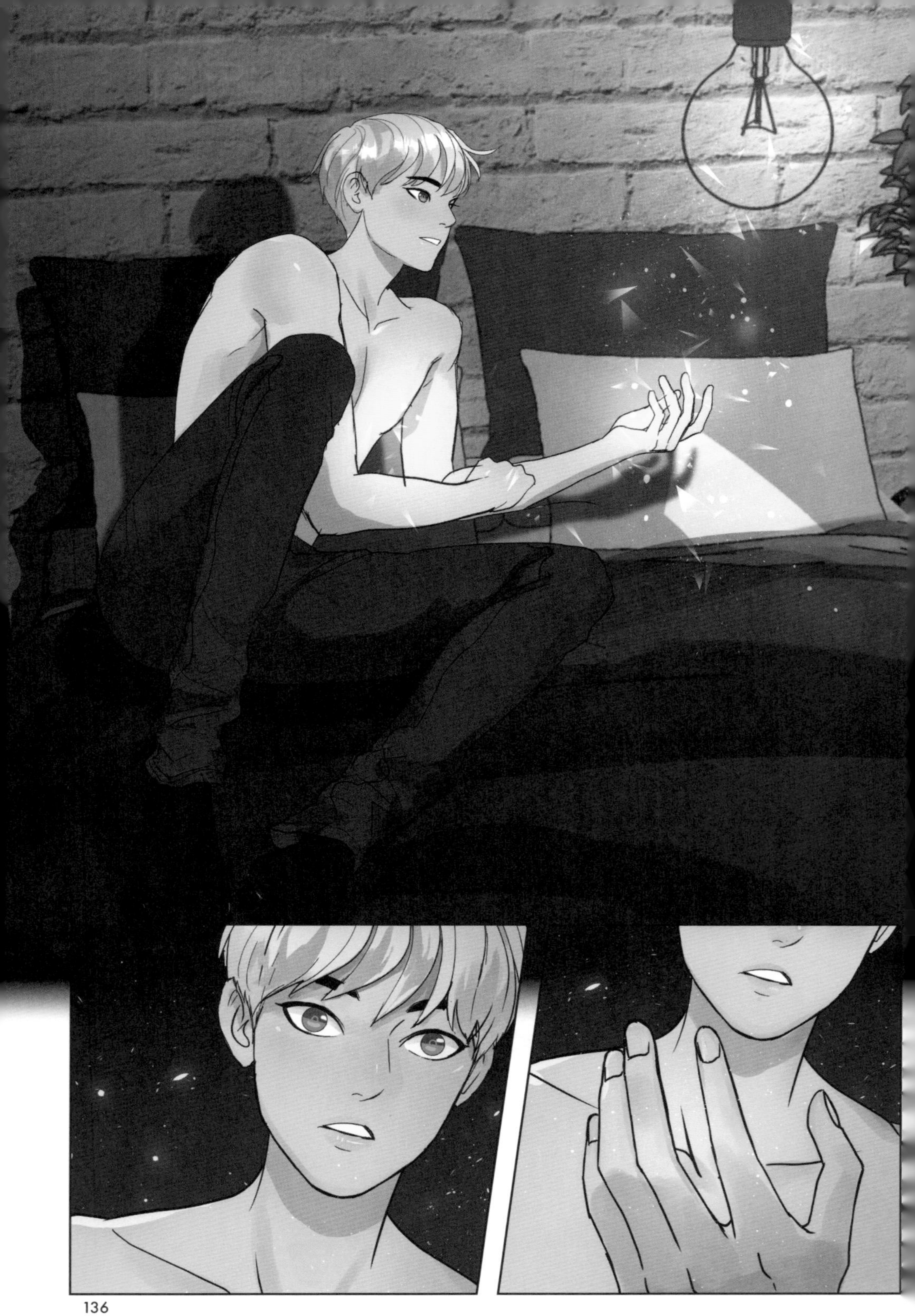

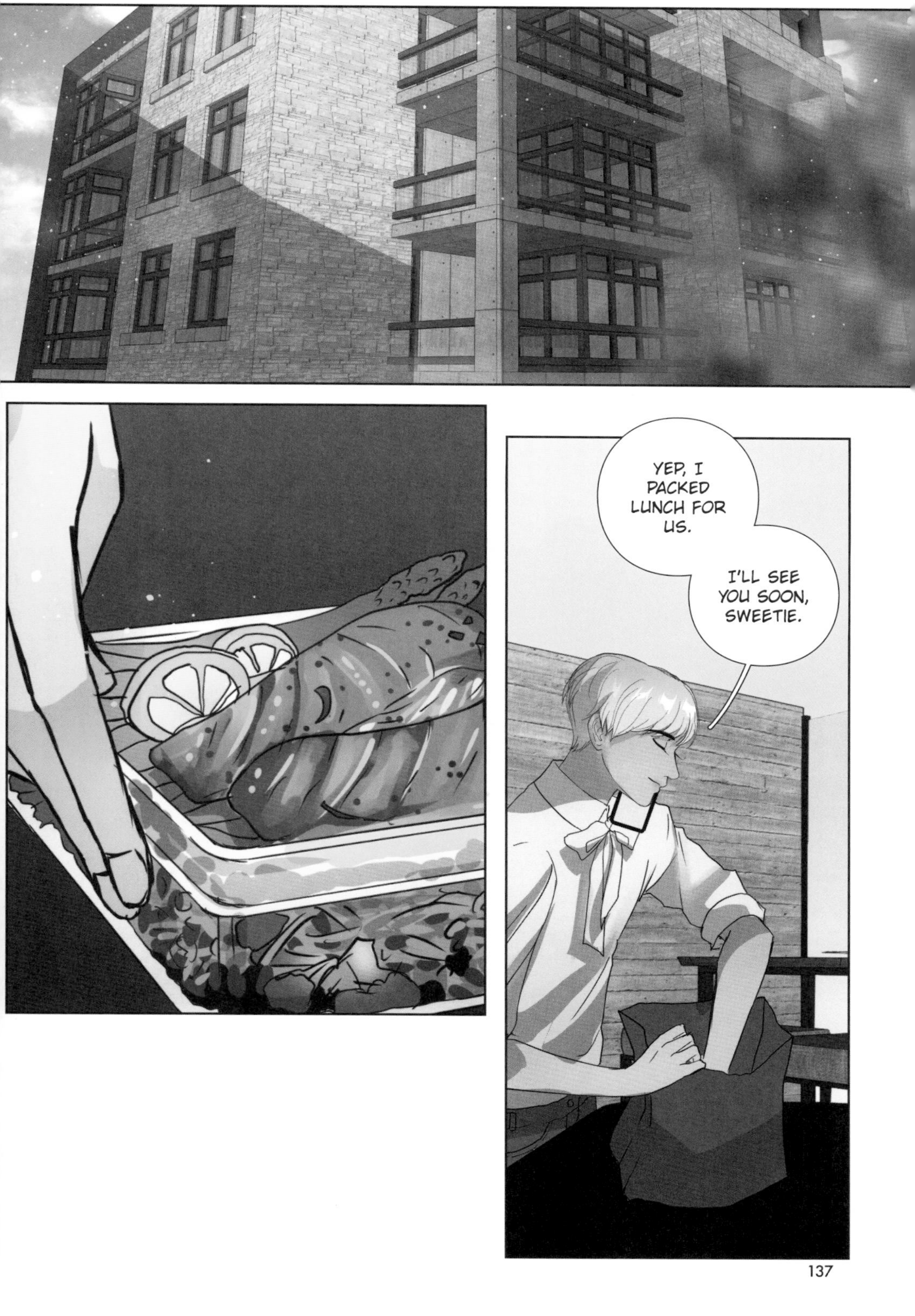
YEP, I PACKED LUNCH FOR US.
I'LL SEE YOU SOON, SWEETIE.

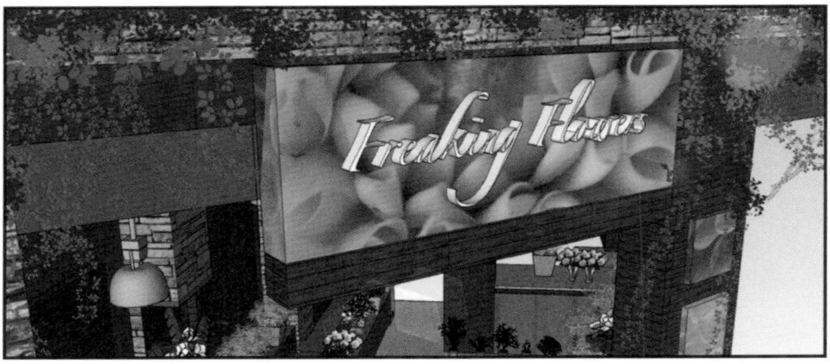
Freaking Flowers

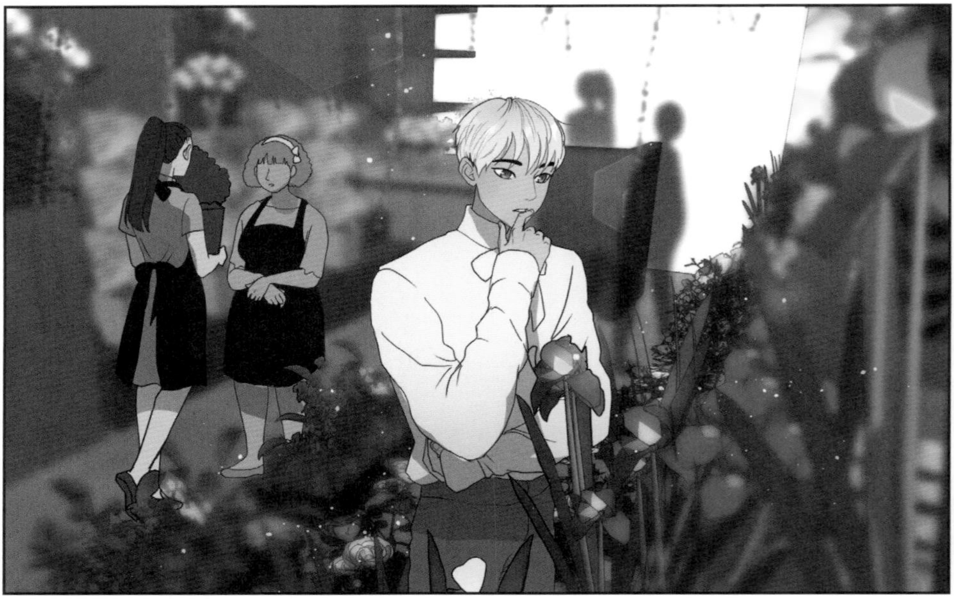

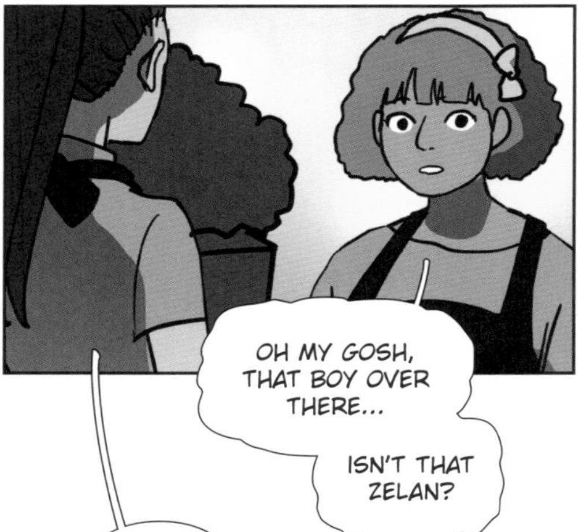
OH MY GOSH, THAT BOY OVER THERE...
ISN'T THAT ZELAN?
WHO?

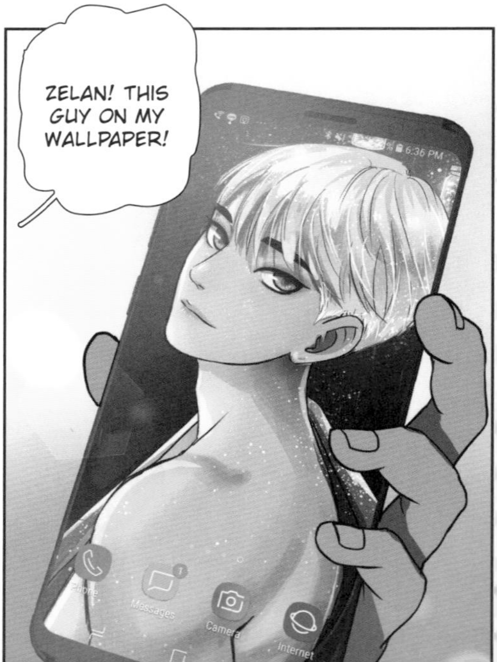
ZELAN! THIS GUY ON MY WALLPAPER!
6:36 PM
Phone
Messages
Camera
Internet

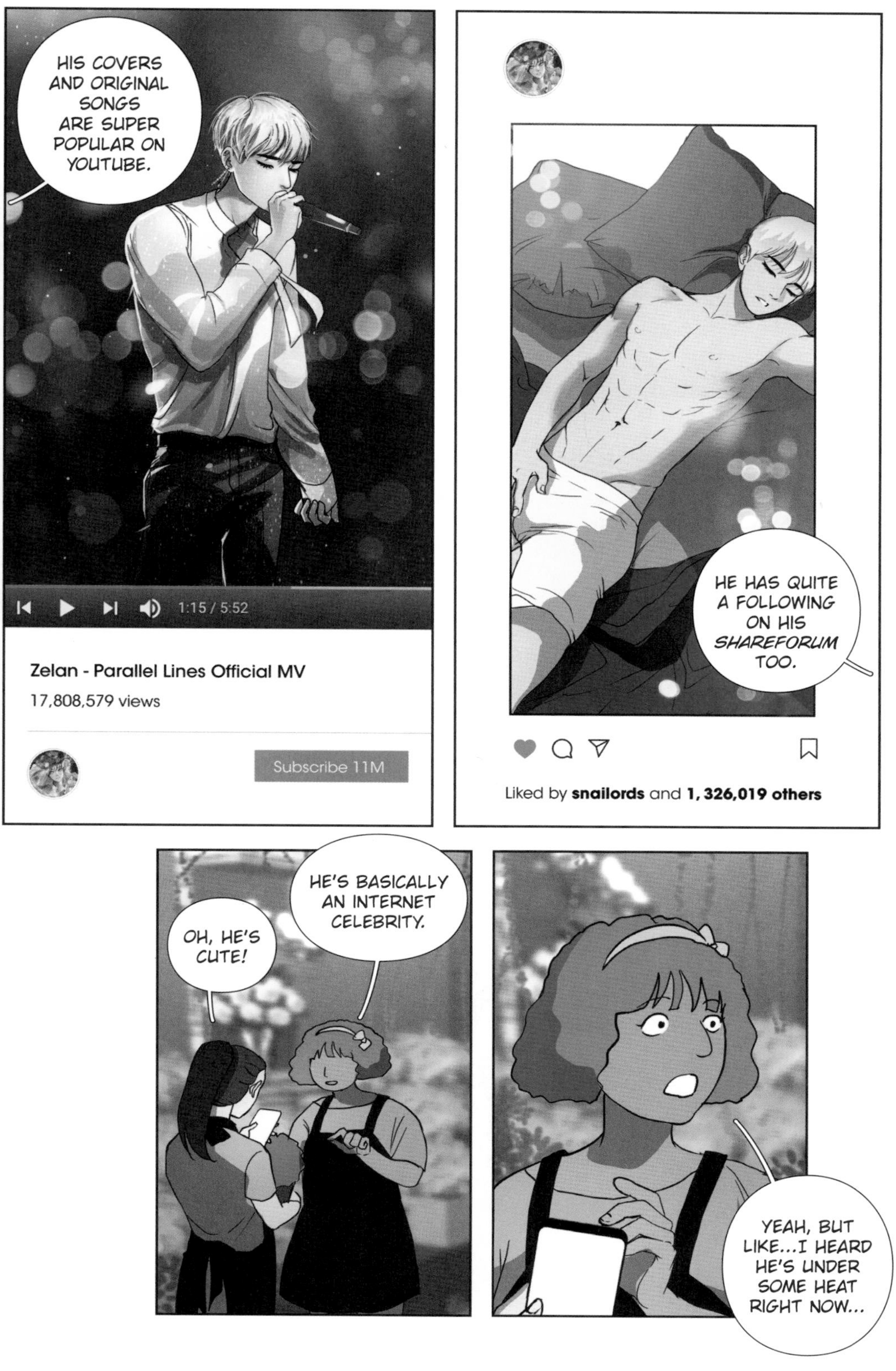
HIS COVERS AND ORIGINAL SONGS ARE SUPER POPULAR ON YOUTUBE.
1:15 / 5:52
Zelan - Parallel Lines Official MV
17,808,579 views
Subscribe 11M
HE HAS QUITE A FOLLOWING ON HIS *SHAREFORUM* TOO.
Liked by **snailords** and **1, 326,019 others**
OH, HE'S CUTE!
HE'S BASICALLY AN INTERNET CELEBRITY.
YEAH, BUT LIKE...I HEARD HE'S UNDER SOME HEAT RIGHT NOW...

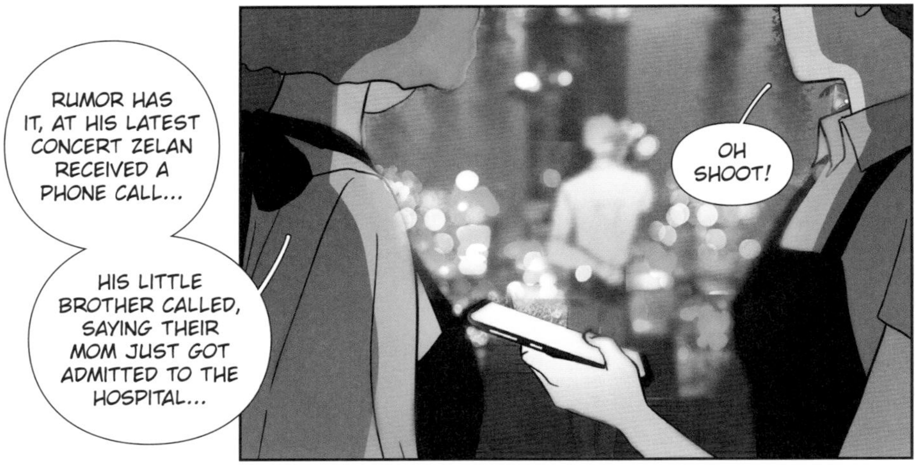
RUMOR HAS IT, AT HIS LATEST CONCERT ZELAN RECEIVED A PHONE CALL...
HIS LITTLE BROTHER CALLED, SAYING THEIR MOM JUST GOT ADMITTED TO THE HOSPITAL...
OH SHOOT!
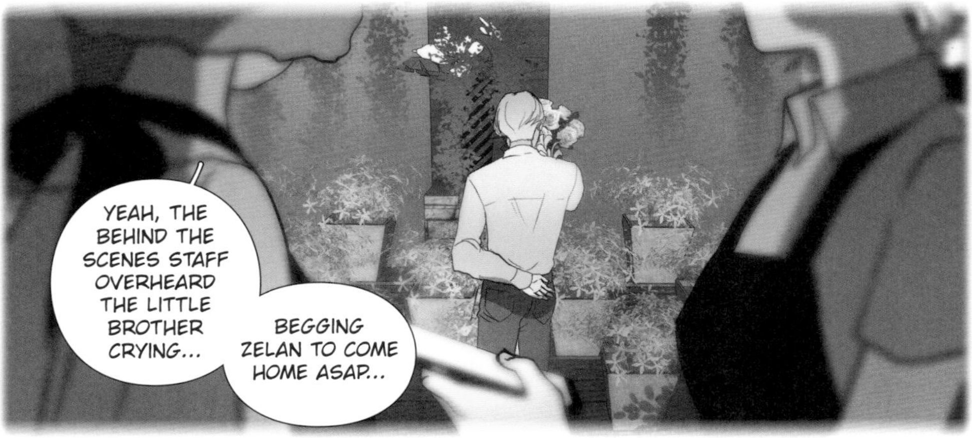
YEAH, THE BEHIND THE SCENES STAFF OVERHEARD THE LITTLE BROTHER CRYING...
BEGGING ZELAN TO COME HOME ASAP...
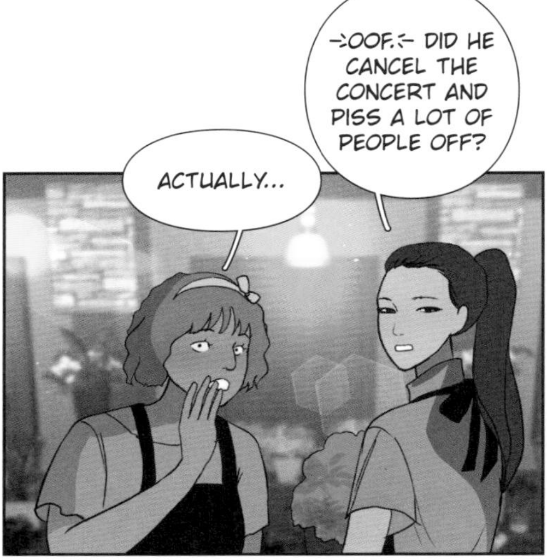
OOF. DID HE CANCEL THE CONCERT AND PISS A LOT OF PEOPLE OFF?
ACTUALLY...
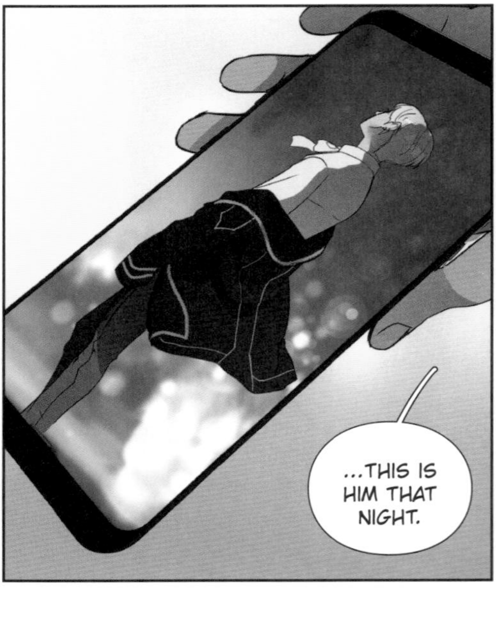
...THIS IS HIM THAT NIGHT.

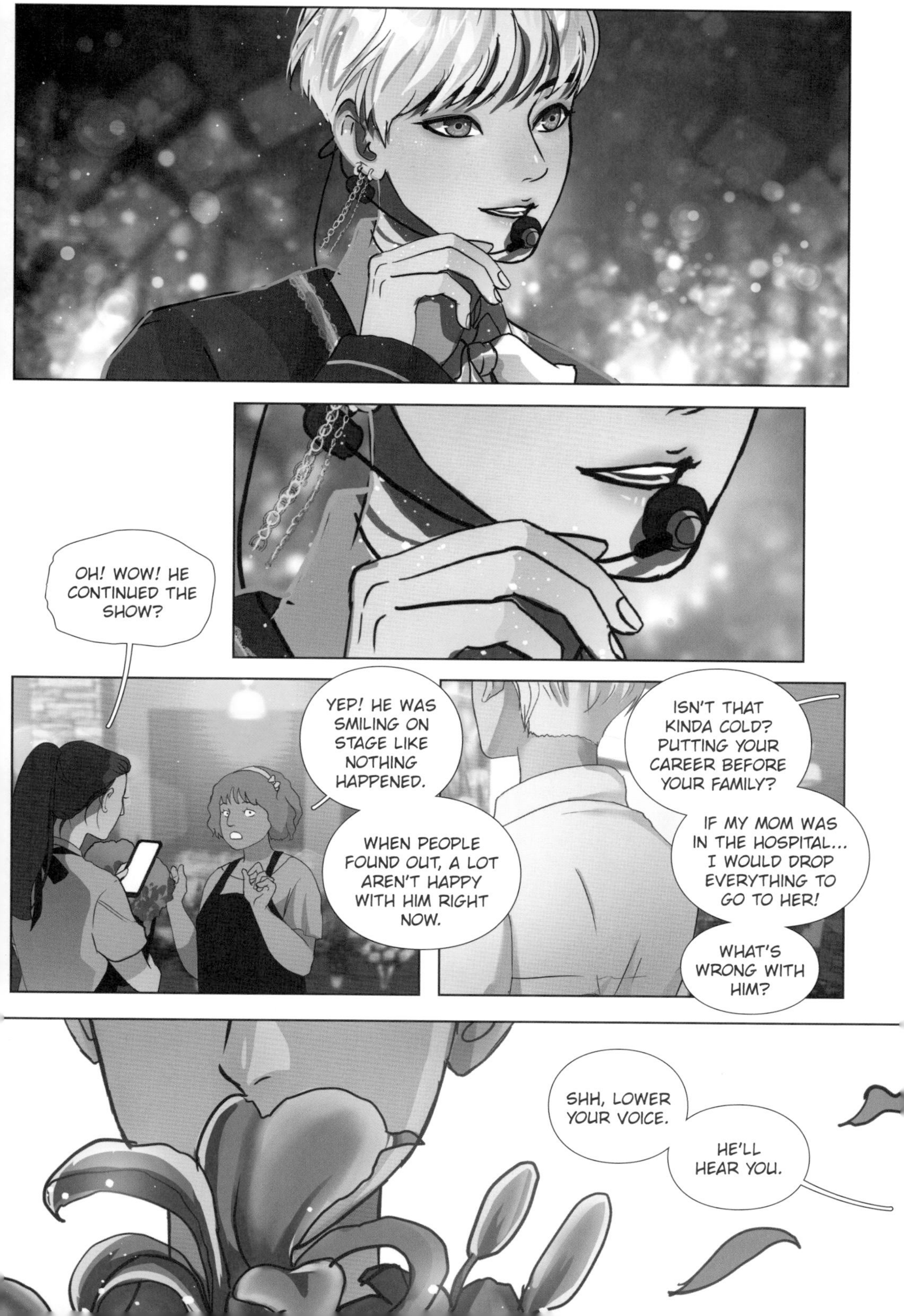
OH! WOW! HE CONTINUED THE SHOW?
YEP! HE WAS SMILING ON STAGE LIKE NOTHING HAPPENED.
WHEN PEOPLE FOUND OUT, A LOT AREN'T HAPPY WITH HIM RIGHT NOW.
ISN'T THAT KINDA COLD? PUTTING YOUR CAREER BEFORE YOUR FAMILY?
IF MY MOM WAS IN THE HOSPITAL... I WOULD DROP EVERYTHING TO GO TO HER!
WHAT'S WRONG WITH HIM?
SHH, LOWER YOUR VOICE.
HE'LL HEAR YOU.

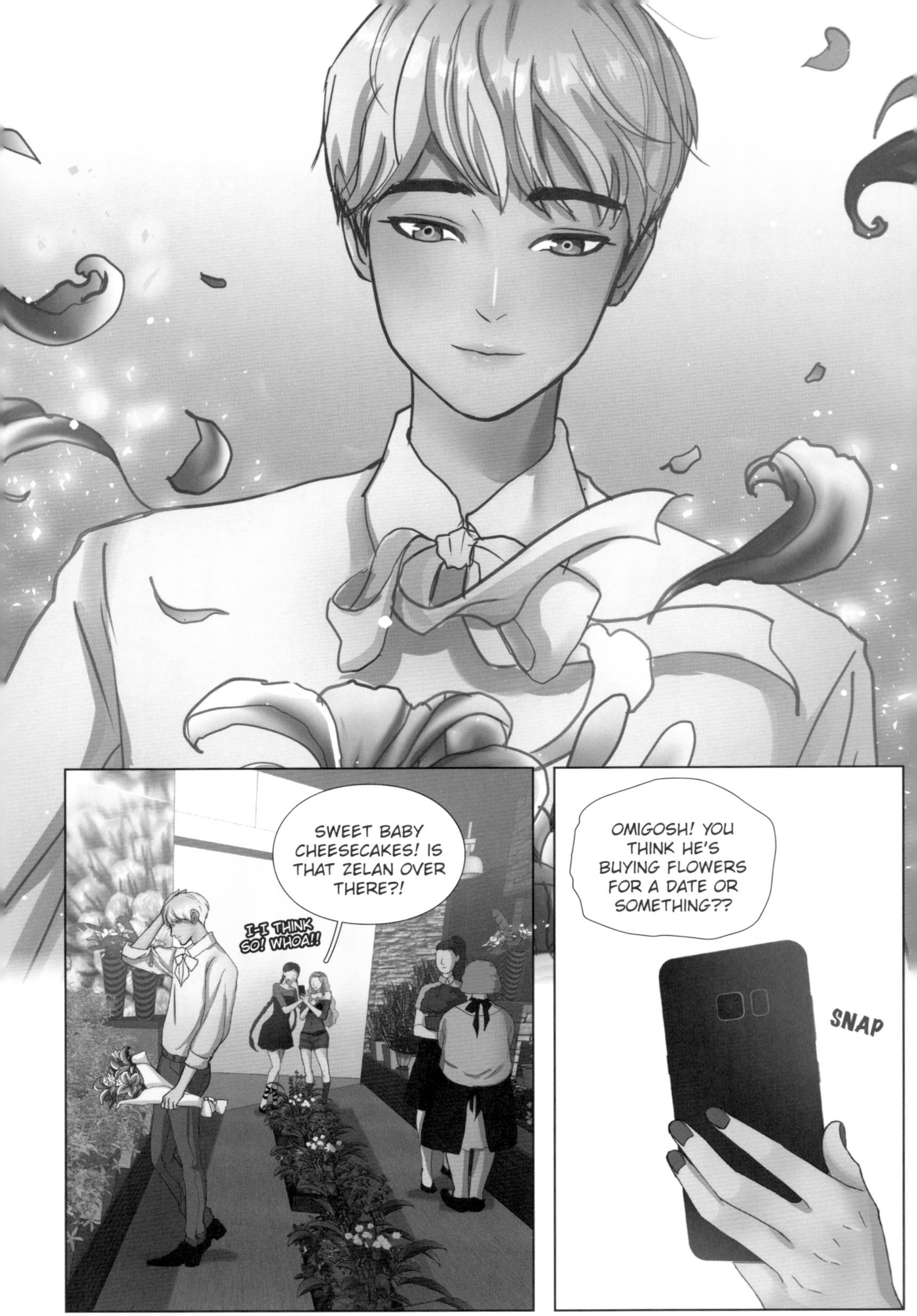
SWEET BABY CHEESECAKES! IS THAT ZELAN OVER THERE?!
I-I THINK SO! WHOA!!
OMIGOSH! YOU THINK HE'S BUYING FLOWERS FOR A DATE OR SOMETHING??
SNAP

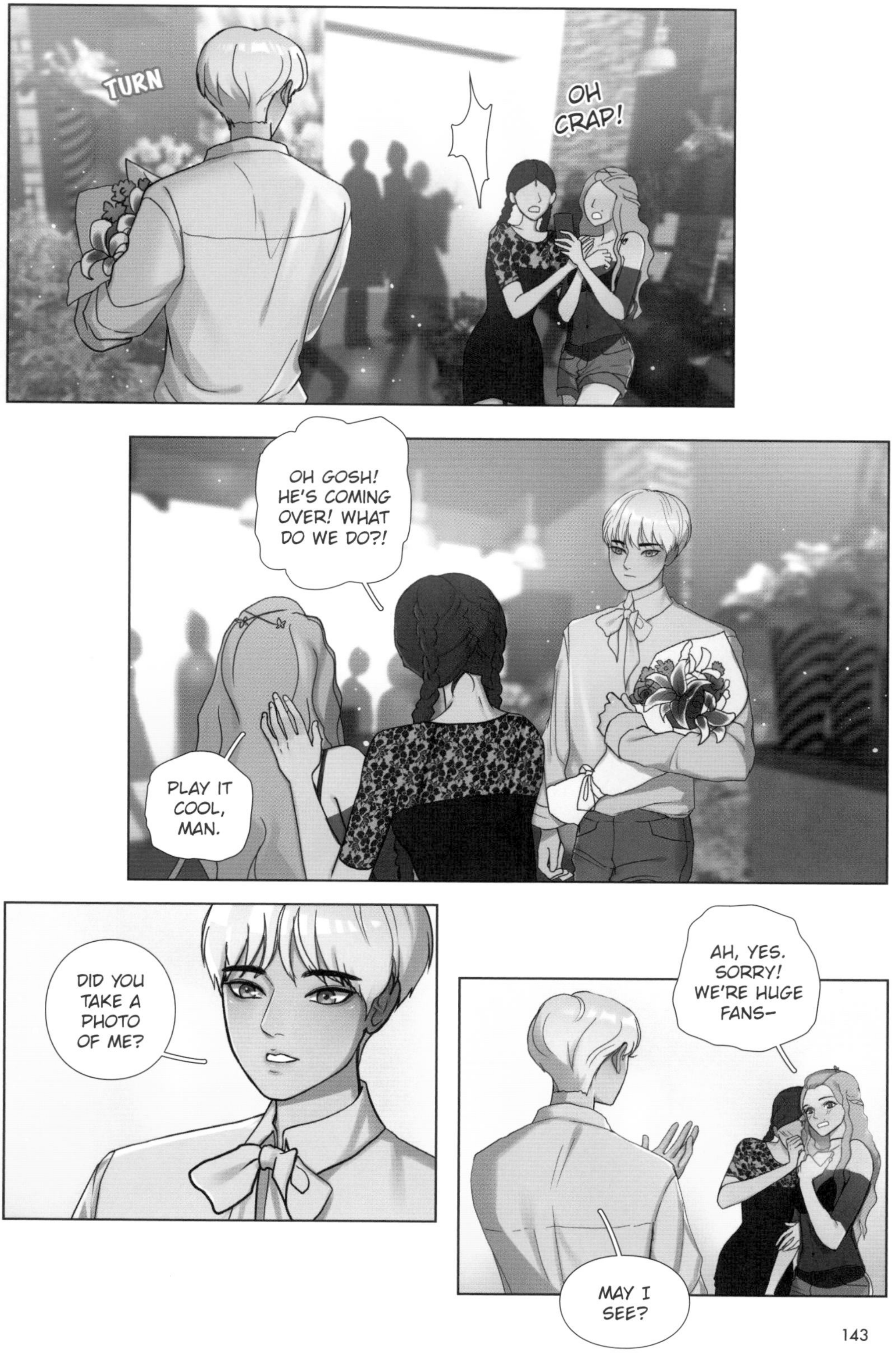
TURN
OH CRAP!
OH GOSH! HE'S COMING OVER! WHAT DO WE DO?!
PLAY IT COOL, MAN.
DID YOU TAKE A PHOTO OF ME?
AH, YES. SORRY! WE'RE HUGE FANS–
MAY I SEE?

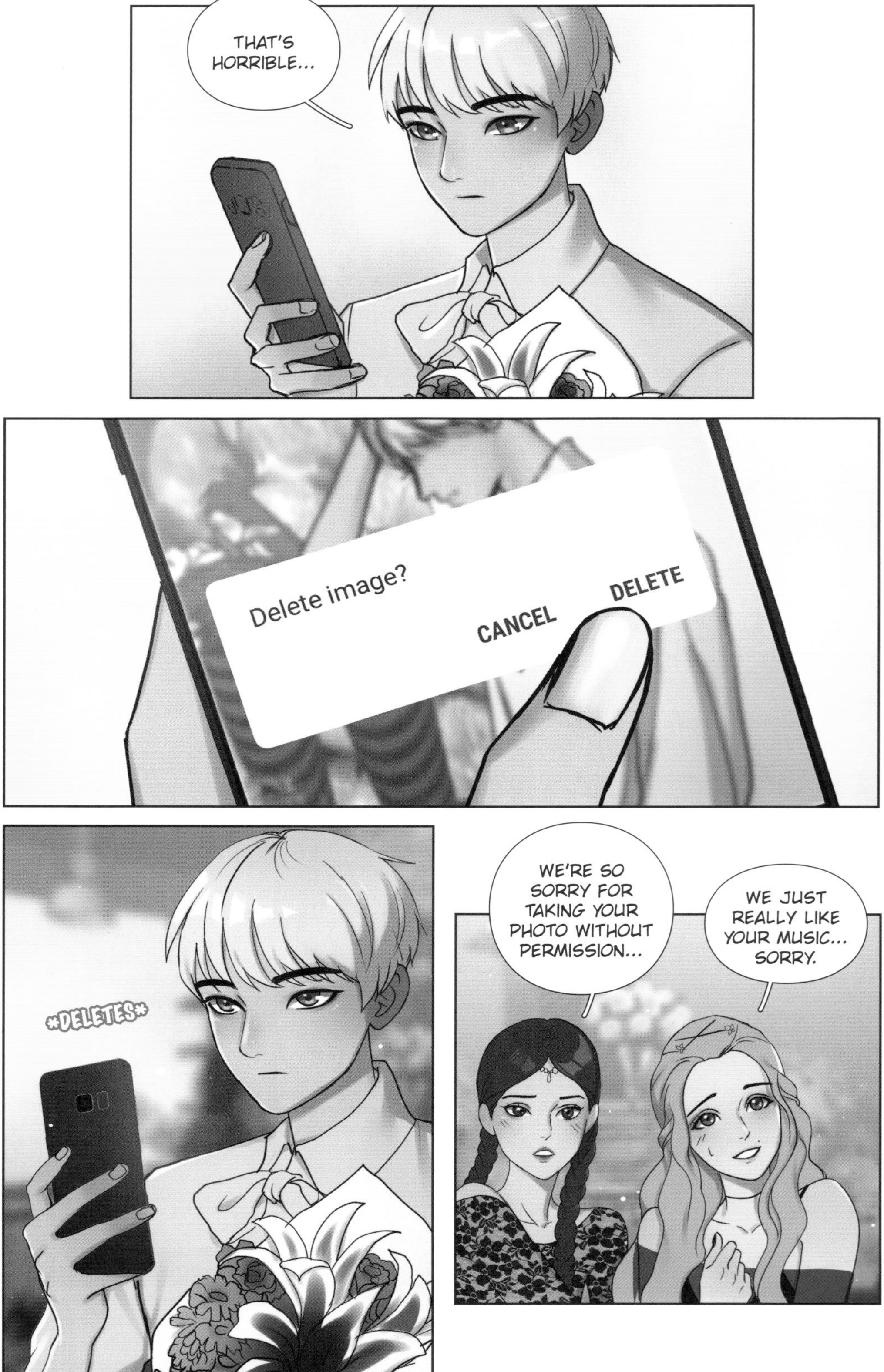
THAT'S HORRIBLE...
Delete image?
CANCEL
DELETE
DELETES
WE'RE SO SORRY FOR TAKING YOUR PHOTO WITHOUT PERMISSION...
WE JUST REALLY LIKE YOUR MUSIC... SORRY.

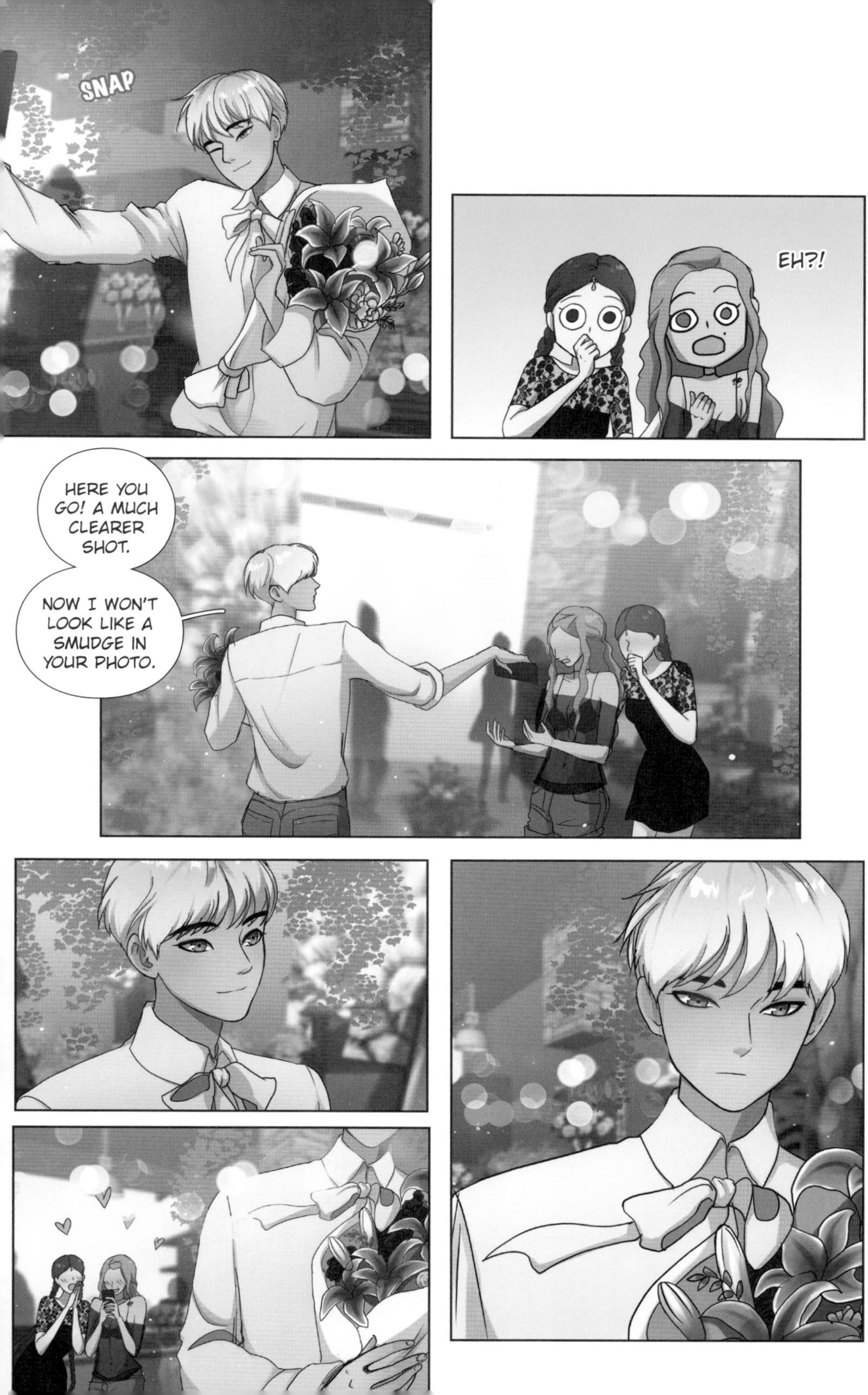
SNAP
EH?!
HERE YOU GO! A MUCH CLEARER SHOT.
NOW I WON'T LOOK LIKE A SMUDGE IN YOUR PHOTO.

HOSPITAL

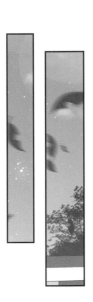

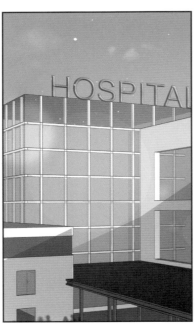

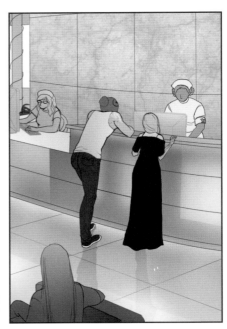

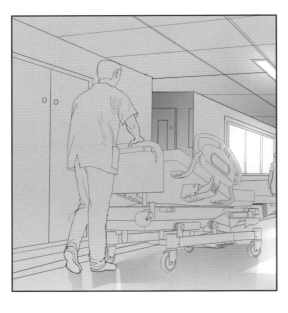

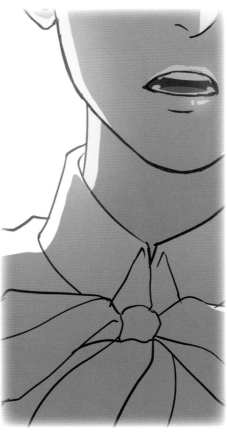

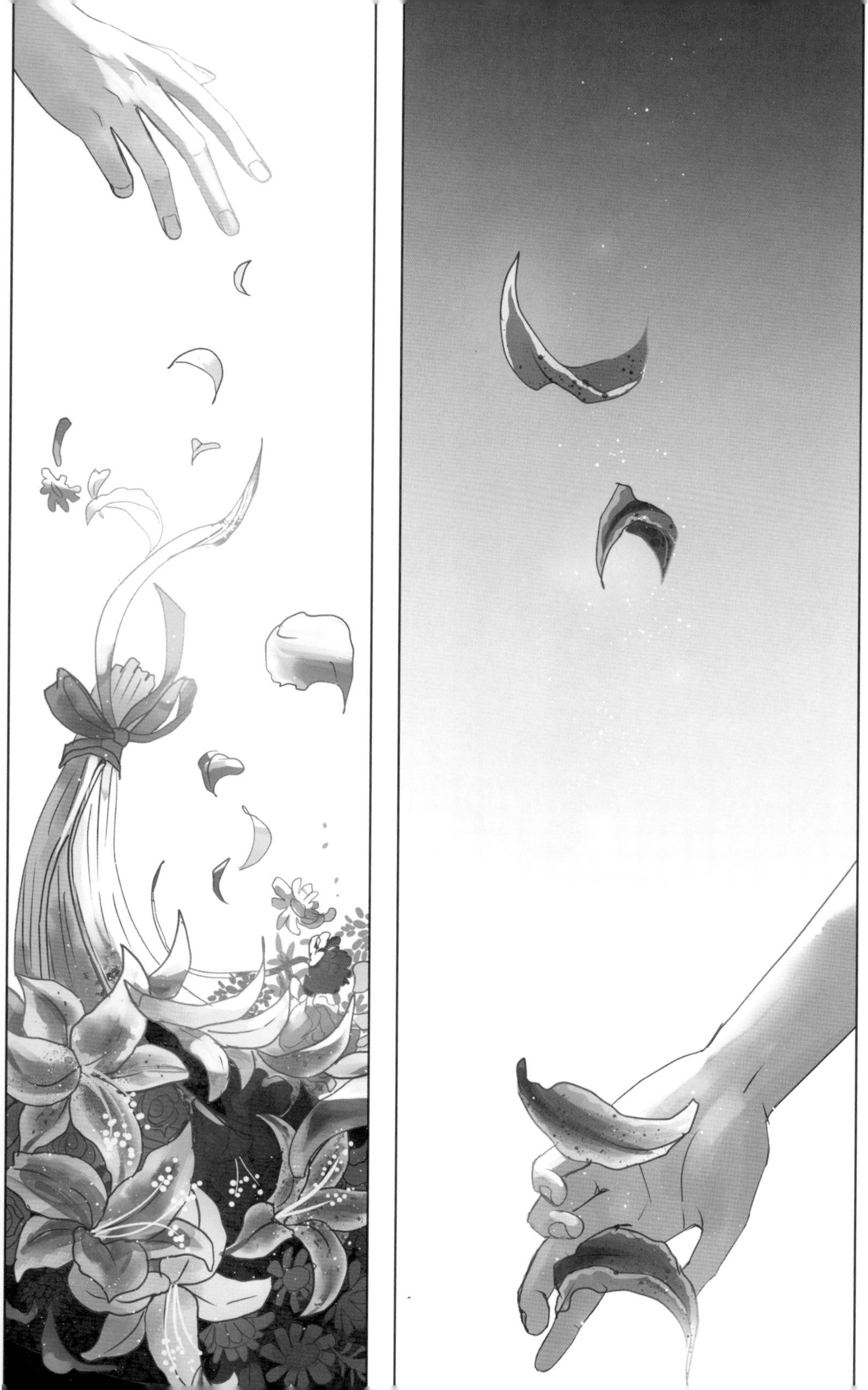

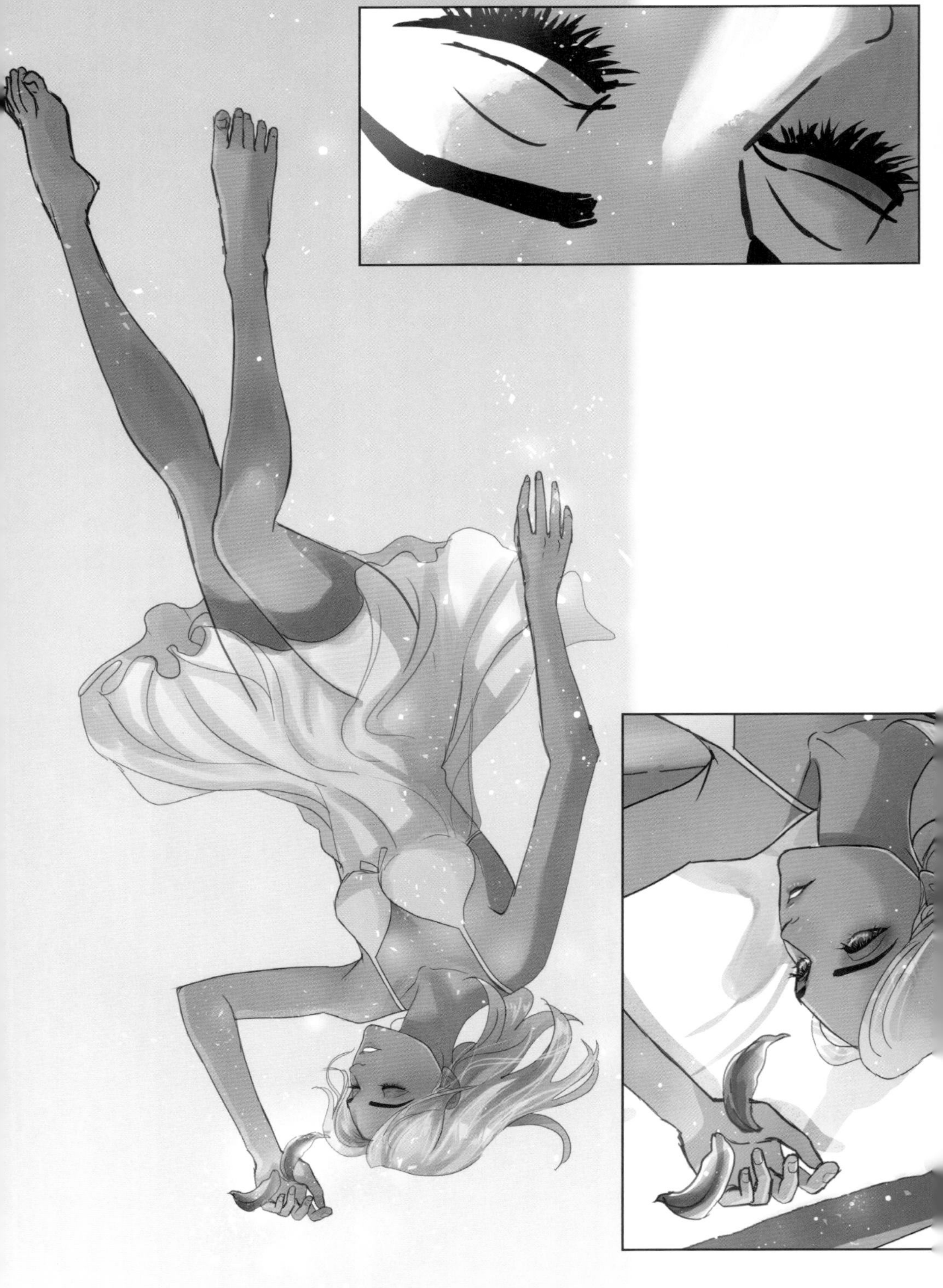

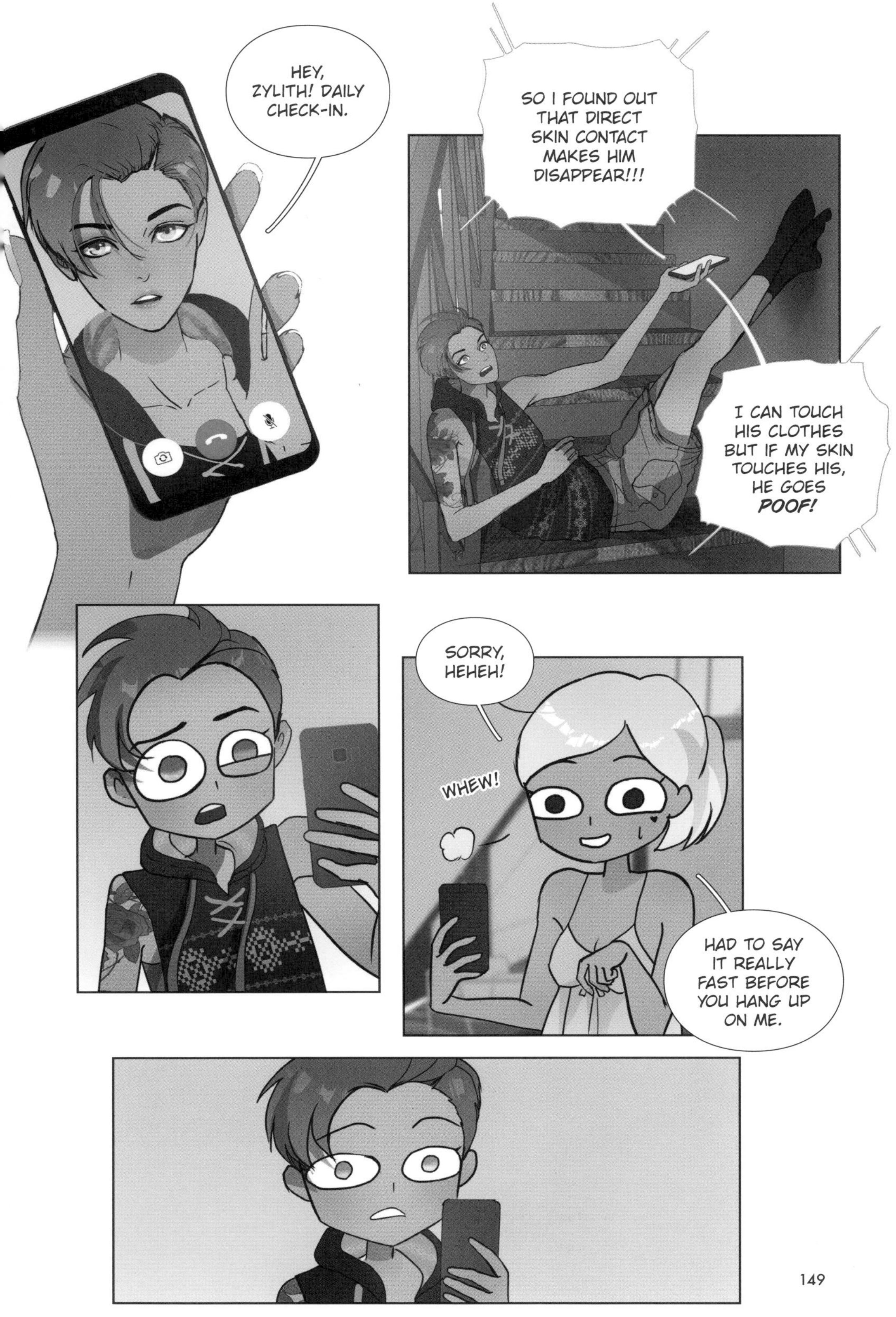

HEY, ZYLITH! DAILY CHECK-IN.
SO I FOUND OUT THAT DIRECT SKIN CONTACT MAKES HIM DISAPPEAR!!!
I CAN TOUCH HIS CLOTHES BUT IF MY SKIN TOUCHES HIS, HE GOES *POOF!*
SORRY, HEHEH!
WHEW!
HAD TO SAY IT REALLY FAST BEFORE YOU HANG UP ON ME.

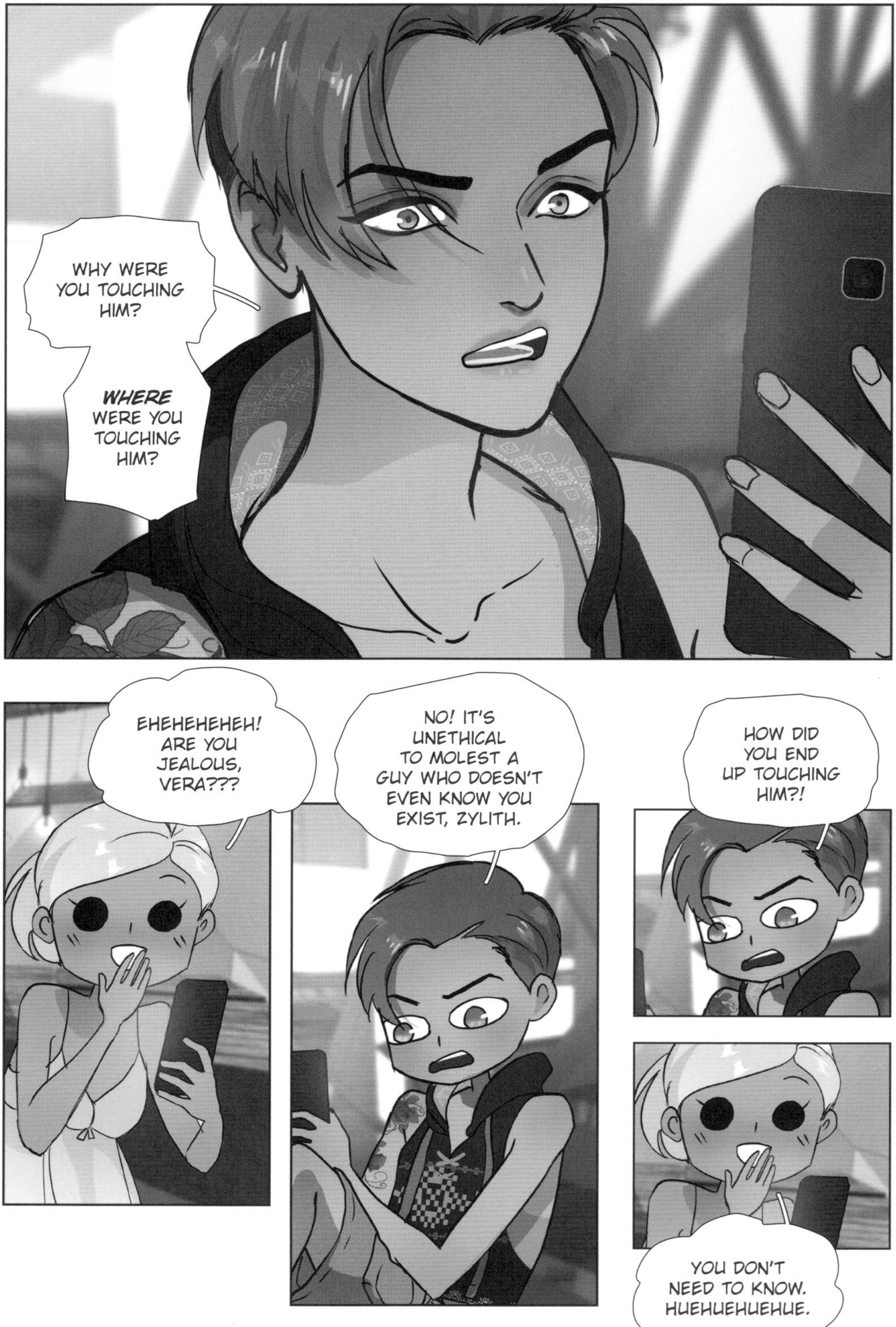
WHY WERE YOU TOUCHING HIM?
WHERE WERE YOU TOUCHING HIM?
EHEHEHEHEH! ARE YOU JEALOUS, VERA???
NO! IT'S UNETHICAL TO MOLEST A GUY WHO DOESN'T EVEN KNOW YOU EXIST, ZYLITH.
HOW DID YOU END UP TOUCHING HIM?!
YOU DON'T NEED TO KNOW. HUEHUEHUEHUE.

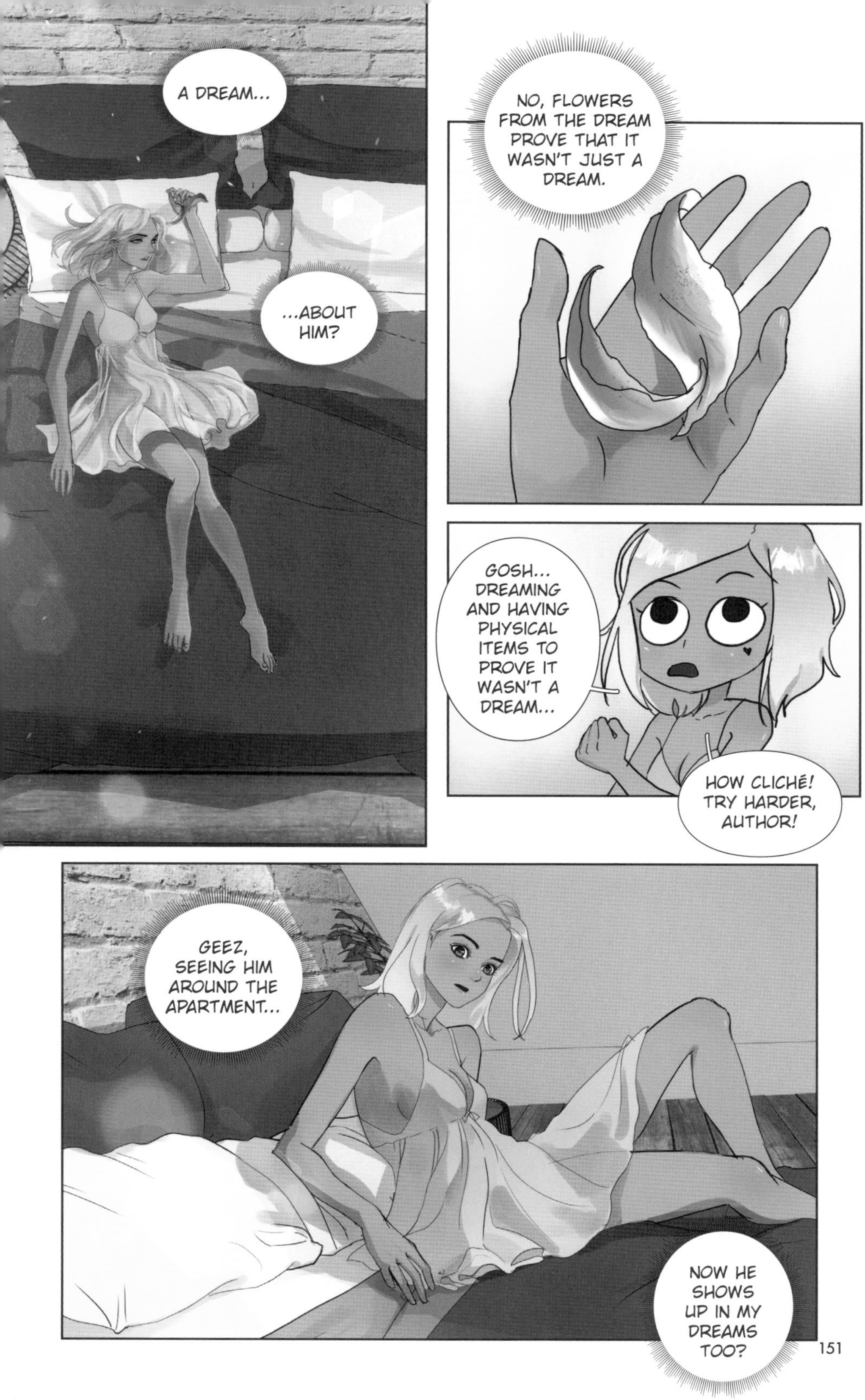
A DREAM...
...ABOUT HIM?
NO, FLOWERS FROM THE DREAM PROVE THAT IT WASN'T JUST A DREAM.
GOSH... DREAMING AND HAVING PHYSICAL ITEMS TO PROVE IT WASN'T A DREAM...
HOW CLICHÉ! TRY HARDER, AUTHOR!
GEEZ, SEEING HIM AROUND THE APARTMENT...
NOW HE SHOWS UP IN MY DREAMS TOO?

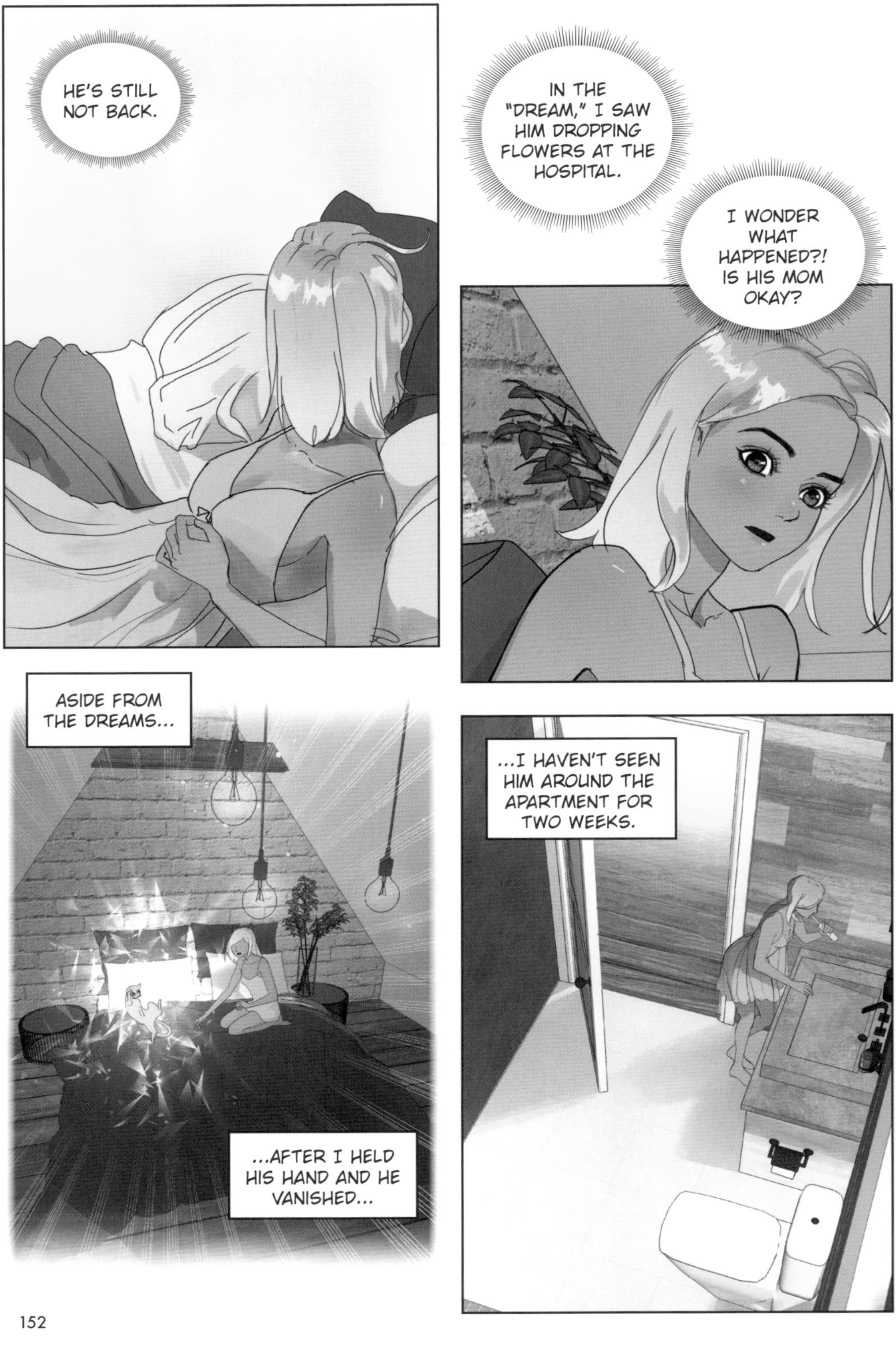
HE'S STILL NOT BACK.
IN THE "DREAM," I SAW HIM DROPPING FLOWERS AT THE HOSPITAL.
I WONDER WHAT HAPPENED?! IS HIS MOM OKAY?
ASIDE FROM THE DREAMS...
...AFTER I HELD HIS HAND AND HE VANISHED...
...I HAVEN'T SEEN HIM AROUND THE APARTMENT FOR TWO WEEKS.

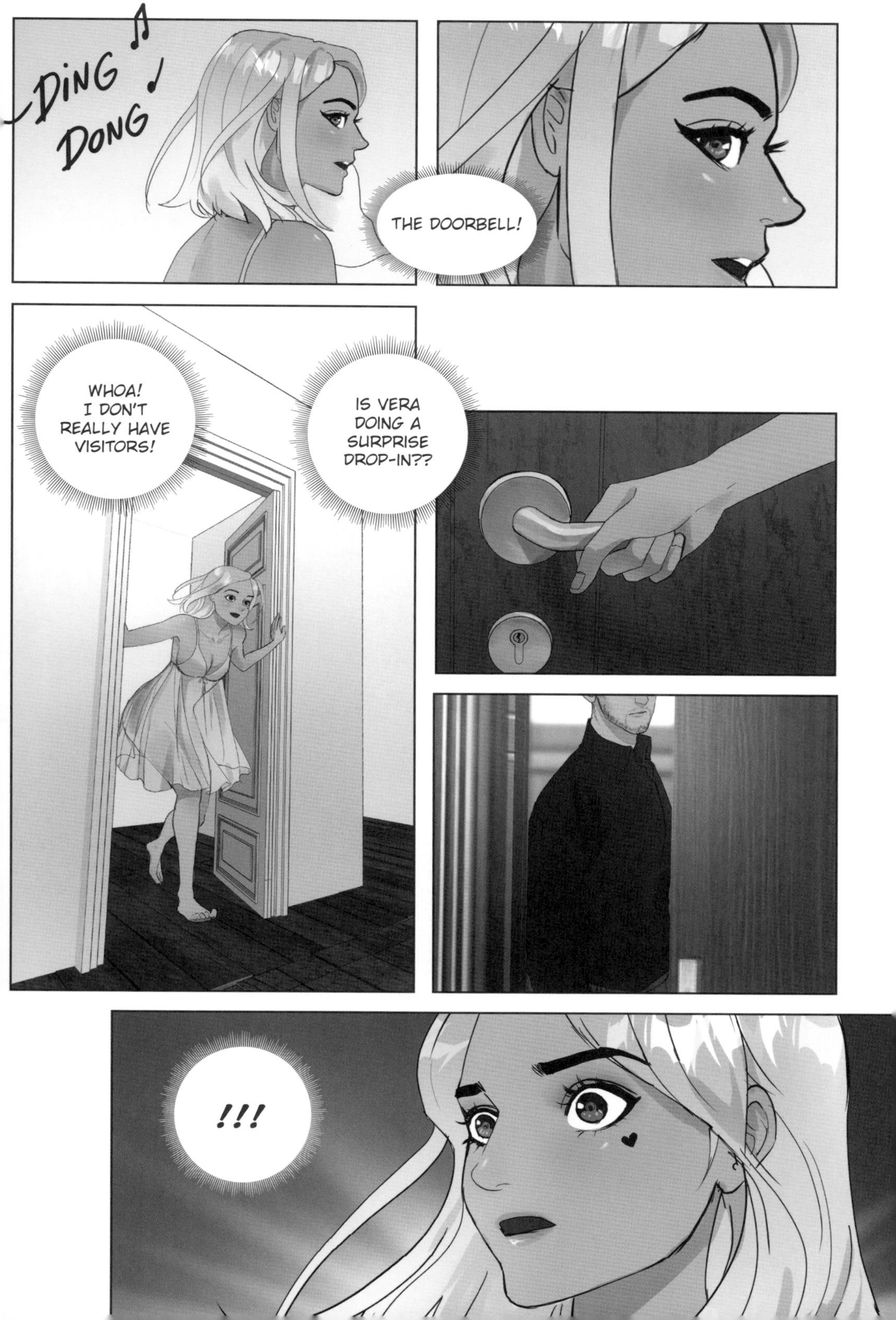
DING DONG
THE DOORBELL!
WHOA! I DON'T REALLY HAVE VISITORS!
IS VERA DOING A SURPRISE DROP-IN??
!!!

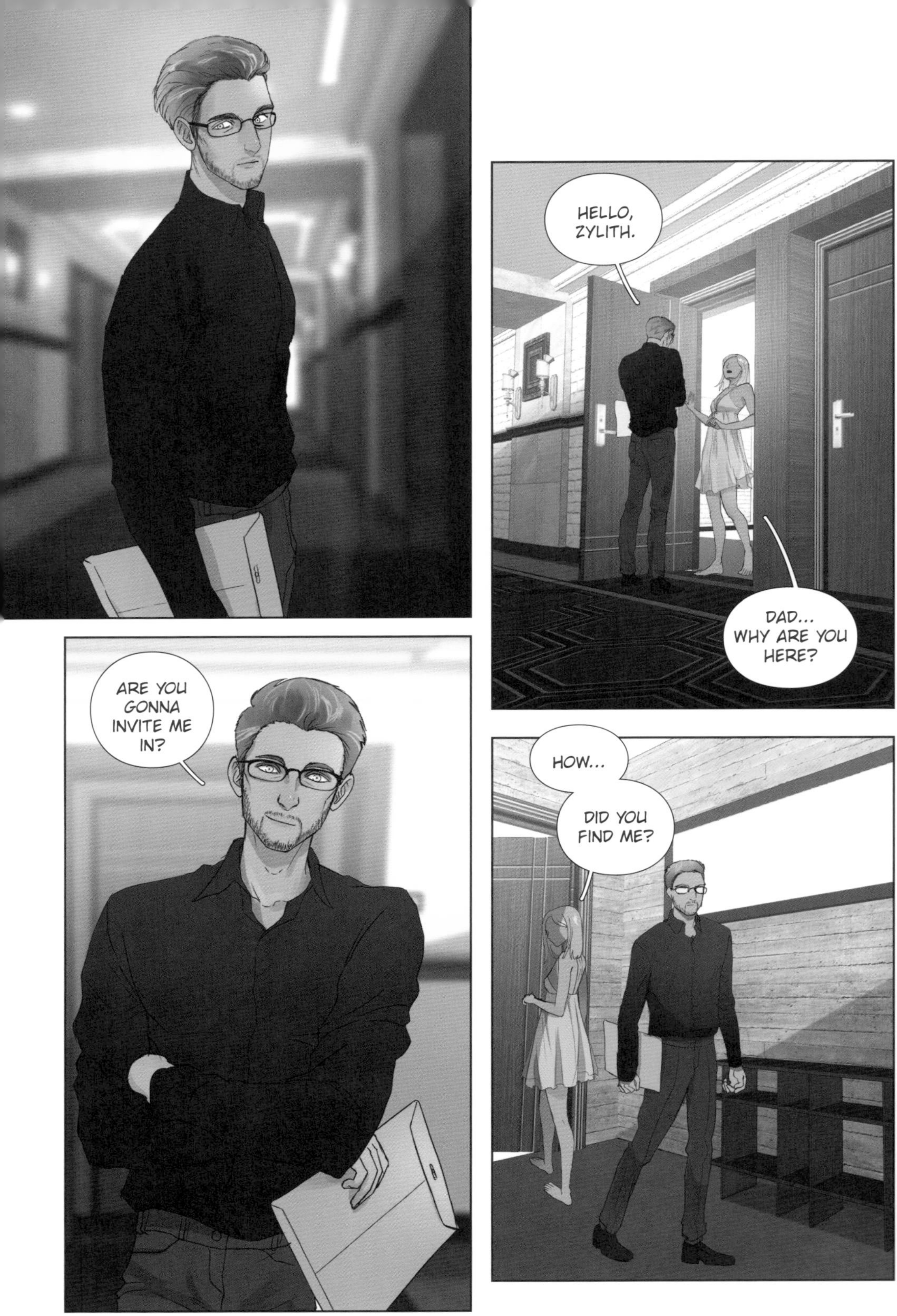
HELLO, ZYLITH.
DAD... WHY ARE YOU HERE?
ARE YOU GONNA INVITE ME IN?
HOW...
DID YOU FIND ME?

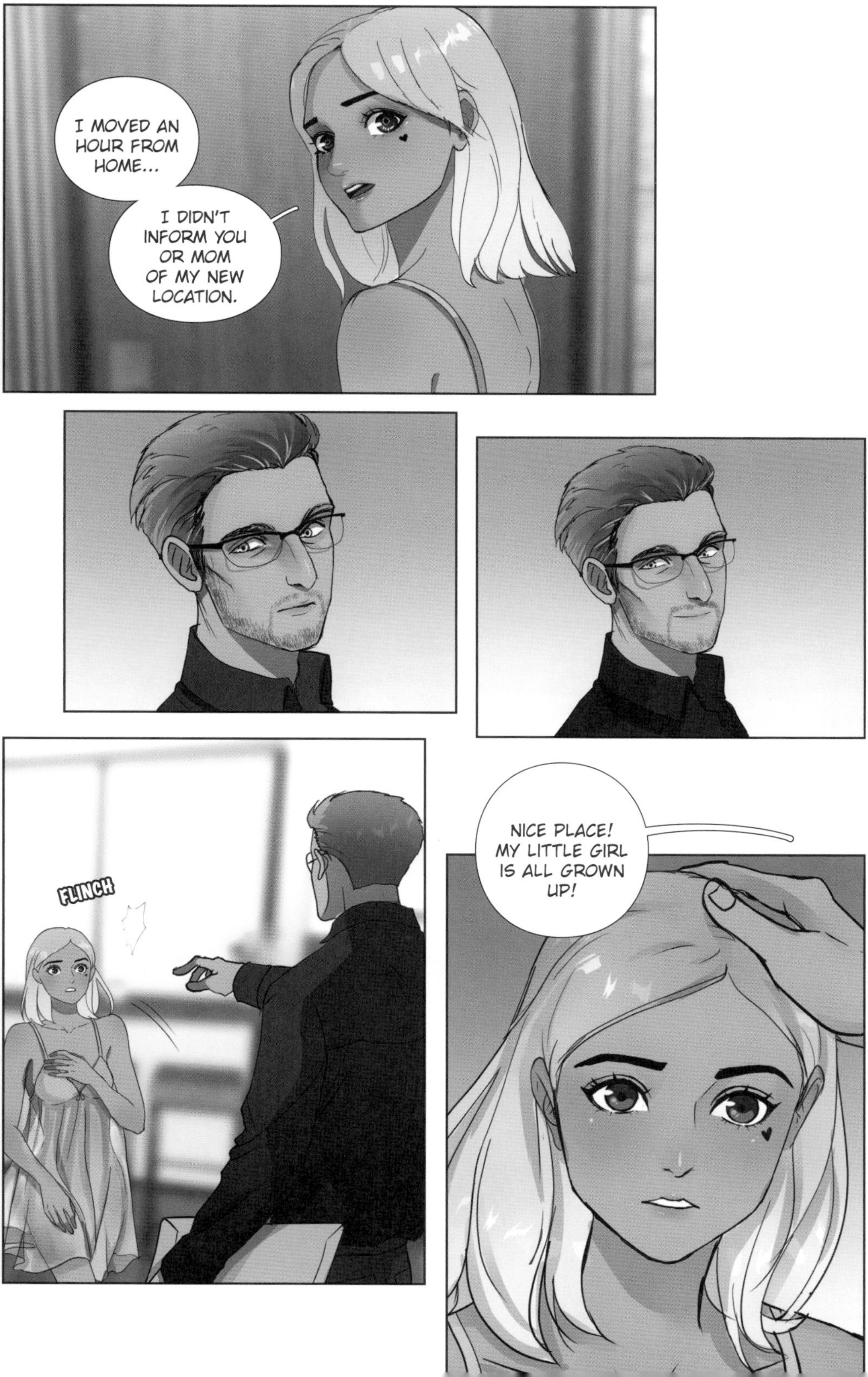
I MOVED AN HOUR FROM HOME...
I DIDN'T INFORM YOU OR MOM OF MY NEW LOCATION.
FLINCH
NICE PLACE! MY LITTLE GIRL IS ALL GROWN UP!

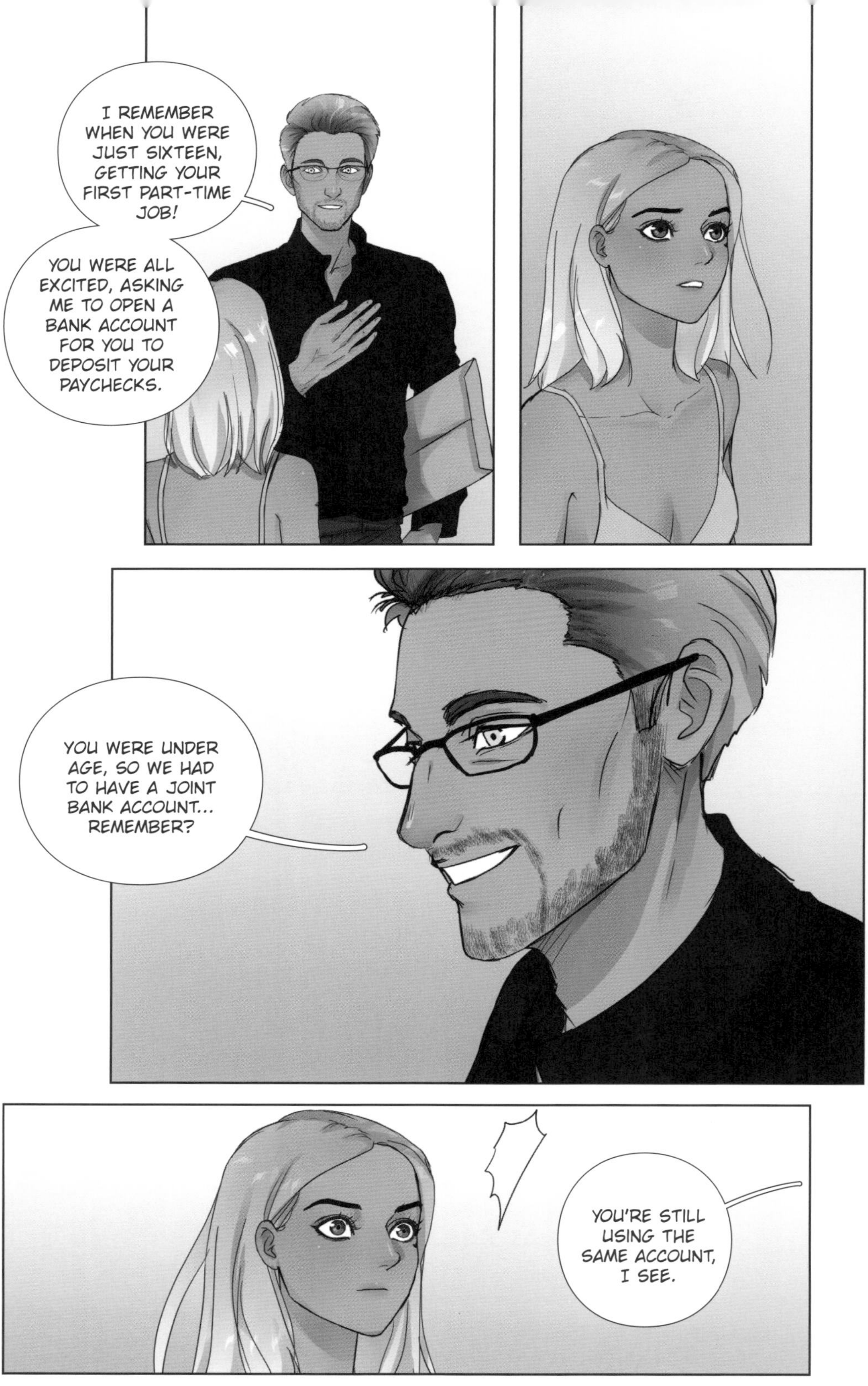
I REMEMBER WHEN YOU WERE JUST SIXTEEN, GETTING YOUR FIRST PART-TIME JOB!
YOU WERE ALL EXCITED, ASKING ME TO OPEN A BANK ACCOUNT FOR YOU TO DEPOSIT YOUR PAYCHECKS.
YOU WERE UNDER AGE, SO WE HAD TO HAVE A JOINT BANK ACCOUNT... REMEMBER?
YOU'RE STILL USING THE SAME ACCOUNT, I SEE.

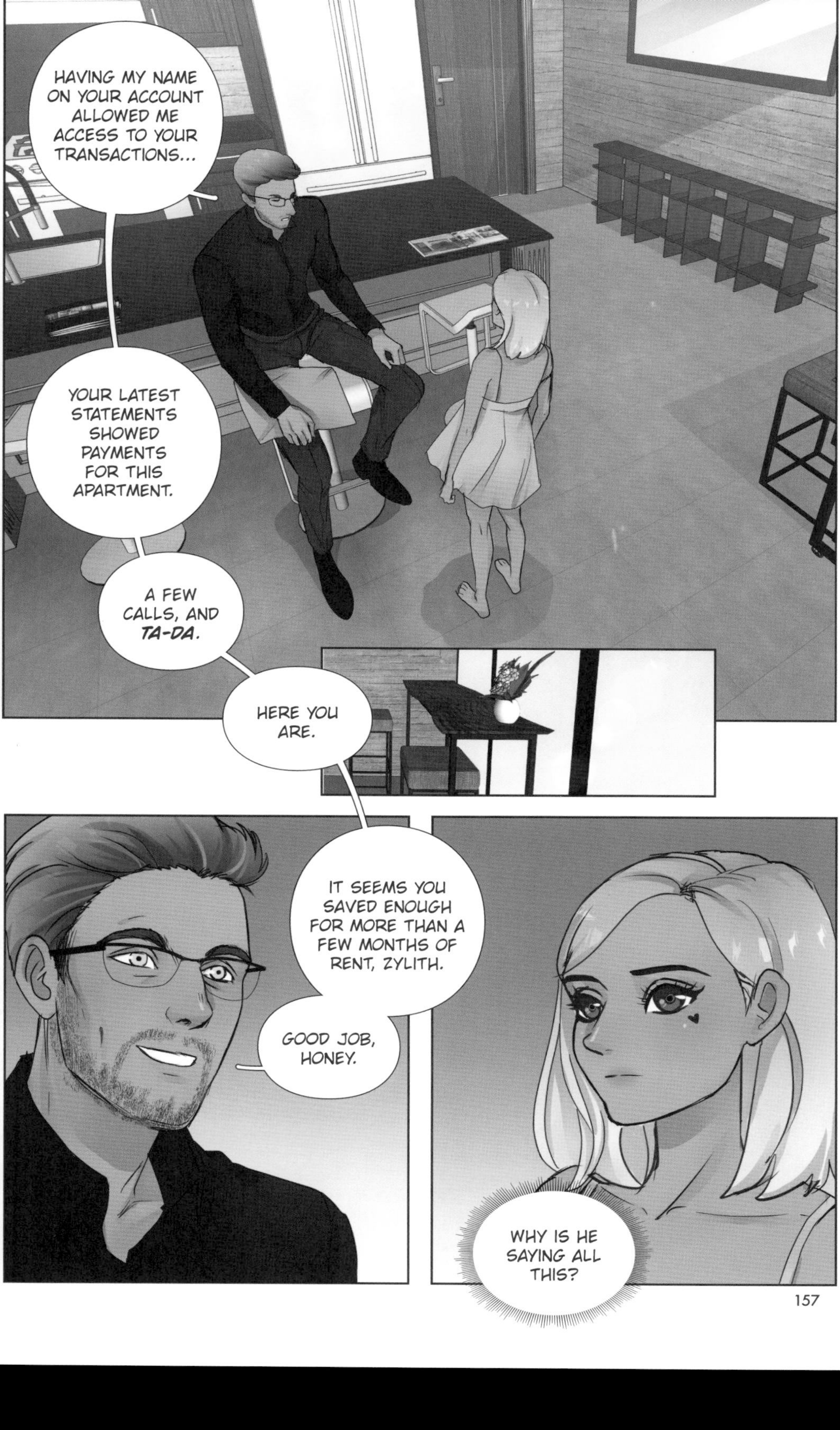

HAVING MY NAME ON YOUR ACCOUNT ALLOWED ME ACCESS TO YOUR TRANSACTIONS...
YOUR LATEST STATEMENTS SHOWED PAYMENTS FOR THIS APARTMENT.
A FEW CALLS, AND *TA-DA*.
HERE YOU ARE.
IT SEEMS YOU SAVED ENOUGH FOR MORE THAN A FEW MONTHS OF RENT, ZYLITH.
GOOD JOB, HONEY.
WHY IS HE SAYING ALL THIS?

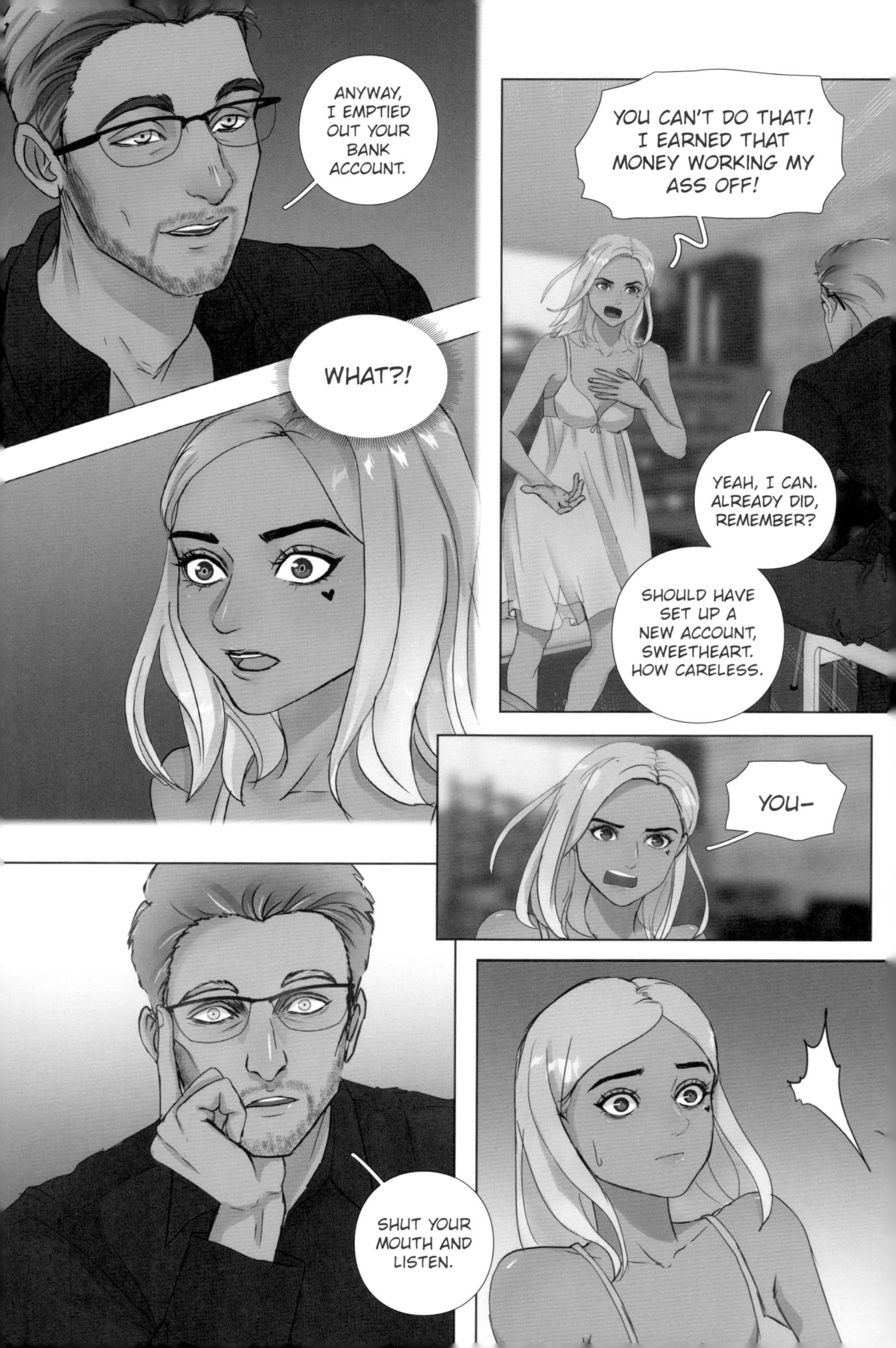
ANYWAY, I EMPTIED OUT YOUR BANK ACCOUNT.
WHAT?!
YOU CAN'T DO THAT! I EARNED THAT MONEY WORKING MY ASS OFF!
YEAH, I CAN. ALREADY DID, REMEMBER?
SHOULD HAVE SET UP A NEW ACCOUNT, SWEETHEART. HOW CARELESS.
YOU-
SHUT YOUR MOUTH AND LISTEN.

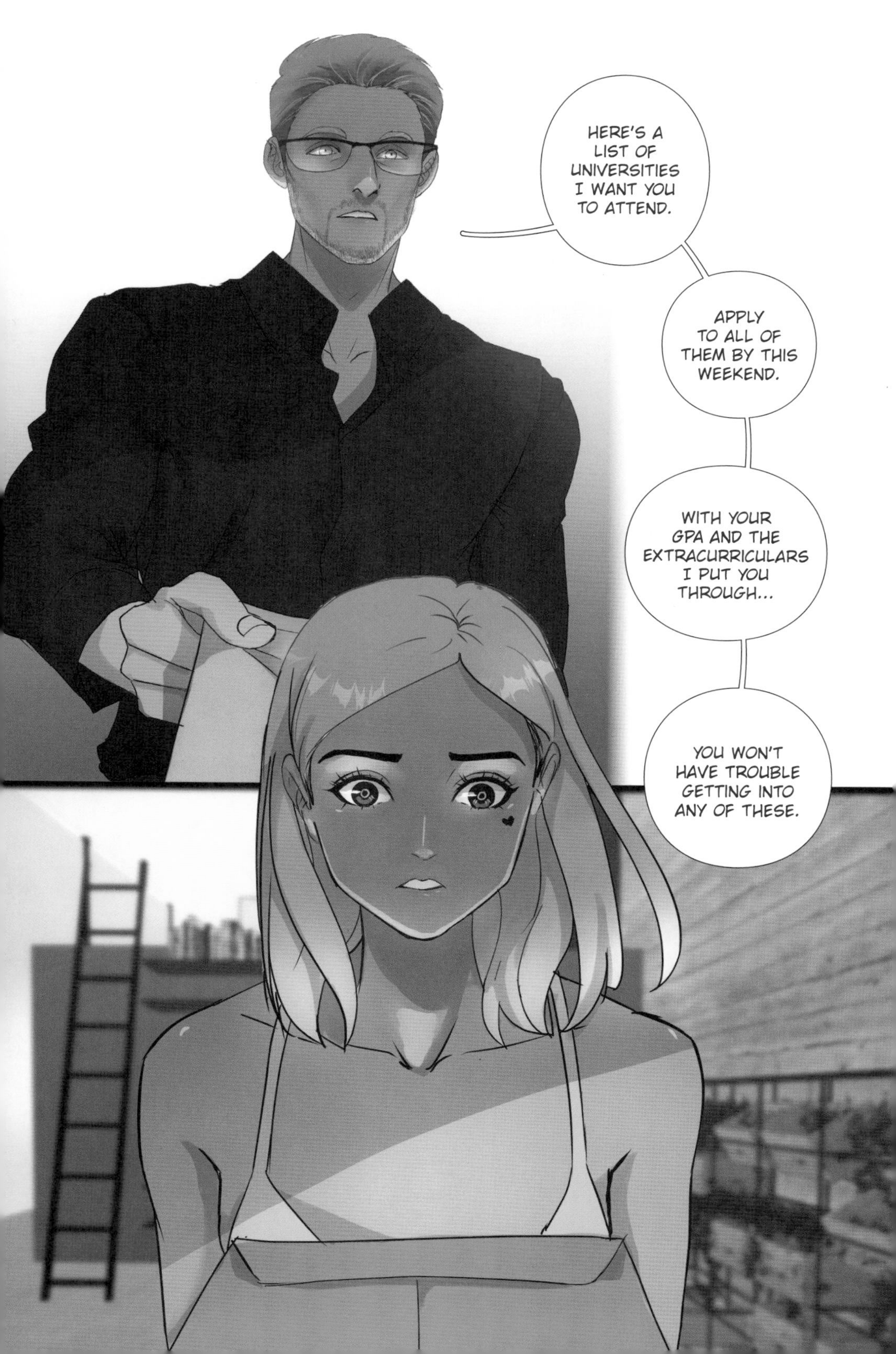
HERE'S A LIST OF UNIVERSITIES I WANT YOU TO ATTEND.
APPLY TO ALL OF THEM BY THIS WEEKEND.
WITH YOUR GPA AND THE EXTRACURRICULARS I PUT YOU THROUGH...
YOU WON'T HAVE TROUBLE GETTING INTO ANY OF THESE.

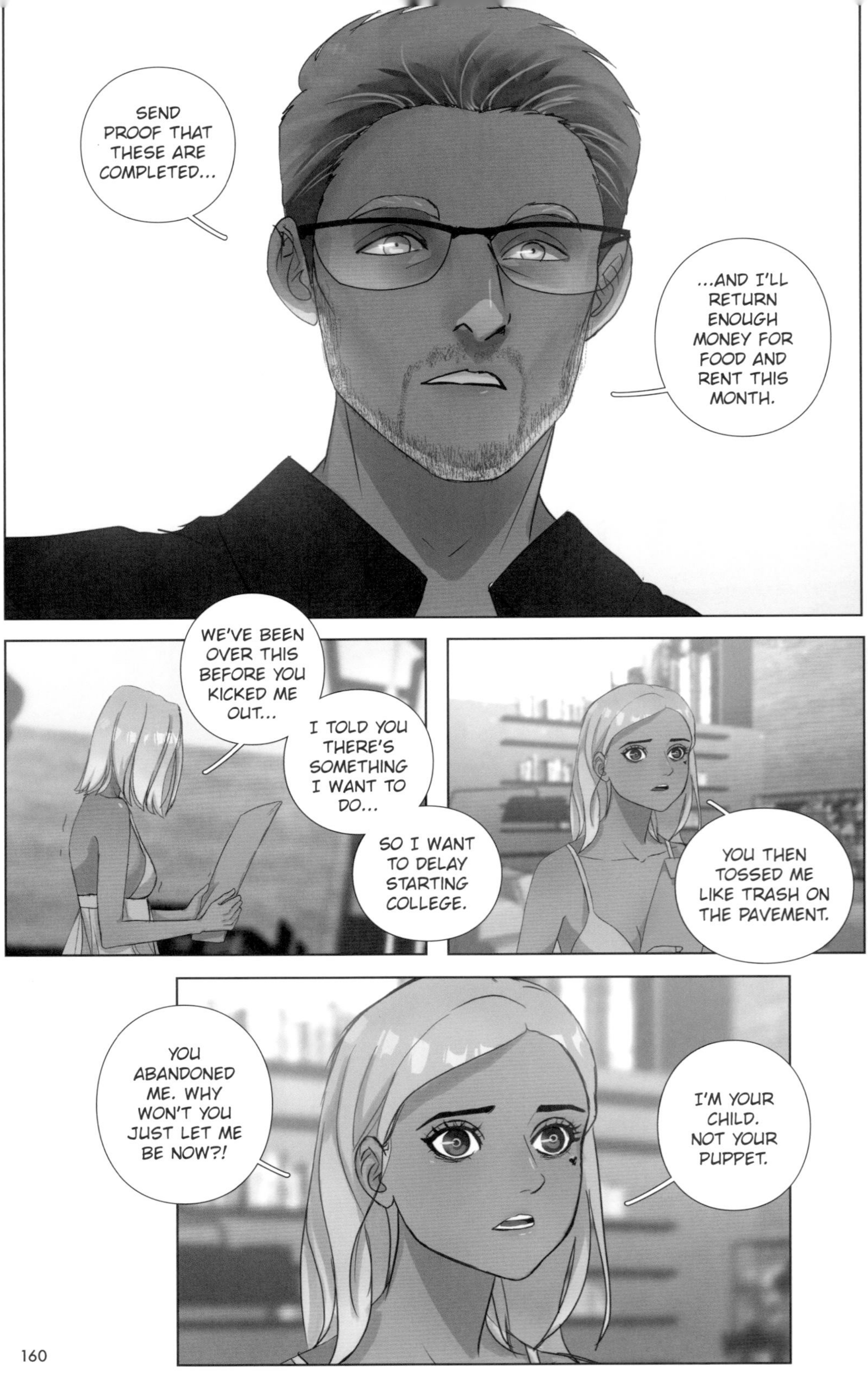
SEND PROOF THAT THESE ARE COMPLETED...
...AND I'LL RETURN ENOUGH MONEY FOR FOOD AND RENT THIS MONTH.
WE'VE BEEN OVER THIS BEFORE YOU KICKED ME OUT...
I TOLD YOU THERE'S SOMETHING I WANT TO DO...
SO I WANT TO DELAY STARTING COLLEGE.
YOU THEN TOSSED ME LIKE TRASH ON THE PAVEMENT.
YOU ABANDONED ME. WHY WON'T YOU JUST LET ME BE NOW?!
I'M YOUR CHILD. NOT YOUR PUPPET.

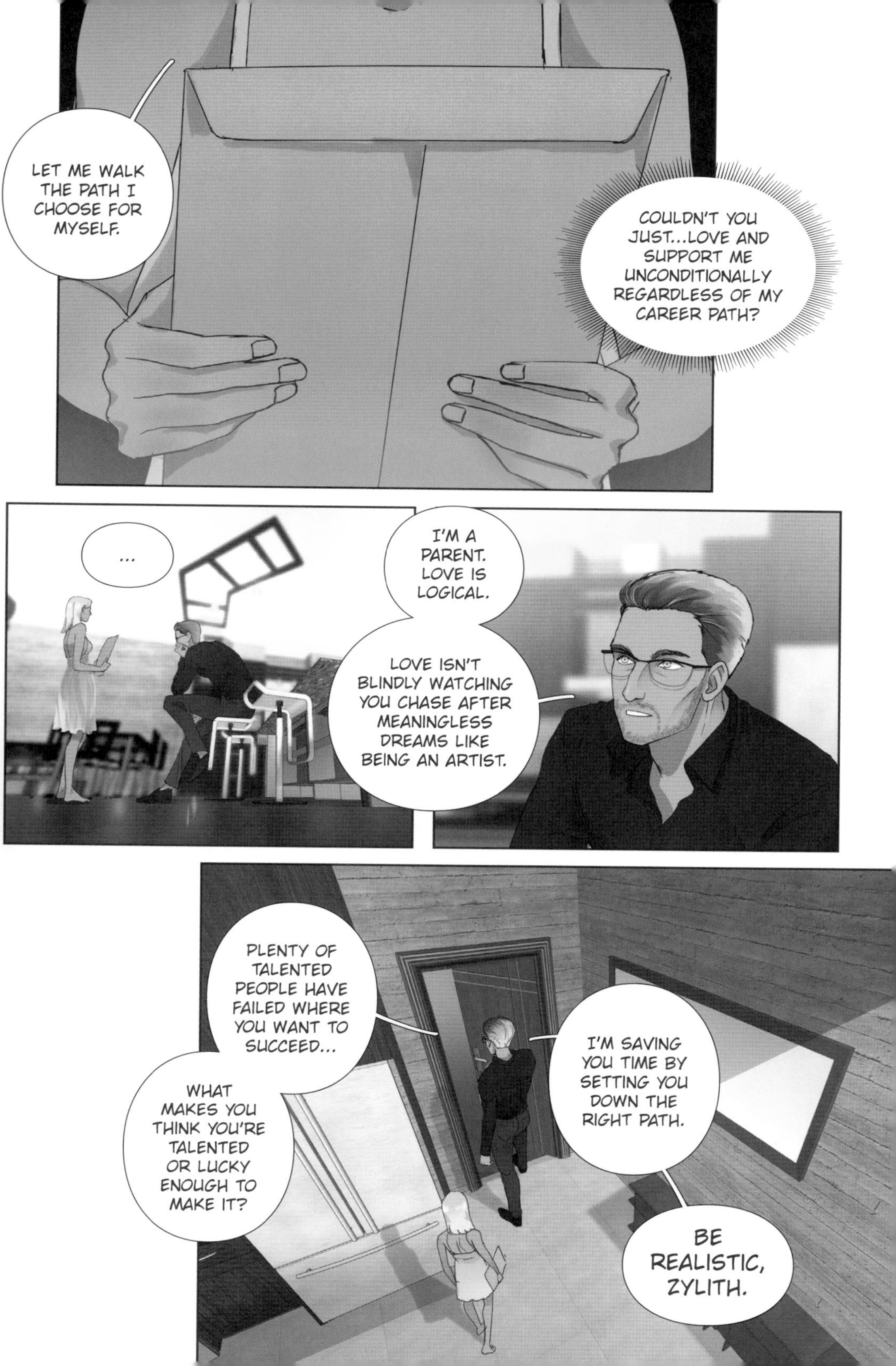
LET ME WALK THE PATH I CHOOSE FOR MYSELF.
COULDN'T YOU JUST...LOVE AND SUPPORT ME UNCONDITIONALLY REGARDLESS OF MY CAREER PATH?
...
I'M A PARENT. LOVE IS LOGICAL.
LOVE ISN'T BLINDLY WATCHING YOU CHASE AFTER MEANINGLESS DREAMS LIKE BEING AN ARTIST.
PLENTY OF TALENTED PEOPLE HAVE FAILED WHERE YOU WANT TO SUCCEED...
WHAT MAKES YOU THINK YOU'RE TALENTED OR LUCKY ENOUGH TO MAKE IT?
I'M SAVING YOU TIME BY SETTING YOU DOWN THE RIGHT PATH.
BE REALISTIC, ZYLITH.

A FEW DAYS LATER...

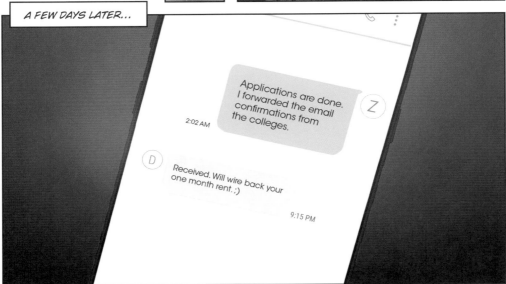

Applications are done. I forwarded the email confirmations from the colleges.

2:02 AM

Received. Will wire back your one month rent. :)

9:15 PM

JUST ONE MONTH? ARE YOU SERIOUS?

162

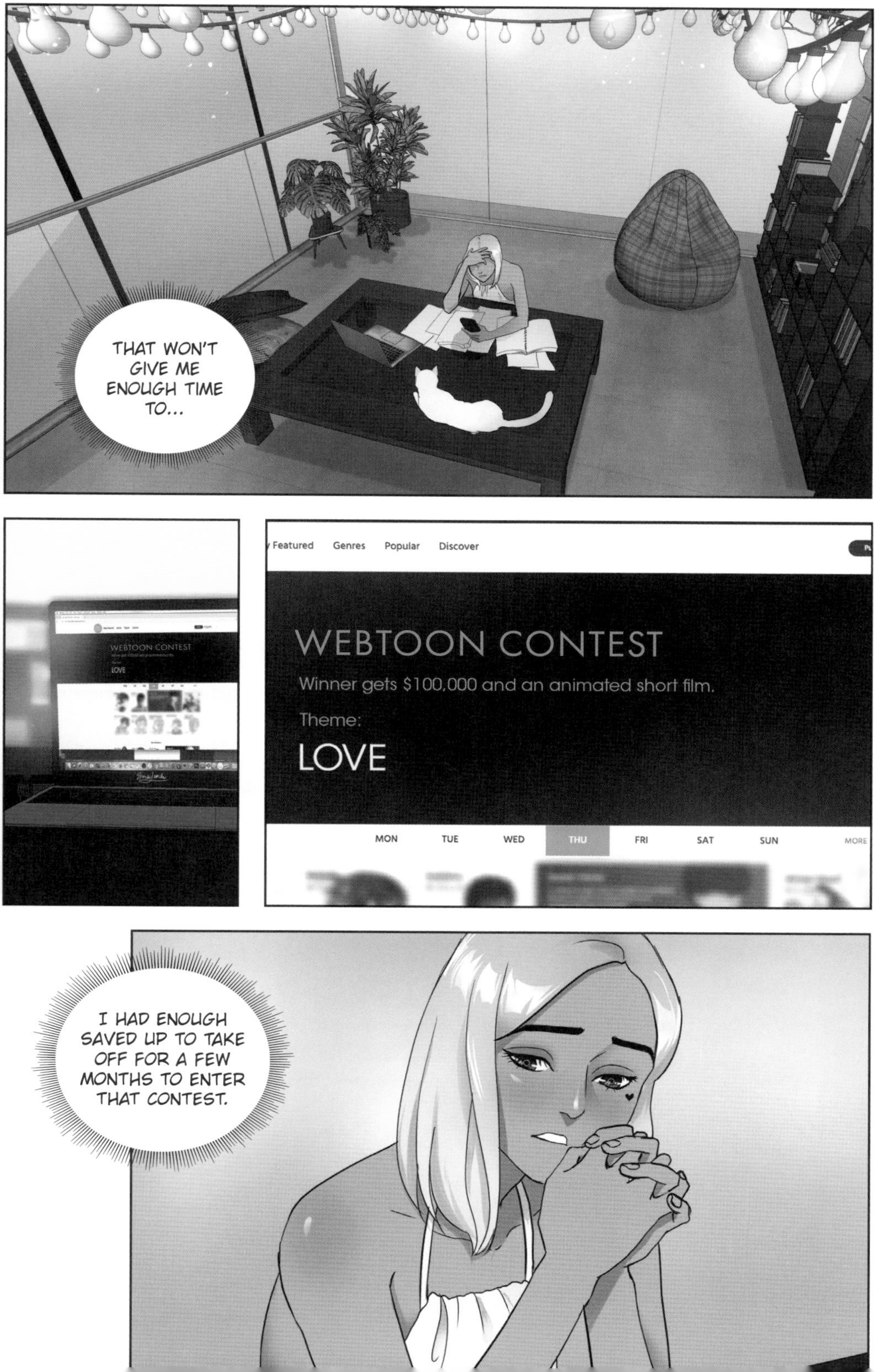
THAT WON'T GIVE ME ENOUGH TIME TO...
Featured Genres Popular Discover
WEBTOON CONTEST
Winner gets $100,000 and an animated short film.
Theme:
LOVE
MON TUE WED THU FRI SAT SUN MORE
I HAD ENOUGH SAVED UP TO TAKE OFF FOR A FEW MONTHS TO ENTER THAT CONTEST.

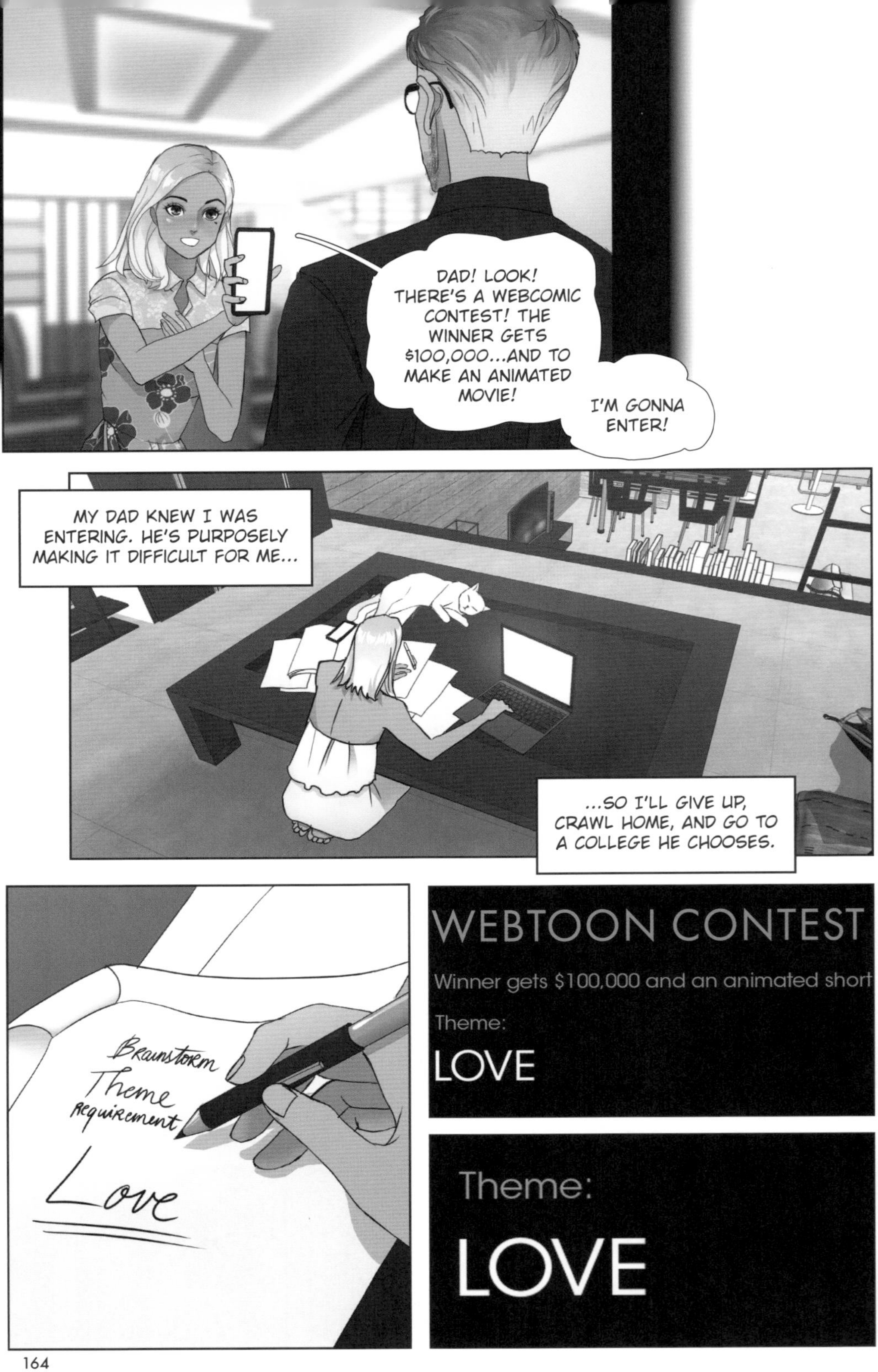
DAD! LOOK! THERE'S A WEBCOMIC CONTEST! THE WINNER GETS $100,000...AND TO MAKE AN ANIMATED MOVIE!
I'M GONNA ENTER!
MY DAD KNEW I WAS ENTERING. HE'S PURPOSELY MAKING IT DIFFICULT FOR ME...
...SO I'LL GIVE UP, CRAWL HOME, AND GO TO A COLLEGE HE CHOOSES.
Brainstorm
Theme
Requirement
Love
WEBTOON CONTEST
Winner gets $100,000 and an animated short
Theme:
LOVE
Theme:
LOVE

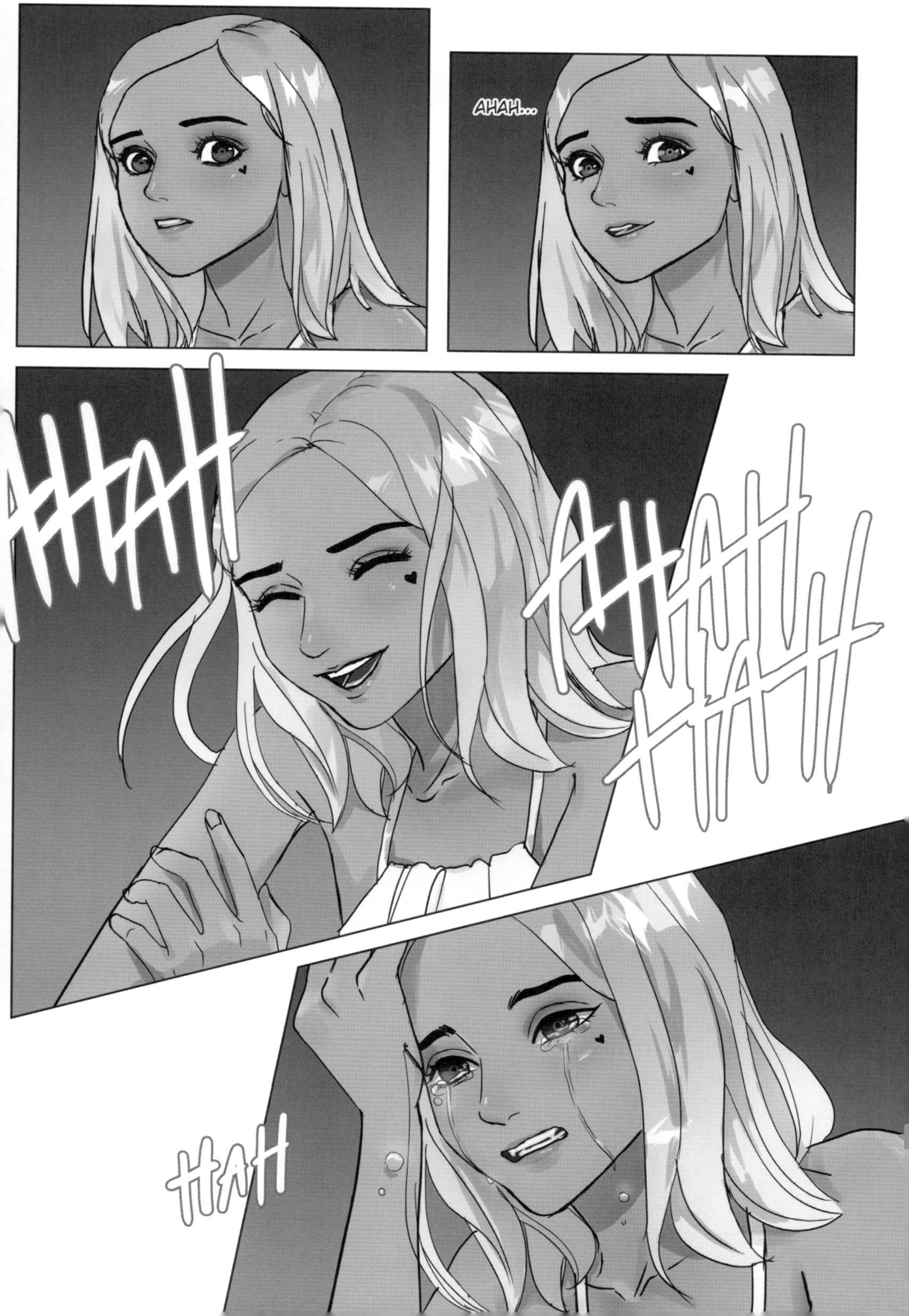
AHAH...
AHAH
AHAH
HAH
HAH

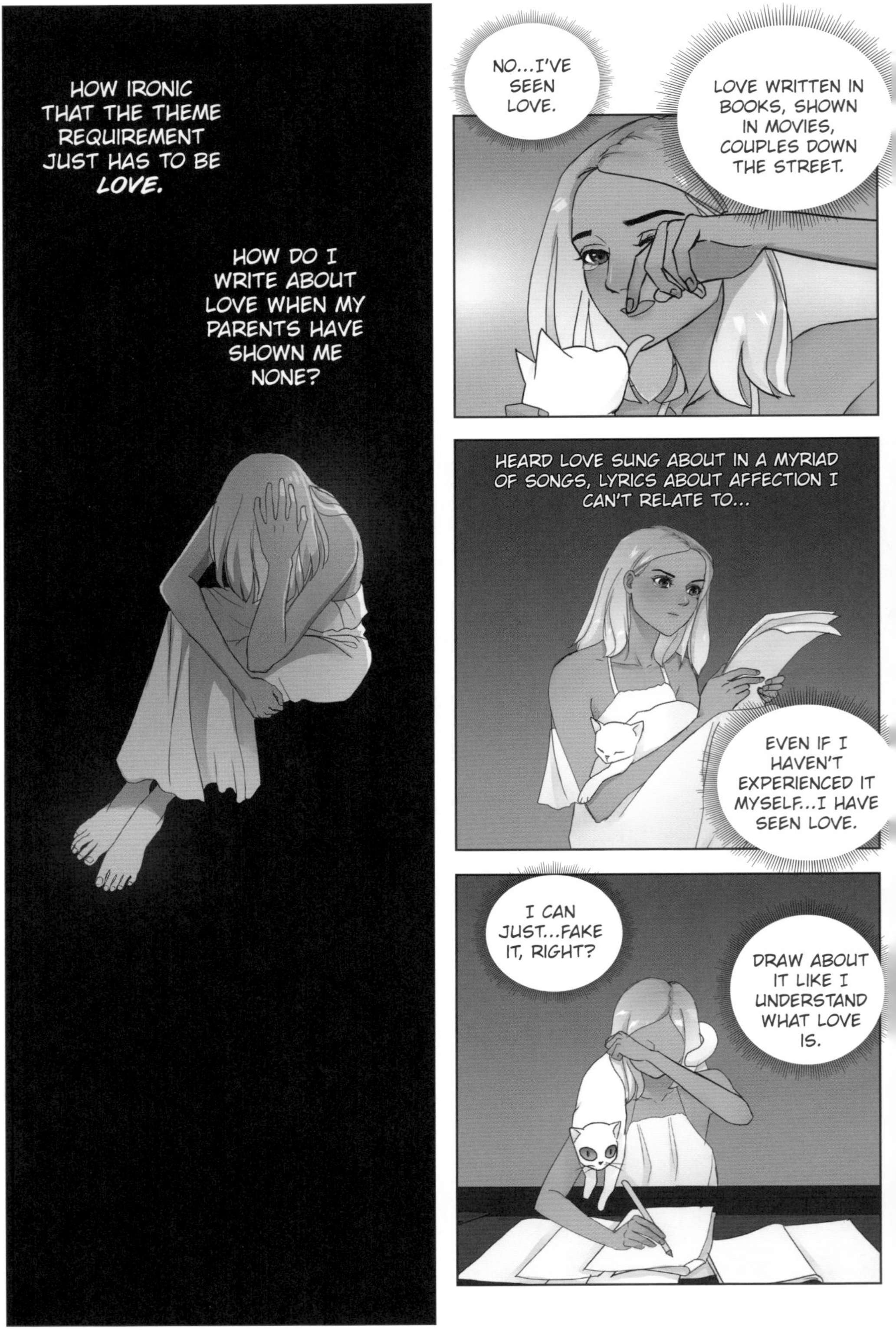
HOW IRONIC THAT THE THEME REQUIREMENT JUST HAS TO BE *LOVE.*
HOW DO I WRITE ABOUT LOVE WHEN MY PARENTS HAVE SHOWN ME NONE?
NO...I'VE SEEN LOVE.
LOVE WRITTEN IN BOOKS, SHOWN IN MOVIES, COUPLES DOWN THE STREET.
HEARD LOVE SUNG ABOUT IN A MYRIAD OF SONGS, LYRICS ABOUT AFFECTION I CAN'T RELATE TO...
EVEN IF I HAVEN'T EXPERIENCED IT MYSELF...I HAVE SEEN LOVE.
I CAN JUST...FAKE IT, RIGHT?
DRAW ABOUT IT LIKE I UNDERSTAND WHAT LOVE IS.

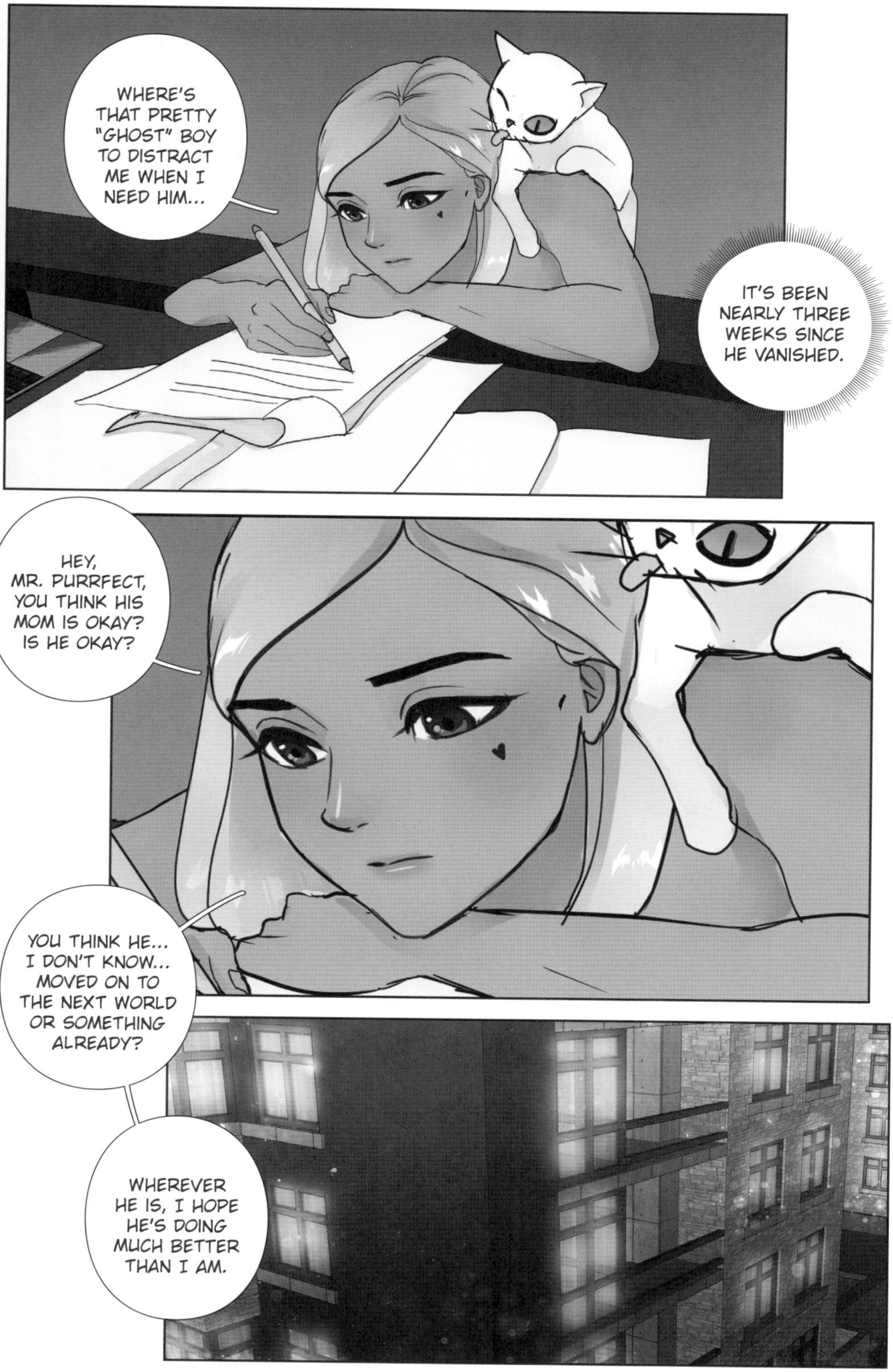
WHERE'S THAT PRETTY "GHOST" BOY TO DISTRACT ME WHEN I NEED HIM...
IT'S BEEN NEARLY THREE WEEKS SINCE HE VANISHED.
HEY, MR. PURRFECT, YOU THINK HIS MOM IS OKAY? IS HE OKAY?
YOU THINK HE... I DON'T KNOW... MOVED ON TO THE NEXT WORLD OR SOMETHING ALREADY?
WHEREVER HE IS, I HOPE HE'S DOING MUCH BETTER THAN I AM.

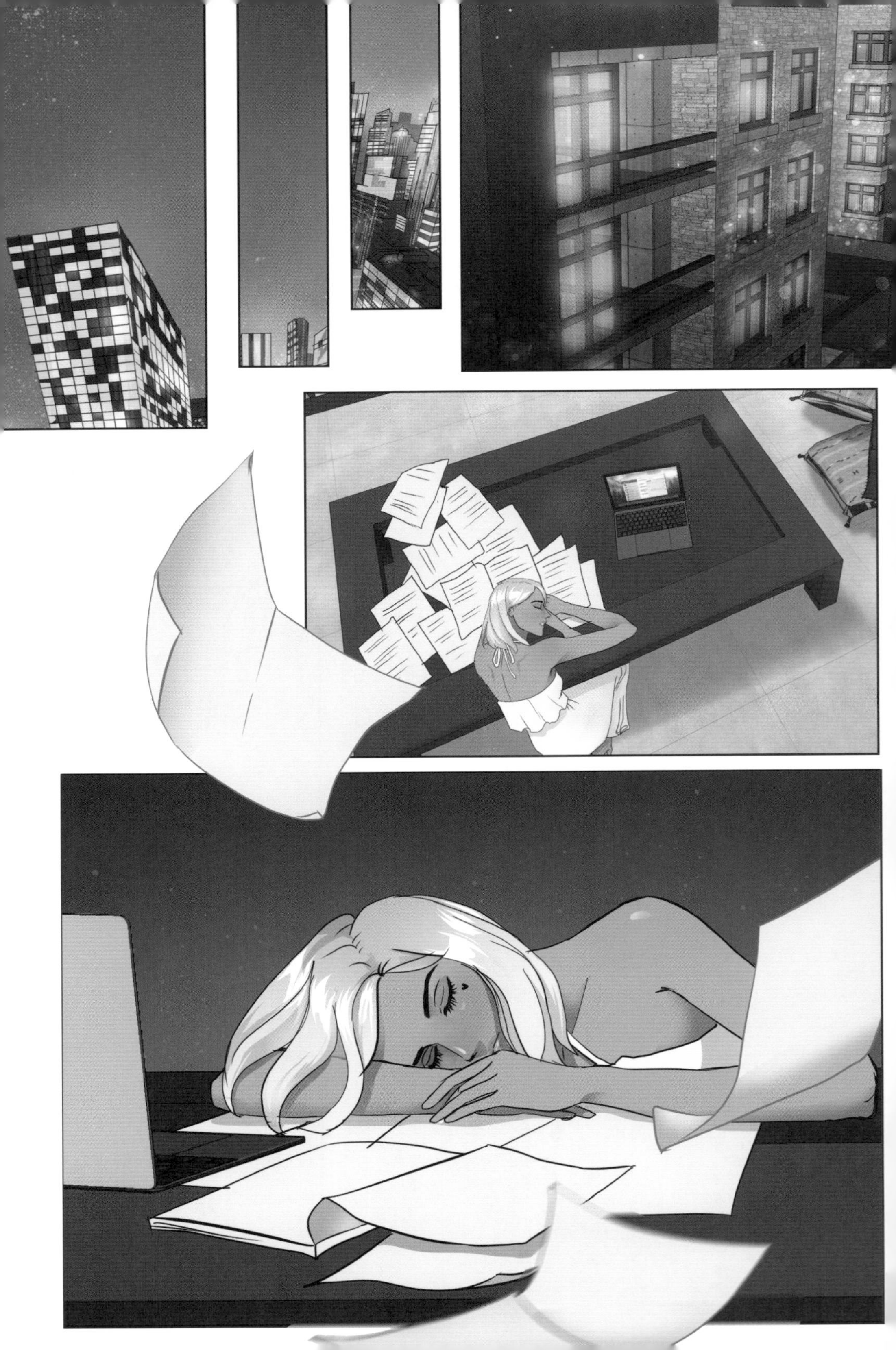

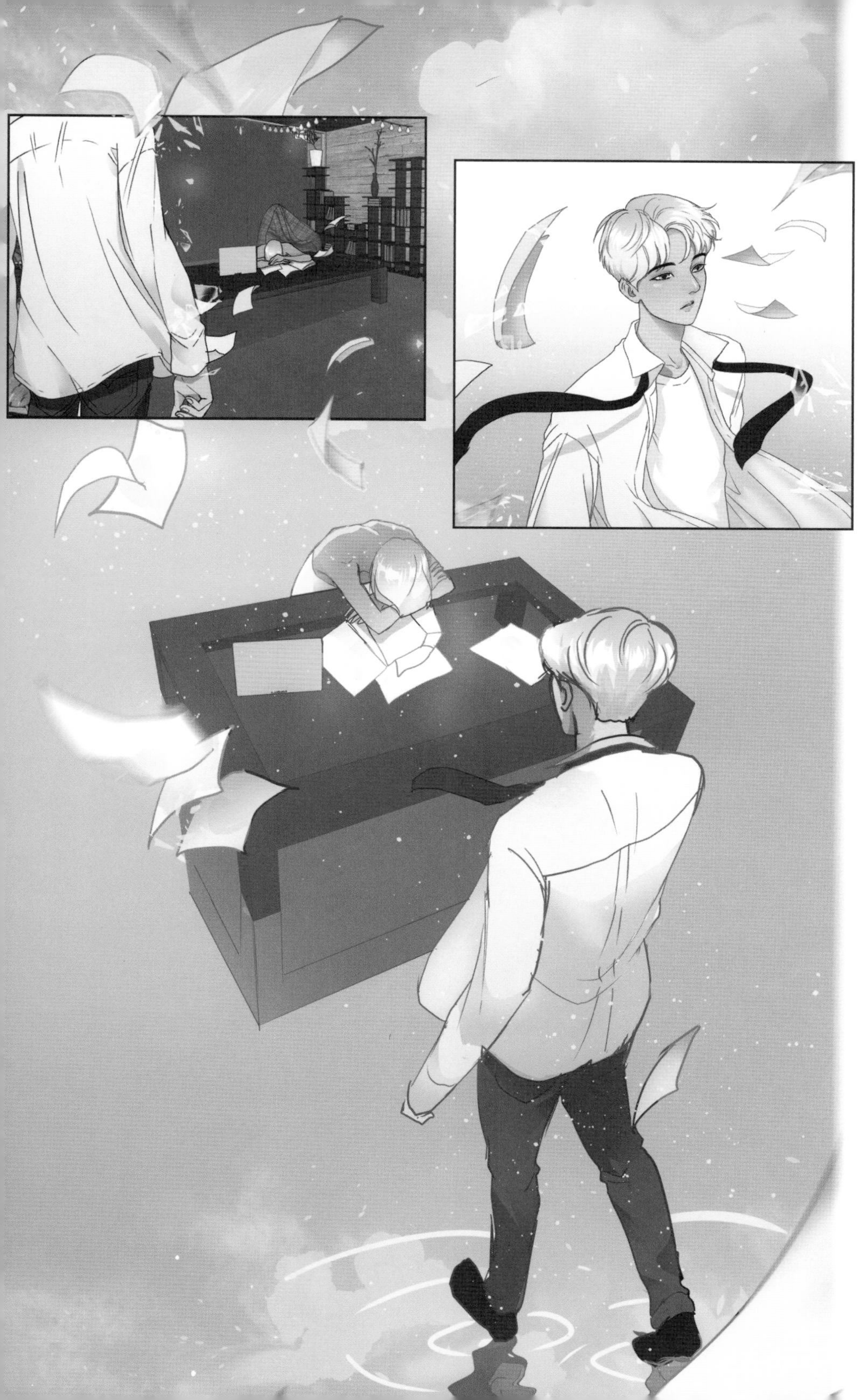

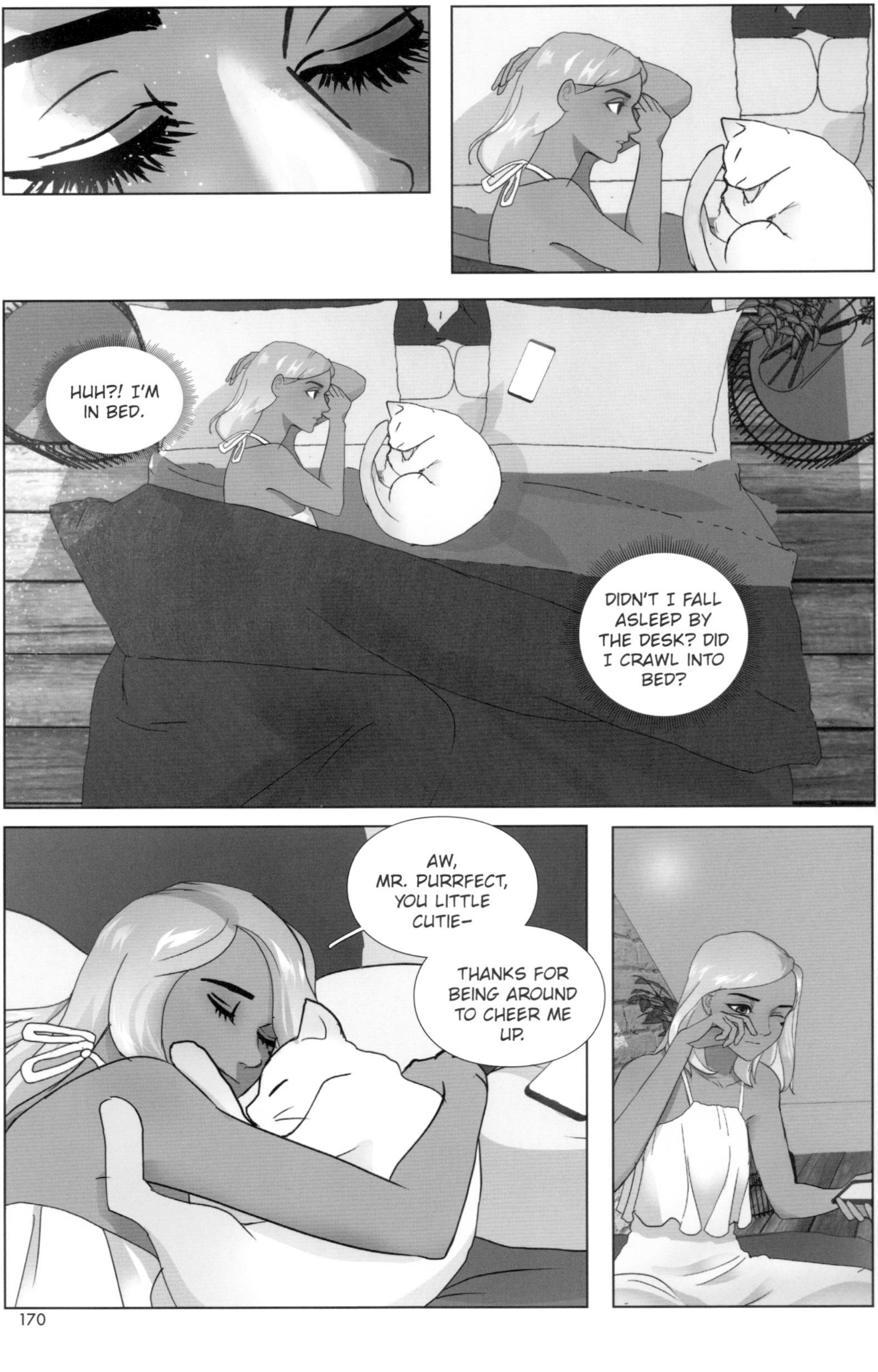
HUH?! I'M IN BED.
DIDN'T I FALL ASLEEP BY THE DESK? DID I CRAWL INTO BED?
AW, MR. PURRFECT, YOU LITTLE CUTIE–
THANKS FOR BEING AROUND TO CHEER ME UP.

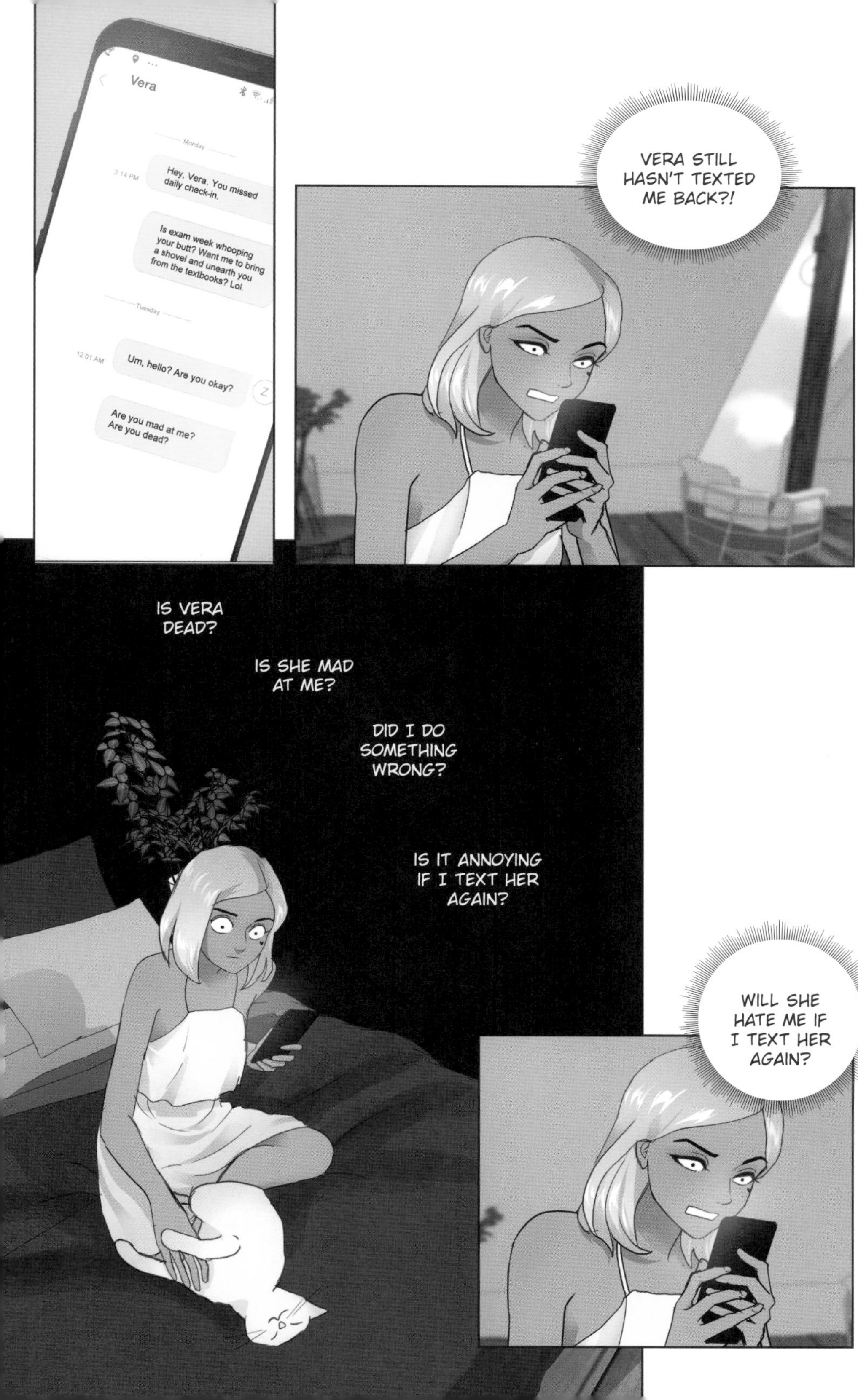

Vera
Monday
3:14 PM
Hey, Vera. You missed daily check-in.
Is exam week whooping your butt? Want me to bring a shovel and unearth you from the textbooks? Lol.
Tuesday
12:01 AM
Um, hello? Are you okay?
Are you mad at me? Are you dead?
VERA STILL HASN'T TEXTED ME BACK?!
IS VERA DEAD?
IS SHE MAD AT ME?
DID I DO SOMETHING WRONG?
IS IT ANNOYING IF I TEXT HER AGAIN?
WILL SHE HATE ME IF I TEXT HER AGAIN?

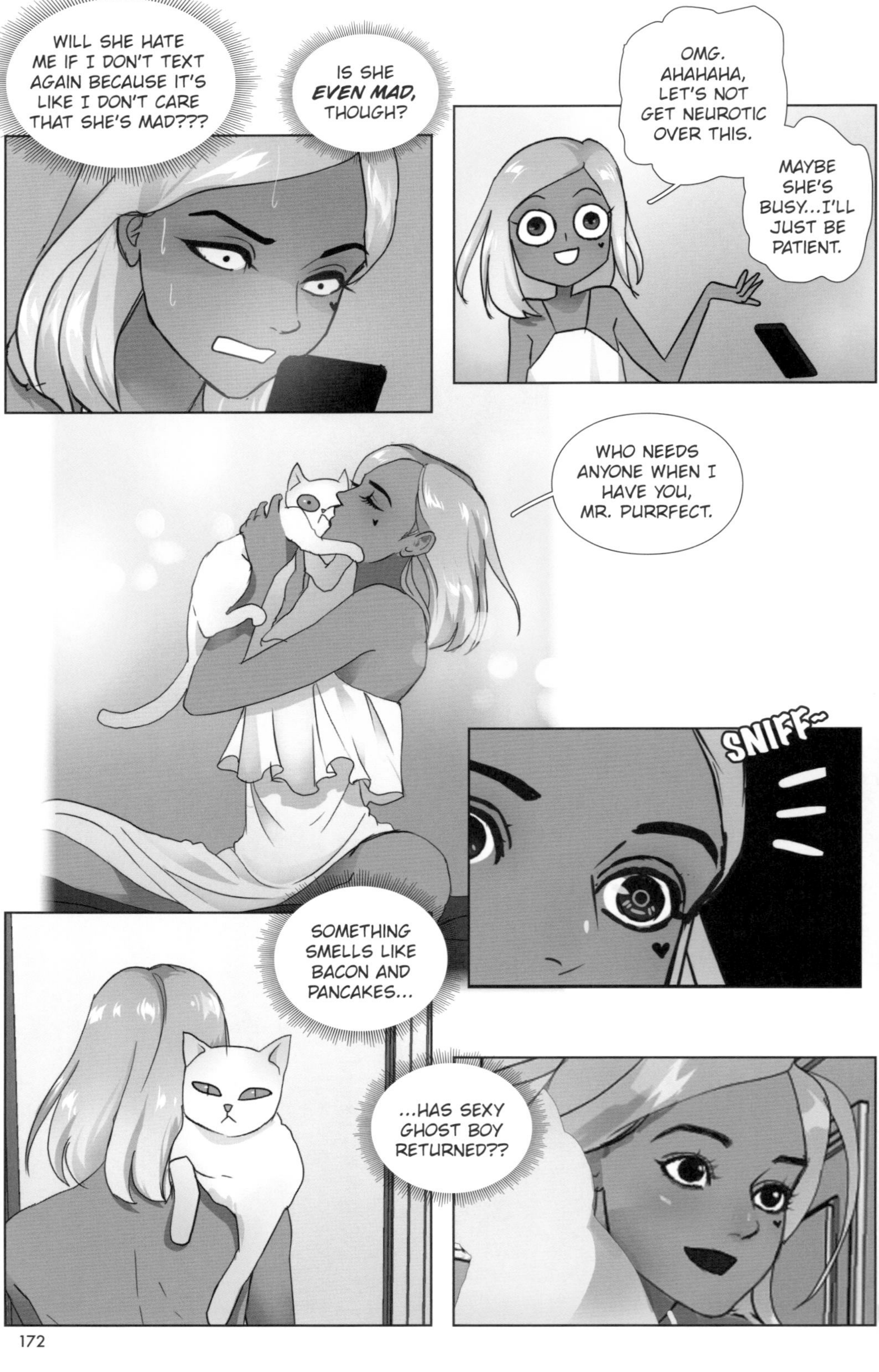
WILL SHE HATE ME IF I DON'T TEXT AGAIN BECAUSE IT'S LIKE I DON'T CARE THAT SHE'S MAD???
IS SHE **EVEN MAD,** THOUGH?
OMG. AHAHAHA, LET'S NOT GET NEUROTIC OVER THIS.
MAYBE SHE'S BUSY...I'LL JUST BE PATIENT.
WHO NEEDS ANYONE WHEN I HAVE YOU, MR. PURRFECT.
SNIFF~
SOMETHING SMELLS LIKE BACON AND PANCAKES...
...HAS SEXY GHOST BOY RETURNED??

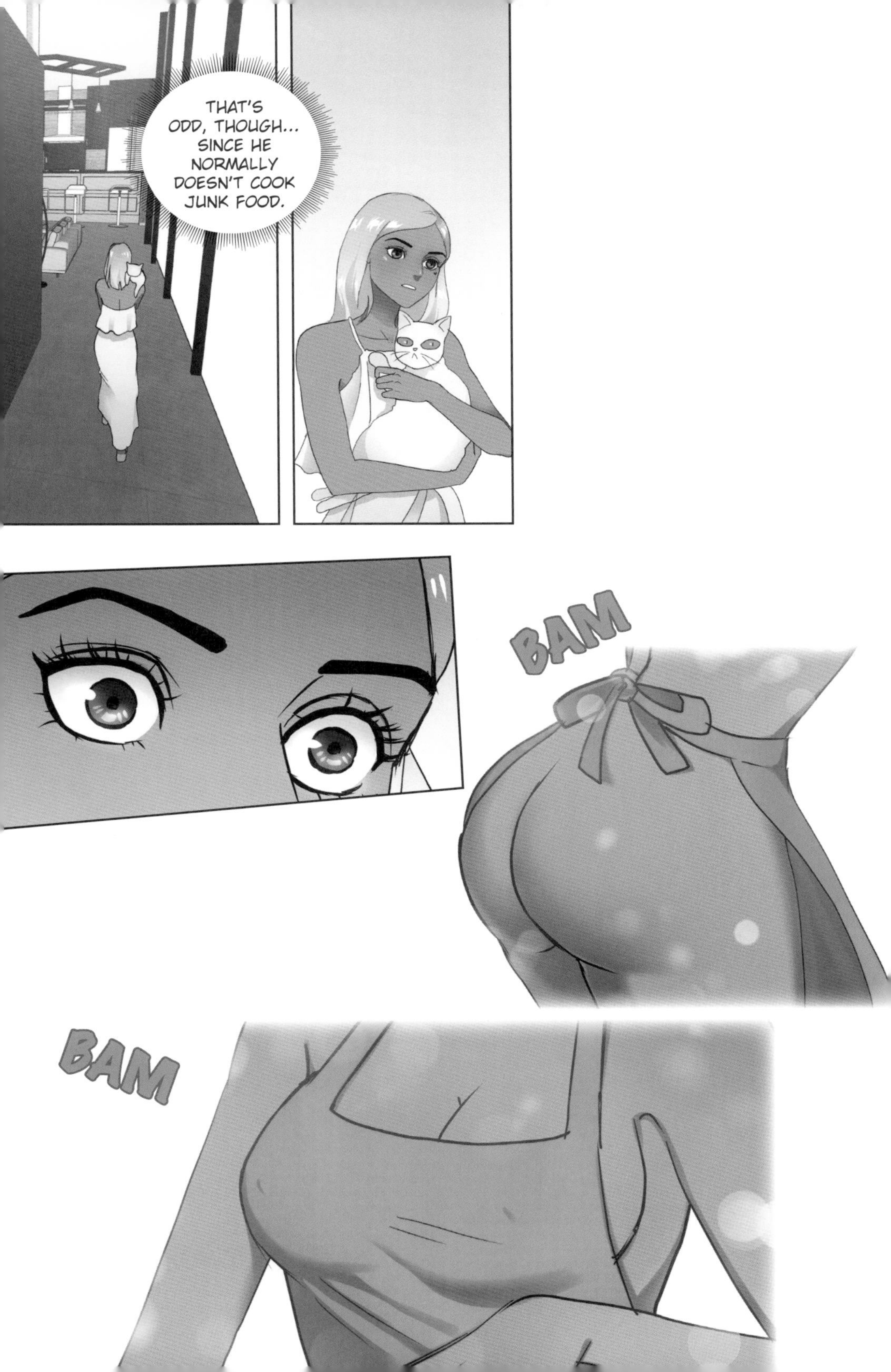
THAT'S ODD, THOUGH... SINCE HE NORMALLY DOESN'T COOK JUNK FOOD.
BAM
BAM

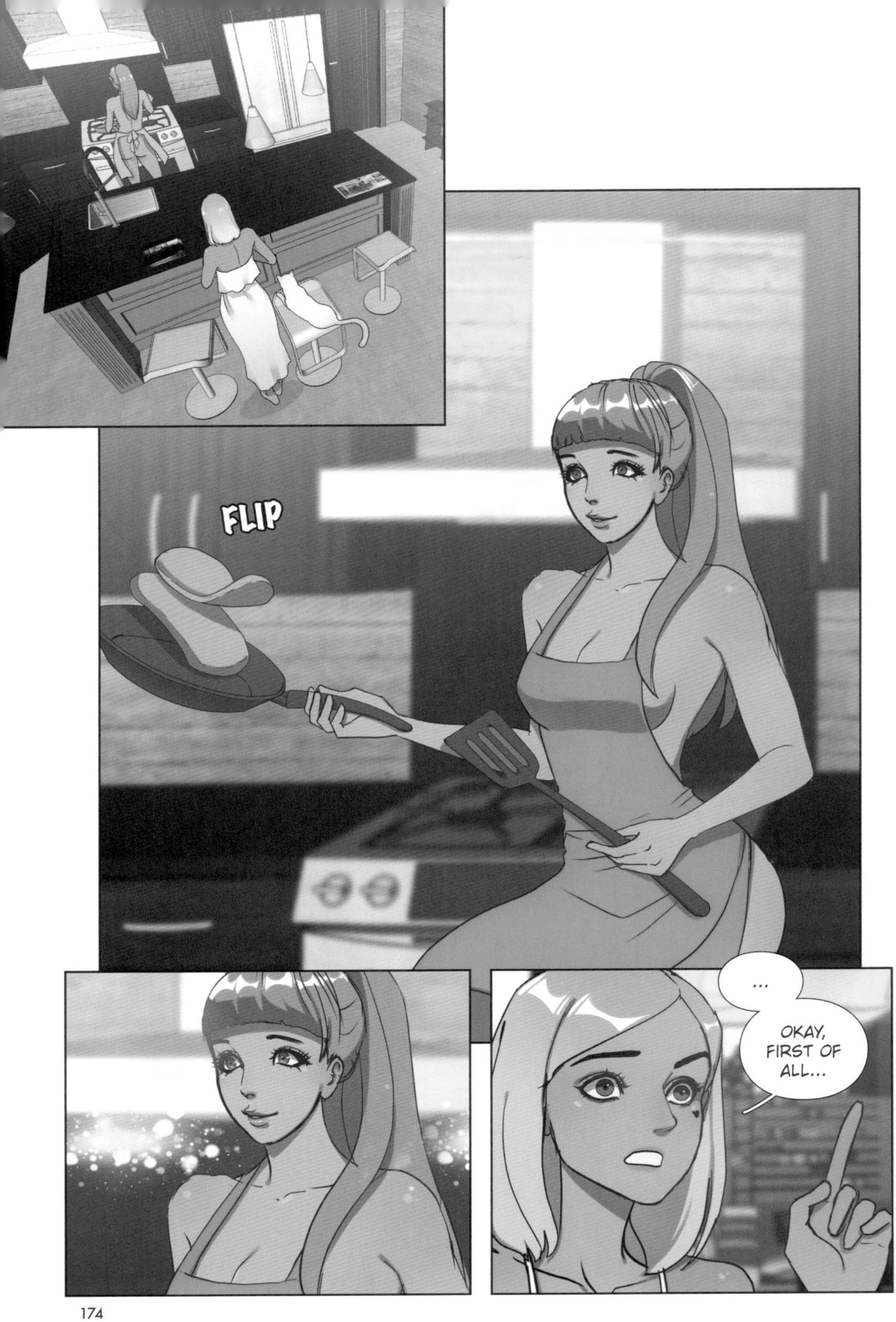
FLIP
...
OKAY, FIRST OF ALL...

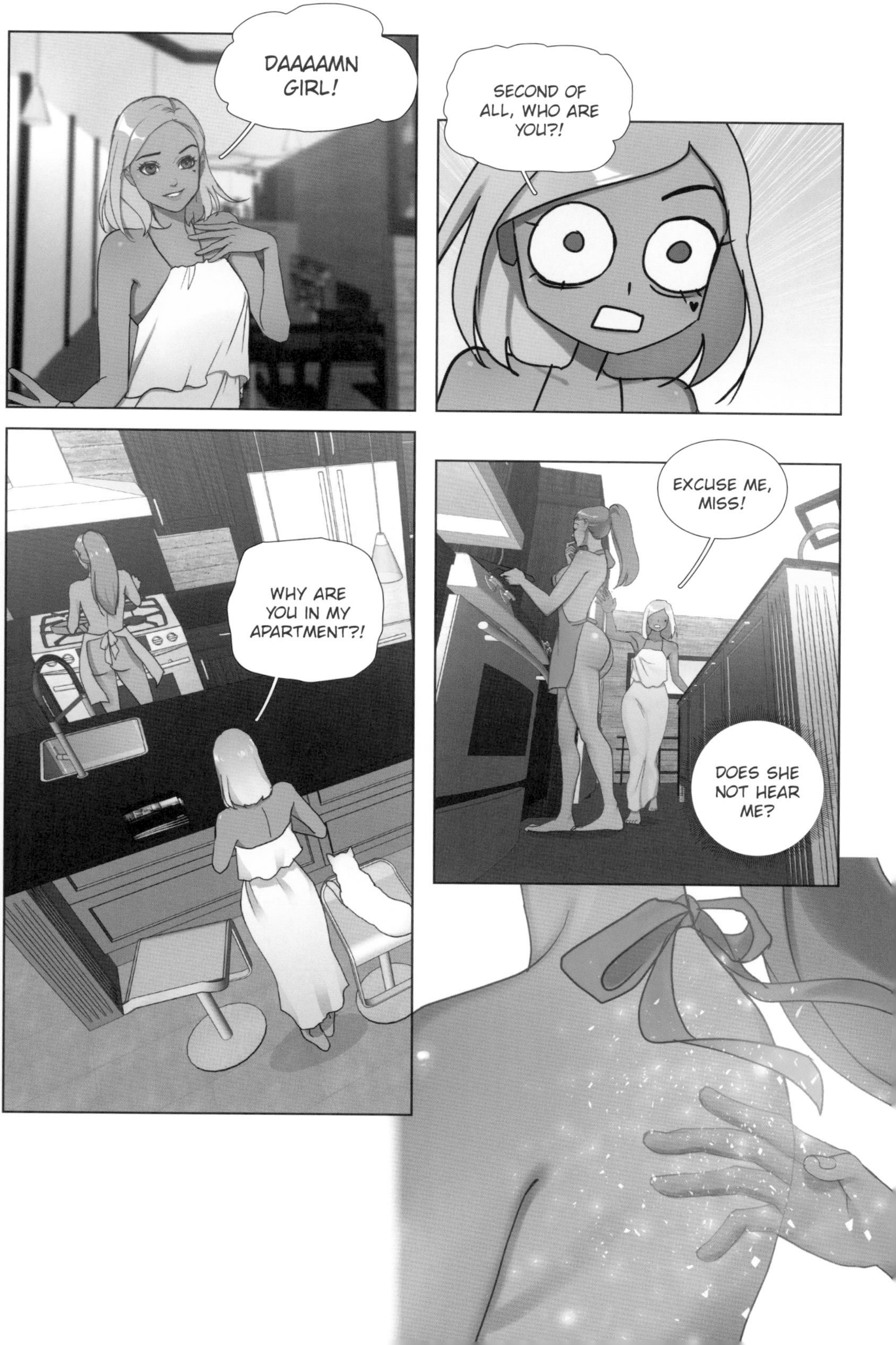
DAAAAMN GIRL!
SECOND OF ALL, WHO ARE YOU?!
WHY ARE YOU IN MY APARTMENT?!
EXCUSE ME, MISS!
DOES SHE NOT HEAR ME?

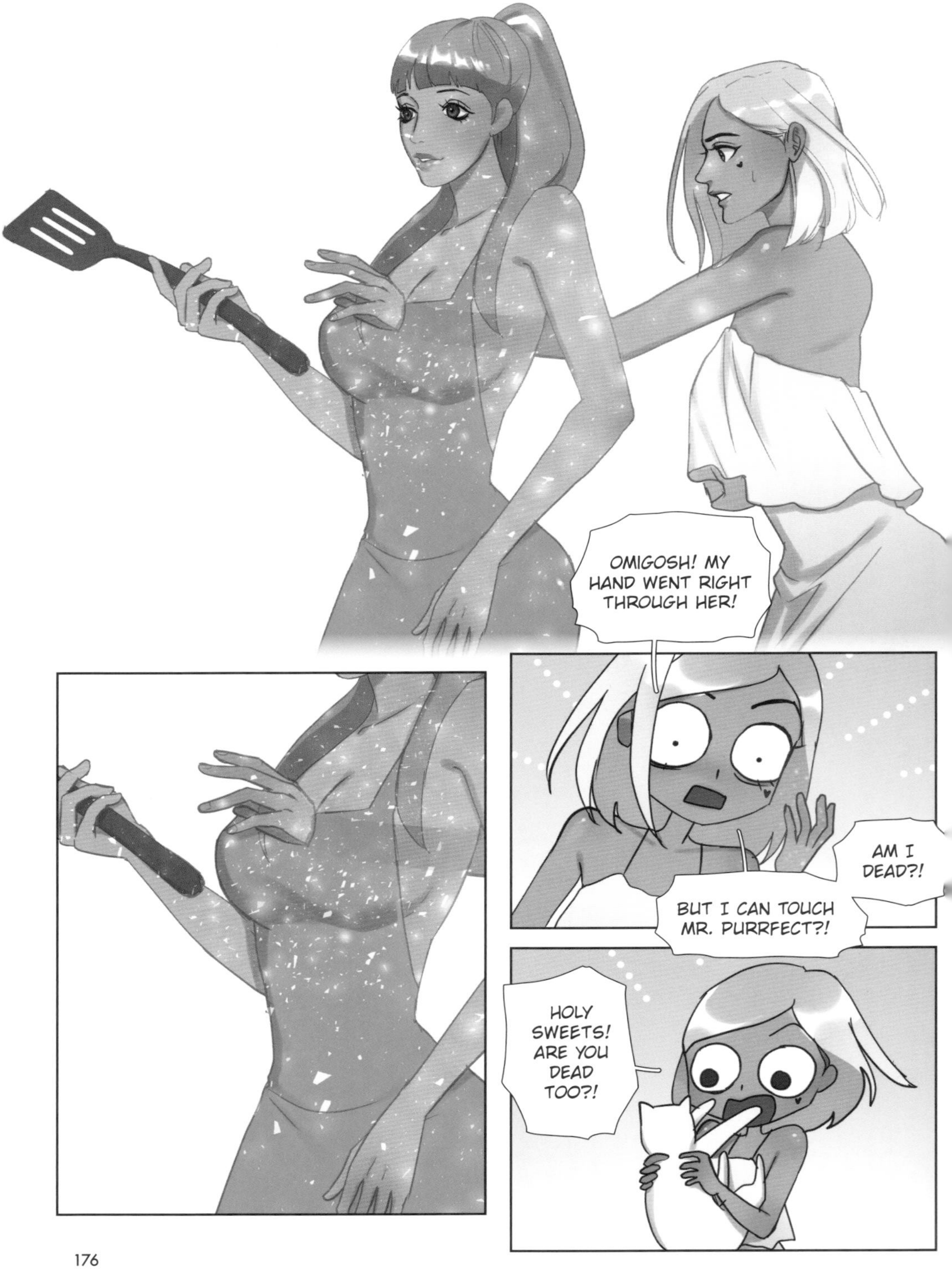
OMIGOSH! MY HAND WENT RIGHT THROUGH HER!
AM I DEAD?!
BUT I CAN TOUCH MR. PURRFECT?!
HOLY SWEETS! ARE YOU DEAD TOO?!

RUSTLE

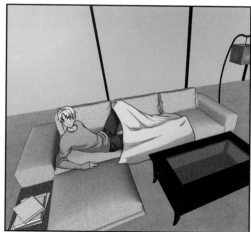

WIPE

ZELAN.

HAS HE BEEN ON THE COUCH THIS WHOLE TIME?

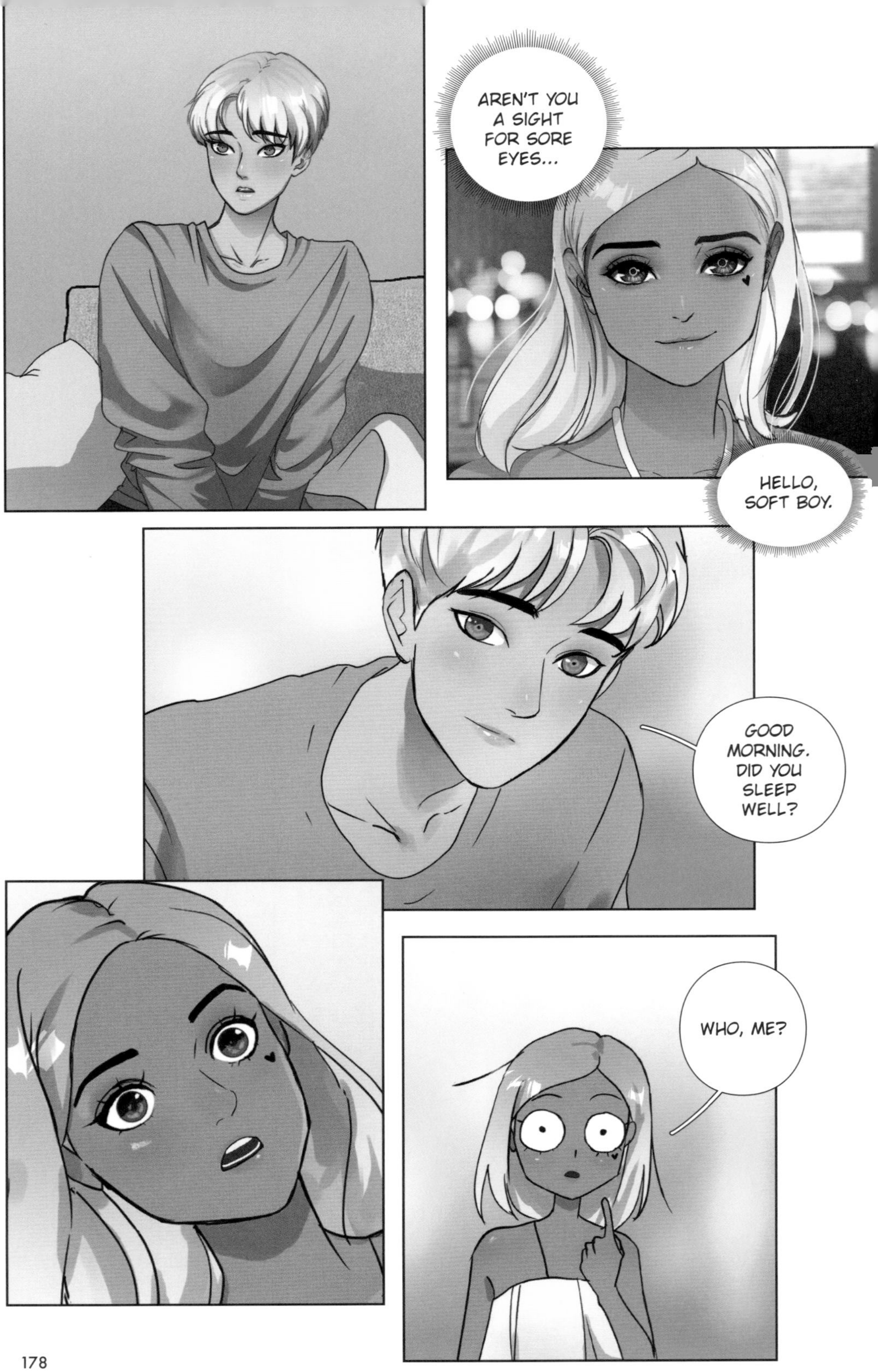
AREN'T YOU A SIGHT FOR SORE EYES...
HELLO, SOFT BOY.
GOOD MORNING. DID YOU SLEEP WELL?
WHO, ME?

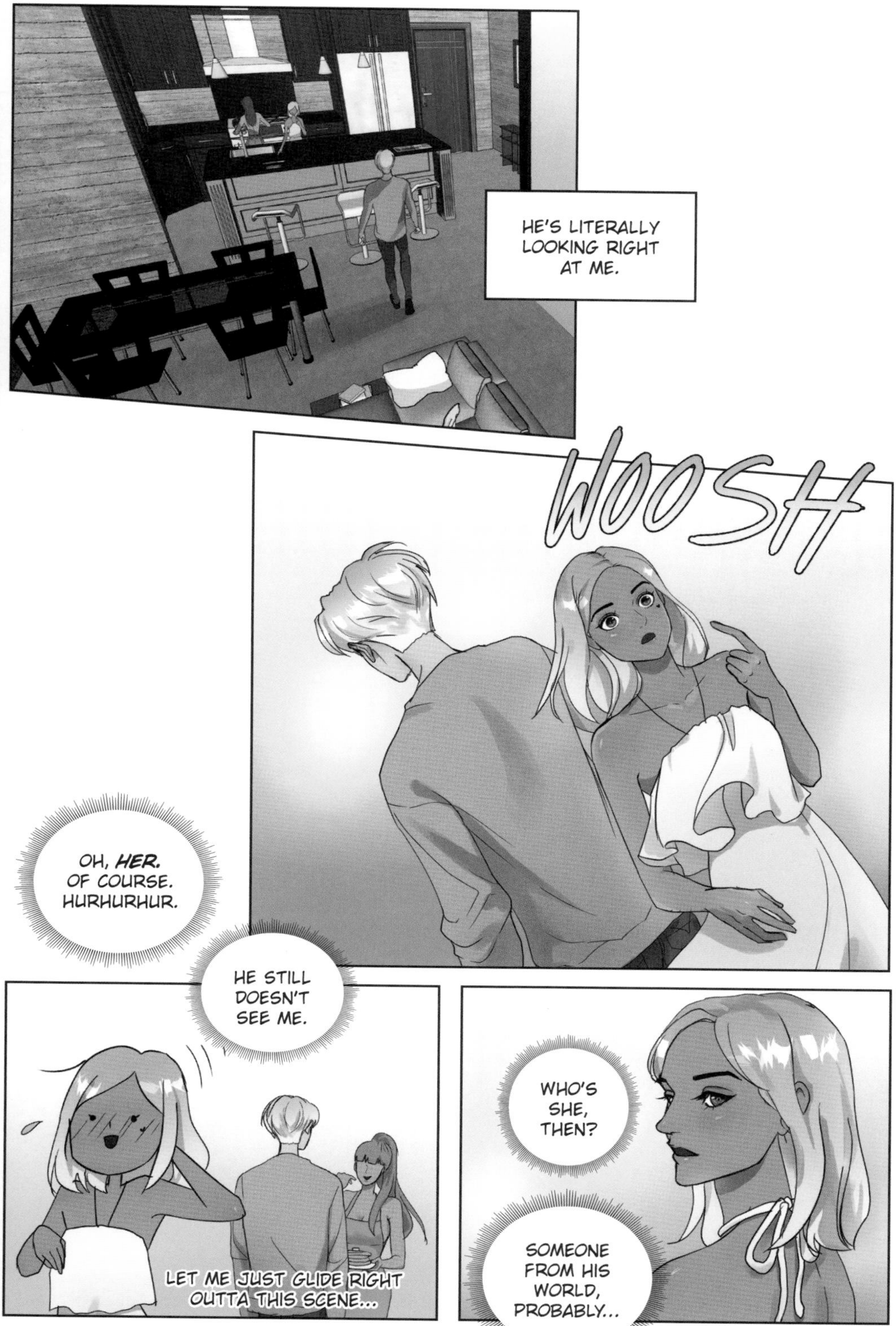
HE'S LITERALLY LOOKING RIGHT AT ME.
WOOSH
OH, HER. OF COURSE. HURHURHUR.
HE STILL DOESN'T SEE ME.
LET ME JUST GLIDE RIGHT OUTTA THIS SCENE...
WHO'S SHE, THEN?
SOMEONE FROM HIS WORLD, PROBABLY...

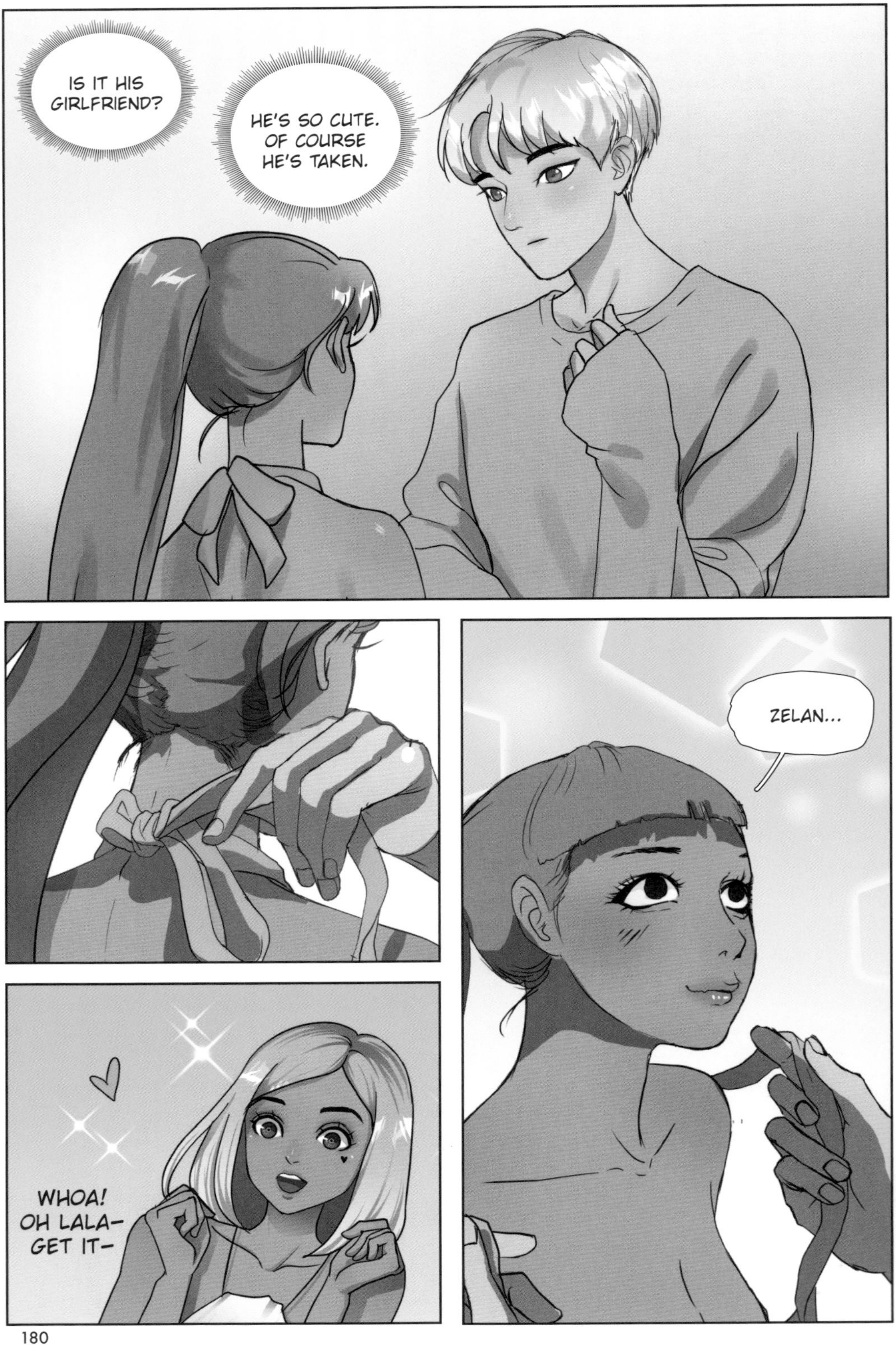
IS IT HIS GIRLFRIEND?
HE'S SO CUTE. OF COURSE HE'S TAKEN.
WHOA! OH LALA– GET IT–
ZELAN...

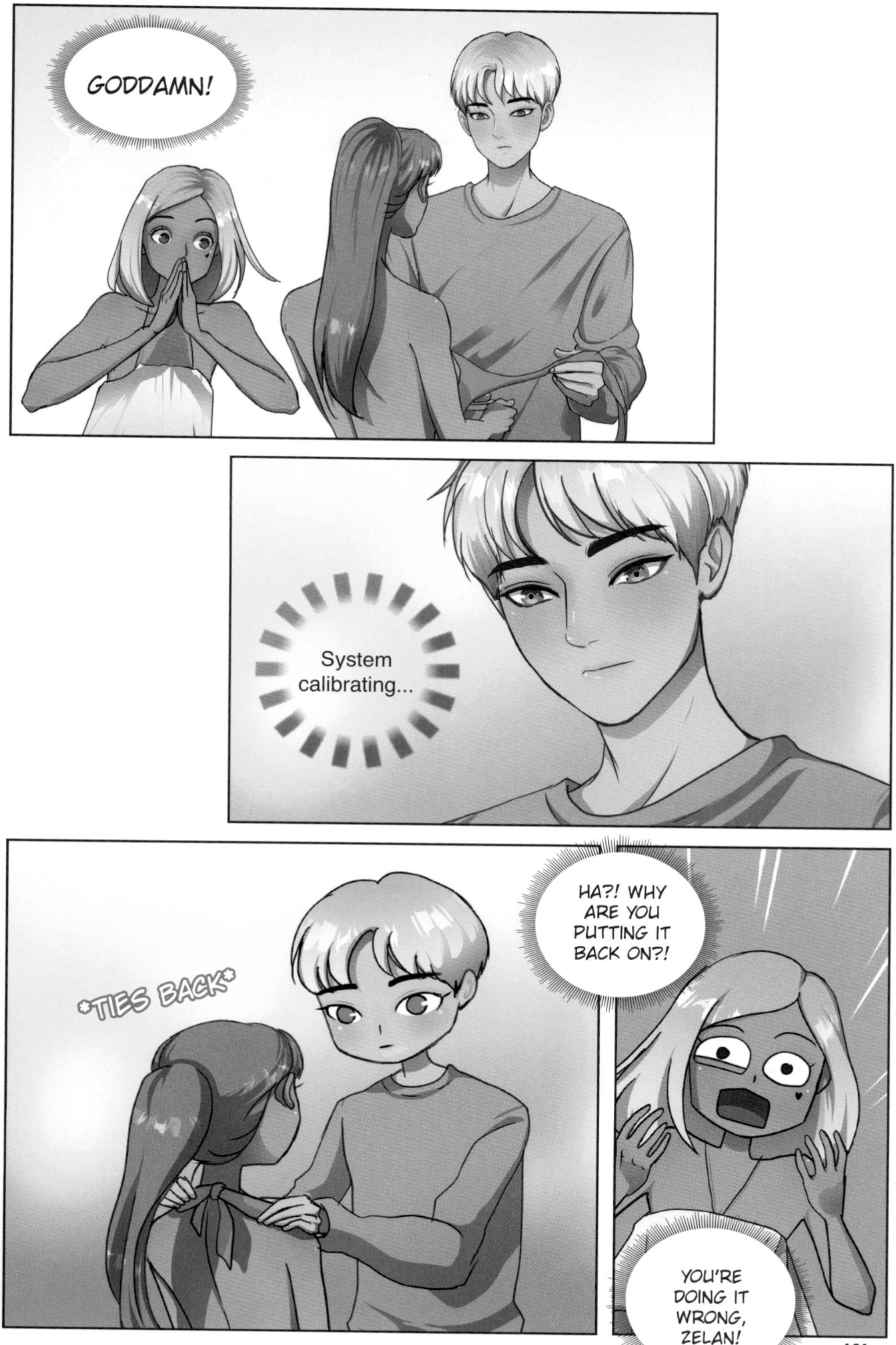
GODDAMN!
System calibrating...
TIES BACK
HA?! WHY ARE YOU PUTTING IT BACK ON?!
YOU'RE DOING IT WRONG, ZELAN!

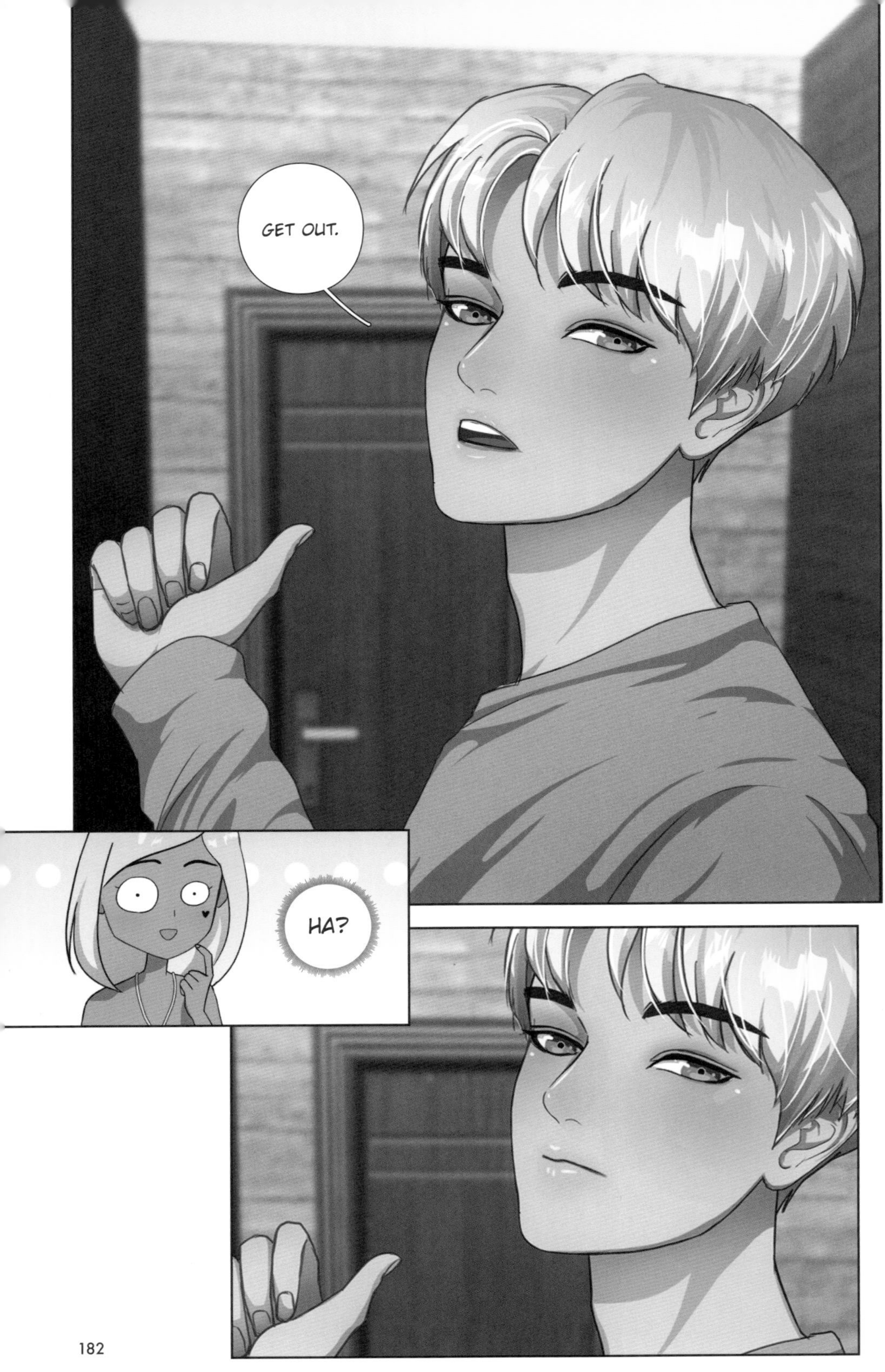
GET OUT.
HA?

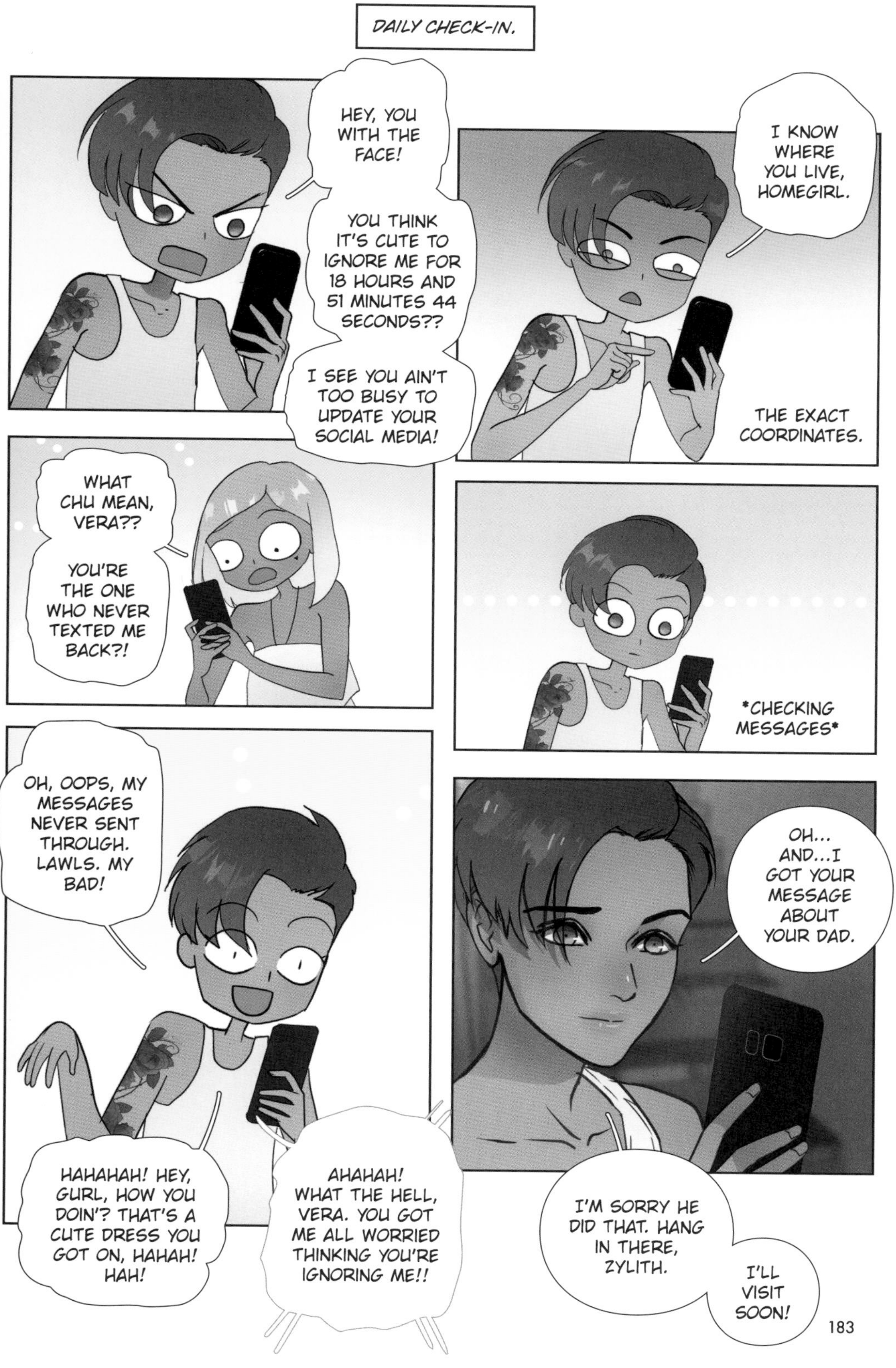
DAILY CHECK-IN.
HEY, YOU WITH THE FACE!
YOU THINK IT'S CUTE TO IGNORE ME FOR 18 HOURS AND 51 MINUTES 44 SECONDS??
I SEE YOU AIN'T TOO BUSY TO UPDATE YOUR SOCIAL MEDIA!
I KNOW WHERE YOU LIVE, HOMEGIRL.
THE EXACT COORDINATES.
WHAT CHU MEAN, VERA??
YOU'RE THE ONE WHO NEVER TEXTED ME BACK?!
CHECKING MESSAGES
OH, OOPS, MY MESSAGES NEVER SENT THROUGH. LAWLS. MY BAD!
HAHAHAH! HEY, GURL, HOW YOU DOIN'? THAT'S A CUTE DRESS YOU GOT ON, HAHAH! HAH!
AHAHAH! WHAT THE HELL, VERA. YOU GOT ME ALL WORRIED THINKING YOU'RE IGNORING ME!!
OH... AND...I GOT YOUR MESSAGE ABOUT YOUR DAD.
I'M SORRY HE DID THAT. HANG IN THERE, ZYLITH.
I'LL VISIT SOON!

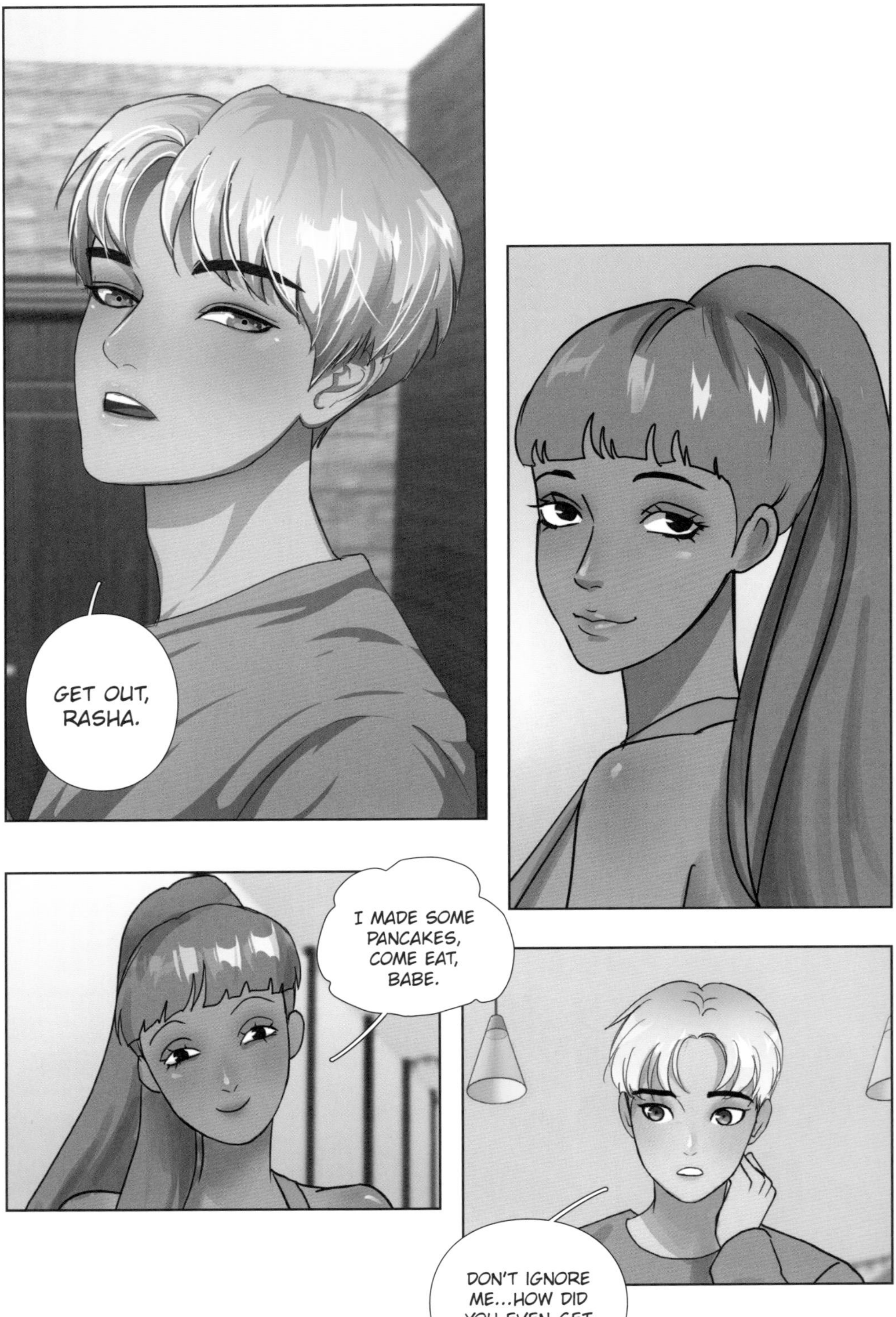
GET OUT, RASHA.
I MADE SOME PANCAKES, COME EAT, BABE.
DON'T IGNORE ME...HOW DID YOU EVEN GET INSIDE?

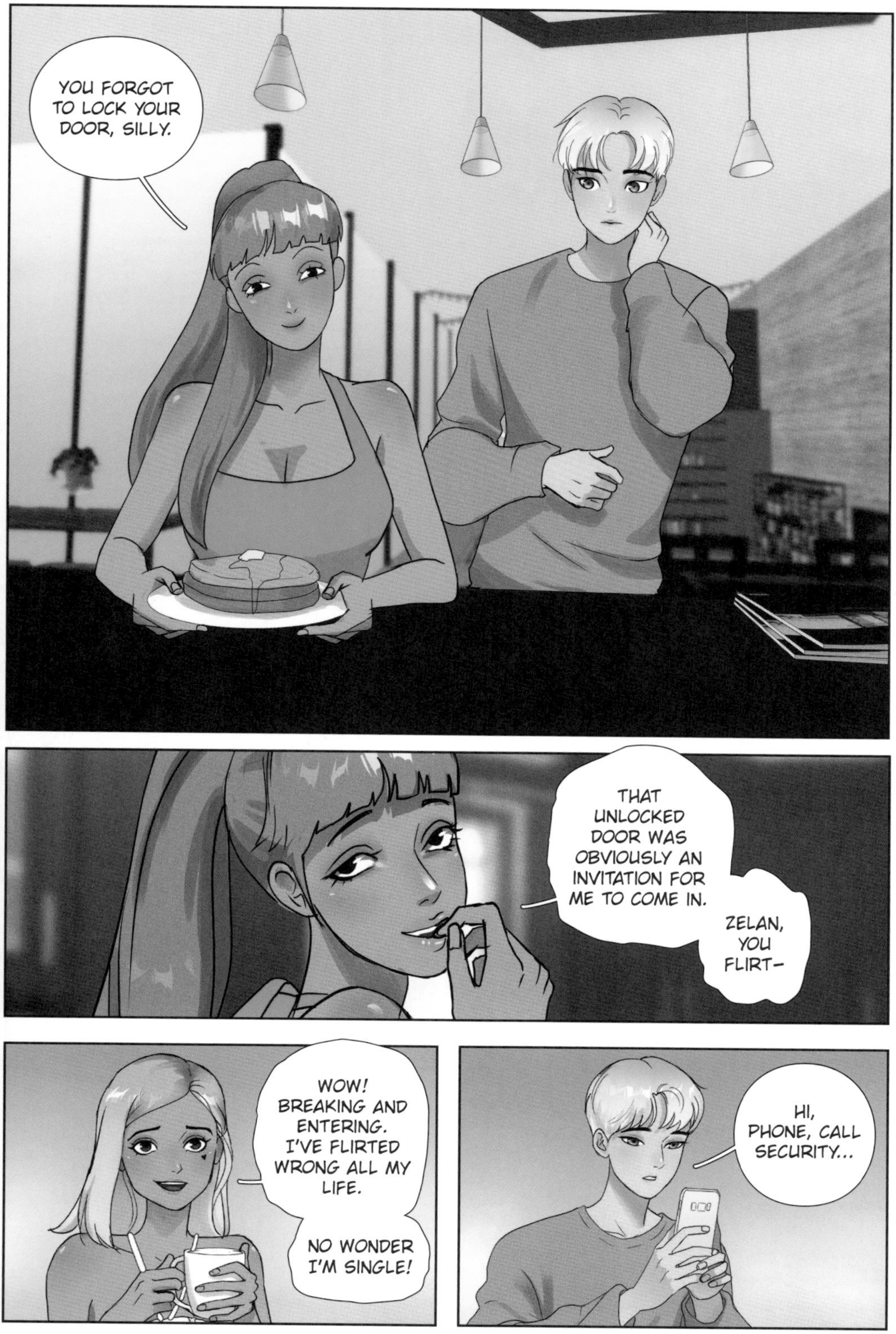
YOU FORGOT TO LOCK YOUR DOOR, SILLY.
THAT UNLOCKED DOOR WAS OBVIOUSLY AN INVITATION FOR ME TO COME IN.
ZELAN, YOU FLIRT–
WOW! BREAKING AND ENTERING. I'VE FLIRTED WRONG ALL MY LIFE.
NO WONDER I'M SINGLE!
HI, PHONE, CALL SECURITY...

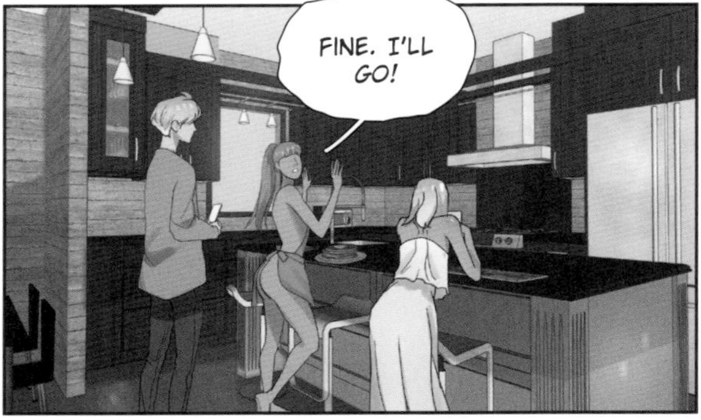
FINE. I'LL GO!

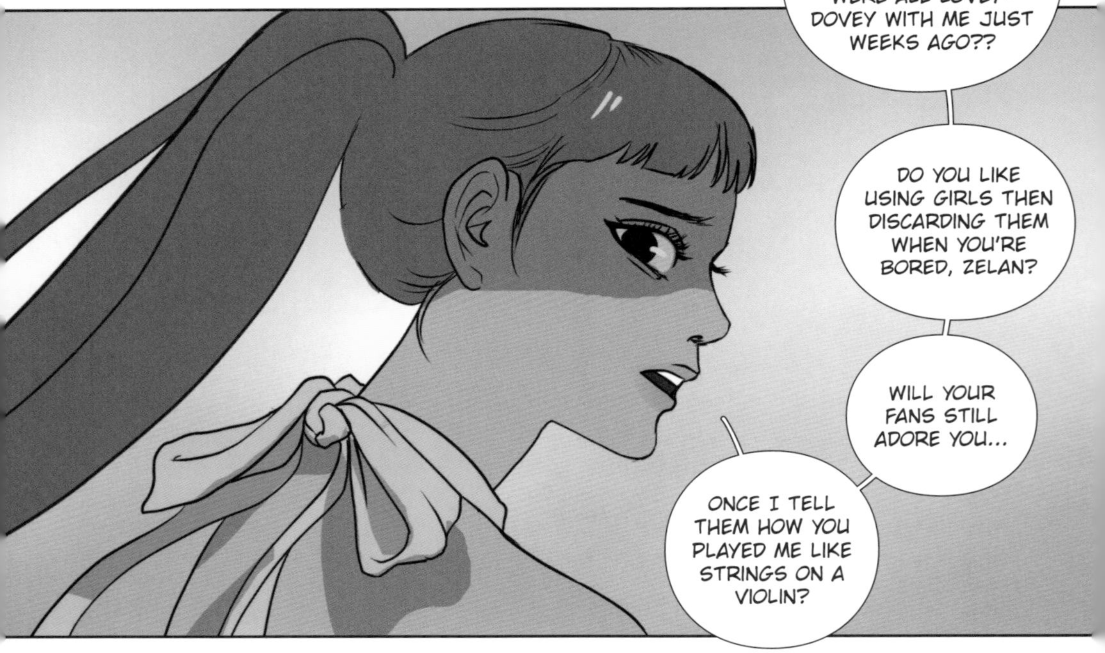
I'M SORRY I BROKE IN.
I DON'T UNDERSTAND WHY YOU'RE SO COLD TO ME NOW...WHEN YOU WERE ALL LOVEY-DOVEY WITH ME JUST WEEKS AGO??
DO YOU LIKE USING GIRLS THEN DISCARDING THEM WHEN YOU'RE BORED, ZELAN?
WILL YOUR FANS STILL ADORE YOU...
ONCE I TELL THEM HOW YOU PLAYED ME LIKE STRINGS ON A VIOLIN?

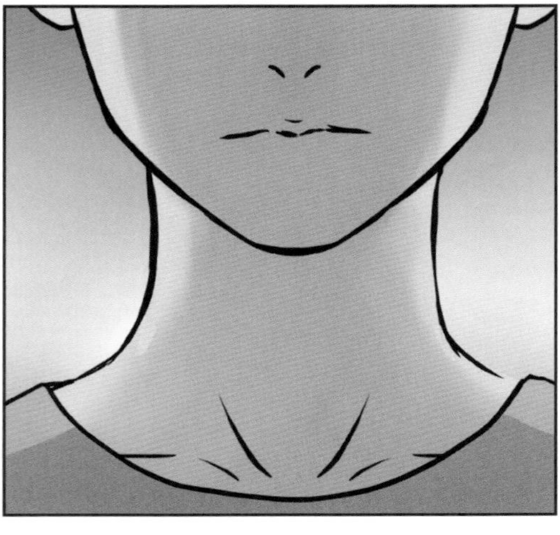

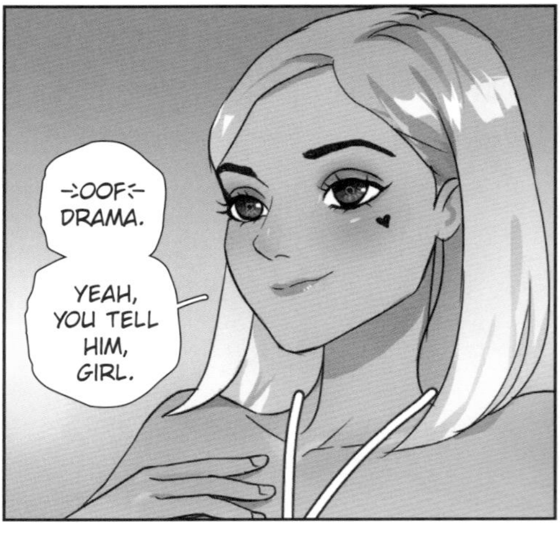
OOF
DRAMA.
YEAH, YOU TELL HIM, GIRL.

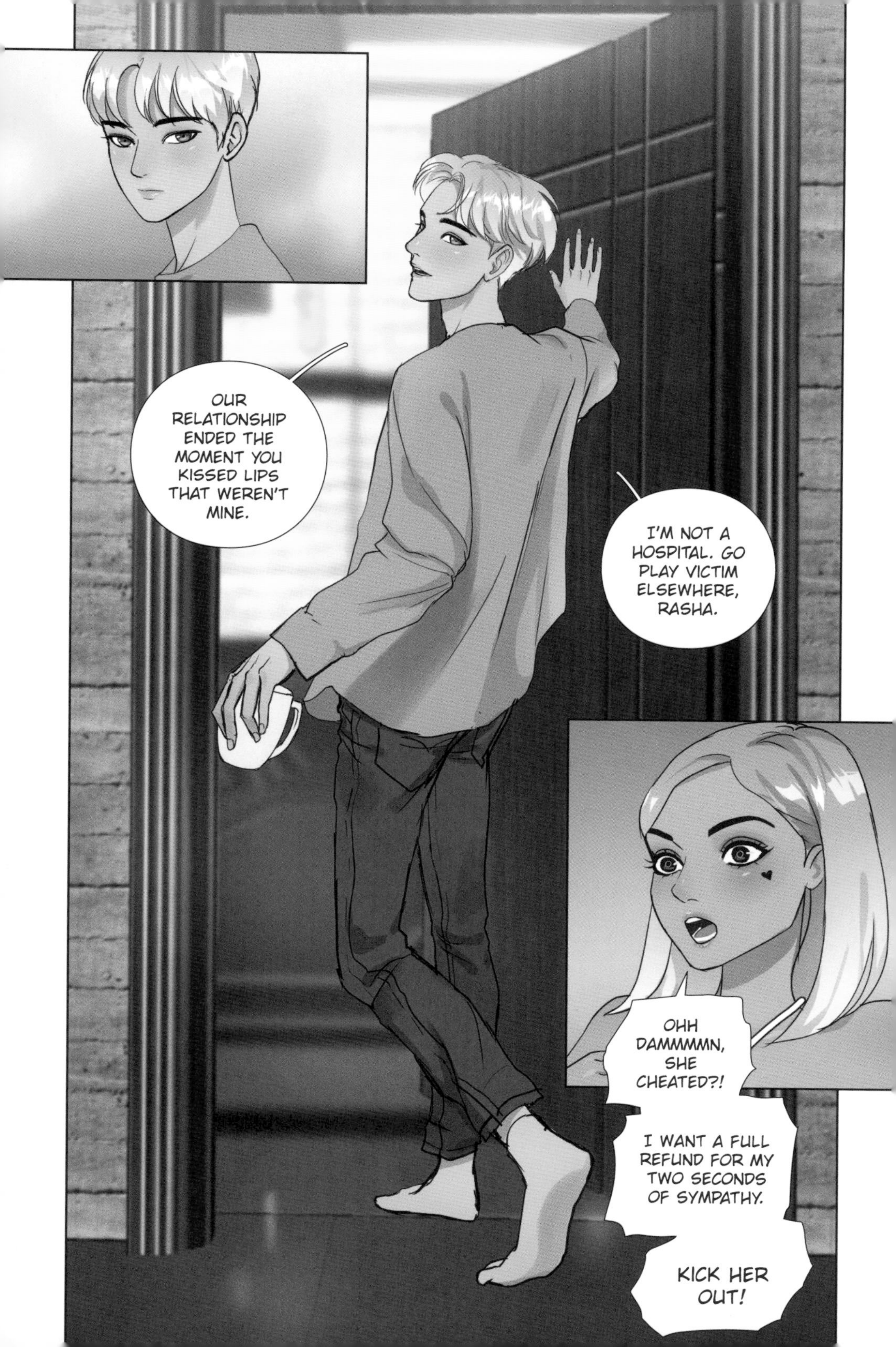
OUR RELATIONSHIP ENDED THE MOMENT YOU KISSED LIPS THAT WEREN'T MINE.
I'M NOT A HOSPITAL. GO PLAY VICTIM ELSEWHERE, RASHA.
OHH DAMMMMN, SHE CHEATED?!
I WANT A FULL REFUND FOR MY TWO SECONDS OF SYMPATHY.
KICK HER OUT!

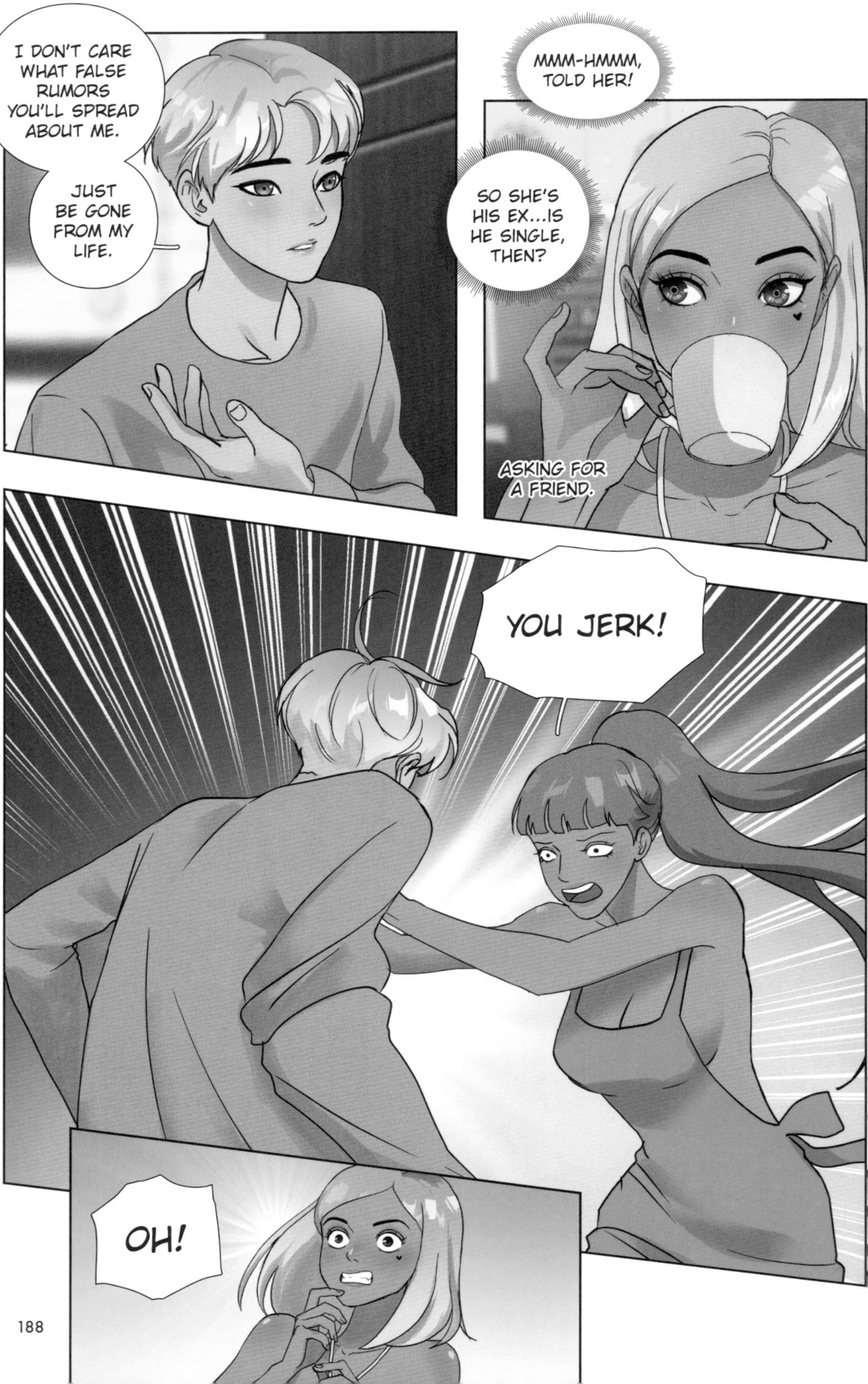
I DON'T CARE WHAT FALSE RUMORS YOU'LL SPREAD ABOUT ME.
JUST BE GONE FROM MY LIFE.
MMM-HMMM, TOLD HER!
SO SHE'S HIS EX...IS HE SINGLE, THEN?
ASKING FOR A FRIEND.
YOU JERK!
OH!

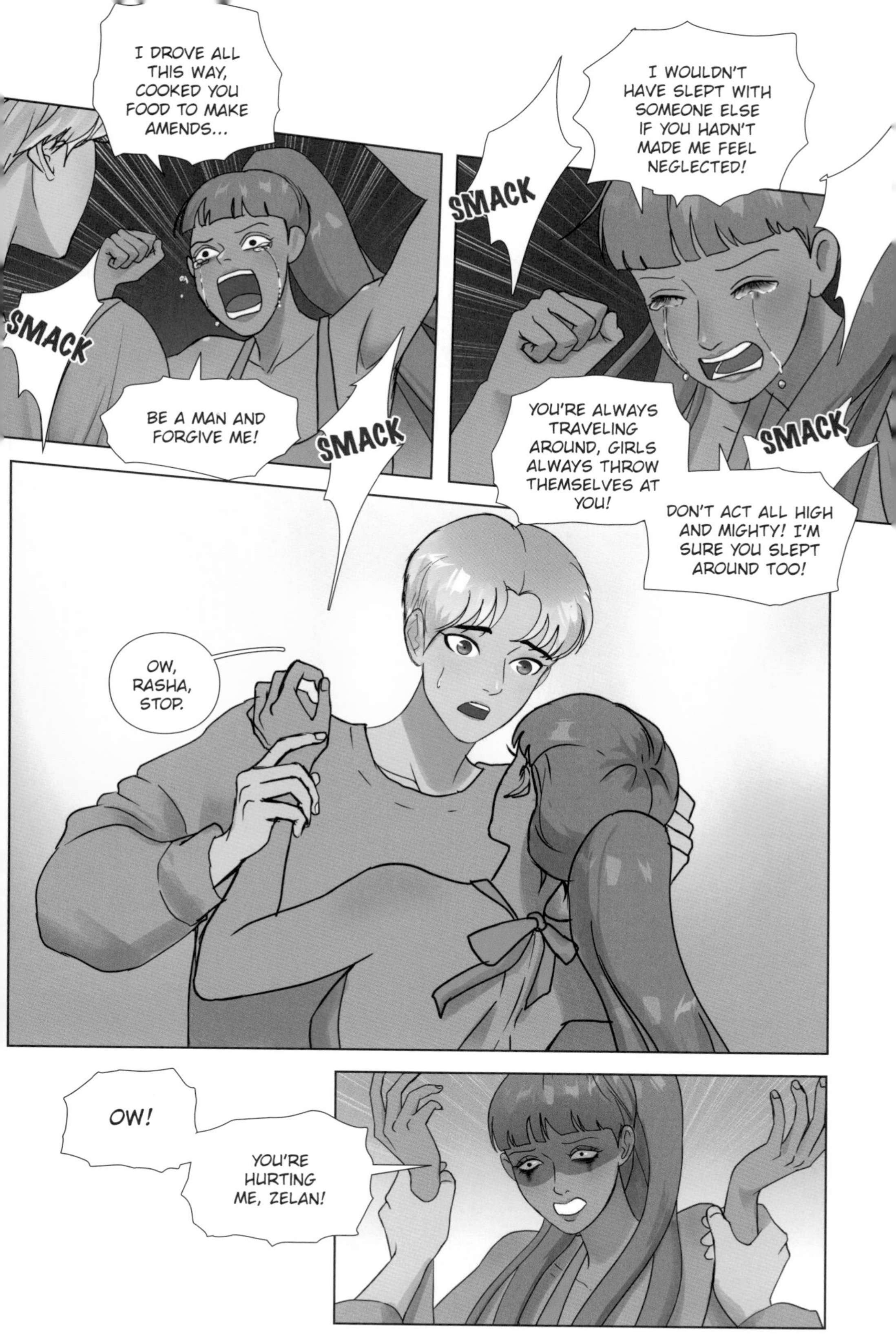

I DROVE ALL THIS WAY, COOKED YOU FOOD TO MAKE AMENDS...
SMACK
BE A MAN AND FORGIVE ME!
SMACK
SMACK
I WOULDN'T HAVE SLEPT WITH SOMEONE ELSE IF YOU HADN'T MADE ME FEEL NEGLECTED!
YOU'RE ALWAYS TRAVELING AROUND, GIRLS ALWAYS THROW THEMSELVES AT YOU!
SMACK
DON'T ACT ALL HIGH AND MIGHTY! I'M SURE YOU SLEPT AROUND TOO!
OW, RASHA, STOP.
OW!
YOU'RE HURTING ME, ZELAN!

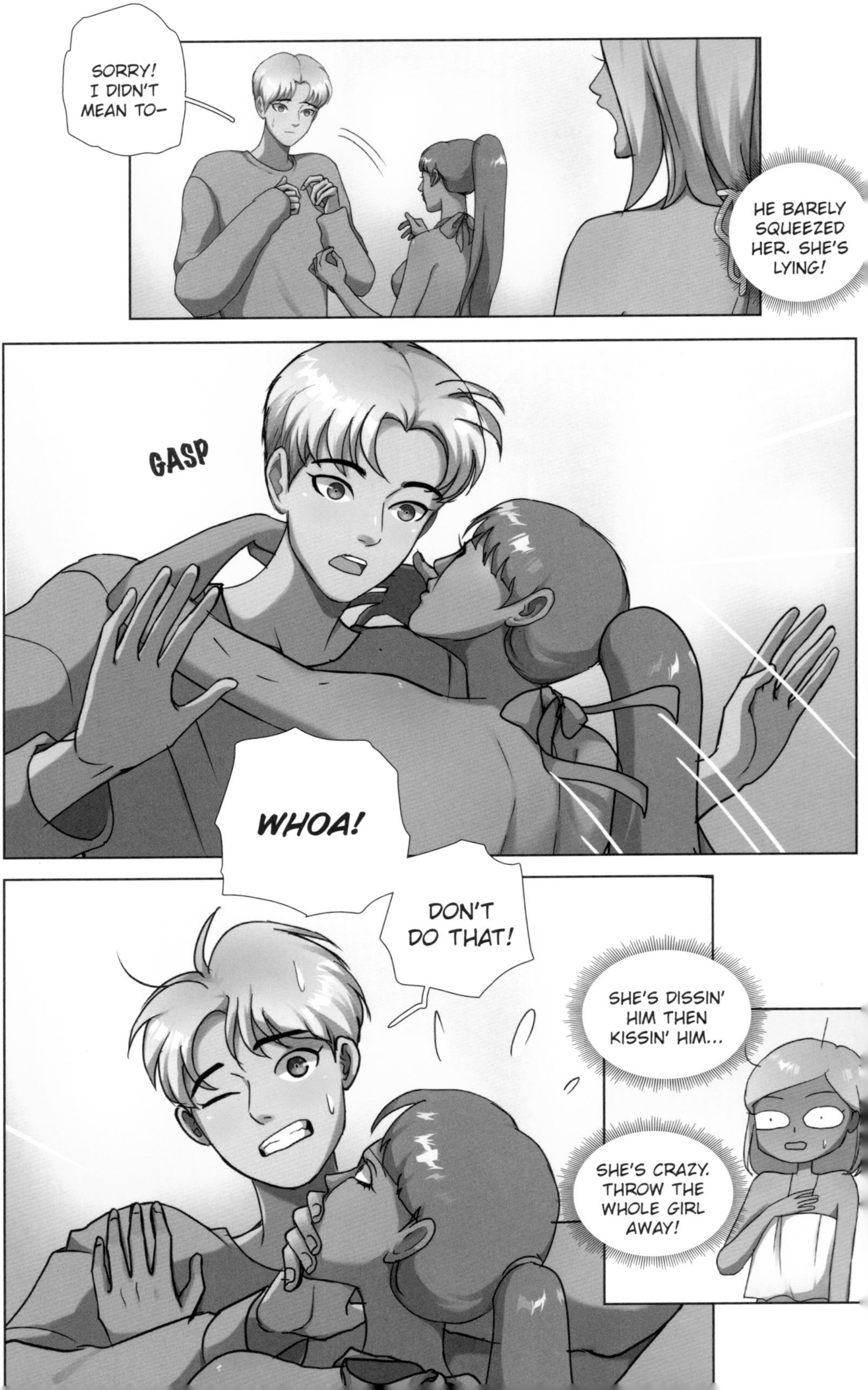
SORRY! I DIDN'T MEAN TO–
HE BARELY SQUEEZED HER. SHE'S LYING!
GASP
WHOA!
DON'T DO THAT!
SHE'S DISSIN' HIM THEN KISSIN' HIM...
SHE'S CRAZY. THROW THE WHOLE GIRL AWAY!

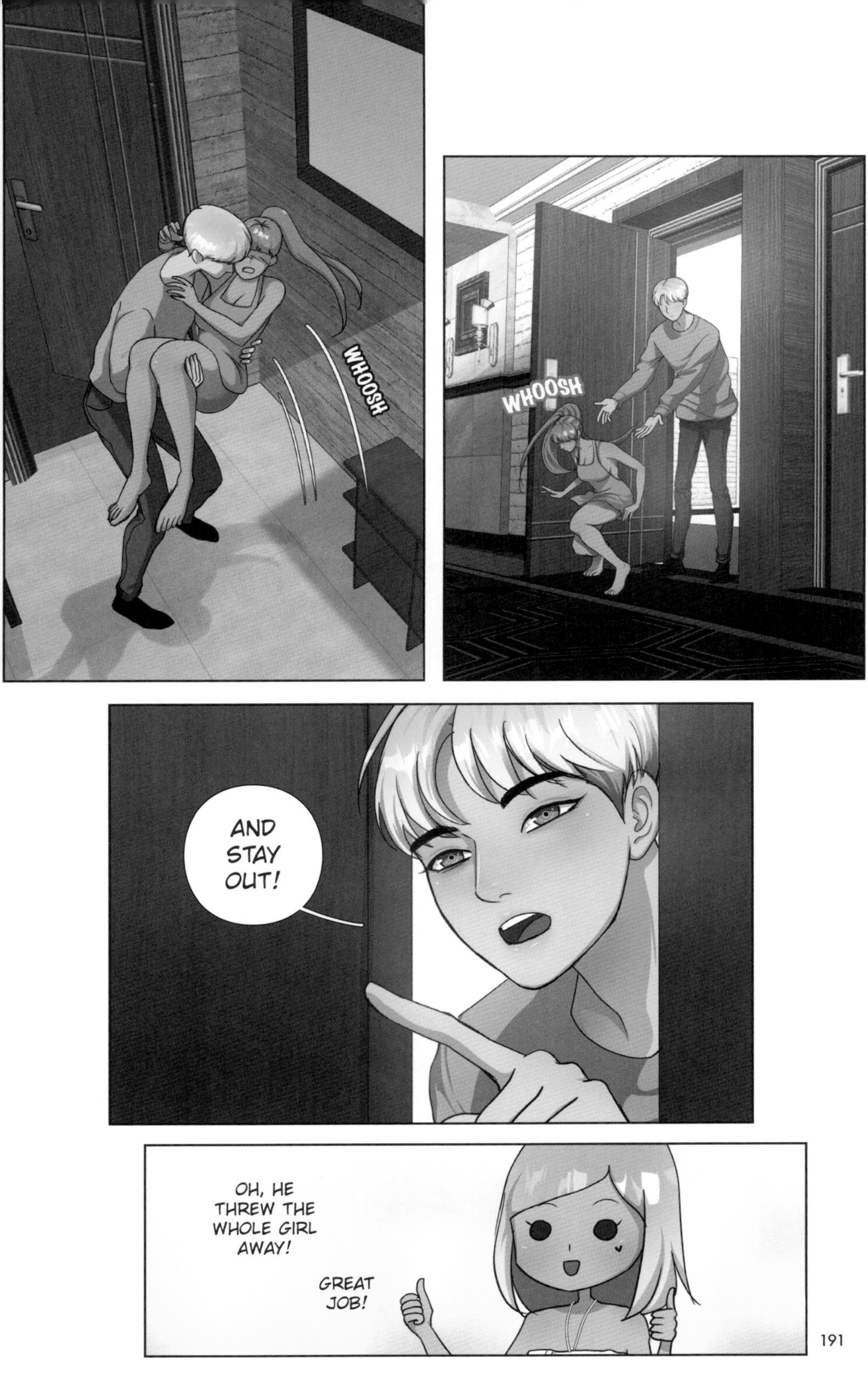
WHOOSH
WHOOSH
AND STAY OUT!
OH, HE THREW THE WHOLE GIRL AWAY!
GREAT JOB!

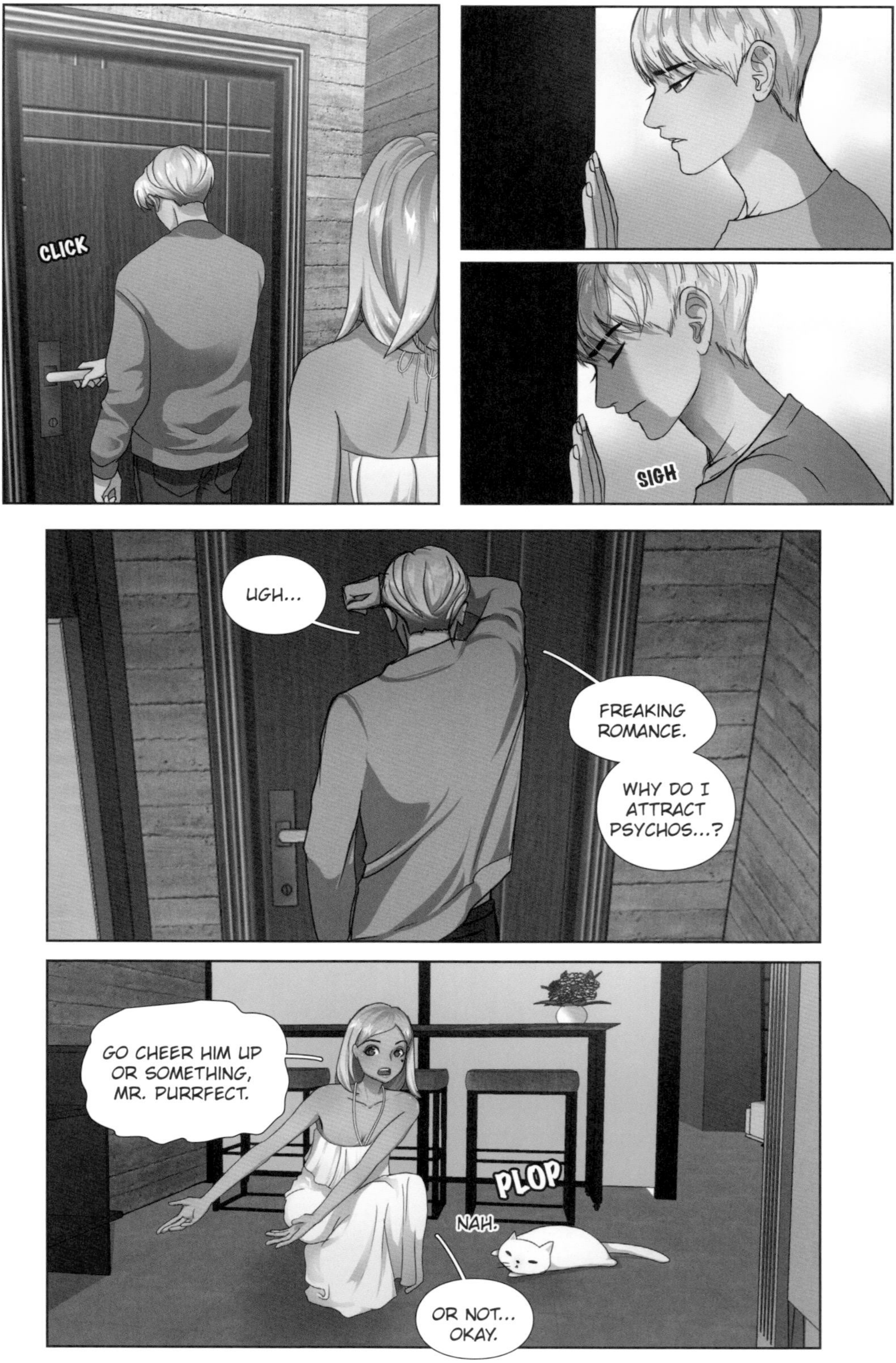
CLICK
SIGH
UGH...
FREAKING ROMANCE.
WHY DO I ATTRACT PSYCHOS...?
GO CHEER HIM UP OR SOMETHING, MR. PURRFECT.
PLOP
NAH.
OR NOT... OKAY.

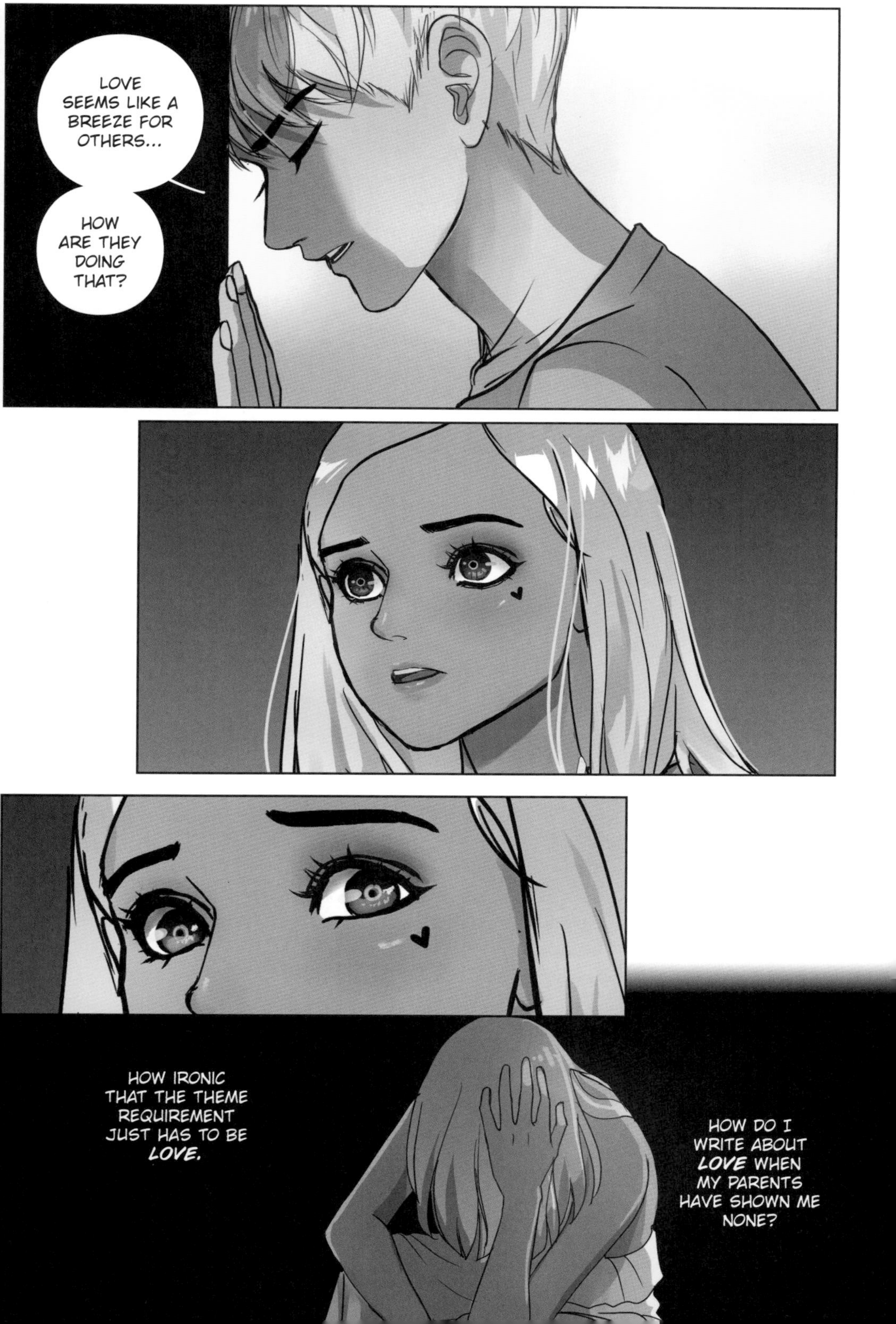
LOVE SEEMS LIKE A BREEZE FOR OTHERS...
HOW ARE THEY DOING THAT?
HOW IRONIC THAT THE THEME REQUIREMENT JUST HAS TO BE ***LOVE.***
HOW DO I WRITE ABOUT ***LOVE*** WHEN MY PARENTS HAVE SHOWN ME NONE?

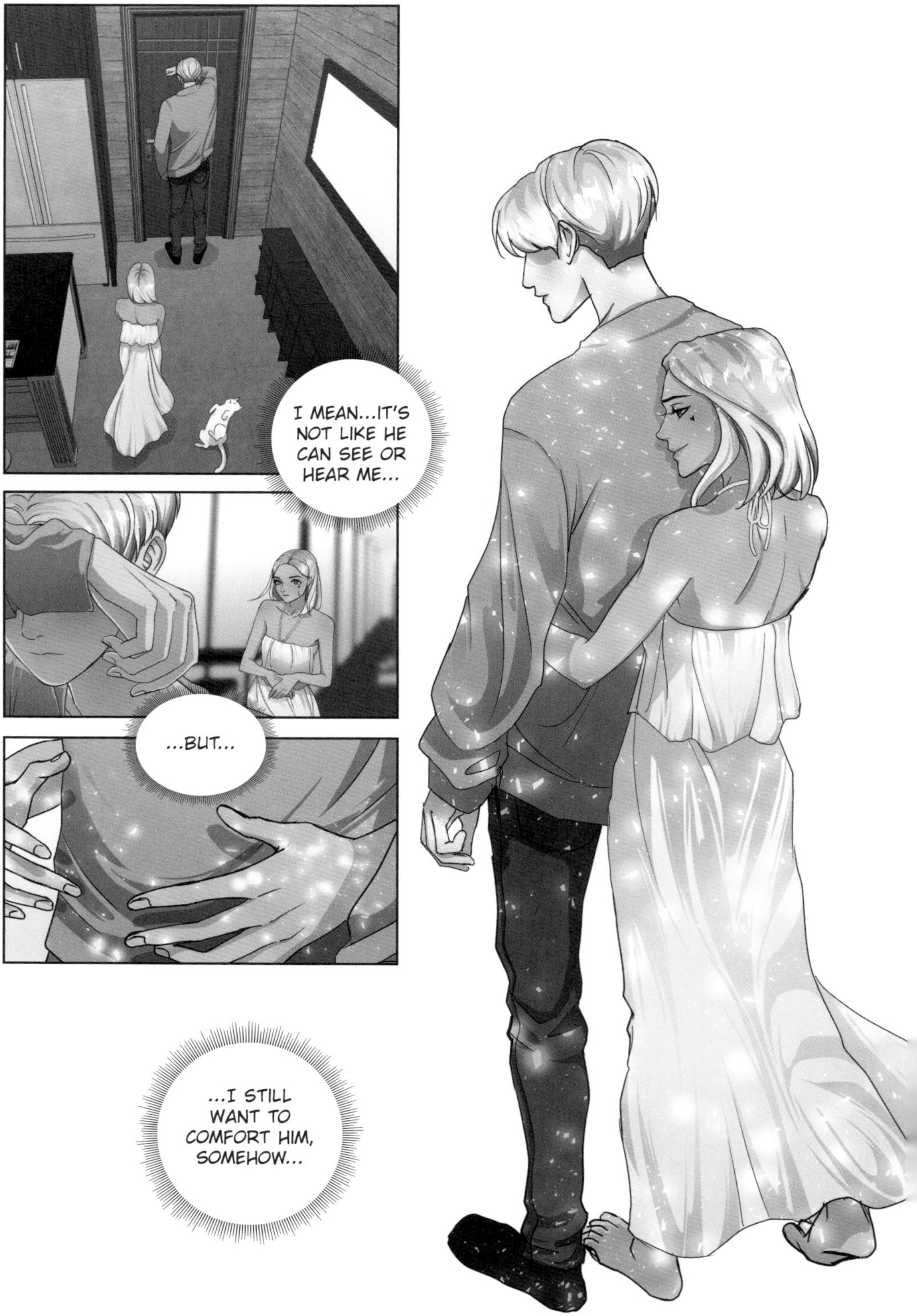
I MEAN...IT'S NOT LIKE HE CAN SEE OR HEAR ME...
...BUT...
...I STILL WANT TO COMFORT HIM, SOMEHOW...

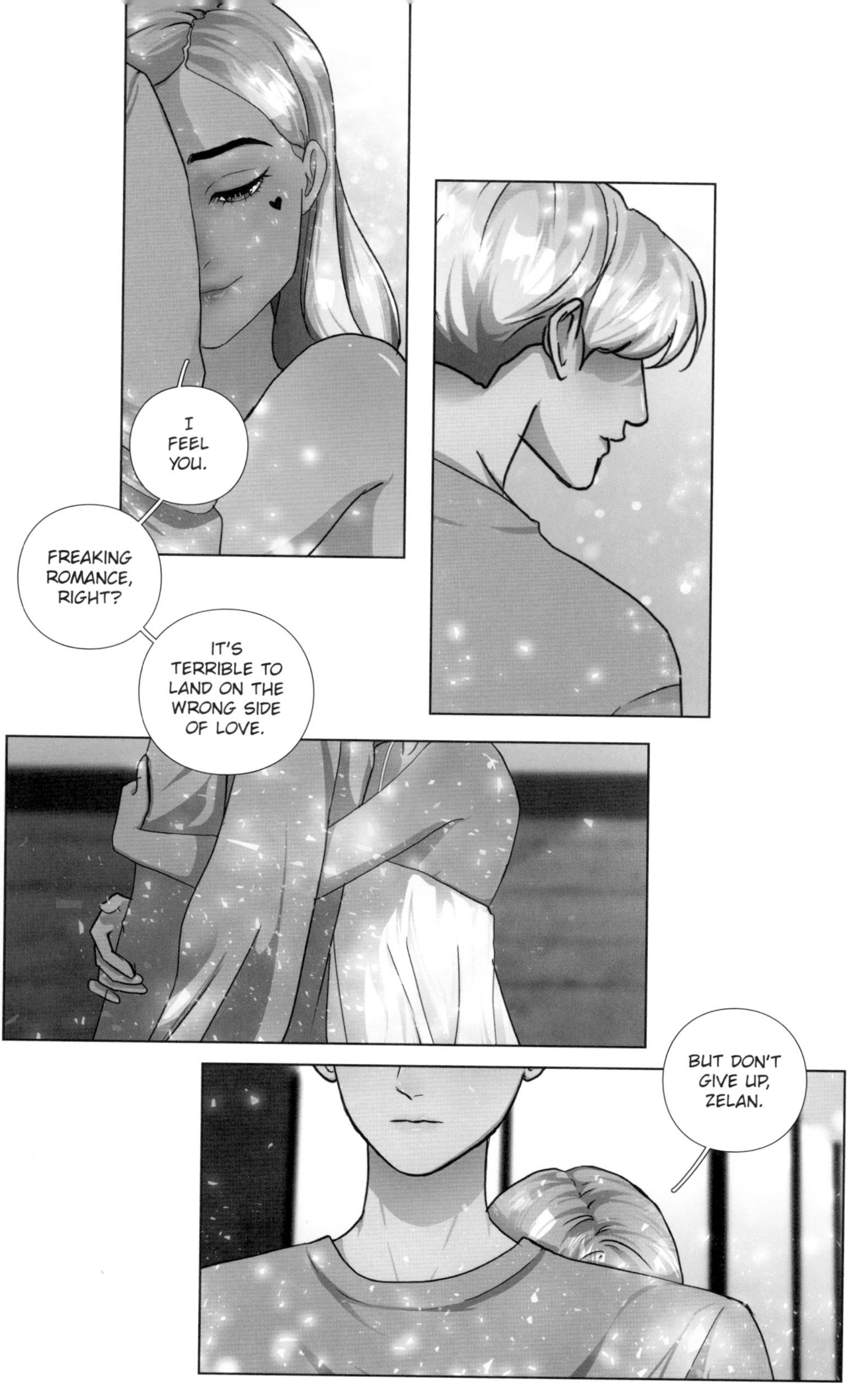
I FEEL YOU.
FREAKING ROMANCE, RIGHT?
IT'S TERRIBLE TO LAND ON THE WRONG SIDE OF LOVE.
BUT DON'T GIVE UP, ZELAN.

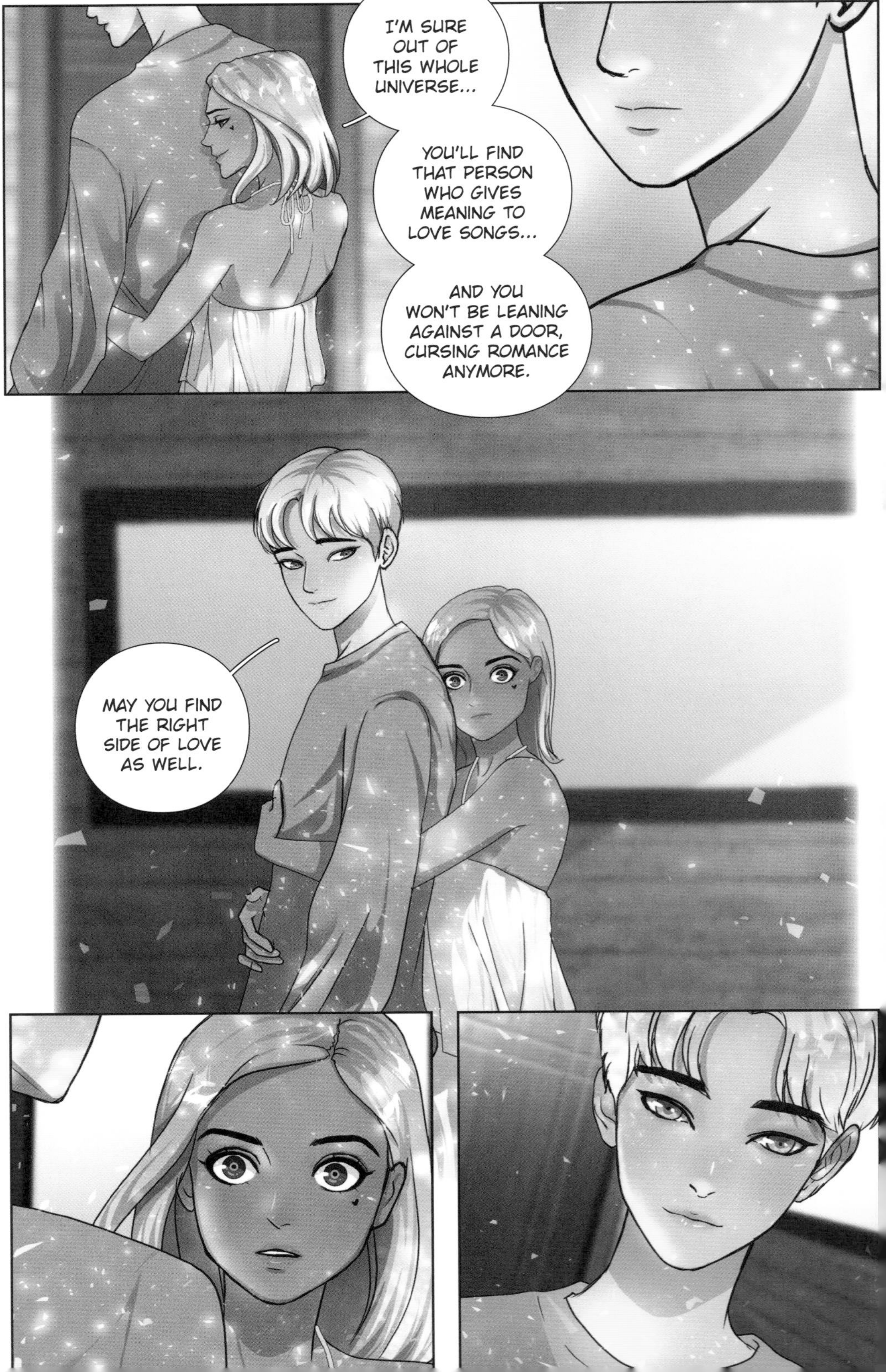
I'M SURE OUT OF THIS WHOLE UNIVERSE...
YOU'LL FIND THAT PERSON WHO GIVES MEANING TO LOVE SONGS...
AND YOU WON'T BE LEANING AGAINST A DOOR, CURSING ROMANCE ANYMORE.
MAY YOU FIND THE RIGHT SIDE OF LOVE AS WELL.

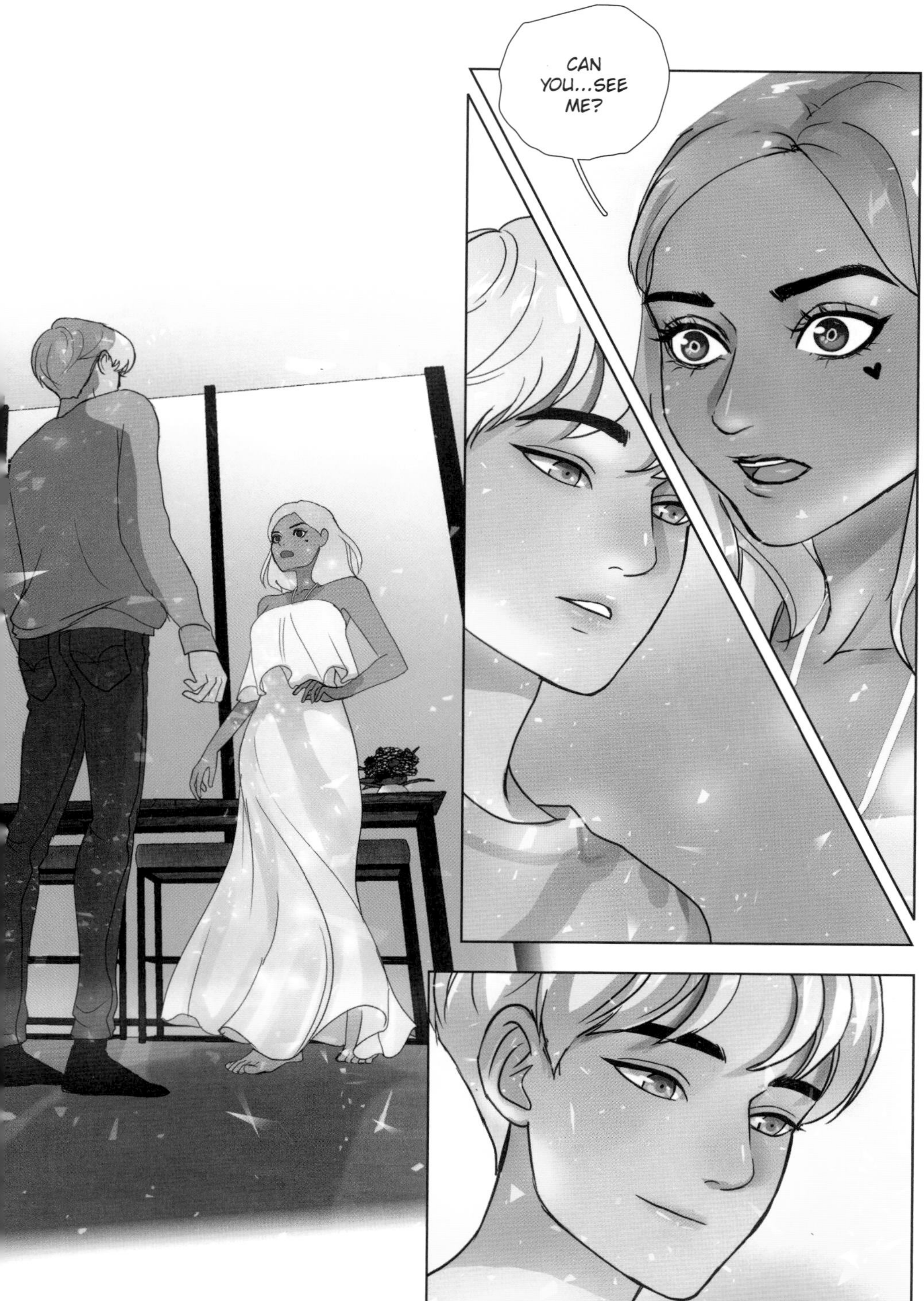
CAN YOU...SEE ME?

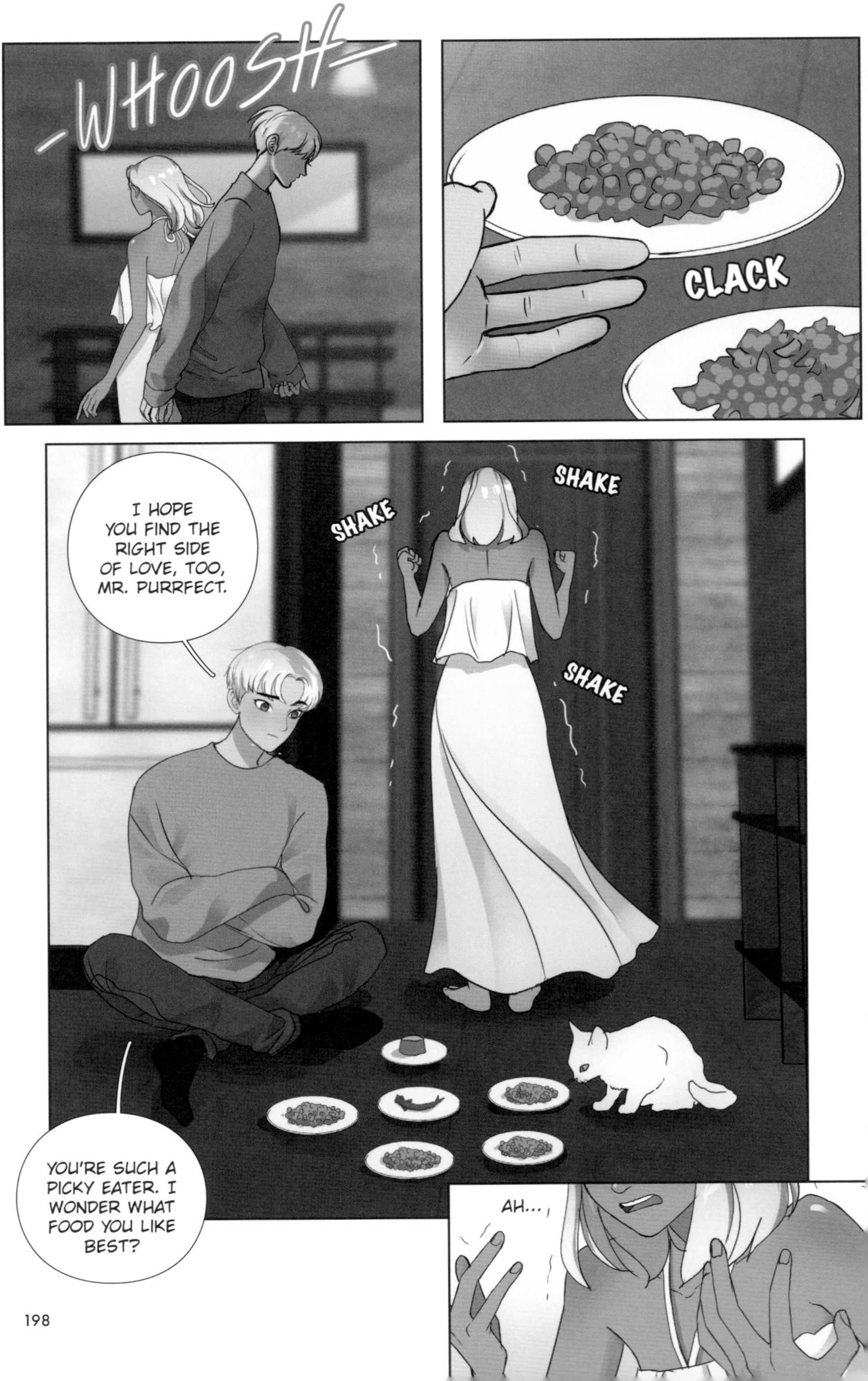
WHOOSH
CLACK
I HOPE YOU FIND THE RIGHT SIDE OF LOVE, TOO, MR. PURRFECT.
SHAKE
SHAKE
SHAKE
YOU'RE SUCH A PICKY EATER. I WONDER WHAT FOOD YOU LIKE BEST?
AH...

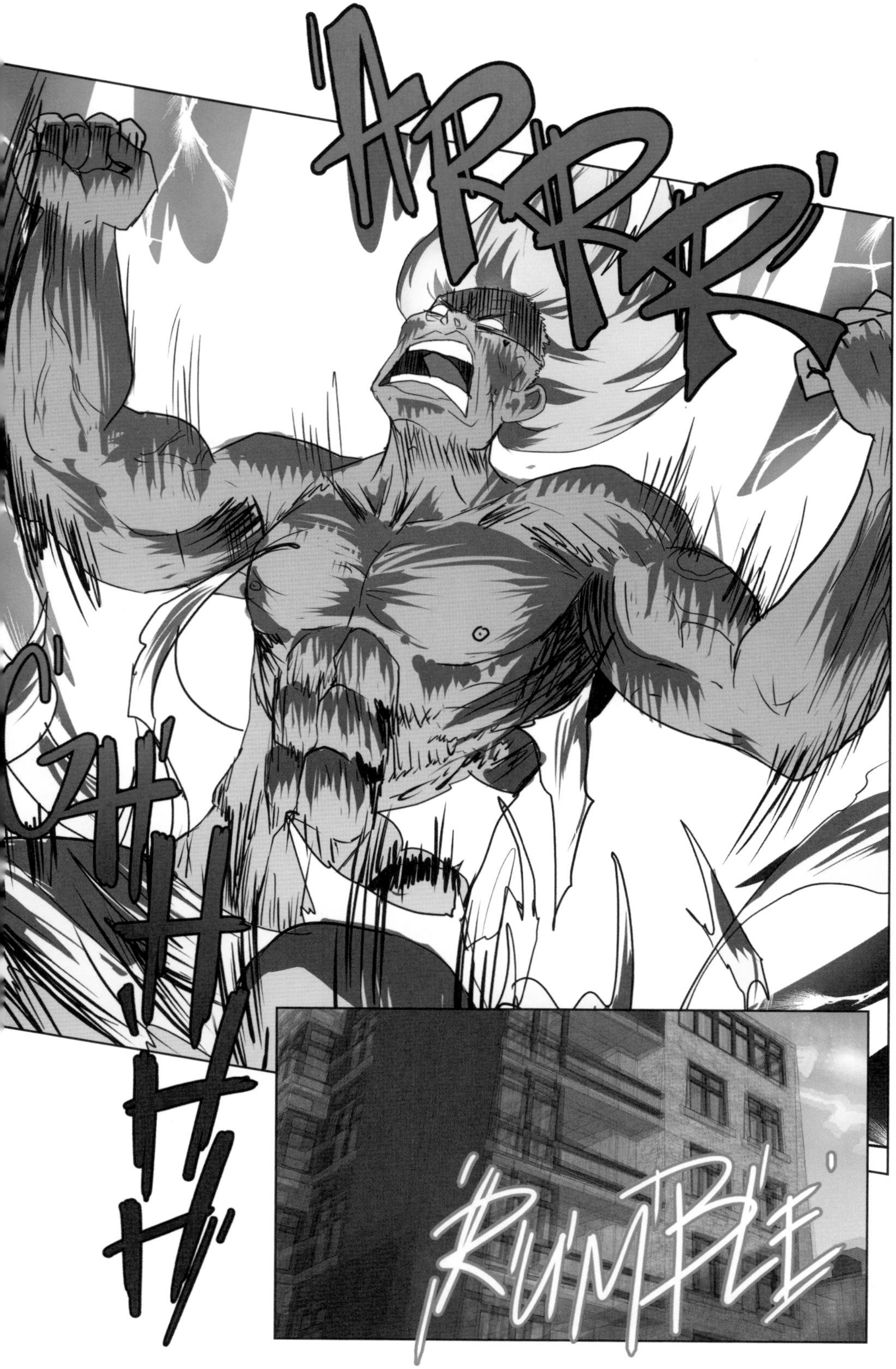
ARRR
RUMBLE

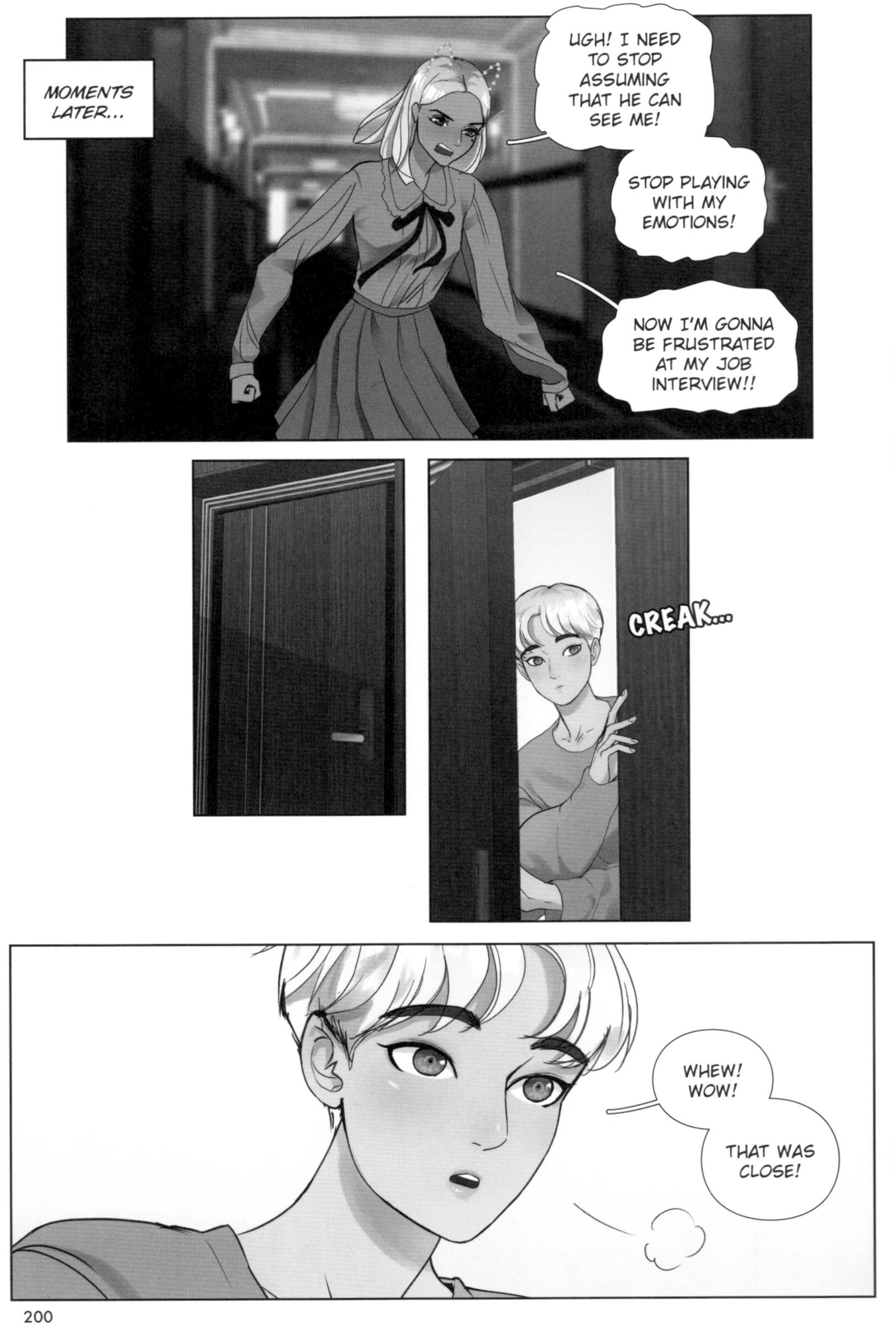
MOMENTS LATER...
UGH! I NEED TO STOP ASSUMING THAT HE CAN SEE ME!
STOP PLAYING WITH MY EMOTIONS!
NOW I'M GONNA BE FRUSTRATED AT MY JOB INTERVIEW!!
CREAK...
WHEW! WOW!
THAT WAS CLOSE!

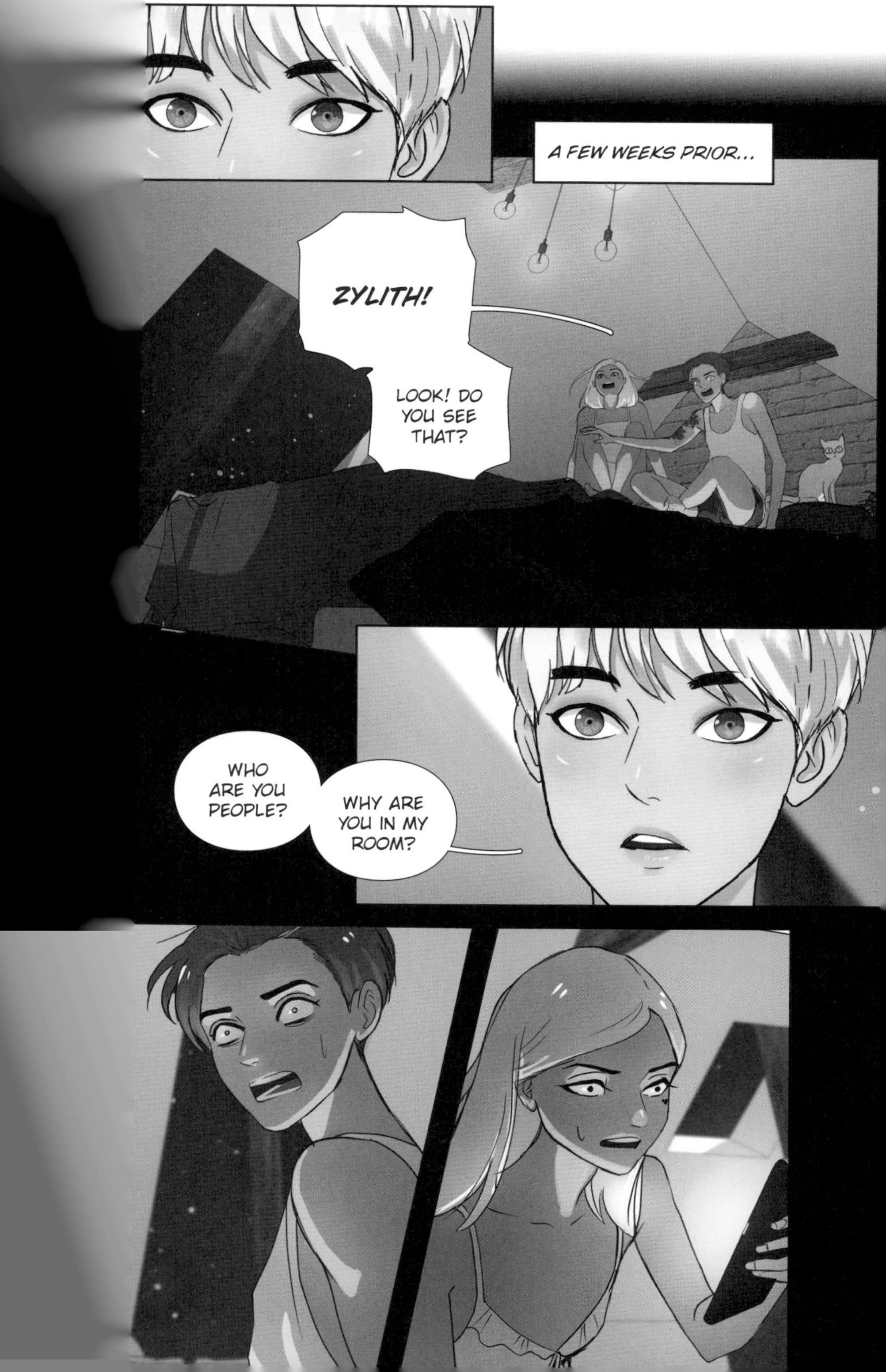
A FEW WEEKS PRIOR...
ZYLITH!
LOOK! DO YOU SEE THAT?
WHO ARE YOU PEOPLE?
WHY ARE YOU IN MY ROOM?

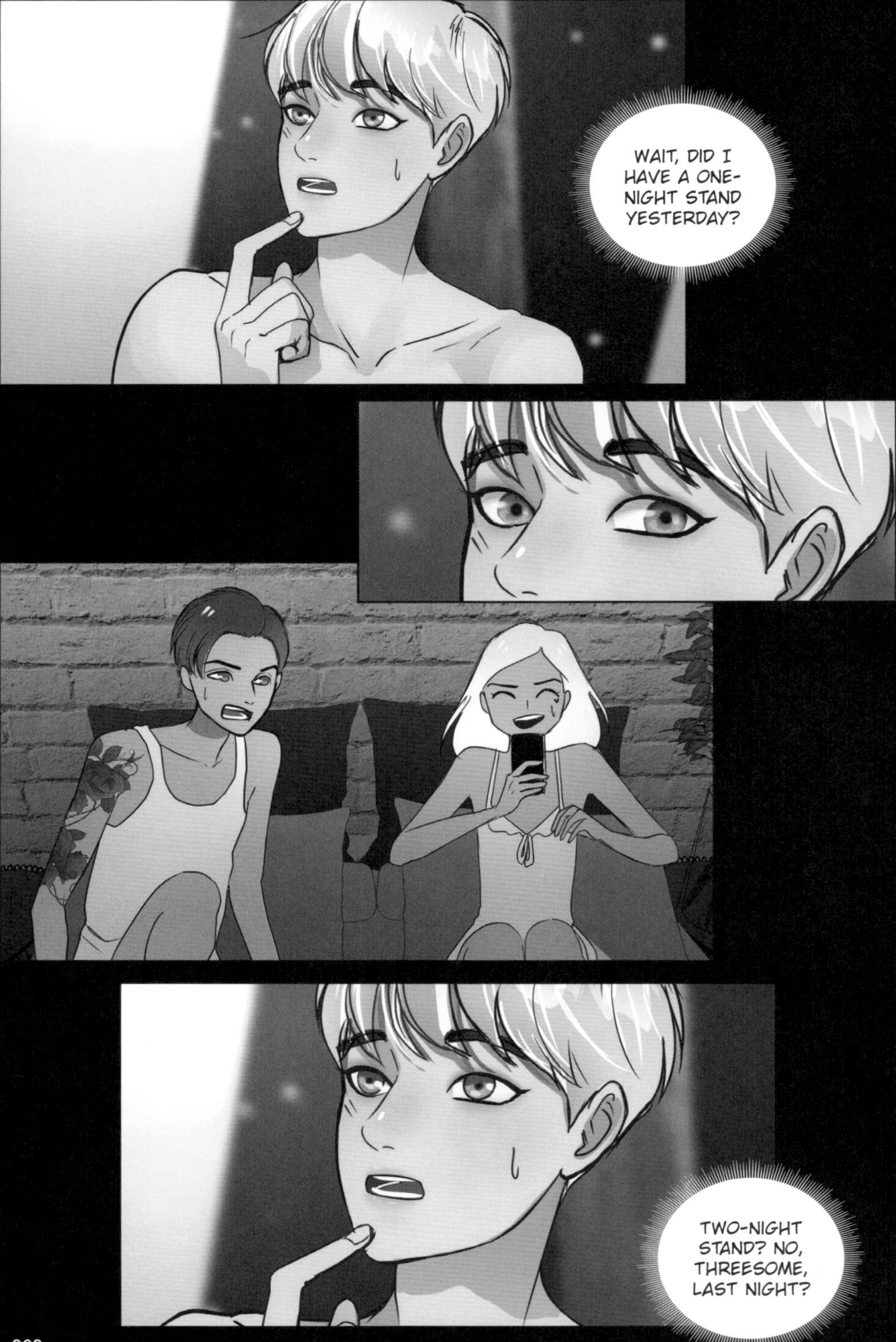
WAIT, DID I HAVE A ONE-NIGHT STAND YESTERDAY?
TWO-NIGHT STAND? NO, THREESOME, LAST NIGHT?

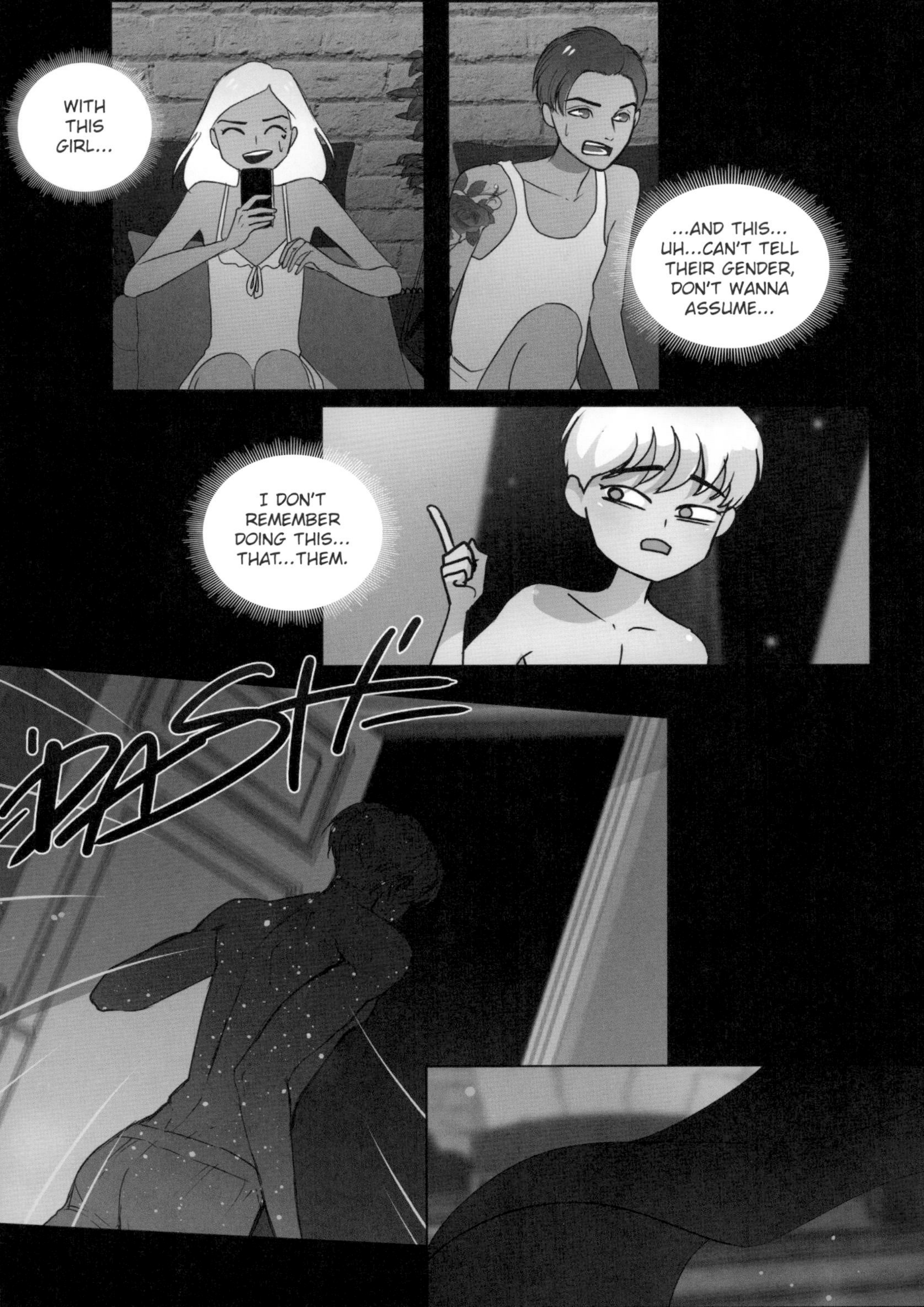
WITH THIS GIRL...
...AND THIS... UH...CAN'T TELL THEIR GENDER, DON'T WANNA ASSUME...
I DON'T REMEMBER DOING THIS... THAT...THEM.
DASH

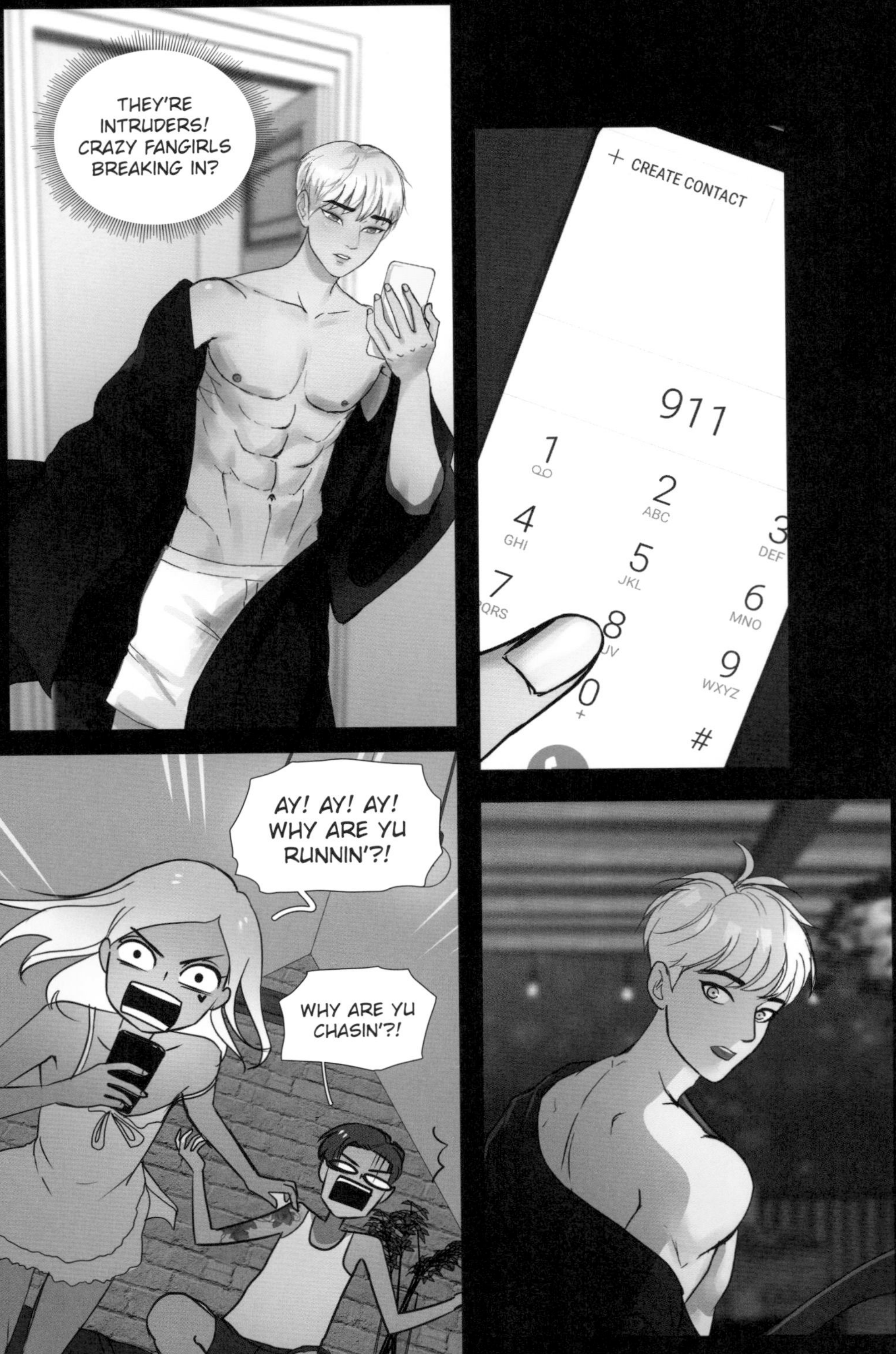
THEY'RE INTRUDERS! CRAZY FANGIRLS BREAKING IN?
+ CREATE CONTACT
911
1
2 ABC
4 GHI
5 JKL
7
6 MNO
9 WXYZ
0 +
#
AY! AY! AY! WHY ARE YU RUNNIN'?!
WHY ARE YU CHASIN'?!

AHAHAHAHAH!
WHAT AM I DOING LAUGHING WITH THE INTRUDERS?
THIS IS HOW PEOPLE DIE IN HORROR MOVIES!
NINE-ONE-ONE, WHAT IS YOUR EMERGENCY?
WAIT!

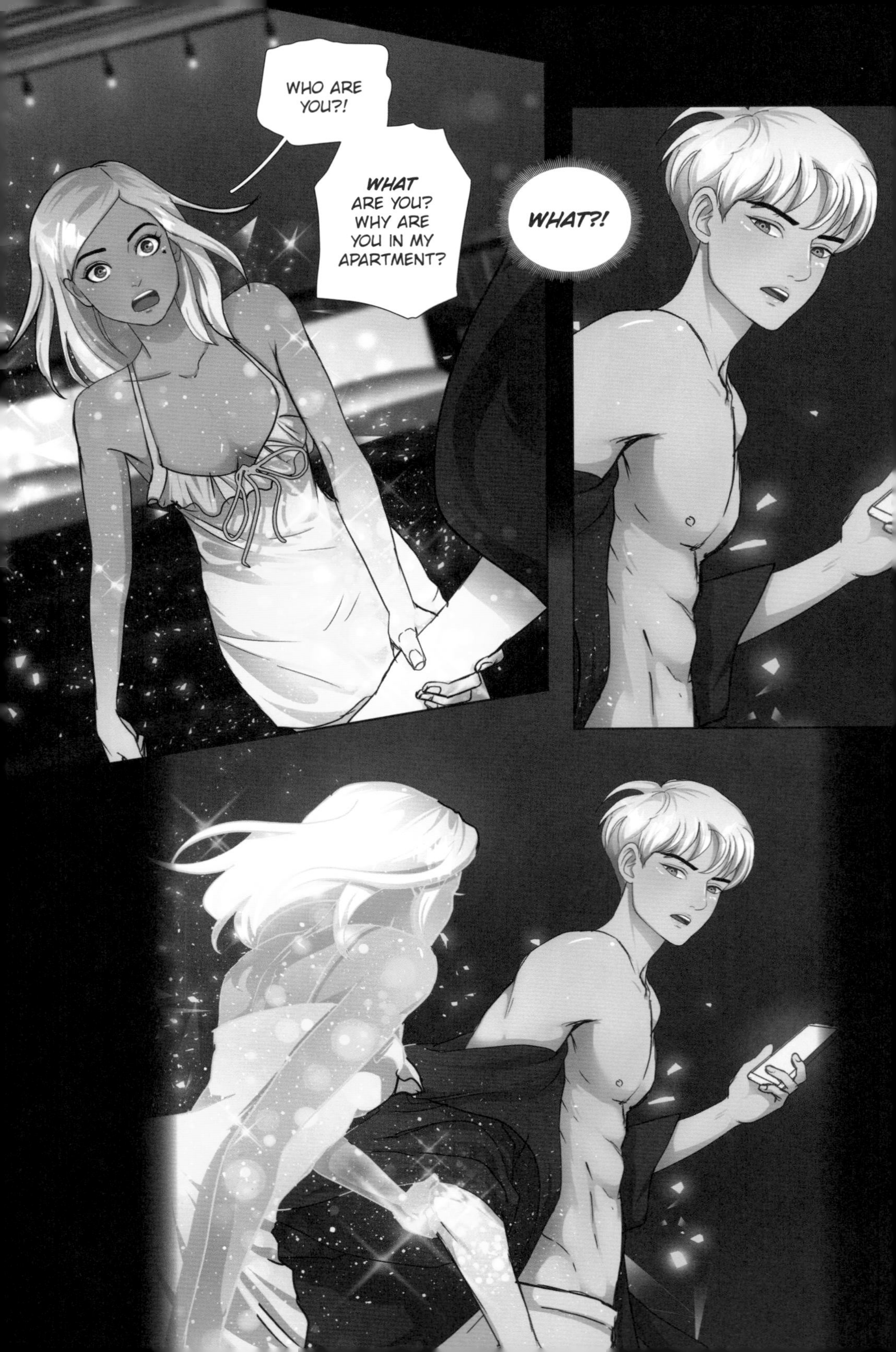
WHO ARE YOU?!
WHAT ARE YOU? WHY ARE YOU IN MY APARTMENT?
WHAT?!

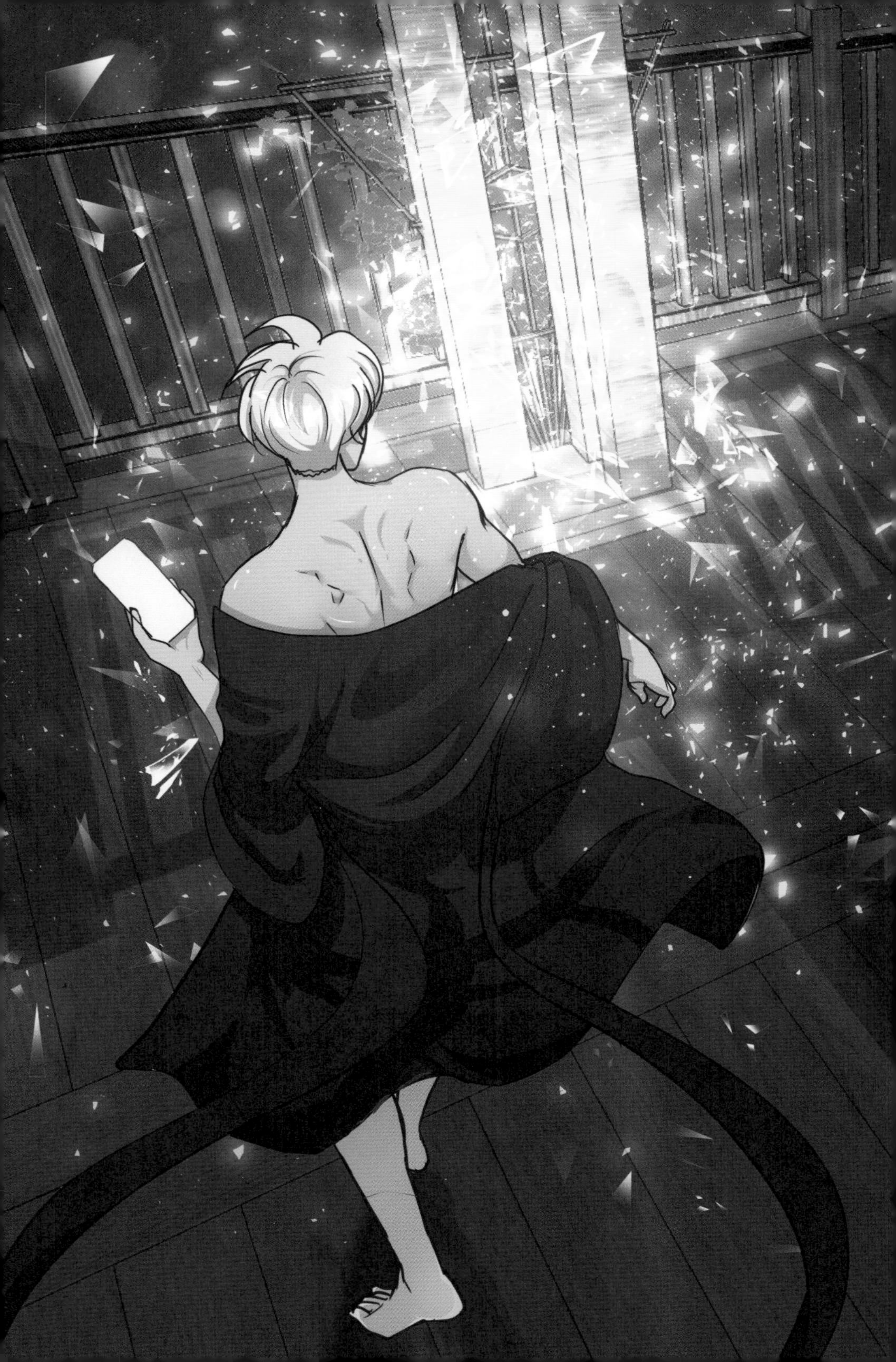

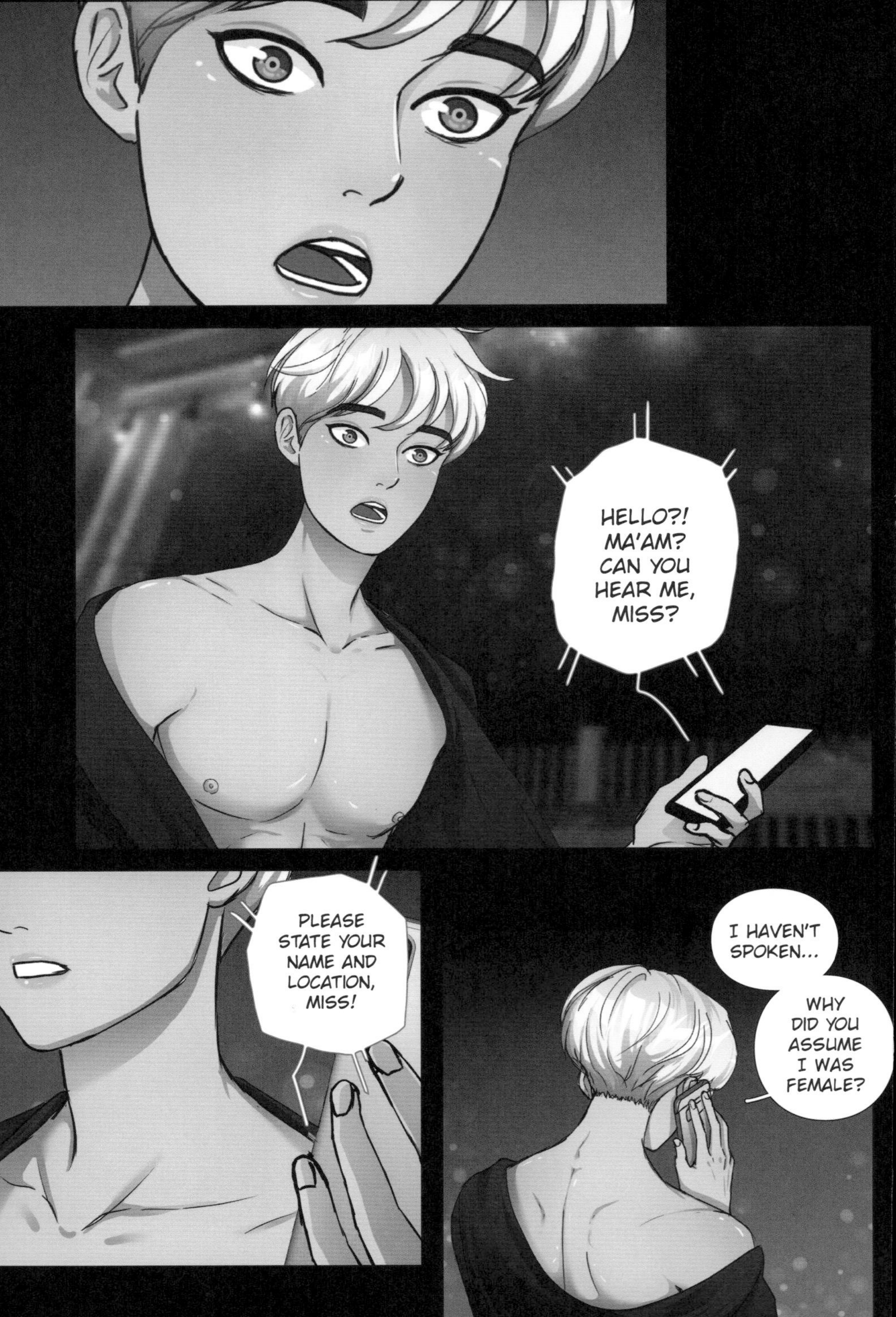
HELLO?! MA'AM? CAN YOU HEAR ME, MISS?
PLEASE STATE YOUR NAME AND LOCATION, MISS!
I HAVEN'T SPOKEN...
WHY DID YOU ASSUME I WAS FEMALE?

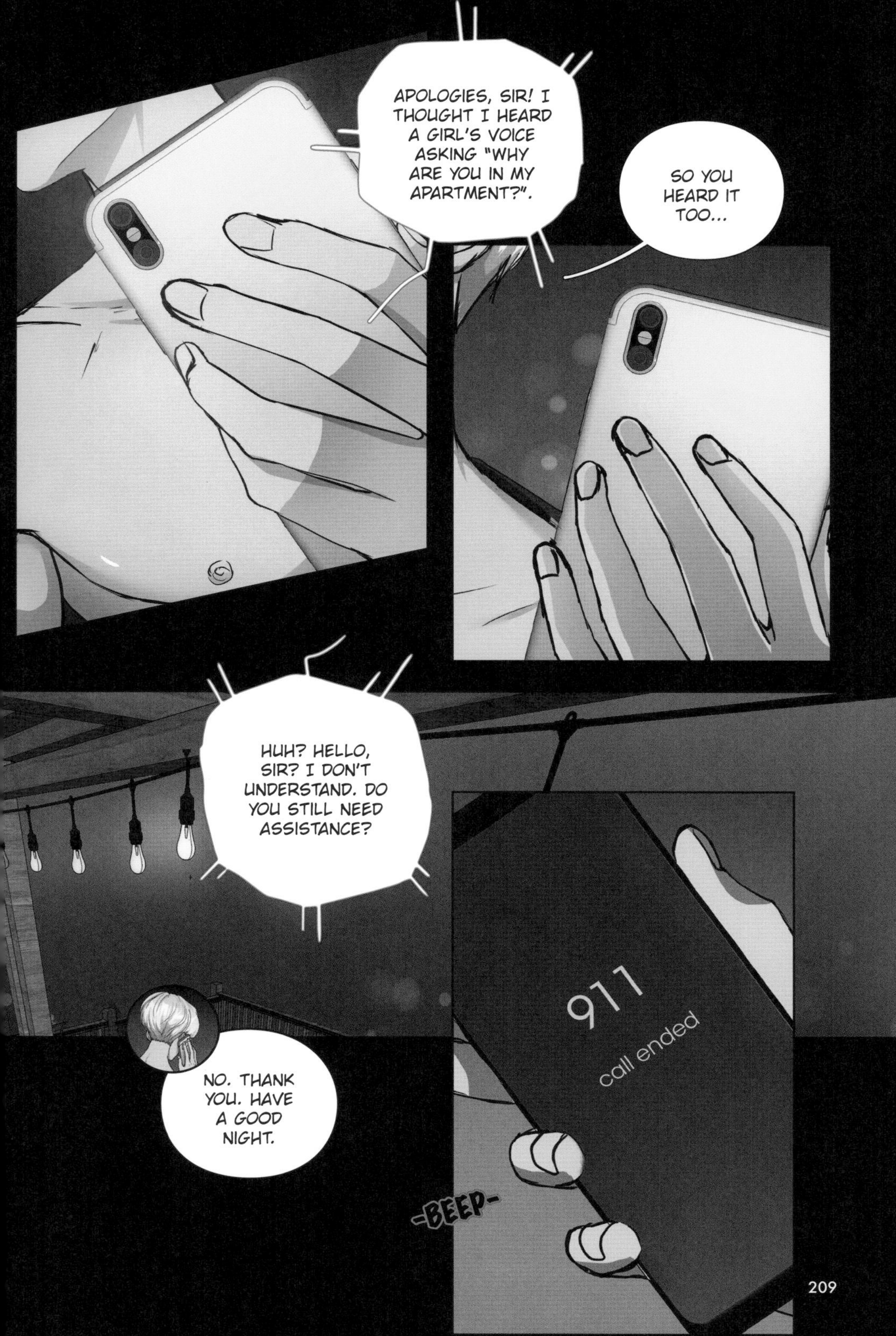
APOLOGIES, SIR! I THOUGHT I HEARD A GIRL'S VOICE ASKING "WHY ARE YOU IN MY APARTMENT?".
SO YOU HEARD IT TOO...
HUH? HELLO, SIR? I DON'T UNDERSTAND. DO YOU STILL NEED ASSISTANCE?
NO. THANK YOU. HAVE A GOOD NIGHT.
911
call ended
-BEEP-

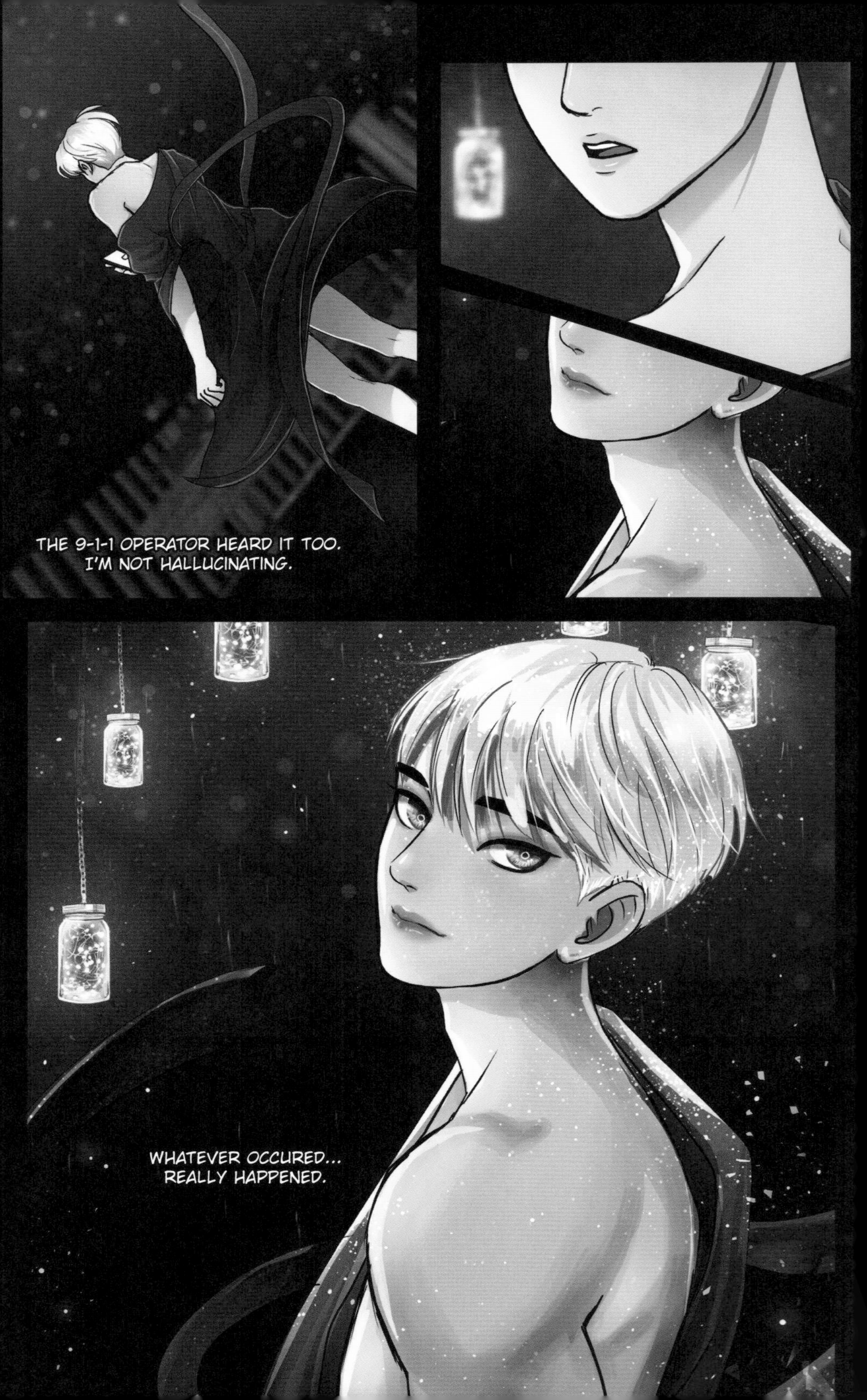
THE 9-1-1 OPERATOR HEARD IT TOO. I'M NOT HALLUCINATING.
WHATEVER OCCURED... REALLY HAPPENED.

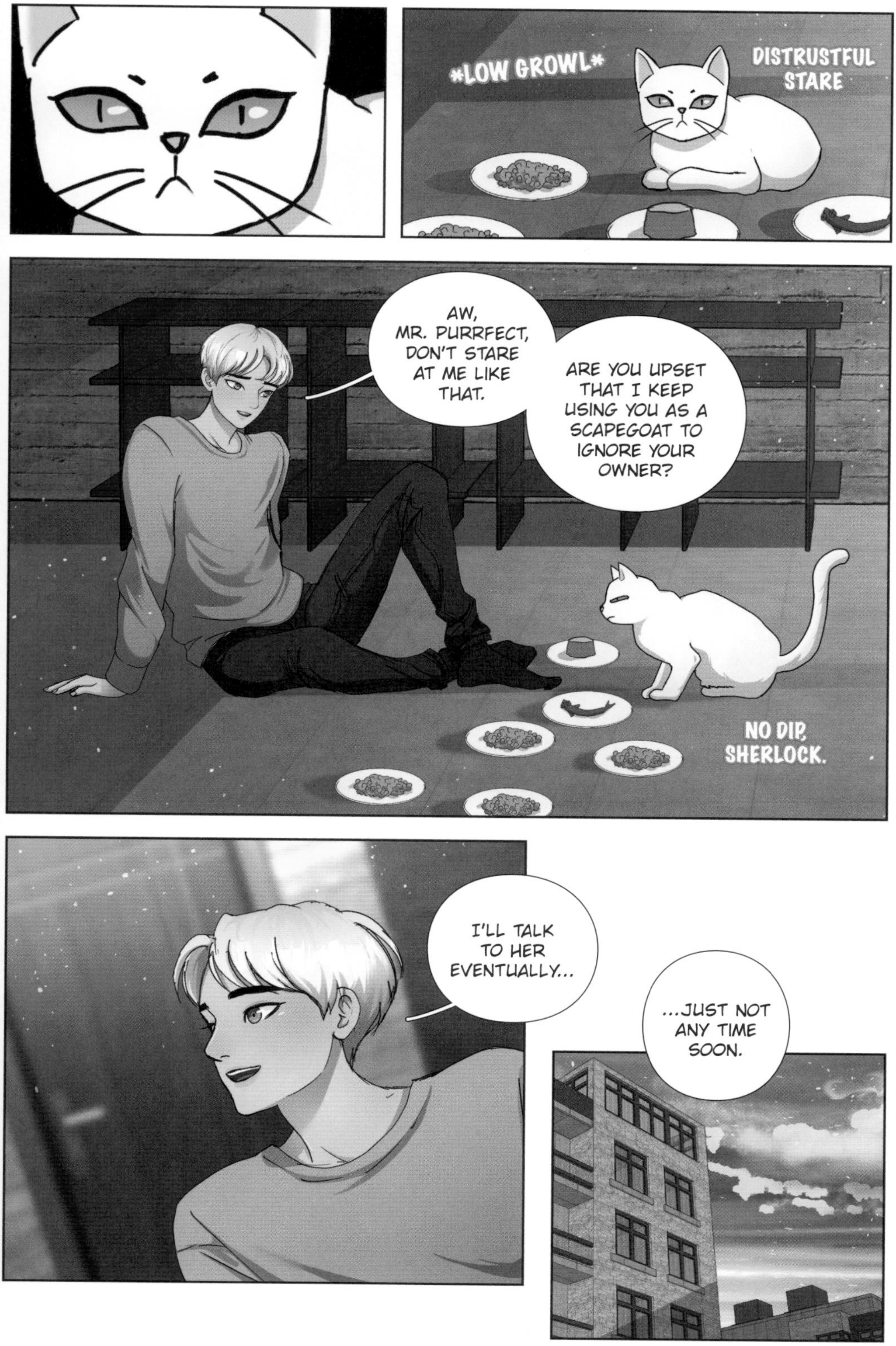
LOW GROWL
DISTRUSTFUL STARE
AW, MR. PURRFECT, DON'T STARE AT ME LIKE THAT.
ARE YOU UPSET THAT I KEEP USING YOU AS A SCAPEGOAT TO IGNORE YOUR OWNER?
NO DIP, SHERLOCK.
I'LL TALK TO HER EVENTUALLY...
...JUST NOT ANY TIME SOON.

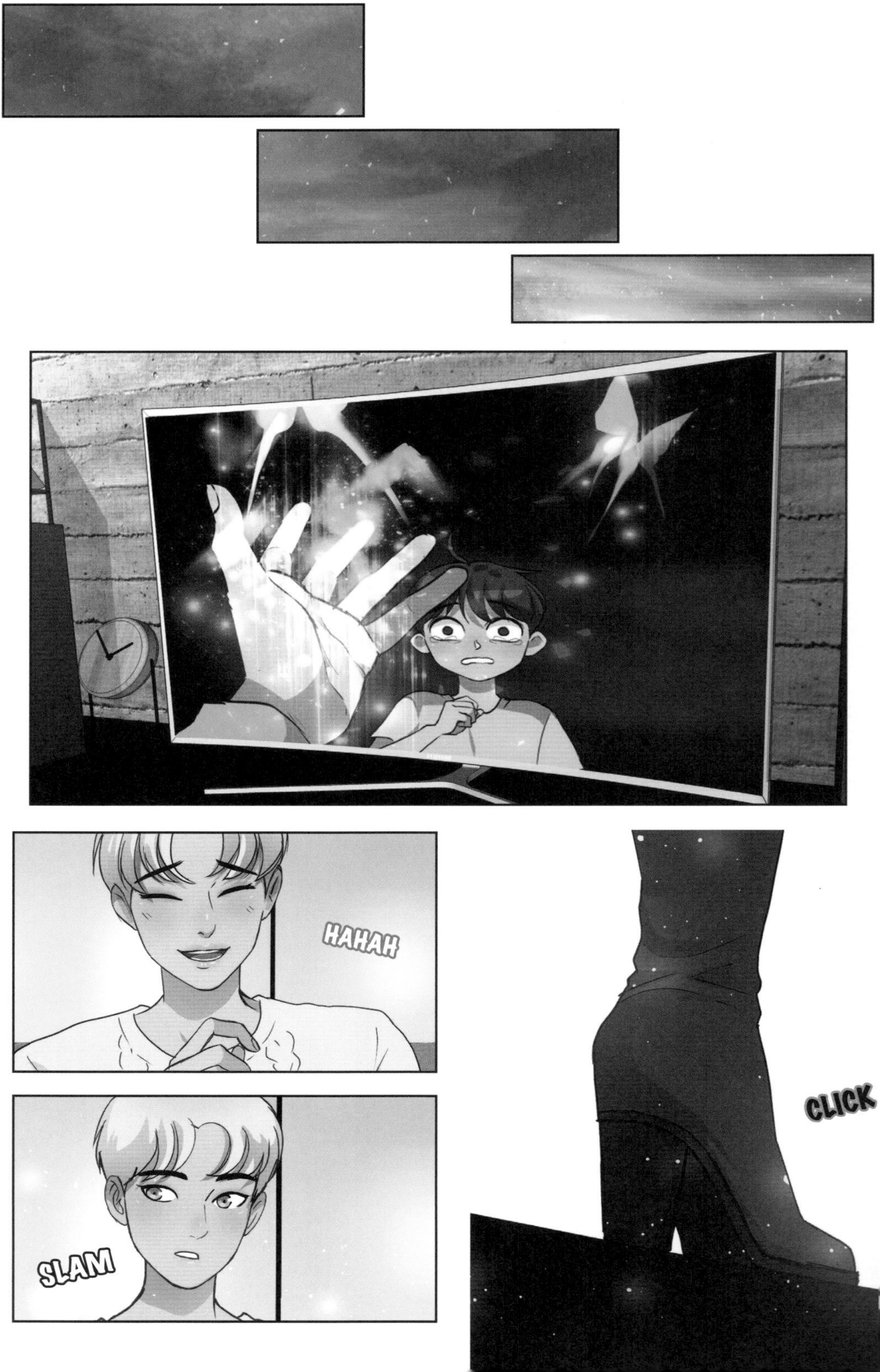
HAHAH
SLAM
CLICK

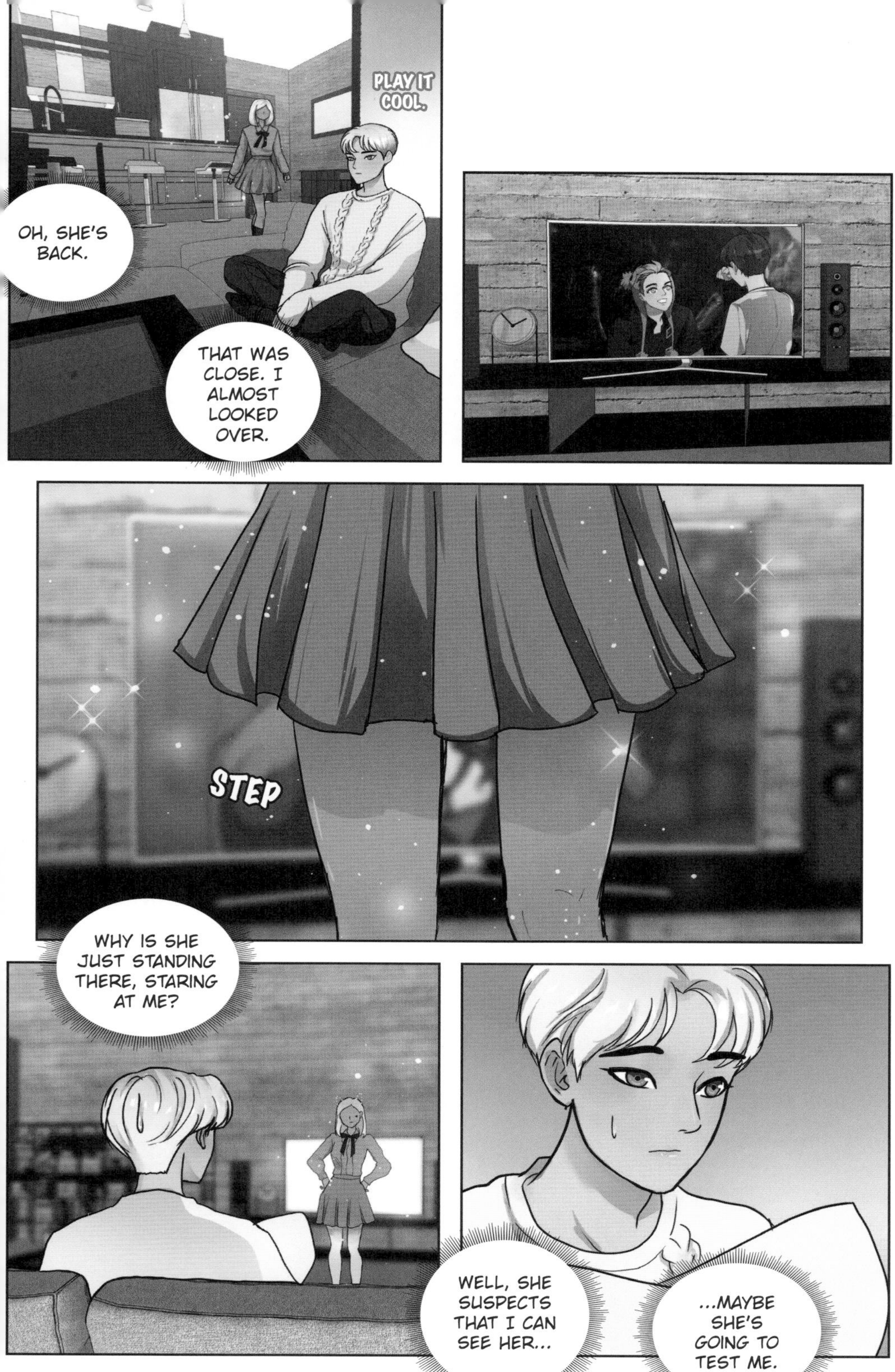
PLAY IT COOL.
OH, SHE'S BACK.
THAT WAS CLOSE. I ALMOST LOOKED OVER.
STEP
WHY IS SHE JUST STANDING THERE, STARING AT ME?
WELL, SHE SUSPECTS THAT I CAN SEE HER...
...MAYBE SHE'S GOING TO TEST ME.

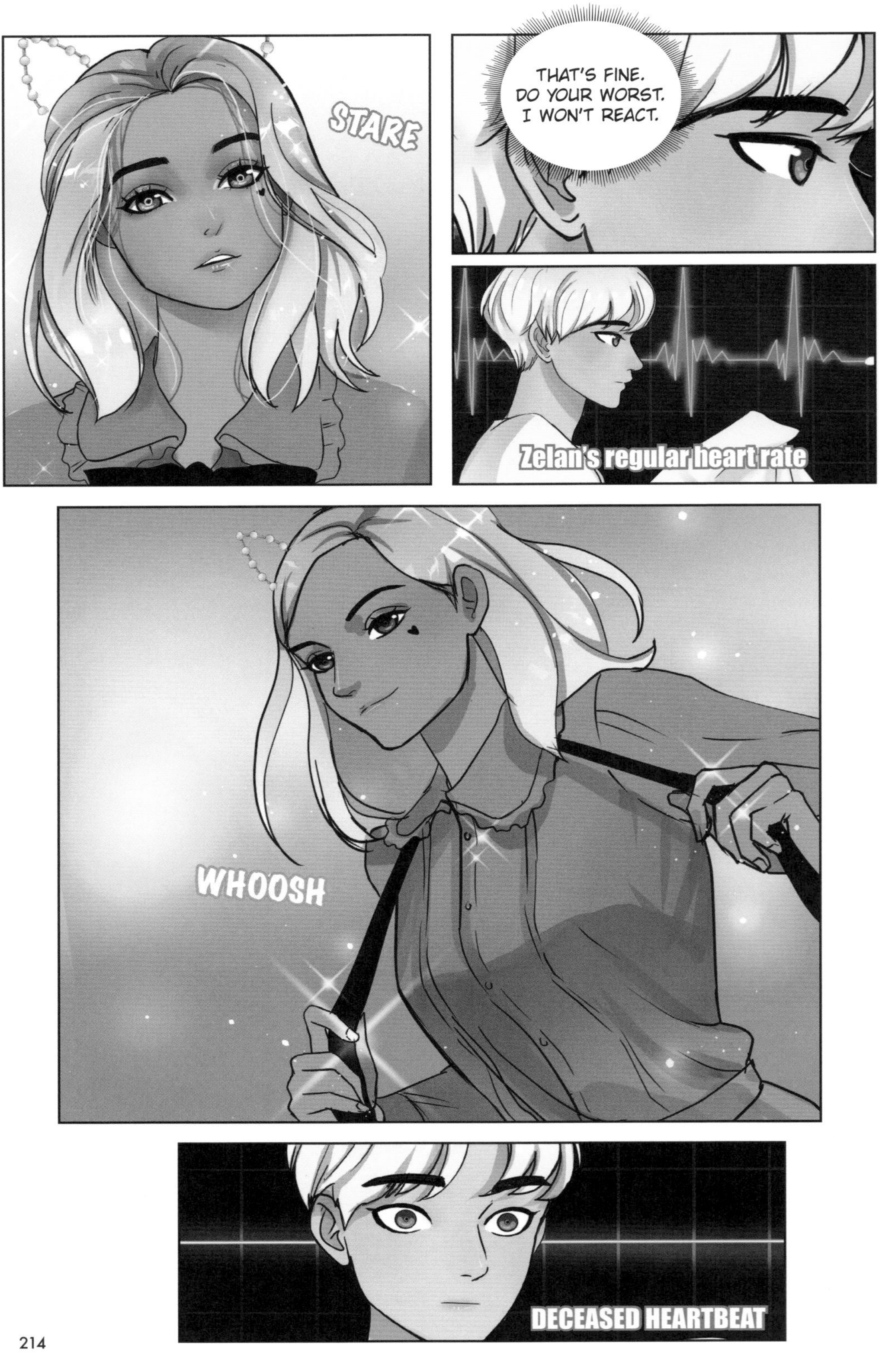
STARE
THAT'S FINE. DO YOUR WORST. I WON'T REACT.
Zelan's regular heart rate
WHOOSH
DECEASED HEARTBEAT

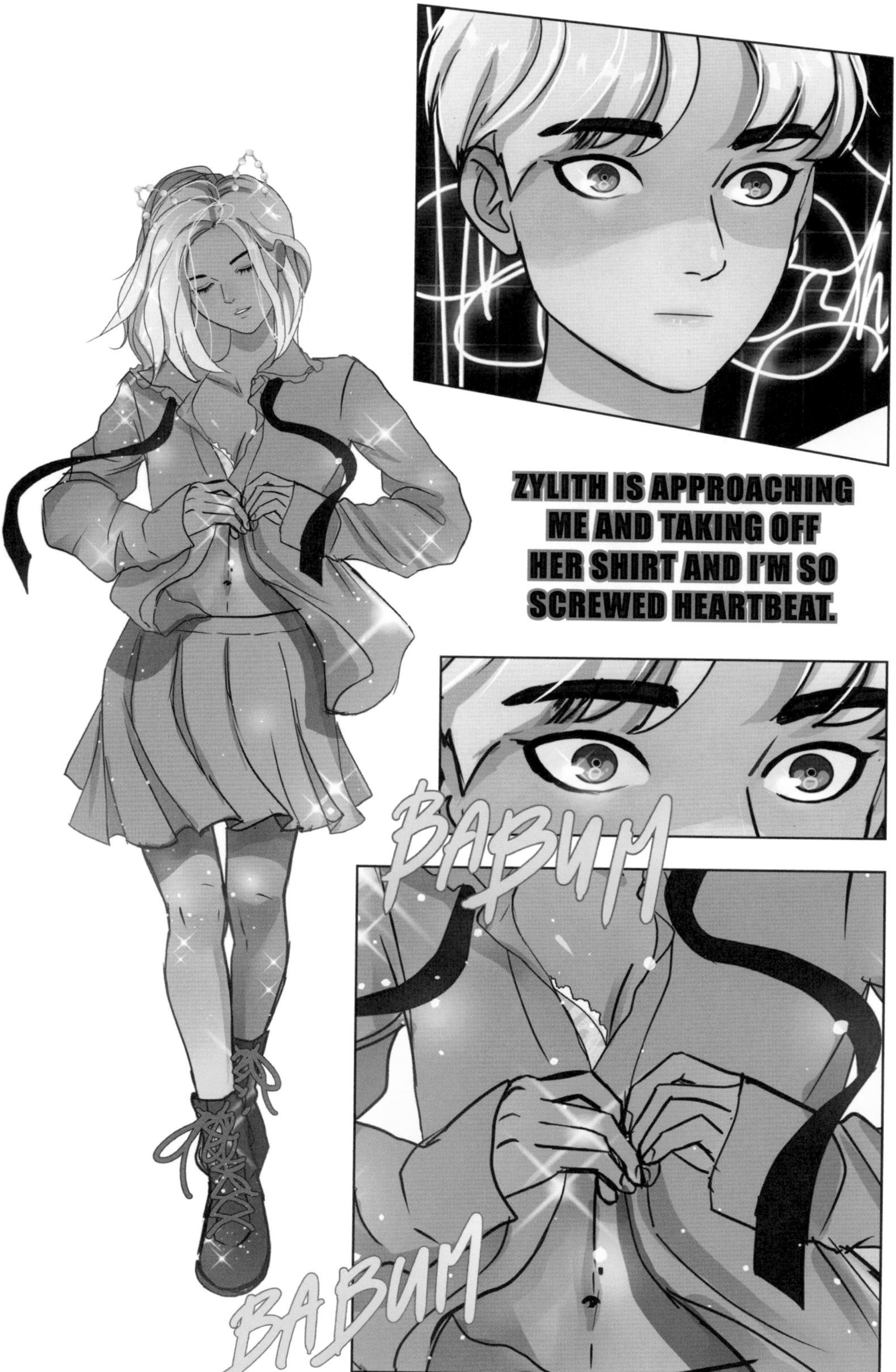
ZYLITH IS APPROACHING ME AND TAKING OFF HER SHIRT AND I'M SO SCREWED HEARTBEAT.
BABUM
BABUM

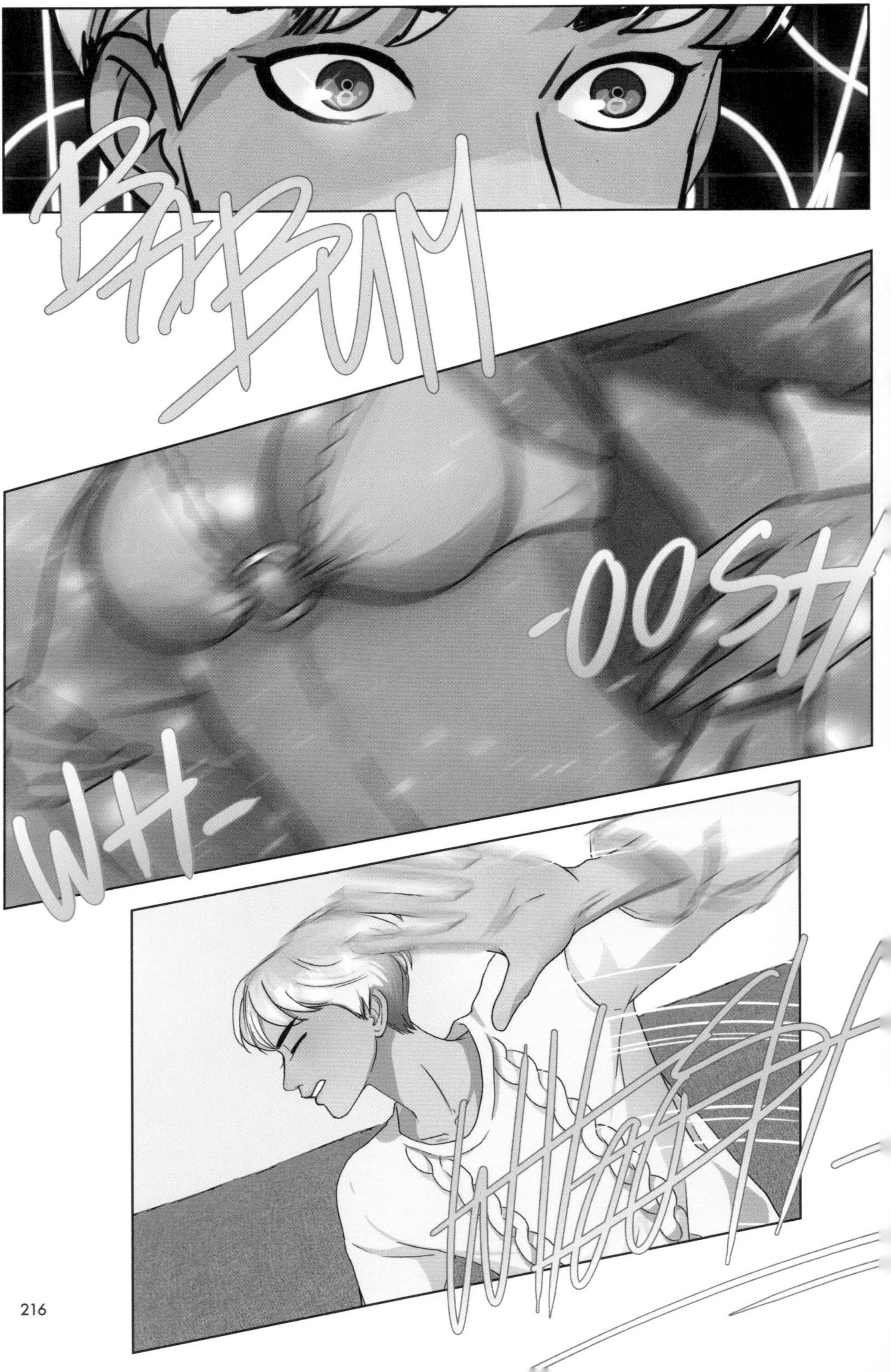
BA-BUM
-OOSH
WH-
WHOOSH-

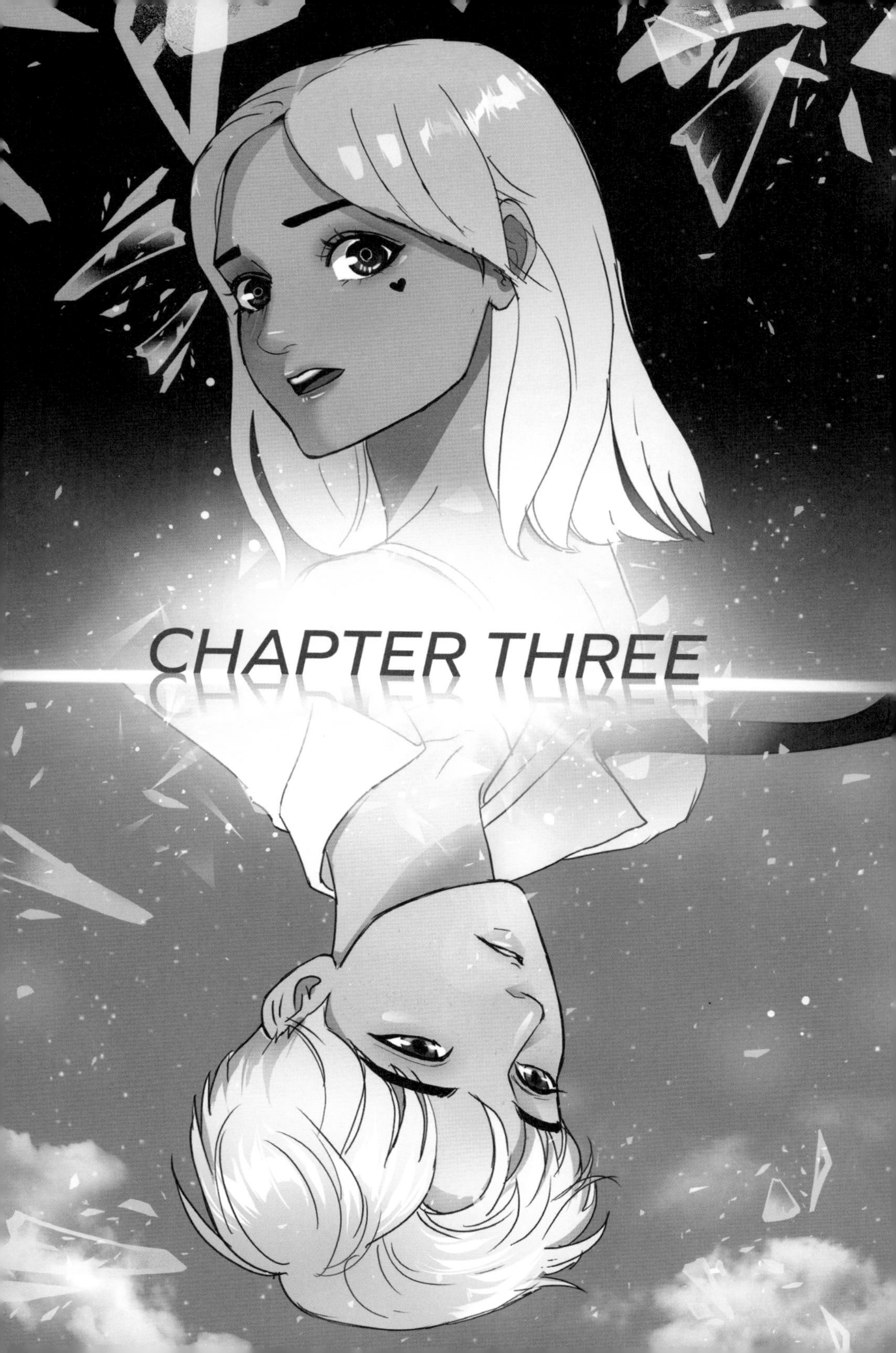
CHAPTER THREE

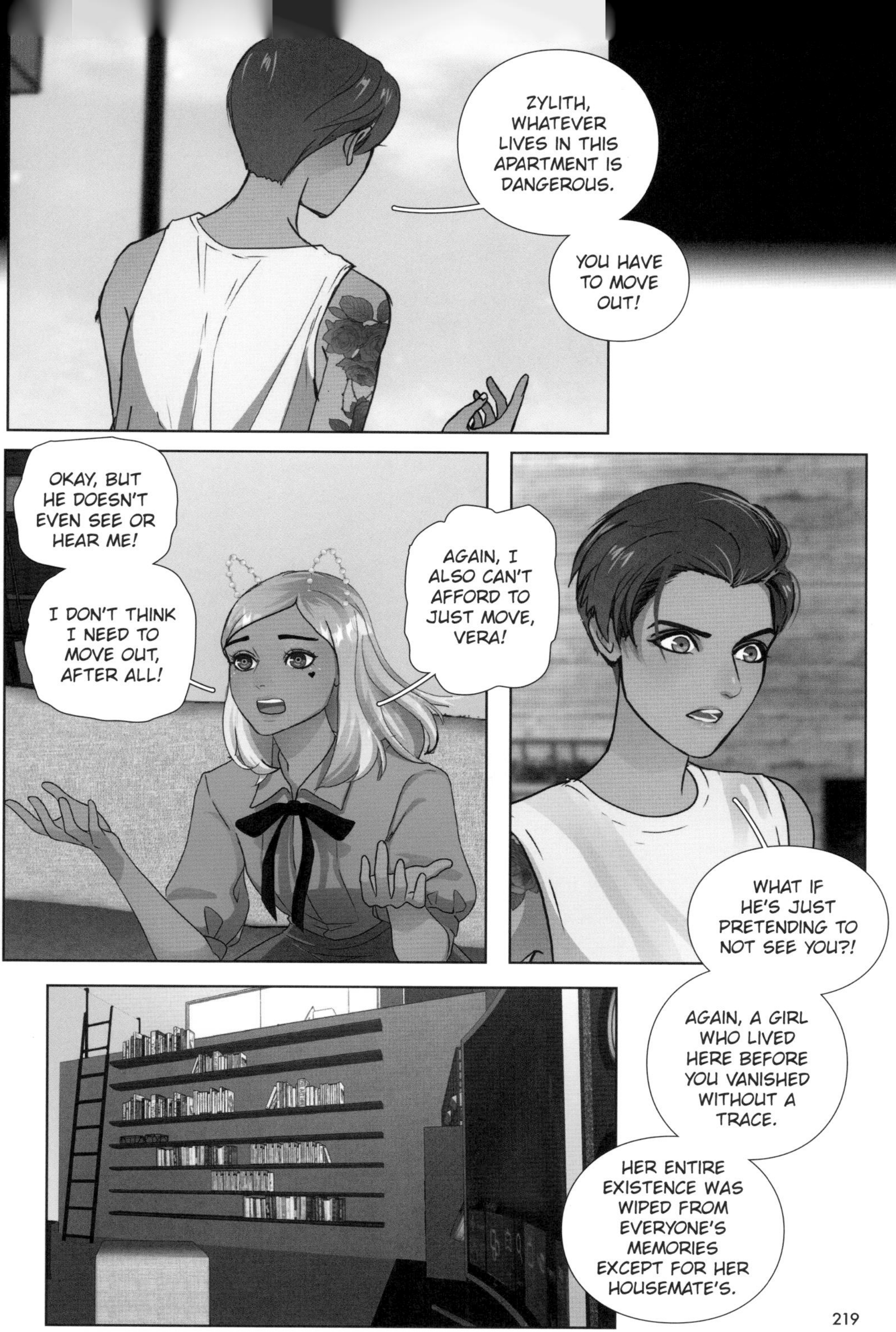
ZYLITH, WHATEVER LIVES IN THIS APARTMENT IS DANGEROUS.
YOU HAVE TO MOVE OUT!
OKAY, BUT HE DOESN'T EVEN SEE OR HEAR ME!
I DON'T THINK I NEED TO MOVE OUT, AFTER ALL!
AGAIN, I ALSO CAN'T AFFORD TO JUST MOVE, VERA!
WHAT IF HE'S JUST PRETENDING TO NOT SEE YOU?!
AGAIN, A GIRL WHO LIVED HERE BEFORE YOU VANISHED WITHOUT A TRACE.
HER ENTIRE EXISTENCE WAS WIPED FROM EVERYONE'S MEMORIES EXCEPT FOR HER HOUSEMATE'S.

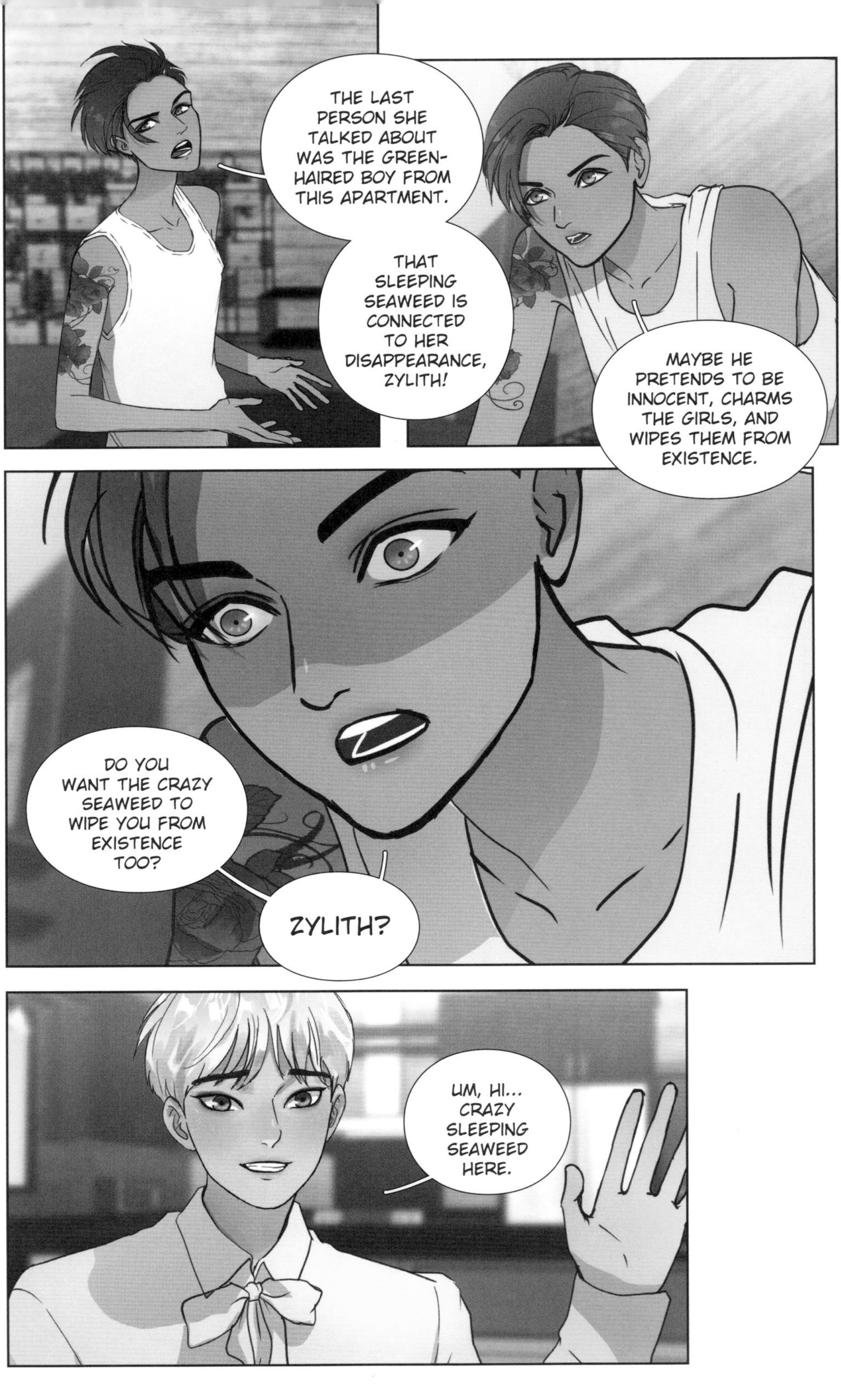
THE LAST PERSON SHE TALKED ABOUT WAS THE GREEN-HAIRED BOY FROM THIS APARTMENT.
THAT SLEEPING SEAWEED IS CONNECTED TO HER DISAPPEARANCE, ZYLITH!
MAYBE HE PRETENDS TO BE INNOCENT, CHARMS THE GIRLS, AND WIPES THEM FROM EXISTENCE.
DO YOU WANT THE CRAZY SEAWEED TO WIPE YOU FROM EXISTENCE TOO?
ZYLITH?
UM, HI... CRAZY SLEEPING SEAWEED HERE.

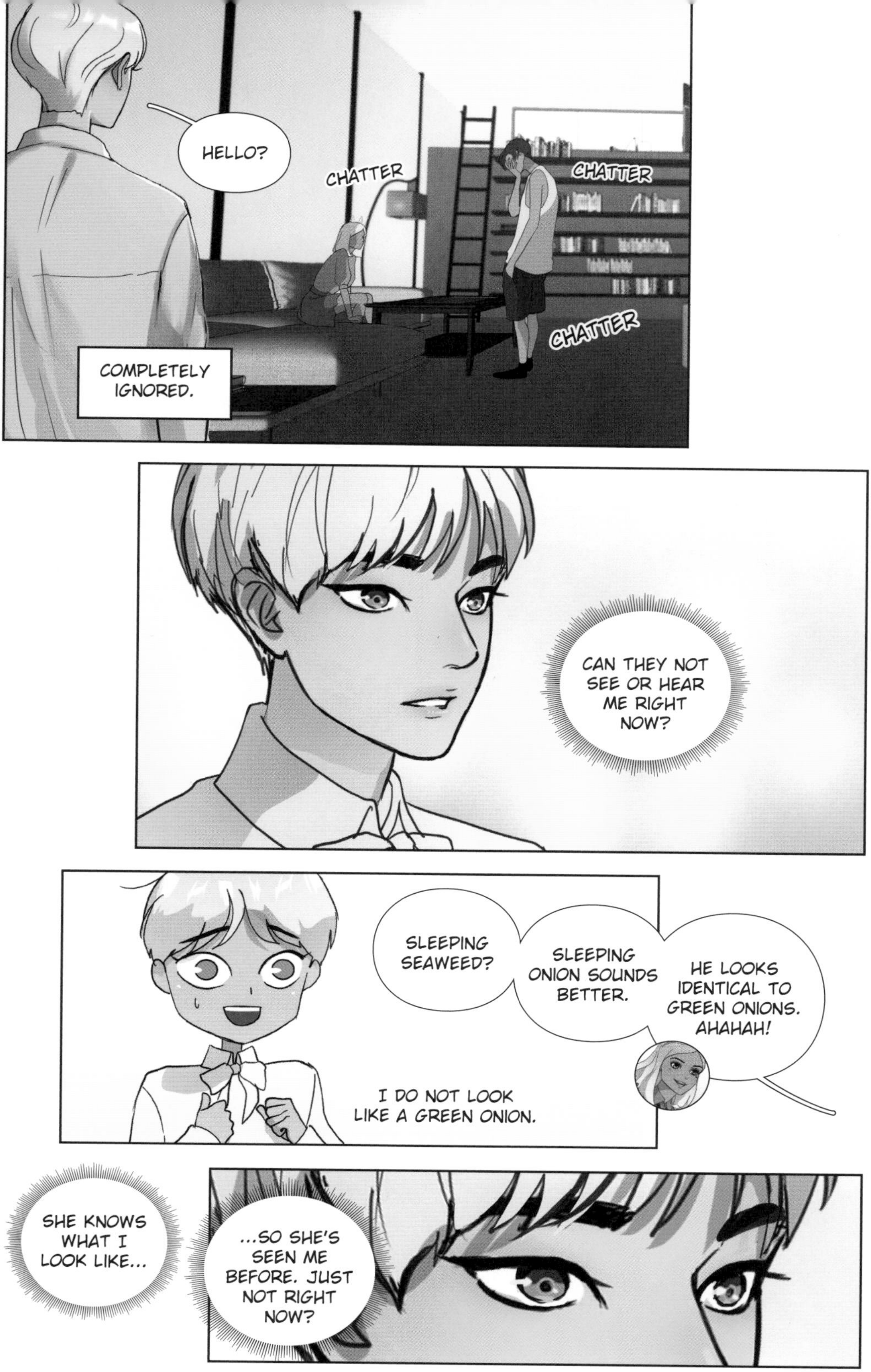
HELLO?
CHATTER
CHATTER
CHATTER
COMPLETELY IGNORED.
CAN THEY NOT SEE OR HEAR ME RIGHT NOW?
SLEEPING SEAWEED?
SLEEPING ONION SOUNDS BETTER.
HE LOOKS IDENTICAL TO GREEN ONIONS. AHAHAH!
I DO NOT LOOK LIKE A GREEN ONION.
SHE KNOWS WHAT I LOOK LIKE...
...SO SHE'S SEEN ME BEFORE. JUST NOT RIGHT NOW?

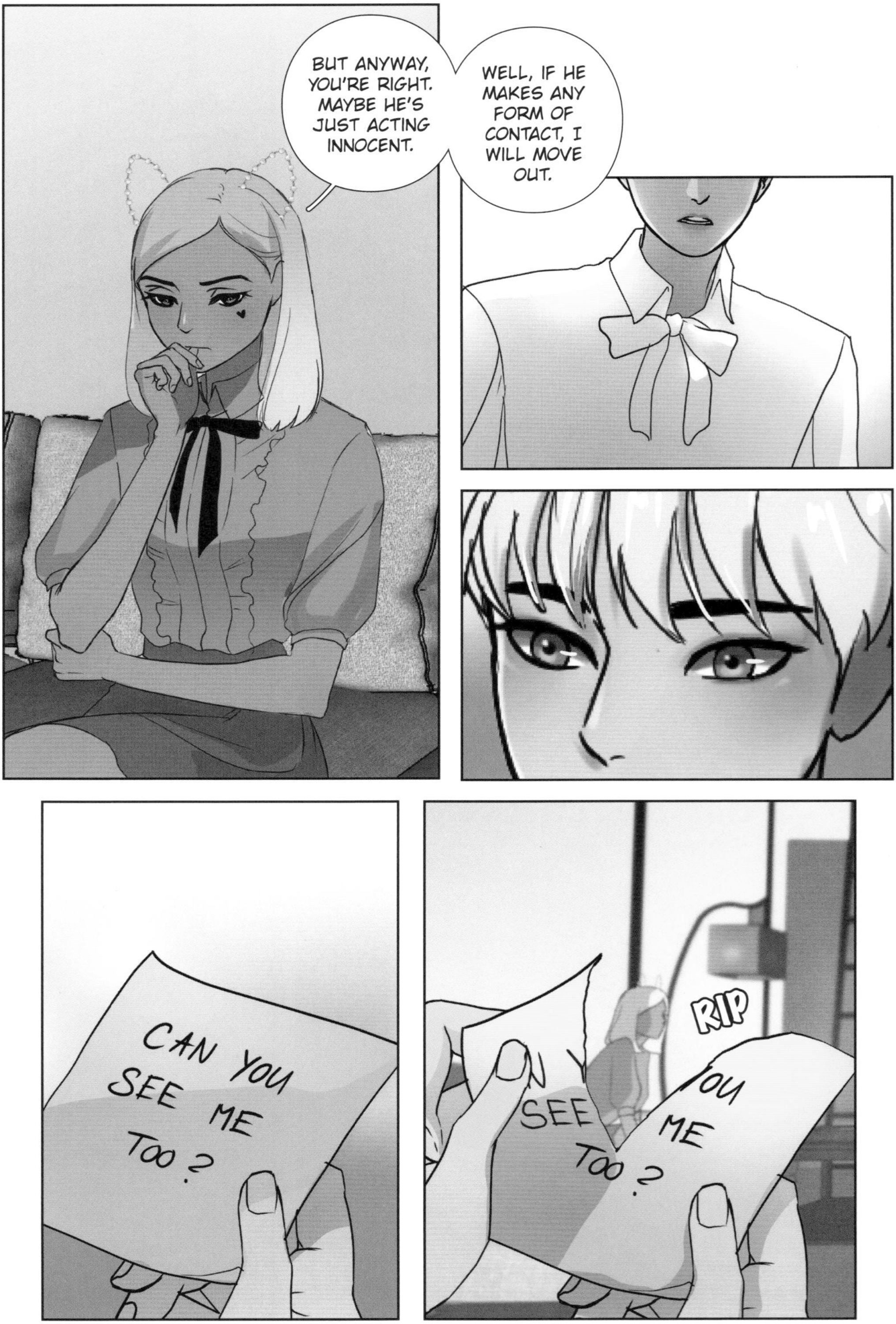

BUT ANYWAY, YOU'RE RIGHT. MAYBE HE'S JUST ACTING INNOCENT.
WELL, IF HE MAKES ANY FORM OF CONTACT, I WILL MOVE OUT.
CAN YOU SEE ME TOO ?
RIP
SEE YOU ME TOO ?

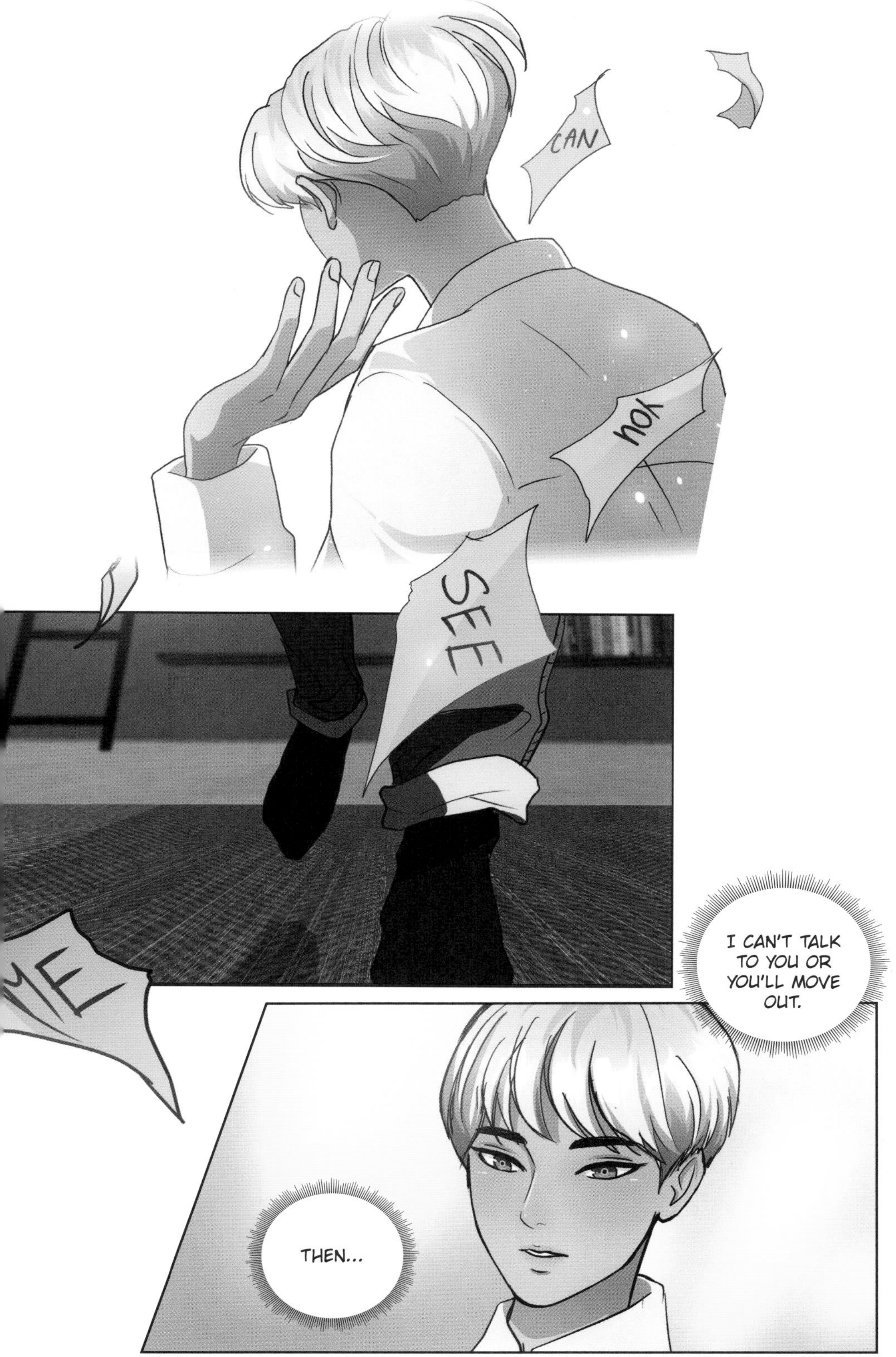
CAN
YOU
SEE
ME
I CAN'T TALK TO YOU OR YOU'LL MOVE OUT.
THEN...

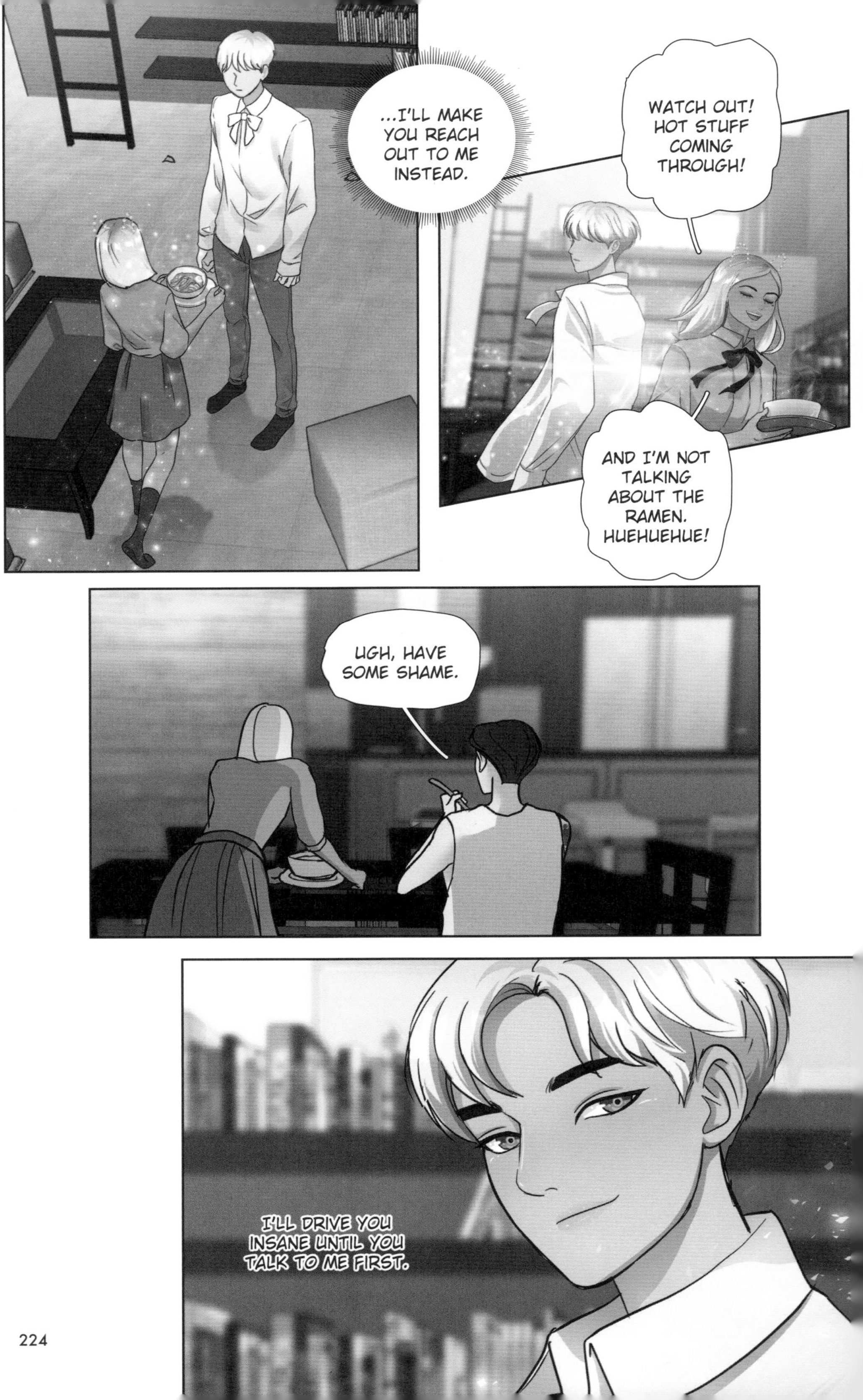
...I'LL MAKE YOU REACH OUT TO ME INSTEAD.
WATCH OUT! HOT STUFF COMING THROUGH!
AND I'M NOT TALKING ABOUT THE RAMEN. HUEHUEHUE!
UGH, HAVE SOME SHAME.
I'LL DRIVE YOU INSANE UNTIL YOU TALK TO ME FIRST.

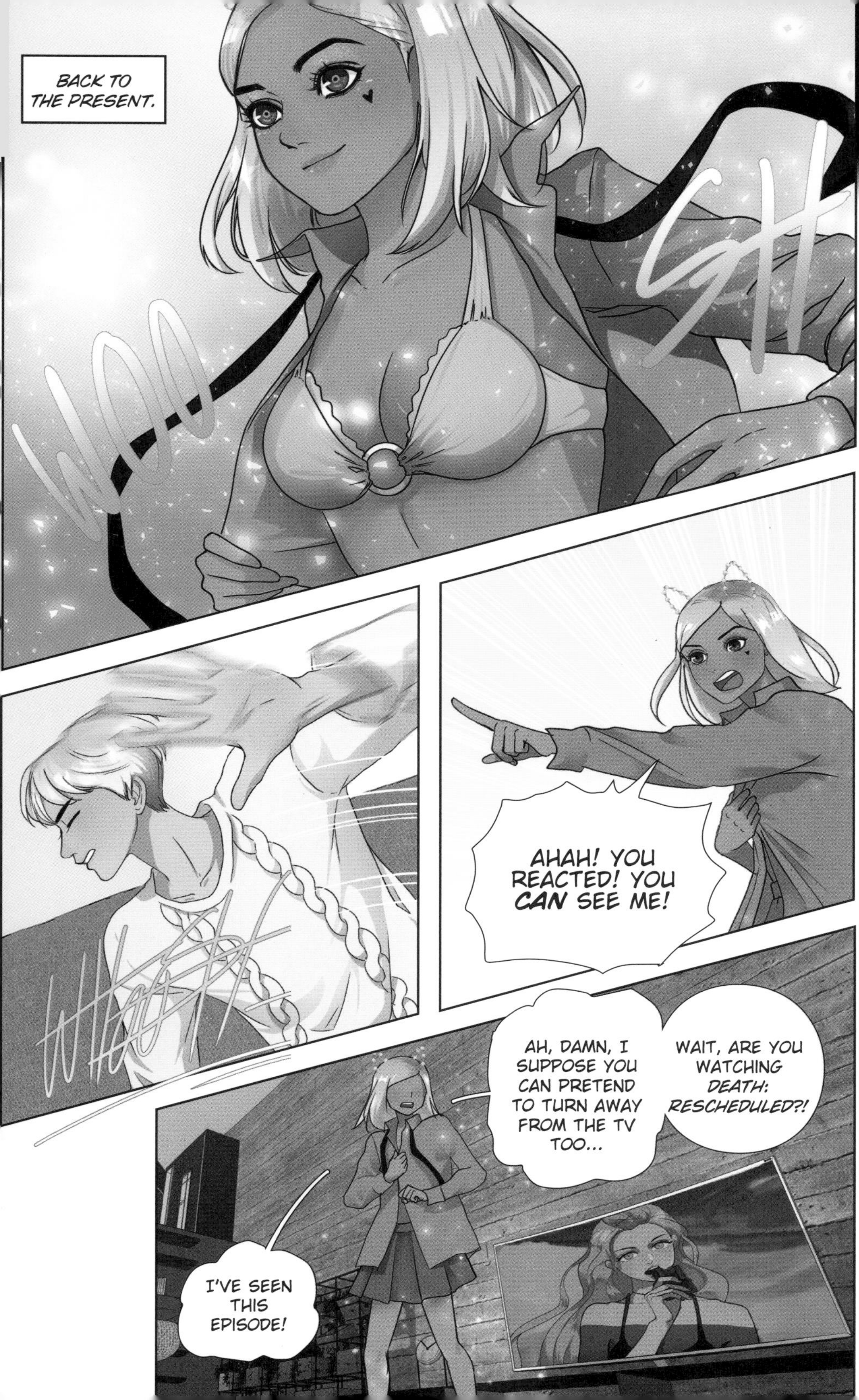
BACK TO THE PRESENT.
WOO
SH
AHAH! YOU REACTED! YOU *CAN* SEE ME!
AH, DAMN, I SUPPOSE YOU CAN PRETEND TO TURN AWAY FROM THE TV TOO...
WAIT, ARE YOU WATCHING *DEATH: RESCHEDULED*?!
I'VE SEEN THIS EPISODE!

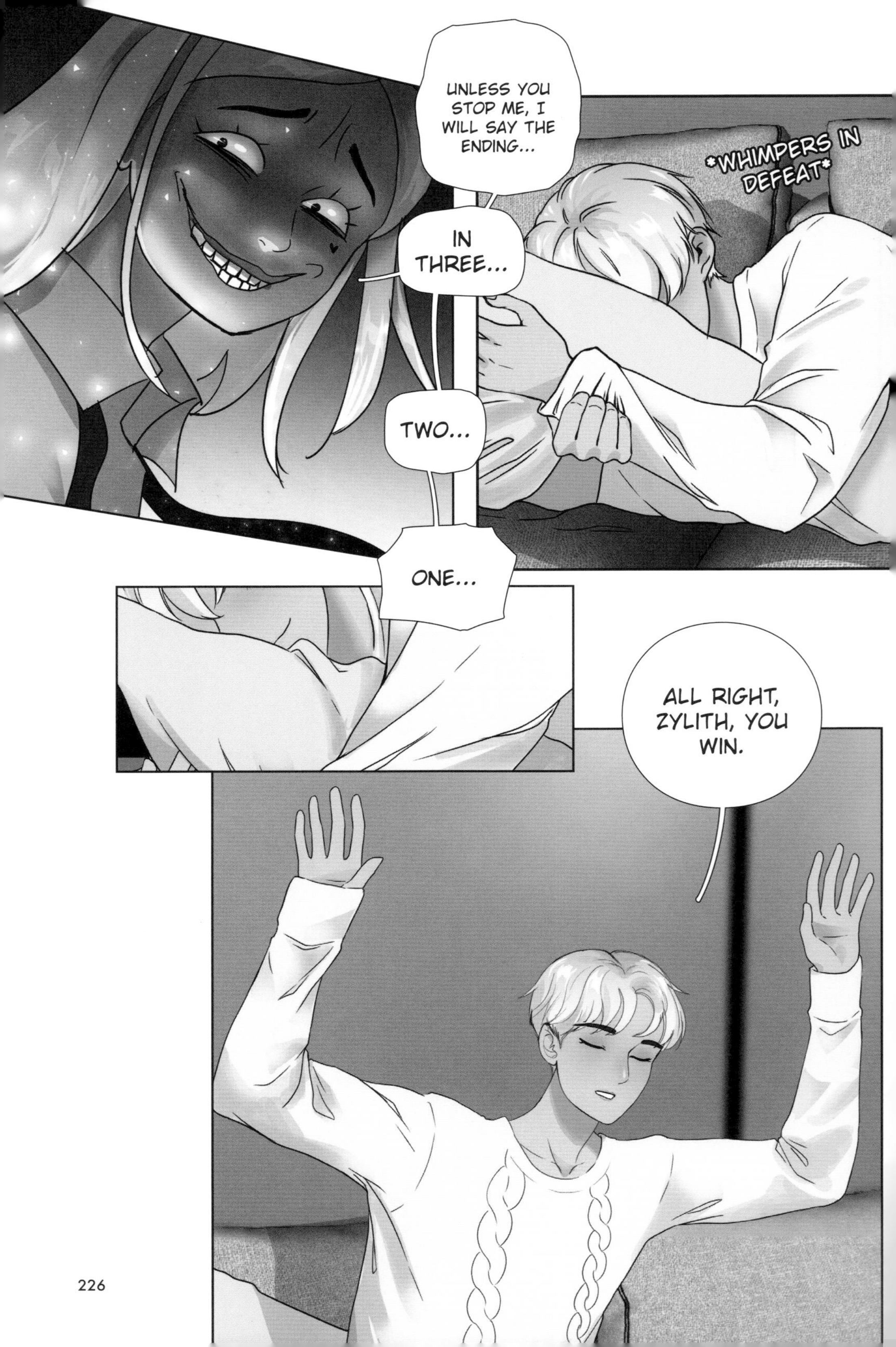
UNLESS YOU STOP ME, I WILL SAY THE ENDING...
IN THREE...
TWO...
ONE...
WHIMPERS IN DEFEAT
ALL RIGHT, ZYLITH, YOU WIN.

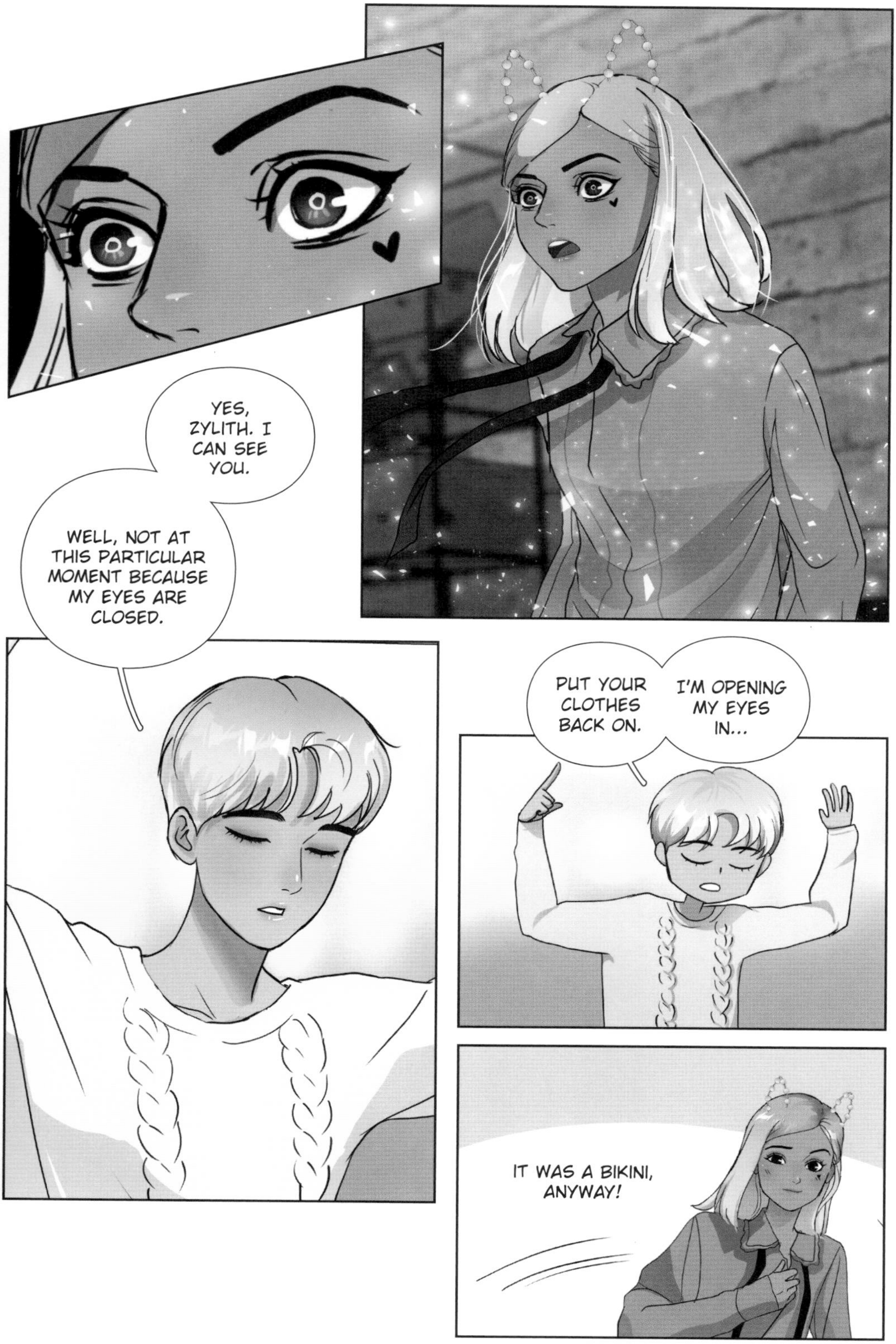
YES, ZYLITH. I CAN SEE YOU.
WELL, NOT AT THIS PARTICULAR MOMENT BECAUSE MY EYES ARE CLOSED.
PUT YOUR CLOTHES BACK ON.
I'M OPENING MY EYES IN...
IT WAS A BIKINI, ANYWAY!

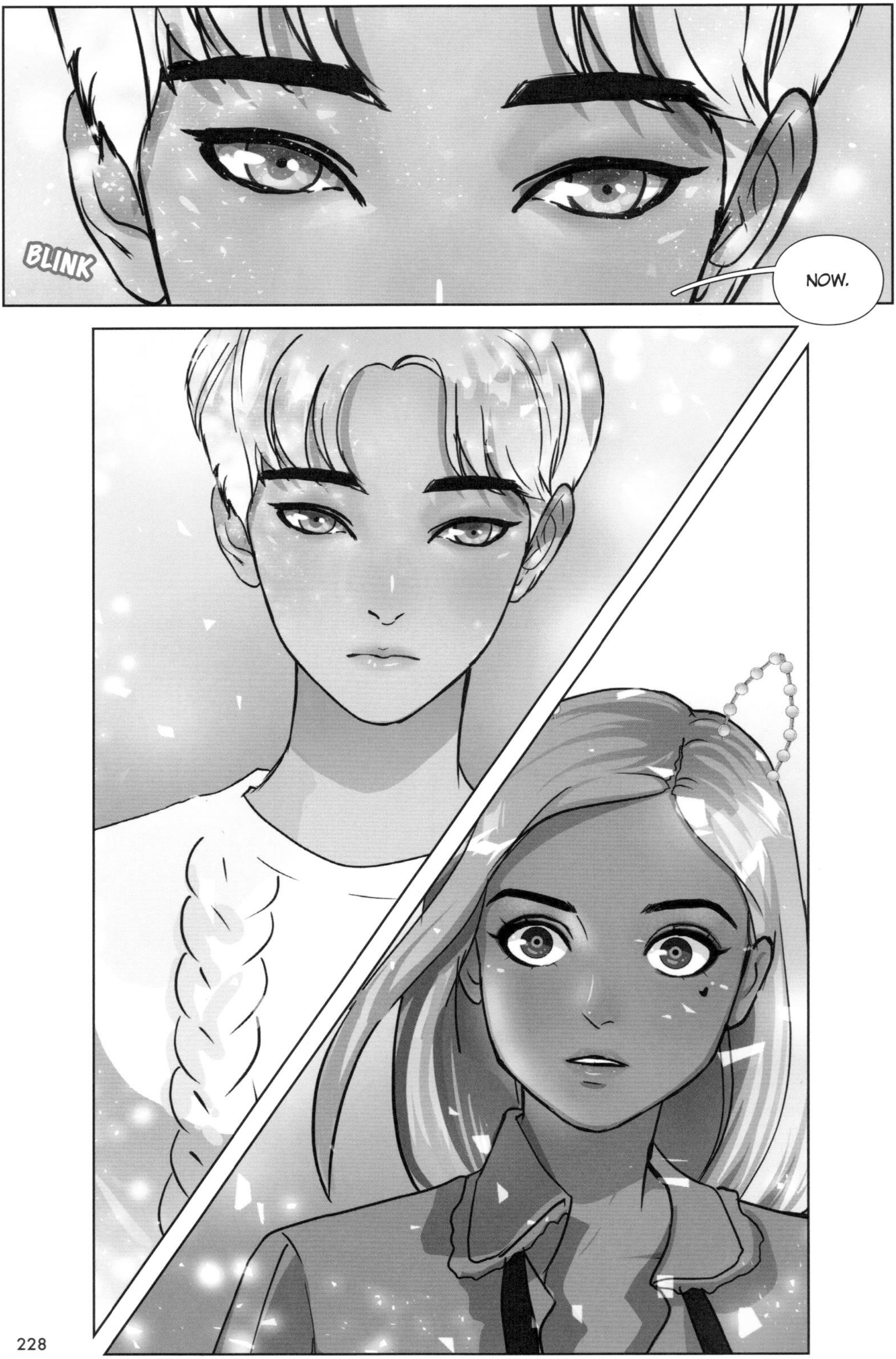
BLINK
NOW.

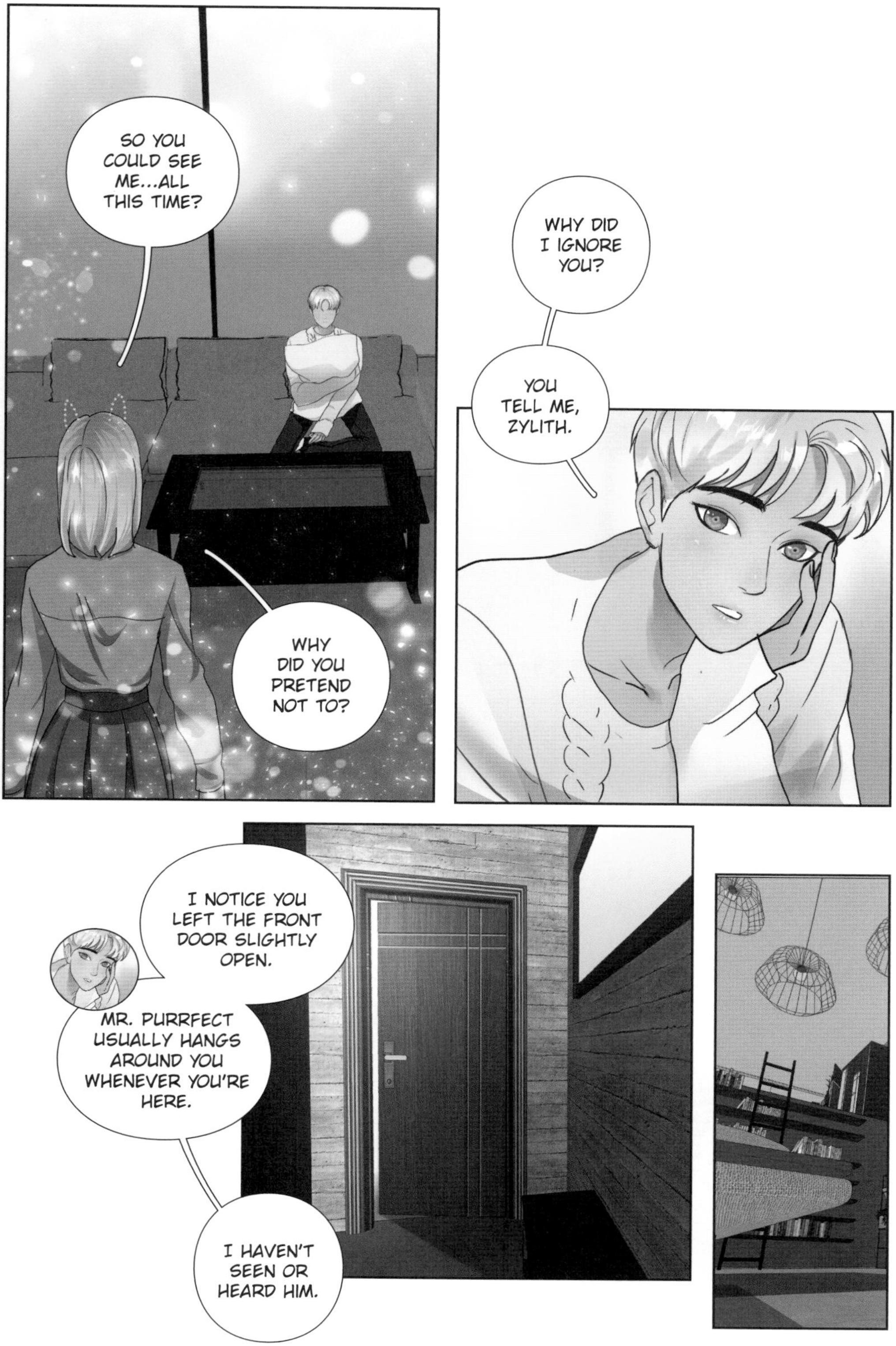
SO YOU COULD SEE ME...ALL THIS TIME?
WHY DID YOU PRETEND NOT TO?
WHY DID I IGNORE YOU?
YOU TELL ME, ZYLITH.
I NOTICE YOU LEFT THE FRONT DOOR SLIGHTLY OPEN.
MR. PURRFECT USUALLY HANGS AROUND YOU WHENEVER YOU'RE HERE.
I HAVEN'T SEEN OR HEARD HIM.

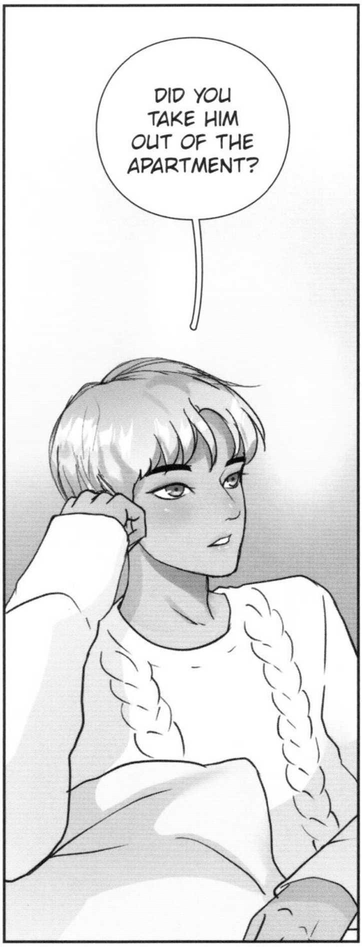
DID YOU TAKE HIM OUT OF THE APARTMENT?

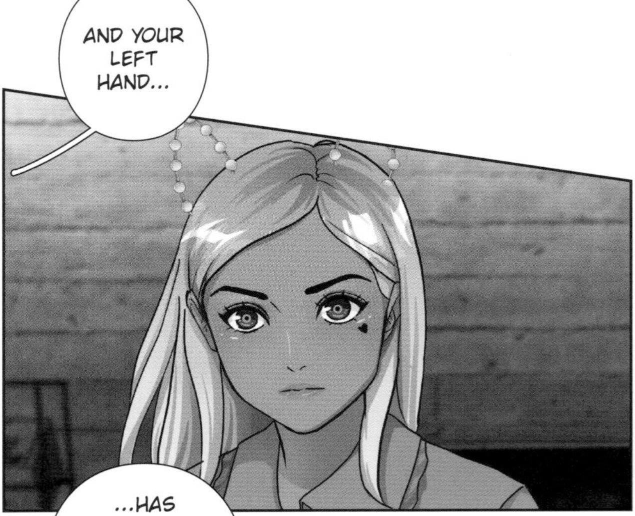
AND YOUR LEFT HAND...

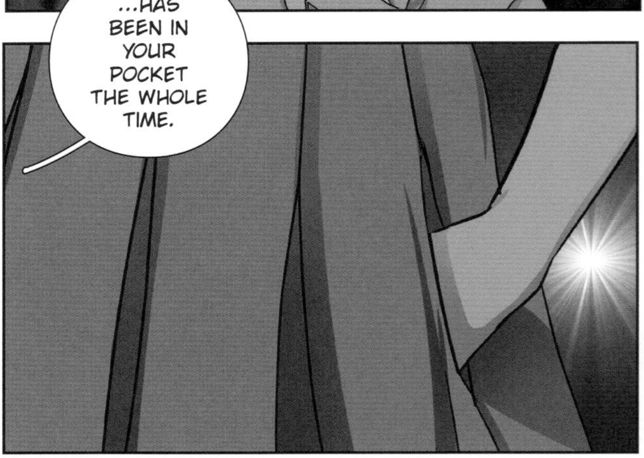
...HAS BEEN IN YOUR POCKET THE WHOLE TIME.

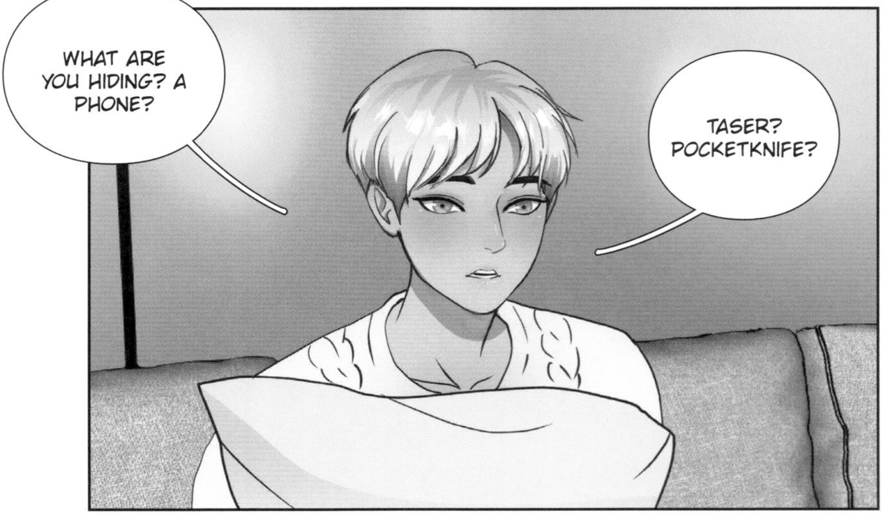
WHAT ARE YOU HIDING? A PHONE?
TASER? POCKETKNIFE?

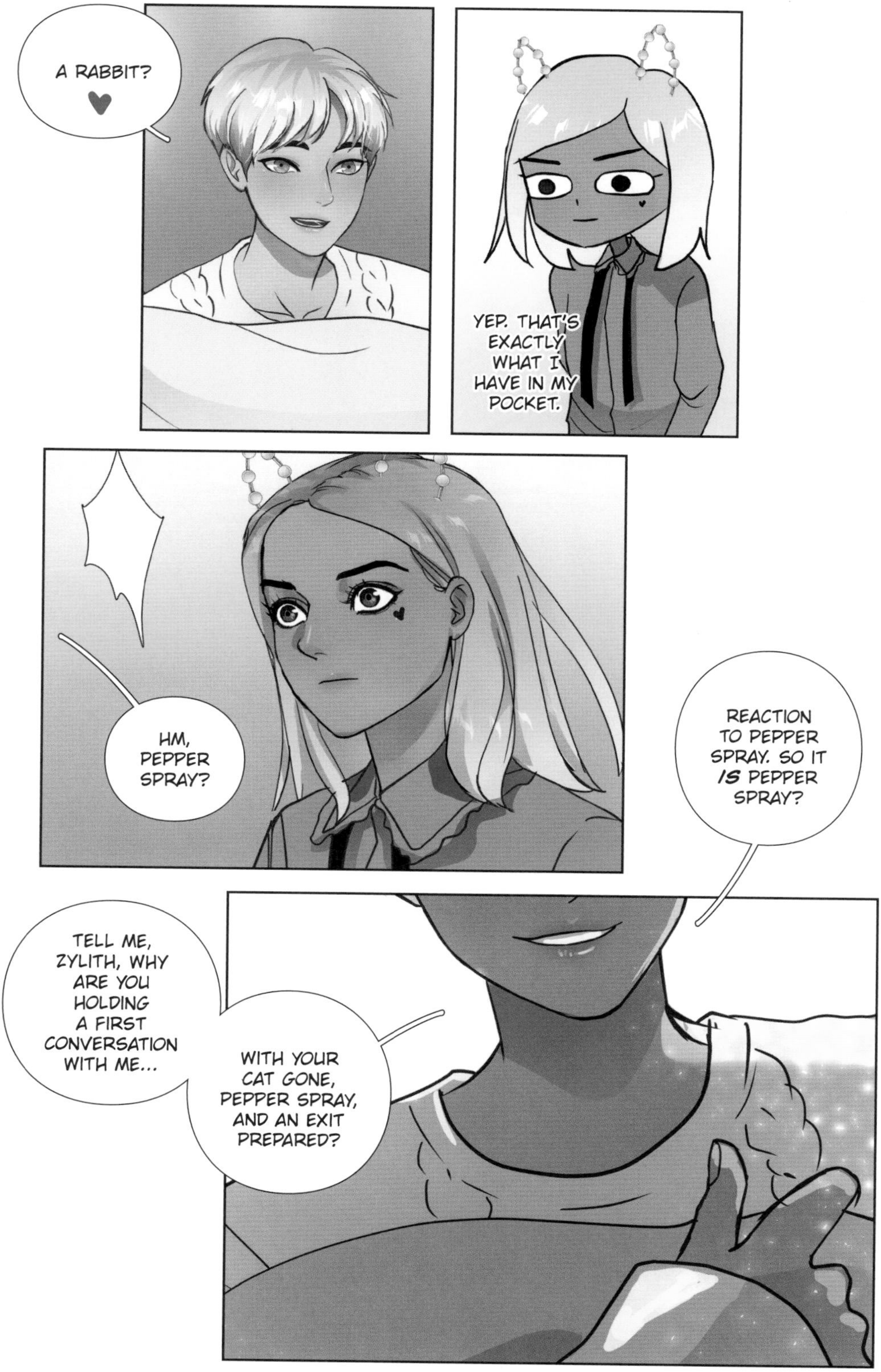
A RABBIT? ♥
YEP. THAT'S EXACTLY WHAT I HAVE IN MY POCKET.
HM, PEPPER SPRAY?
REACTION TO PEPPER SPRAY. SO IT *IS* PEPPER SPRAY?
TELL ME, ZYLITH, WHY ARE YOU HOLDING A FIRST CONVERSATION WITH ME...
WITH YOUR CAT GONE, PEPPER SPRAY, AND AN EXIT PREPARED?

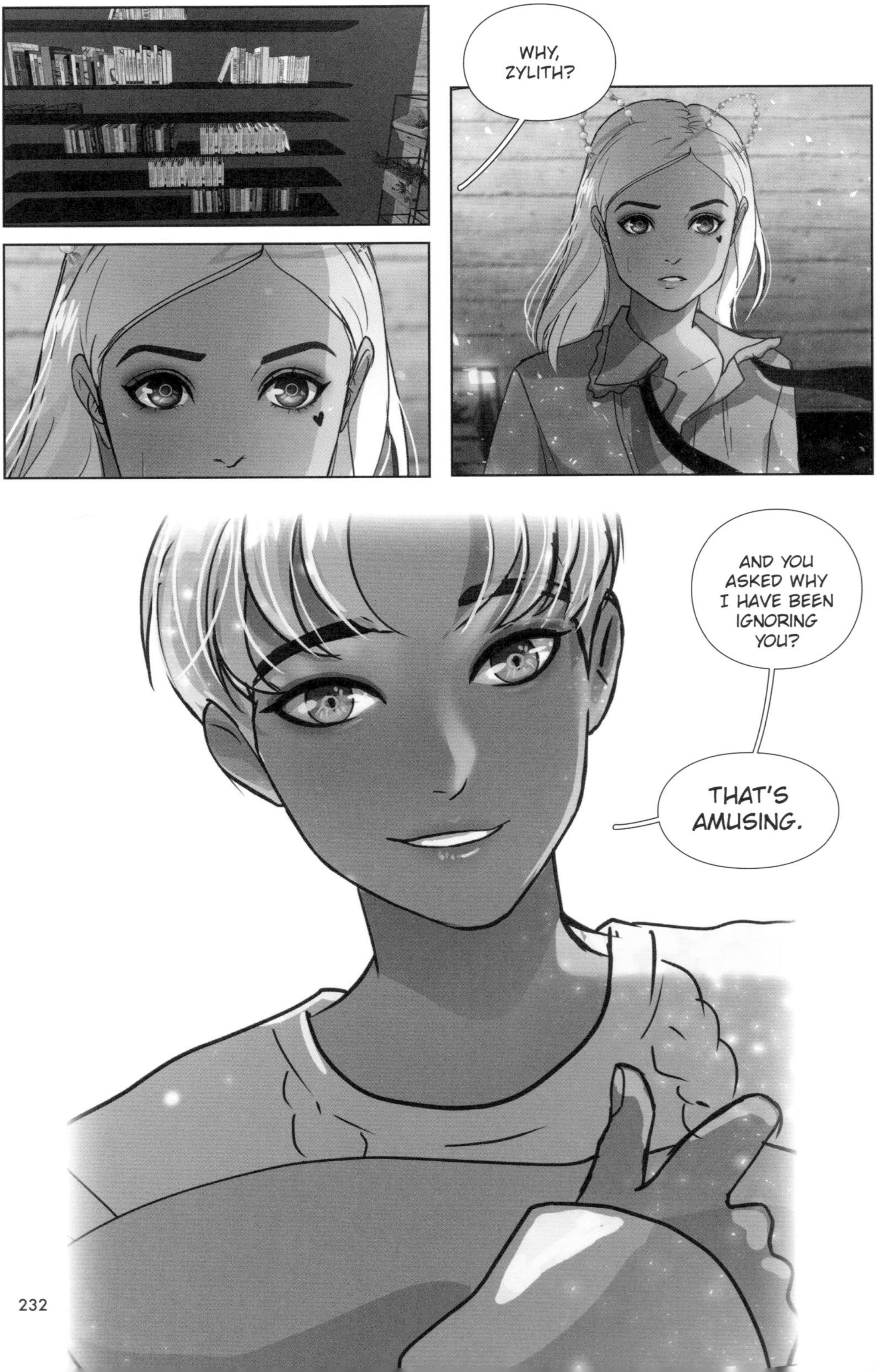
WHY, ZYLITH?
AND YOU ASKED WHY I HAVE BEEN IGNORING YOU?
THAT'S AMUSING.

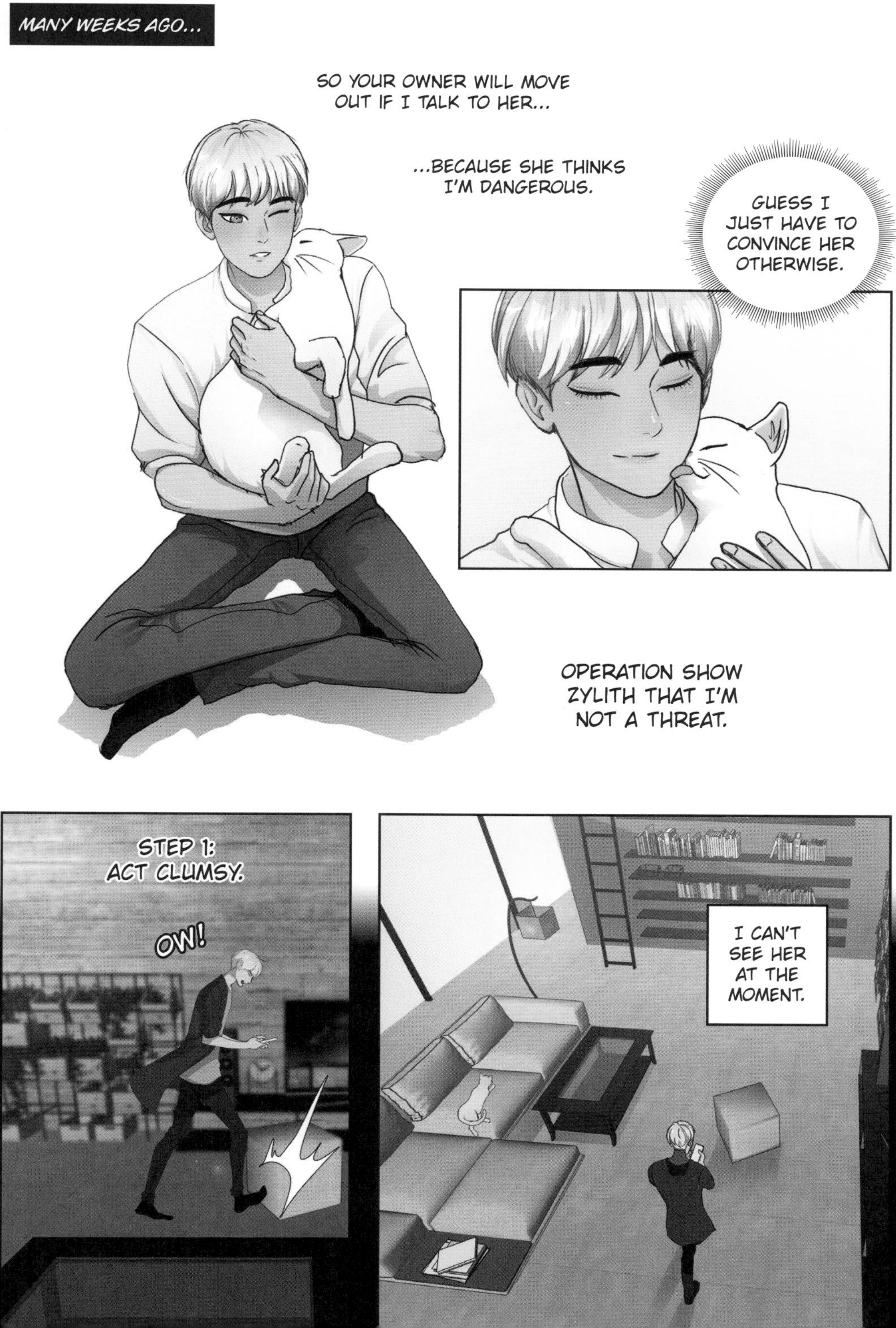
MANY WEEKS AGO...
SO YOUR OWNER WILL MOVE OUT IF I TALK TO HER...
...BECAUSE SHE THINKS I'M DANGEROUS.
GUESS I JUST HAVE TO CONVINCE HER OTHERWISE.
OPERATION SHOW ZYLITH THAT I'M NOT A THREAT.
STEP 1: ACT CLUMSY.
OW!
I CAN'T SEE HER AT THE MOMENT.

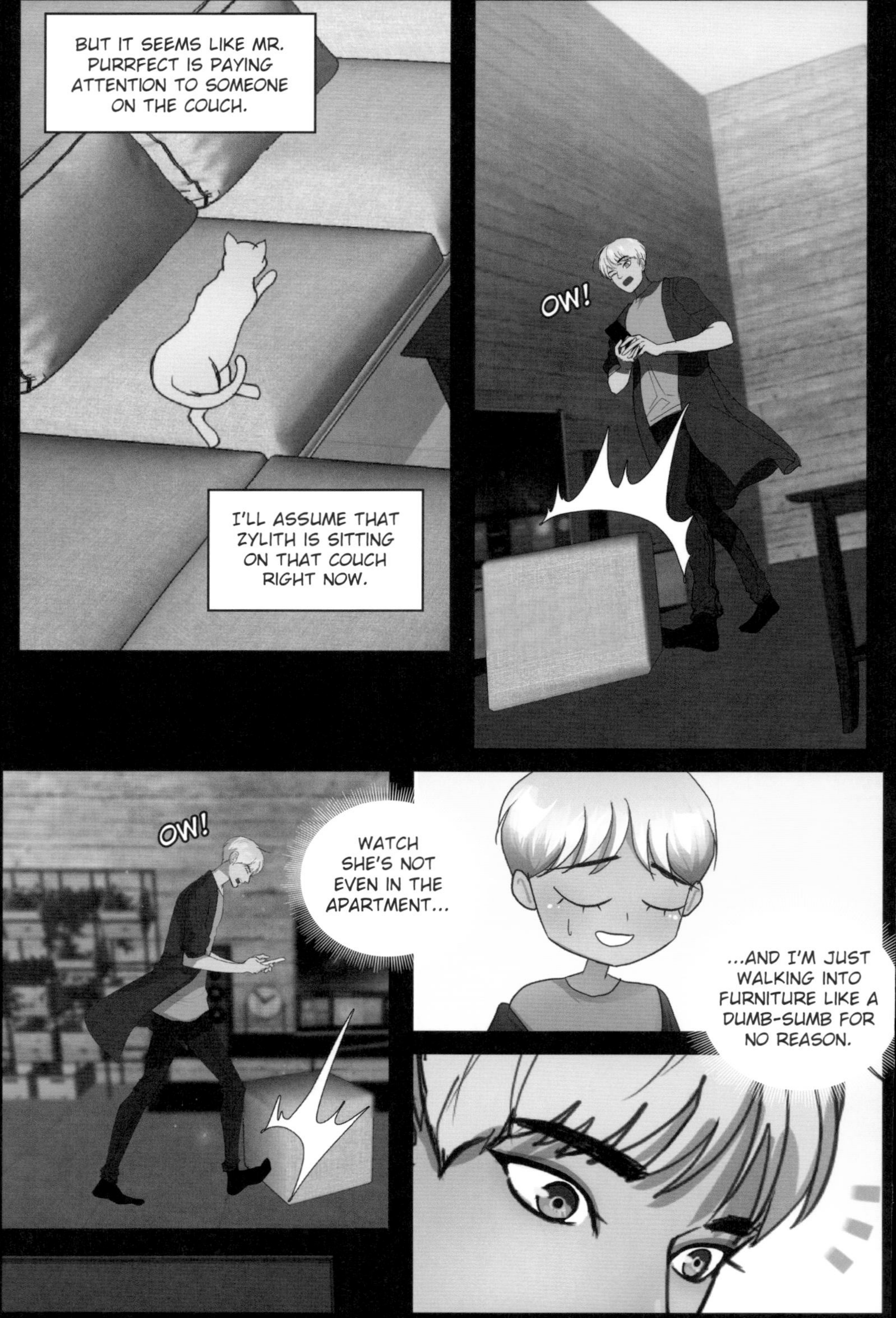

BUT IT SEEMS LIKE MR. PURRFECT IS PAYING ATTENTION TO SOMEONE ON THE COUCH.
I'LL ASSUME THAT ZYLITH IS SITTING ON THAT COUCH RIGHT NOW.
OW!
OW!
WATCH SHE'S NOT EVEN IN THE APARTMENT...
...AND I'M JUST WALKING INTO FURNITURE LIKE A DUMB-SUMB FOR NO REASON.

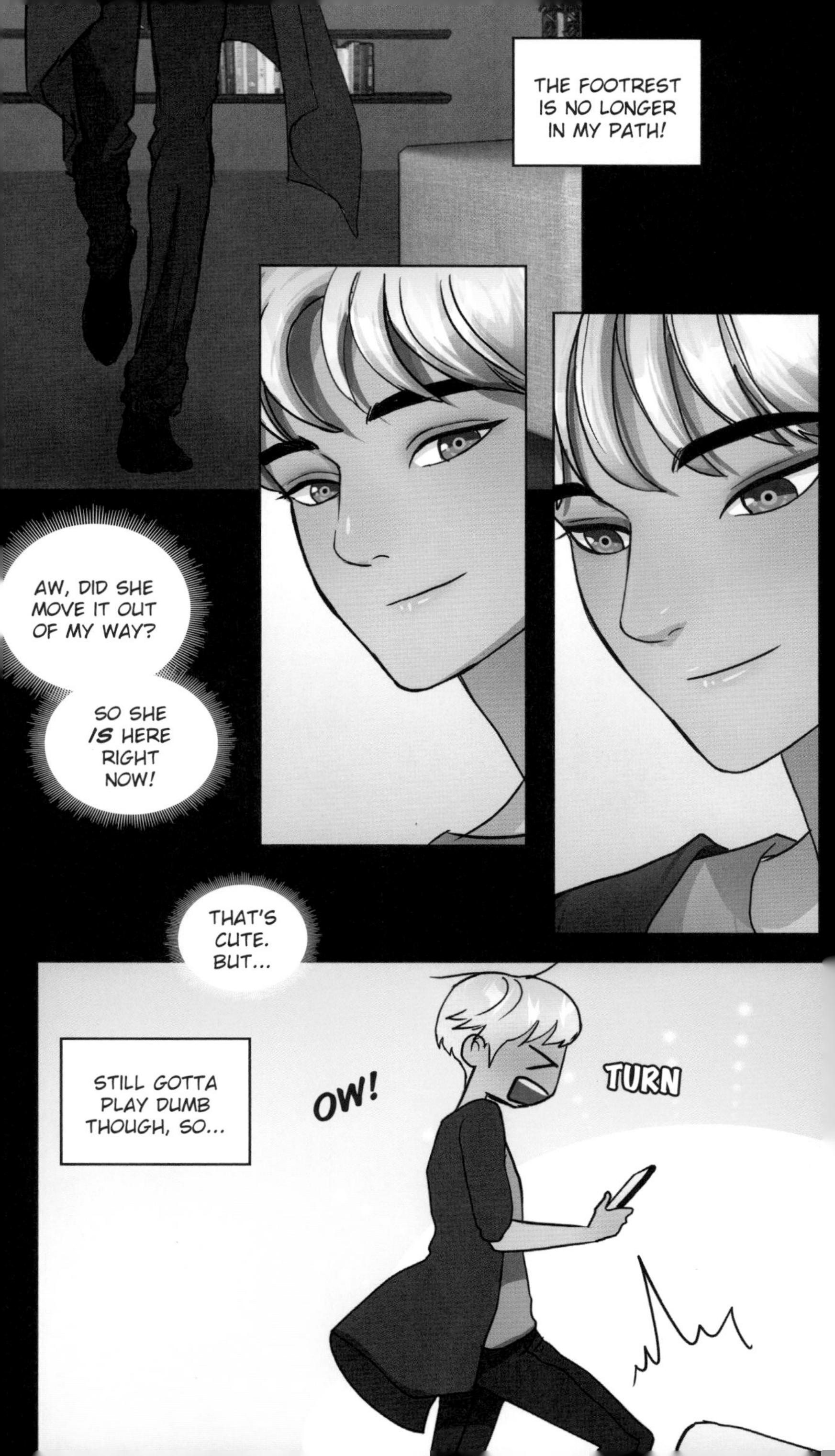
THE FOOTREST IS NO LONGER IN MY PATH!
AW, DID SHE MOVE IT OUT OF MY WAY?
SO SHE *IS* HERE RIGHT NOW!
THAT'S CUTE. BUT...
STILL GOTTA PLAY DUMB THOUGH, SO...
OW!
TURN

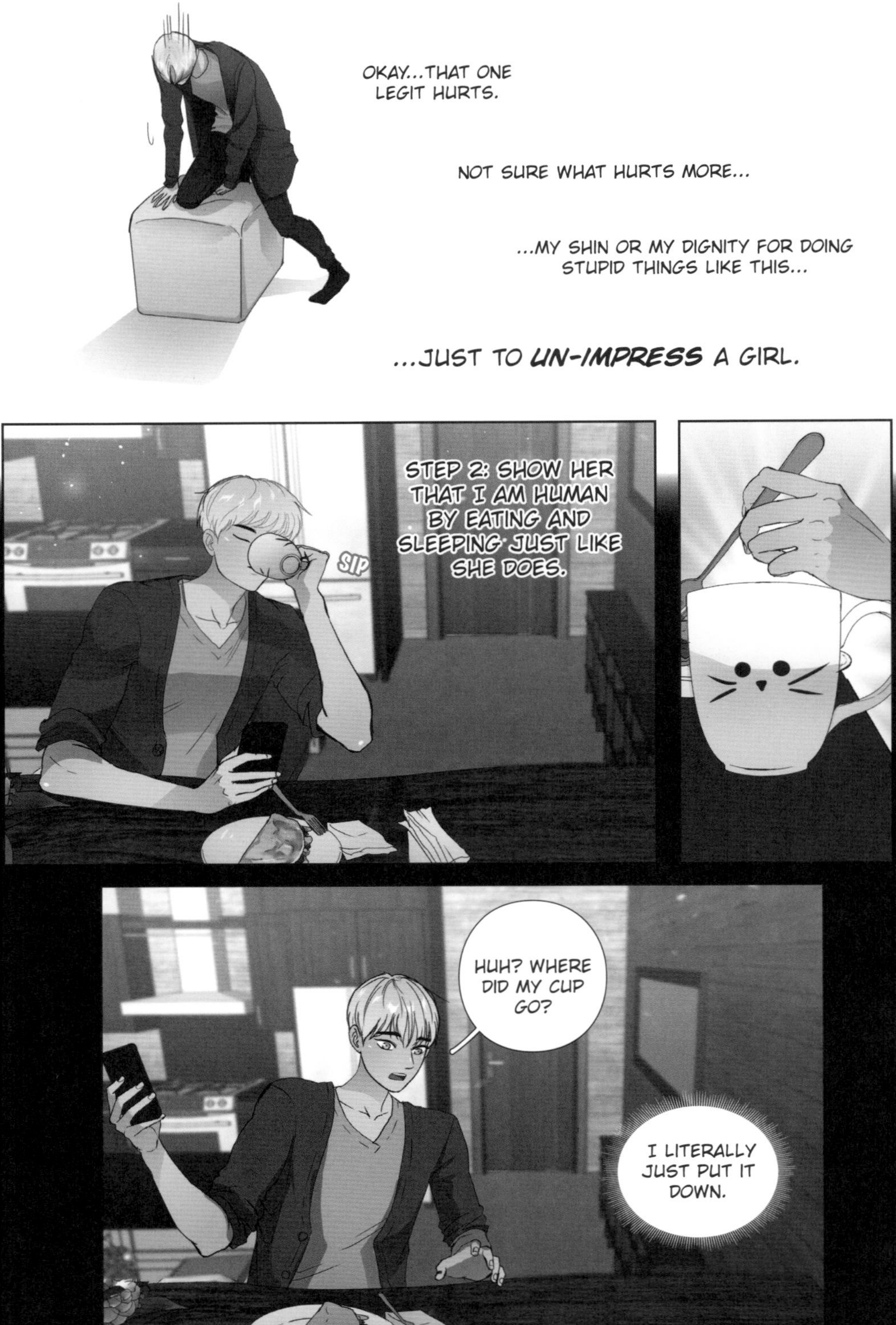
OKAY...THAT ONE LEGIT HURTS.
NOT SURE WHAT HURTS MORE...
...MY SHIN OR MY DIGNITY FOR DOING STUPID THINGS LIKE THIS...
...JUST TO UN-IMPRESS A GIRL.
STEP 2: SHOW HER THAT I AM HUMAN BY EATING AND SLEEPING JUST LIKE SHE DOES.
SIP
HUH? WHERE DID MY CUP GO?
I LITERALLY JUST PUT IT DOWN.

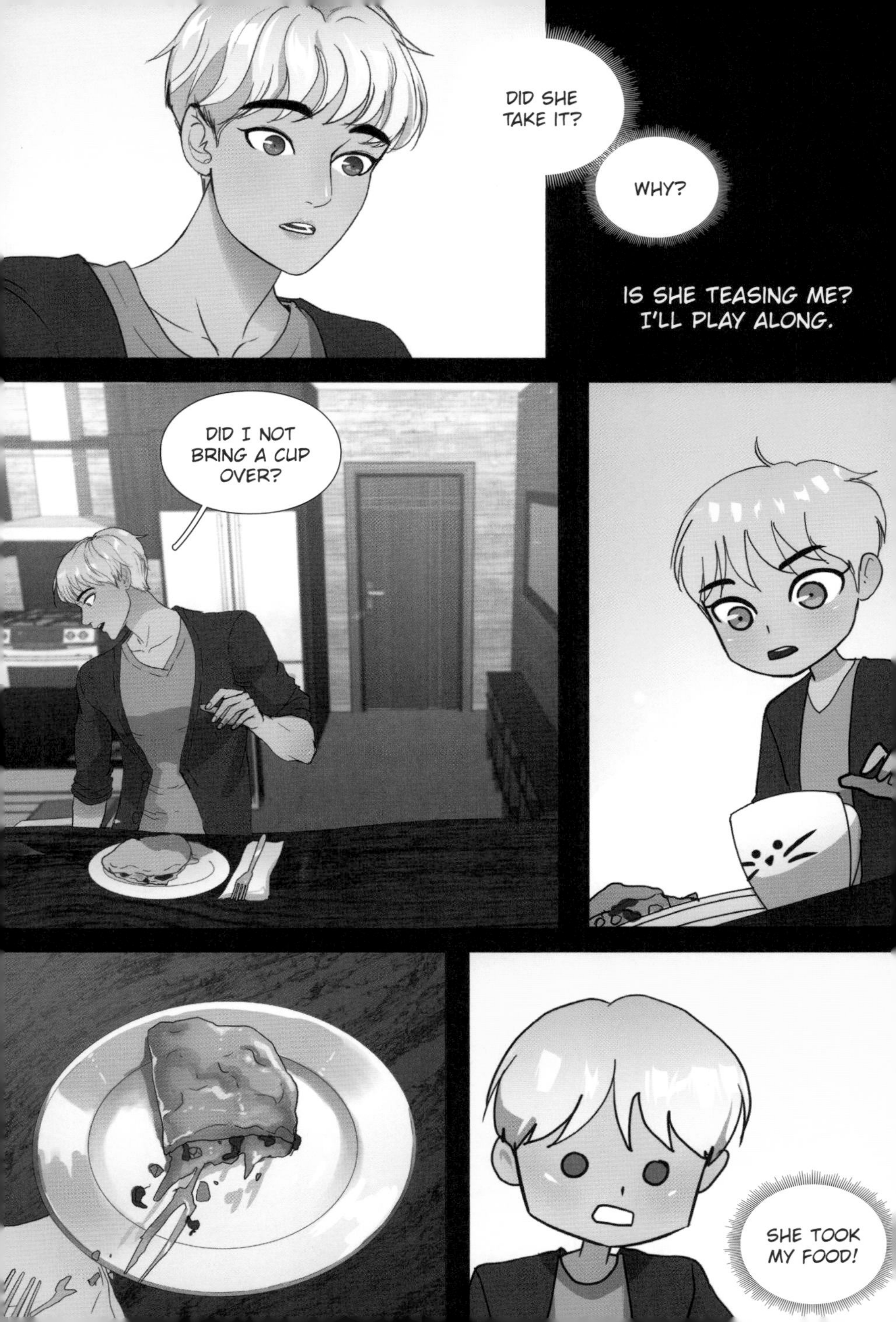
DID SHE TAKE IT?
WHY?
IS SHE TEASING ME? I'LL PLAY ALONG.
DID I NOT BRING A CUP OVER?
SHE TOOK MY FOOD!

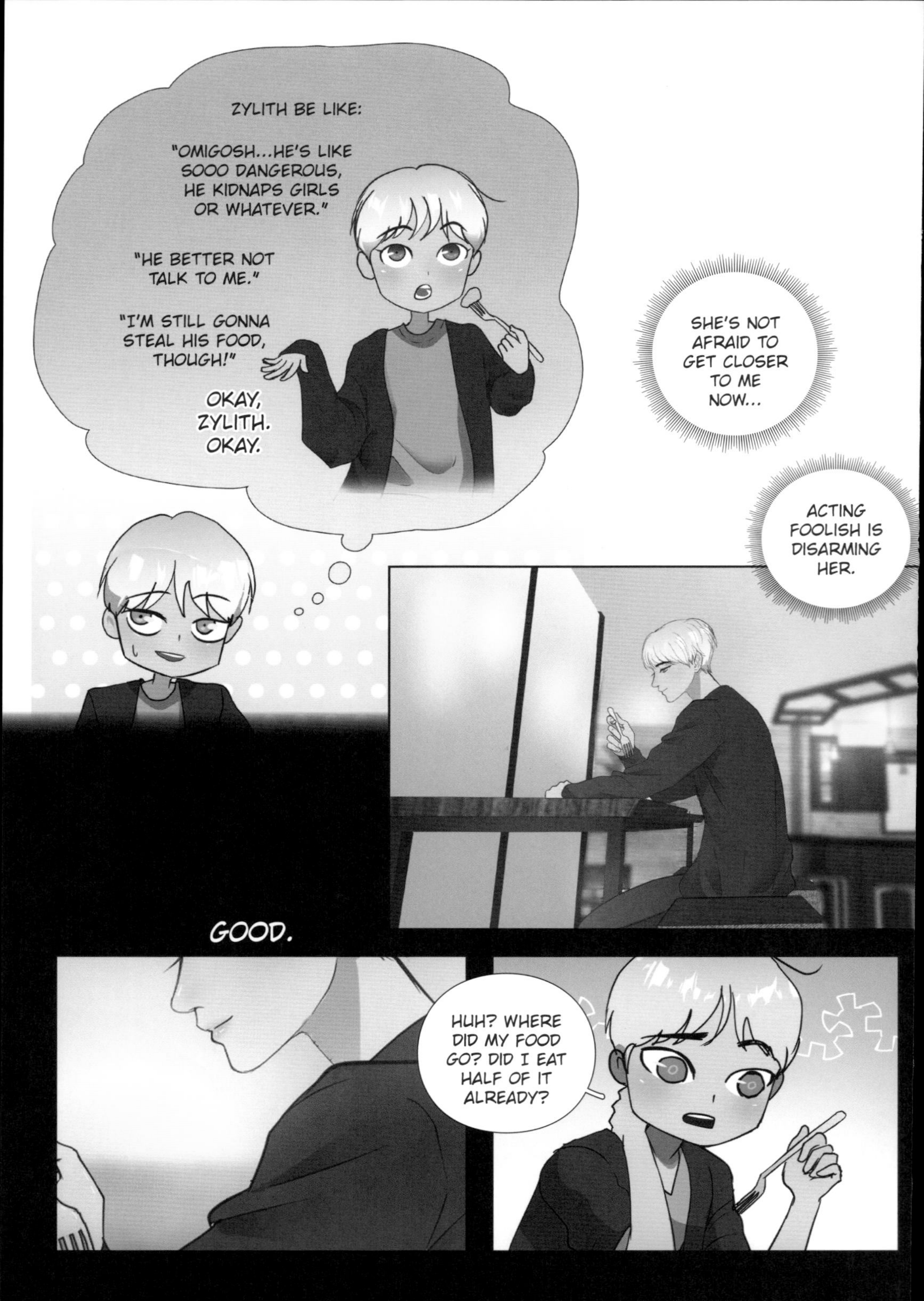
ZYLITH BE LIKE:
"OMIGOSH...HE'S LIKE SOOO DANGEROUS, HE KIDNAPS GIRLS OR WHATEVER."
"HE BETTER NOT TALK TO ME."
"I'M STILL GONNA STEAL HIS FOOD, THOUGH!"
OKAY, ZYLITH. OKAY.
SHE'S NOT AFRAID TO GET CLOSER TO ME NOW...
ACTING FOOLISH IS DISARMING HER.
GOOD.
HUH? WHERE DID MY FOOD GO? DID I EAT HALF OF IT ALREADY?
PLAYING DUMB CONTINUES...

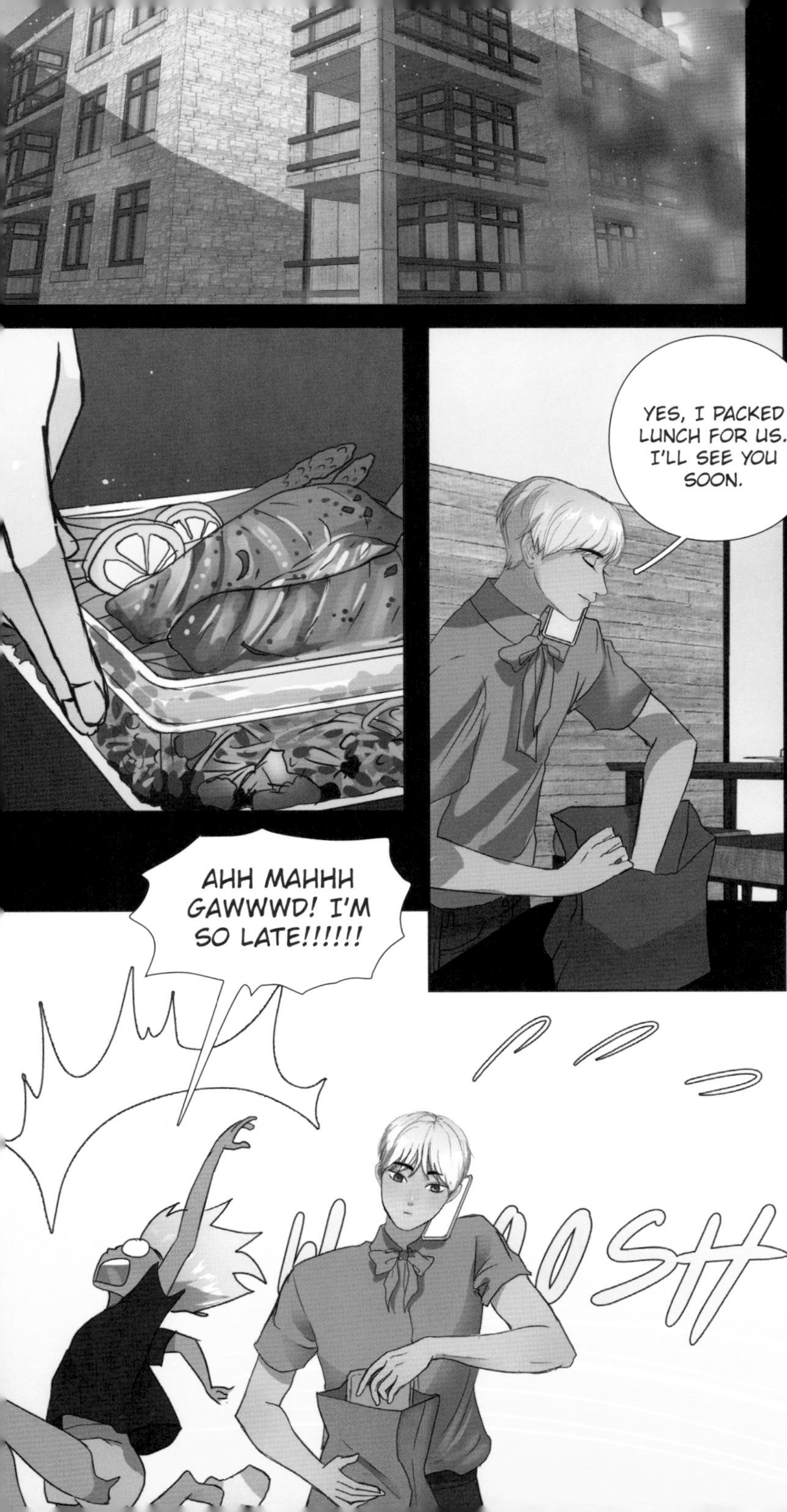
YES, I PACKED LUNCH FOR US. I'LL SEE YOU SOON.
AHH MAHHH GAWWWD! I'M SO LATE!!!!!!

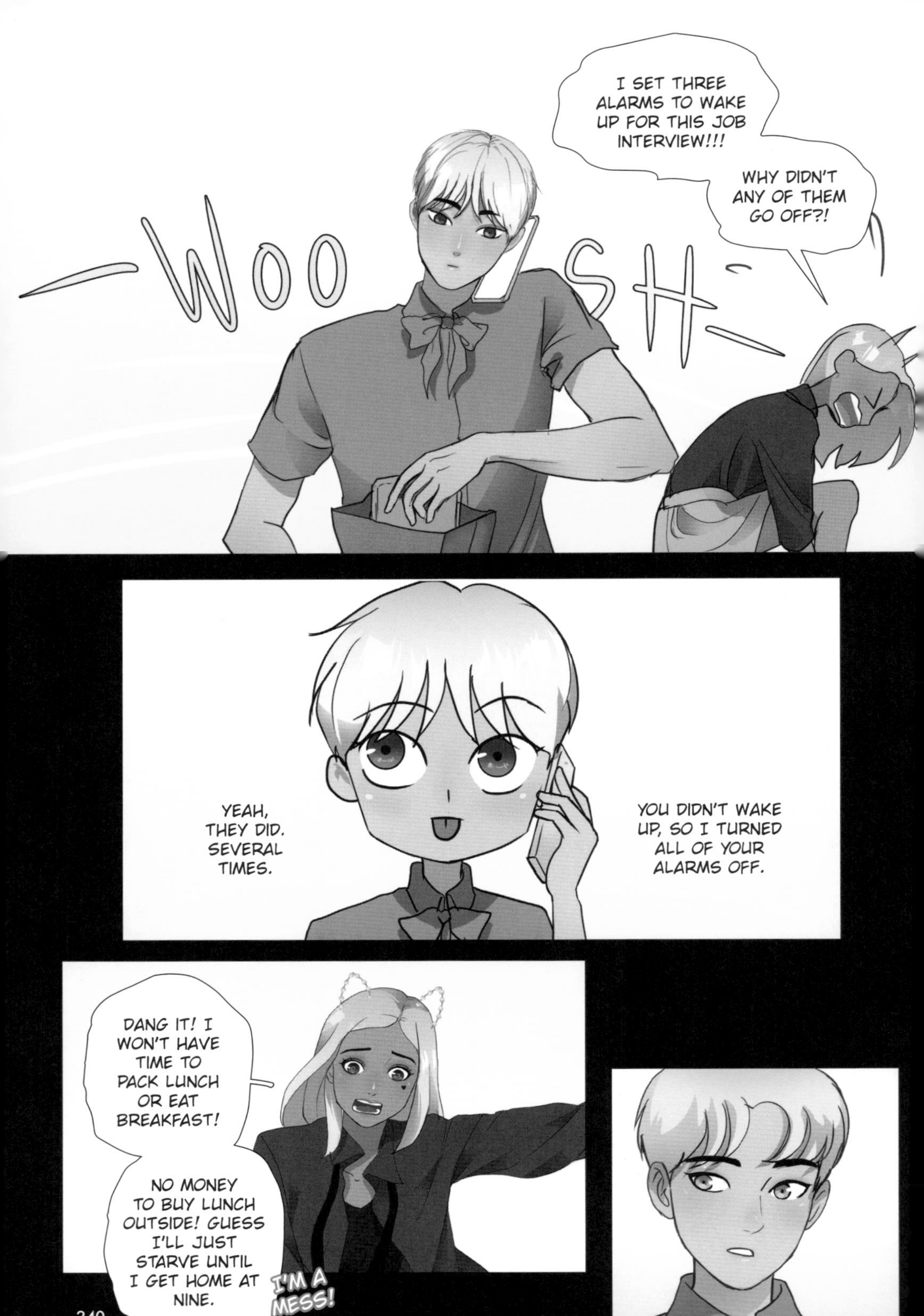
I SET THREE ALARMS TO WAKE UP FOR THIS JOB INTERVIEW!!!
WHY DIDN'T ANY OF THEM GO OFF?!
WOOSH
YEAH, THEY DID. SEVERAL TIMES.
YOU DIDN'T WAKE UP, SO I TURNED ALL OF YOUR ALARMS OFF.
DANG IT! I WON'T HAVE TIME TO PACK LUNCH OR EAT BREAKFAST!
NO MONEY TO BUY LUNCH OUTSIDE! GUESS I'LL JUST STARVE UNTIL I GET HOME AT NINE.
I'M A MESS!

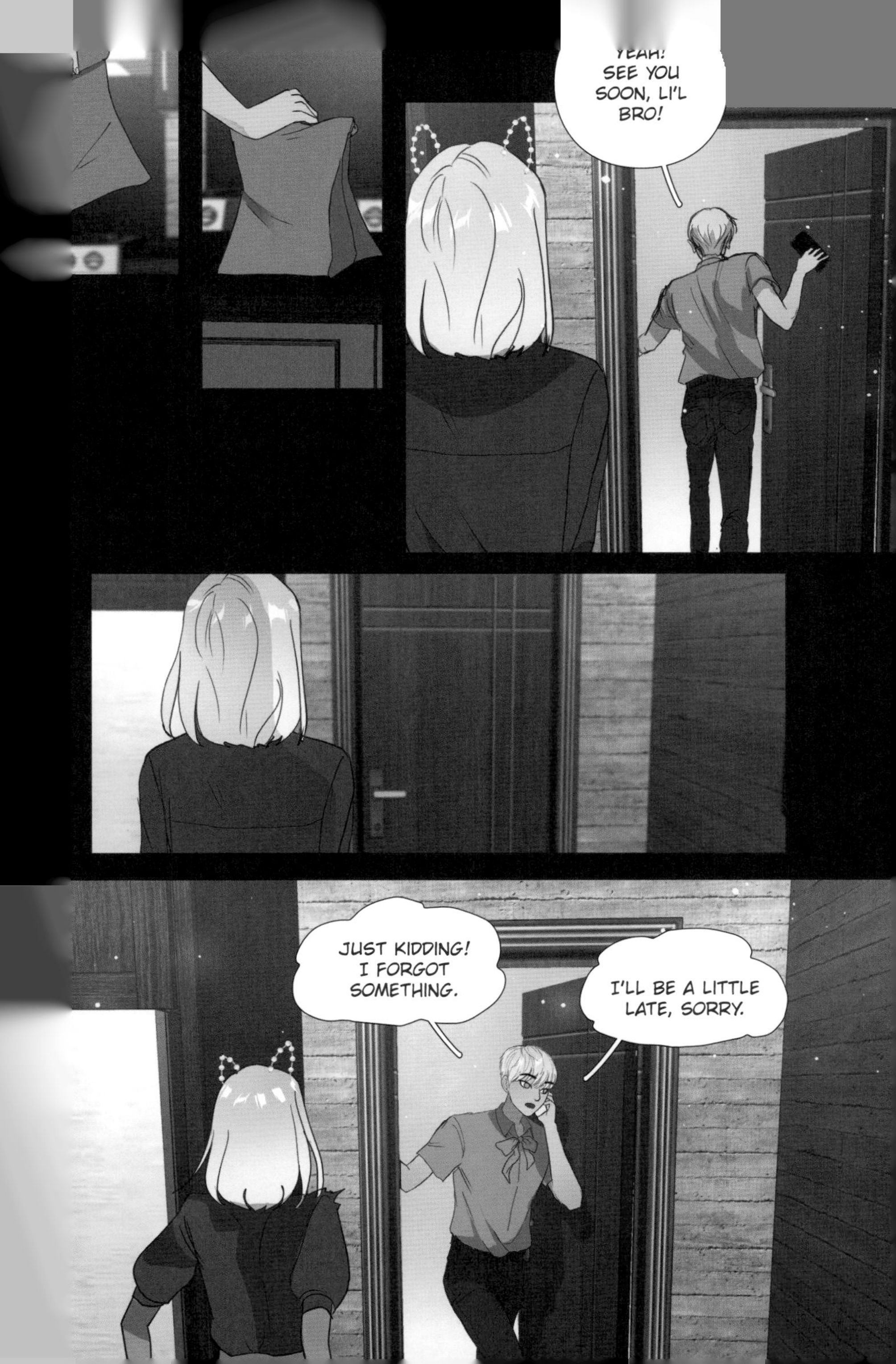
YEAH! SEE YOU SOON, LI'L BRO!
JUST KIDDING! I FORGOT SOMETHING.
I'LL BE A LITTLE LATE, SORRY.

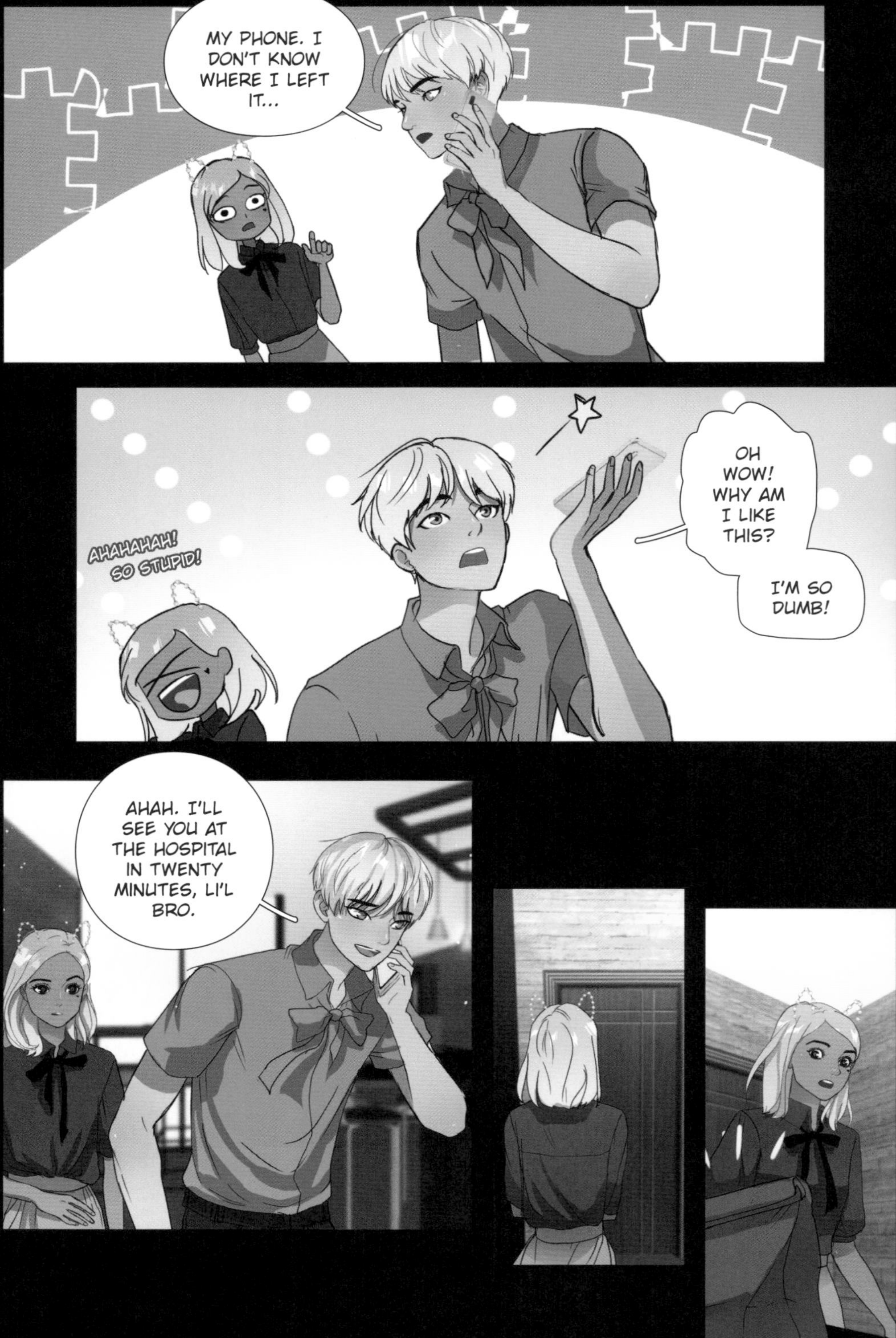
MY PHONE. I DON'T KNOW WHERE I LEFT IT...
AHAHAHAH! SO STUPID!
OH WOW! WHY AM I LIKE THIS?
I'M SO DUMB!
AHAH. I'LL SEE YOU AT THE HOSPITAL IN TWENTY MINUTES, LI'L BRO.

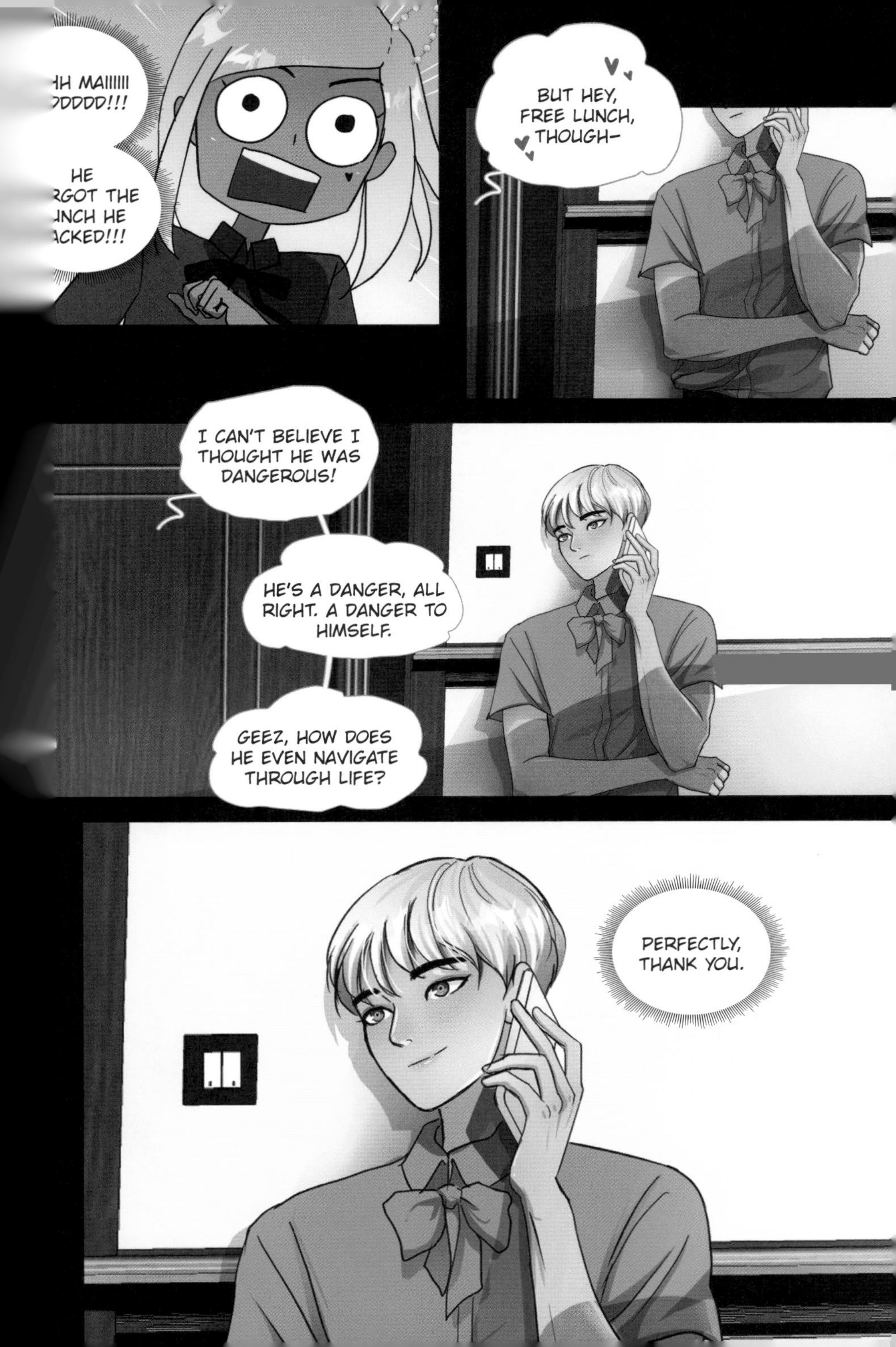
HH MAIIIIII DDDDD!!!
HE RGOT THE NCH HE ACKED!!!
BUT HEY, FREE LUNCH, THOUGH–
I CAN'T BELIEVE I THOUGHT HE WAS DANGEROUS!
HE'S A DANGER, ALL RIGHT. A DANGER TO HIMSELF.
GEEZ, HOW DOES HE EVEN NAVIGATE THROUGH LIFE?
PERFECTLY, THANK YOU.

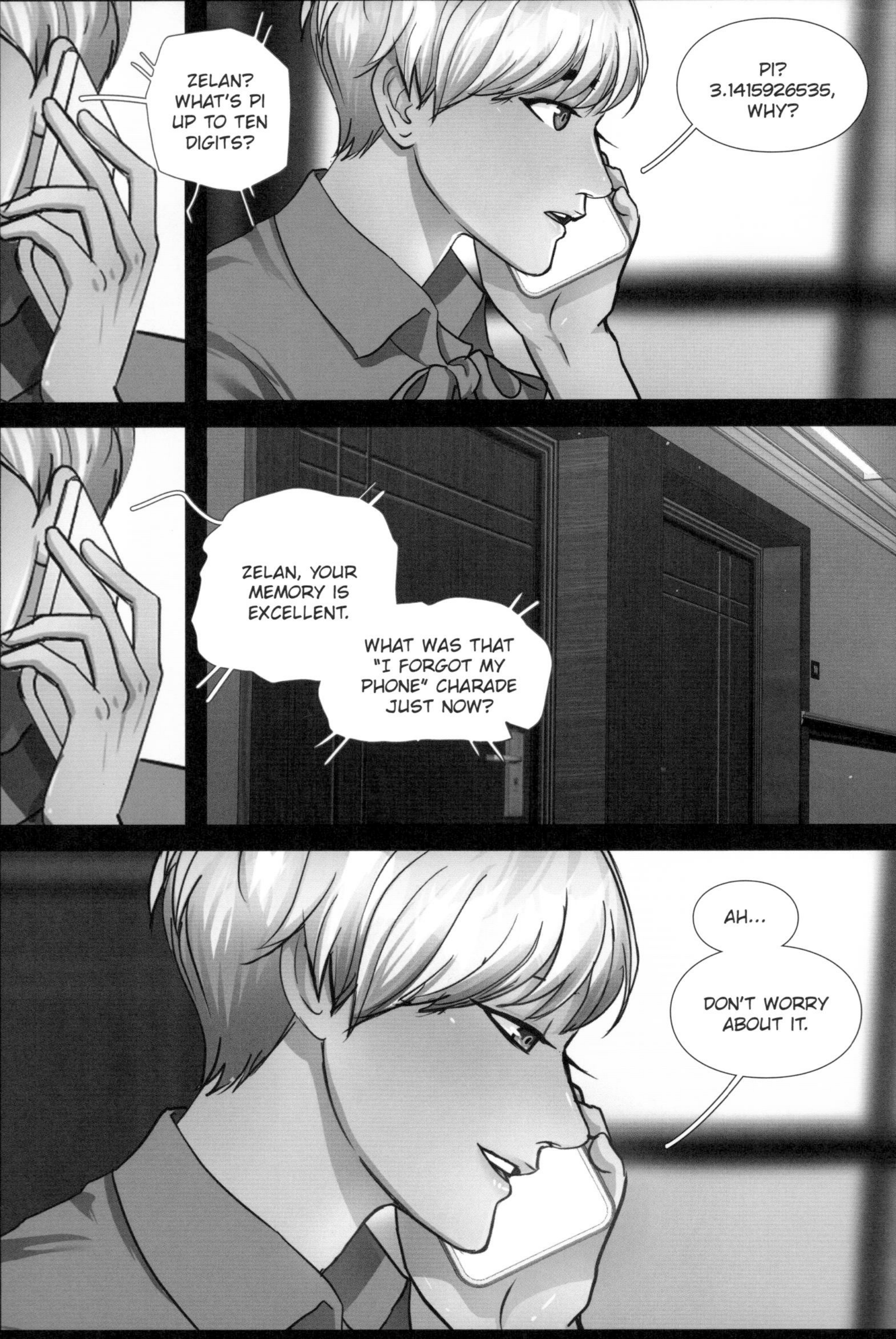
ZELAN? WHAT'S PI UP TO TEN DIGITS?
PI? 3.1415926535, WHY?
ZELAN, YOUR MEMORY IS EXCELLENT.
WHAT WAS THAT "I FORGOT MY PHONE" CHARADE JUST NOW?
AH...
DON'T WORRY ABOUT IT.

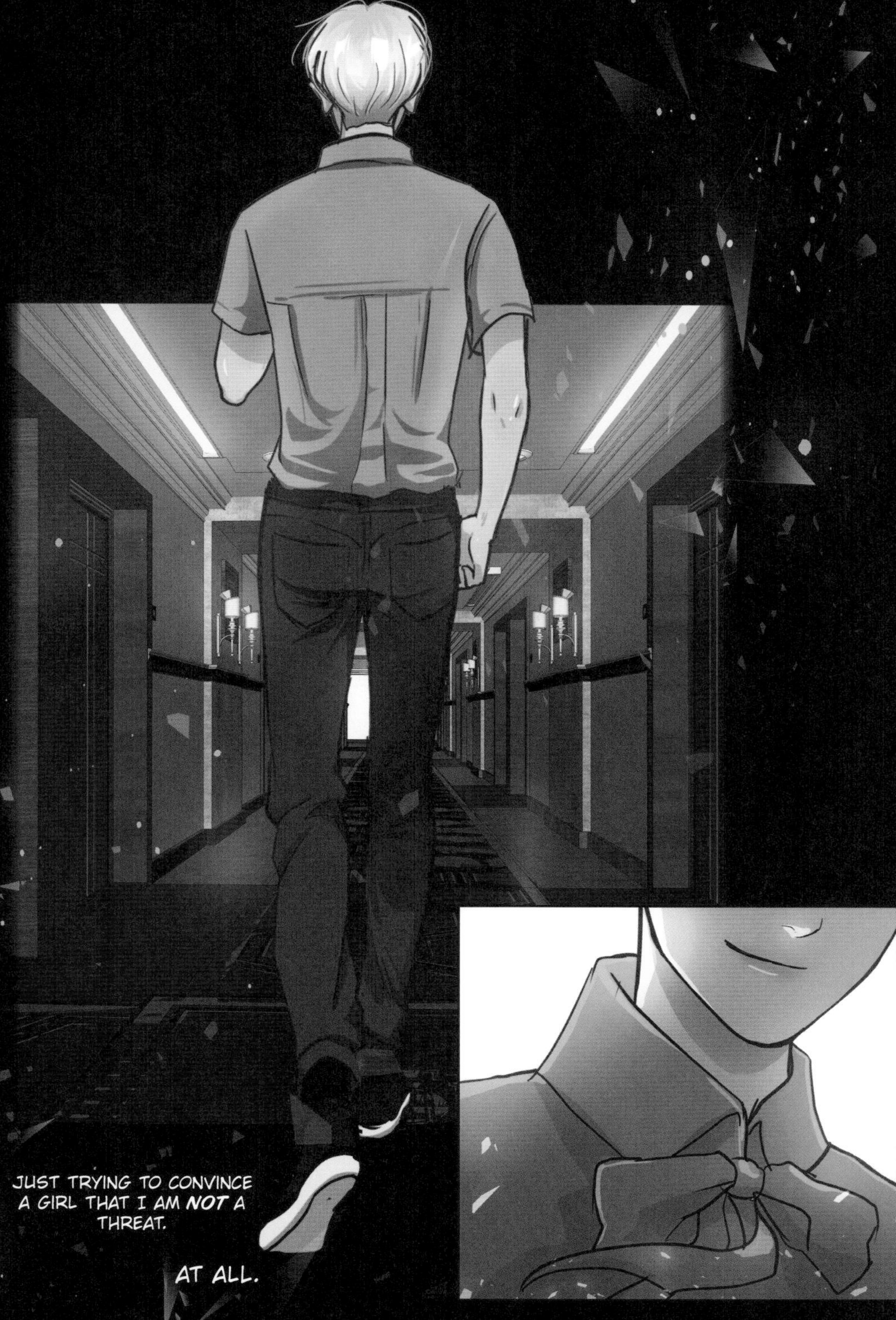
JUST TRYING TO CONVINCE A GIRL THAT I AM **NOT** A THREAT.
AT ALL.

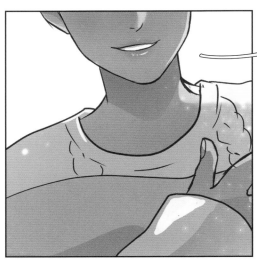

TELL ME, ZYLITH. WHY ARE YOU HOLDING A FIRST CONVERSATION WITH ME...

WITH YOUR CAT GONE, PEPPER SPRAY, AND AN EXIT PREPARED?

AND YOU ASKED WHY *I* HAVE BEEN IGNORING YOU?

THAT'S AMUSING.

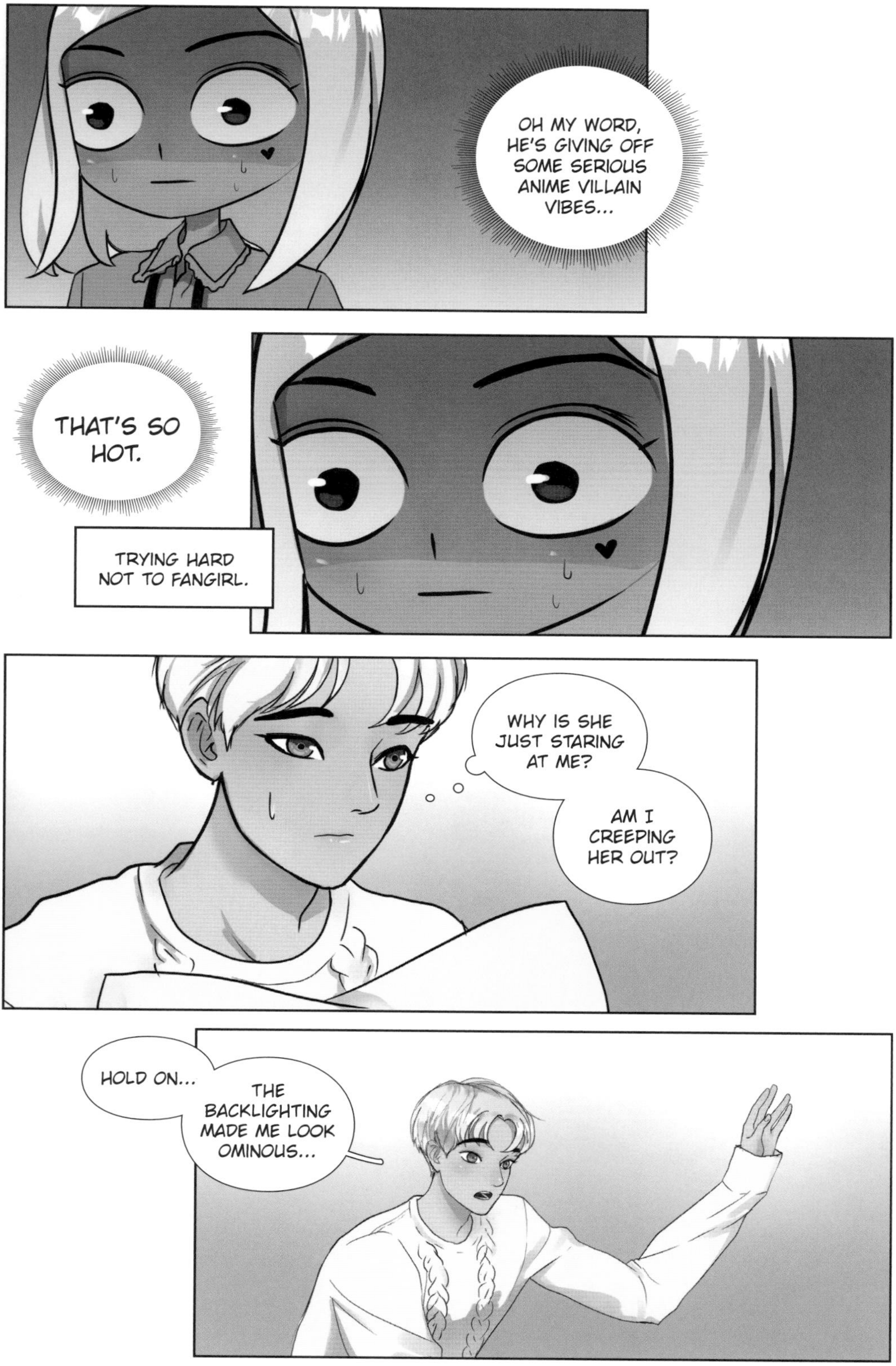
OH MY WORD, HE'S GIVING OFF SOME SERIOUS ANIME VILLAIN VIBES...
THAT'S SO HOT.
TRYING HARD NOT TO FANGIRL.
WHY IS SHE JUST STARING AT ME?
AM I CREEPING HER OUT?
HOLD ON...
THE BACKLIGHTING MADE ME LOOK OMINOUS...

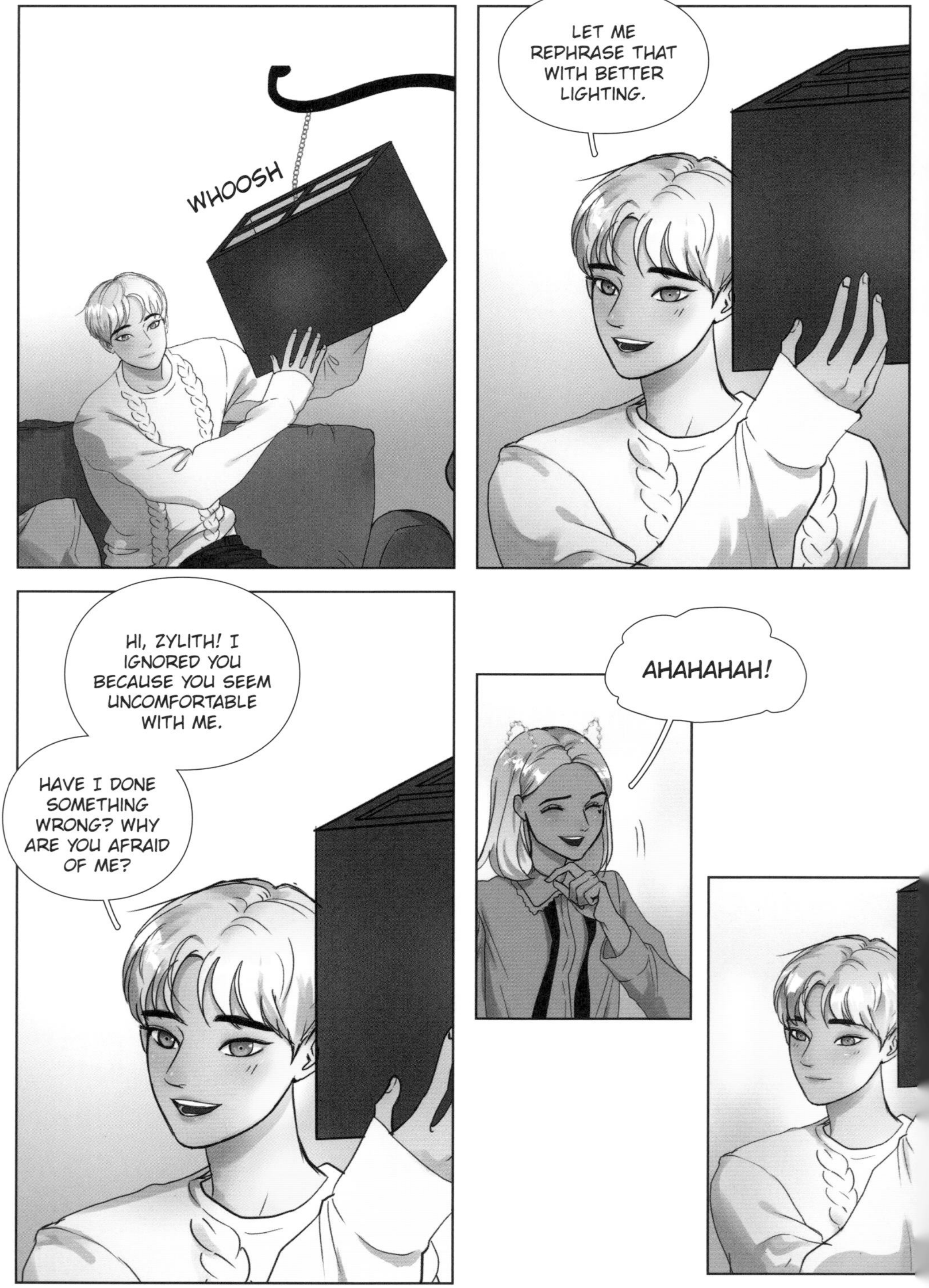

WHOOSH
LET ME REPHRASE THAT WITH BETTER LIGHTING.
HI, ZYLITH! I IGNORED YOU BECAUSE YOU SEEM UNCOMFORTABLE WITH ME.
HAVE I DONE SOMETHING WRONG? WHY ARE YOU AFRAID OF ME?
AHAHAHAH!

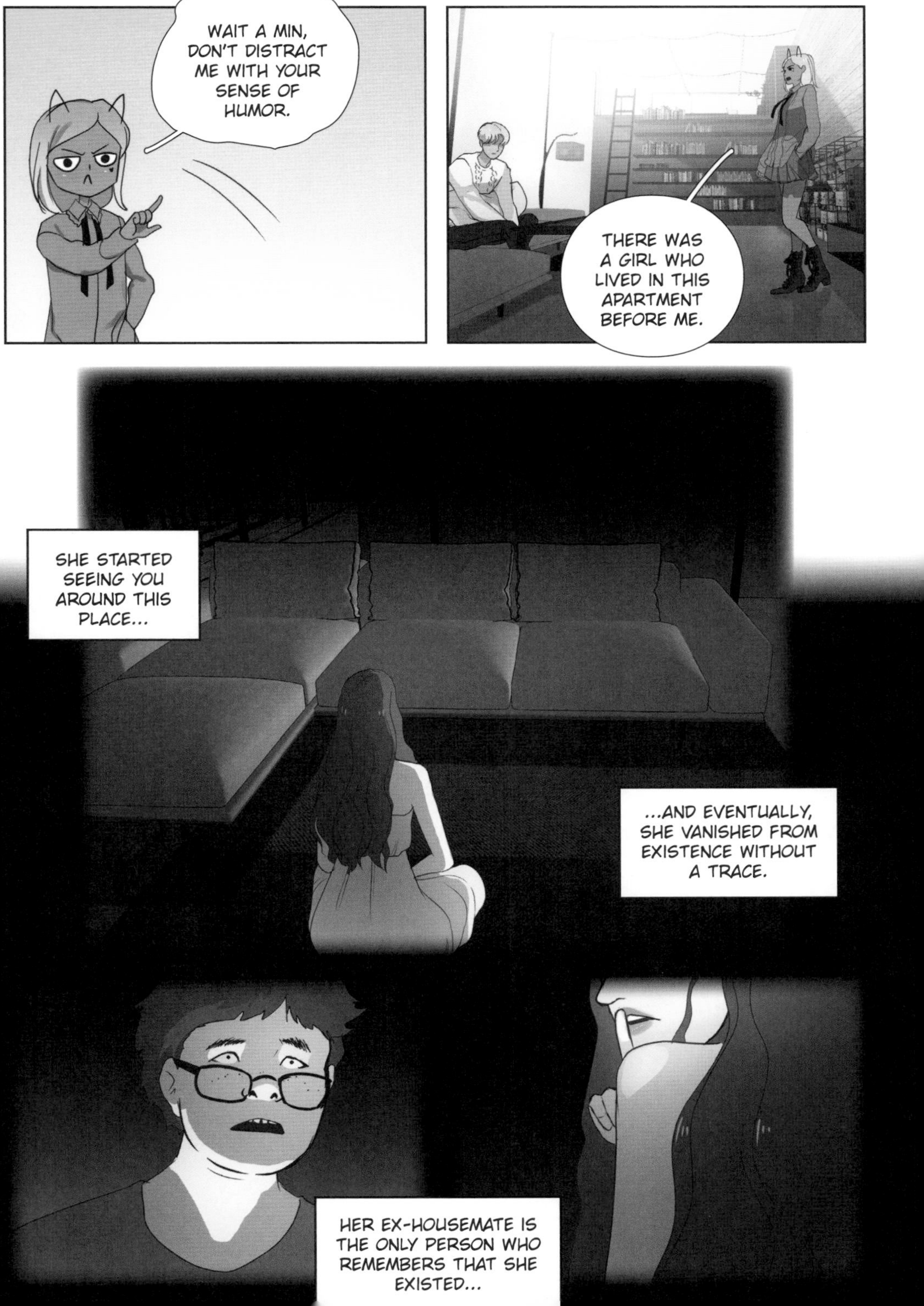
WAIT A MIN, DON'T DISTRACT ME WITH YOUR SENSE OF HUMOR.
THERE WAS A GIRL WHO LIVED IN THIS APARTMENT BEFORE ME.
SHE STARTED SEEING YOU AROUND THIS PLACE...
...AND EVENTUALLY, SHE VANISHED FROM EXISTENCE WITHOUT A TRACE.
HER EX-HOUSEMATE IS THE ONLY PERSON WHO REMEMBERS THAT SHE EXISTED...

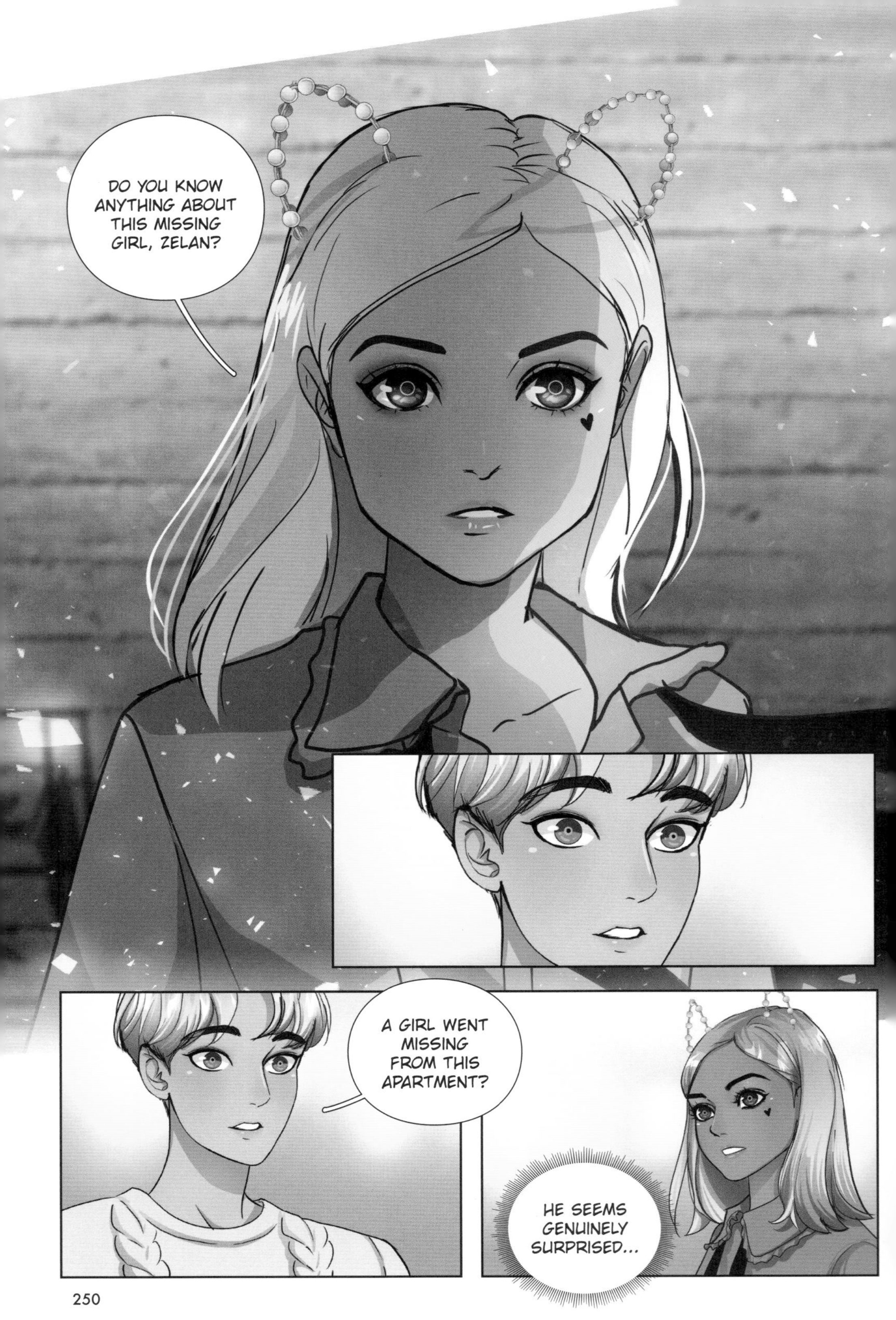
DO YOU KNOW ANYTHING ABOUT THIS MISSING GIRL, ZELAN?
A GIRL WENT MISSING FROM THIS APARTMENT?
HE SEEMS GENUINELY SURPRISED...

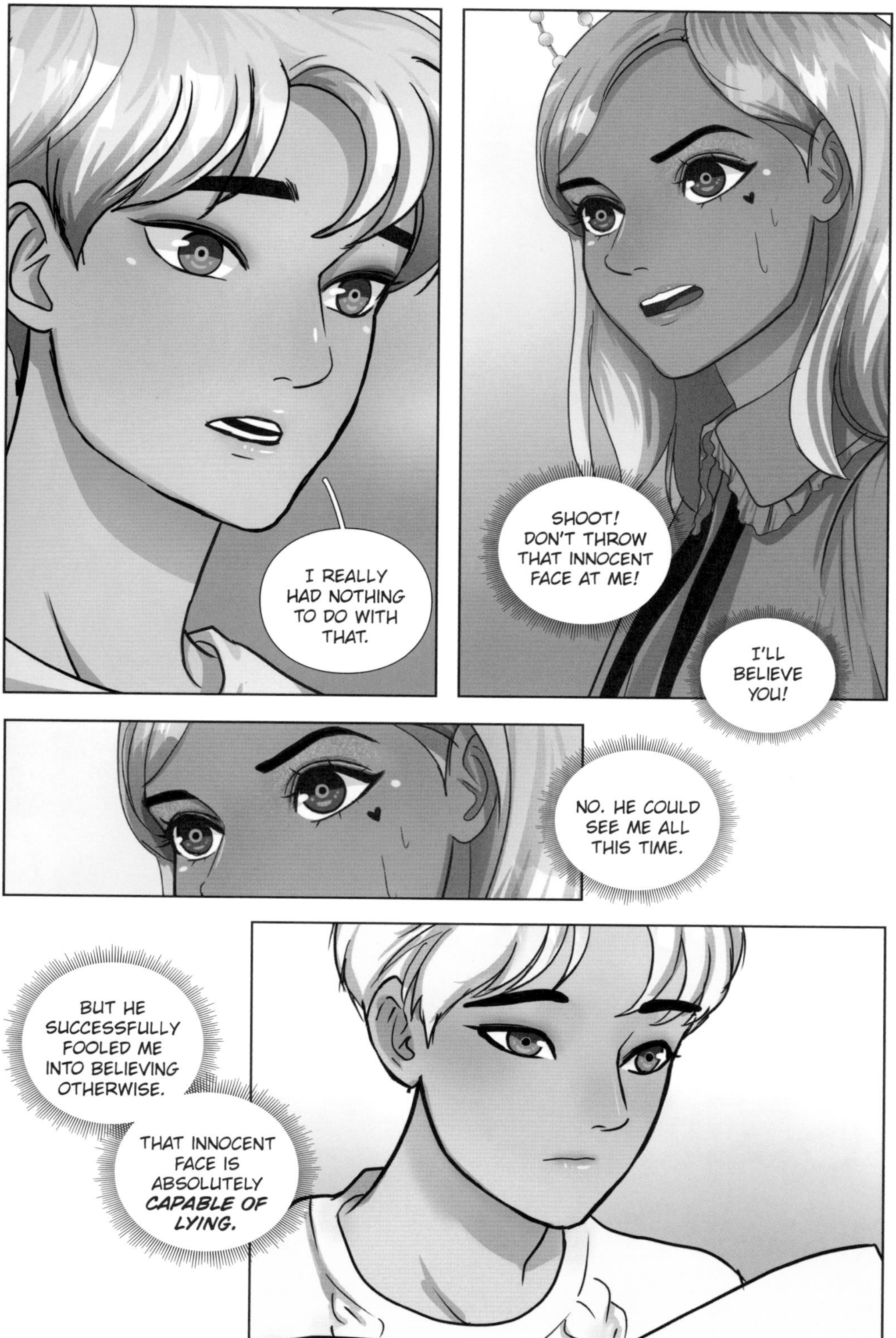
I REALLY HAD NOTHING TO DO WITH THAT.
SHOOT! DON'T THROW THAT INNOCENT FACE AT ME!
I'LL BELIEVE YOU!
NO. HE COULD SEE ME ALL THIS TIME.
BUT HE SUCCESSFULLY FOOLED ME INTO BELIEVING OTHERWISE.
THAT INNOCENT FACE IS ABSOLUTELY ***CAPABLE OF LYING.***

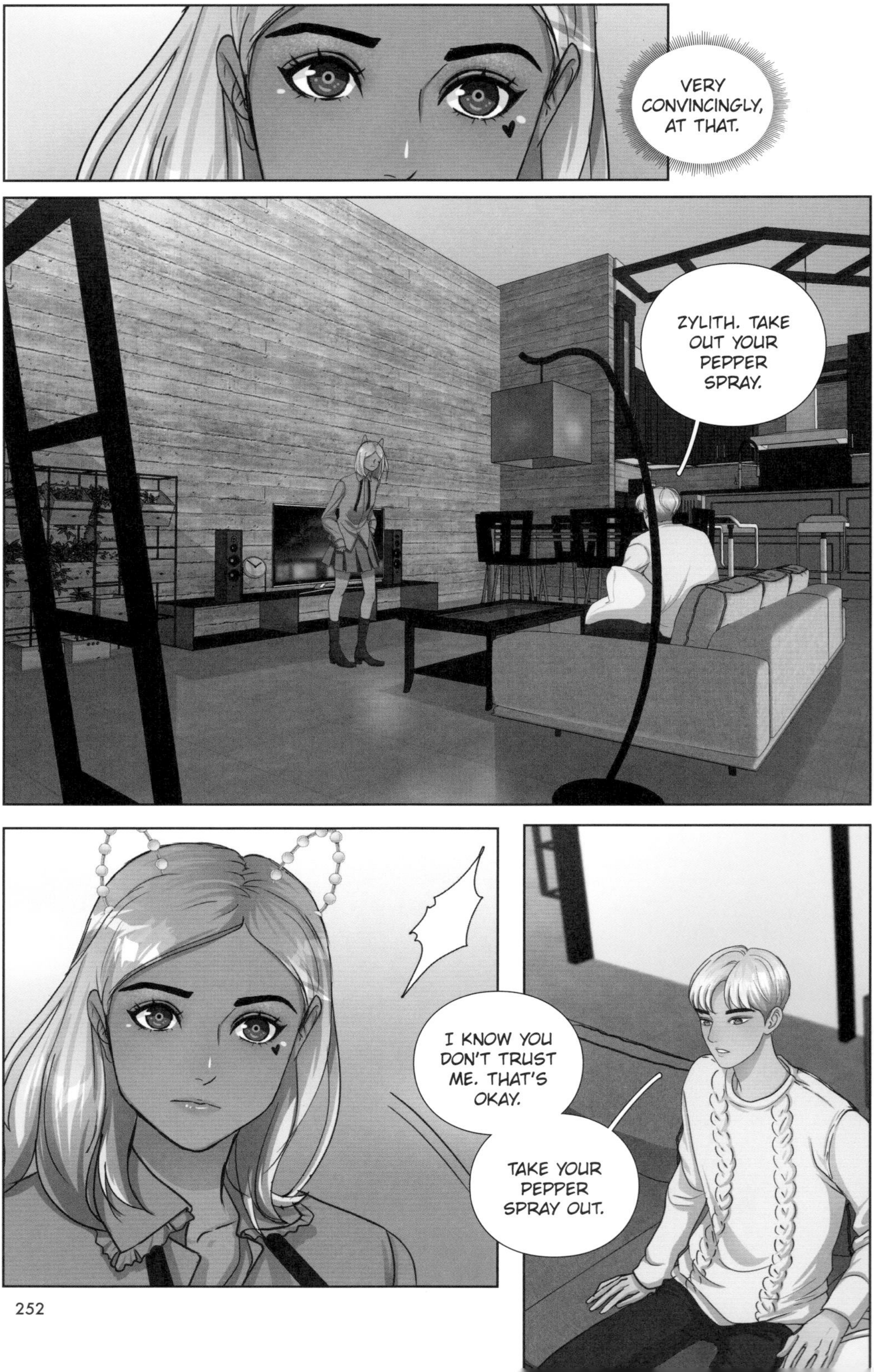
VERY CONVINCINGLY, AT THAT.
ZYLITH. TAKE OUT YOUR PEPPER SPRAY.
I KNOW YOU DON'T TRUST ME. THAT'S OKAY.
TAKE YOUR PEPPER SPRAY OUT.

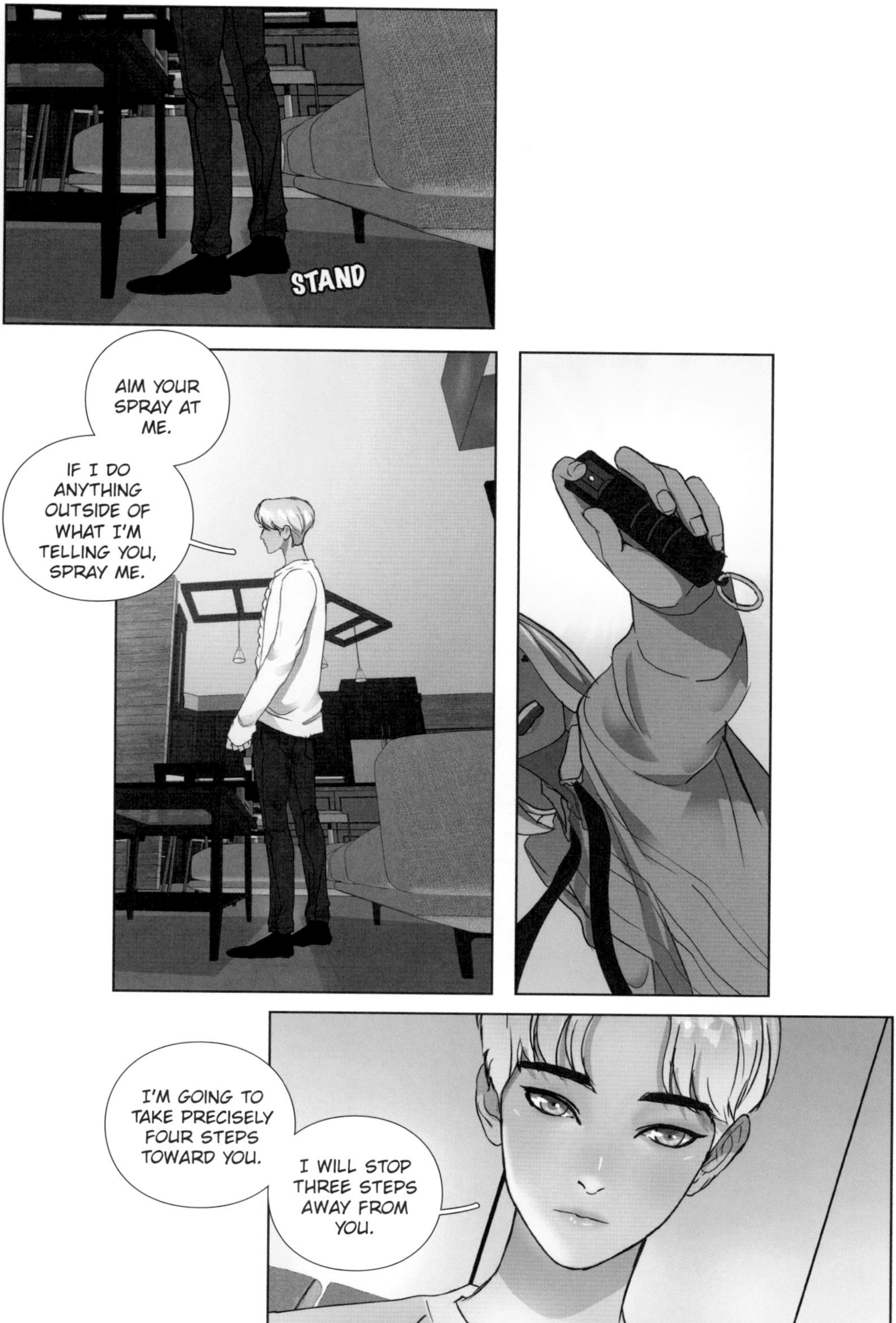
STAND
AIM YOUR SPRAY AT ME.
IF I DO ANYTHING OUTSIDE OF WHAT I'M TELLING YOU, SPRAY ME.
I'M GOING TO TAKE PRECISELY FOUR STEPS TOWARD YOU.
I WILL STOP THREE STEPS AWAY FROM YOU.

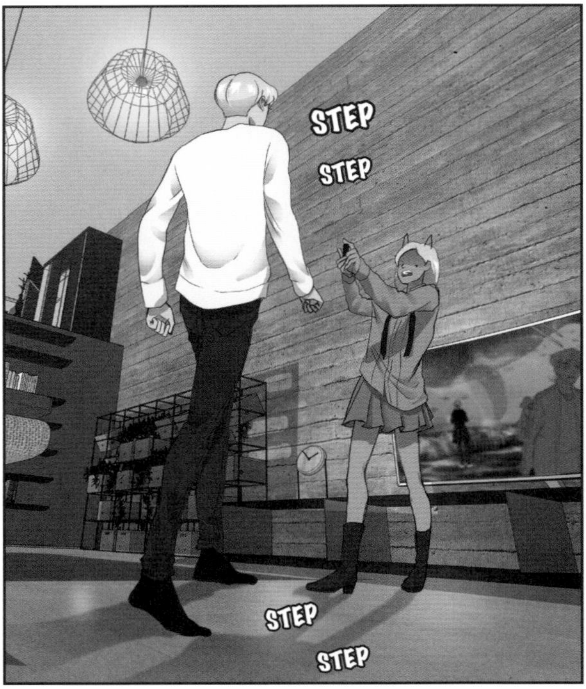
STEP
STEP
STEP
STEP

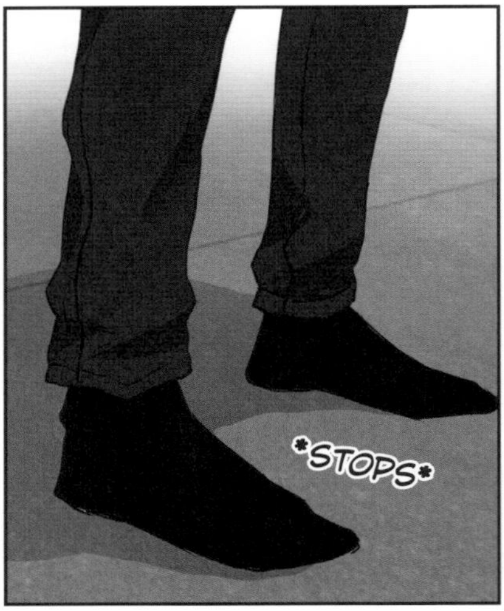
STOPS

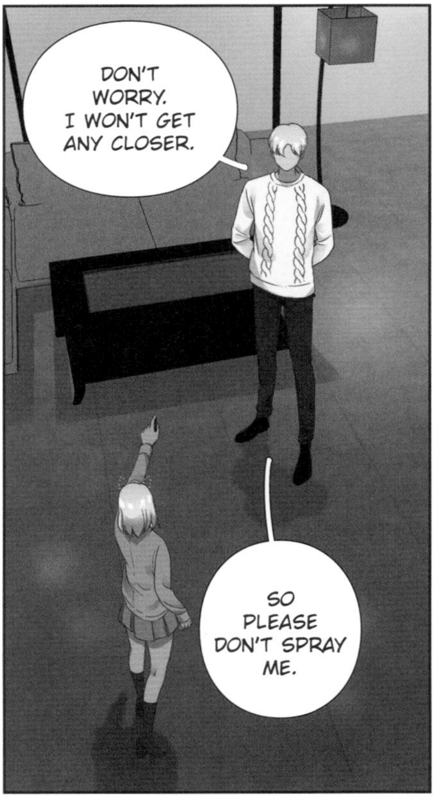
DON'T WORRY. I WON'T GET ANY CLOSER.
SO PLEASE DON'T SPRAY ME.

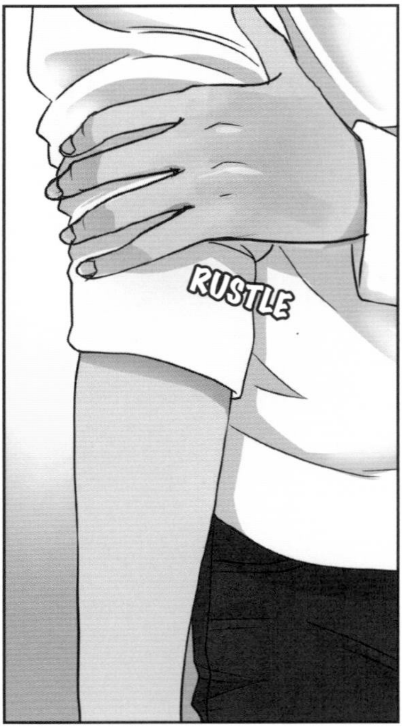
RUSTLE

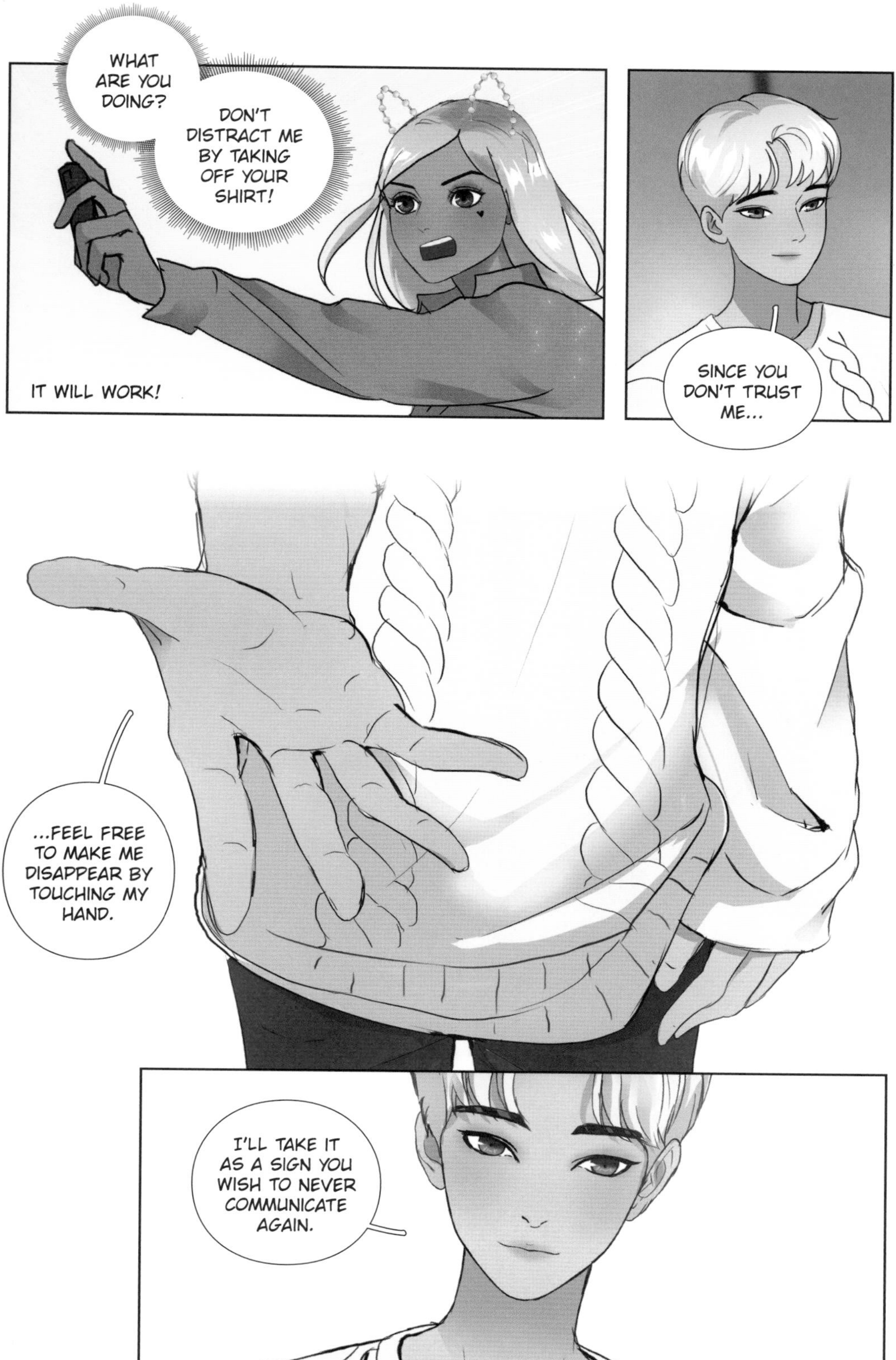

WHAT ARE YOU DOING?
DON'T DISTRACT ME BY TAKING OFF YOUR SHIRT!
IT WILL WORK!
SINCE YOU DON'T TRUST ME...
...FEEL FREE TO MAKE ME DISAPPEAR BY TOUCHING MY HAND.
I'LL TAKE IT AS A SIGN YOU WISH TO NEVER COMMUNICATE AGAIN.

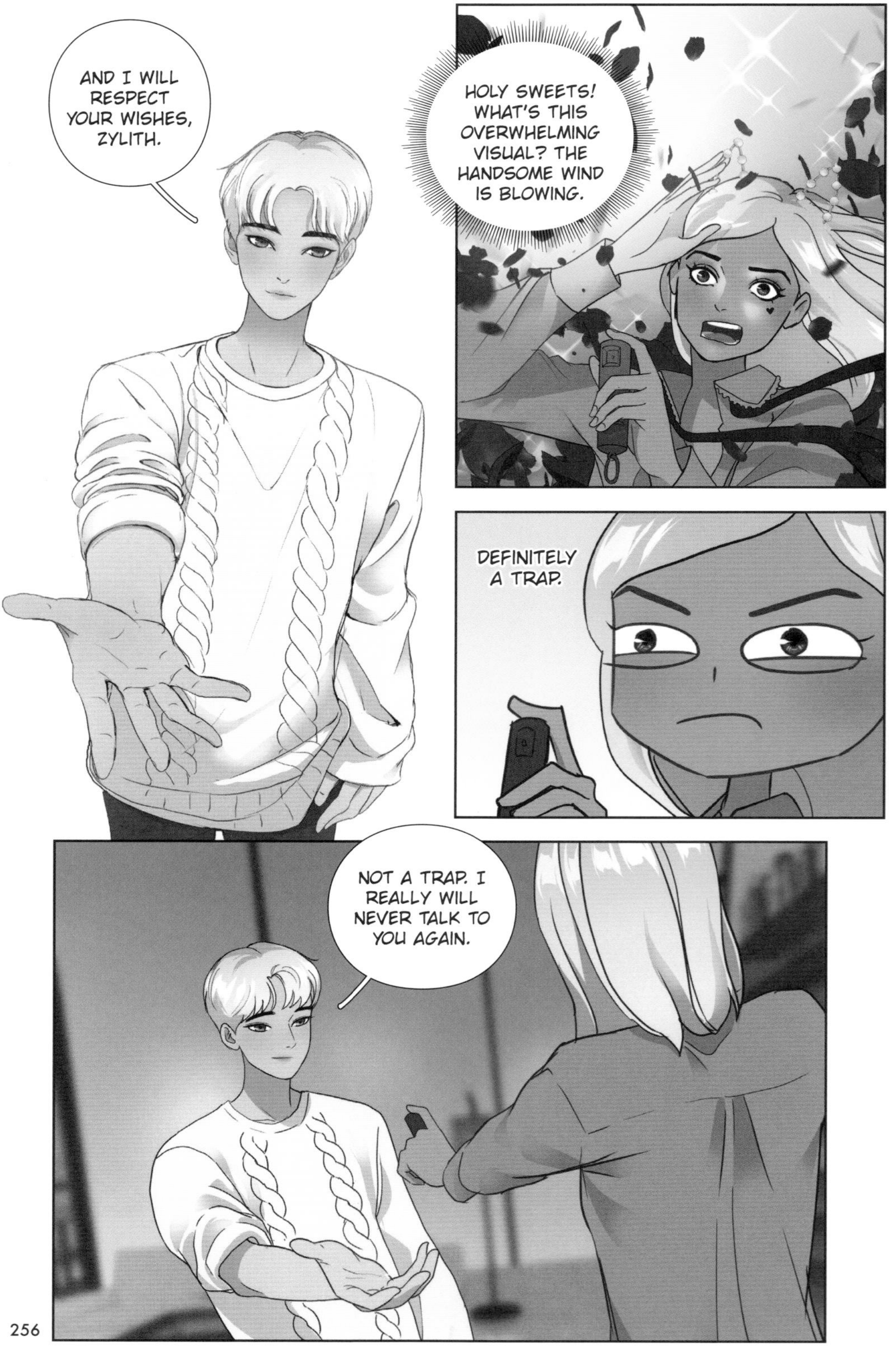
AND I WILL RESPECT YOUR WISHES, ZYLITH.
HOLY SWEETS! WHAT'S THIS OVERWHELMING VISUAL? THE HANDSOME WIND IS BLOWING.
DEFINITELY A TRAP.
NOT A TRAP. I REALLY WILL NEVER TALK TO YOU AGAIN.

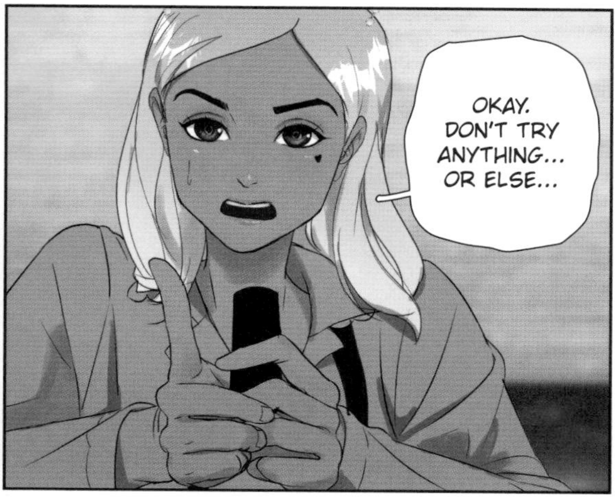
OKAY. DON'T TRY ANYTHING... OR ELSE...

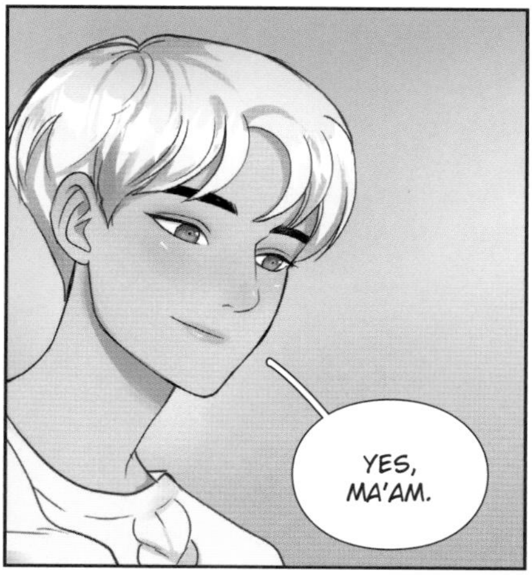
YES, MA'AM.

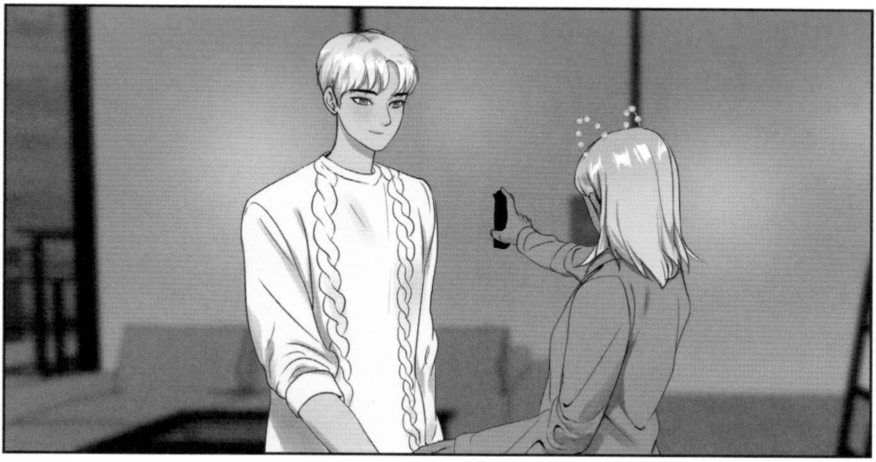

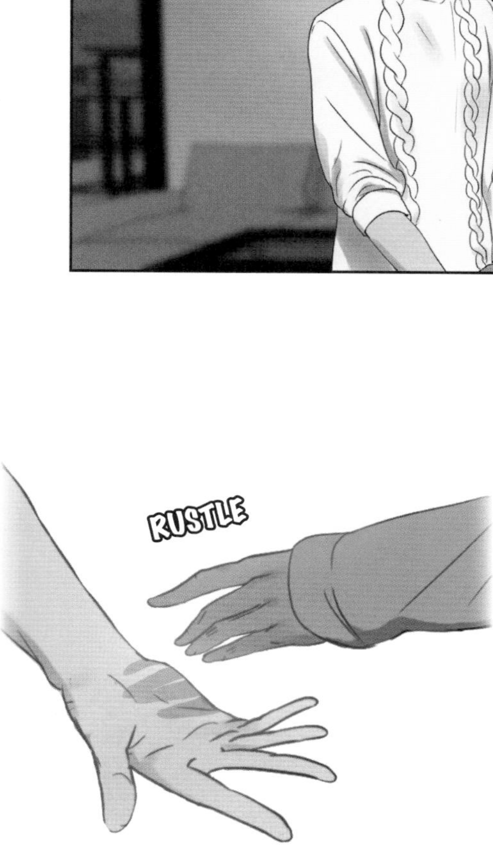
RUSTLE

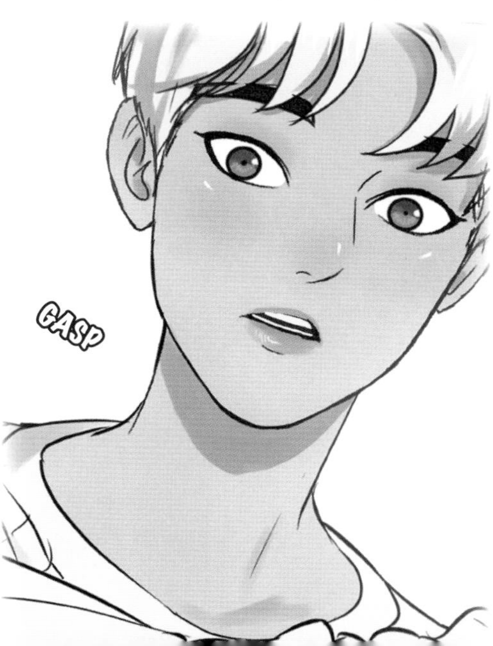
GASP

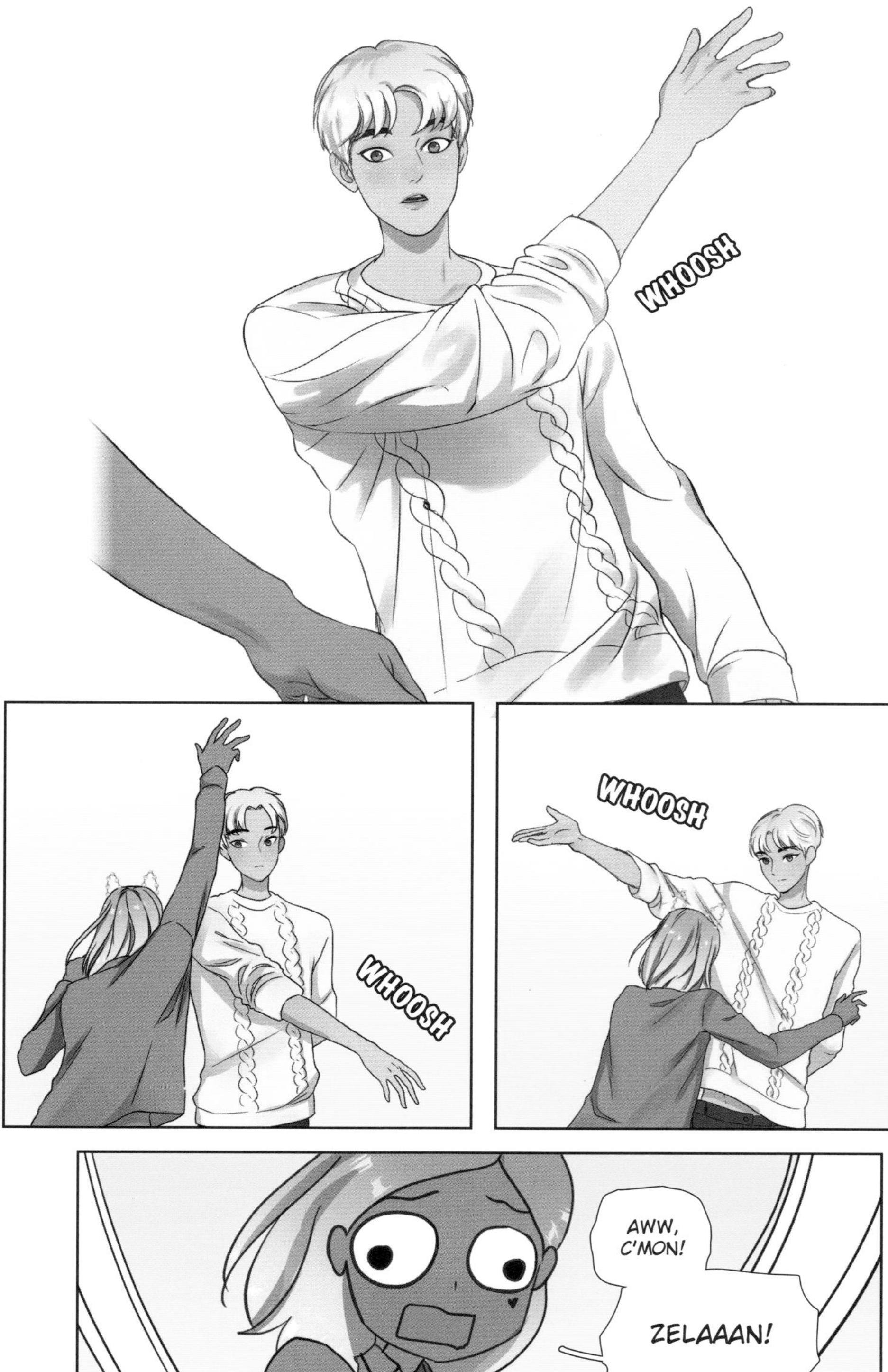
WHOOSH
WHOOSH
WHOOSH
AWW, C'MON!
ZELAAAN!

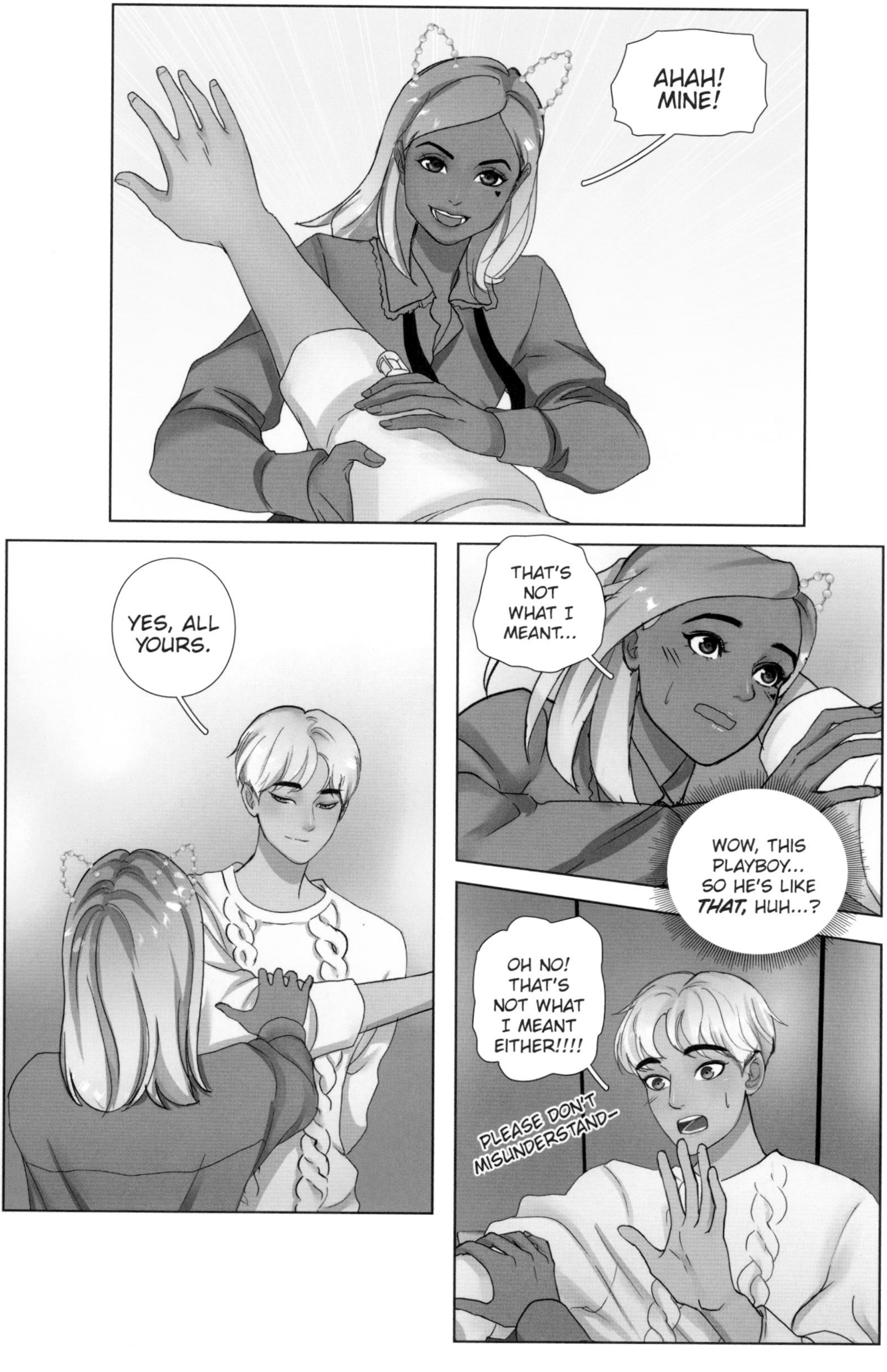
AHAH! MINE!
YES, ALL YOURS.
THAT'S NOT WHAT I MEANT...
WOW, THIS PLAYBOY... SO HE'S LIKE *THAT,* HUH...?
OH NO! THAT'S NOT WHAT I MEANT EITHER!!!!
PLEASE DON'T MISUNDERSTAND—

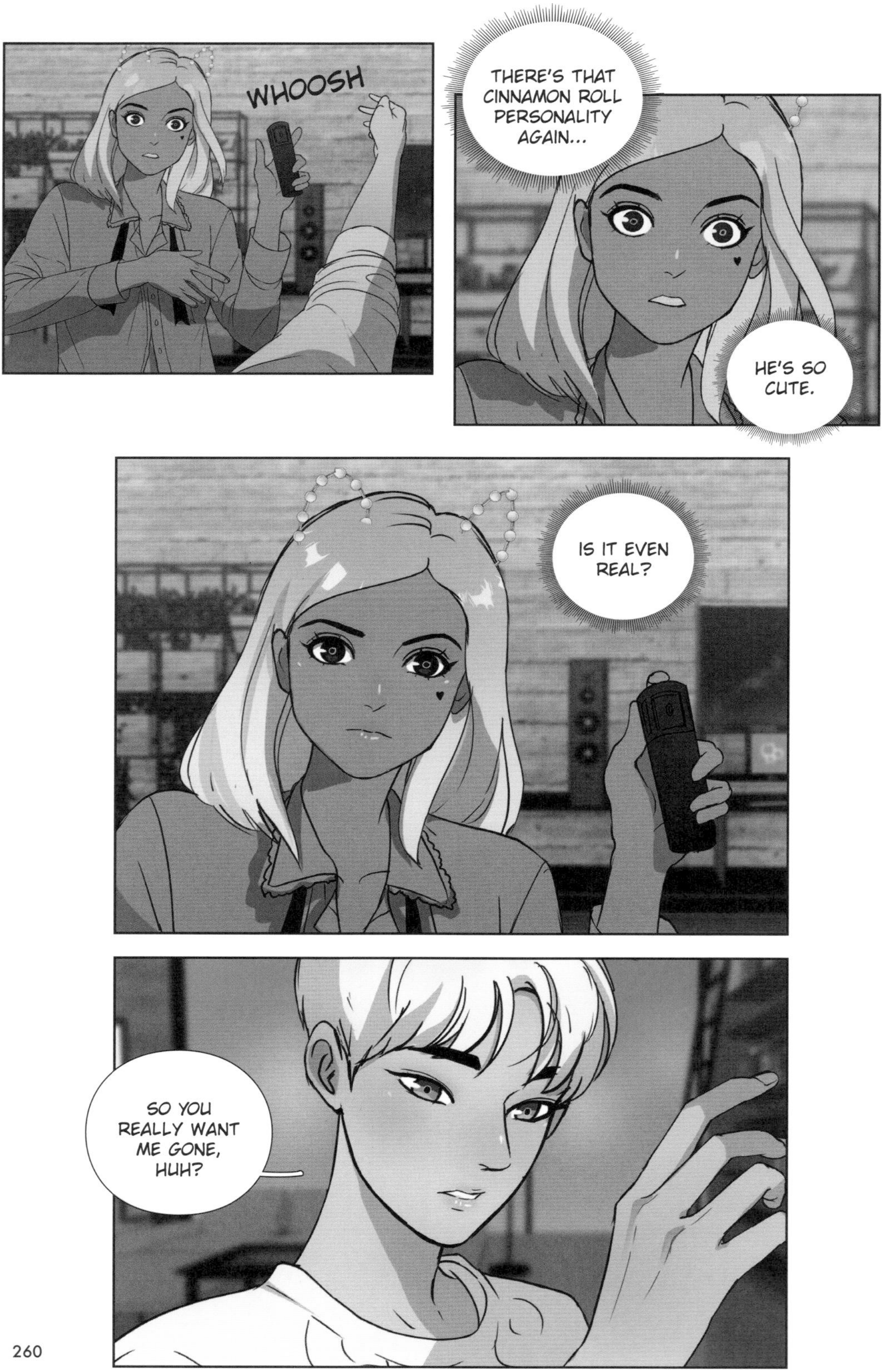
WHOOSH
THERE'S THAT CINNAMON ROLL PERSONALITY AGAIN...
HE'S SO CUTE.
IS IT EVEN REAL?
SO YOU REALLY WANT ME GONE, HUH?

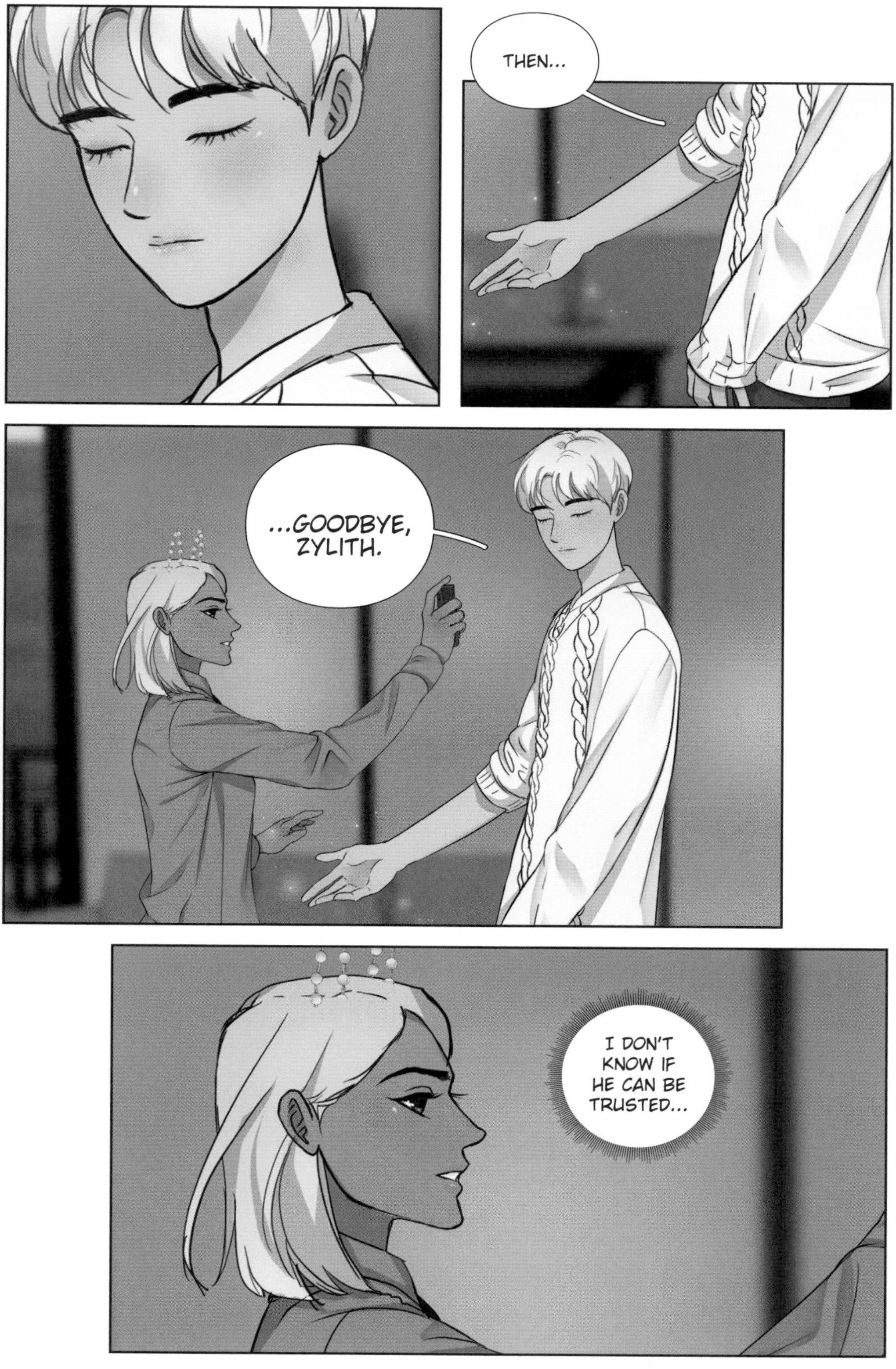
THEN...
...GOODBYE, ZYLITH.
I DON'T KNOW IF HE CAN BE TRUSTED...

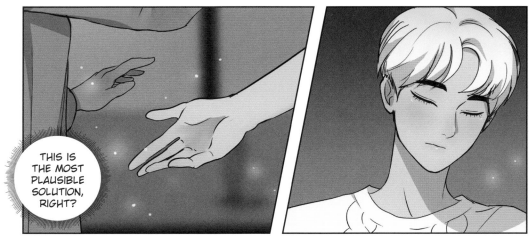

THIS IS THE MOST PLAUSIBLE SOLUTION, RIGHT?

RUSTLE

SHAKE

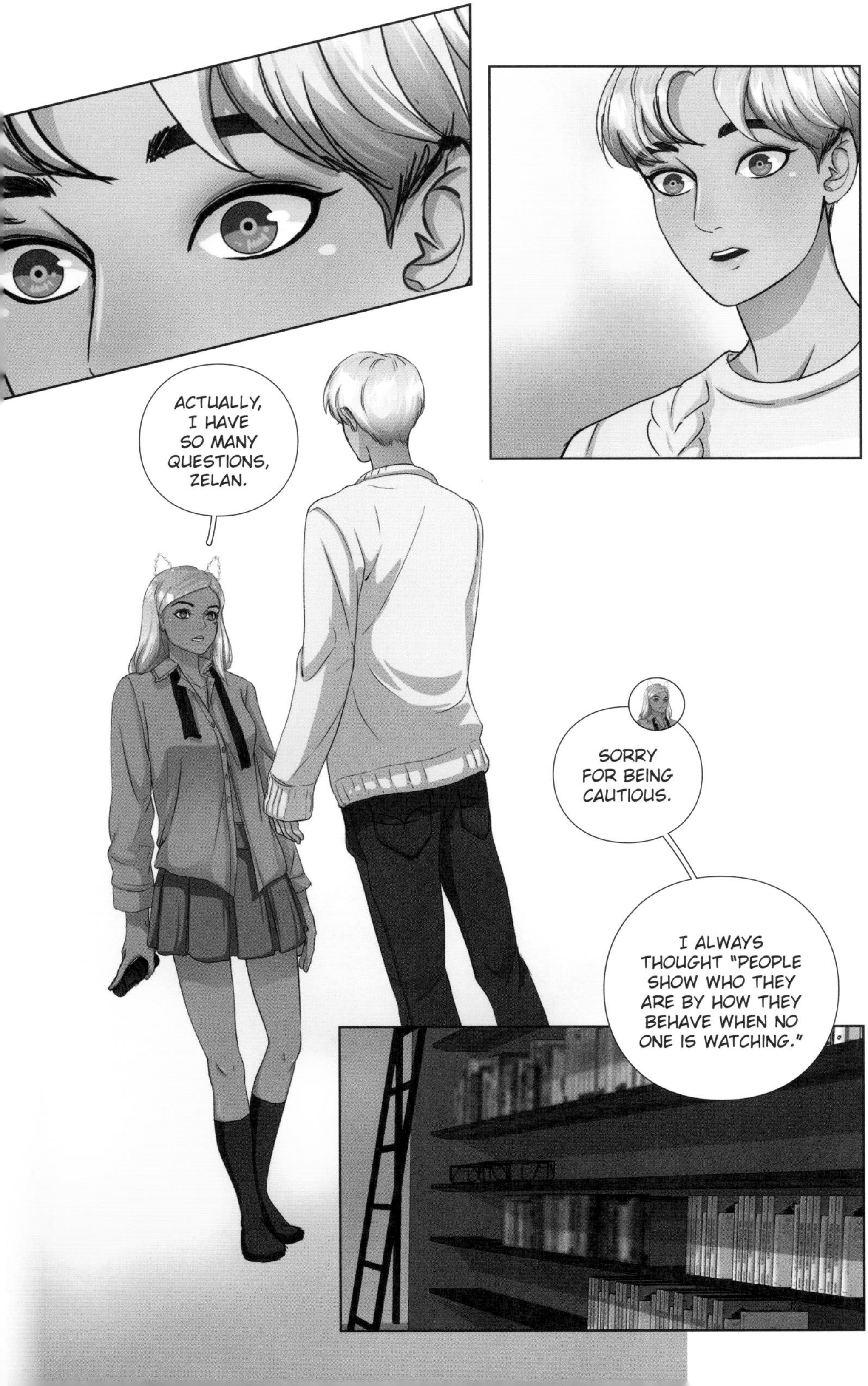

ACTUALLY, I HAVE SO MANY QUESTIONS, ZELAN.
SORRY FOR BEING CAUTIOUS.
I ALWAYS THOUGHT "PEOPLE SHOW WHO THEY ARE BY HOW THEY BEHAVE WHEN NO ONE IS WATCHING."

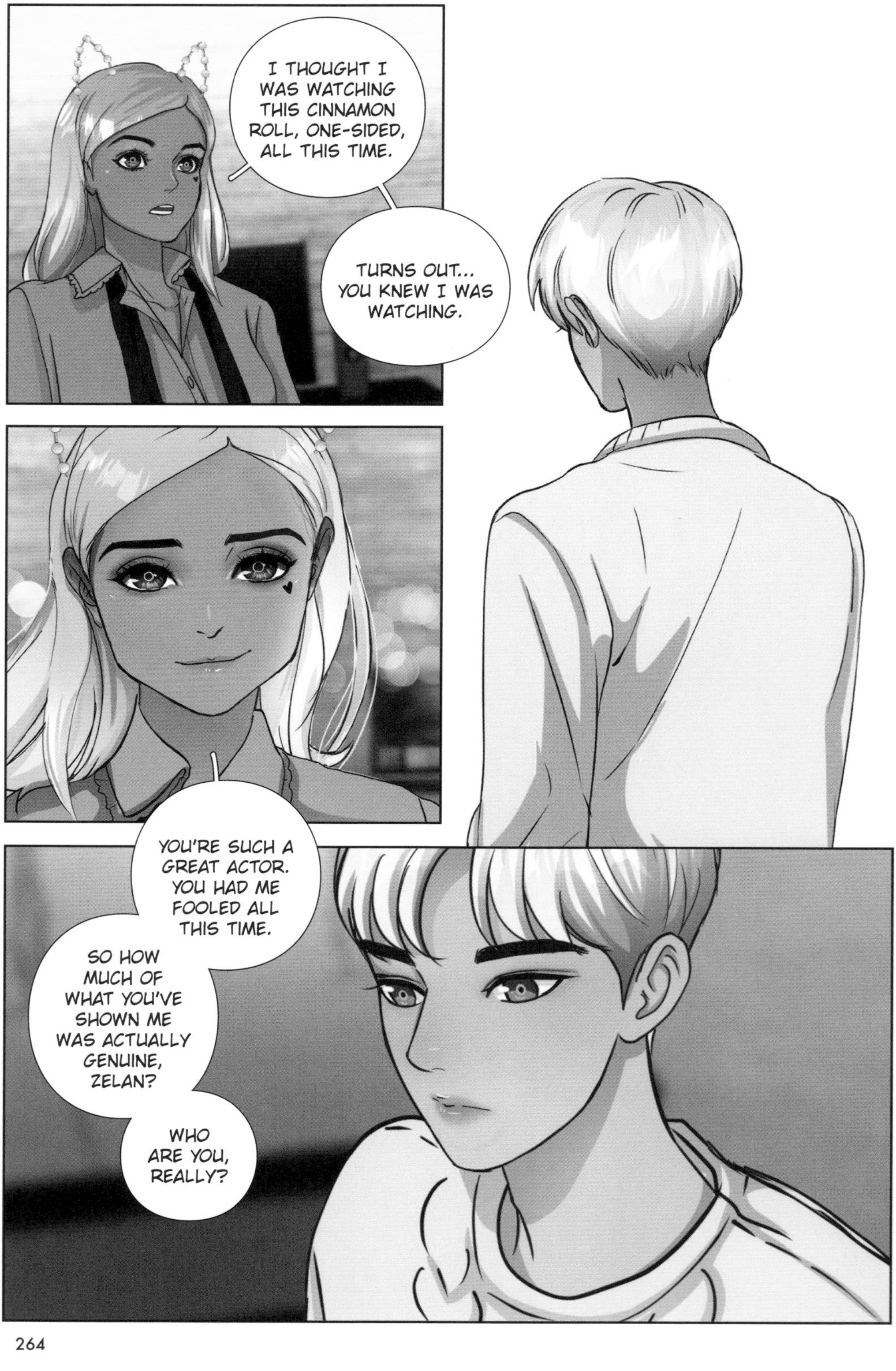
I THOUGHT I WAS WATCHING THIS CINNAMON ROLL, ONE-SIDED, ALL THIS TIME.
TURNS OUT... YOU KNEW I WAS WATCHING.
YOU'RE SUCH A GREAT ACTOR. YOU HAD ME FOOLED ALL THIS TIME.
SO HOW MUCH OF WHAT YOU'VE SHOWN ME WAS ACTUALLY GENUINE, ZELAN?
WHO ARE YOU, REALLY?

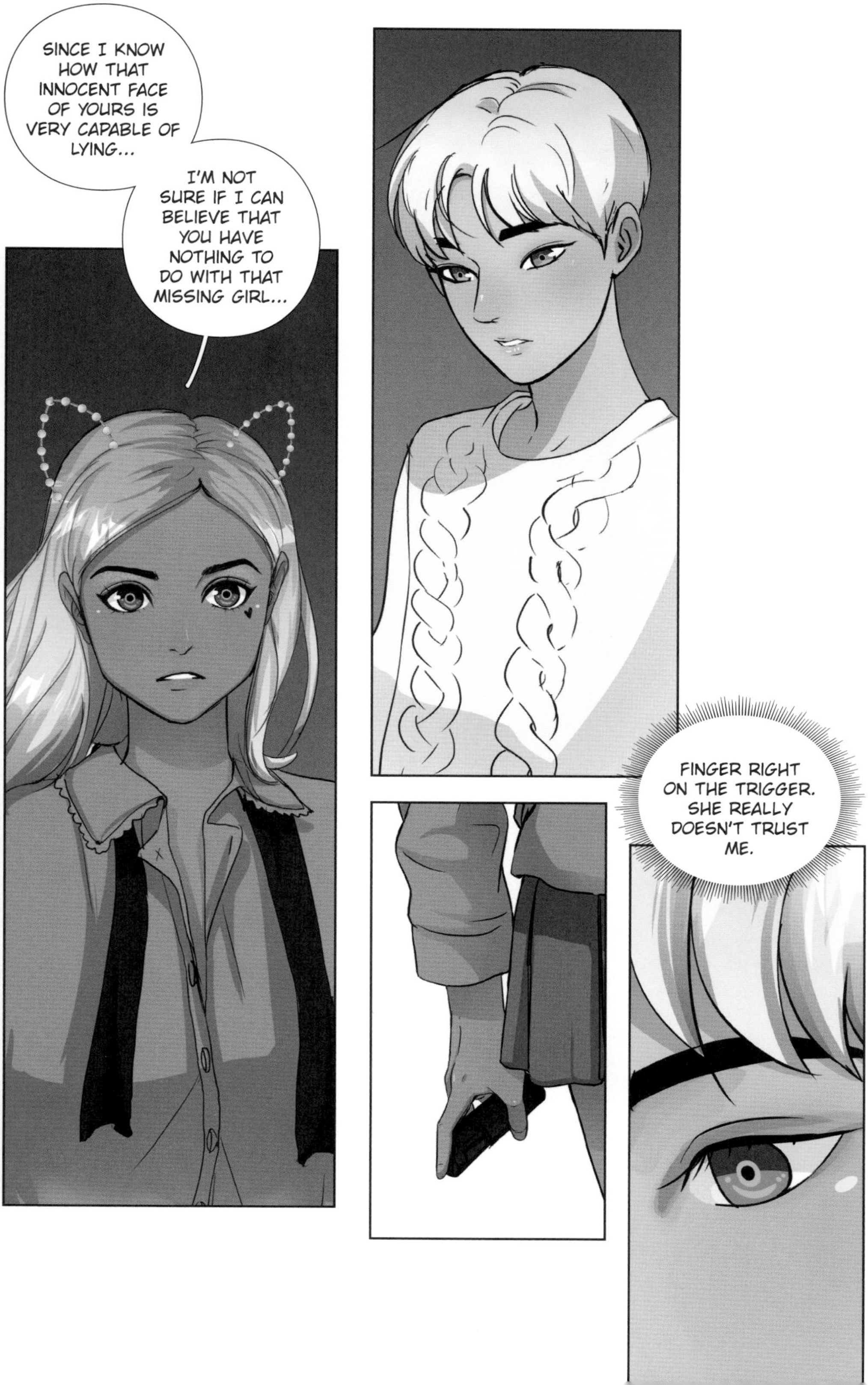
SINCE I KNOW HOW THAT INNOCENT FACE OF YOURS IS VERY CAPABLE OF LYING...
I'M NOT SURE IF I CAN BELIEVE THAT YOU HAVE NOTHING TO DO WITH THAT MISSING GIRL...
FINGER RIGHT ON THE TRIGGER. SHE REALLY DOESN'T TRUST ME.

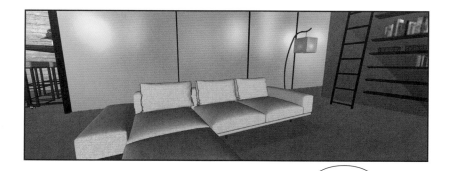

SO LET'S TALK...

THEN I'LL DECIDE WHETHER I EVER WANT TO TALK TO YOU AGAIN.

ALL RIGHT, LET'S START WITH THAT MISSING GIRL.

I THINK I ACTUALLY CAN PROVE MY INNOCENCE...

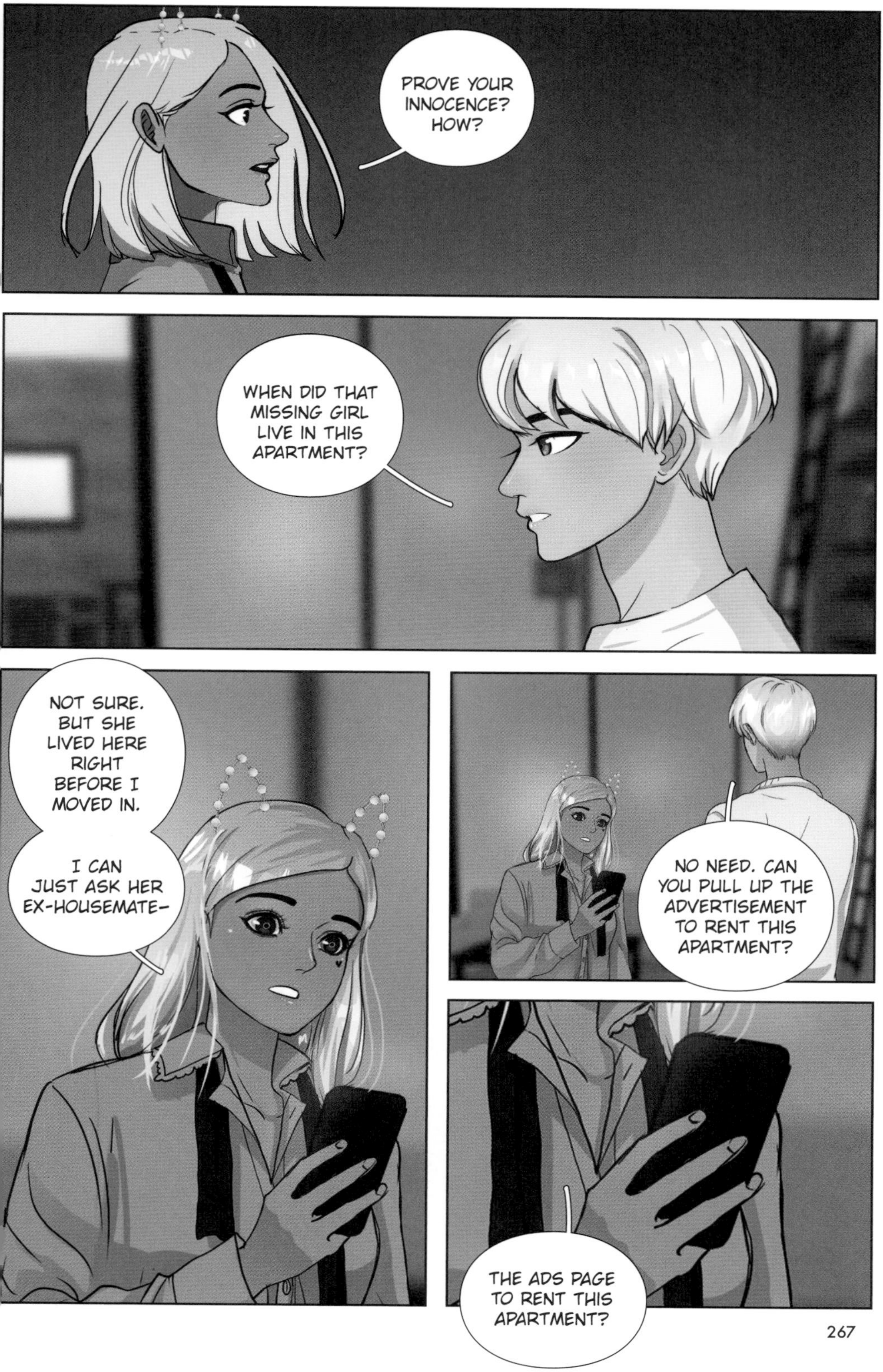
PROVE YOUR INNOCENCE? HOW?
WHEN DID THAT MISSING GIRL LIVE IN THIS APARTMENT?
NOT SURE. BUT SHE LIVED HERE RIGHT BEFORE I MOVED IN.
I CAN JUST ASK HER EX-HOUSEMATE-
NO NEED. CAN YOU PULL UP THE ADVERTISEMENT TO RENT THIS APARTMENT?
THE ADS PAGE TO RENT THIS APARTMENT?

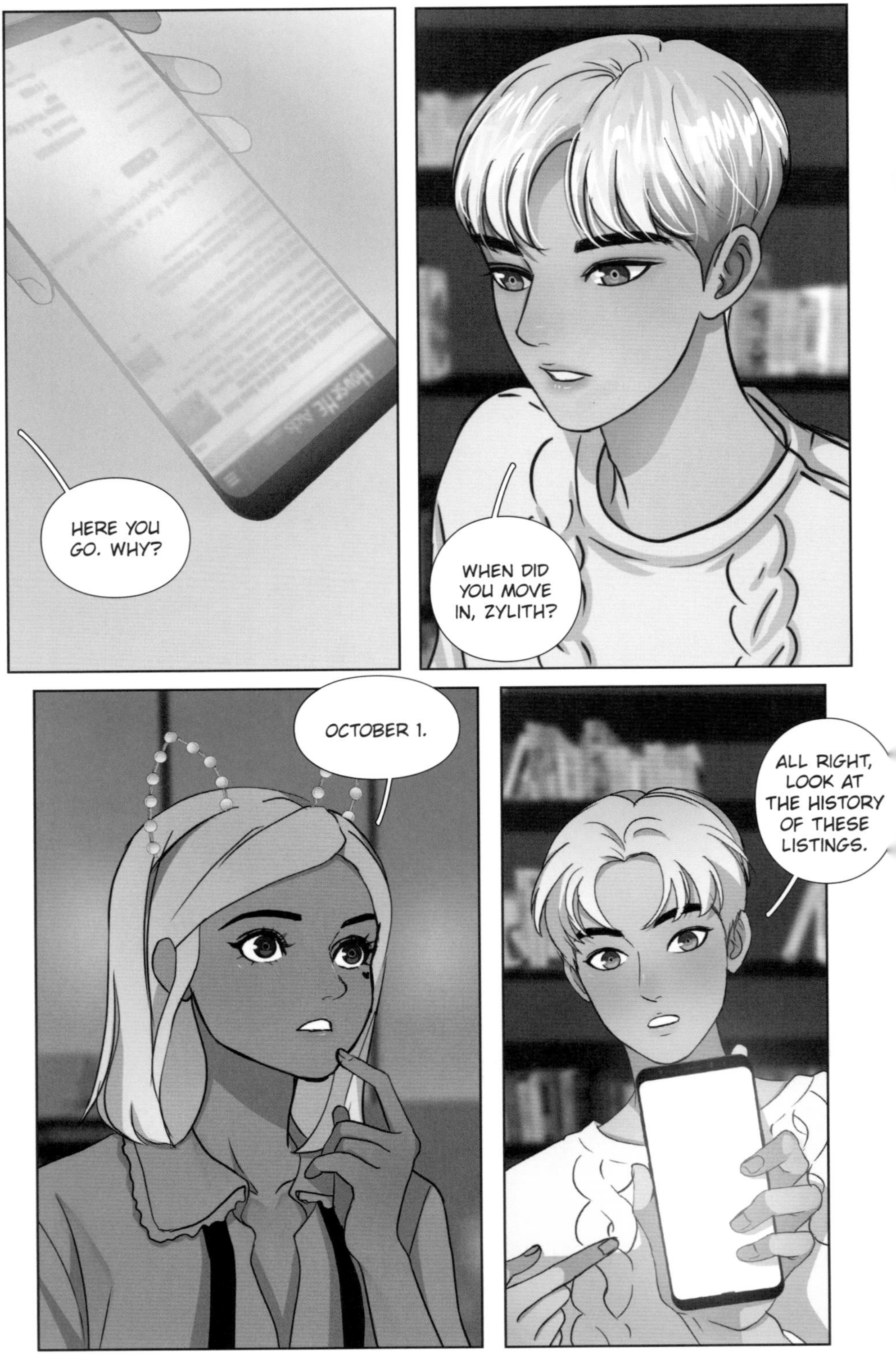
HERE YOU GO. WHY?
WHEN DID YOU MOVE IN, ZYLITH?
OCTOBER 1.
ALL RIGHT, LOOK AT THE HISTORY OF THESE LISTINGS.

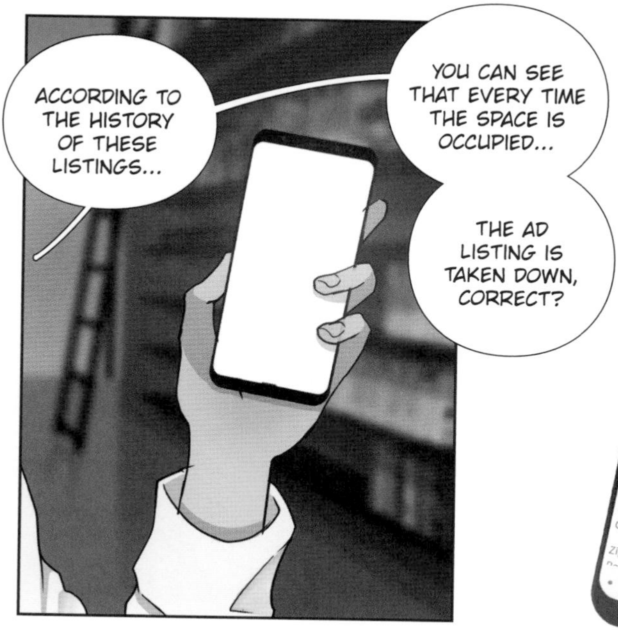
ACCORDING TO THE HISTORY OF THESE LISTINGS...
YOU CAN SEE THAT EVERY TIME THE SPACE IS OCCUPIED...
THE AD LISTING IS TAKEN DOWN, CORRECT?

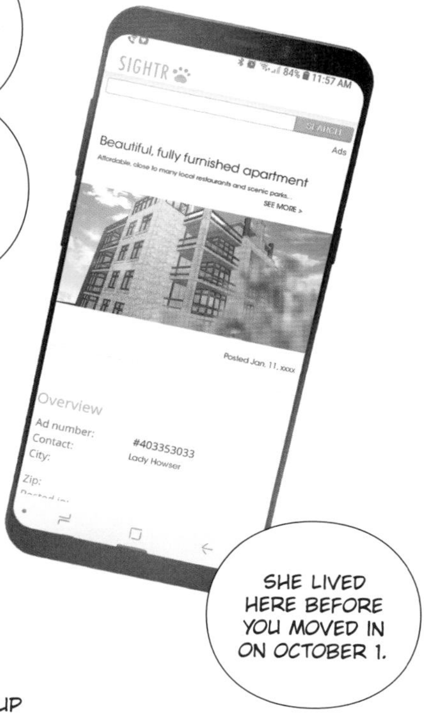
SIGHTR
SEARCH
Ads
Beautiful, fully furnished apartment
Affordable, close to many local restaurants and scenic parks...
SEE MORE >
Posted Jan. 11, xxxx
Overview
Ad number:
Contact:
City:
#403353033
Lady Howser
Zip:
SHE LIVED HERE BEFORE YOU MOVED IN ON OCTOBER 1.

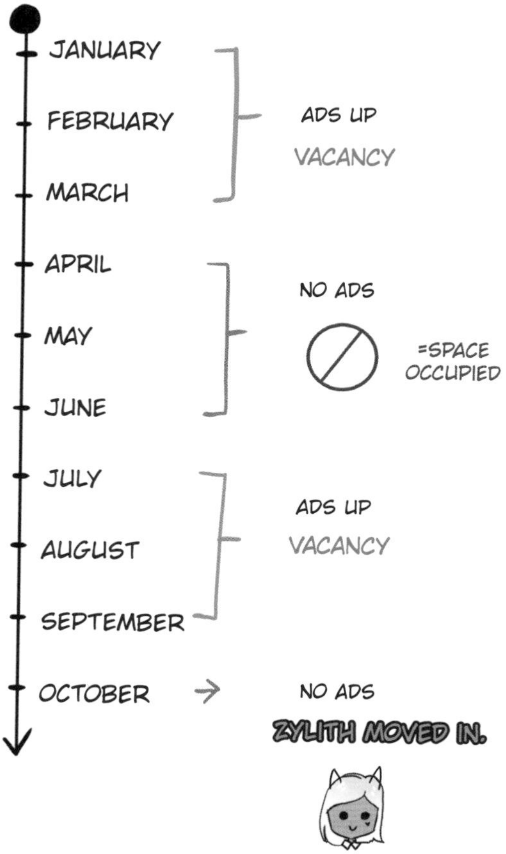
JANUARY
FEBRUARY
MARCH
ADS UP
VACANCY
APRIL
MAY
JUNE
NO ADS
=SPACE OCCUPIED
JULY
AUGUST
SEPTEMBER
ADS UP
VACANCY
OCTOBER
NO ADS
ZYLITH MOVED IN.

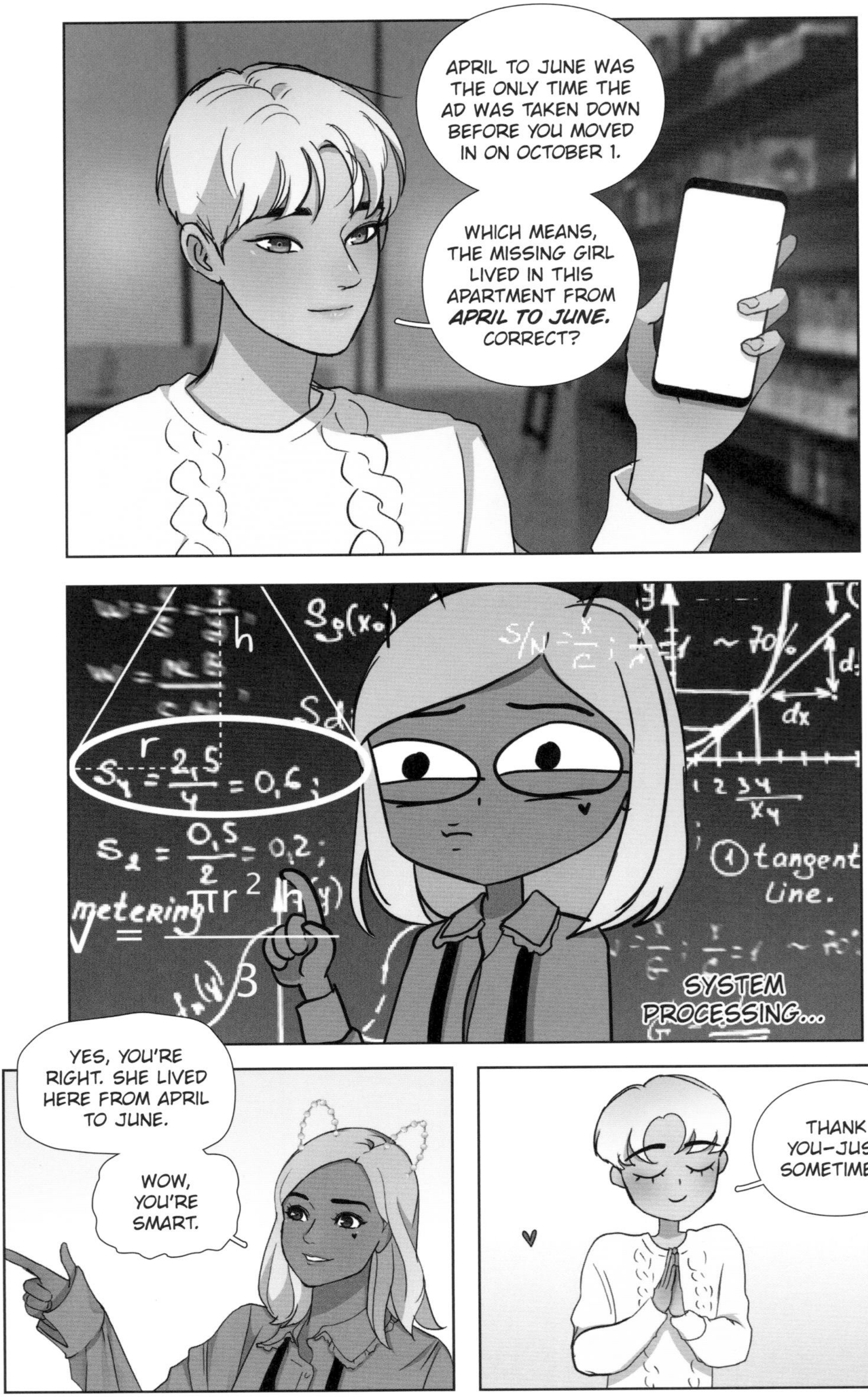
APRIL TO JUNE WAS THE ONLY TIME THE AD WAS TAKEN DOWN BEFORE YOU MOVED IN ON OCTOBER 1.
WHICH MEANS, THE MISSING GIRL LIVED IN THIS APARTMENT FROM ***APRIL TO JUNE.*** CORRECT?
SYSTEM PROCESSING...
YES, YOU'RE RIGHT. SHE LIVED HERE FROM APRIL TO JUNE.
WOW, YOU'RE SMART.
THANK YOU—JUST SOMETIMES.

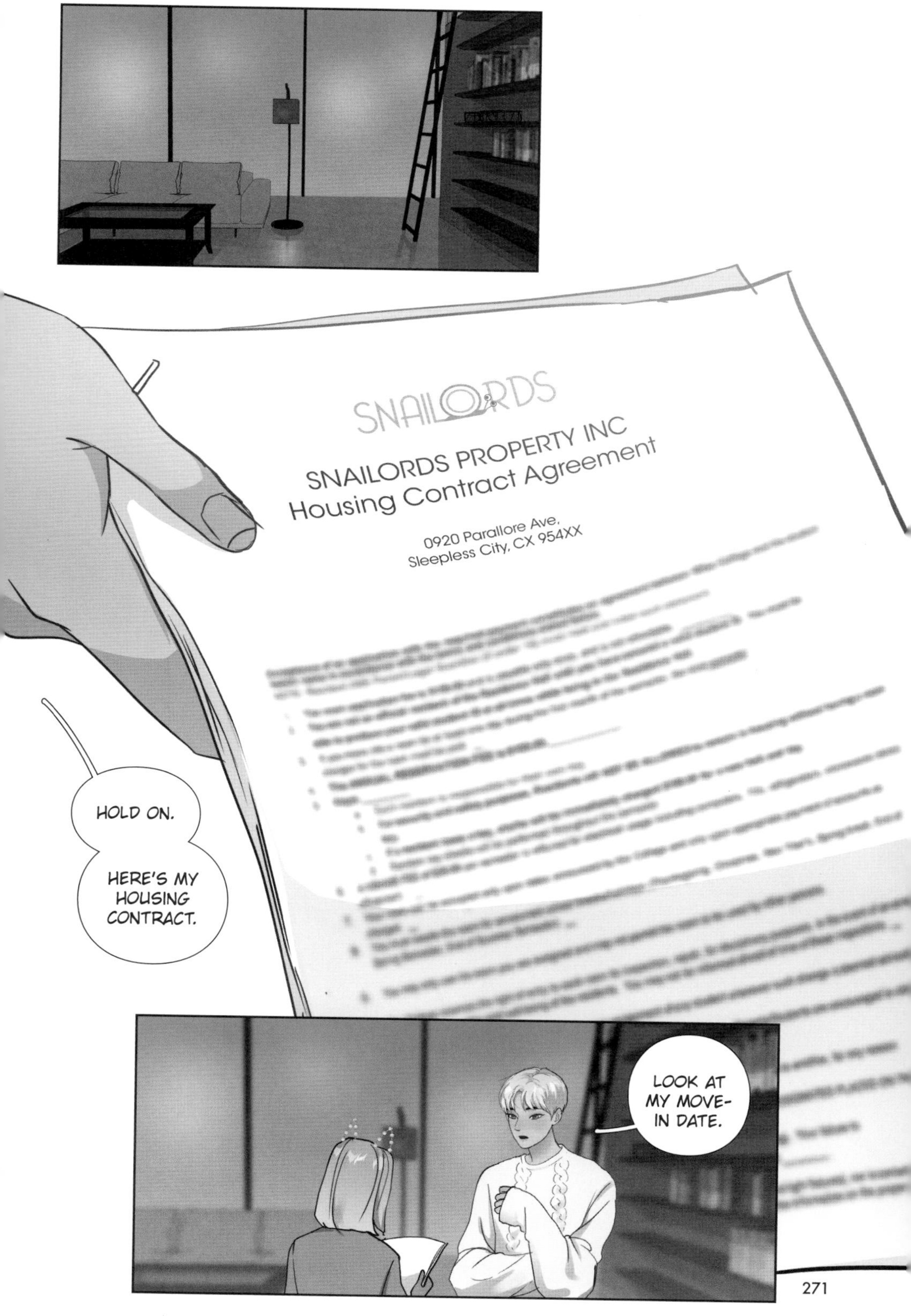
SNAILORDS
SNAILORDS PROPERTY INC
Housing Contract Agreement
0920 Parallore Ave,
Sleepless City, CX 954XX
HOLD ON.
HERE'S MY HOUSING CONTRACT.
LOOK AT MY MOVE-IN DATE.

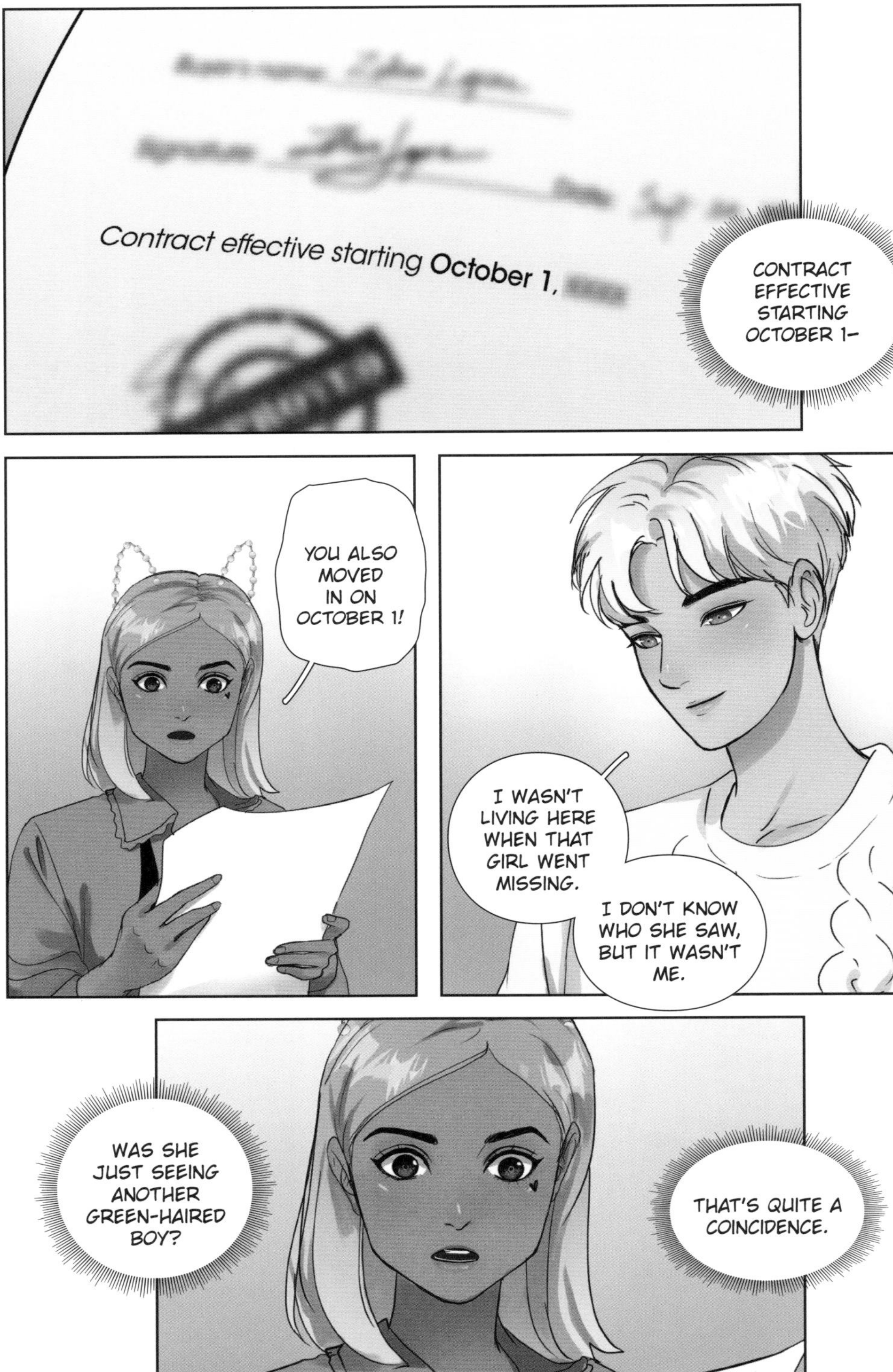
Contract effective starting October 1,
CONTRACT EFFECTIVE STARTING OCTOBER 1–
YOU ALSO MOVED IN ON OCTOBER 1!
I WASN'T LIVING HERE WHEN THAT GIRL WENT MISSING.
I DON'T KNOW WHO SHE SAW, BUT IT WASN'T ME.
WAS SHE JUST SEEING ANOTHER GREEN-HAIRED BOY?
THAT'S QUITE A COINCIDENCE.

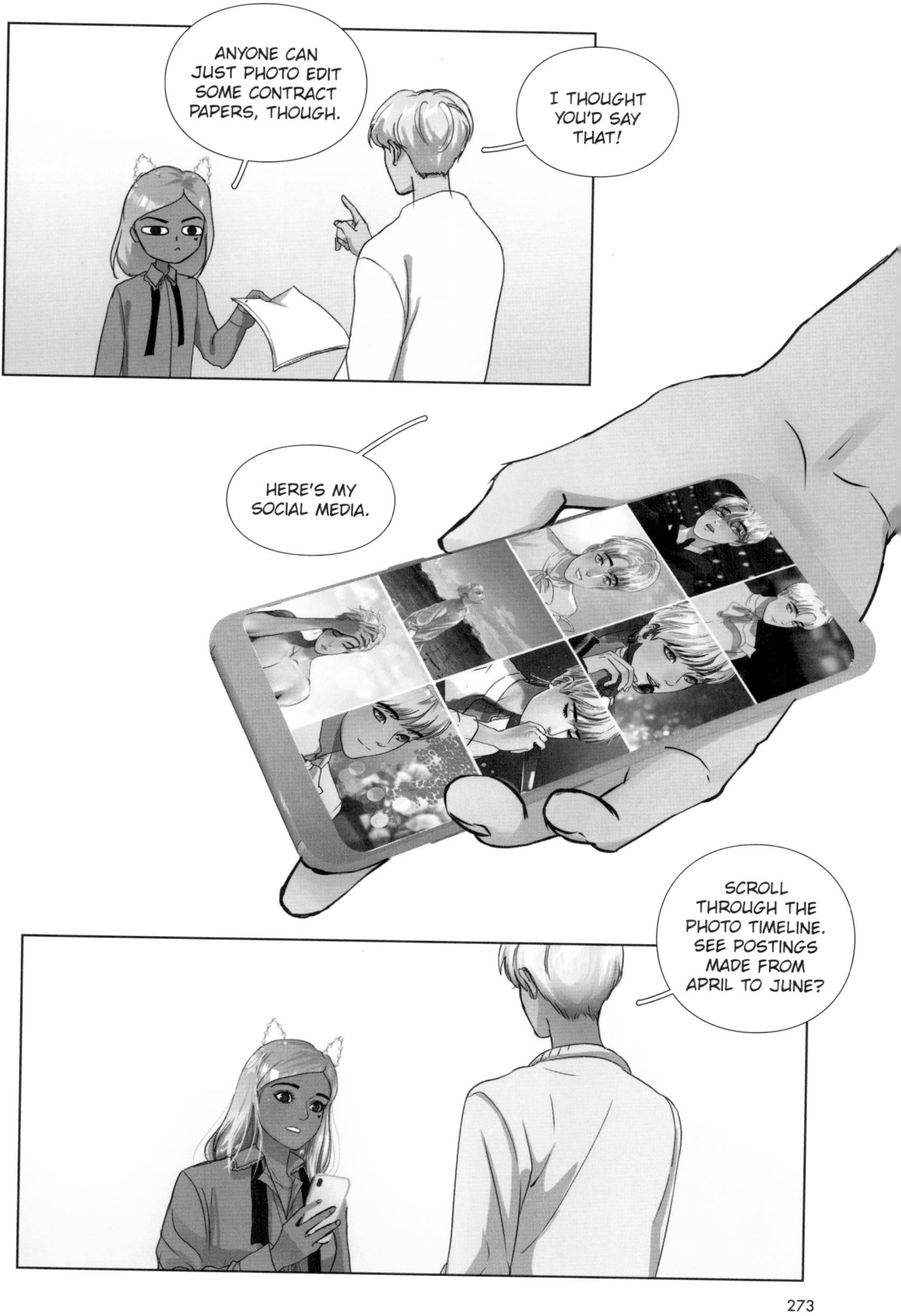
ANYONE CAN JUST PHOTO EDIT SOME CONTRACT PAPERS, THOUGH.
I THOUGHT YOU'D SAY THAT!
HERE'S MY SOCIAL MEDIA.
SCROLL THROUGH THE PHOTO TIMELINE. SEE POSTINGS MADE FROM APRIL TO JUNE?

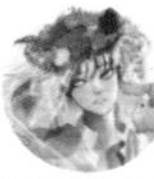

Zelan_Lycas

Tokyo, Japan

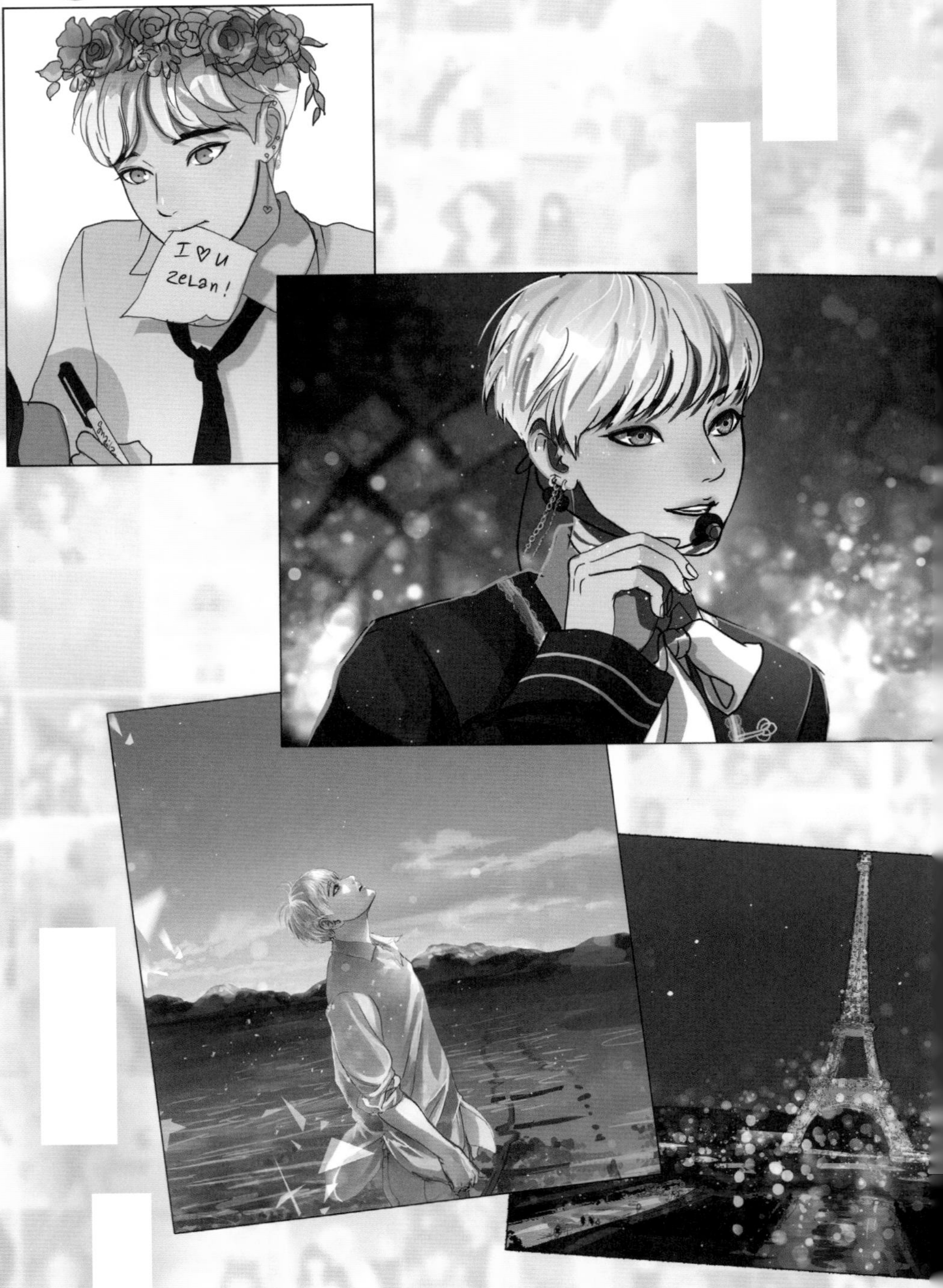
I ♥ U
zeLan!

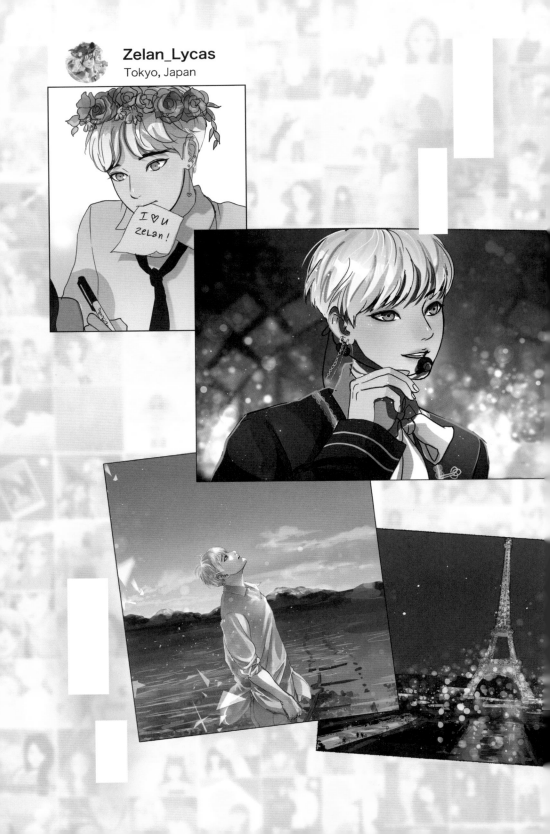

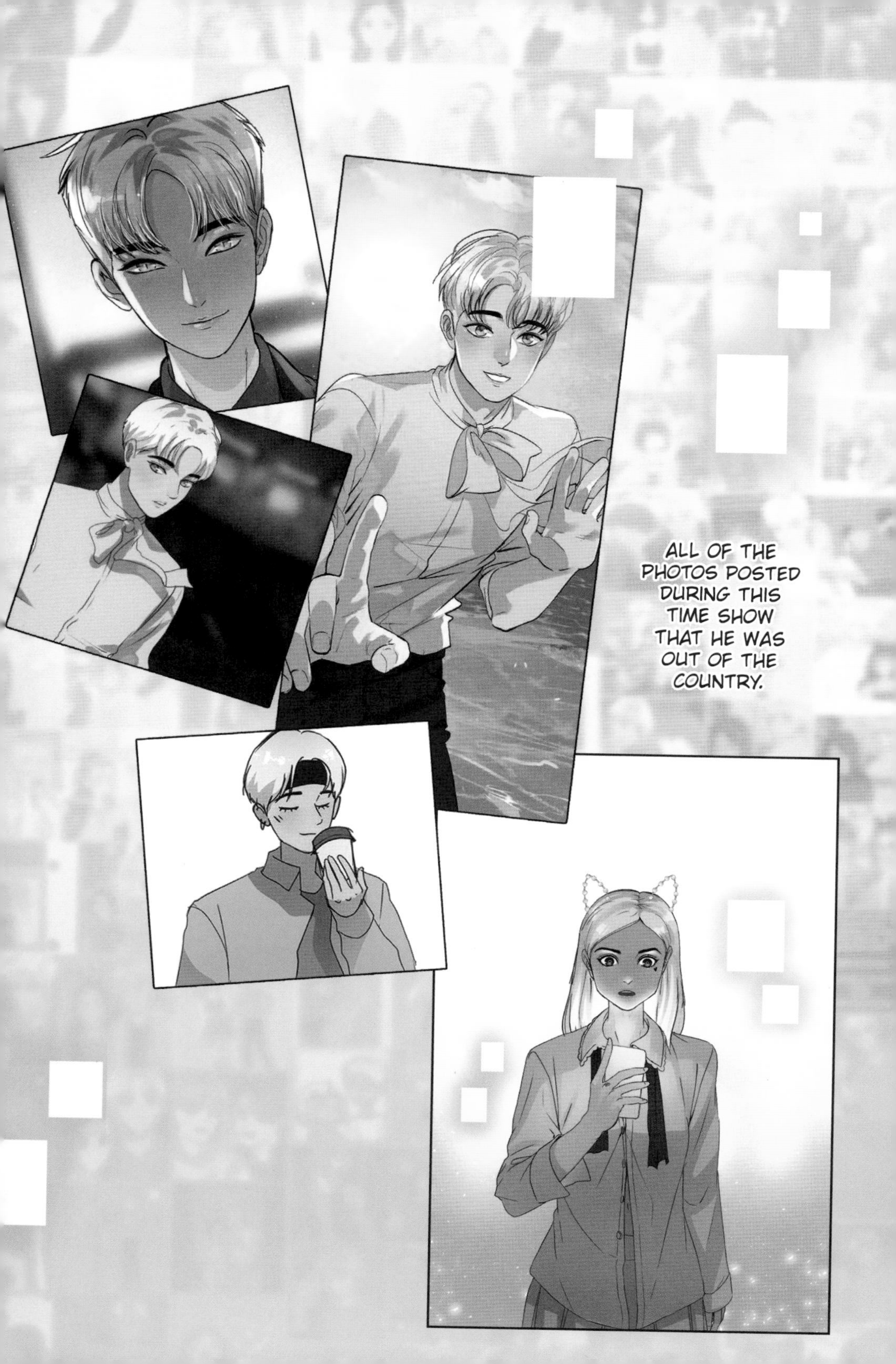
ALL OF THE PHOTOS POSTED DURING THIS TIME SHOW THAT HE WAS OUT OF THE COUNTRY.

snailords

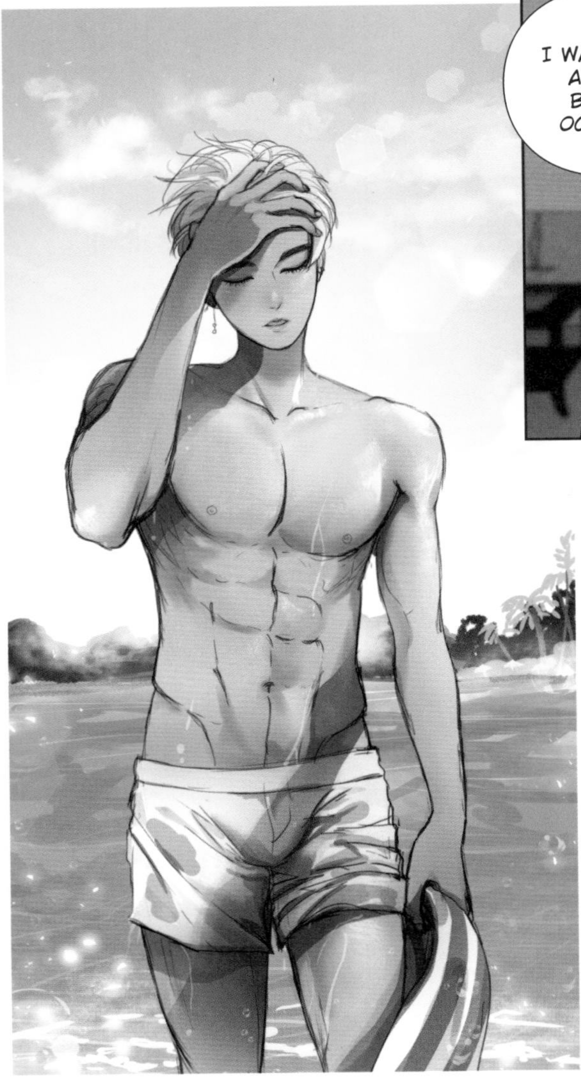

37,171 views • Liked by θλλαμcορπερ and νεύμαοσ

snailords What kinda seaweed is this? Cuz DAMN DADDY! That's not the beach, that's my drool...y'all.

YOU CAN ALSO SEE MY TAGGED PHOTOS FROM FANS WHO RAN INTO ME.

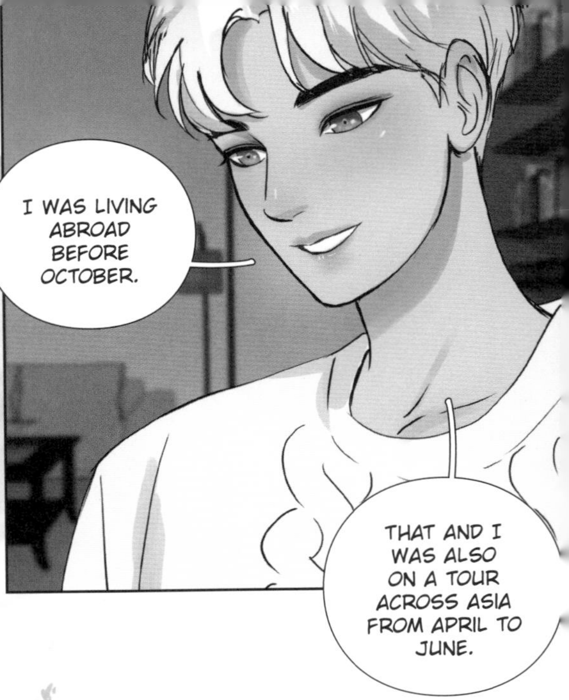
I WAS LIVING ABROAD BEFORE OCTOBER.
THAT AND I WAS ALSO ON A TOUR ACROSS ASIA FROM APRIL TO JUNE.

επίσημοχάος
Seoul, S Korea

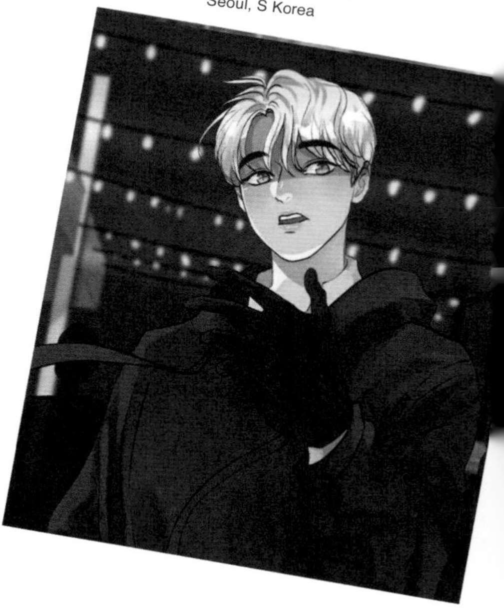

AND SEE, THE LOCATIONS THAT THEY TAGGED ME IN WERE ALL IN ASIA.

επίσημ • Follow   Kyoto, Japan

CONSTANT VIDEOS, PICTURES, AND SHOWS PROVING THAT I WAS OUT OF THE COUNTRY.

I BARELY HAD TIME TO BREATHE LET ALONE KIDNAP SOME GIRL.

HO I MET #foundzelan
nstaRSTRUCK

επίσημοχάος
Hong Kong

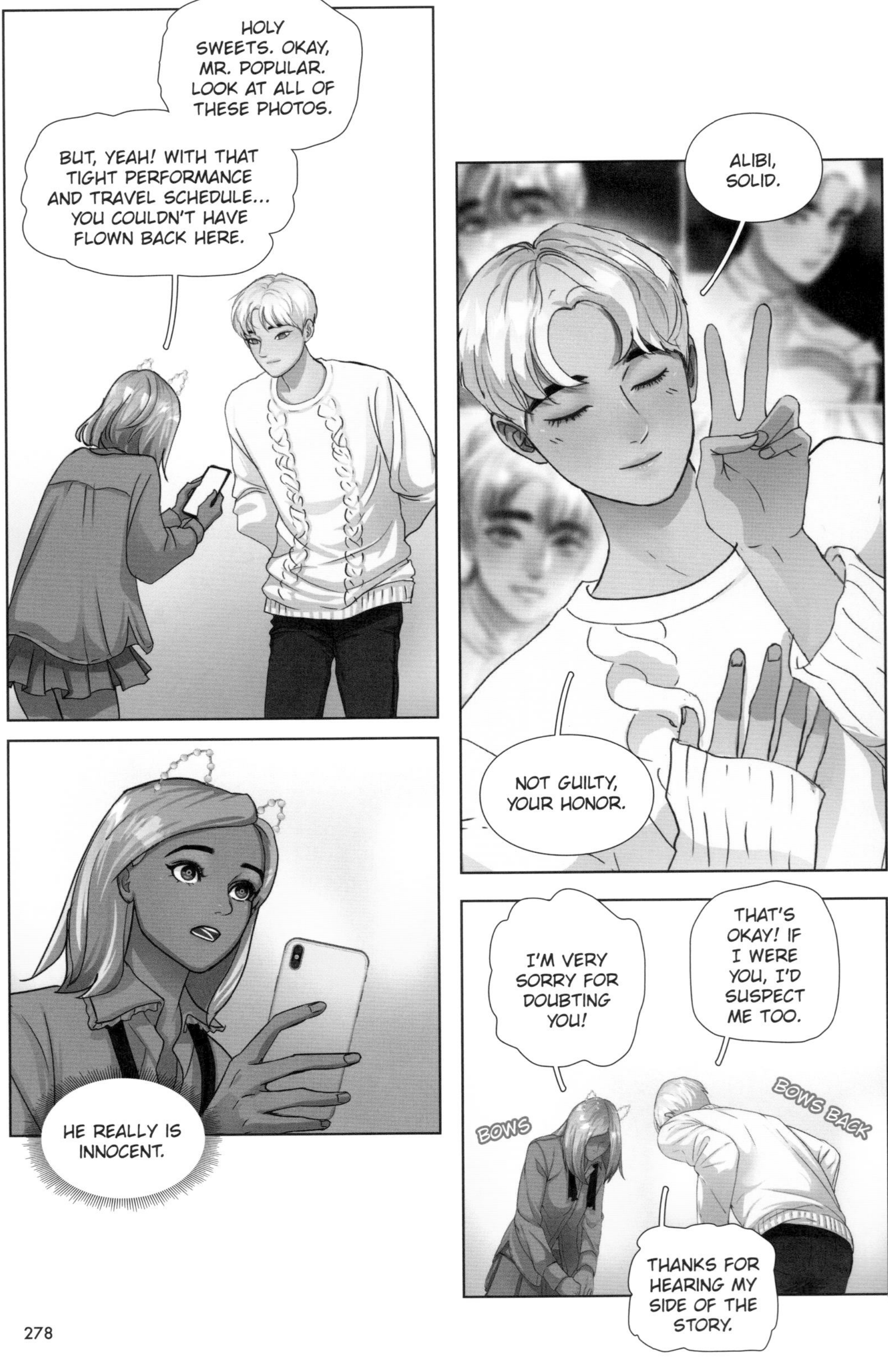
HOLY SWEETS. OKAY, MR. POPULAR. LOOK AT ALL OF THESE PHOTOS.
BUT, YEAH! WITH THAT TIGHT PERFORMANCE AND TRAVEL SCHEDULE... YOU COULDN'T HAVE FLOWN BACK HERE.
ALIBI, SOLID.
NOT GUILTY, YOUR HONOR.
HE REALLY IS INNOCENT.
I'M VERY SORRY FOR DOUBTING YOU!
THAT'S OKAY! IF I WERE YOU, I'D SUSPECT ME TOO.
BOWS
BOWS BACK
THANKS FOR HEARING MY SIDE OF THE STORY.

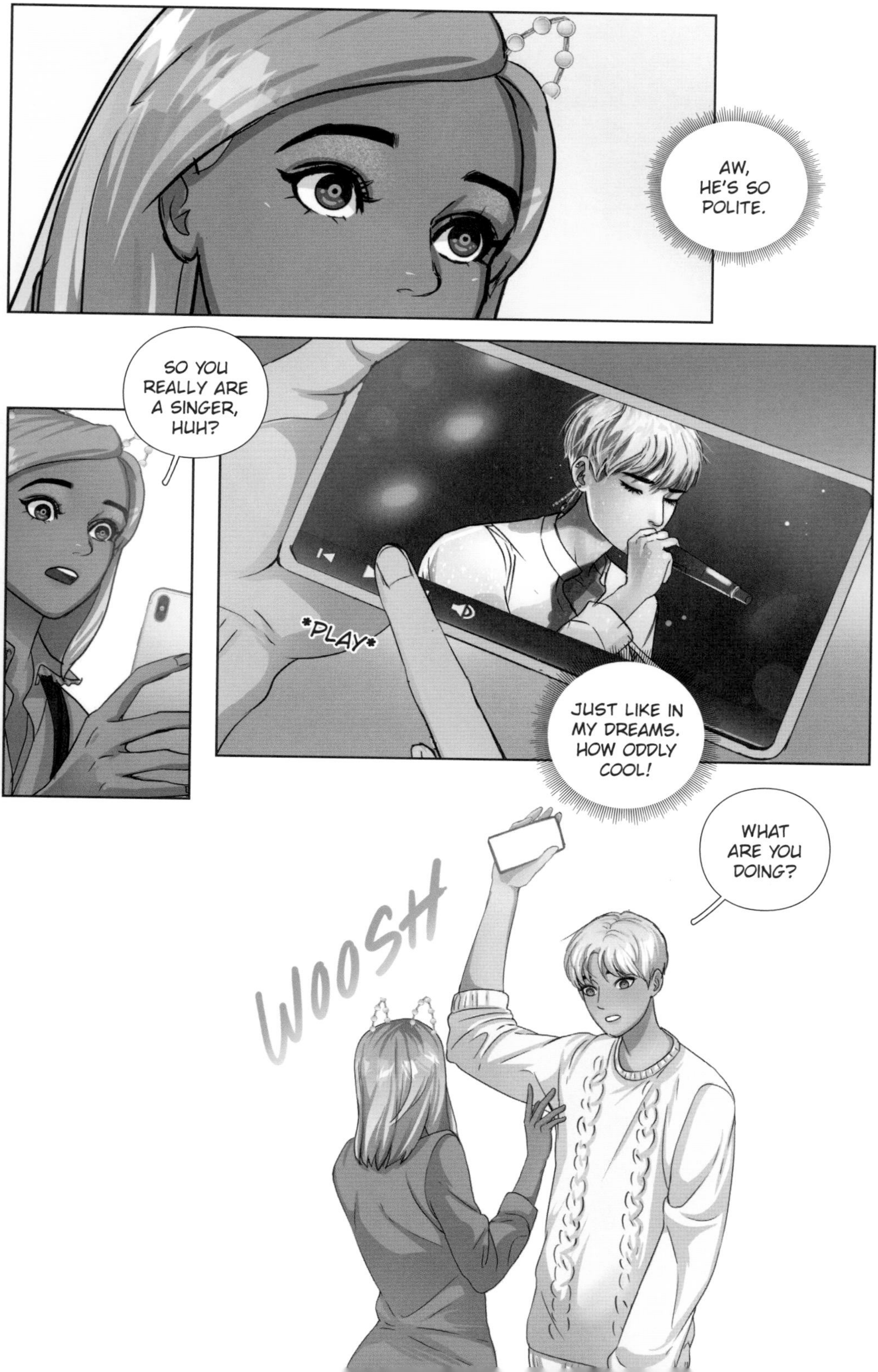
AW, HE'S SO POLITE.
SO YOU REALLY ARE A SINGER, HUH?
PLAY
JUST LIKE IN MY DREAMS. HOW ODDLY COOL!
WHAT ARE YOU DOING?
WOOSH

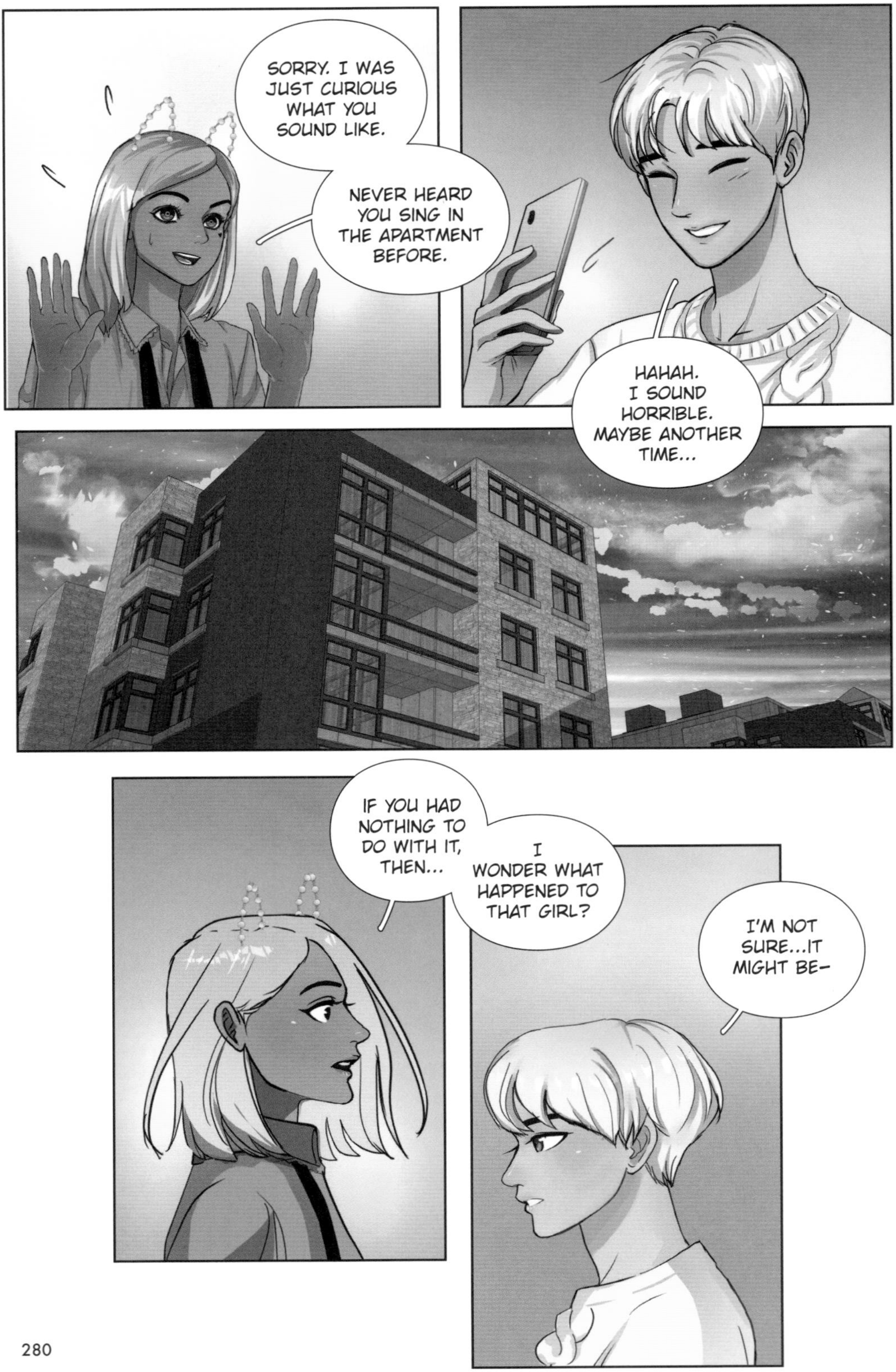
SORRY. I WAS JUST CURIOUS WHAT YOU SOUND LIKE.
NEVER HEARD YOU SING IN THE APARTMENT BEFORE.
HAHAH. I SOUND HORRIBLE. MAYBE ANOTHER TIME...
IF YOU HAD NOTHING TO DO WITH IT, THEN...
I WONDER WHAT HAPPENED TO THAT GIRL?
I'M NOT SURE...IT MIGHT BE-

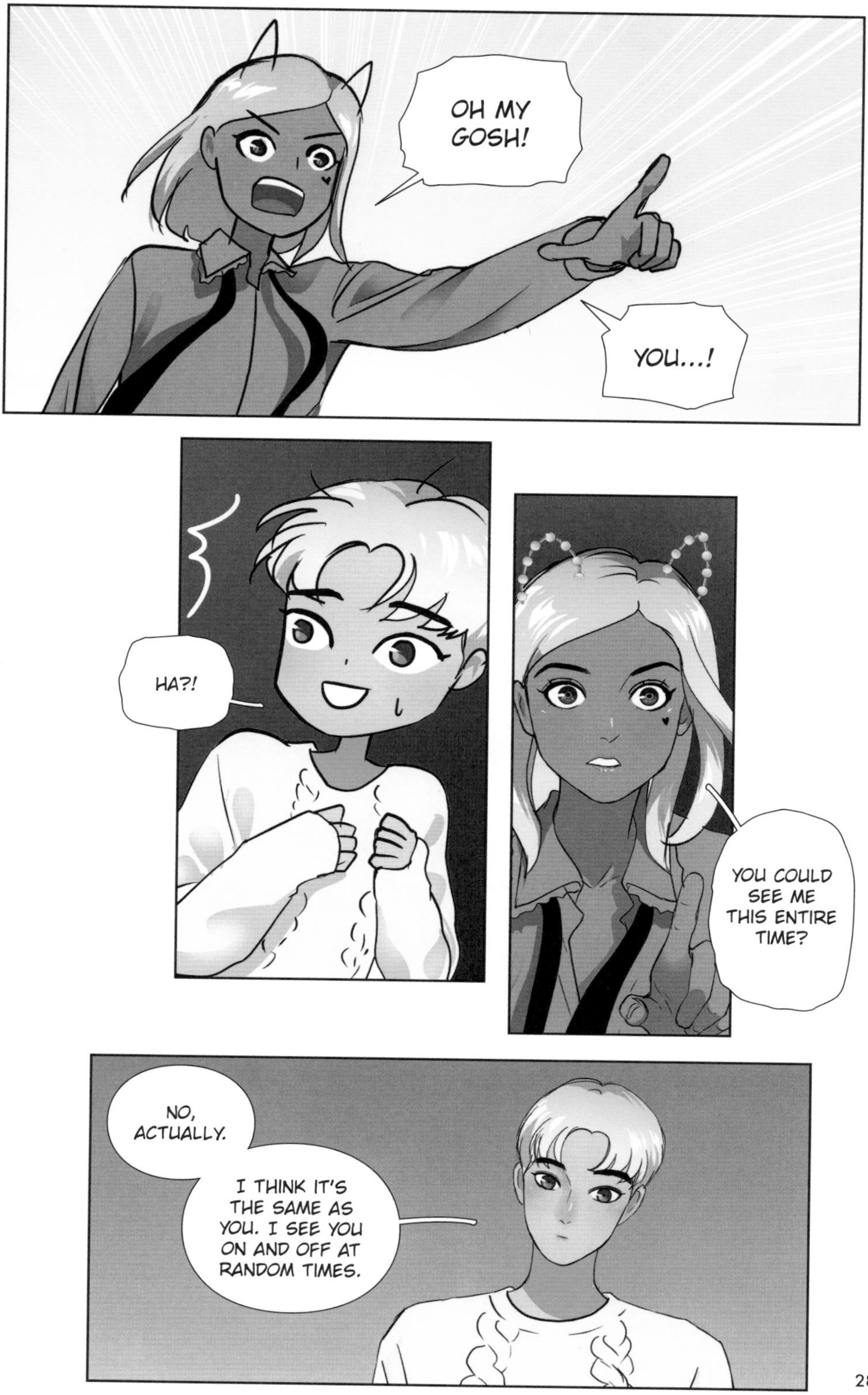
OH MY GOSH!
YOU...!
HA?!
YOU COULD SEE ME THIS ENTIRE TIME?
NO, ACTUALLY.
I THINK IT'S THE SAME AS YOU. I SEE YOU ON AND OFF AT RANDOM TIMES.

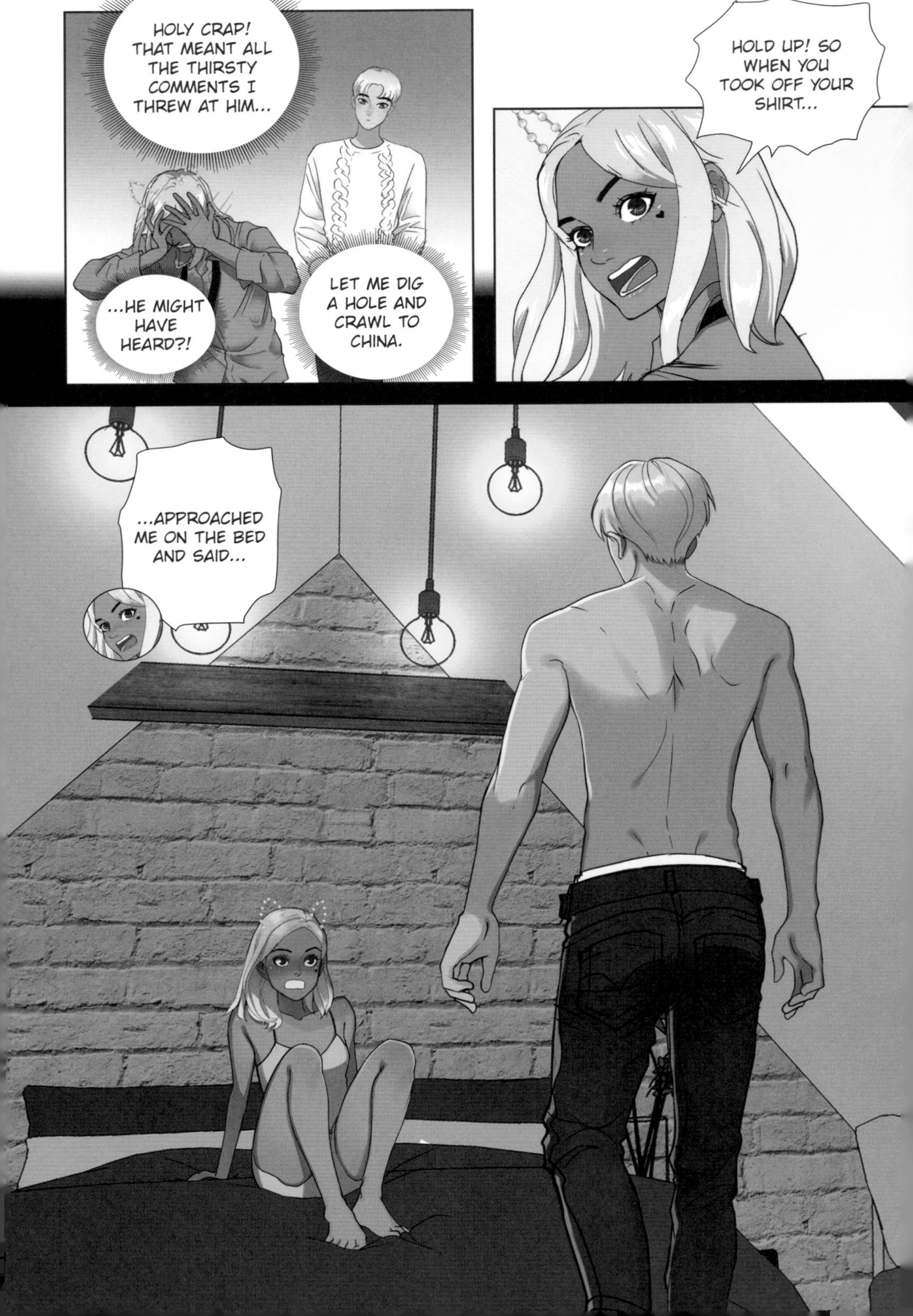
HOLY CRAP! THAT MEANT ALL THE THIRSTY COMMENTS I THREW AT HIM...
...HE MIGHT HAVE HEARD?!
LET ME DIG A HOLE AND CRAWL TO CHINA.
HOLD UP! SO WHEN YOU TOOK OFF YOUR SHIRT...
...APPROACHED ME ON THE BED AND SAID...

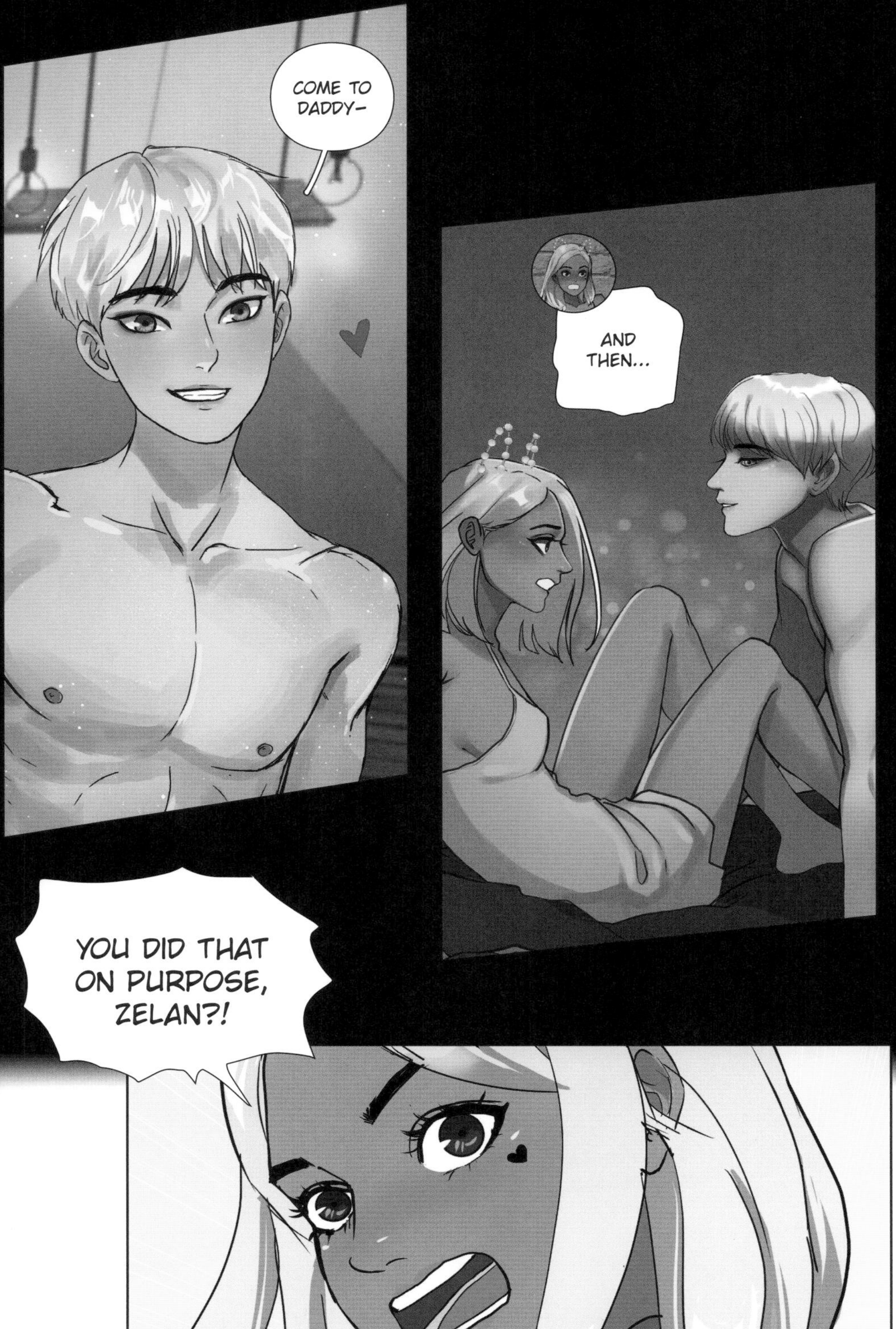
COME TO DADDY-
AND THEN...
YOU DID THAT ON PURPOSE, ZELAN?!

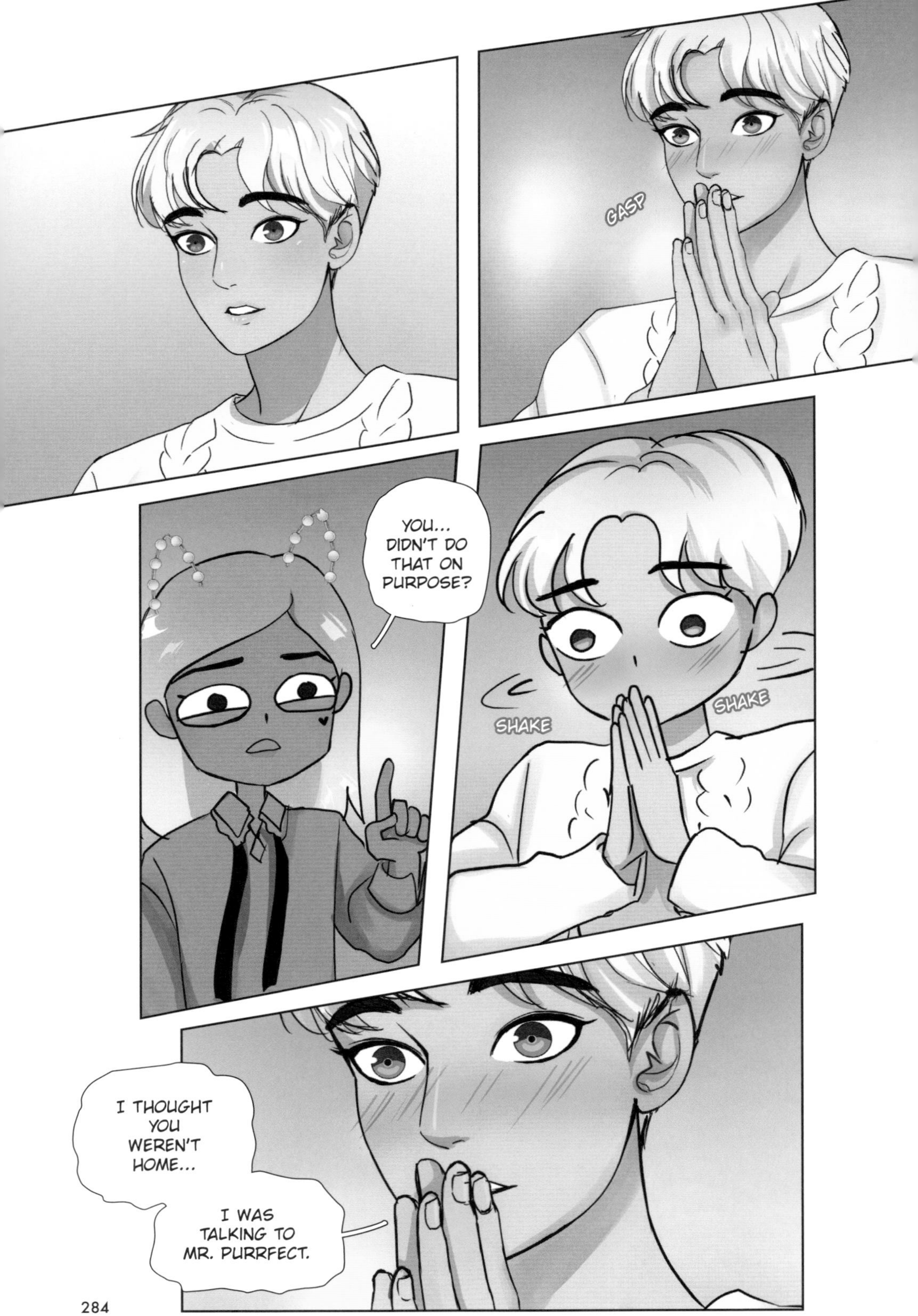
GASP
YOU... DIDN'T DO THAT ON PURPOSE?
SHAKE
SHAKE
I THOUGHT YOU WEREN'T HOME...
I WAS TALKING TO MR. PURRFECT.

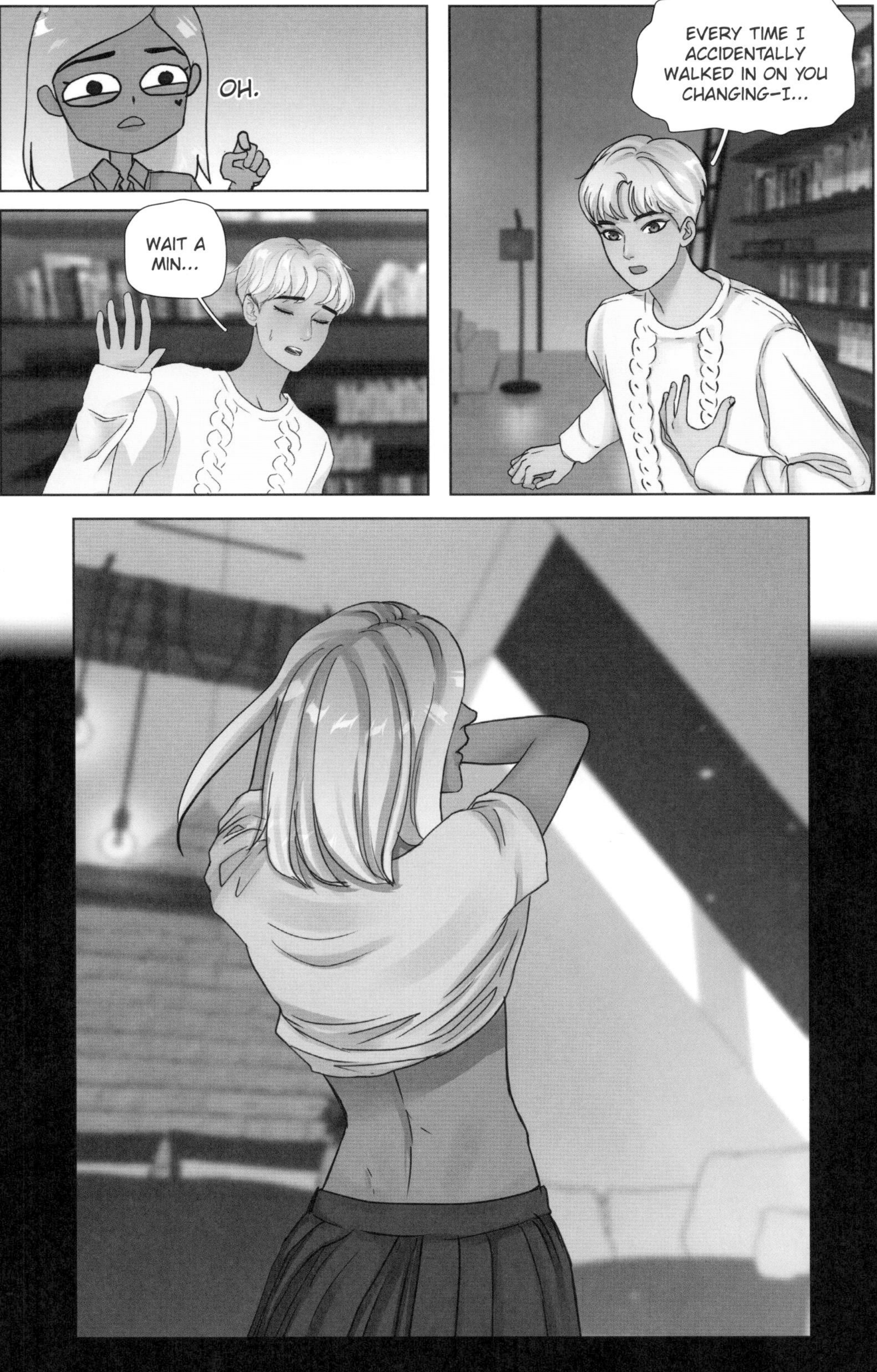
OH.
WAIT A MIN...
EVERY TIME I ACCIDENTALLY WALKED IN ON YOU CHANGING—I...

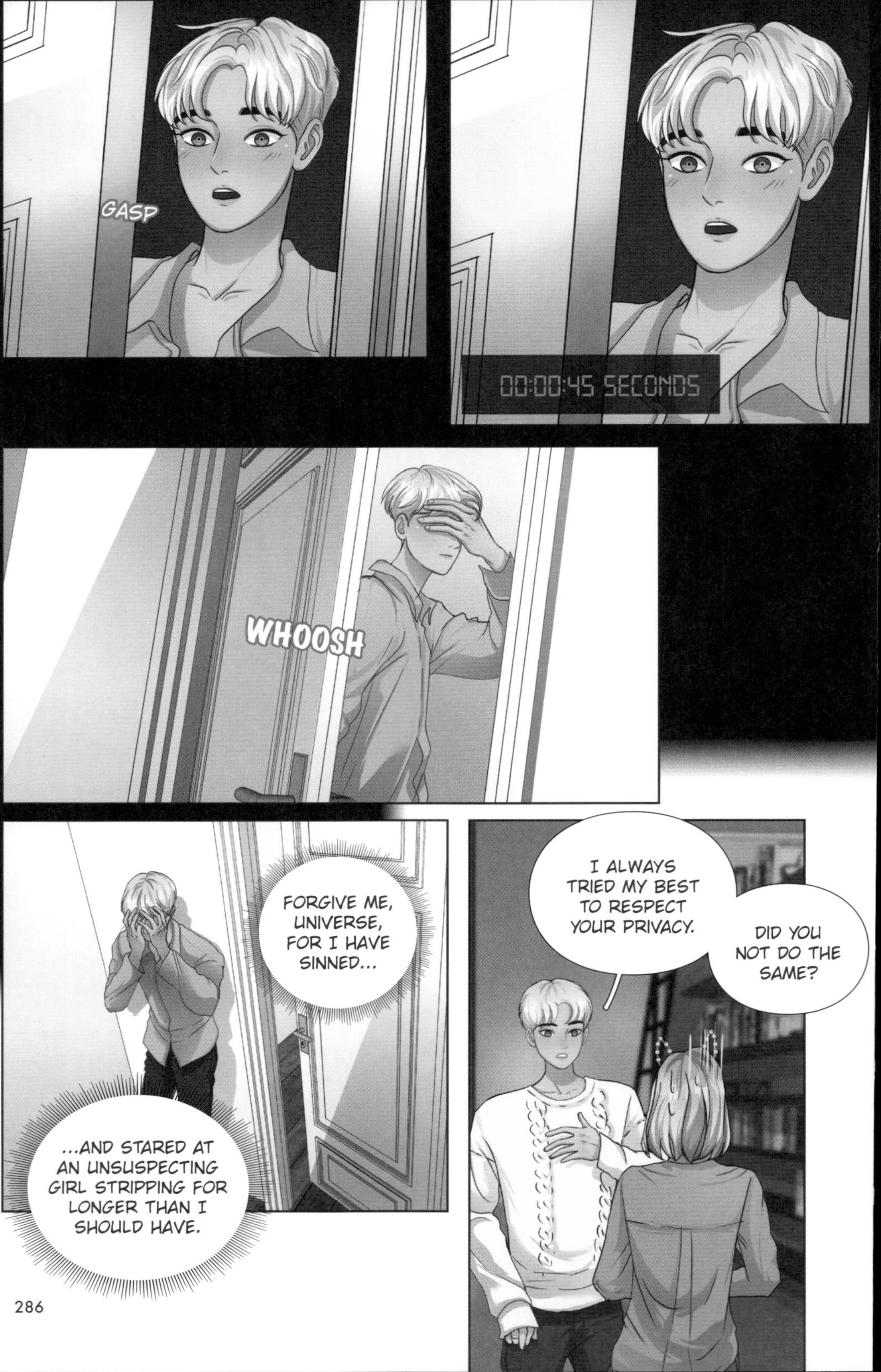
GASP
00:00:45 SECONDS
WHOOSH
FORGIVE ME, UNIVERSE, FOR I HAVE SINNED...
...AND STARED AT AN UNSUSPECTING GIRL STRIPPING FOR LONGER THAN I SHOULD HAVE.
I ALWAYS TRIED MY BEST TO RESPECT YOUR PRIVACY.
DID YOU NOT DO THE SAME?

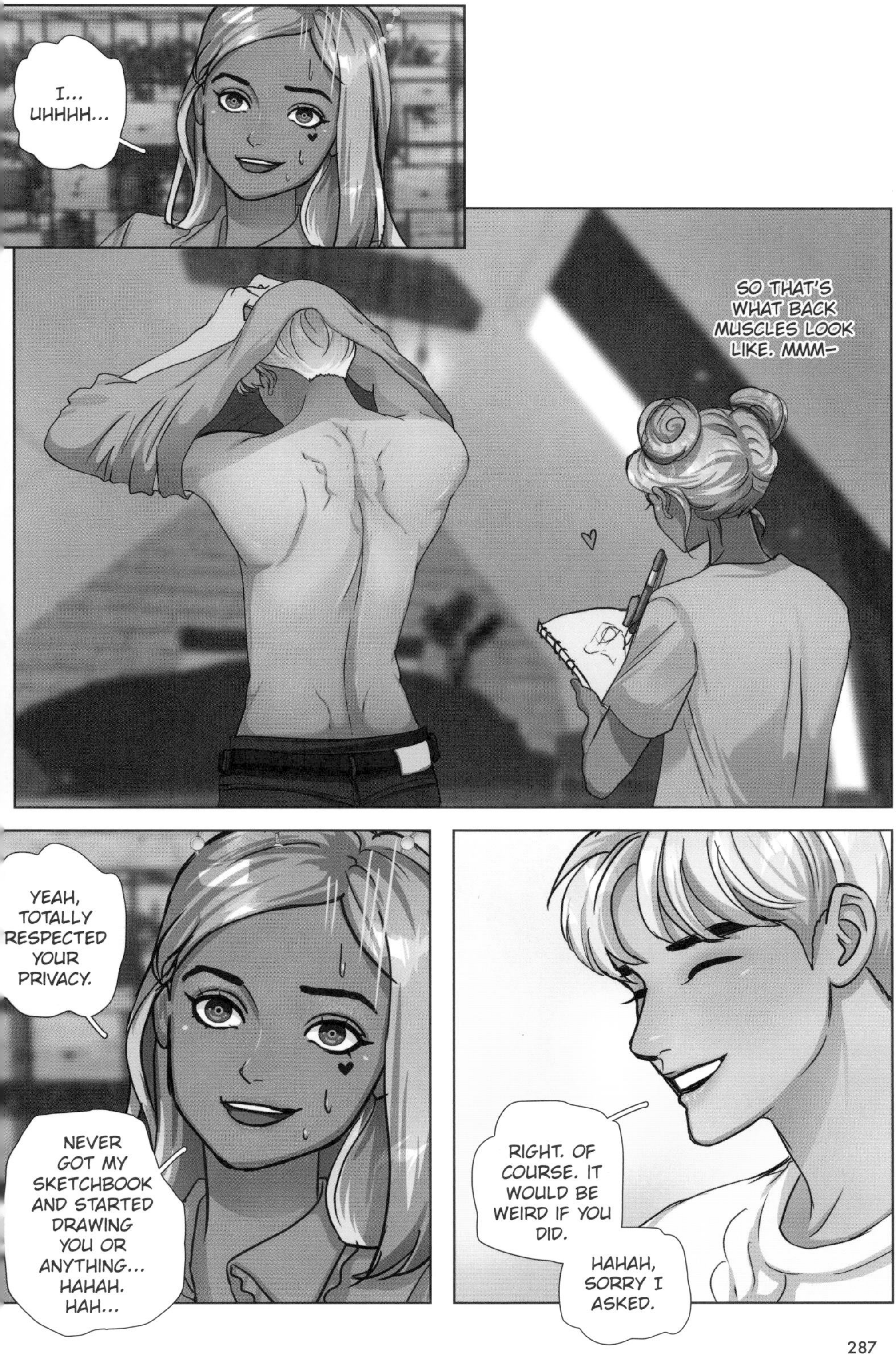
I... UHHHH...
SO THAT'S WHAT BACK MUSCLES LOOK LIKE. MMM–
YEAH, TOTALLY RESPECTED YOUR PRIVACY.
NEVER GOT MY SKETCHBOOK AND STARTED DRAWING YOU OR ANYTHING... HAHAH. HAH...
RIGHT. OF COURSE. IT WOULD BE WEIRD IF YOU DID.
HAHAH, SORRY I ASKED.

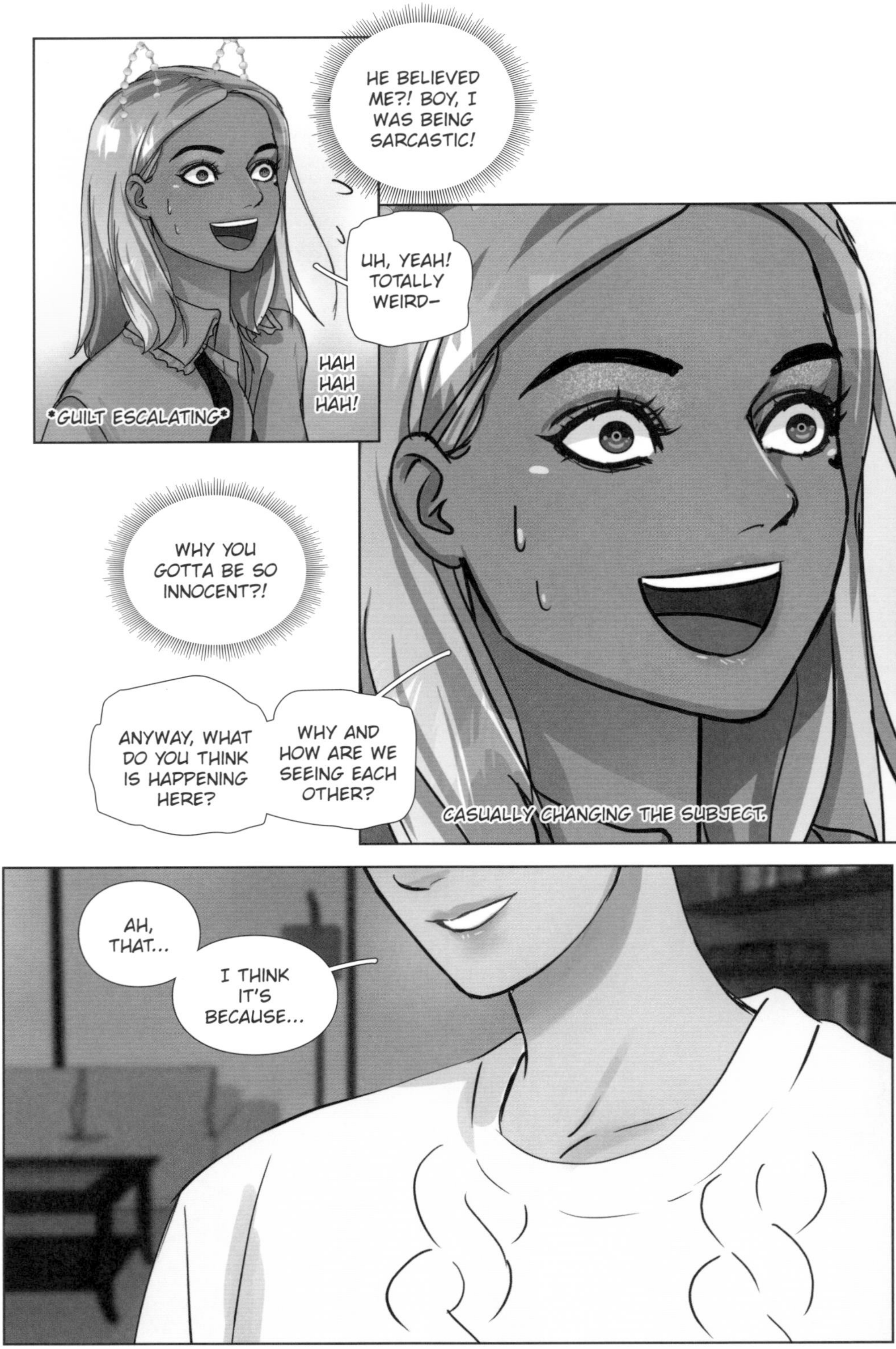
HE BELIEVED ME?! BOY, I WAS BEING SARCASTIC!
UH, YEAH! TOTALLY WEIRD—
HAH HAH HAH!
GUILT ESCALATING
WHY YOU GOTTA BE SO INNOCENT?!
ANYWAY, WHAT DO YOU THINK IS HAPPENING HERE?
WHY AND HOW ARE WE SEEING EACH OTHER?
CASUALLY CHANGING THE SUBJECT.
AH, THAT...
I THINK IT'S BECAUSE...

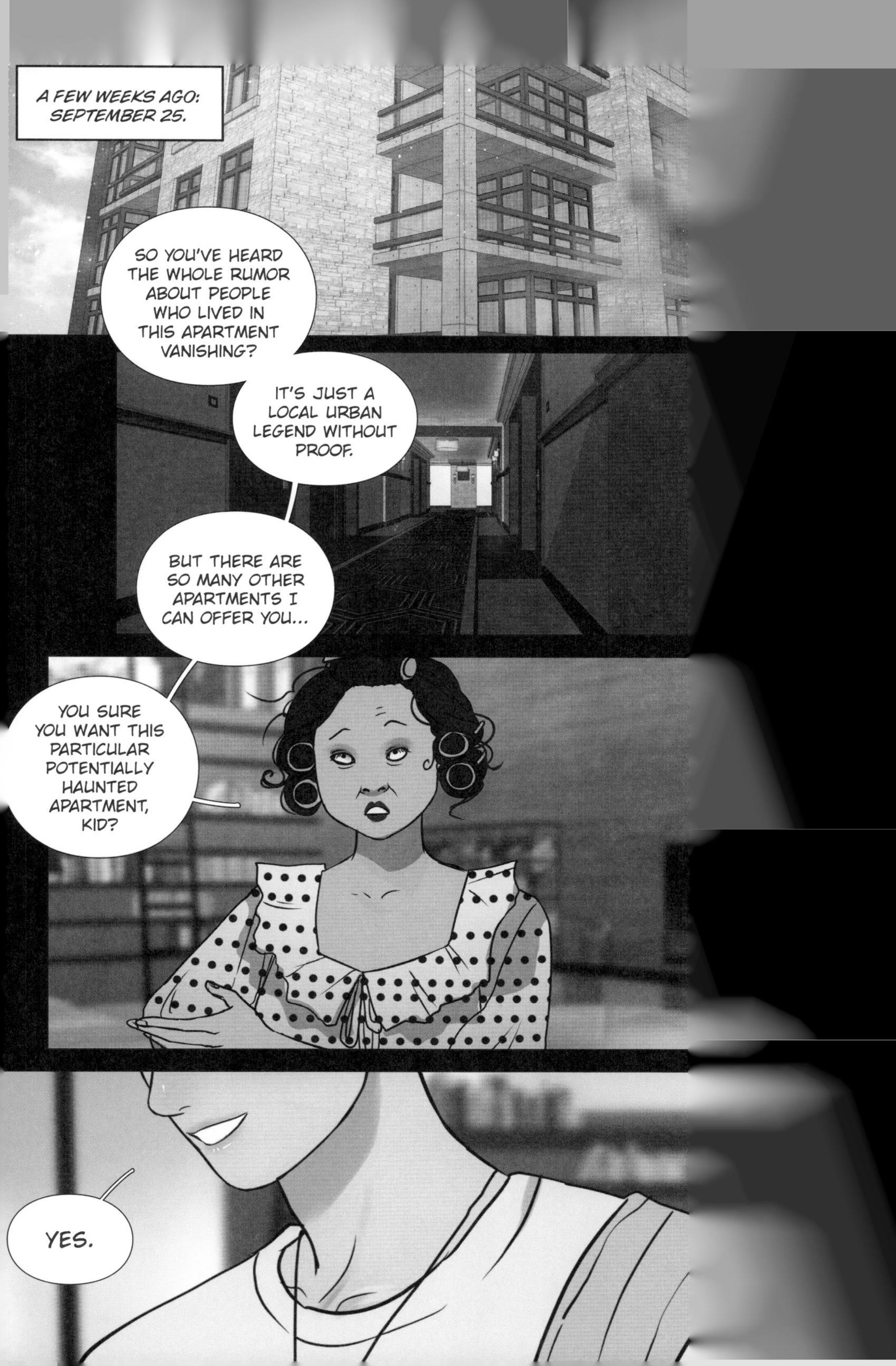
A FEW WEEKS AGO: SEPTEMBER 25.
SO YOU'VE HEARD THE WHOLE RUMOR ABOUT PEOPLE WHO LIVED IN THIS APARTMENT VANISHING?
IT'S JUST A LOCAL URBAN LEGEND WITHOUT PROOF.
BUT THERE ARE SO MANY OTHER APARTMENTS I CAN OFFER YOU...
YOU SURE YOU WANT THIS PARTICULAR POTENTIALLY HAUNTED APARTMENT, KID?
YES.

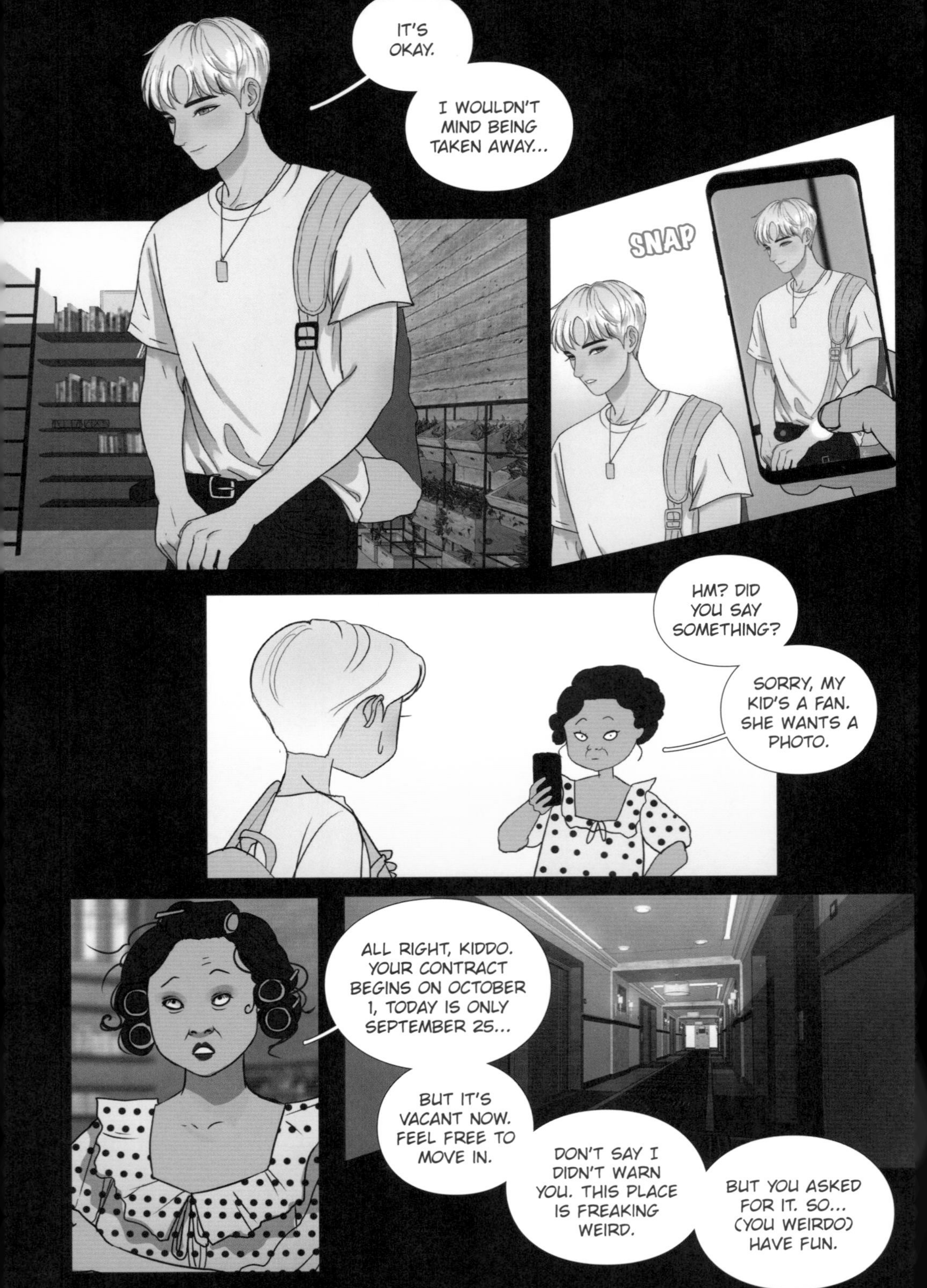
IT'S OKAY.
I WOULDN'T MIND BEING TAKEN AWAY...
SNAP
HM? DID YOU SAY SOMETHING?
SORRY, MY KID'S A FAN. SHE WANTS A PHOTO.
ALL RIGHT, KIDDO. YOUR CONTRACT BEGINS ON OCTOBER 1, TODAY IS ONLY SEPTEMBER 25...
BUT IT'S VACANT NOW. FEEL FREE TO MOVE IN.
DON'T SAY I DIDN'T WARN YOU. THIS PLACE IS FREAKING WEIRD.
BUT YOU ASKED FOR IT. SO... (YOU WEIRDO) HAVE FUN.

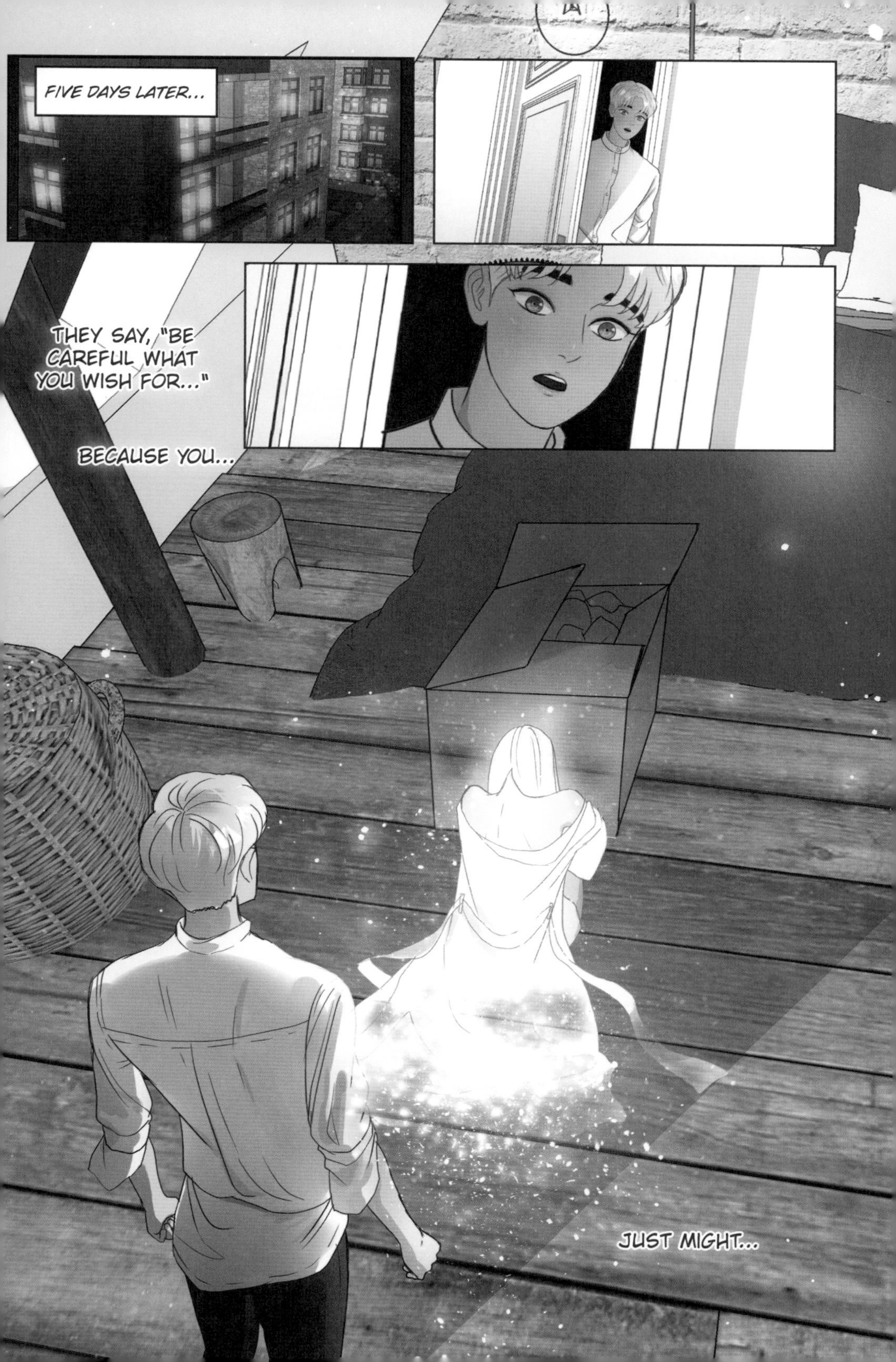
FIVE DAYS LATER...
THEY SAY, "BE CAREFUL WHAT YOU WISH FOR..."
BECAUSE YOU...
JUST MIGHT...

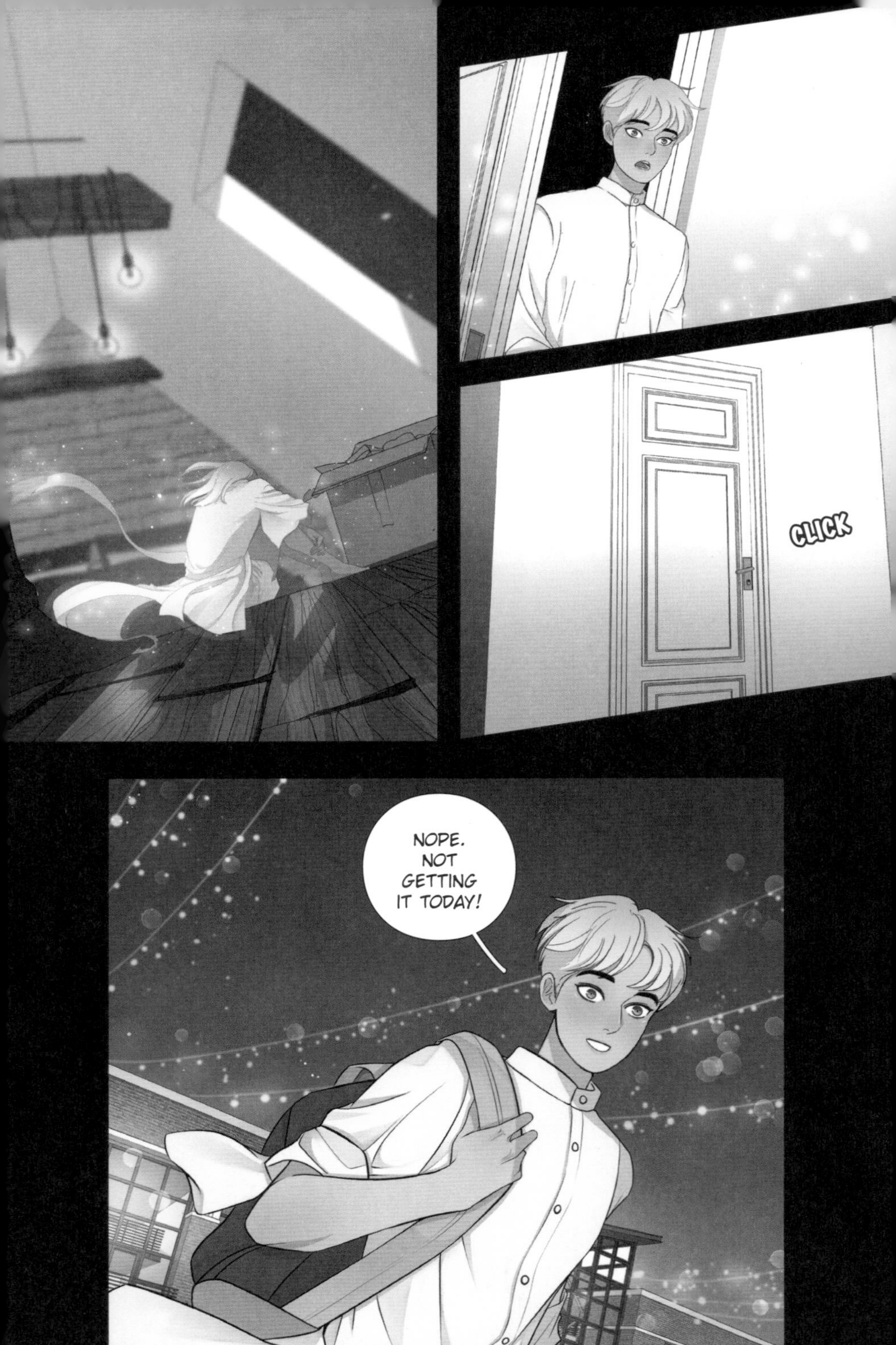
CLICK
NOPE. NOT GETTING IT TODAY!

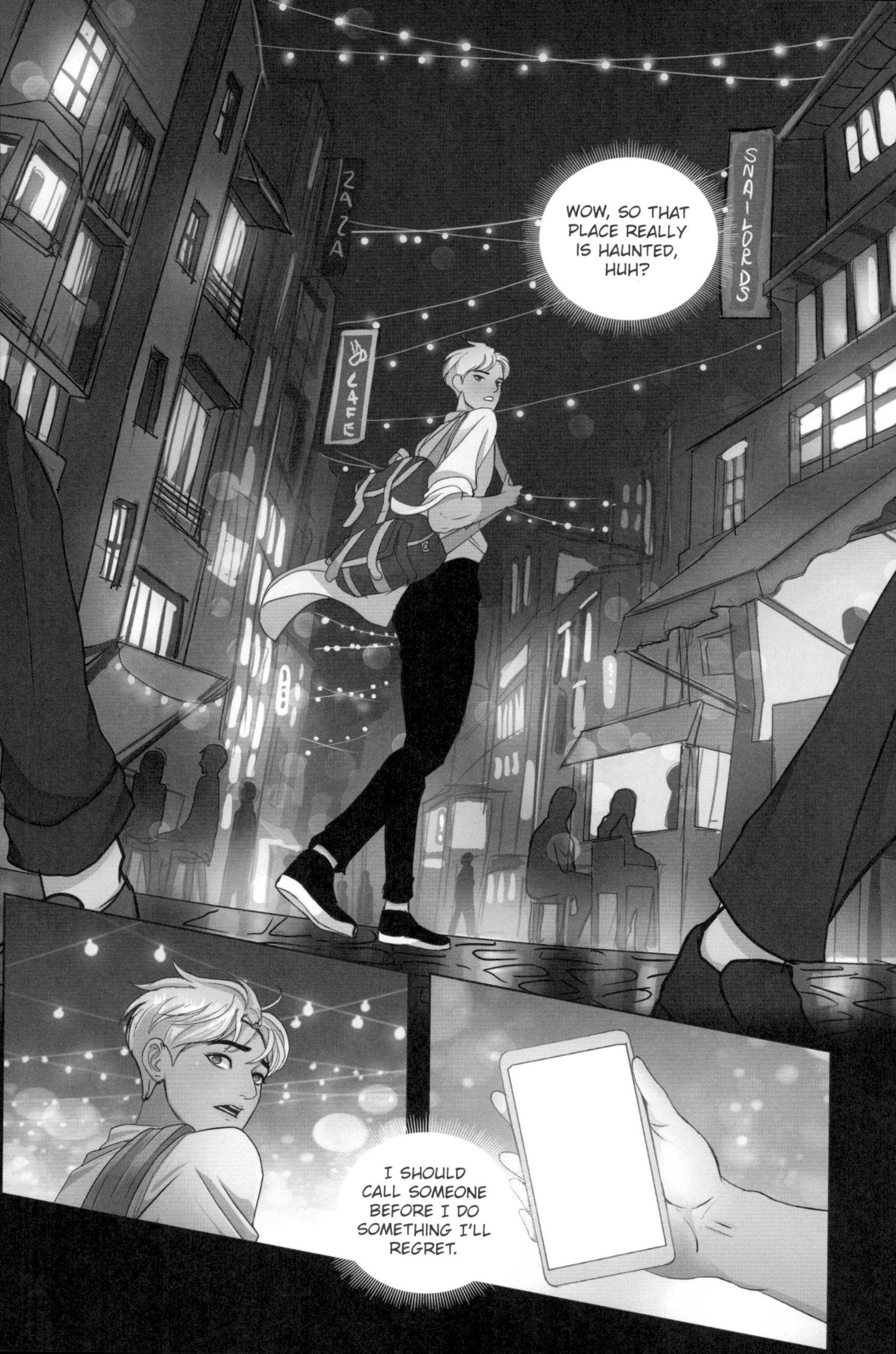
ZAZA
CAFE
SNAILORDS
WOW, SO THAT PLACE REALLY IS HAUNTED, HUH?
I SHOULD CALL SOMEONE BEFORE I DO SOMETHING I'LL REGRET.

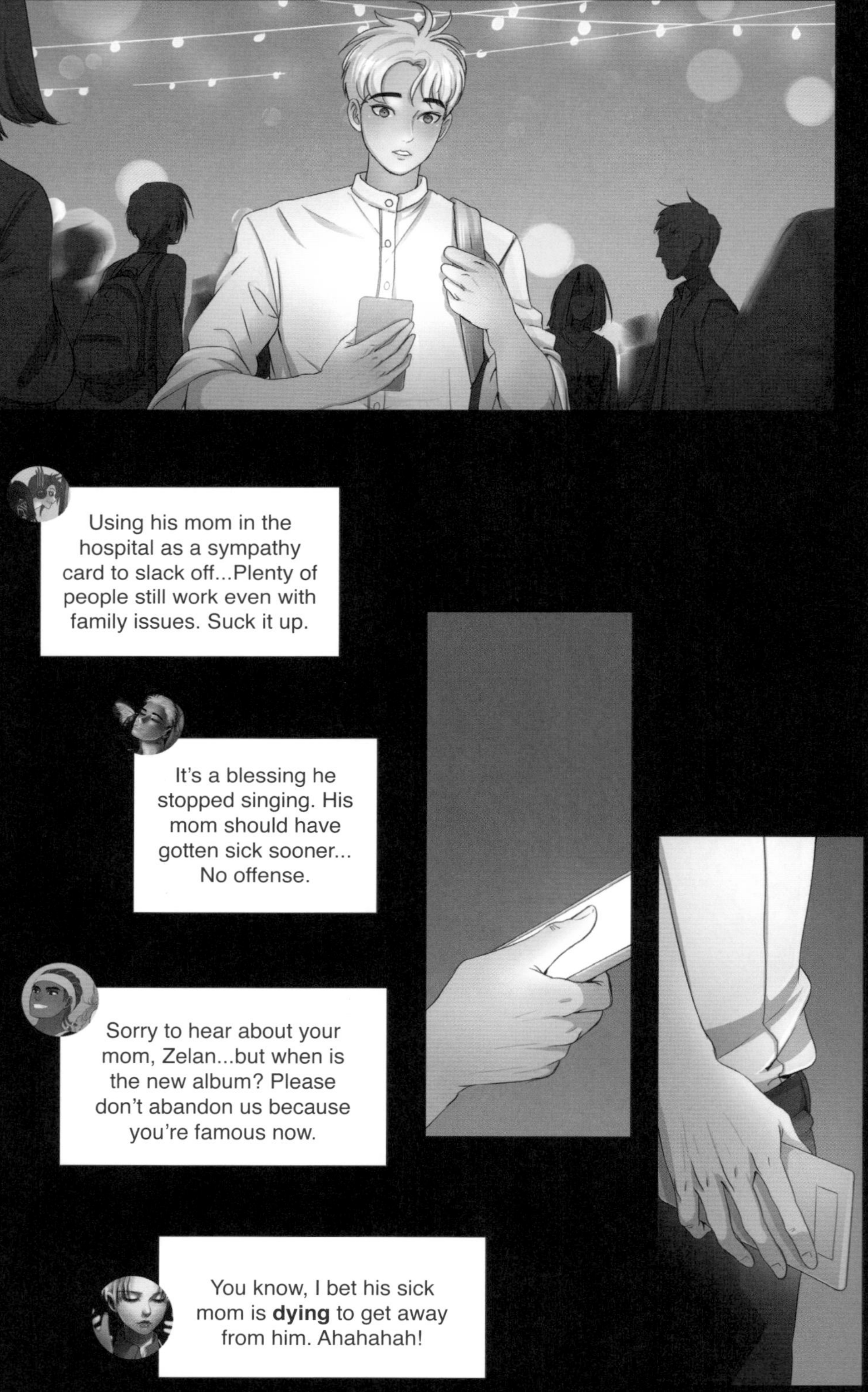
Using his mom in the hospital as a sympathy card to slack off...Plenty of people still work even with family issues. Suck it up.
It’s a blessing he stopped singing. His mom should have gotten sick sooner... No offense.
Sorry to hear about your mom, Zelan...but when is the new album? Please don’t abandon us because you’re famous now.
You know, I bet his sick mom is **dying** to get away from him. Ahahahah!

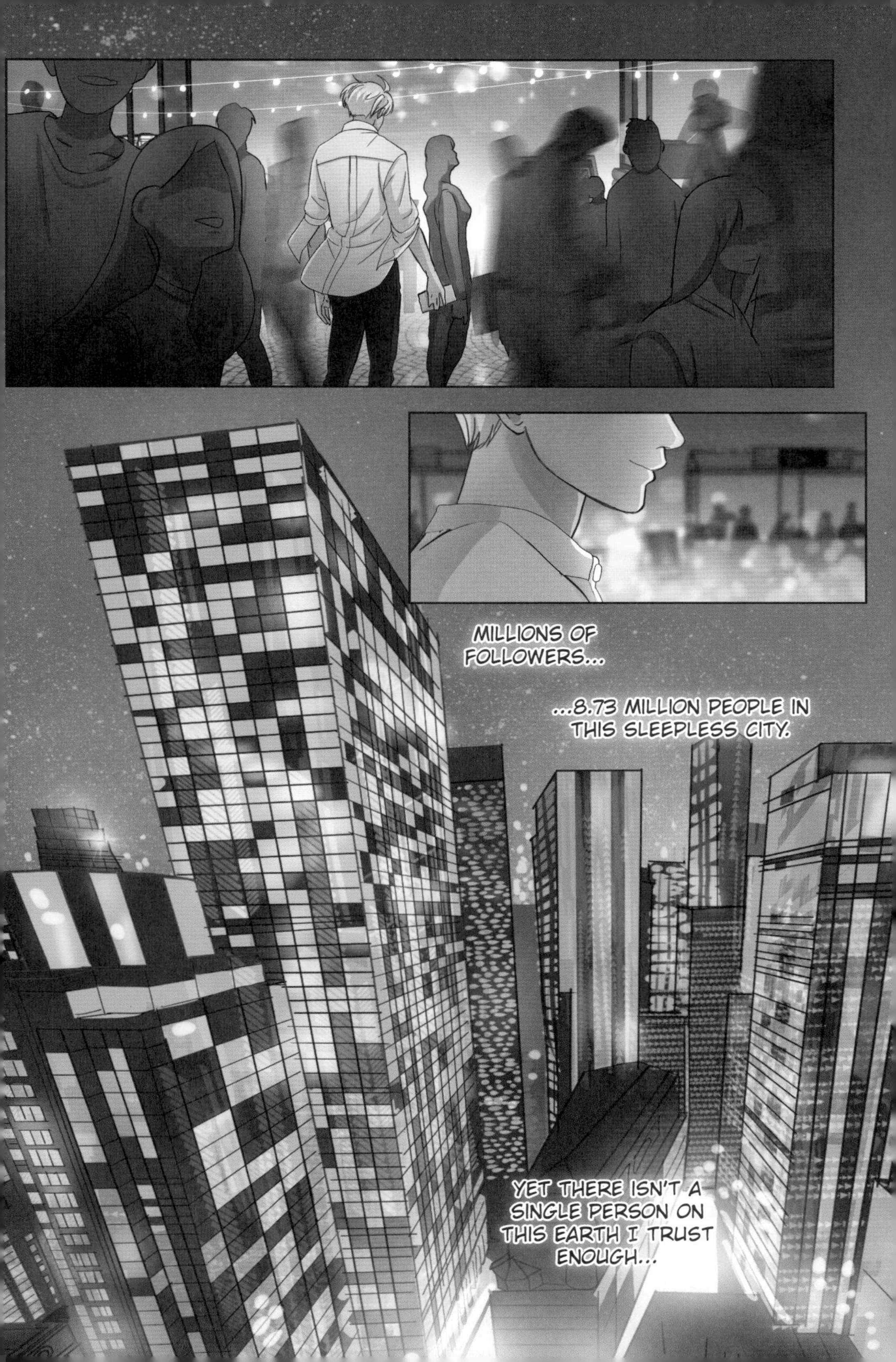
MILLIONS OF FOLLOWERS...
...8.73 MILLION PEOPLE IN THIS SLEEPLESS CITY.
YET THERE ISN'T A SINGLE PERSON ON THIS EARTH I TRUST ENOUGH...

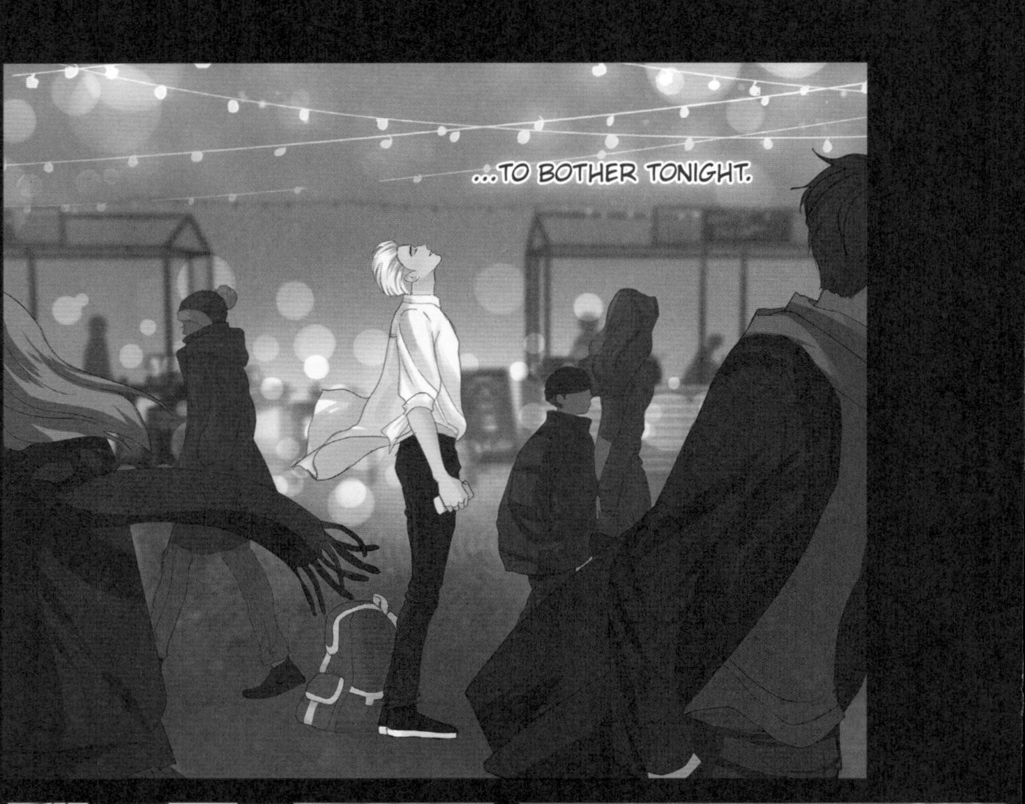
...TO BOTHER TONIGHT.

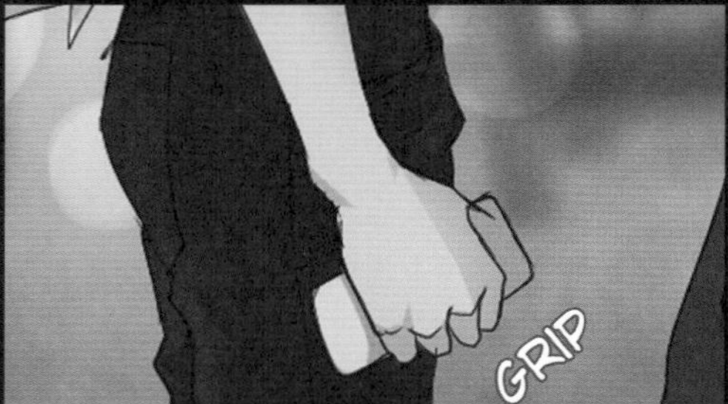
GRIP

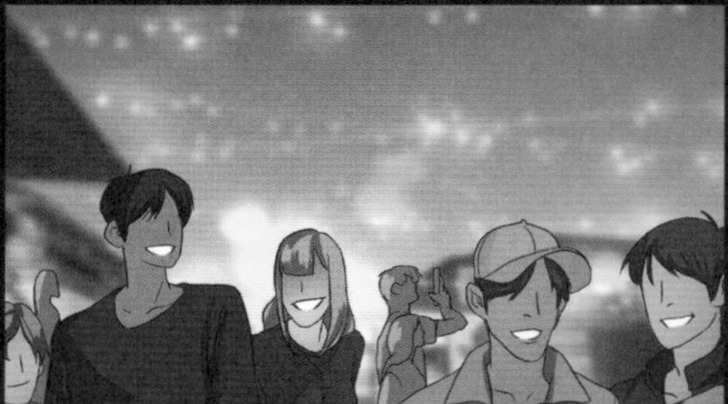

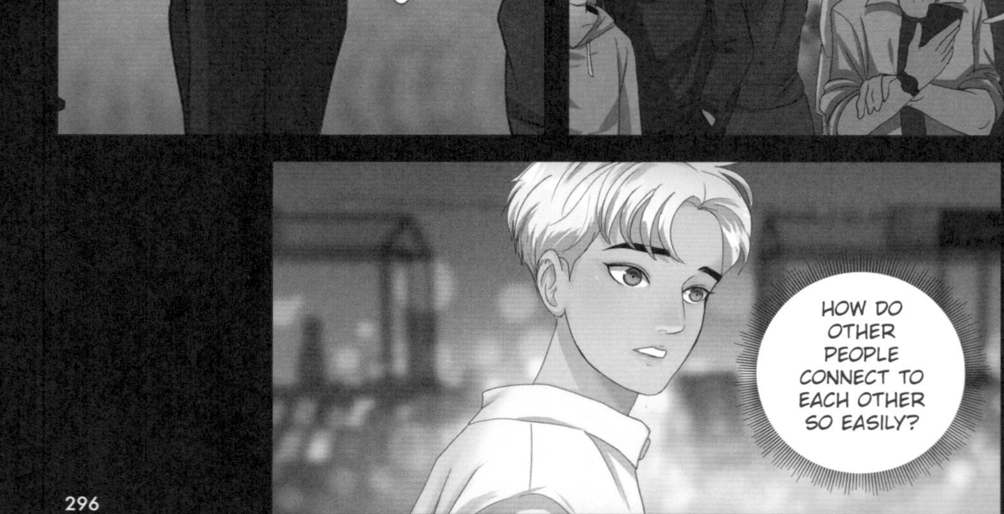
HOW DO OTHER PEOPLE CONNECT TO EACH OTHER SO EASILY?

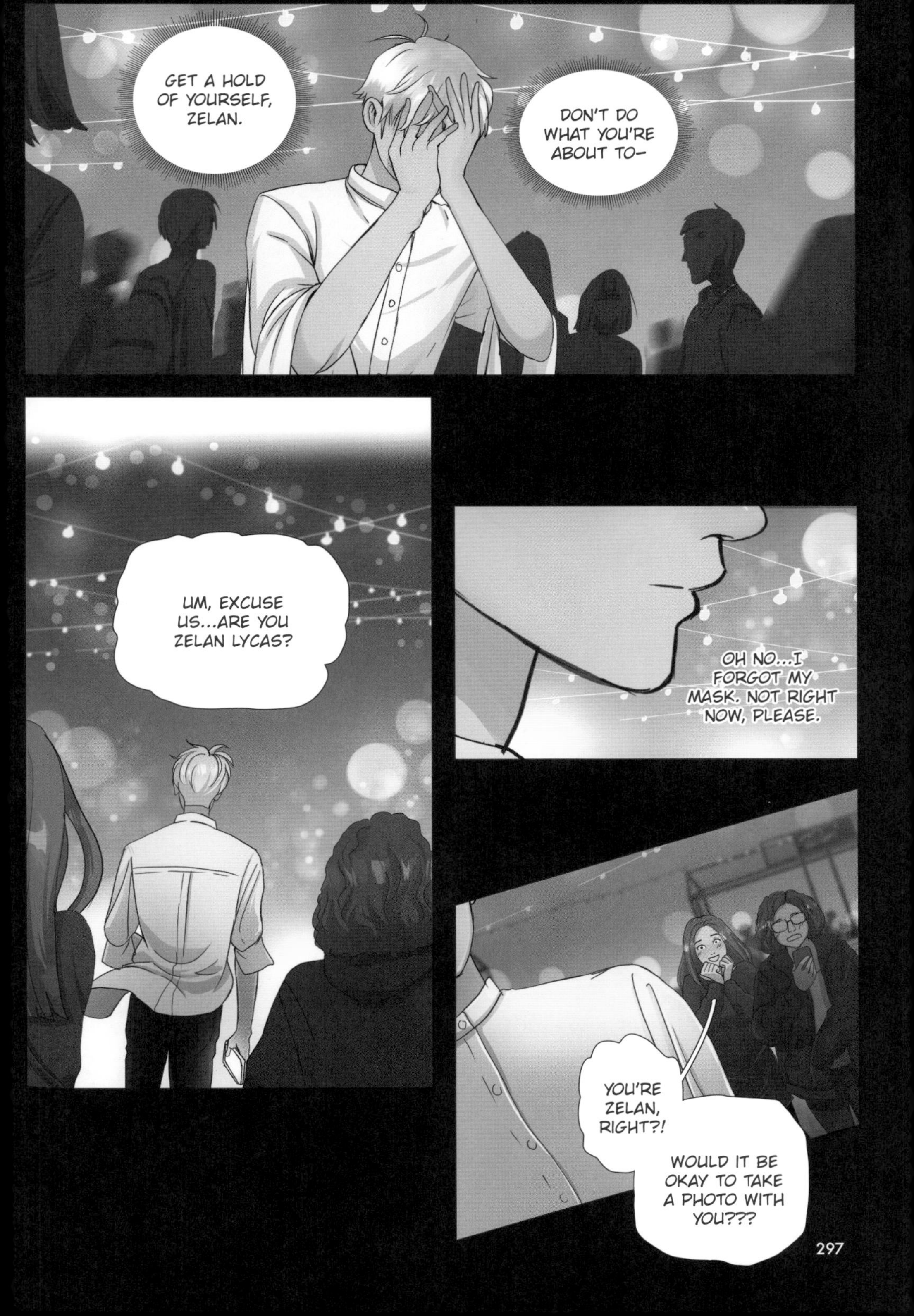
GET A HOLD OF YOURSELF, ZELAN.
DON'T DO WHAT YOU'RE ABOUT TO-
UM, EXCUSE US...ARE YOU ZELAN LYCAS?
OH NO...I FORGOT MY MASK. NOT RIGHT NOW, PLEASE.
YOU'RE ZELAN, RIGHT?!
WOULD IT BE OKAY TO TAKE A PHOTO WITH YOU???

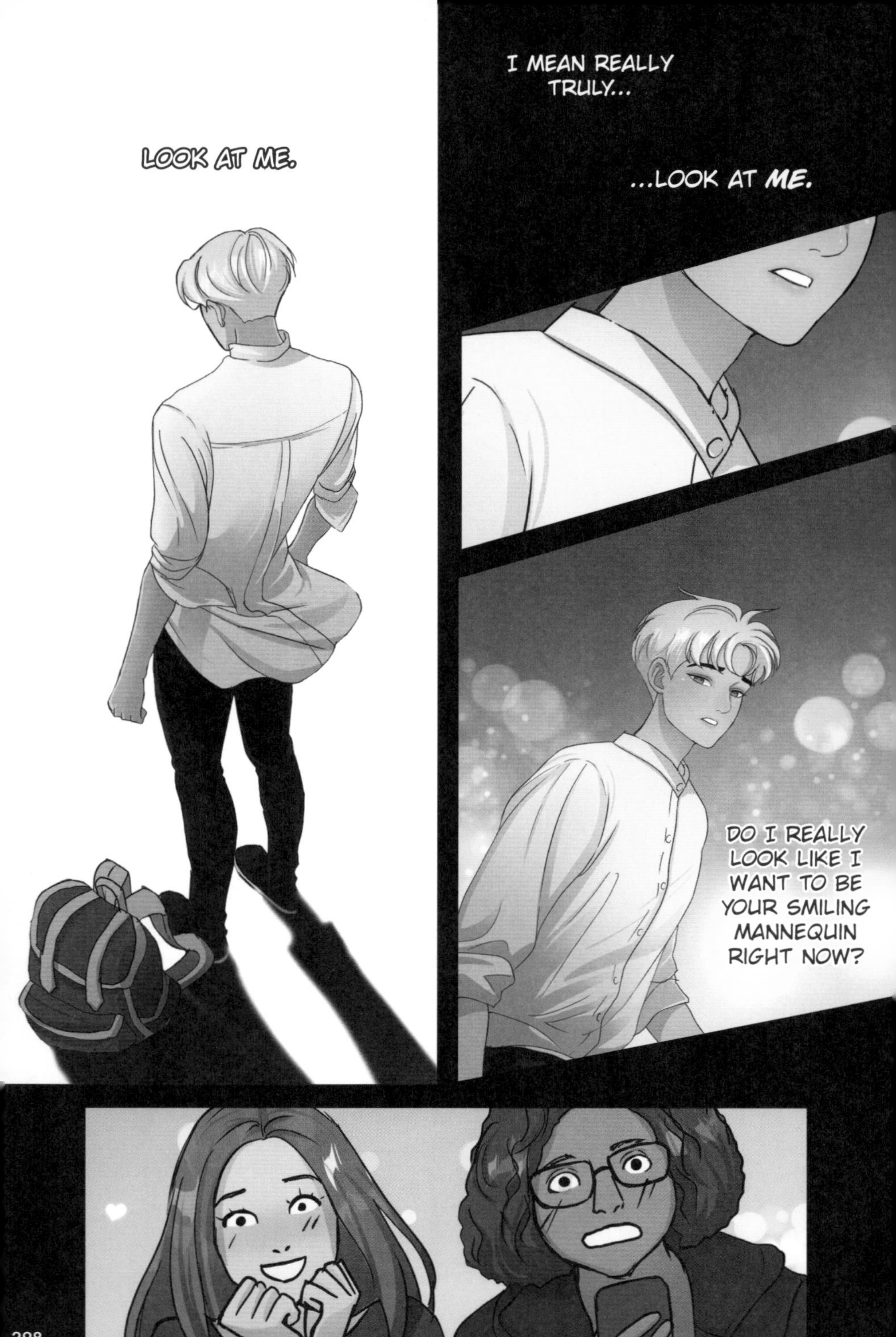
LOOK AT ME.
I MEAN REALLY TRULY...
...LOOK AT ME.
DO I REALLY LOOK LIKE I WANT TO BE YOUR SMILING MANNEQUIN RIGHT NOW?

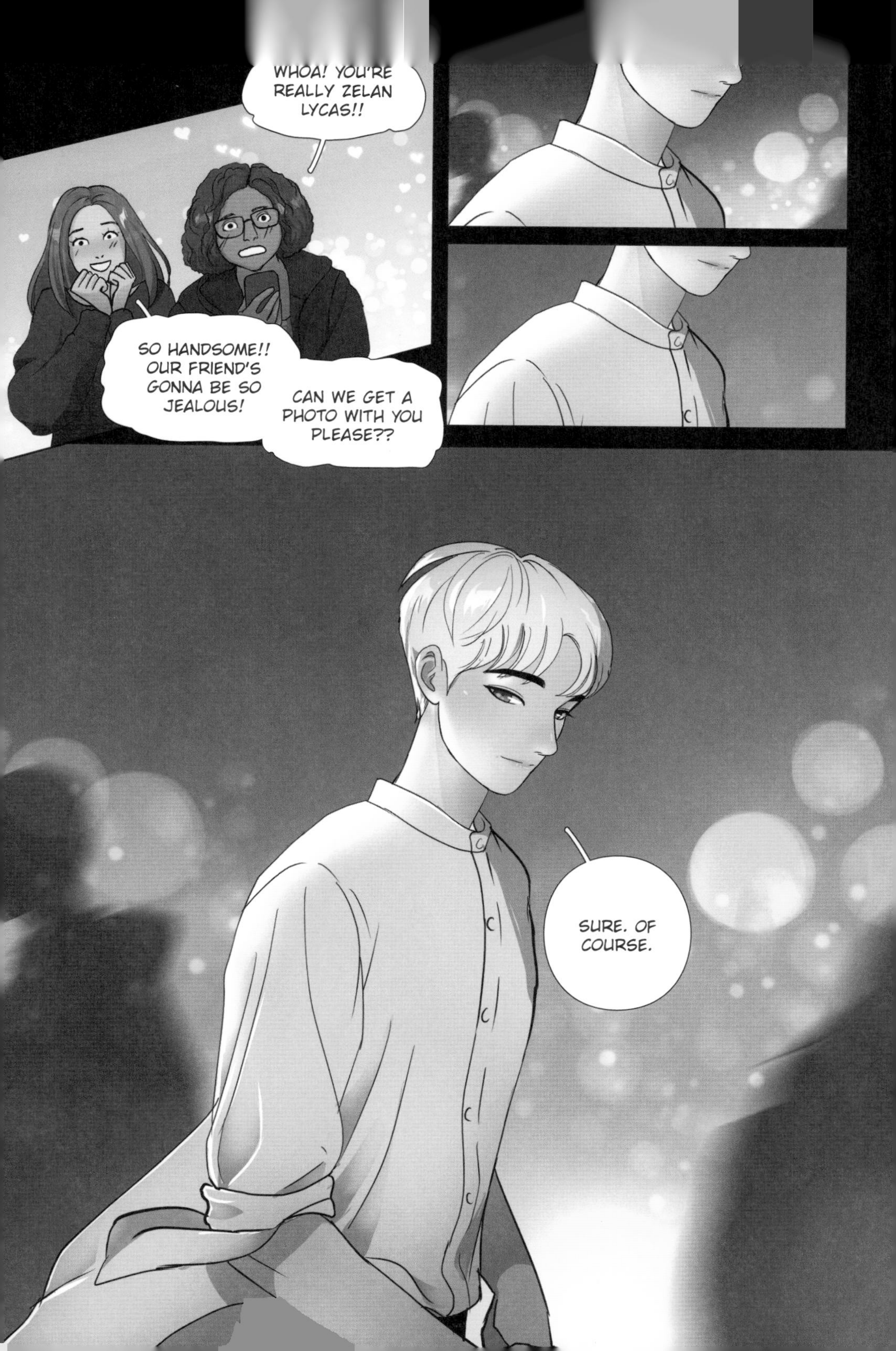
WHOA! YOU'RE REALLY ZELAN LYCAS!!
SO HANDSOME!! OUR FRIEND'S GONNA BE SO JEALOUS!
CAN WE GET A PHOTO WITH YOU PLEASE??
SURE. OF COURSE.

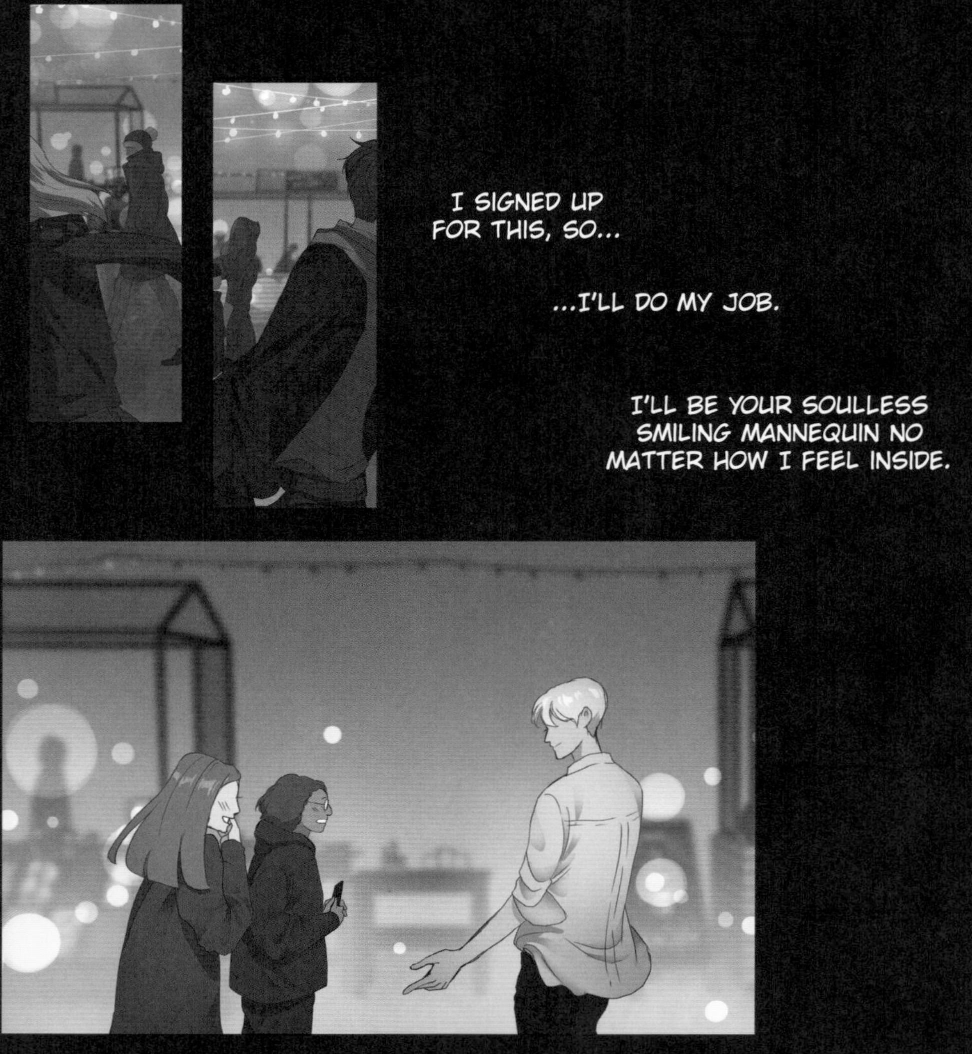
I SIGNED UP FOR THIS, SO...
...I'LL DO MY JOB.
I'LL BE YOUR SOULLESS SMILING MANNEQUIN NO MATTER HOW I FEEL INSIDE.
I-I CAN'T BELIEVE WE WERE L-LUCKY ENOUGH TO RUN INTO YOU...
...Y-YOU HAVEN'T BEEN ACTIVE ON SOCIAL MEDIA FOR A WHILE...
I WAS SAD BE-BECAUSE I REALLY MISS YOUR POSTS!!

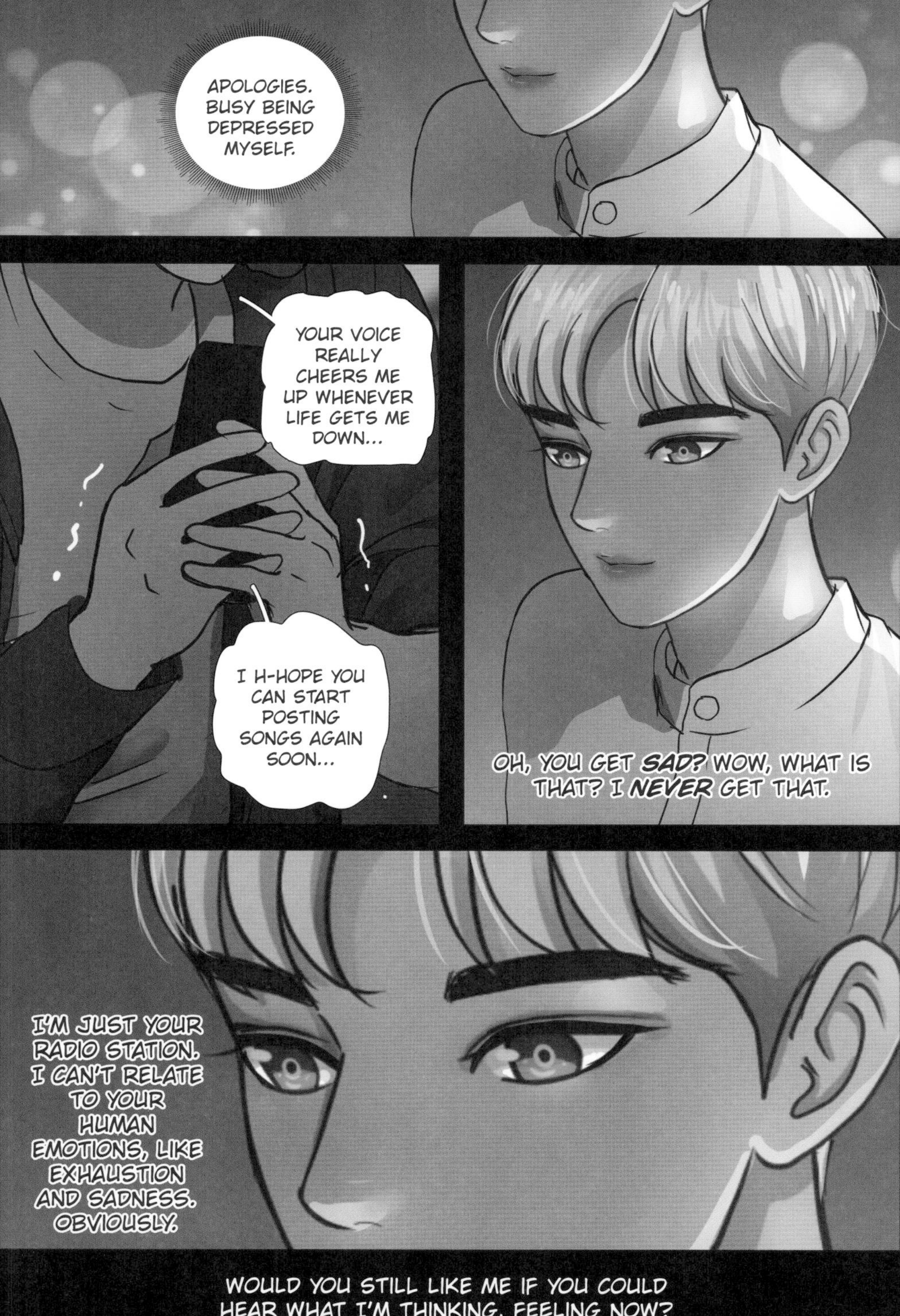
APOLOGIES. BUSY BEING DEPRESSED MYSELF.
YOUR VOICE REALLY CHEERS ME UP WHENEVER LIFE GETS ME DOWN...
I H-HOPE YOU CAN START POSTING SONGS AGAIN SOON...
OH, YOU GET SAD? WOW, WHAT IS THAT? I NEVER GET THAT.
I'M JUST YOUR RADIO STATION. I CAN'T RELATE TO YOUR HUMAN EMOTIONS, LIKE EXHAUSTION AND SADNESS. OBVIOUSLY.
WOULD YOU STILL LIKE ME IF YOU COULD HEAR WHAT I'M THINKING, FEELING NOW?

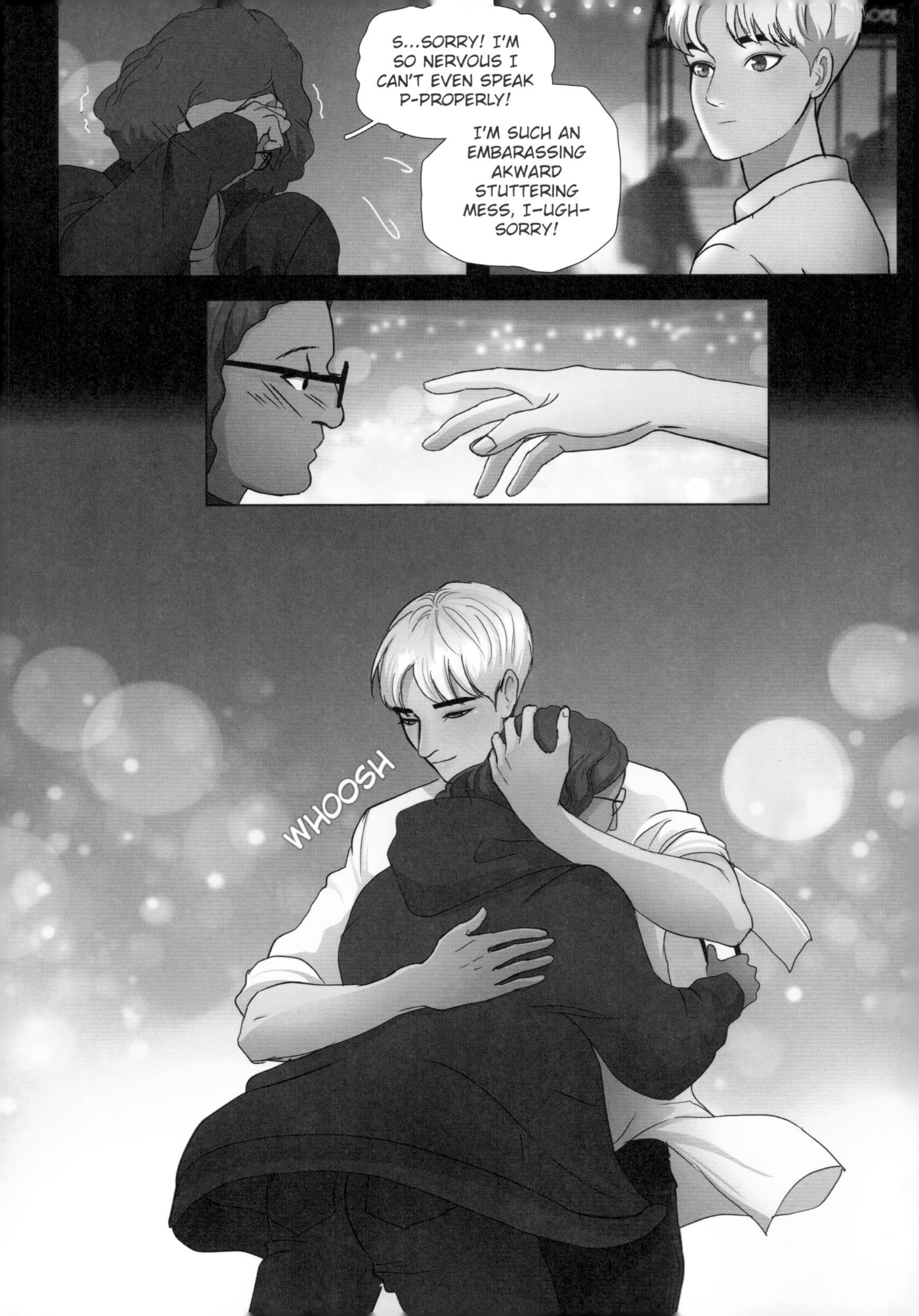
S...SORRY! I'M SO NERVOUS I CAN'T EVEN SPEAK P-PROPERLY!
I'M SUCH AN EMBARASSING AKWARD STUTTERING MESS, I-UGH- SORRY!
WHOOSH

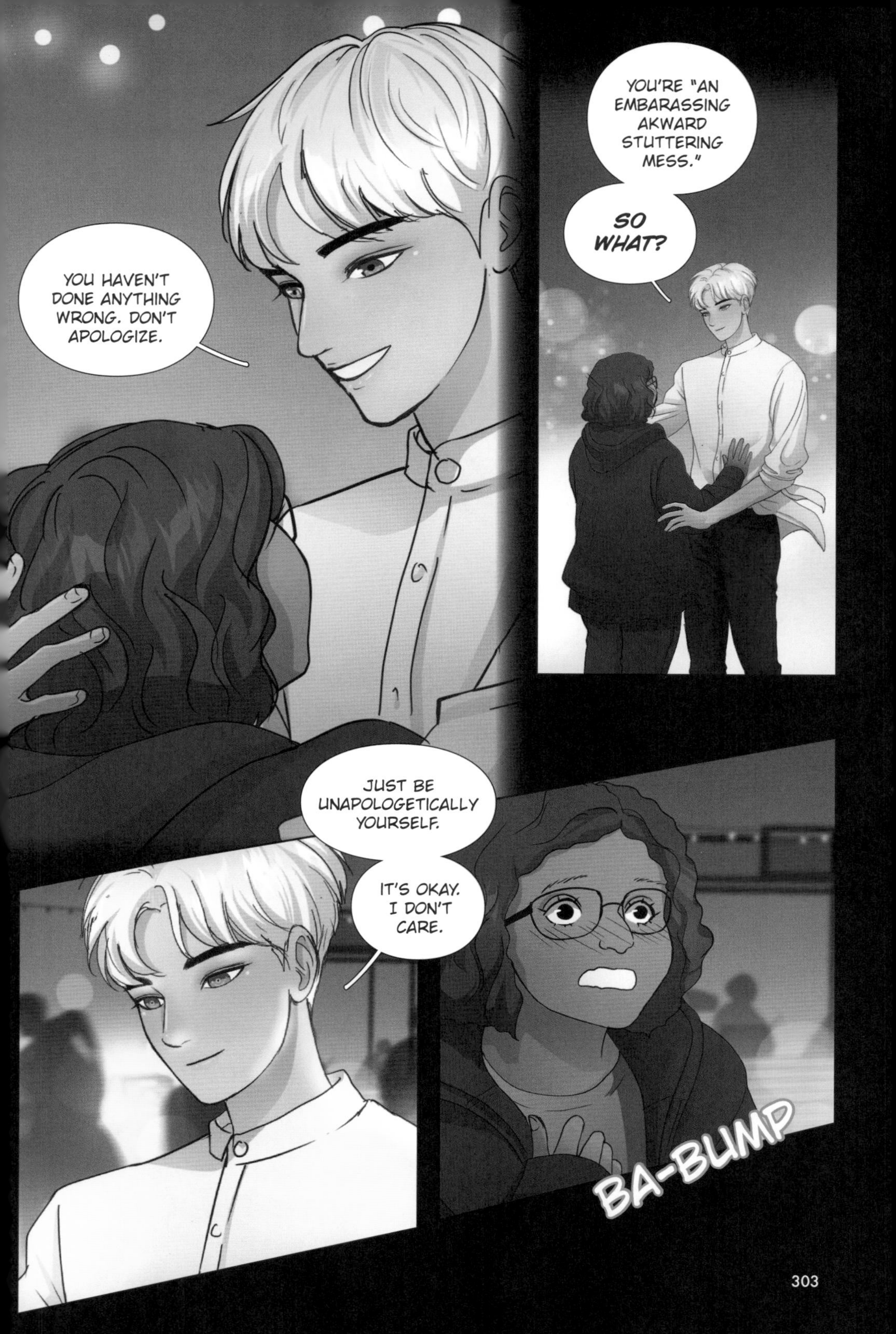
YOU HAVEN'T DONE ANYTHING WRONG. DON'T APOLOGIZE.
YOU'RE "AN EMBARASSING AKWARD STUTTERING MESS."
SO WHAT?
JUST BE UNAPOLOGETICALLY YOURSELF.
IT'S OKAY. I DON'T CARE.
BA-BUMP

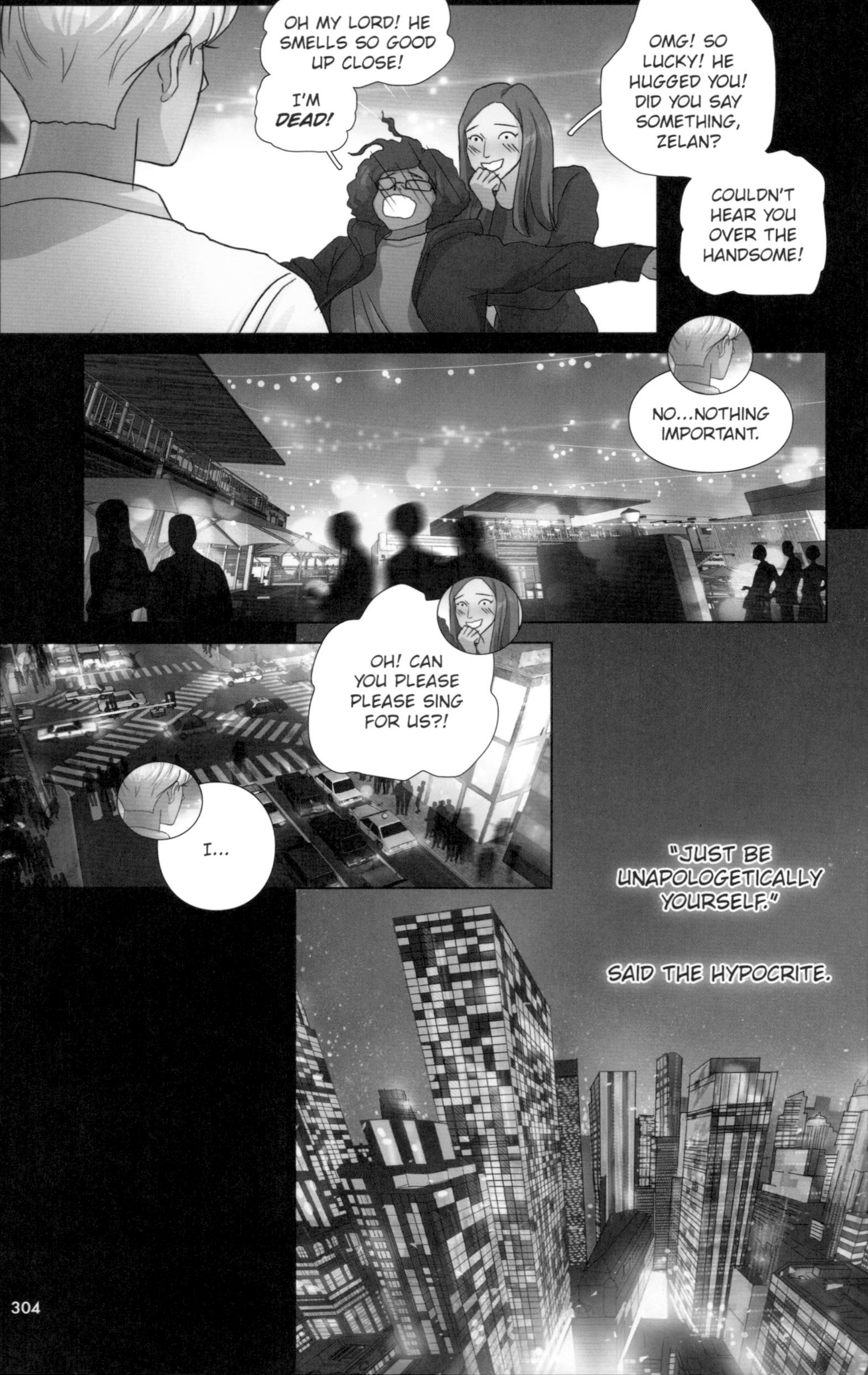
OH MY LORD! HE SMELLS SO GOOD UP CLOSE!
I'M *DEAD!*
OMG! SO LUCKY! HE HUGGED YOU! DID YOU SAY SOMETHING, ZELAN?
COULDN'T HEAR YOU OVER THE HANDSOME!
NO...NOTHING IMPORTANT.
OH! CAN YOU PLEASE PLEASE SING FOR US?!
I...
"JUST BE UNAPOLOGETICALLY YOURSELF."
SAID THE HYPOCRITE.

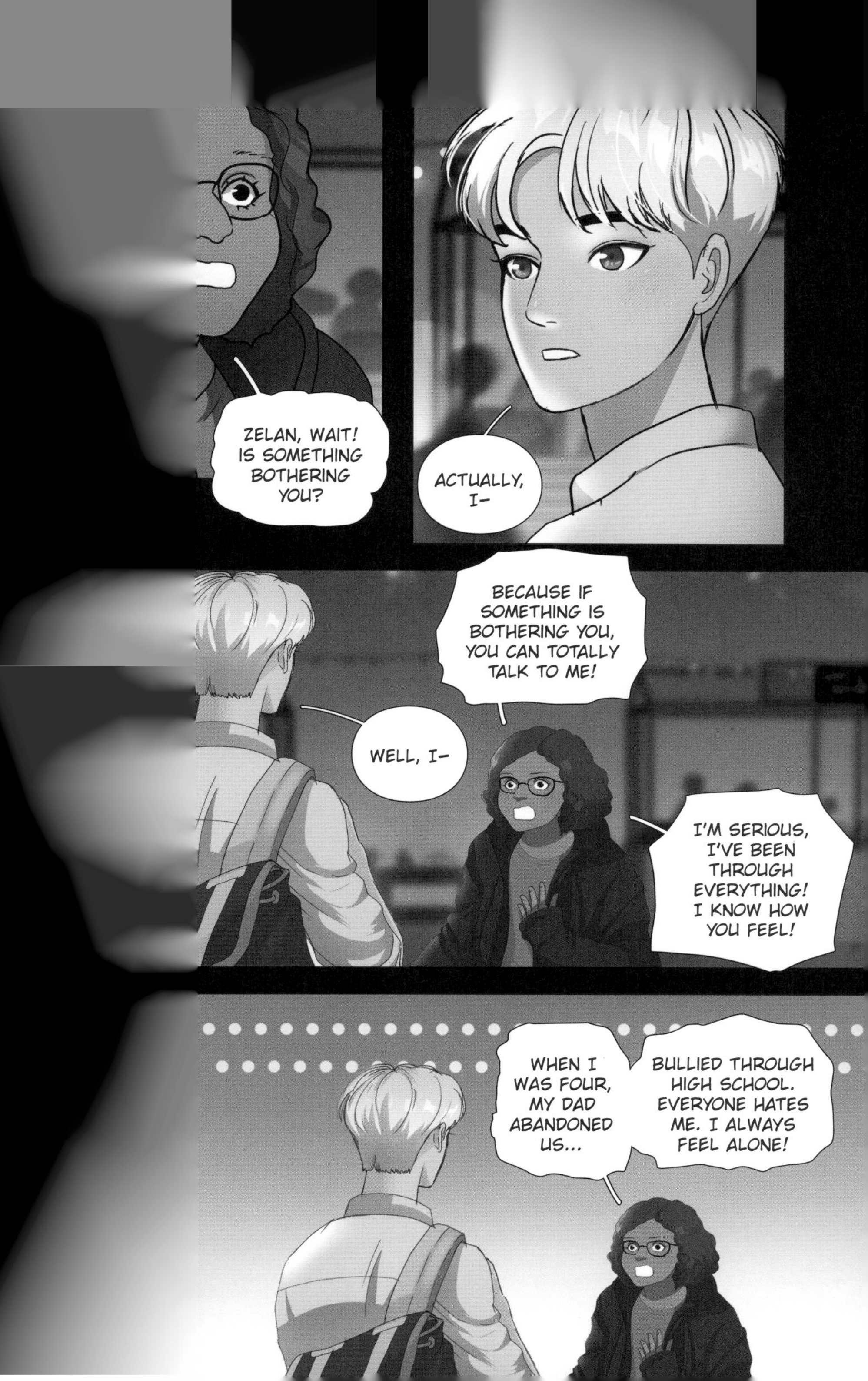
ZELAN, WAIT! IS SOMETHING BOTHERING YOU?
ACTUALLY, I–
BECAUSE IF SOMETHING IS BOTHERING YOU, YOU CAN TOTALLY TALK TO ME!
WELL, I–
I'M SERIOUS, I'VE BEEN THROUGH EVERYTHING! I KNOW HOW YOU FEEL!
WHEN I WAS FOUR, MY DAD ABANDONED US...
BULLIED THROUGH HIGH SCHOOL. EVERYONE HATES ME. I ALWAYS FEEL ALONE!

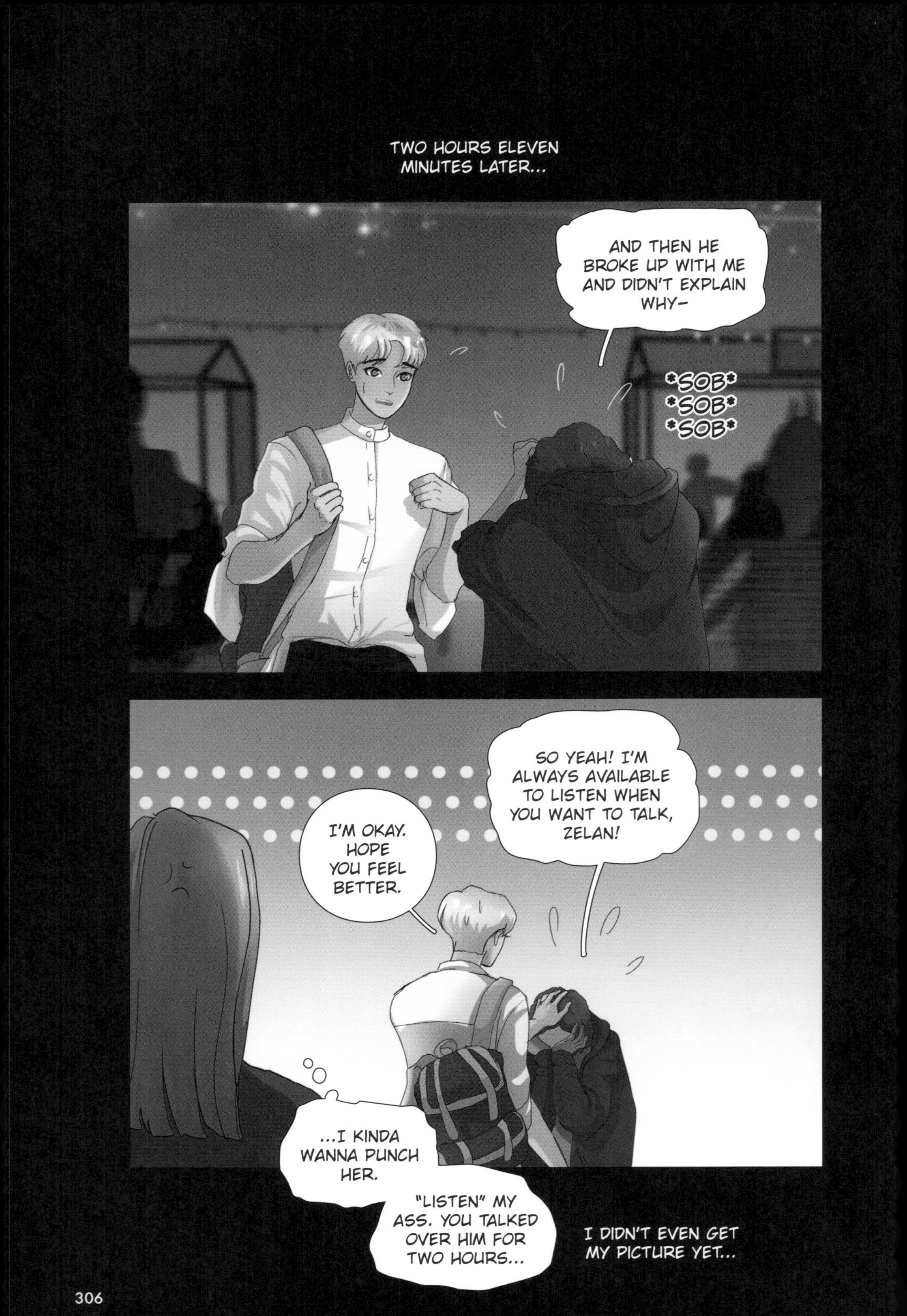
TWO HOURS ELEVEN MINUTES LATER...
AND THEN HE BROKE UP WITH ME AND DIDN'T EXPLAIN WHY–
SOB *SOB* *SOB*
I'M OKAY. HOPE YOU FEEL BETTER.
SO YEAH! I'M ALWAYS AVAILABLE TO LISTEN WHEN YOU WANT TO TALK, ZELAN!
...I KINDA WANNA PUNCH HER.
"LISTEN" MY ASS. YOU TALKED OVER HIM FOR TWO HOURS...
I DIDN'T EVEN GET MY PICTURE YET...

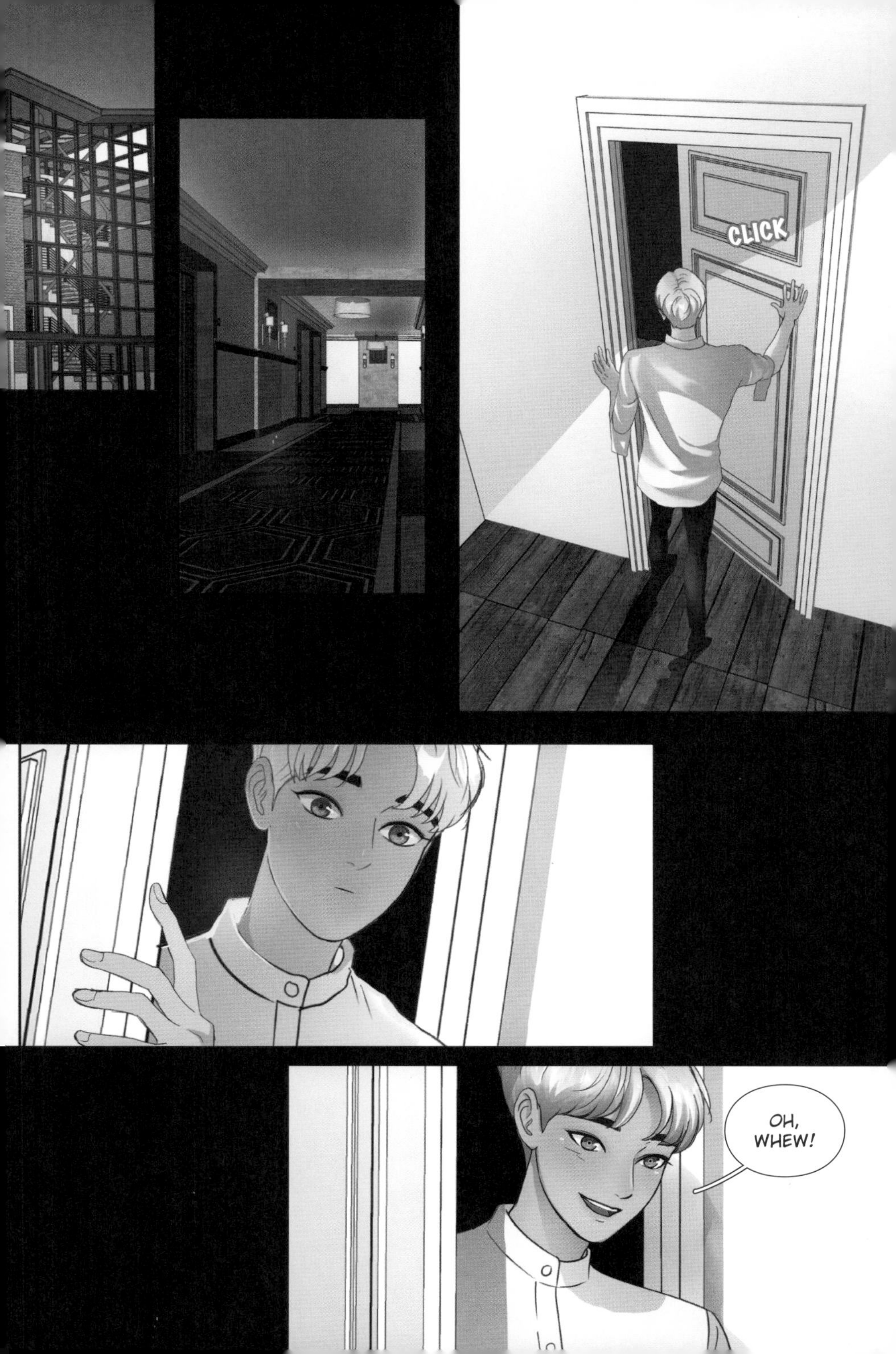
CLICK
OH, WHEW!

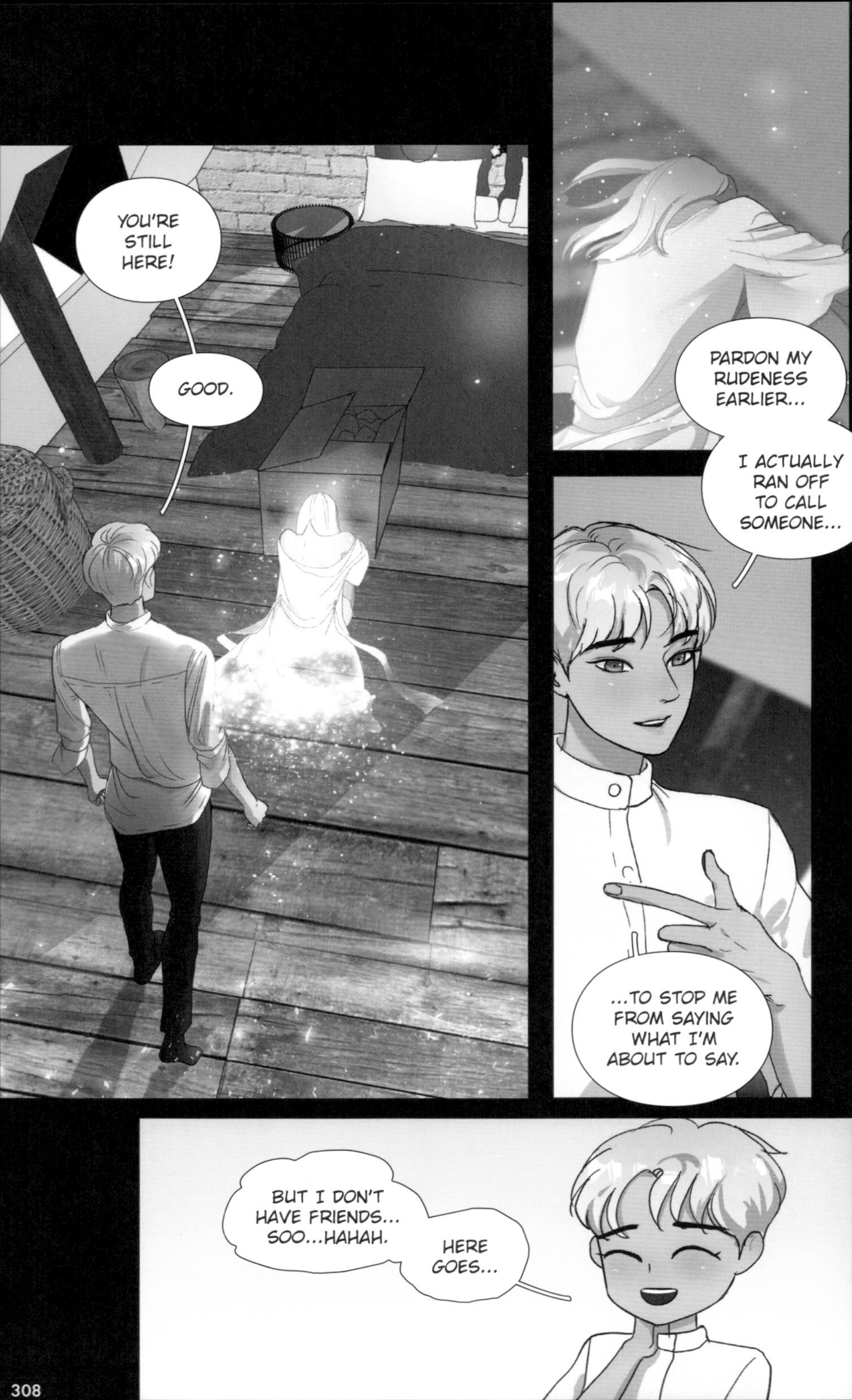

YOU'RE STILL HERE!
GOOD.
PARDON MY RUDENESS EARLIER...
I ACTUALLY RAN OFF TO CALL SOMEONE...
...TO STOP ME FROM SAYING WHAT I'M ABOUT TO SAY.
BUT I DON'T HAVE FRIENDS... SOO...HAHAH.
HERE GOES...

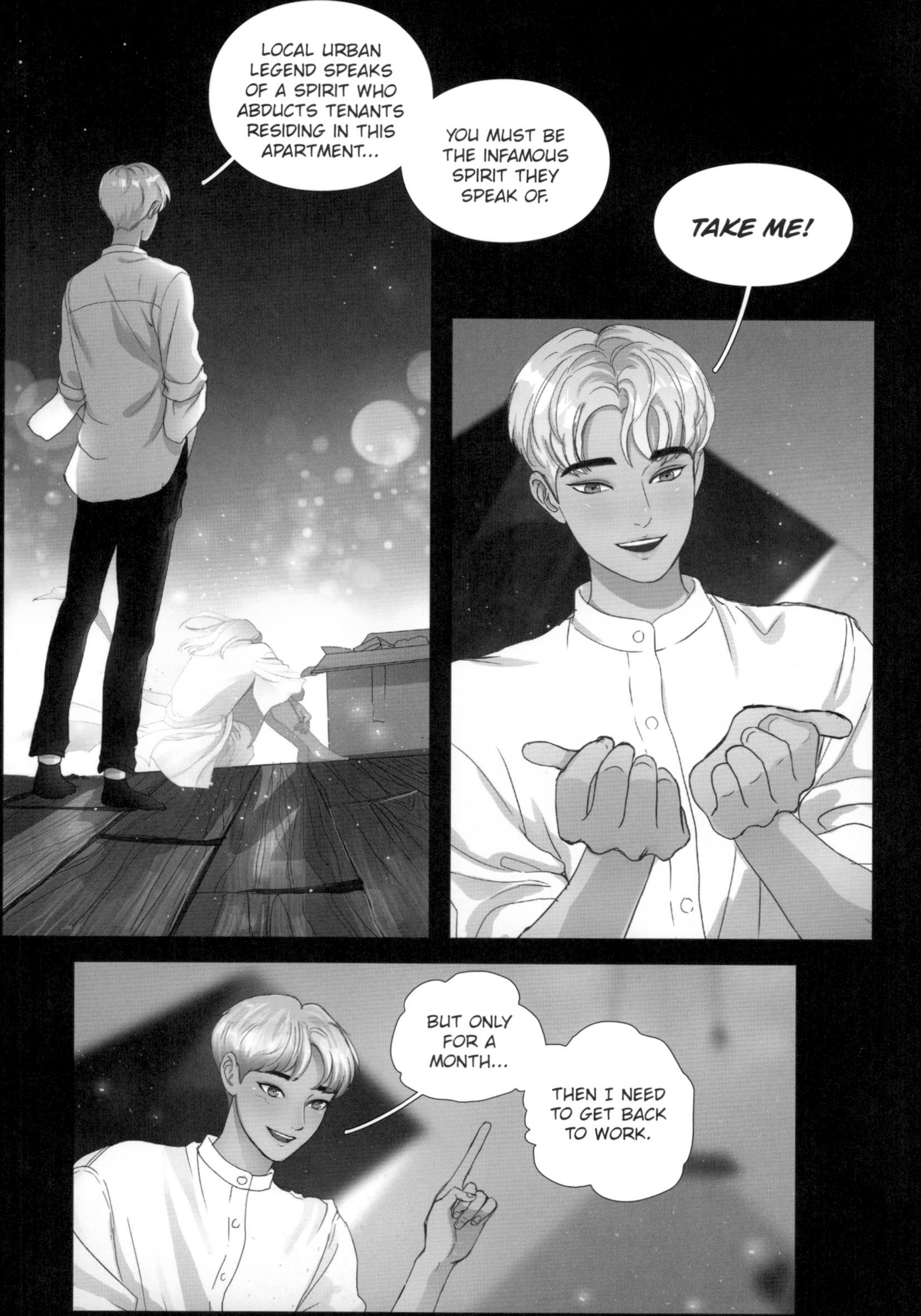
LOCAL URBAN LEGEND SPEAKS OF A SPIRIT WHO ABDUCTS TENANTS RESIDING IN THIS APARTMENT...
YOU MUST BE THE INFAMOUS SPIRIT THEY SPEAK OF.
TAKE ME!
BUT ONLY FOR A MONTH...
THEN I NEED TO GET BACK TO WORK.

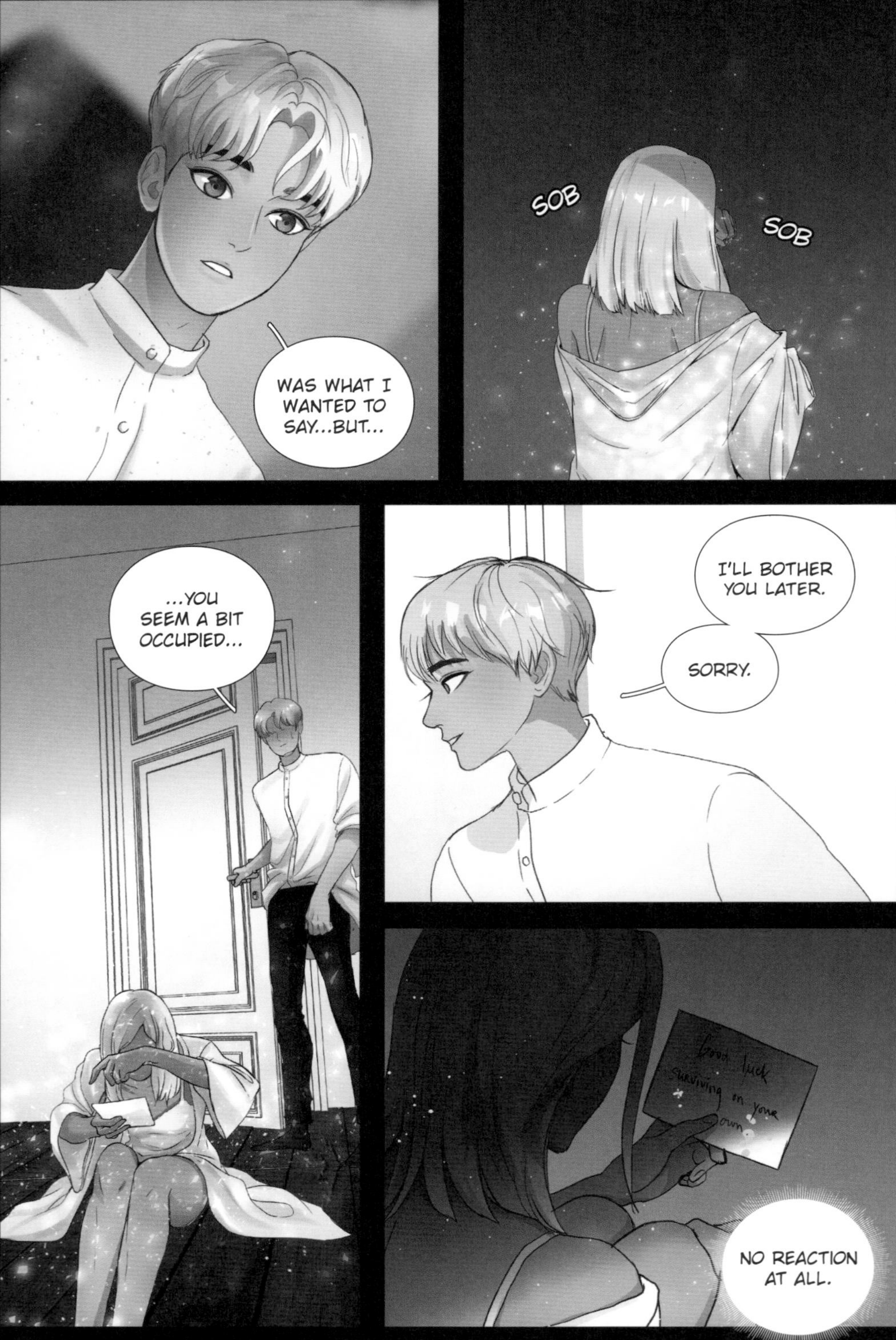
WAS WHAT I WANTED TO SAY...BUT...
SOB
SOB
...YOU SEEM A BIT OCCUPIED...
I'LL BOTHER YOU LATER.
SORRY.
Good luck Surviving on your own.
NO REACTION AT ALL.

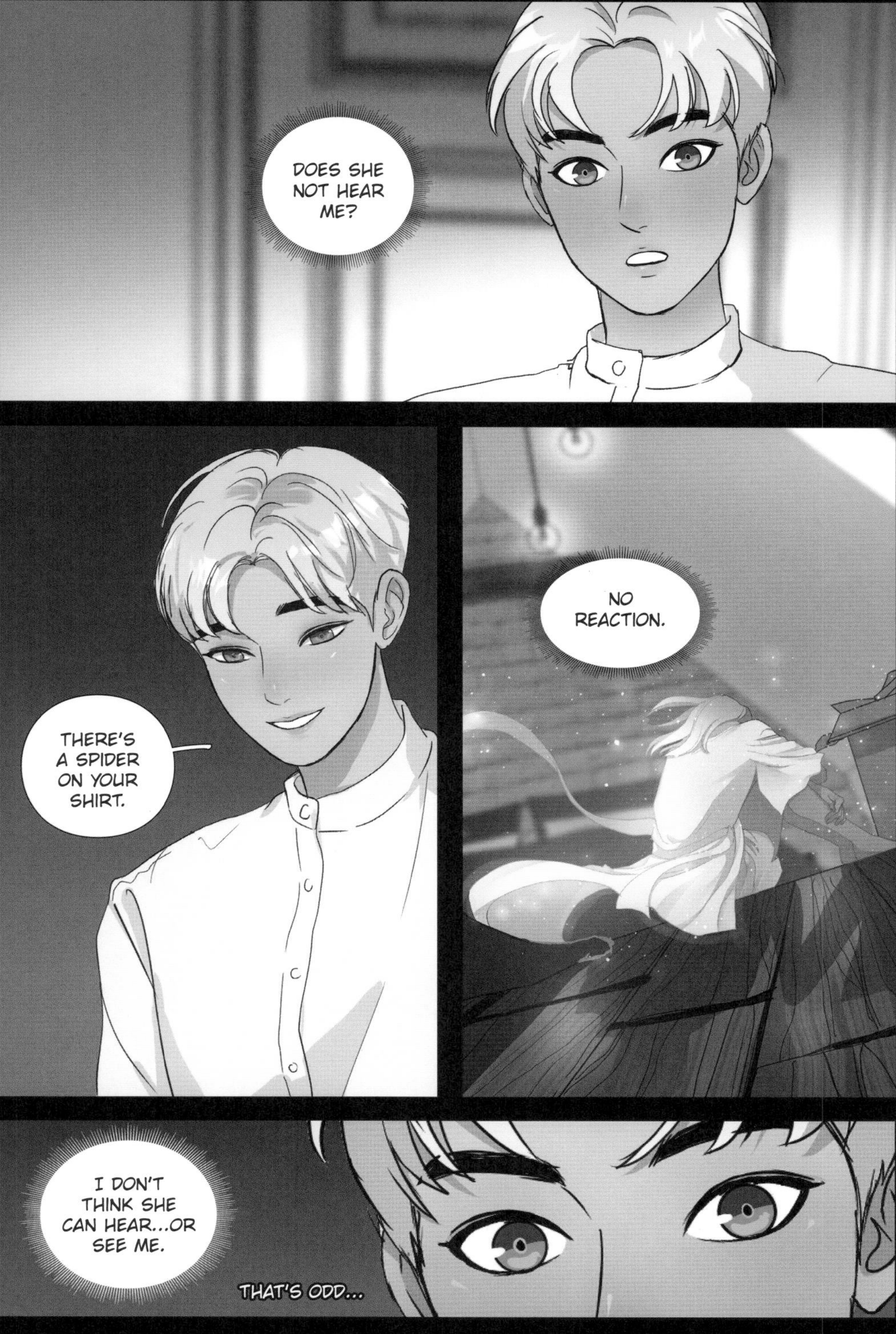
DOES SHE NOT HEAR ME?
THERE'S A SPIDER ON YOUR SHIRT.
NO REACTION.
I DON'T THINK SHE CAN HEAR...OR SEE ME.
THAT'S ODD...

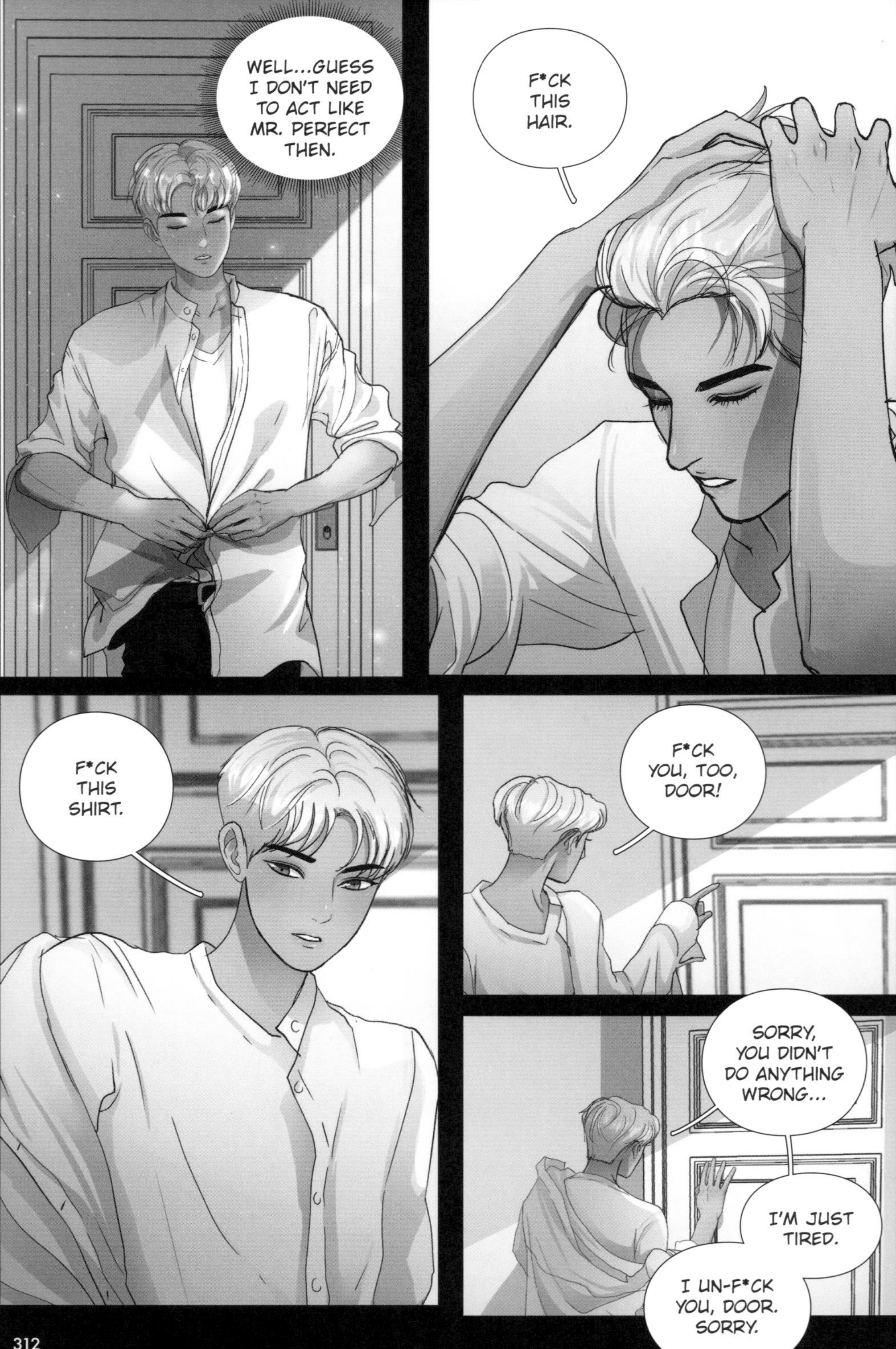
WELL...GUESS I DON'T NEED TO ACT LIKE MR. PERFECT THEN.
F*CK THIS HAIR.
F*CK THIS SHIRT.
F*CK YOU, TOO, DOOR!
SORRY, YOU DIDN'T DO ANYTHING WRONG...
I'M JUST TIRED.
I UN-F*CK YOU, DOOR. SORRY.

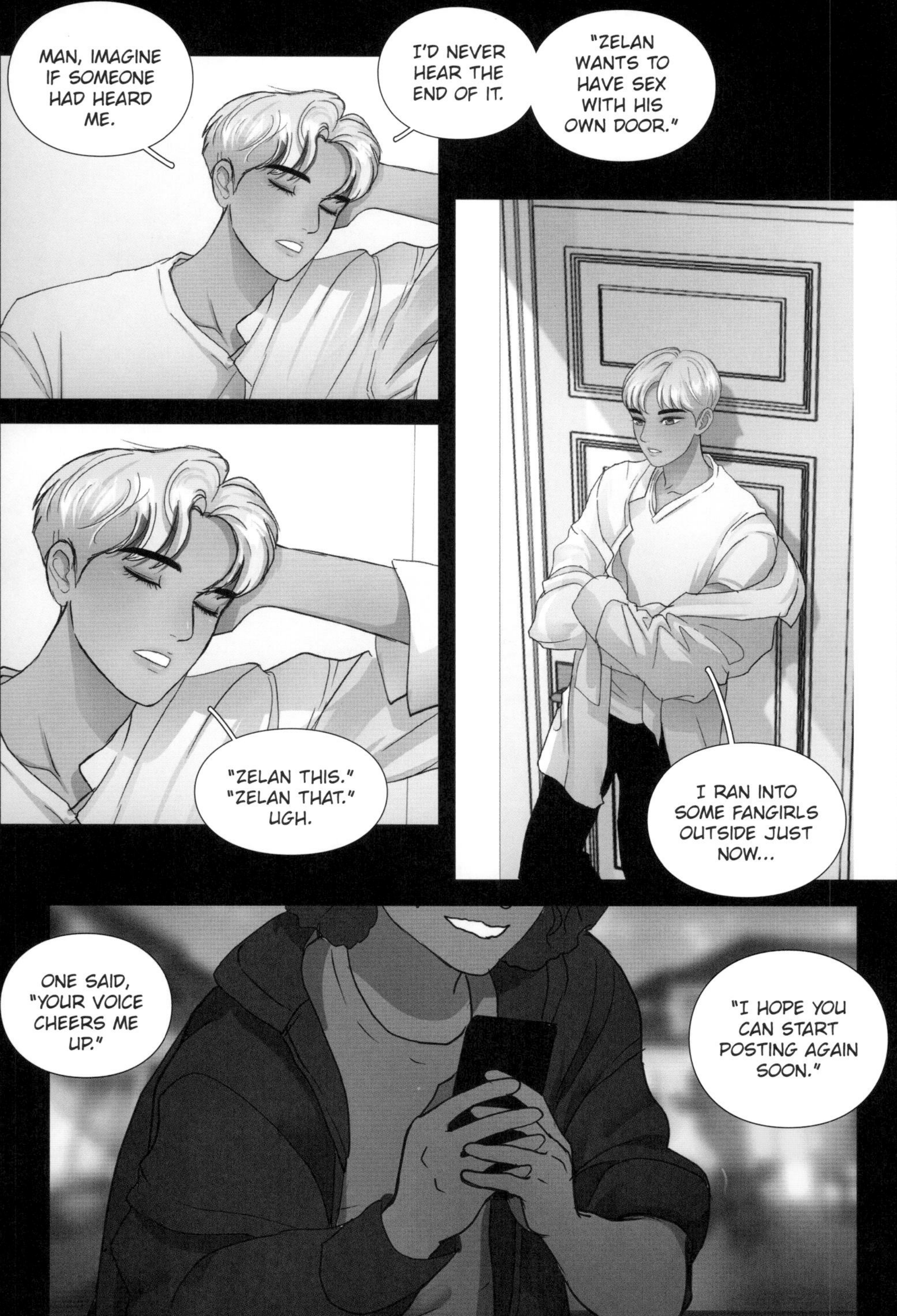
MAN, IMAGINE IF SOMEONE HAD HEARD ME.
I'D NEVER HEAR THE END OF IT.
"ZELAN WANTS TO HAVE SEX WITH HIS OWN DOOR."
"ZELAN THIS." "ZELAN THAT." UGH.
I RAN INTO SOME FANGIRLS OUTSIDE JUST NOW...
ONE SAID, "YOUR VOICE CHEERS ME UP."
"I HOPE YOU CAN START POSTING AGAIN SOON."

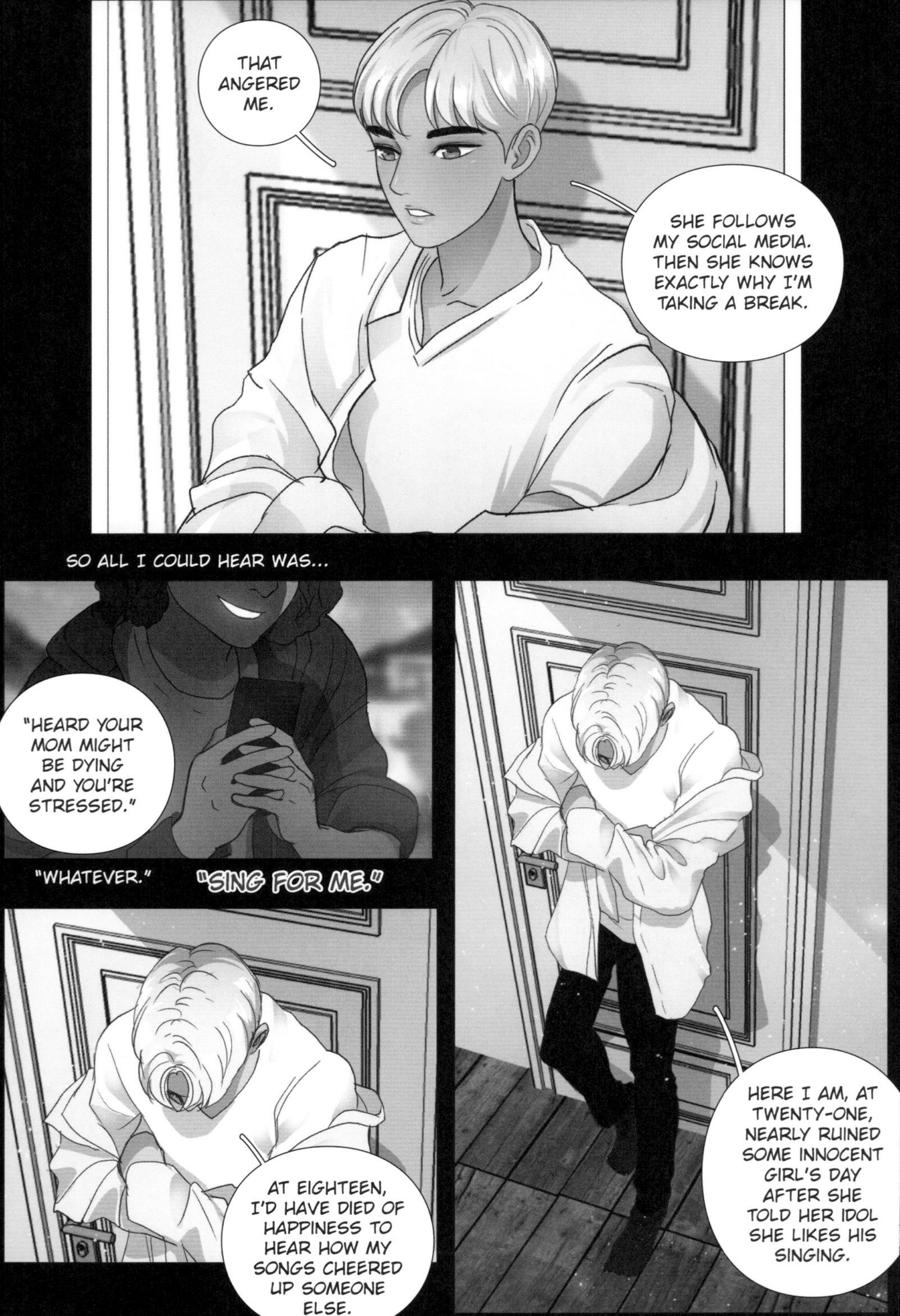
THAT ANGERED ME.
SHE FOLLOWS MY SOCIAL MEDIA. THEN SHE KNOWS EXACTLY WHY I'M TAKING A BREAK.
SO ALL I COULD HEAR WAS...
"HEARD YOUR MOM MIGHT BE DYING AND YOU'RE STRESSED."
"WHATEVER."
"SING FOR ME."
AT EIGHTEEN, I'D HAVE DIED OF HAPPINESS TO HEAR HOW MY SONGS CHEERED UP SOMEONE ELSE.
HERE I AM, AT TWENTY-ONE, NEARLY RUINED SOME INNOCENT GIRL'S DAY AFTER SHE TOLD HER IDOL SHE LIKES HIS SINGING.

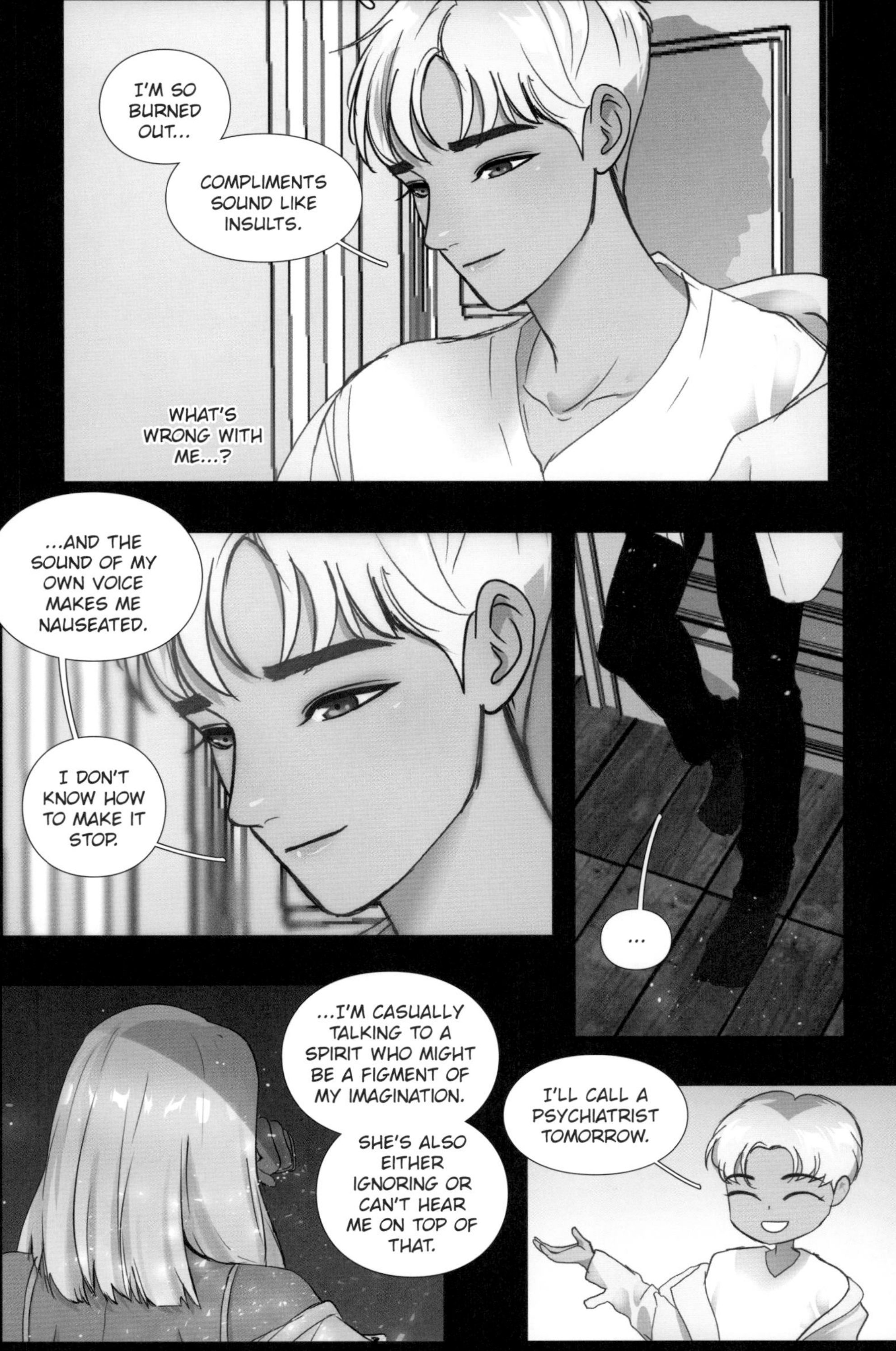
I'M SO BURNED OUT...
COMPLIMENTS SOUND LIKE INSULTS.
WHAT'S WRONG WITH ME...?
...AND THE SOUND OF MY OWN VOICE MAKES ME NAUSEATED.
I DON'T KNOW HOW TO MAKE IT STOP.
...
...I'M CASUALLY TALKING TO A SPIRIT WHO MIGHT BE A FIGMENT OF MY IMAGINATION.
SHE'S ALSO EITHER IGNORING OR CAN'T HEAR ME ON TOP OF THAT.
I'LL CALL A PSYCHIATRIST TOMORROW.

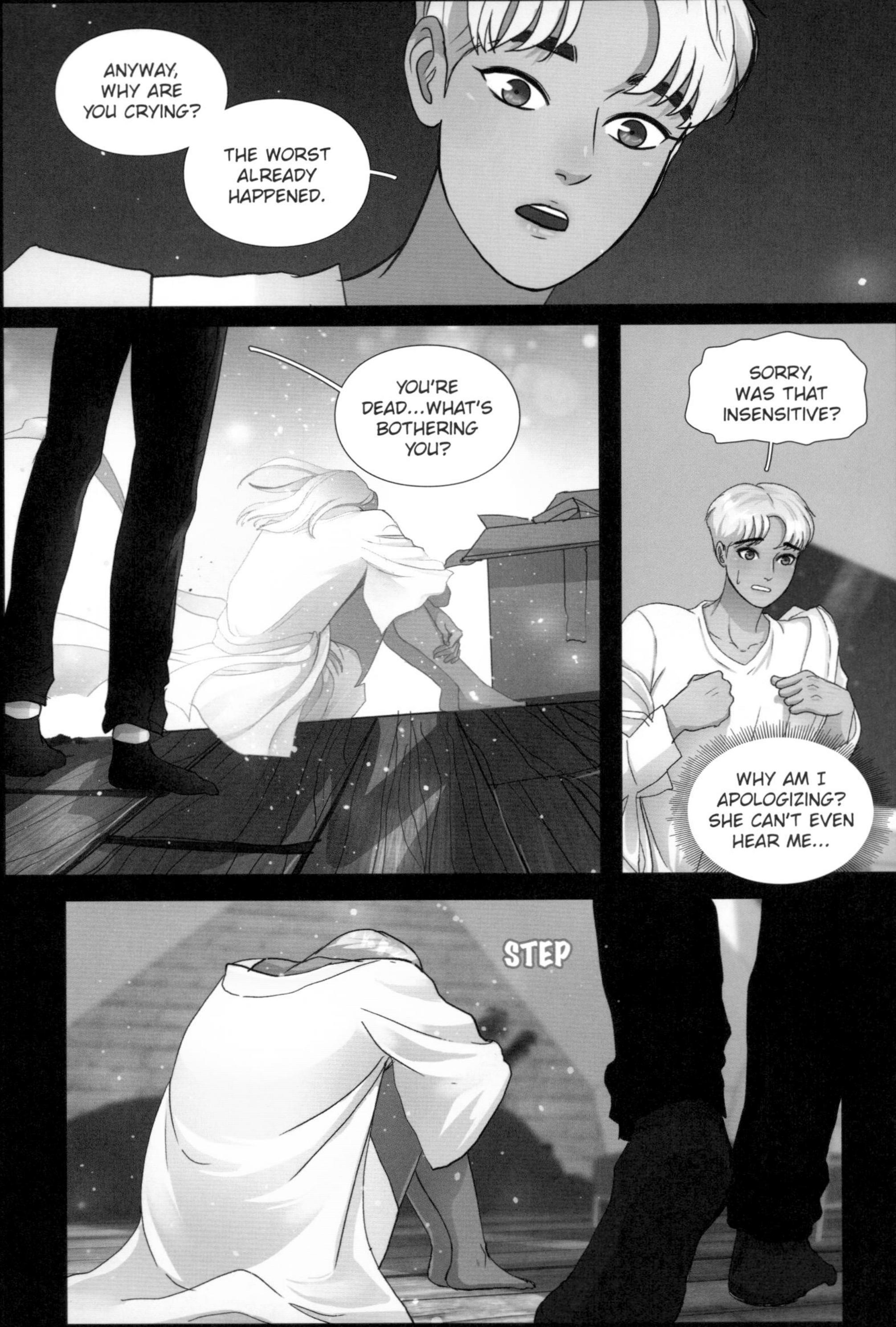
ANYWAY, WHY ARE YOU CRYING?
THE WORST ALREADY HAPPENED.
YOU'RE DEAD...WHAT'S BOTHERING YOU?
SORRY, WAS THAT INSENSITIVE?
WHY AM I APOLOGIZING? SHE CAN'T EVEN HEAR ME...
STEP

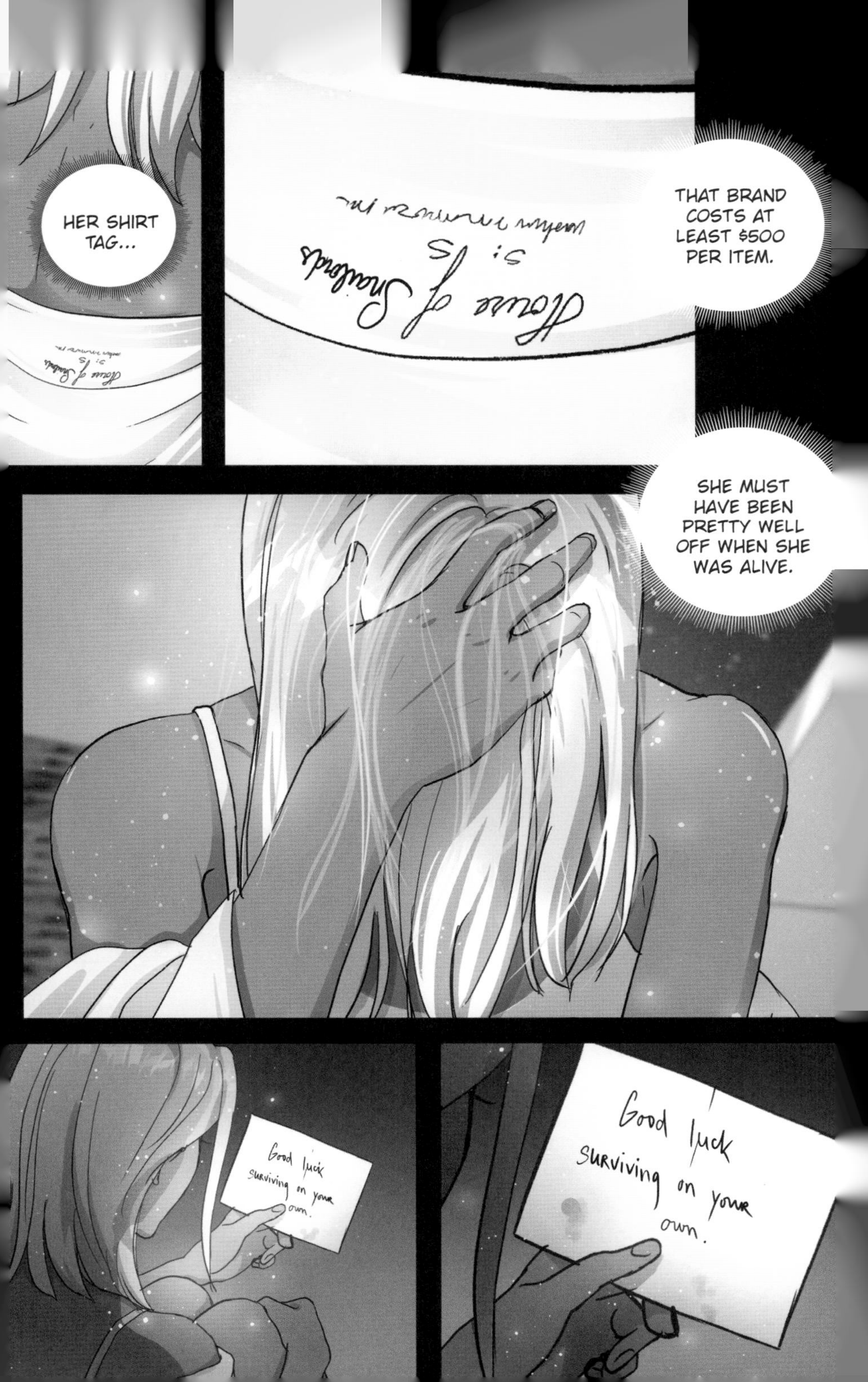
HER SHIRT TAG...
THAT BRAND COSTS AT LEAST $500 PER ITEM.
SHE MUST HAVE BEEN PRETTY WELL OFF WHEN SHE WAS ALIVE.
Good luck surviving on your own.
Good luck surviving on your own.

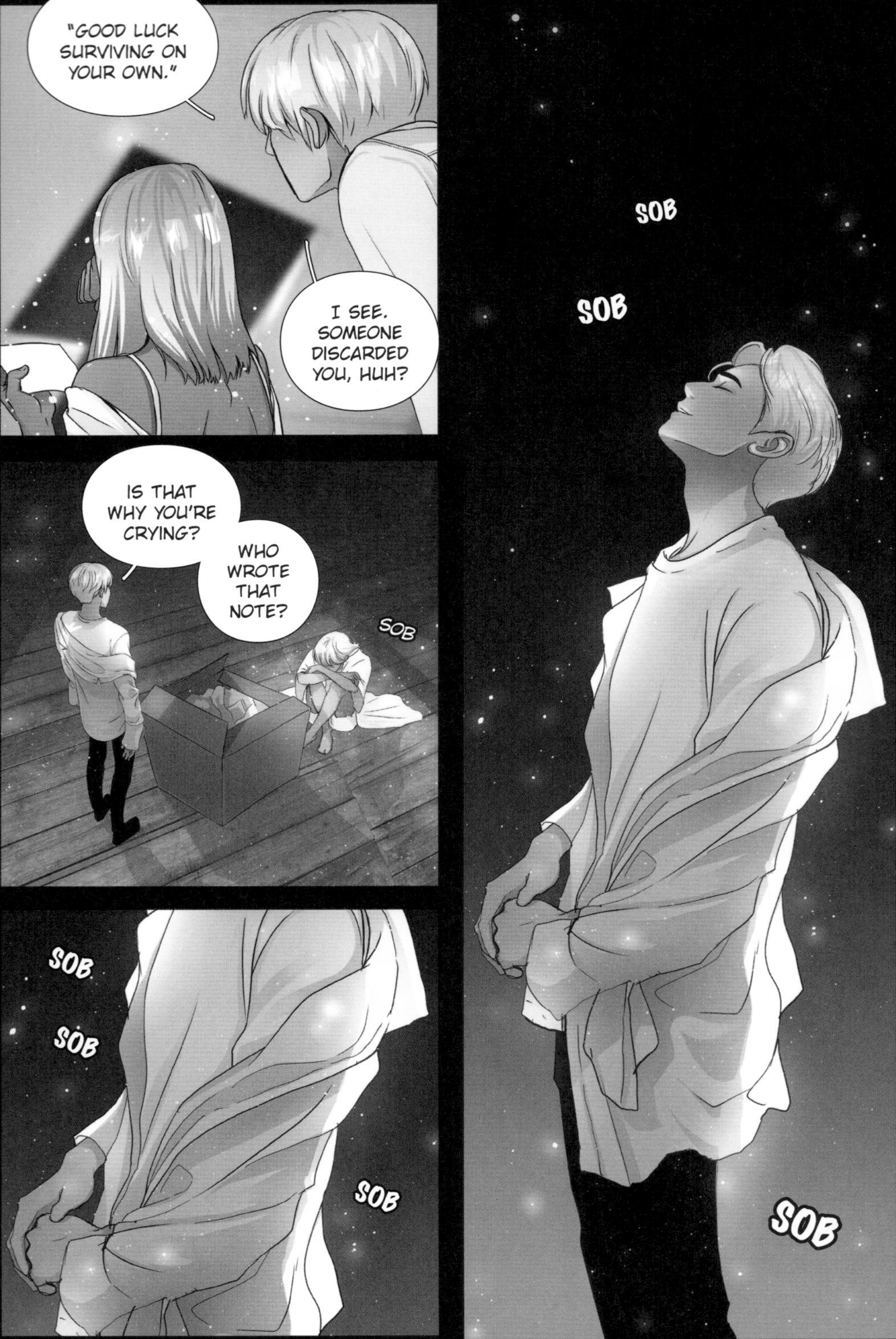
"GOOD LUCK SURVIVING ON YOUR OWN."
I SEE. SOMEONE DISCARDED YOU, HUH?
IS THAT WHY YOU'RE CRYING?
WHO WROTE THAT NOTE?
SOB
SOB
SOB
SOB
SOB
SOB
SOB

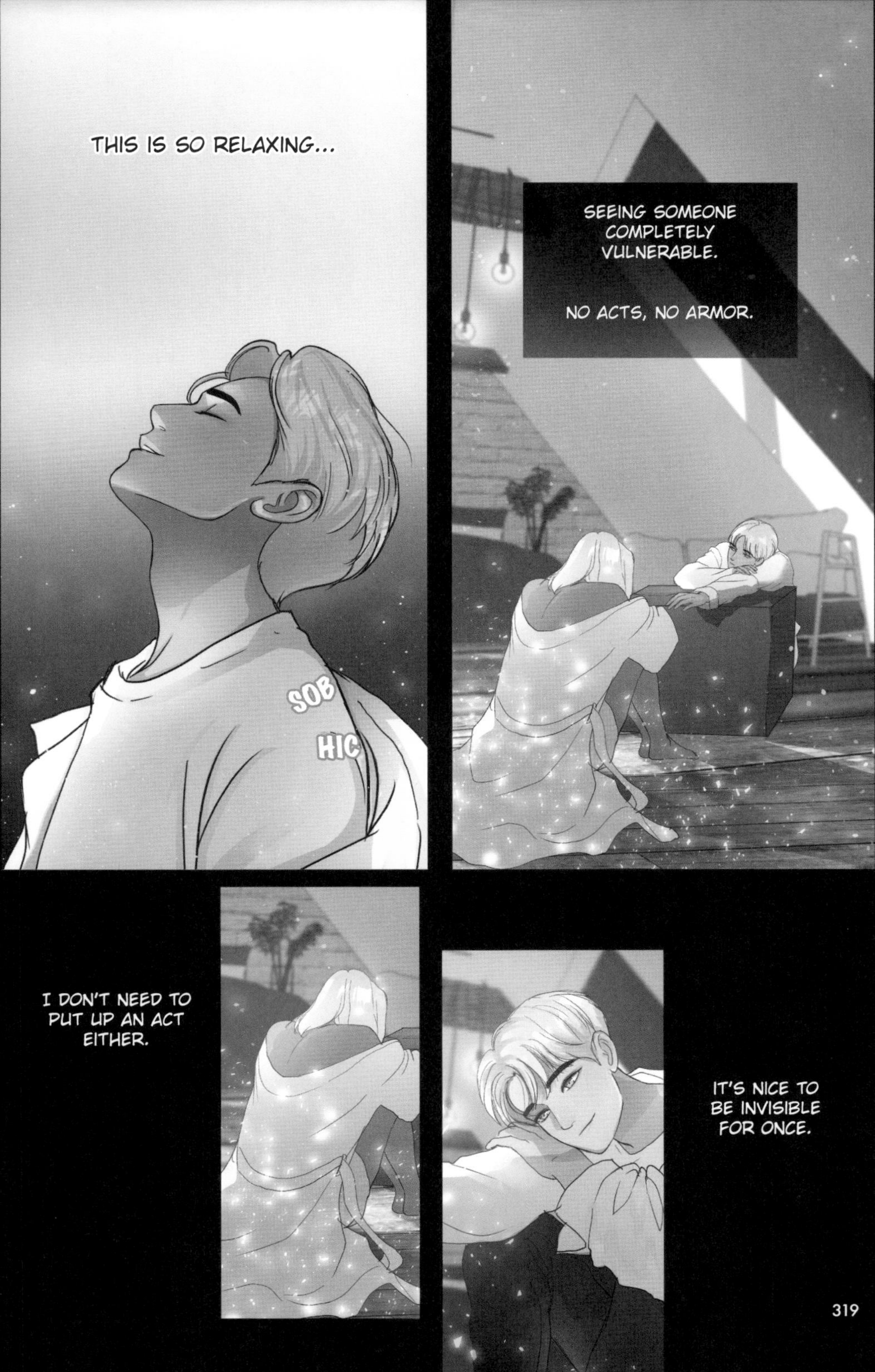
THIS IS SO RELAXING...
SOB
HIC
SEEING SOMEONE COMPLETELY VULNERABLE.
NO ACTS, NO ARMOR.
I DON'T NEED TO PUT UP AN ACT EITHER.
IT'S NICE TO BE INVISIBLE FOR ONCE.

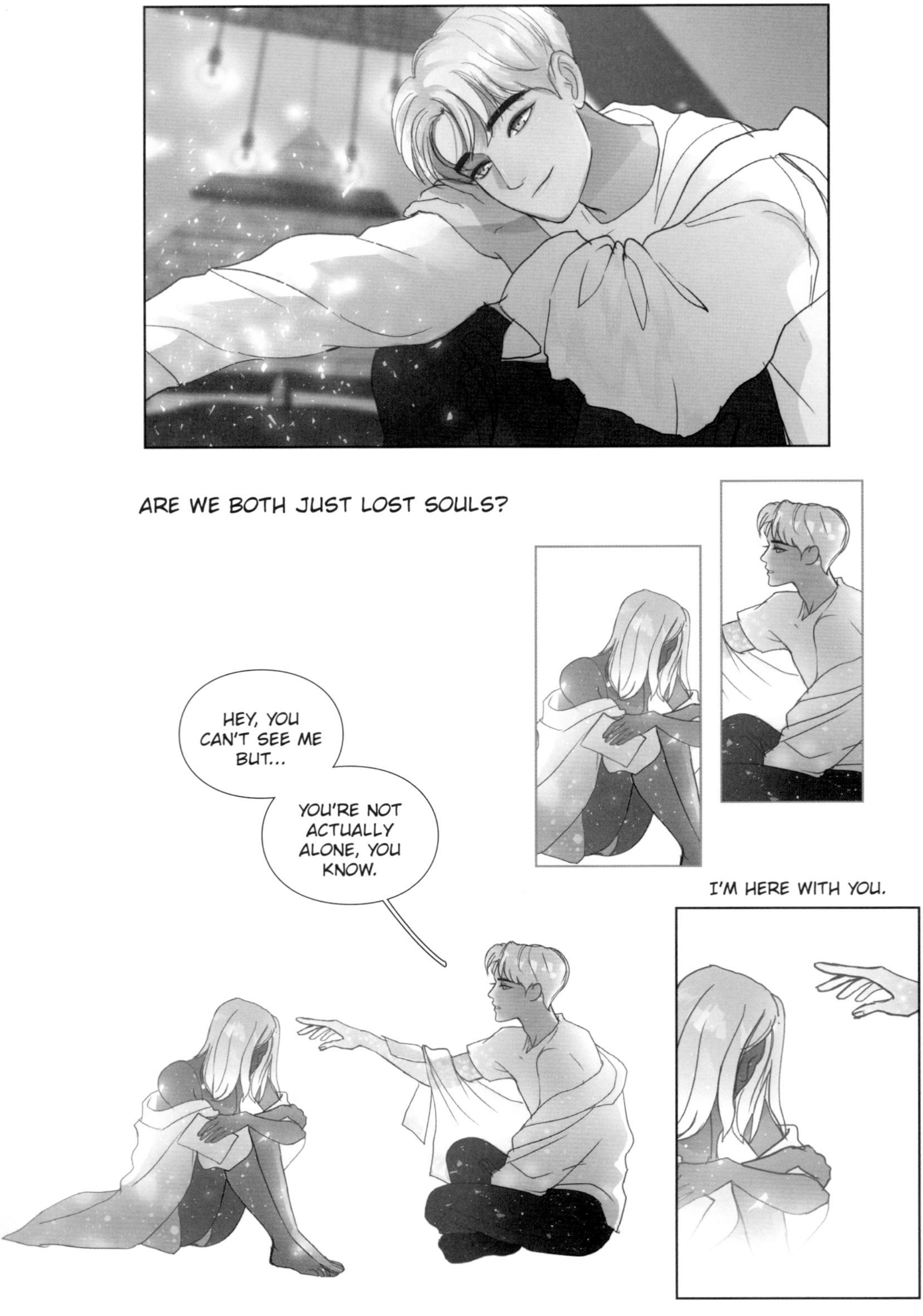
ARE WE BOTH JUST LOST SOULS?
HEY, YOU CAN'T SEE ME BUT...
YOU'RE NOT ACTUALLY ALONE, YOU KNOW.
I'M HERE WITH YOU.

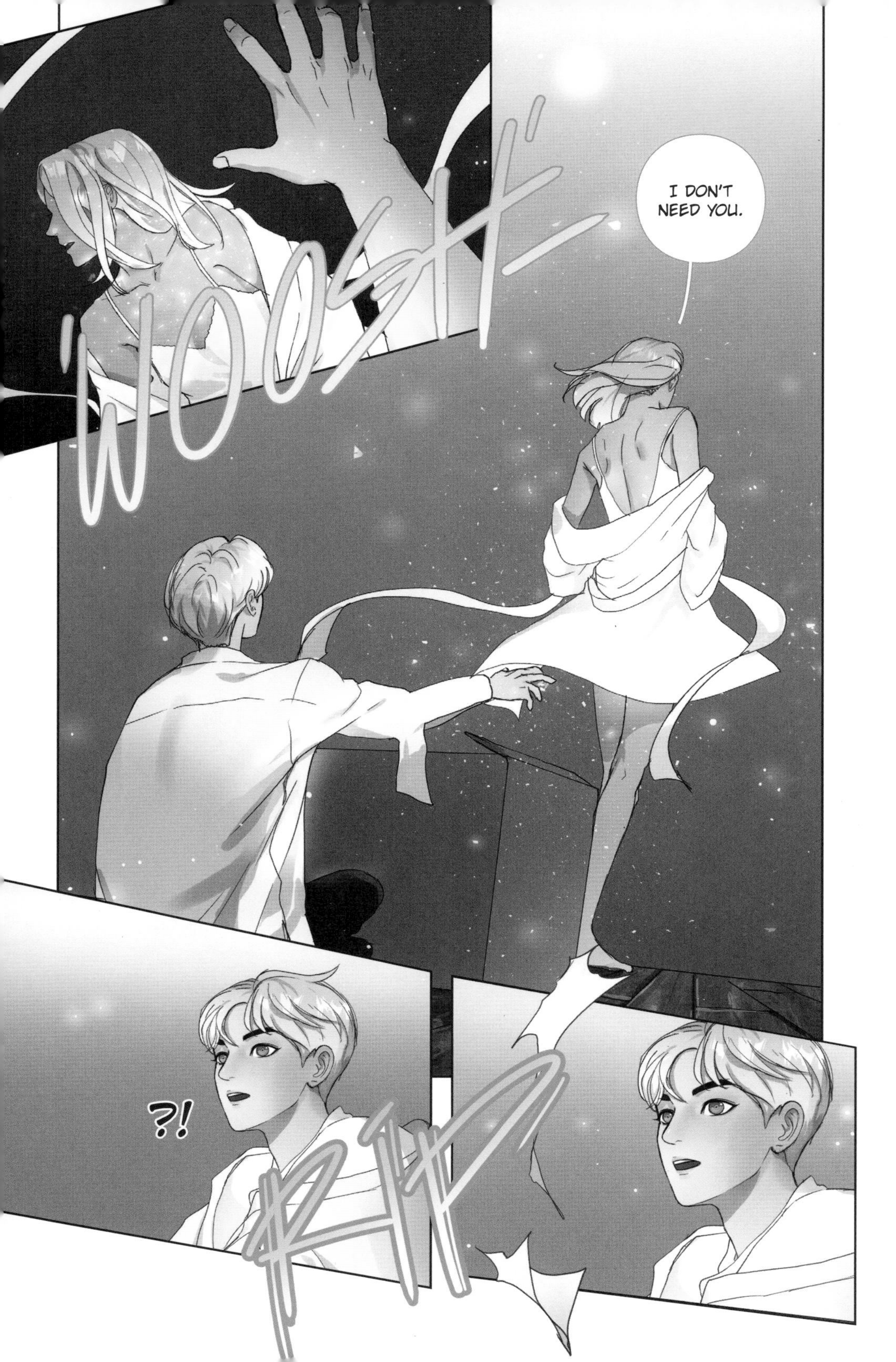
WOOSH
I DON'T NEED YOU.
?!
RIP

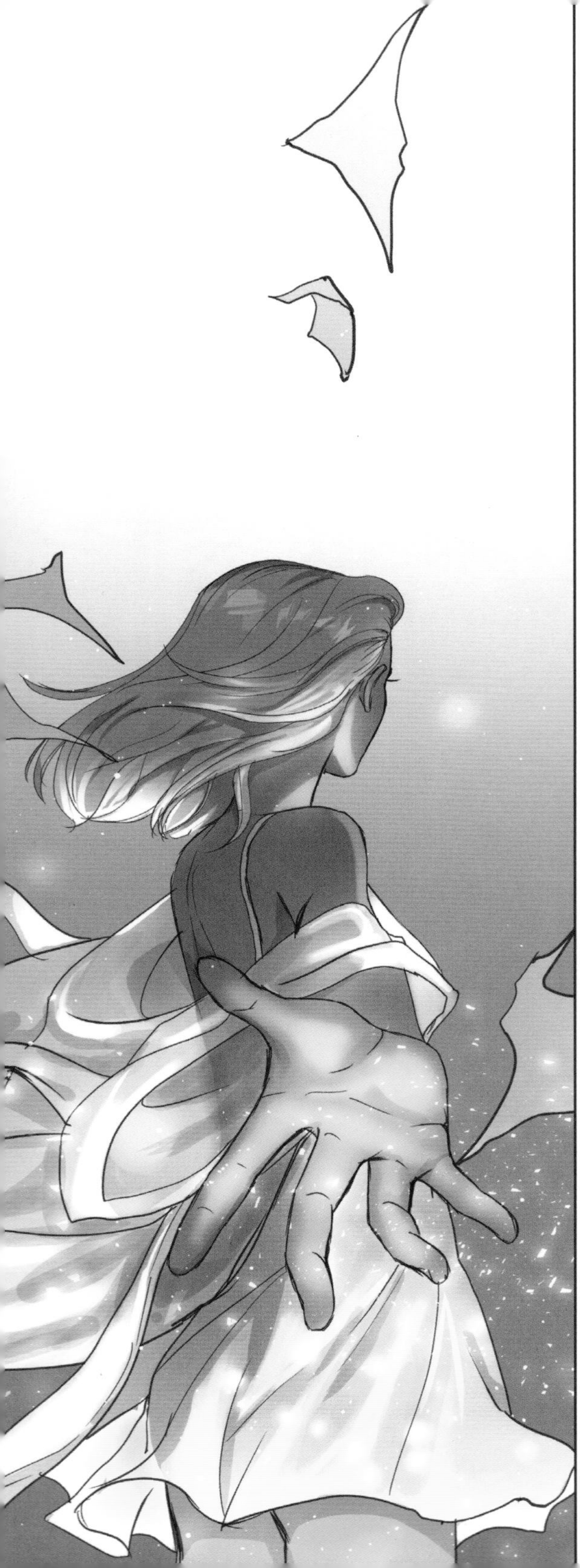

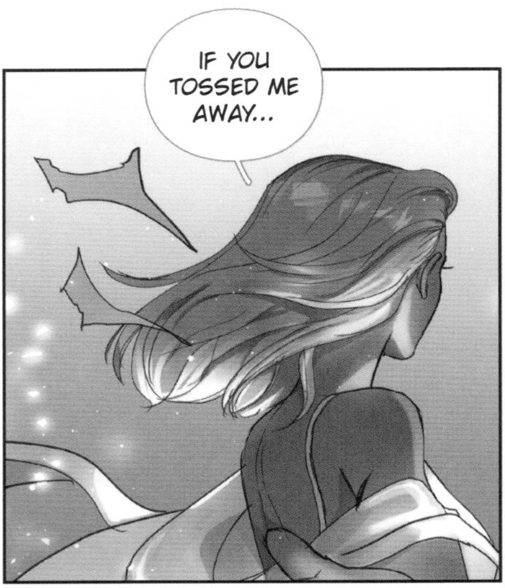
IF YOU TOSSED ME AWAY...

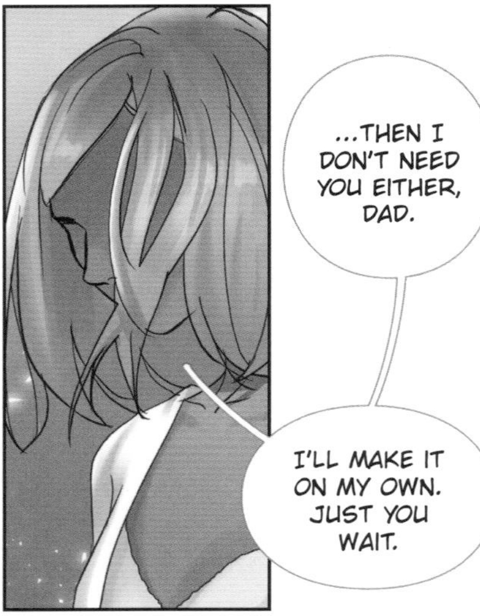
...THEN I DON'T NEED YOU EITHER, DAD.
I'LL MAKE IT ON MY OWN. JUST YOU WAIT.

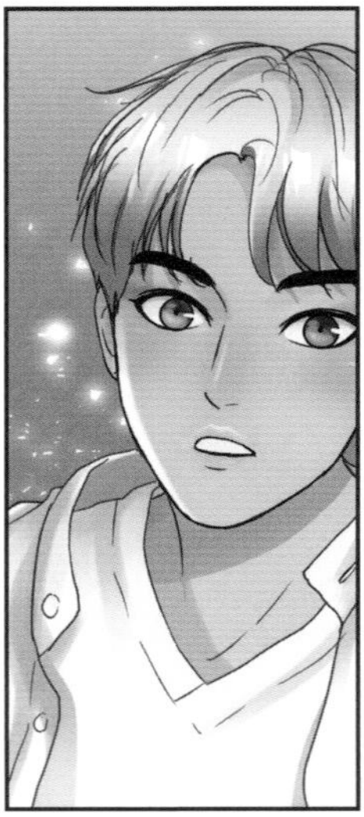

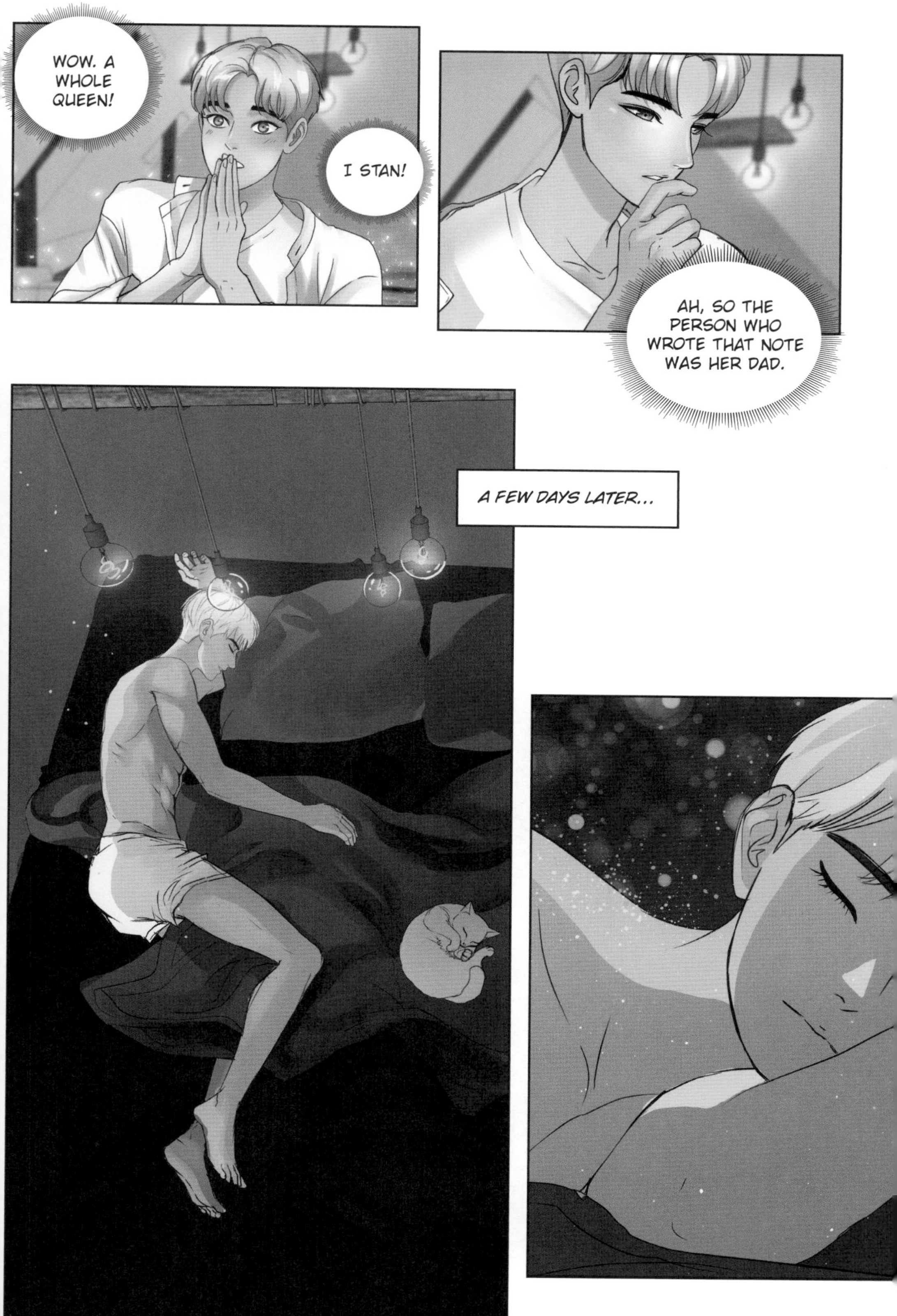
WOW. A WHOLE QUEEN!
I STAN!
AH, SO THE PERSON WHO WROTE THAT NOTE WAS HER DAD.
A FEW DAYS LATER...

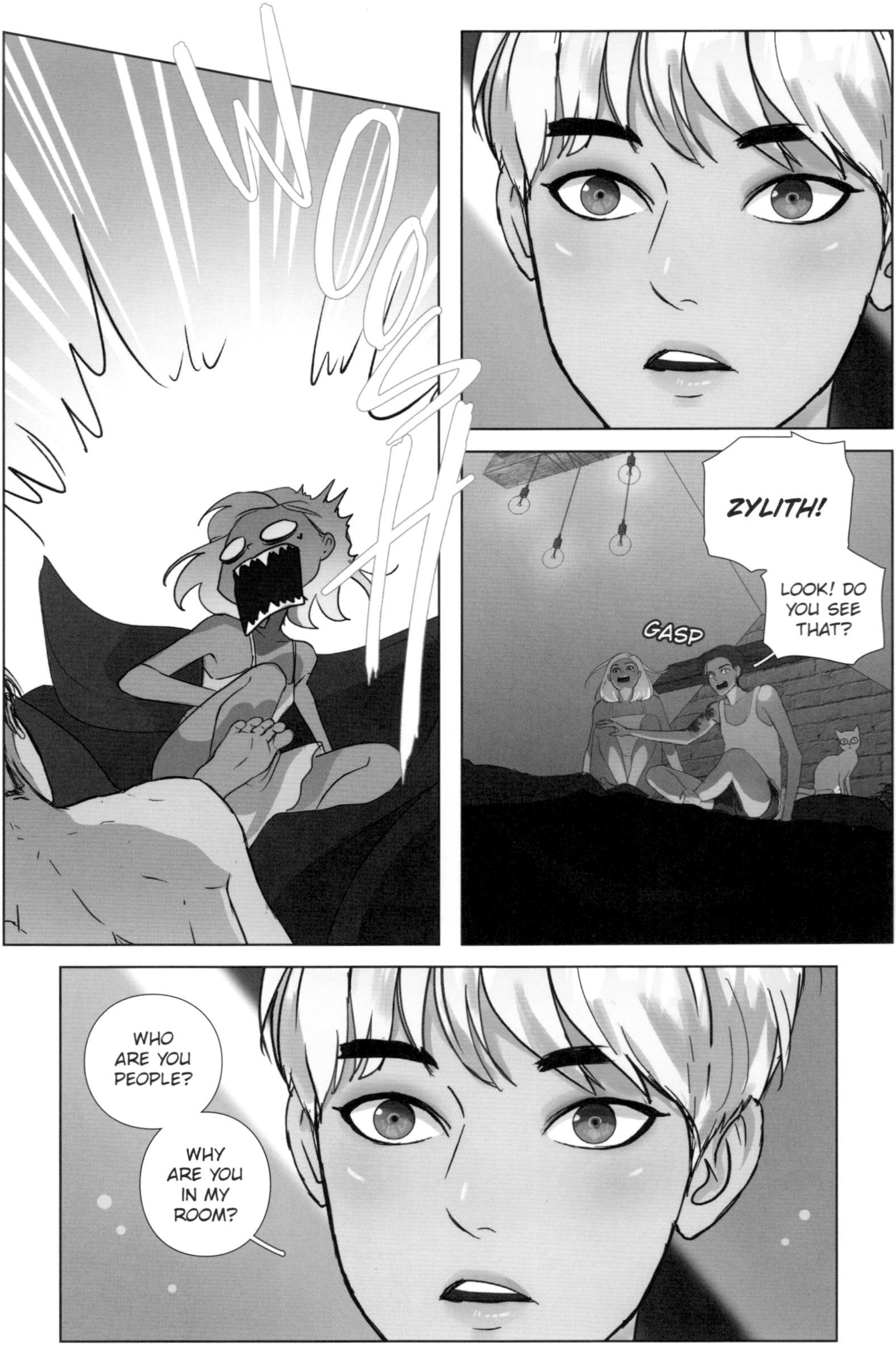
WOOOSH
ZYLITH!
LOOK! DO YOU SEE THAT?
GASP
WHO ARE YOU PEOPLE?
WHY ARE YOU IN MY ROOM?

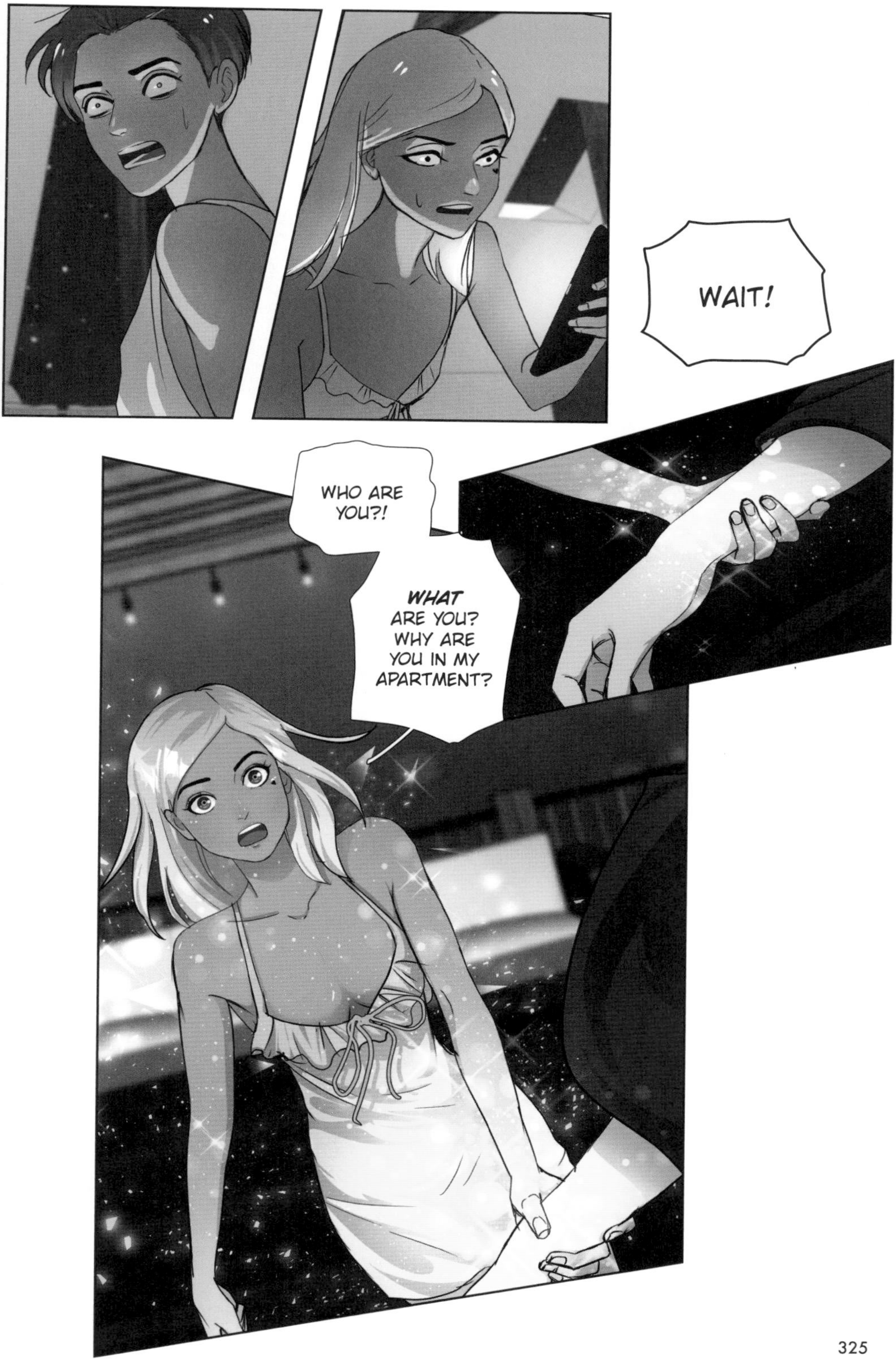
WAIT!
WHO ARE YOU?!
WHAT ARE YOU? WHY ARE YOU IN MY APARTMENT?

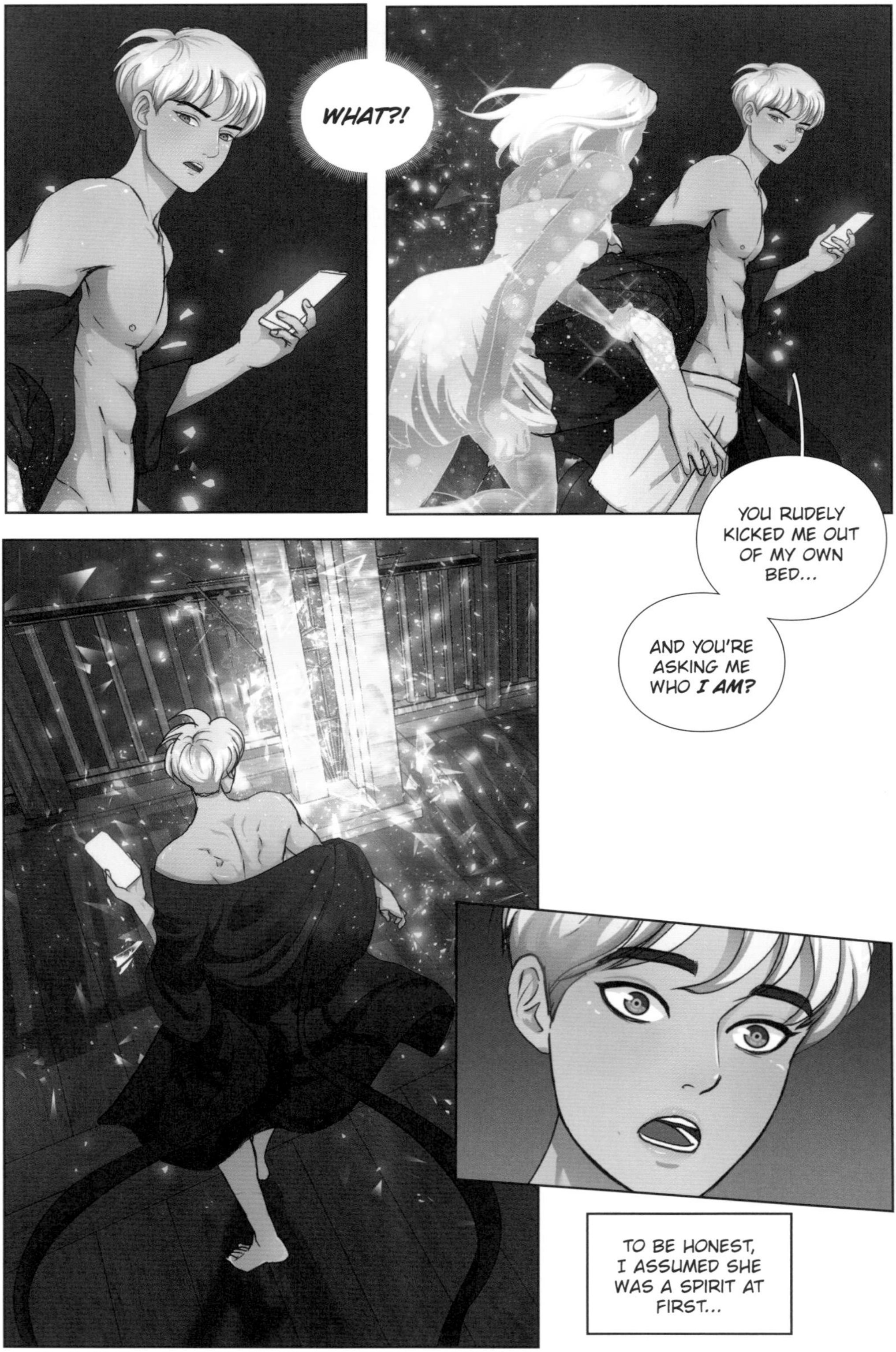
WHAT?!
YOU RUDELY KICKED ME OUT OF MY OWN BED...
AND YOU'RE ASKING ME WHO ***I AM?***
TO BE HONEST, I ASSUMED SHE WAS A SPIRIT AT FIRST...

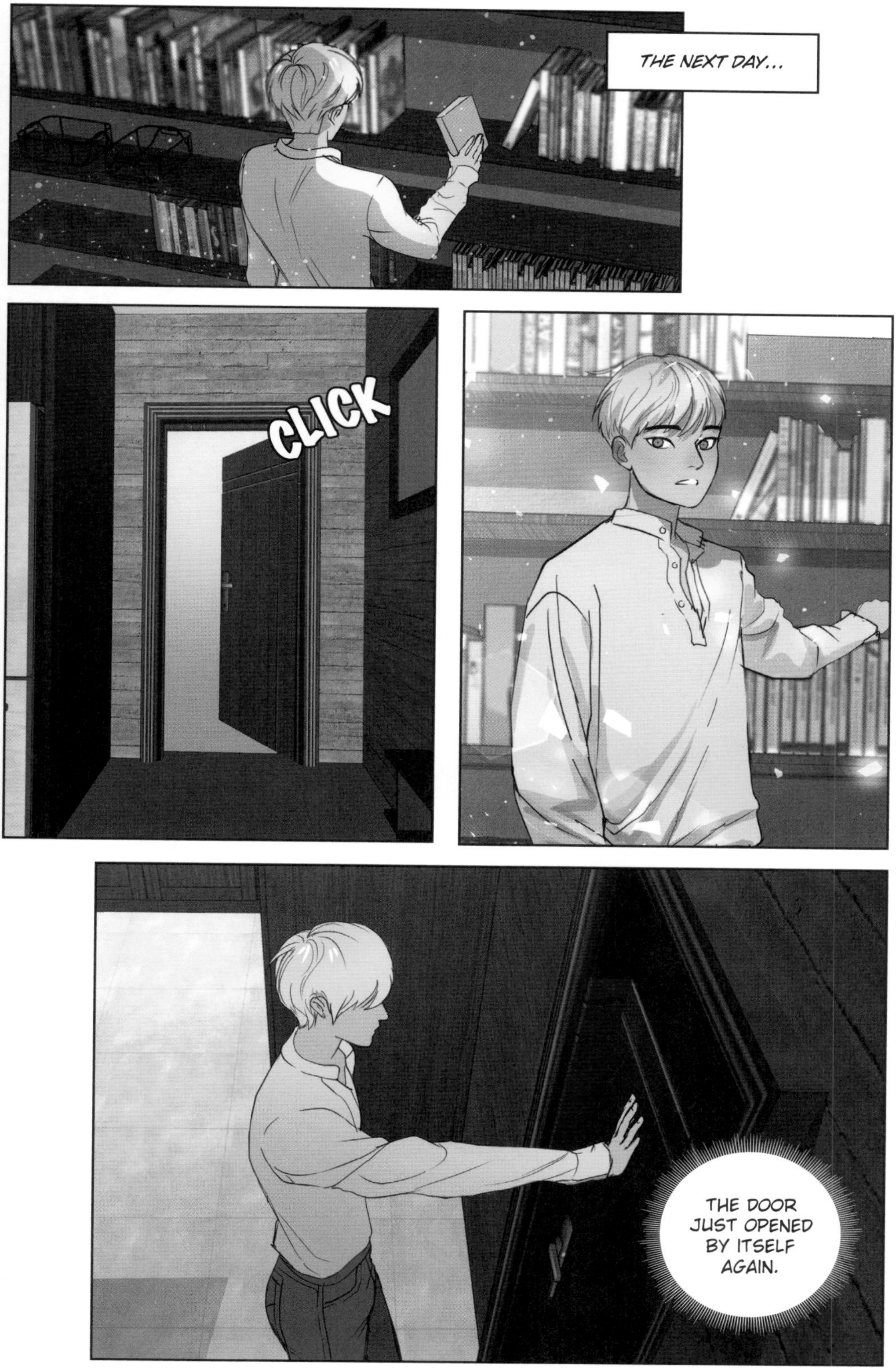
THE NEXT DAY...
CLICK
THE DOOR JUST OPENED BY ITSELF AGAIN.

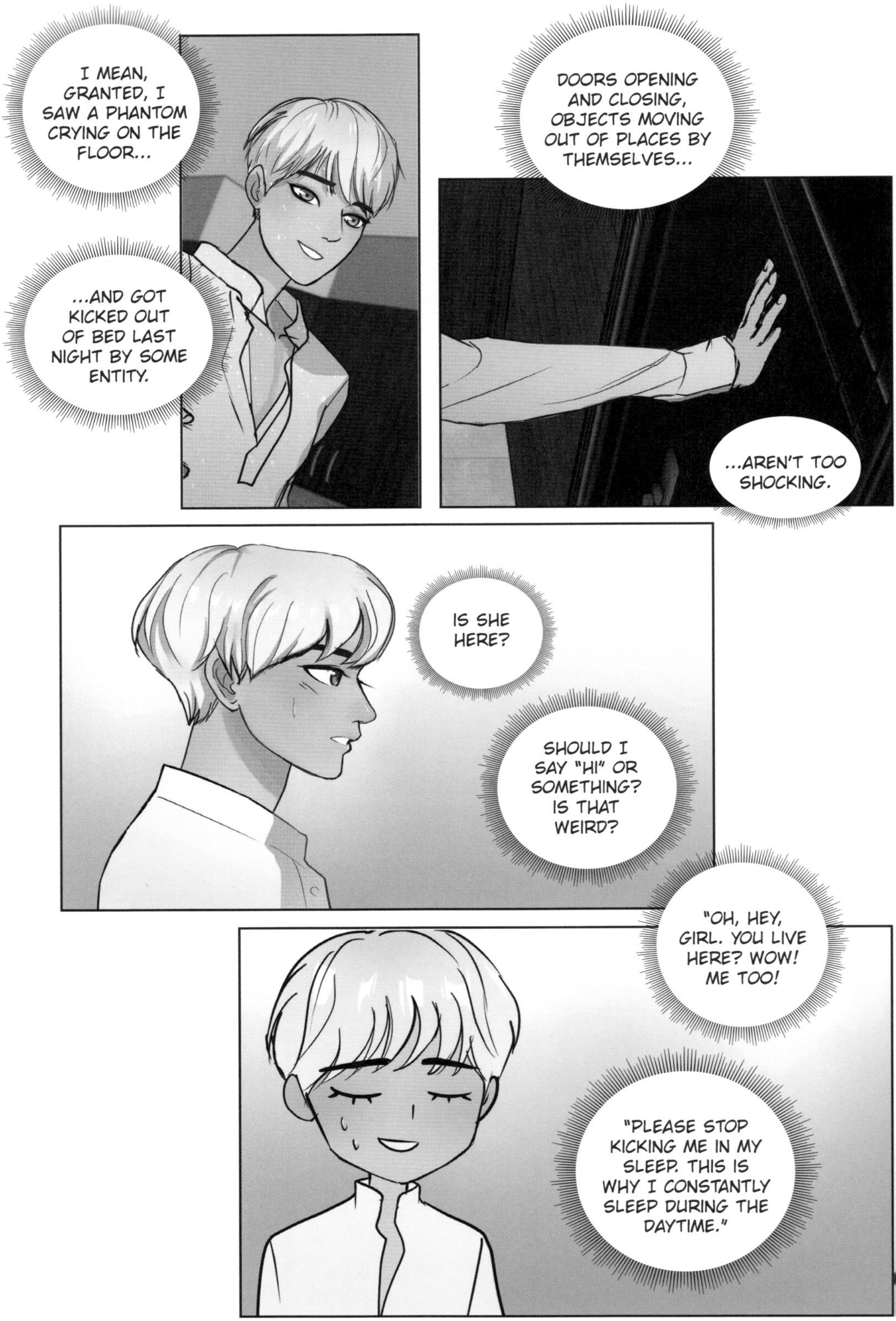
I MEAN, GRANTED, I SAW A PHANTOM CRYING ON THE FLOOR...
...AND GOT KICKED OUT OF BED LAST NIGHT BY SOME ENTITY.
DOORS OPENING AND CLOSING, OBJECTS MOVING OUT OF PLACES BY THEMSELVES...
...AREN'T TOO SHOCKING.
IS SHE HERE?
SHOULD I SAY "HI" OR SOMETHING? IS THAT WEIRD?
"OH, HEY, GIRL. YOU LIVE HERE? WOW! ME TOO!
"PLEASE STOP KICKING ME IN MY SLEEP. THIS IS WHY I CONSTANTLY SLEEP DURING THE DAYTIME."

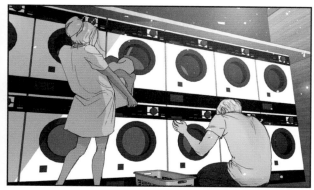

GRADUALLY, IT SEEMED I WAS SEEING SLICES OF HER LIFE.

THE MORE I WATCHED...THE LESS I THOUGHT SHE WAS JUST A MERE SPIRIT SHARING THIS SPACE.

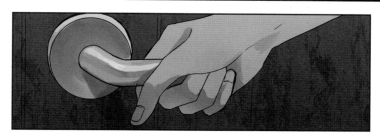

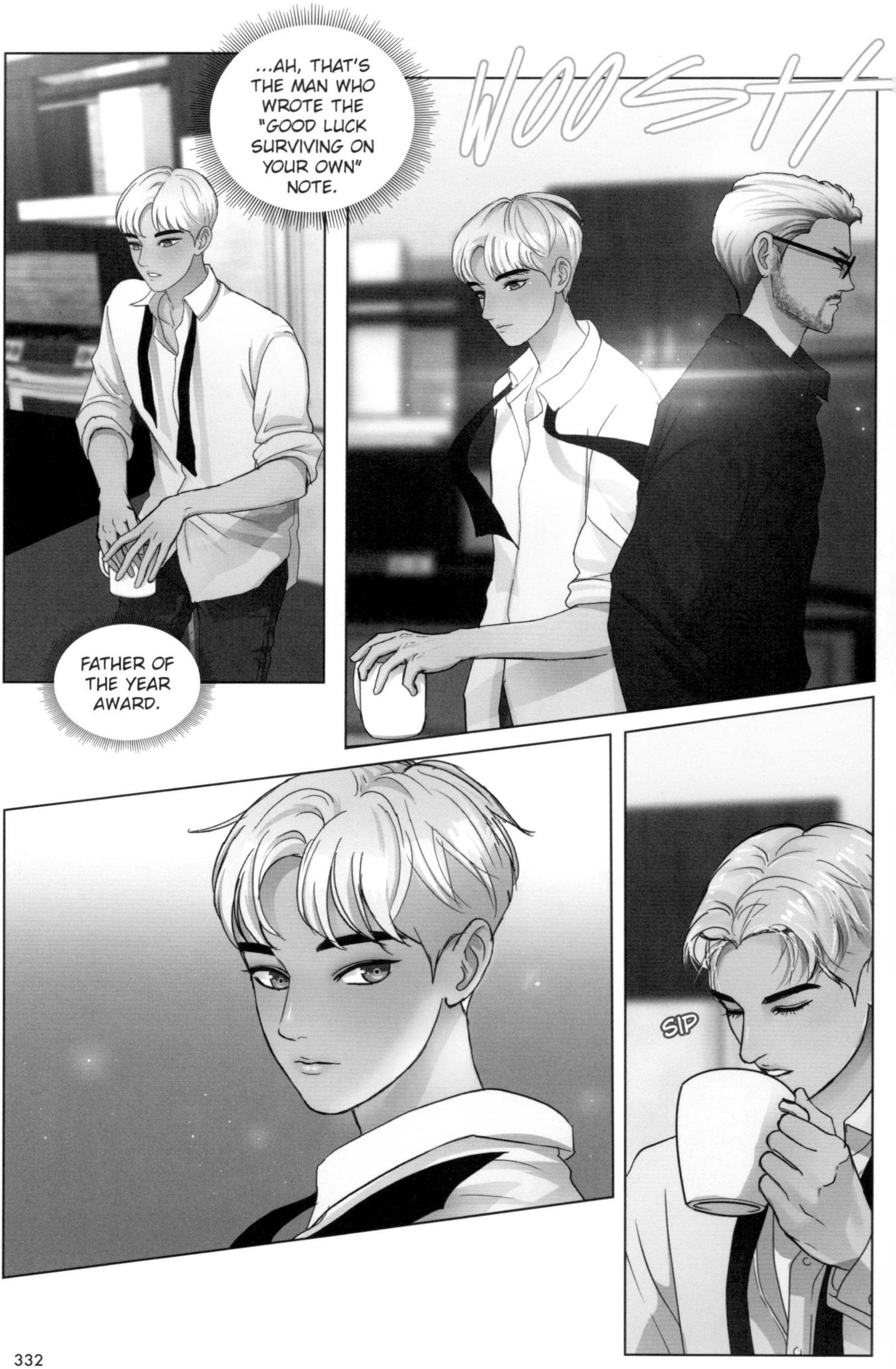
...AH, THAT'S THE MAN WHO WROTE THE "GOOD LUCK SURVIVING ON YOUR OWN" NOTE.
FATHER OF THE YEAR AWARD.
WOOSH
SIP

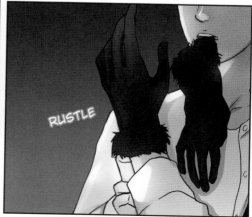

RUSTLE

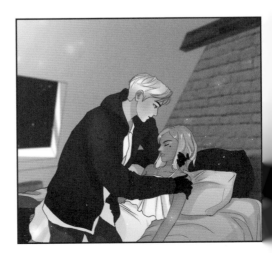

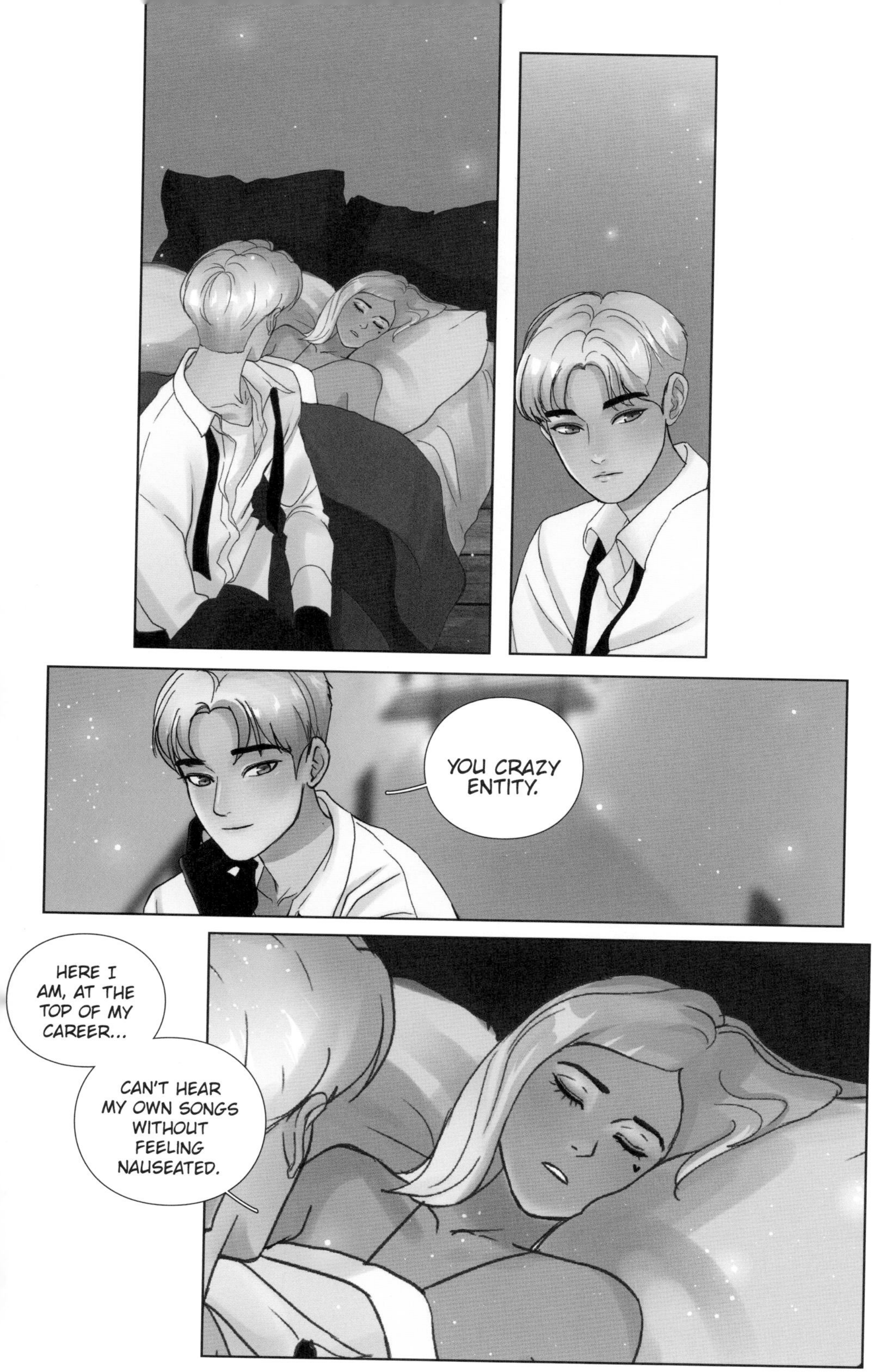
YOU CRAZY ENTITY.
HERE I AM, AT THE TOP OF MY CAREER...
CAN'T HEAR MY OWN SONGS WITHOUT FEELING NAUSEATED.

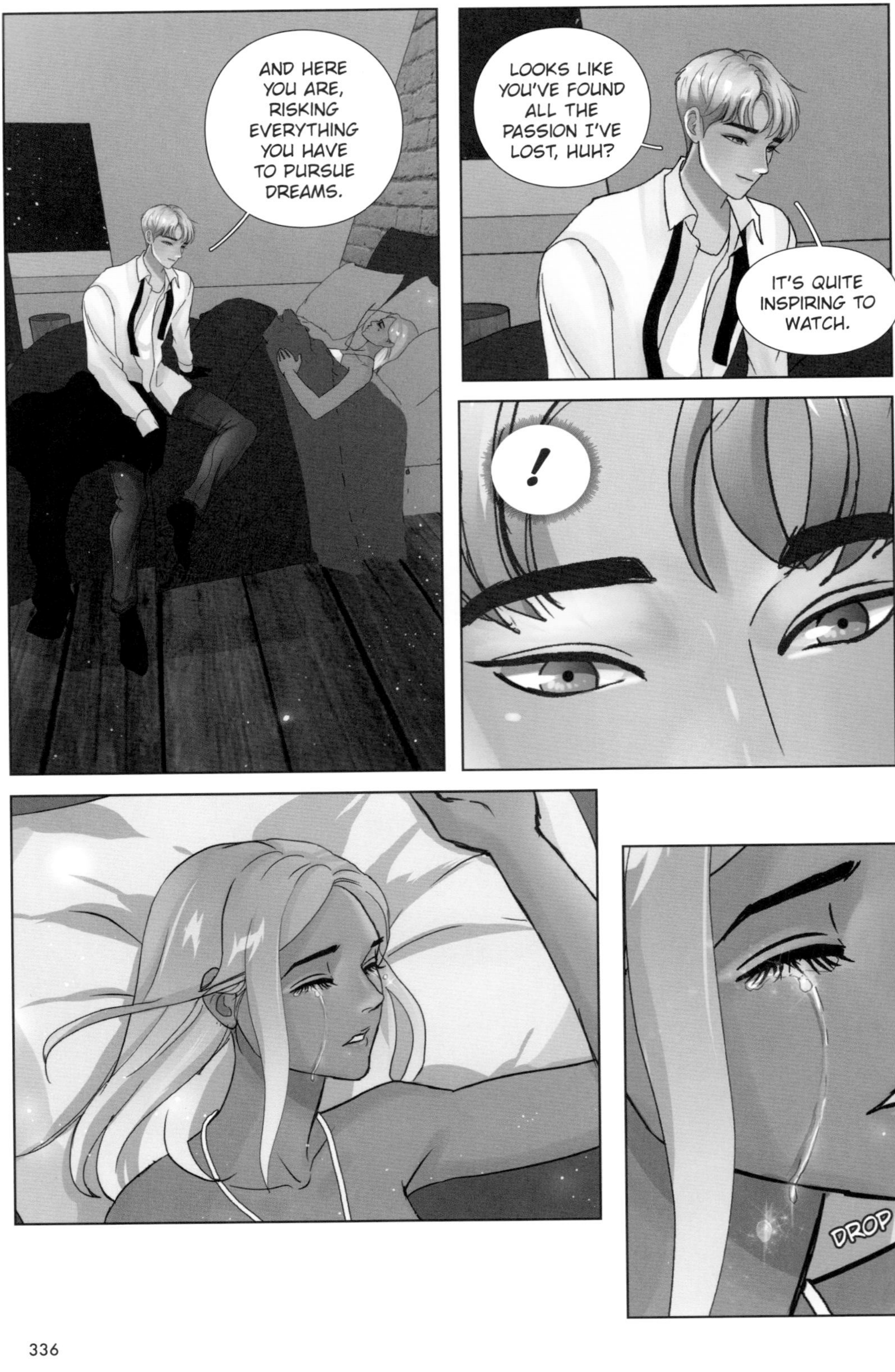
AND HERE YOU ARE, RISKING EVERYTHING YOU HAVE TO PURSUE DREAMS.
LOOKS LIKE YOU'VE FOUND ALL THE PASSION I'VE LOST, HUH?
IT'S QUITE INSPIRING TO WATCH.
!
DROP

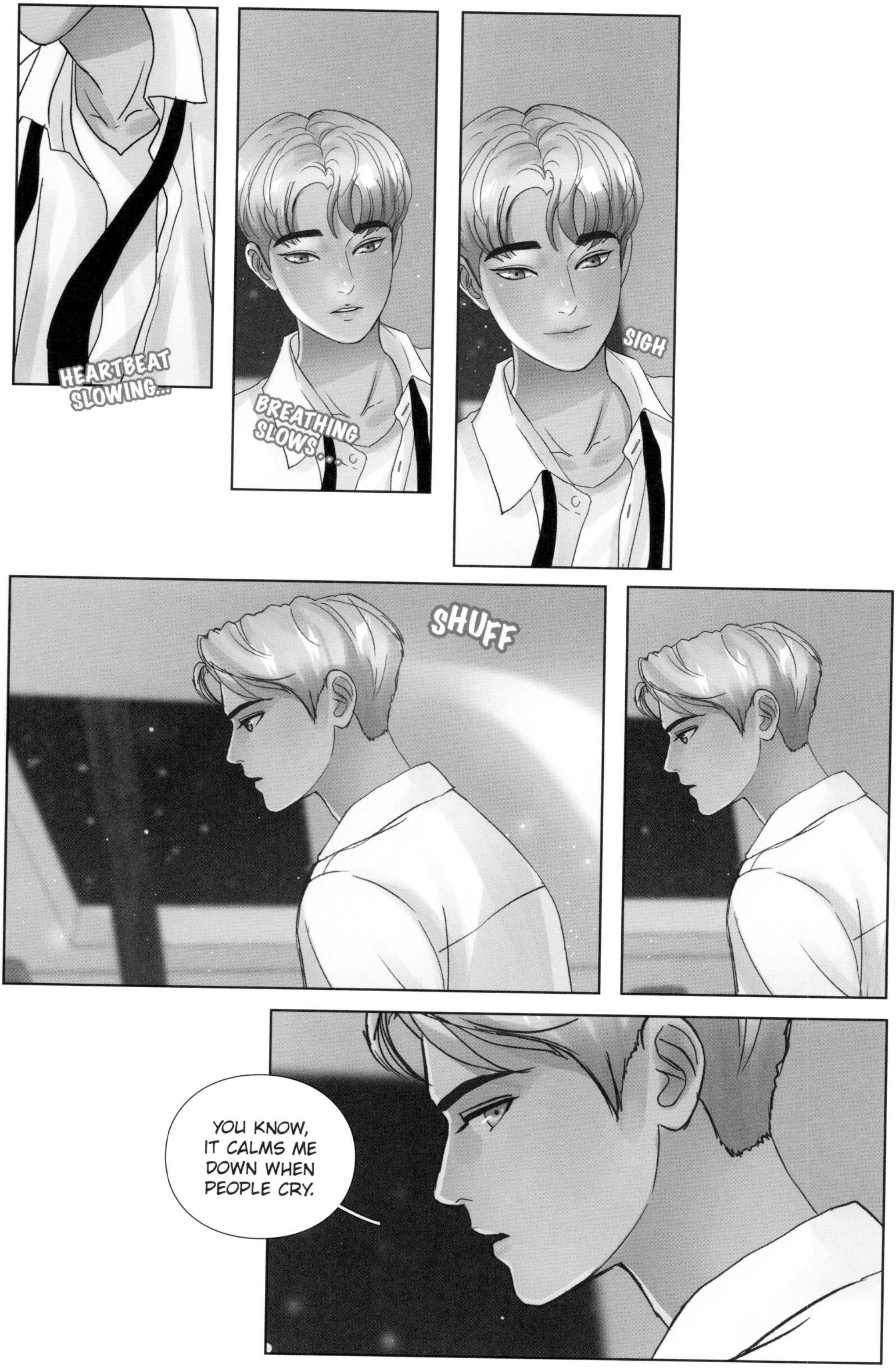
HEARTBEAT SLOWING...
BREATHING SLOWS...
SIGH
SHUFF
YOU KNOW, IT CALMS ME DOWN WHEN PEOPLE CRY.

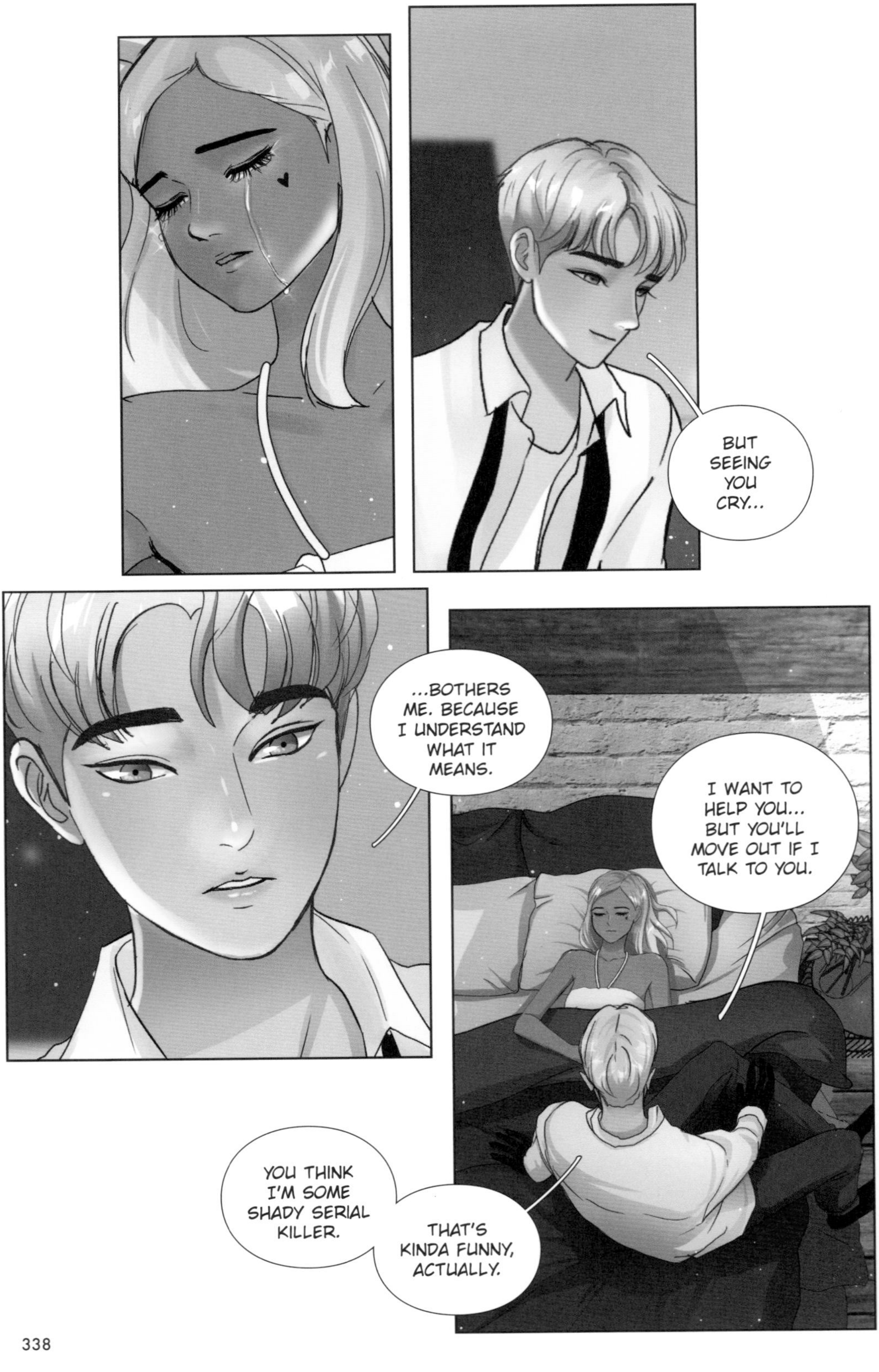

BUT SEEING YOU CRY...
...BOTHERS ME. BECAUSE I UNDERSTAND WHAT IT MEANS.
I WANT TO HELP YOU... BUT YOU'LL MOVE OUT IF I TALK TO YOU.
YOU THINK I'M SOME SHADY SERIAL KILLER.
THAT'S KINDA FUNNY, ACTUALLY.

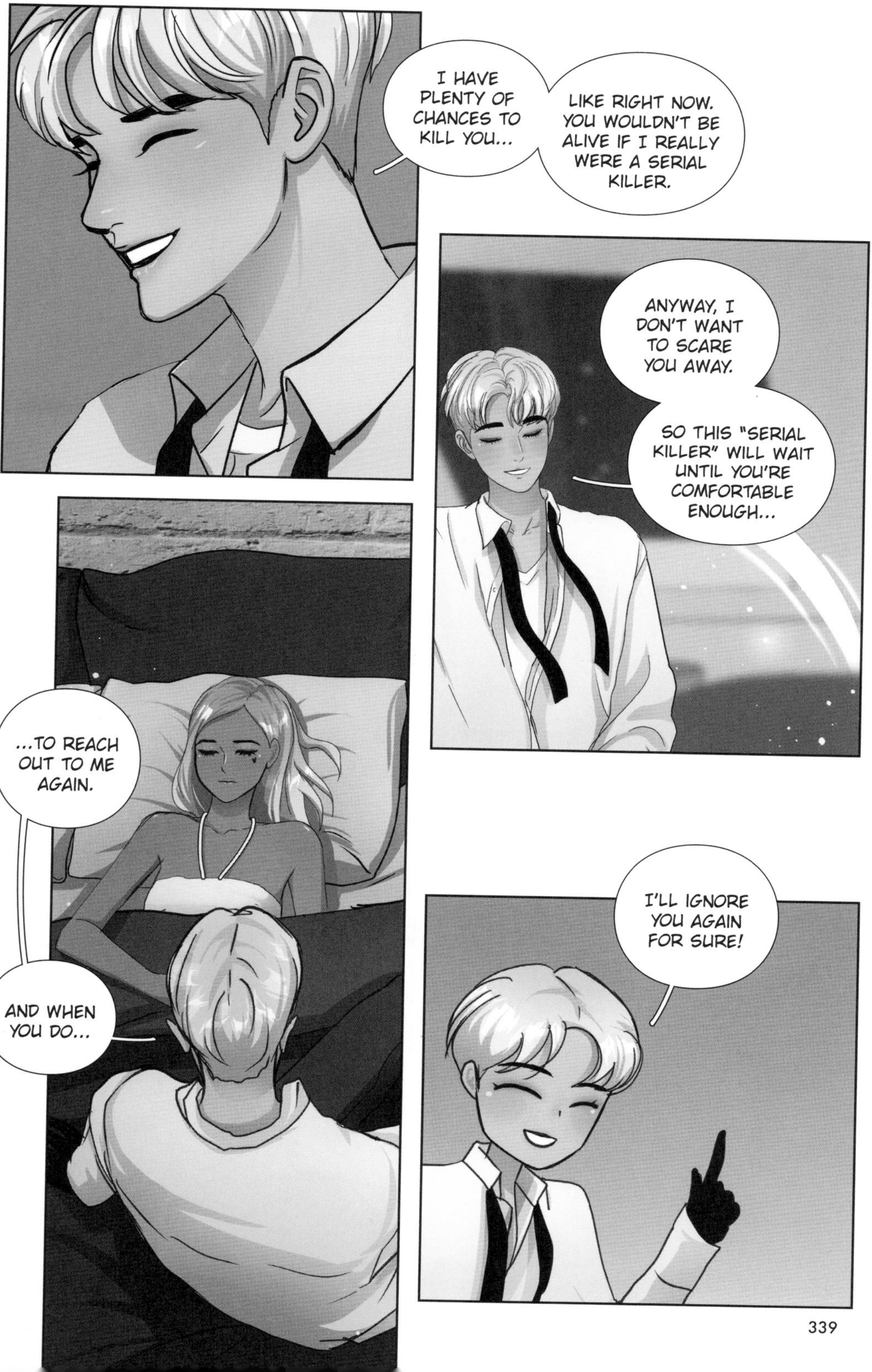

I HAVE PLENTY OF CHANCES TO KILL YOU...
LIKE RIGHT NOW. YOU WOULDN'T BE ALIVE IF I REALLY WERE A SERIAL KILLER.
ANYWAY, I DON'T WANT TO SCARE YOU AWAY.
SO THIS "SERIAL KILLER" WILL WAIT UNTIL YOU'RE COMFORTABLE ENOUGH...
...TO REACH OUT TO ME AGAIN.
AND WHEN YOU DO...
I'LL IGNORE YOU AGAIN FOR SURE!

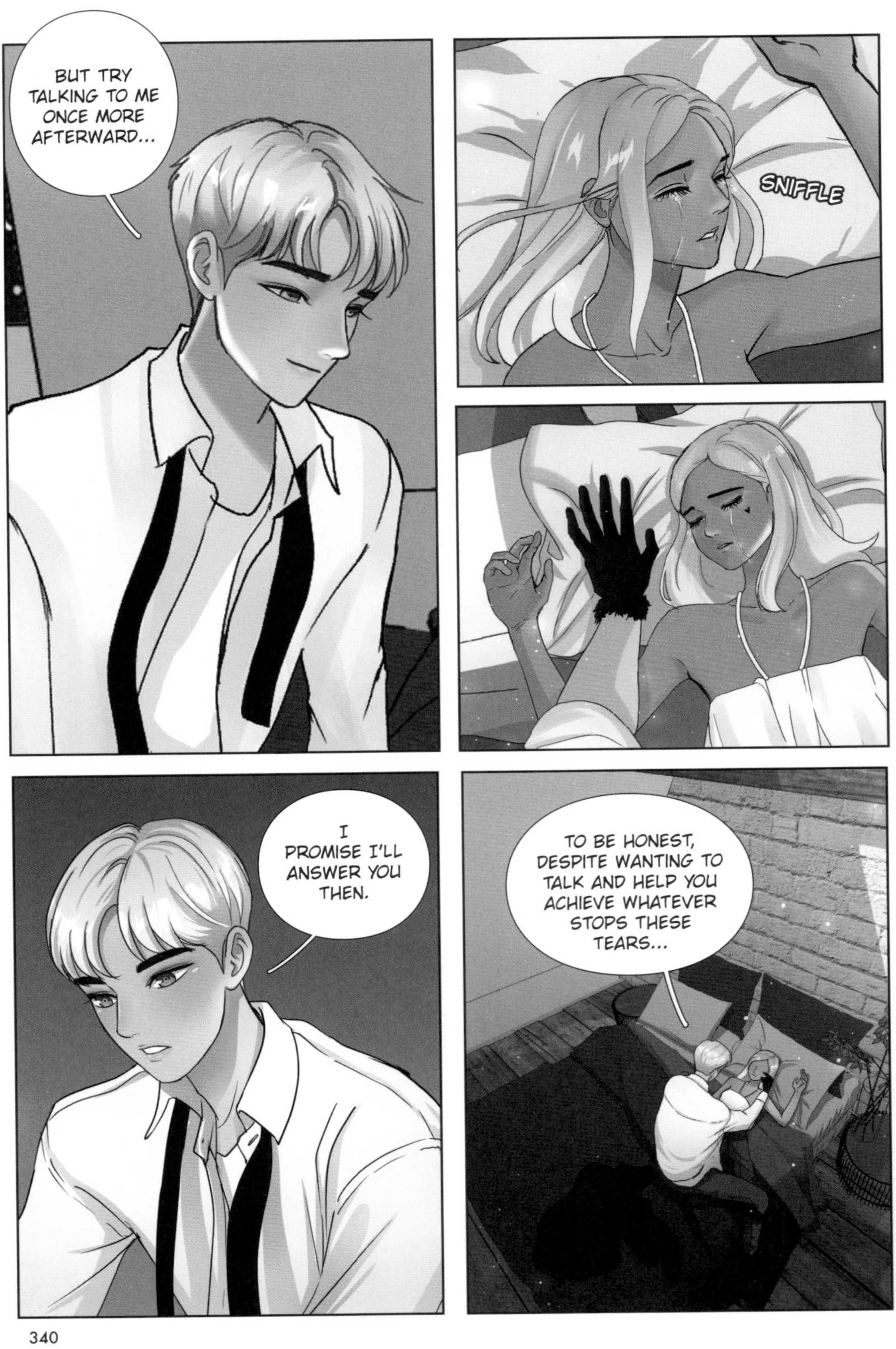
BUT TRY TALKING TO ME ONCE MORE AFTERWARD...
SNIFFLE
I PROMISE I'LL ANSWER YOU THEN.
TO BE HONEST, DESPITE WANTING TO TALK AND HELP YOU ACHIEVE WHATEVER STOPS THESE TEARS...

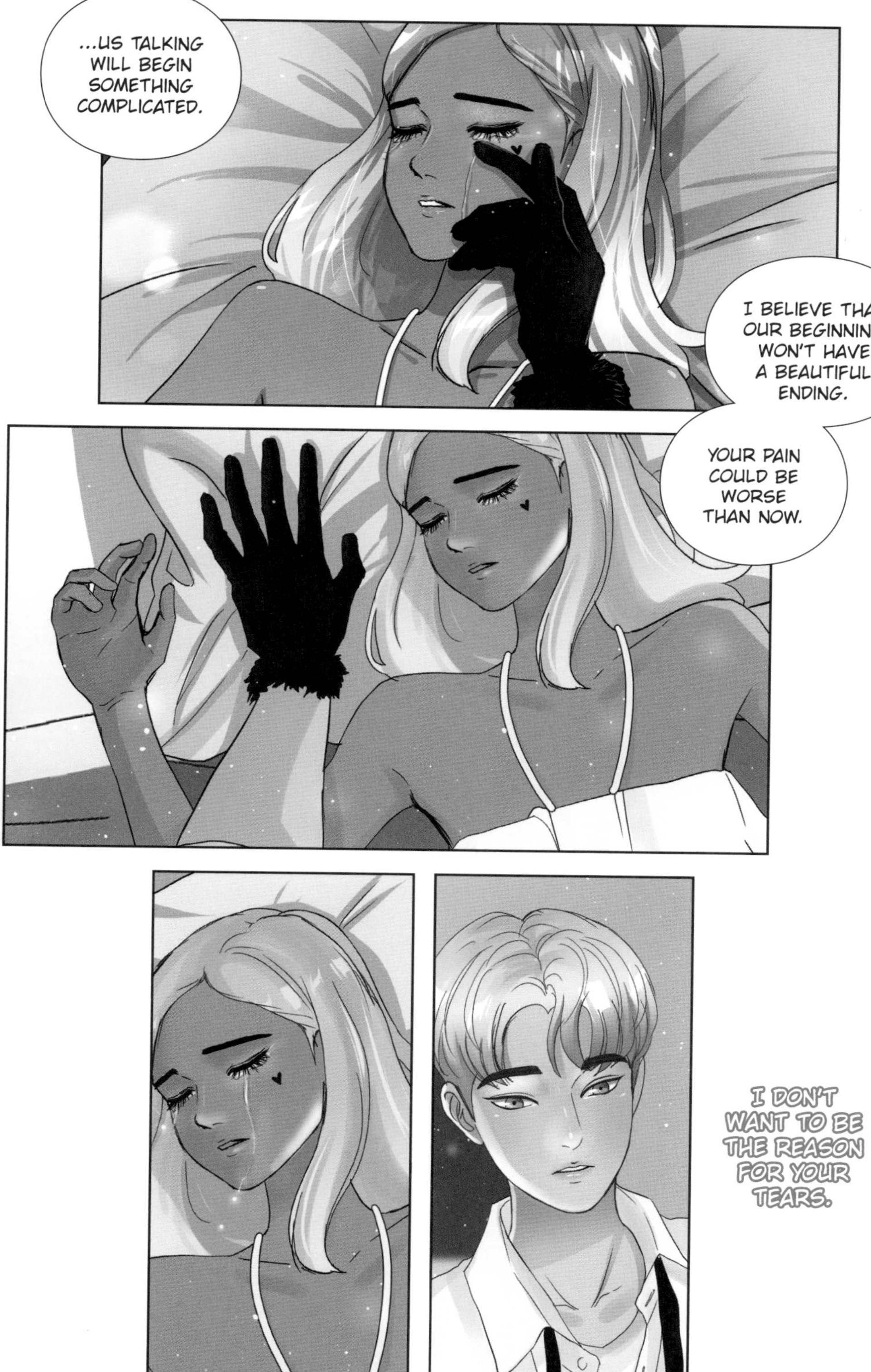
...US TALKING WILL BEGIN SOMETHING COMPLICATED.
I BELIEVE THAT OUR BEGINNING WON'T HAVE A BEAUTIFUL ENDING.
YOUR PAIN COULD BE WORSE THAN NOW.
I DON'T WANT TO BE THE REASON FOR YOUR TEARS.

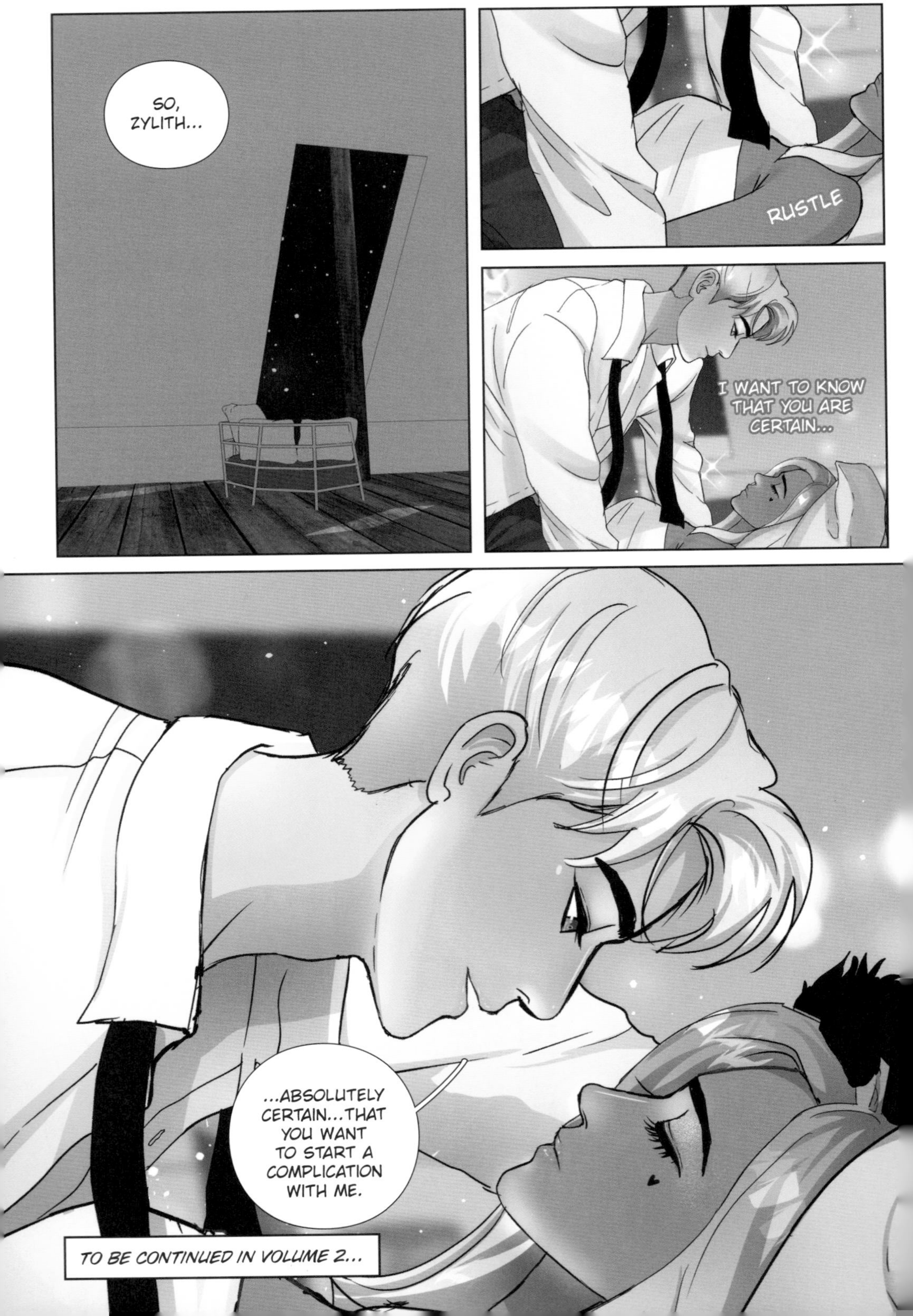
SO, ZYLITH...
RUSTLE
I WANT TO KNOW THAT YOU ARE CERTAIN...
...ABSOLUTELY CERTAIN...THAT YOU WANT TO START A COMPLICATION WITH ME.
TO BE CONTINUED IN VOLUME 2...

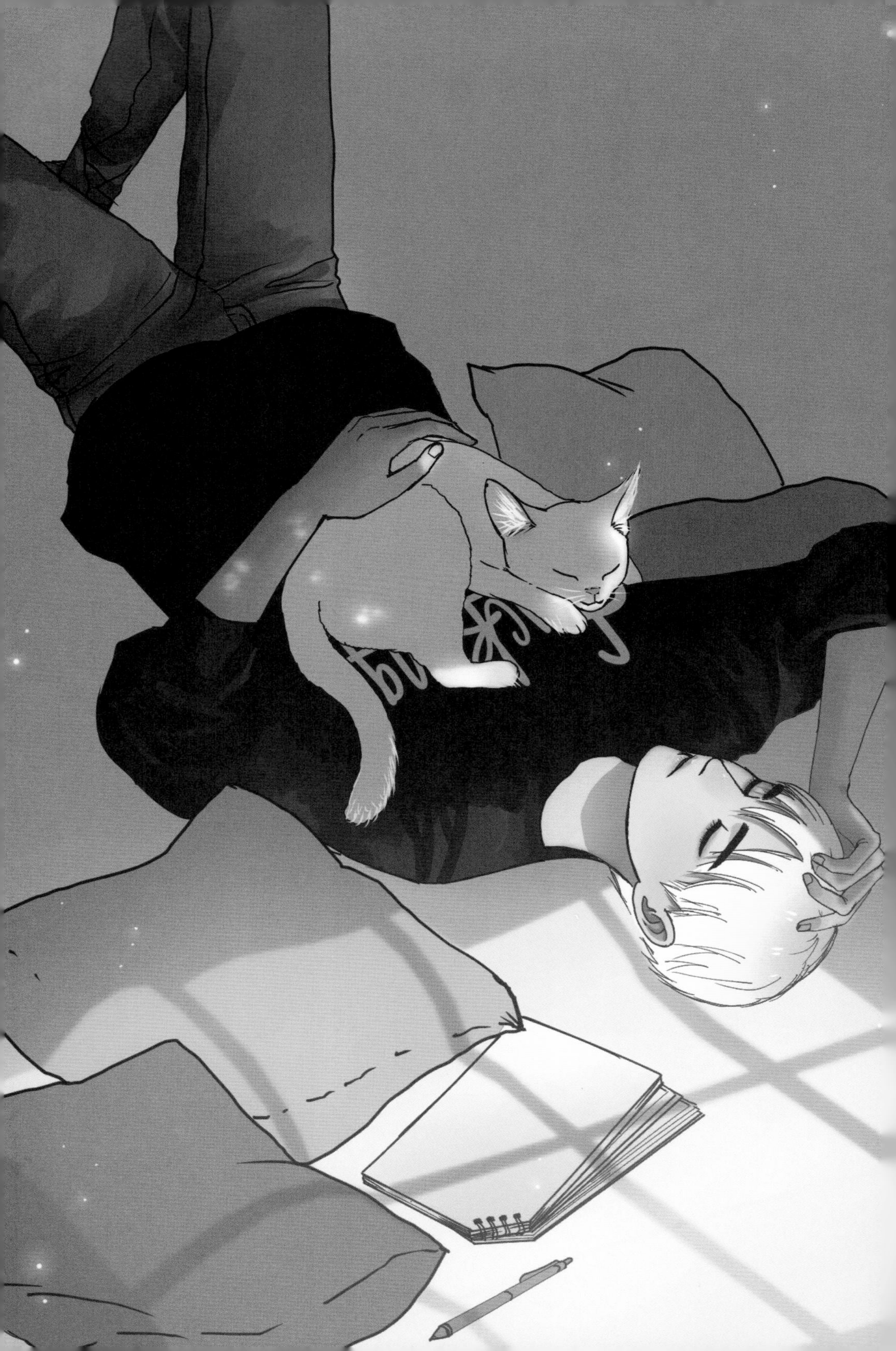

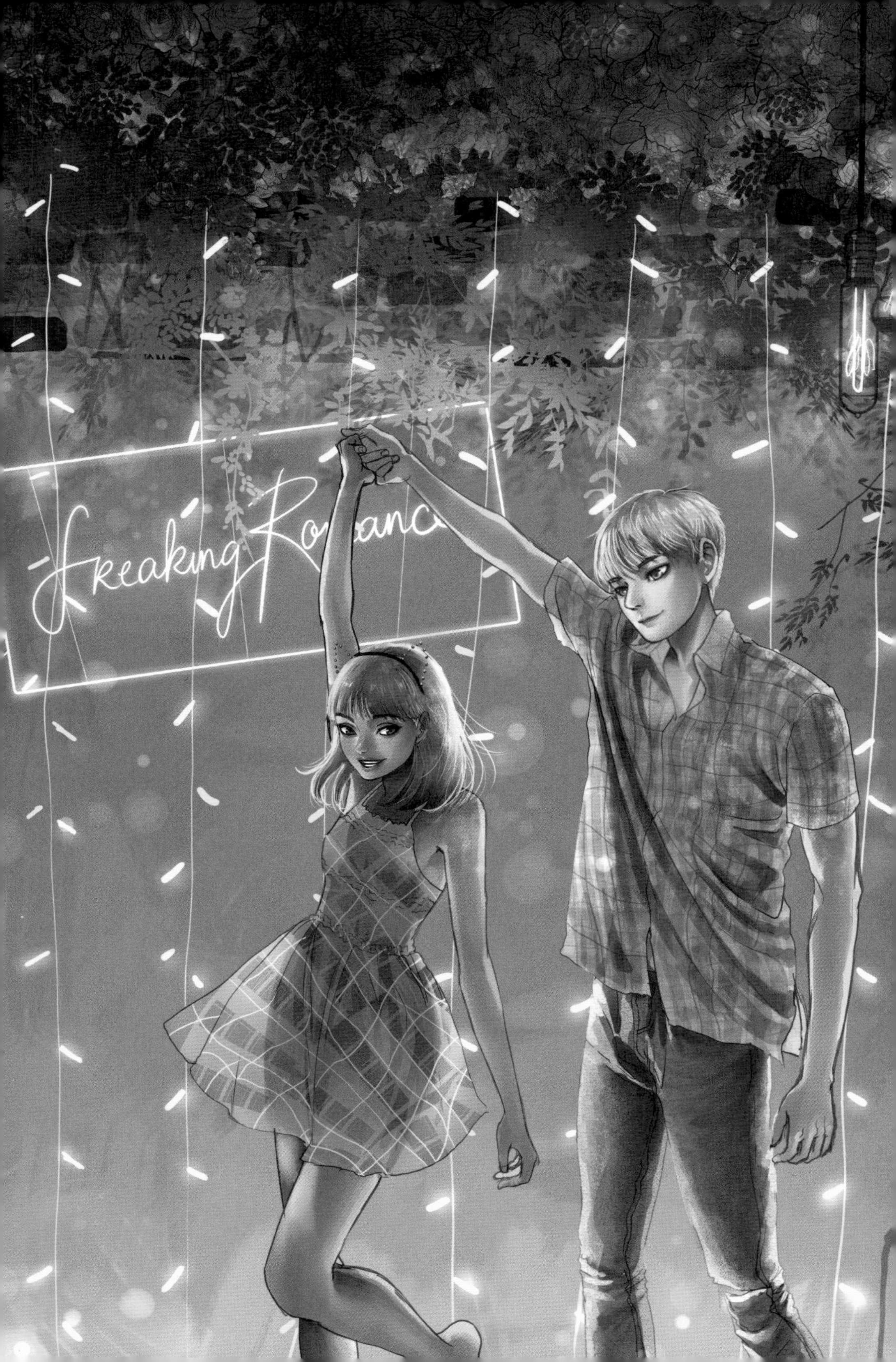
Freaking

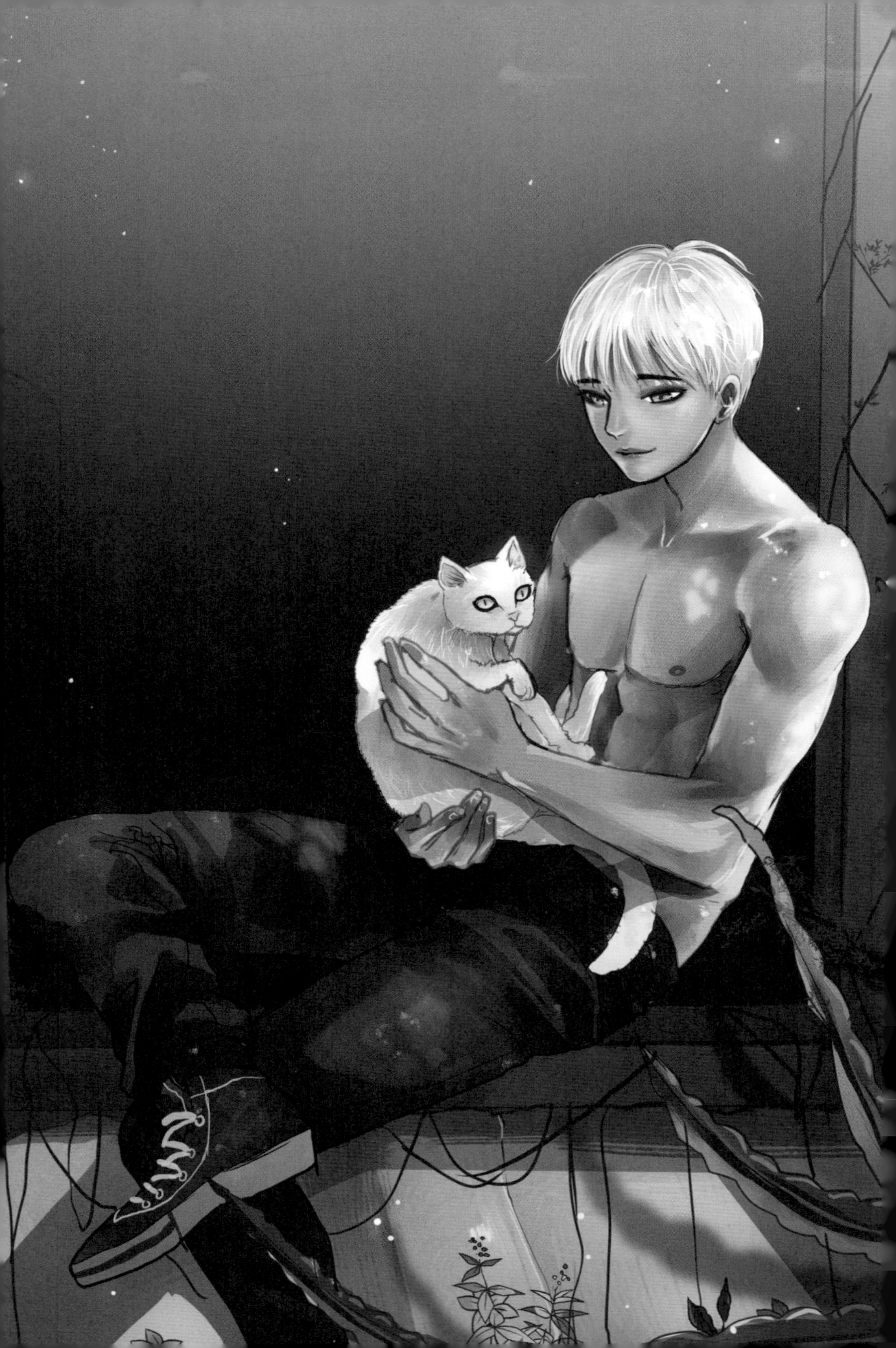

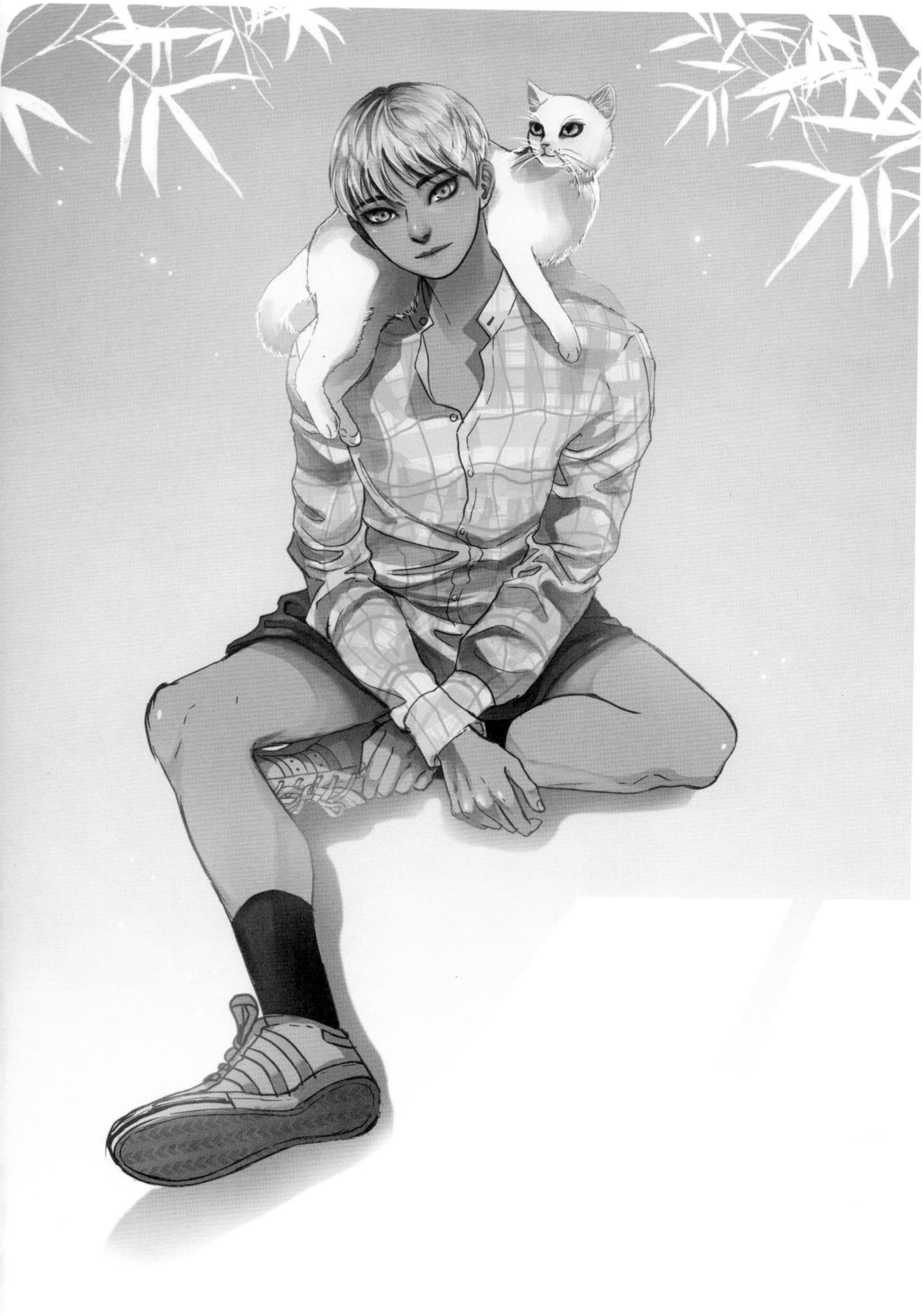

snailords
Aidyn Arroyal

SNAILORDS

Aidyn Arroyal aka Snailords (he/they) is a manga, comic, and WEBTOON artist. He's best known for his romance WEBTOON series *Freaking Romance* (completed) and thriller WEBTOON series *Death: Rescheduled* (ongoing).

He is also the creator of *Snailogy* and *Snailed It*, two slice-of-life comics series.